IN THE MAELSTROM

IN THE
MAELSTROM

THE WAFFEN-SS "GALICIA" DIVISION AND ITS LEGACY

MYROSLAV SHKANDRIJ

MCGILL-QUEEN'S UNIVERSITY PRESS

Montreal & Kingston • London • Chicago

© McGill-Queen's University Press 2023

ISBN 978-0-2280-1652-6 (cloth)
ISBN 978-0-2280-1653-3 (paper)
ISBN 978-0-2280-1654-0 (ePDF)

Legal deposit first quarter 2023
Bibliothèque nationale du Québec

Printed in Canada on acid-free paper that is 100% ancient forest free (100% post-consumer recycled), processed chlorine free

McGill-Queen's University Press gratefully acknowledges the financial contributions of the Canadian Foundation for Ukrainian Studies and the Ukrainian Studies Fund toward the publication of this volume.

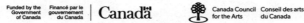

We acknowledge the support of the Canada Council for the Arts.
Nous remercions le Conseil des arts du Canada de son soutien.

LIBRARY AND ARCHIVES CANADA CATALOGUING IN PUBLICATION

Title: In the maelstrom : the Waffen-SS "Galicia" Division and its legacy / Myroslav Shkandrij.
Names: Shkandrij, Myroslav, 1950– author.
Description: Includes bibliographical references and index.
Identifiers: Canadiana (print) 20220447659 | Canadiana (ebook) 20220447896
    ISBN 9780228016526 (cloth) | ISBN 9780228016533 (paper)
    ISBN 9780228016540 (ePDF)
Subjects: LCSH: Waffen-SS. Grenadier-Division, 14.—History. | LCSH: Waffen-SS. Grenadier-Division, 14.—Recruiting, enlistment, etc. | LCSH: World War, 1939–1945—Regimental histories—Germany. | LCSH: World War, 1939–1945—Regimental histories—Ukraine. | LCSH: World War, 1939–1945—Personal narratives, Ukrainian.
Classification: LCC D757.85 .S55 2023 | DDC 940.54/1343—dc23

CONTENTS

Figures   vii

Glossary and Abbreviations   xi

Preface   xvii

Acknowledgments   xix

Note on Usage   xxi

Notes on Political and Military Figures   xxiii

Maps follow page   xxx

Introduction   3

PART ONE | MOTIVES

1   Genesis and Reasons for Volunteering   15

2   Collaborators and Co-operators   31

3   Kubijovyč, Pankivskyi, and the Ukrainian Central Committee   45

4   Military Training: Propaganda, Chaplains, and Relations with Germans   59

PART TWO | ACTIONS

5   Beyersdorff Battle Group, February–March, 1944   85

6   District of Lublin as War Theatre: Battalions, Guards, and Mutinies   93

7   Galician ss Volunteer Regiments   102

8   Slovakia, Slovenia, Austria, and the Ukrainian National Army, 1944–45   121

9   Youth Soldiers, Women, and Nurses   142

PART THREE | CAMPS

10 Bellaria and the Repatriation Campaign, 1945   161

11 Rimini, 1945–47   177

12 United Kingdom, 1947–49   197

PART FOUR | STORIES

13 Stories of Captured Men: Interrogations 1944–54 and Interviews 1987–2012   211

14 Émigré Press and the Patriot Image, 1951–74   230

15 Poetry and Memoirs   244

16 Popular Fiction   264

PART FIVE | REAPPRAISALS

17 Commissions of Inquiry and Postwar Trials   281

18 Reasons Recalled: Last Interviews, 1987–2012   298

19 Accomplices, Traitors, and Foes: Three Narrative Perspectives   314

20 Monuments and Memory   326

21 Conclusion   345

Notes   351
References   389
Index   415

Figures

1.1 Volunteers marching in the parade, Lviv, 28 April 1943. Courtesy Ukrainian Canadian Research and Documentation Centre. 22

1.2 Women holding the Galicia Division emblem, Lviv, 28 April 1943. Courtesy Ukrainian Canadian Research and Documentation Centre. 22

1.3 Women in the parade. Lviv, 28 April 1943. Courtesy Ukrainian Canadian Research and Documentation Centre. 23

1.4 Men and women in the parade. Lviv, 28 April 1943. Courtesy Ukrainian Canadian Research and Documentation Centre. 25

1.5 Governor Wächter salutes volunteers, Lviv, 28 April 1943. Courtesy Ukrainian Canadian Research and Documentation Centre. 26

1.6 Wächter and Bisantz, Lviv, 28 April, 1943. Author's archive. 26

4.1 Galicia troops in camouflage before Brody, July 1943. Petro Markevych with members of his company. Courtesy Ukrainian Canadian Research and Documentation Centre. 66

8.1 Returning from church service in Slovakia, 1944. Courtesy Ukrainian Canadian Research and Documentation Centre. 123

8.2 At the front by a bunker, Gleichenberg, Austria, April 1945. Left to right: Roman Hankevych, Smuk, Yaroslav Rudyi, N.N., Stefan Maier, Solodkyi, N.N., Volodymyr Motyka (with back turned). Courtesy the estate of B. Maciw. 133

8.3 General Pavlo Shandruk. Courtesy the estate of B. Maciw. 133

9.1 Youth "recruits" with Wächter, Bisantz, and the Division's reporter Stepan Konrad, Przeworsk (Ukr: Perevorsk). Courtesy Ukrainian Canadian Research and Documentation Centre. 144

9.2 Youth being taught to assemble a rifle in Malta, Austria, 1944. Courtesy Ukrainian Canadian Research and Documentation Centre. 148

viii • Figures

9.3 Study session for youth. Malta, Austria, 1944. Courtesy Ukrainian Canadian Research and Documentation Centre. 148

9.4 Woman operating searchlight. From Zelenyi, *Ukrainske iunatstvo*, 1965. Courtesy Ukrainian Canadian Research and Documentation Centre. 151

9.5 Woman in anti-aircraft force. From Zelenyi, *Ukrainske iunatstvo*, 1965. Courtesy Ukrainian Canadian Research and Documentation Centre. 151

9.6 Armbands for groups in the "Youth ss." Ukrainians were separated into Galicia and Ukraine groups. Other groups: Estonia, Latvia, Lithuania, Belarus, Russia, and Volga and Crimean Tatars. The central diamond in each armband was used as a badge on caps. Courtesy Ukrainian Canadian Research and Documentation Centre. 153

9.7 Reverend Severyn Saprun conducts mass near anti-aircraft gun, Vienna, 6 January 1944. Courtesy the estate of B. Maciw. 155

11.1 Judging an athletic competition, Rimini. Courtesy Ukrainian Canadian Research and Documentation Centre. 180

11.2 Blessing Easter baskets, 21 April 1946. Courtesy the estate of B. Maciw. 180

11.3 Ukrainian commanders with nurses from the Riccione camp. Courtesy Ukrainian Historical and Educational Center. 182

11.4 Final high school exams in the theatre built by the Division's veterans, 30 July 1946. Courtesy the estate of B. Maciw. 184

11.5 Stamp produced in Rimini, 1946, "Ukrainian Camp Post Italy." Designed by Stepan Dytso. 189

11.6 Stamp produced in Rimini, 1946. Designed by Dmytro Dudynskyi. 189

11.7 Stamp produced in Rimini, 1946. Designed by Stepan Dytso. The figure symbolizes labour. Monte Titano is in the background. 189

11.8 Stamp produced in Rimini, 1946. Designed by Dmytro Dudynskyi. 189

11.9 Stamp produced in Rimini, 1946. Designed by Sviatoslav Yatsushko. It commemorates Metropolitan Andrei Sheptytskyi. 189

11.10 Stamp produced in Rimini, 1946. Designed by Sviatoslav Yatsushko. It commemorates the anniversary of the Lviv Uprising on 1 November 1918. 189

Figures · **ix**

11.11 Theatre performance, Rimini. Francuzenko in female role in Borys Hrinchenko's *Na iasni zori*, 1946. Courtesy Ukrainian Historical and Educational Center. 190

11.12 Blessing the flag, 9,000 participants. Rimini, 25 May 1946. Courtesy the estate of B. Maciw. 192

12.1 Writers and editors of camp publications shortly before leaving Rimini for the UK. Author's archive. 201

12.2 Lodge Moor Camp, Sheffield. Author's archive. 201

12.3 "1976 Our Last POW." Copied by a Division POW from a painting left on the wall of Barrack D5, POW Camp 17, by German POWs, 1947. Author's archive. 202

14.1 Front page of *Visti bratstva kol. Voiakiv 1 UD UNA*, July 1951, depicting Battle of Brody. Heading: "Glory to the fighters at Brody!" Caption: "You will win a Ukrainian State or die in the struggle for her. Yevhen Konovalets." 232

16.1 General Mykhailo Krat. From Orest Slupchynskyi's *Zibralasia Kumpaniia* (1946). The caption reads: "He led us to the camp, like Moses led sons of the kahal – Moses brought the stones … He got the rank of general." 265

16.2 Portrait of the writer Oleksii Devlad (Zaporozhets) by Volodymyr Kaplun, Rimini camp, 1946. From Zaporozhets-Devlad, *V odvichnii borotbi*, 1955. Courtesy Ukrainian Canadian Research and Documentation Centre. 265

20.1 Cemetery in Cervia where 39 Division soldiers who died in Italy were buried. They are now reburied in Passo della Futa. Courtesy Ukrainian Historical and Educational Center. 327

20.2 Inscription on Cervia monument: "To fighters for Ukraine's freedom." This monument is now embedded in the crypt in Passo della Futa. Courtesy Ukrainian Historical and Educational Center. 327

20.3 Monument to all fallen Ukrainian soldiers in St Andrew's Cemetery, South Bound Brook, New Jersey. Author's archive. 329

20.4 Base of monument to fallen soldiers in South Bound Brook, showing the UNA's emblem (lion) next to the UNR's emblem (Petliura Cross). Author's archive. 329

20.5 Mykola Francuzenko (Frantsuzhenko) interviewing Jack Palance, with Ulas Samchuk in foreground. At the unveiling of the Shevchenko monument, Washington, 1964. Francuzenko worked for Voice of

x • Figures

America and Radio Free Europe. Courtesy Ukrainian Historical and Educational Center. 330

20.6 Monument to the Division's soldiers in St Volodymyr Cemetery, Oakville, Ontario. Courtesy Andrij Maleckyj. 331

20.7 Monument to General Andrei Vlasov in Nanuet, New Jersey, with the ROA emblem and flag. Author's archive. 339

20.8 Close up of Vlasov monument showing three flags. Carved into the side are the words "To those who fell in the struggle for a free Russia." Author's archive. 339

20.9 Monument to the Russian Corps, Nanuet, New Jersey. Author's archive. 340

20.10 Reburial of a Division soldier's remains. Chervone, 19 July 2015. From Ihor Ivankiv et al., eds., *Ukrainska dyviziia "Halychyna" Lvivshchyna: Istoriia, spohady, svitlyny* (Lviv : Dukhovna vis, 2016), 497. 343

20.11 Anniversary of Brody. Chervone, 24 July 2005. Left to right: Mykhailo Mulyk, Volodymyr Malkosh, Yurii Ferentsevych, Ivan Mamchur. From Ihor Ivankiv et al., eds., *Ukrainska dyviziia "Halychyna" Lvivshchyna: Istoriia, spohady, svitlyny* (Lviv: Dukhovna vis, 2016), 476. 343

Glossary and Abbreviations

AAV	Archivio Apostolico Vaticano, Vatican City
AK	Home Army (Armia Krajowa), Polish underground resistance
AL	People's Army (Armia Ludowa), a communist partisan group
AO	Archives of Ontario, Toronto
APL	Archiwum Panstwowe w Lublinie, Lublin
AUSBUTO	Arkhiv Upravlinnia Sluzhby Bezpeky Ukrainy v Ternopilskii Oblast (Archive of the Administration of the Security Service of Ukraine in Ternopil Oblast)
BA-KO	Bundesarkhiv, Berlin (formerly German Military Archive, Koblenz)
BA-L	Budesarkhiv Aussenstelle Ludwigsberg
BCh	Peasants' Battalions (Bataliony Chłopskie), partially integrated into the AK
BSRN	The Military Union of Russian People (Boevoi Soiuz Russkogo Naroda)
BUK	Ukrainian Battalion (Bataillon Ukrainien)
CURB	Central Ukrainian Relief Bureau
DP	displaced person
FFI	French Forces of the Interior (Forces Françaises de l'Interieur)
Gestapo	Secret State Police (Geheime Statspolizei), fought the state's political enemies.
GG	General Government (Generalgouvernement), after 1939 included four districts (Warsaw, Lublin, Radom, and Kraków) of what had been pre-war Poland, and after 1942 a fifth district (Galicia).

xii • Glossary and Abbreviations

GPU
: State Political Directorate (Gosudarstvennoe Politicheskoe Upravlenie), state security police 1922–34, forerunner of KGB. The Ukrainian abbreviation is DPU. The organization's headquarters were in Moscow and its full title was OGPU (Joint State Political Directorate).

Gulag
: Main Directorate of Camps (Glavnoe Upravlenie Lagerei), the agency in charge of the network of corrective labour camps that was spread mainly over the territory of Russia.

HDASBU
: Halyzevyi Derzhavnyi Arkhiv Sluzhby Bezpeky Ukrainy (State Archive of the Security Service of Ukraine), Kyiv.

Holodomor
: The Great Famine of 1932–34, a term meaning "death by starvation."

HSSPF
: Higher ss and Police Leader (Höherer ss- und Polizeiführer), coordinated any action with more than one agency of the ss and police. The districts of the GG (Warsaw, Radom, Kraków, Lublin, Galicia) had SSPFs who controlled the Secret Police and Order Police at the district level.

IHRC
: Immigration History Research Center, University of Minnesota

IMT
: International Military Tribunal, Nuremberg, 1945–46

KGB
: Committee of State Security (Komitet Gosudarstvennoi Bezopasnosti) from 1954

Komsomol
: Communist Youth League (Kommunisticheskii Soiuz Molodezhi)

KONR
: Committee for the Liberation of the Peoples of Russia (Komitet osvobozhdeniia narodov Rossii)

Kurkul
: (Russ: *kulak*) An ideological label supposedly for rich farmers, applied in 1930 to anyone who resisted collectivization.

LAC
: Library and Archives Canada, Ottawa

MGB
: Ministry of State Security (Ministerstvo Gosudarstvennoi Bezopasnosti), conducted espionage from 1946 to 1953.

MI6
: Military Intelligence, Branch 6, British intelligence linked to Foreign Office.

Glossary and Abbreviations • xiii

MVD	Ministry of Internal Affairs (Ministerstvo Vnutrennykh Del), secret political police from 1946, absorbed NKGB and NKVD. Superseded by KGB in 1954.
NA/PRO	National Archive (formerly Public Records Office), London
NAUS	National Archives of the United States, Washington
NCO	non-commissioned officer
NKGB	People's Commissariat of State Security (Narodnyi Kommissariat Gosudarstvennoi Bezopasnosti) became KGB in 1954.
NKVD	People's Commissariat of Internal Affairs (Narodnyi Komissariat Vnutrennikh Del), from 1934, later MVD
NOW	National Military Organization (Narodowa Organizacja Wojskowa)
NSDAP	National Socialist German Workers Party (Nationalsozialistische Deutsche Arbeiterpartei)
NSZ	People's Armed Forces (Narodowe Siły Zbrojne)
Orpo	Order Police (Ordnungspolizei)
OSI	Office of Special Investigations
Ostministerium	Reich Ministry for the Occupied Eastern Territories (Reichministerium für die besetzten Ostgebiete) headed by Alfred Rosenberg from 1941
OUN-B	Organization of Ukrainian Nationalists-Bandera faction (Orhanizatsiia Ukrainskykh Natsionalistiv)
OUN-M	Organization of Ukrainian Nationalists-Melnyk faction (Orhanizatsiia Ukrainskykh Natsionalistiv)
PAA	Provincial Archives of Alberta, Edmonton
PISM	Polish Institute and Sikorski Museum, London
POW	prisoner of war
RNNA	Russian National Patriotic Army (Russkaia Natsionalnaia Narodnaia Armiia)
ROA	Russian Liberation Army (Russkaia Osvoboditelnaia Armiia)
RONA	Russian National Army of Liberation (Russkaia Osvoboditelnaia Narodnaia Armiia)
RSHA	Reich Main Security Office of the SS (Reichssicherheitshauptamt), in which Gestapo, criminal police, and SD were unofficially combined in 1936

xiv · Glossary and Abbreviations

RUSHA	Race and Settlement Main Office (Rasse- und Siedlungshauptamt)
SA	Storm Troopers of the Nazi Party (Sturmabteilungen)
SB	Security Service of the OUN-B (Sluzhba Bezpeky)
SD	Security Service of the SS intelligence (Sicherheitsdienst der SS)
SEP	surrendered enemy personnel
SMERSH	Counter-intelligence unit within the Red Army during Second World War. Name derived from a phrase translated as "death to spies"
SS	Protection Squadrons (Schutzstaffel). Paramilitary organization created in 1929 and expanded into Himmler's armed service
Sipo	The Security Police (Sicherheitspolizei), which contained the Gestapo, SD, and criminal police, often described as "SS" or "SD-men"
SUB	Union of Ukrainians in Great Britain (Soiuz Ukraintsiv u Velykii Brytanii)
TsDAVOV	Tsentralnyi derzhavnyi arkhiv vyshchykh orhaniv vlady i upravlinnia Ukrainy (Central State Archive of Higher Organs of Power), Kyiv
UCCA	Ukrainian Congress Committee of America
UCRDC	Ukrainian Canadian Research and Documentation Centre, Toronto
UDK	Ukrainian Aid Committee (Ukrainskyi Dopomohovyi Komitet)
UHA	Ukrainian Galician Army (Ukrainska Halytska Armiia)
UHVR	Ukraine's Supreme Liberation Council (Ukrainska Holovna Vyzvolna Rada)
UKK	Ukrainian Regional Committee (Ukrainskyi Kraiovyi Komitet)
ULS	Ukrainian Legion of Self-Defence (Ukrainskyi Lehion Samooborony)
UNA	Ukrainian National Army (Ukrainska Natsionalna Armiia)
UNDO	Ukrainian National Democratic Association (Ukrainske Nationalno-Demokratychne Obiednannia)

Glossary and Abbreviations • **xv**

UNK	Ukrainian National Committee (Ukrainskyi Natsionalnyi Komitet)
UNR	Ukrainian People's Republic (Ukrainska Narodna Respublika). Proclaimed by the Central Rada in its Third Universal on 20 November 1917, declared independence in its Fourth Universal on 22 January 1918, proclaimed a constitution on 29 April 1918. The Directory of the UNR ousted Hetman Pavlo Skoropadsky's German-installed regime in December 1918.
UNS	Ukrainian People's Self-Defence (Ukrainska Narodna Smooborona), renamed UPA in 1943
UOT	Ukrainian Educational Society (Ukrainske Osvitnie Tovarystvo)
UPA	Ukrainian Insurgent Army (Ukrainska Povstanska Armiia)
URDP	Ukrainian Revolutionary Democratic Party (Ukainska Revoliutsiina Demokratychna Partiia)
USHMM	United States Holocaust Memorial Museum Archive, Washington
UTsK	Ukrainian Central Committee (Ukrainskyi Tsentralnyi Komitet)
UVO	Ukrainian Military Organization (Ukrainska Viiskova Orhanizatsiia)
UVV	Ukrainian Liberation Army (Ukrainske Vyzvolne Viisko)
VUAN	All-Ukrainian Academy of Sciences (Vseukrainska Akademiia Nauk)
WiN	Freedom and Independence (Wolność i Niezawisłość)
ZWZ	Union of Armed Struggle (Związek Walki Zbrojnej)

Preface

While growing up in the UK in the 1950s and 1960s, and then studying in Canada in the 1970s, the Waffen-ss "Galicia" Division was a topic of discussion among my fellow students and friends. The milieu in which I moved at the time was radically leftist, but this did not prevent conversations with a wide range of individuals, including veterans of the Division. There was plenty of common ground in the diaspora, which then closely followed cultural and political developments in the Soviet Union and protested the arrest of dissidents. In the 1980s, when the media began describing the Division's veterans as mass murderers and war criminals, who apparently met in secret covens to plot a fascist takeover of Ukraine, this did not square with my personal experience, knowledge of history, or, for that matter, with common sense. Newspaper accounts at the time described the Division as a monolith, ignored differences within the diaspora community, and showed no interest in what the veterans had experienced. Instead, the coverage revelled in a nightmarish image of monsters "living next door." The present text came out of a desire, which no doubt first arose at that time, to examine the facts and present a more accurate and realistic picture. Moreover, I have always had a personal interest in the formation. My father volunteered for the Division and was sent for officer training before he joined the force in Slovakia in late 1944. While in a British internment camp in Rimini he began publishing poetry under the pseudonym Bohdan Bora. My mother Olga (née Poloziuk) was from a part of the Donetsk oblast that is presently under Russian occupation. As a teenager she was sent as an Ostarbeiter (slave labourer) to work on a German farm for two years. My parents married in the UK in 1949.

The Division is a contentious topic that has been the subject of polemics for several decades. Debates have taken place over what motivated individuals to join the Waffen-ss, war crimes they may have committed, their relationship to the Holocaust, and their release from pow camps in 1949. These polemics are embedded in historical contexts: the anti-Soviet guerrilla war of 1944–45, the Cold War, Russian colonialism and Ukraine's emancipatory struggle, the role of the diaspora, and Russian-Ukrainian relations after the declaration of independence in 1991. The final three chapters look at the way different contexts have generated competing perspectives.

In the Maelstrom makes substantial use of memoirs and documents to explain why individuals entered the force, to outline the political situation and the options that were available, and the reasoning – sometimes myopic and sometimes insightful – that governed their behaviour. Given the general abhorrence of military men in German uniforms during the Second World War, some readers might find information from a number of sources disconcerting. As will be discovered, individuals found themselves in the force for various reasons and had illuminating stories to tell. The book begins by reviewing the facts as presented in the most reliable accounts, draws on various archival sources, and records different perspectives.

Acknowledgments

The list of people who offered help and advice while I was writing the book is a long one, and I wish to collectively thank everyone. For reading portions of the book and offering comments I am grateful to Yaroslav Hrytsak, Damian Markowski, Łukasz Adamski, Olha Poliukhovych, Reverend Athanasius McVay, Oksana Dudko, Roman Waschuk, Andrij Maleckyj, Bohdan Figol, and two anonymous manuscript reviewers. For steering the book through the editing process I wish to thank Richard Ratzlaff. Individuals who found materials, or offered them from personal archives, include Michael Melnyk, Olesya Khromeychuk, Liliana Hentosh, Myron Momryk, Alti Rodal, Motria Shuhan, Darlene Zeleney, Bohdan Vitvitsky, Lubomyr Luciuk, Frank Sysyn, Olga Bertelsen, John-Paul Himka, Petro Kormylo, Martin Rapak, and Yaroslaw Botiuk. Several veterans of the Division provided information, among them Wasyl Veryha, Roman Kolisnyk, and Orest Slupchynskyj. Darian Picklyk kindly produced the maps. I owe a special debt to archivists and librarians, in particular James Kominowski and Orest Martynowych at the University of Manitoba; Irodia Wynnyckyj and Bozhena Gembatiuk at the Ukrainian Canadian Research and Documentation Centre; Michael Andrec at the Ukrainian Historical and Educational Center, Somerset, New Jersey; Ksenya Kiebuzinski at the University of Toronto; and the staff at Library and Archives Canada, Archives of Ontario, Polish Institute and Sikorski Museum, Shevchenko Library and Archive in London, National Archive in London, Archives of the Security Service of Ukraine in Kyiv and Ternopil, Central State Archive of Higher Organs of Power in Kyiv, the Immigrant History Research Center at the University of Minnesota, and the Hoover Institution Library and Archives at Stanford University.

Along the way many conversations sustained my interest in the topic and provided encouragement. To list every individual would be impossible, but I would like to express gratitude in particular to Roman Senkus,

Jurij Fedyk, Roman Serbyn, Leo and Marco Iwanytskyj, Anhelyna Szuch, Marta Baziuk, Helena Derkatsch Maciw, Anna Ortynskyj, Halyna Hryn, Oksana Zakydalska, Bohdan Klid, Jars Balan, Mark Minenko, Alexandra Chyczij, Eugene Cholkan, and Myroslaw Trutiak. It is my pleasure to thank Natalia Obraztsova, Alexandra Shkandrij, Martin Michalak, Yulia Ivaniuk, Yulia Kravchenko, and Emma Mikuska-Tinman, who assisted me in the research. My first reader, as always, was my wife Natalka Chomiak, to whom I am hugely indebted for many insights and constant support.

I would like to acknowledge the *Kyiv-Mohyla Humanities Journal* for allowing me to adapt passages from the article "The Ukrainian 'Galicia' Division: From Familiar to Unexplored Avenues of Research," 6 (2019): 1–23. The Social Sciences and Humanities Research Council of Canada and the University of Manitoba generously provided the research funding that allowed this book to be written.

Note on Usage

I use a modified Library of Congress transliteration system for Russian and Ukrainian, but to approximate English usage I give the initial letter in personal and place names as a "Y": Yevhen, Yosyp. Place names are given according to the language of the country in which they are now located, but I retain established English usage in a few cases: Moscow, Warsaw, Prague. Since in the twentieth century place names changed under different states and governments, a previous name is sometimes added for purposes of identification. When places figure prominently in both Polish and Ukrainian literature on the subject, both are provided, with that of the country in which they are now located coming first.

Personal names are sometimes recorded differently in archives, usually because the individual adopted a different spelling upon immigrating. In these cases, transliteration from the original Cyrillic is generally retained in the text and bibliography, but the later spelling is provided in any references.

Most readers will not be familiar with commissioned ranks in the Waffen-ss. Moreover, German figures often held more than one rank during their careers. To complicate matters, ranks in the ss differed from those in the regular German army and the Waffen-ss. Among themselves Ukrainians in the Division used their own terminology, which became official practice when the force was renamed the Ukrainian National Army (UNA) in the last weeks of the war. For these reasons English-language equivalents or near-equivalents are used in the text to identify higher ranks, but the German terms are provided in the notes on military and political figures. The higher ranks in the Waffen-ss were: Untersturmführer (2nd Lieutenant); Obersturmführer (Lieutenant); Hauptsturmführer (Captain); Sturmbannführer (Major); Obersturmbannführer (Lieutenant Colonel); Oberführer (Colonel); Brigadeführer (Major General); Gruppenführer (Lieutenant General); Obergruppenführer (General). In the Waffen-ss Galicia the highest rank allowed Ukrainians was Hauptsturmführer, even though some men had achieved a higher rank in the armies of the Ukrainian People's Republic, Russia, Poland, or the Soviet Union. The exceptions were Mykola Paliienko and Yevhen Pobohushchyi (Evhen Pobihushtchyj), who held the rank of Waffen-Sturmbannführer (Major). The only men at Waffen-Hauptsturmführer (Captain) rank were Mykhailo Brygidyr, Volodymyr Kozak (Kosak), Ivan Rembalovych, Dmytro Paliiv, and Dmytro Ferkuniak. The prefix "Waffen-" signified that, as Ukrainians, they were not members of the ss. The ranks of all German officers, with the exception of the Operations Officer Major Wolf Dietrich Heike, were preceded by the prefix "ss-" to designate membership in the ss.[1]

The ethnically mixed lands of prewar Poland immediately west of the Curzon Line (the Lublin, Przemyśl, and Lemko regions) are sometimes referred to as "Zakerzonie" (Pol) or "Zakerzonnia" (Ukr). The latter term is used in quotation marks to designate this band of territories because it is frequently invoked in Ukrainian literature but was never an administrative region.

Notes on Political and Military Figures

ANDERS, WŁADYSŁAW. General (1892–1970). Served in Russian army during the First World War and in Polish army during Polish-Soviet war 1919–21. As a Polish general was captured by the Soviets in 1939, imprisoned and tortured. Released in 1941 to create the 2nd Polish Corps, recruited largely from Poles deported to Siberia. Anders Army, as it was known, passed under British command in Palestine, fought in Italy, notably at Monte Cassino. A member of the Polish government in exile in London, he married Irena Jarosiewicz (stage name Renata Bogdańska), a Ukrainian, in 1948.

ANTONESCU, ION. Marshall (1882–1946). Statesman and dictator of Romania's pro-Nazi government. Minister of defence in 1937. Appointed prime minister with absolute powers 4 September 1940. Joined the Axis powers. Briefly brought fascist Iron Guard to power as his partner but suppressed the organization after criminal excesses of 1941. Toppled by coup d'état in August 1944 led by King Michael. Executed as a war criminal in 1946.

ARLT, FRITZ. SS-Obersturmbannführer (Major) (1912–2004). Considered an SS expert on racial policies, wrote dissertations at the universities of Leipzig and Breslau (Wrocław) on the cultural and political anthropology of Jews, claiming that sexual inclinations were a product of their traditions. From 1939 helped implement Nazi policy in the GG. In 1944 planned recruitment from non-Russian nationalities and was assigned as liaison with the Galicia Division. From 1954 to 1975 served as a director of the German Red Cross, the Köln German Industrial Institute (Deutsches Industrie-Institut), and advisor to the German government.

BACH-ZELEWSKI, ERICH VON DEM. SS-Brigadeführer (Lieutenant General) (1899–1972). Resettled 18,000–20,000 Poles from Żywiec county (Silesia) in 1940. Became HSSPF for Silesia. Served as SS and police leader in Belarus, oversaw Einsatzgruppe B in Riga and Minsk. Conducted anti-partisan warfare in 1942–43. Chief of partisan warfare and commander of an army corps, responsible for murder of 35,000 civilians in Riga and over 200,000 in what is today Belarus and eastern Poland. Commanded troops fighting Warsaw Uprising in 1944. Units under him killed 200,000 civilians, more than 65,000 in mass executions. In exchange for testimony at Nuremberg Trials, never faced trial for any war crimes. Left prison in 1949. In 1951 sentenced to two years in labour camp for the murder of political opponents in the early 1930s but did not serve time. In 1958 sentenced to four and a half years for having killed a German officer. In 1961 sentenced to an additional ten years in home custody for the murder of ten German communists in the 1930s. None of these sentences relate to role in Poland or Holocaust. Died in prison.

BERGER, GOTTLOB. SS-Obergruppenführer and General der Waffen-SS (Lieutenant General) (1896–1975). Head of the RSHA. Responsible for SS recruiting during the war. Extended Waffen-SS recruiting to "Germanic" volunteers from Scandinavia and Western Europe, to Volksdeutsche (ethnic Germans) outside the Reich, and finally to other peoples. Tried and convicted by Nuremberg Military Tribunal, sentenced to twenty-five years imprisonment. Released after six and a half years.

BISANTZ, ALFRED. Oberst (Colonel) (1890–1951). An officer in the Austro-Hungarian Army, then in the UHA. An Abwehr liaison officer with the OUN. From 1943, head of the Galicia Division's Military Board. In 1945 arrested in Vienna by Soviet counterintelligence, sentenced to Siberia, shot in 1951 or died in the Gulag in 1953.

CANARIS, WILHELM. Admiral (1887–1945) Director of Abwehr (German military intelligence) from January 1935 to February 1944. Hanged on 9 April 1944 for his part in the July 1944 plot against Hitler.

DALUEGE, KURT. SS-Oberstgruppenführer (General) (1897–1946). From 1934 to 1942 chief of Order Police (Ordnungspolizei or Orpo). Heydrich's successor as protector of Bohemia-Moravia, where he initiated a wave of terror. Hanged in Prague on 20 October 1946.

D'ALQUEN, GUNTER. SS-Standartenführer (Brigadier General) (1910–1998). Himmler's propagandist, first editor of Das Schwarze Korps, official newspaper of the SS from 1935. Head of armed forces propaganda section at the end of the war and of the propaganda formation SS-Standarte Kurt Eggers.

Notes on Political and Military Figures • **XXV**

DARRÉ, WALTHER RICHARD. SS-Obergruppenführer (Honorary General) (1895–1953). Early friend of Himmler and founder of Race and Settlement Main Office, or RUSHA, minister of agriculture 1933–42. Leading Nazi ideologist, provided justification for "Drang nach Osten" and "Lebensraum" theories. Tried at Nuremberg, sentenced to seven years in prison, released in 1950. Died in hospital of liver cancer.

DIRLEWANGER, OSKAR. SS-Oberführer (Major General) (1895–1945?). Commander of notorious brigade of ex-convicts, protégé of Gottlob Berger. His Sonderkommando Dirlewanger brigade killed over 30,000 Belarusian civilians. During the Warsaw Uprising participated in the Wola massacre, in which some 40,000 civilians were killed, disappeared in May 1945, reportedly died in Allied custody.

FRANK, HANS. SA-Obergruppenführer (General) (1900–1946). Reichskommissar of Justice in 1933, governor of the GG (occupied Poland) after 1939 with headquarters in Kraków. Captured by US troops in 1945, tried by International Military Tribunal at Nuremberg, executed 16 October 1946.

FREITAG, FRITZ. SS-Brigadeführer (Brigade Leader) and Generalmajor der Waffen-SS (General) (1894–1945). Served in First World War, then in police service. After invasion of Poland, as a police colonel organized rear security in Belarus and assisted the Einsatzgruppen in destroying Jewish populations. Commanded 2nd SS Police Infantry Regiment, SS Cavalry Division Florian Geyer, 2nd SS Infantry Brigade, and 4th SS Police Division. From 1943 commanded Waffen-SS Galicia Division. Shot himself on 10 May 1945.

GEHLEN, REINHARD. Wehrmacht Generalleutnant (Major General) (1902–1979). Chief of military intelligence for Wehrmacht's Foreign Armies East. From 1946 to 1956 created Gehlen Organization, an espionage network that employed former officers in the SS and was affiliated with the CIA. From 1956 to 1968 was president of West Germany's Federal Intelligence Service.

GLOBOČNIK, ODILO. SS-Gruppenführer (Major General) (1904–1945). Official in the Gestapo from 1933, later in police department of Ministry of Interior and during the war in the Abwehr. HSSPF for the Lublin district. Played leading role in Operation Reinhard, which organized murder of over 1 million Jews in the district. Committed suicide after being captured by British soldiers

HEYDRICH, REINHARD. SS-Obergruppenführer (General) (1904–1942). From September 1939 head of RSHA, including Gestapo, Kripo, and SD. Founding head of SD charged with neutralizing resistance to Nazi Party. An architect of the Holocaust, directly responsible for Einsatzgruppen. Shot by assassin in Prague on 27 May 1942, died a week later.

HIMMLER, HEINRICH. Reichsführer-SS (1900–1945). Head of Reich political police in 1933, head of German police in 1936, head of Waffen-SS, minister of interior in 1943, commander in chief of replacement army in July 1944 and of Vistula armies December 1944–March 1945. Committed suicide at British interrogation centre on 23 May 1945.

HOFMANN, OTTO. SS-Obergruppenfürer (General) (1896–1982). Head of SS Race and Settlement Main Office (RUSHA). Participated in "Germanization" of territories taken from Poland and Soviet Union. Sentenced to twenty-five years in 1948, pardoned in 1954, worked as a clerk.

HÖFLE, HERMANN. SS-Sturmbannführer (Major) (1911–1962). Austrian-born deputy to Globočnik in Operation Reinhard, managed deportation of Jews to the GG, arrested in 1945, released in 1947. Fled to Italy following an extradition request by Poland. Lived as a free man until arrested in 1961, committed suicide in prison before trial began.

HORTHY, MIKLOS (NIKOLAUS) VON NAGYBANIA. Admiral (1868–1957). Regent of Kingdom of Hungary 1919–44. Supported Hitler's invasion of Soviet Union in 1941 and rewarded with certain areas ceded to neighbours at Treaty of Trianon in 1920. After German invasion in March 1944, forced to abdicate in October 1944 and interned. Appeared as witness at Nuremberg in 1948, settled in Portugal.

JOST, HEINZ. SS-Brigadeführer (Major General) (1904–1964). Chief of Amt VI (Office VI) of SD foreign intelligence 1939–42; commanded Einsatzgruppe A in 1942, operating in Baltic and Belarus; liaison officer of Southern Army Group Headquarters; forced to enlist in Waffen-SS as an untersturmführer (2nd lieutenant) in 1944. Arrested in 1945, sentenced at Nuremberg to life imprisonment. Released after sentence was reviewed in 1951, worked as a real estate agent.

KAMINSKI, BRONISLAV. Waffen-Brigadeführer der SS (Major General) (1899–1944). Russian deserter who formed anti-partisan brigade. Established a civil administration in Lokot near Briansk in 1941 with help of German-controlled militia. Commander of SS Sturmbrigade RONA (known as Kaminski Brigade), which by 1943 had 12,000 men. Later incorporated into the Waffen-ss as 29th Waffen-Grenadier-Division der ss (russische Nr. 1). Participated in suppressing Warsaw Uprising, killing nearly 10,000 in the Ochota district. Executed by Himmler in September 1944 for stealing property.

KATZMANN, FRIEDRICH (FRITZ). ss-Standartenführer (Colonel) (1906–1957). HSSPF in District of Radom, chief executor of Operation Reinhard. Sent to what was then Lemberg (Pol: Lwów. Ukr: Lviv) in July 1941 and became HSSPR for Galicia district. In 1941–42 created a ghetto in the city and personally directed the killing of 55,000 to 65,000 Jews and mass deportations to camps. Lived in Germany under an assumed name until his death in 1957.

KOCH, ERICH. SA-Obergruppenführer (General) (1896–1986). Gauleiter of East Prussia from 1930 to 1945, Reichkommissar of Ukraine from 1941 to 1944, Reichskommissar Ostland from September 1944. Convicted in 1959 of war crimes and sentenced to death, commuted to life imprisonment.

KOPPE, WILHELM KARL HEINRICH. ss-Obergruppenführer (General) and General der Waffen-ss (1896–1975). In 1939 appointed HSSPF in GG. Responsible for execution and deportation of Poles and Polish Jews from Poznań area, and for euthanasia program that executed mental patients. In January 1942 attended the Wannsee Conference, involved in operations of Chełmno extermination camp. In 1945 went underground and became the director of a chocolate factory in Bonn. Arrested in 1960, released on bail in 1962, tried in 1964 as an accessory in the murder of 145,000 people, released in 1966 on medical grounds and prosecution dropped. Polish request for extradition was denied.

KÖSTRING, ERNST-AUGUST. Diplomat (1876–1953). Born in Moscow, son of a diplomat, raised in St Petersburg, fluent in Russian. Served in Prussian War Ministry in 1919. Military attaché to Russia and Lithuania from 1935. Involved in Molotov-Ribbentrop Pact of 1939. Recruited Soviet POWs for war effort; created national legions among Armenians, Georgians, and Karachai Muslims; helped create Vlasov's ROA. Surrendered to US Army in 1945, released in 1947. With Corliss Lamont co-authored The Peoples of the Soviet Union (New York: Harcourt, Brace and Company, 1946), which was used by US Army.

KRAT, MYKHAILO. Brigadier General (1892–1979). Served with distinction in Russian army during the First World War, then as a colonel in the UNR army. After release from internment, lived in Poland. Appointed staff xxviii • Notes on Political and Military Figures

officer of the UNA (the renamed Galicia Division) in 1944–45, interned in Italy, where he was promoted to rank of brigadier general by the UNR government in exile. Immigrated to the US.

KRÜGER, FRIEDRICH-WILHELM. SA-Obergruppenführer (General) (1894–1945). Himmler's delegate in the GG as HSSPF. Coordinated mass shooting of Polish intelligentsia in first weeks of war, deported 184 professors of Krakow's Jagiellonian University to Sachsenhausen concentration camp, supervised Operation Harvest Festival (Erntefest) in District of Lublin in November 1943 during which 83,000 Jews were killed. Drove out 116,000 Polish villagers in Operation Zamość. Dismissed on 9 November 1943 because of disagreement with Hans Frank and replaced by Wilhelm Koppe. Served with Waffen-SS Division Prinz Eugen in Yugoslavia. Committed suicide in Upper Austria.

KUBIJOVYČ, VOLODYMYR (1900–1985). Born in Poland's Lemko territory, served in the UHA, graduated in geography from Kraków's Jagiellonian University and produced detailed maps of Carpathian region. Headed the UTSK from March 1940. After the war edited the ten-volume Entsyklopediia ukrainoznavstva (Encyclopedia of Ukraine, 1949–84), the two-volume Ukraine a Concise Encyclopedia (1963 and 1971), and helped prepare the Encyclopedia of Ukraine (1984–93).

LAHOUSEN, ERWIN HEINRICH RENÉ VON. Brigadeführer (Major General) in Army (1897–1955). Member of interwar Austrian counter-intelligence service, joined Abwehr in 1938, head of its Section II under Admiral Canaris. Handled sabotage aspects of invasion of Poland in 1939. Plotted to assassinate Hitler on 13 March 1943 and 20 July 1944. Testified for prosecution at Nuremberg Trials.

MOLOTOV, VIACHESLAV (neé Skriabin) (1890–1986). Stalin's protégé, member of the Politburo from 1926, chairman of the Council of People's Commissars from 1930 and responsible for the requisitioning of grain from Ukraine during the Great Famine (Holodomor). people's commissar for external affairs from 1939 and minister of foreign affairs from 1946 to 1949 and from 1953 to 1956. Defended Stalin's policies and legacy until his death.

MÜLLER, HEINRICH. SS-Gruppenführer (General) (1900–1945?). Chief of Gestapo 1934–45 and of Central Emigration Agency under Heydrich's command, but delegated day-to-day administration to Adolph Eichmann. Sometimes lauded the Stalinist system as superior to Nazism and admired the Soviet police. Last seen in Hitler's bunker 1 May 1945, one day after Hitler's suicide.

PALIIV, DMYTRO. Hauptsturmführer (Captain) (1896–1944). An officer in the Ukrainian Sich Riflemen, on the military committee that organized the uprising in Lviv on 1 November 1918, served as adjutant to General Myron Tarnavskyi of the UHA. In interwar years a founding member of UVO, edited several periodicals, elected to Polish parliament (Sejm), spent three years in Polish jails, founded Front Natsionalnoi Iednosti (Front of National Unity) party. Served as an adjutant to General Freitag, and was killed at Brody.

PANKIVSKYI, KOST (1897–1974). A prominent lawyer in Lwów/Lemberg (Lviv), from September 1941 headed the Ukrainian Regional Committee (UKK), which existed as an independent organization in Galicia until 28 February 1942, then was Kubijovyc's deputy in the UTSK. Served as vice-president of the UNR government in exile from 1945 to 1949, immigrated to US in 1949.

PETLIURA, SYMON (1879–1926). A journalist and member of the underground socialist movement prior to the 1917 Revolution, became secretary for military affairs in the Central Rada 1917, member and then leader of the Directory government 1918–19, then head of the UNR and commander in chief of its army. Signed an alliance with the Polish government in 1920 and participated in the Polish-Bolshevik war. Assassinated in Paris, probably by a Soviet agent.

POBIHUSHCHYI, YEVHEN (pseudonym Ren) Sturmbannführer (Major) and Polkovnyk (Colonel) (1901–1995). Served in the UHA, then as a contract officer (lieutenant) in the Polish army. In 1941 commanded the "Roland" military unit, and in 1942 Schutzmannschaft Battalion 201, which fought Soviet partisans on the territory of today's Belarus. Joined the Division and served as a commander of the 29th Regiment. Promoted to colonel (polkovnyk) in the UNA. After the war was active in the émigré community in Germany.

RIBBENTROP, JOACHIM VON. SS General (1893–1946). Ambassador to United Kingdom 1936–38, Reich foreign minister 1938–45; hanged at Nuremberg 16 October 1946.

ROSENBERG, ALFRED ERNST. SS General (1893–1946). Chief of foreign political section in Nazi Party office 1930–41 and of Ostministerium (Reich Ministry for Occupied Eastern Territories) from April 1941; minister of foreign affairs 1938–45; tried and hanged in Nuremberg 16 October 1945.

SAUKEL, FRIEDRICH (FRITZ) CHRISTOPHE. SA-Gruppenführer (Lieutenant General) (1894–1946). Plenipotentiary for labour recruitment from March 1942, conducted slave raids in Ukraine and other occupied countries; tried and hanged in Nuremberg on 16 October 1945.

SHANDRUK, PAVLO (PAWŁO SZANDRUK). General (1889–1979). Served with distinction in Russian army during the First World War, then as a UNR general. POW in Poland, then served as a colonel in Polish army. In 1939 saved a Polish infantry brigade from annihilation, for which he was awarded the Virtuti Militari decoration after the war. Imprisoned by Germans, interrogated by Gestapo, worked as a civilian in Poland helping members of Polish underground from 1940 to 1944. The UNR government in exile appointed him general of the UNA, whose surrender to the Americans and British he oversaw in 1945.

SKOROPADSKYI, PAVLO (1873–1945). Proclaimed Hetman of Ukraine at the end of April 1918 after a German coup d'état. Left with the withdrawing German army in December 1918.

VLASOV, ANDREI. General (1901–1946). Captured as a Red Army general in 1942, raised a Russian army (ROA) for the Germans. Over 100,000 former Soviet citizens wore the ROA patch, but Vlasov personally commanded only two divisions. At the war's end changed sides and helped the Prague uprising against the Germans. Handed over to Soviet forces and hanged in Moscow on 2 August 1946.

WÄCHTER, BARON OTTO GUSTAV VON. SS-Gruppenführer (Lieutenant General) (1901–1949). Lawyer and member of the SS from 1930, participated in the failed plot to overthrow the Austrian government in 1934. State secretary in Vienna 1938, governor of Kraków district 1939–41 and Galicia district 1942–44, head of German military administration in the puppet Republic of Salò in Italy 1944, responsible for non-German forces in RSHA. Evaded Allied authorities for four years by hiding in the Austrian Alps, died in Rome's Santo Spirito Hospital in 1949. Responsible for expelling Jews from Kraków 1940–41 and for sending over 430,000 Jews from Lemberg (Lviv) to their deaths 1942–43.

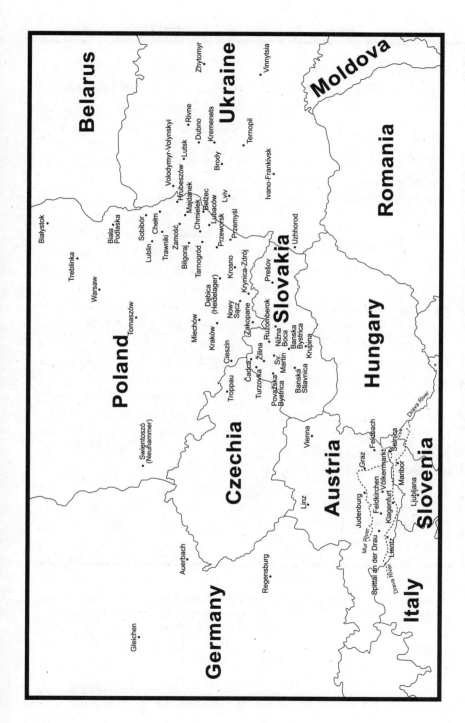

Map 1 Central and Eastern European cities and towns mentioned in the book. Map create by Darian Picklyk.

Map 2 Ukrainians west of the Curzon Line (in "Zakerzonnia"), showing regions that Kubijovyč claimed were predominantly or partially Ukrainian. Map created by Darian Picklyk from Volodymyr Kubijovyč, *Ukraintsi v heneralnii hubernii 1939-1945*. Chicago, 1975.

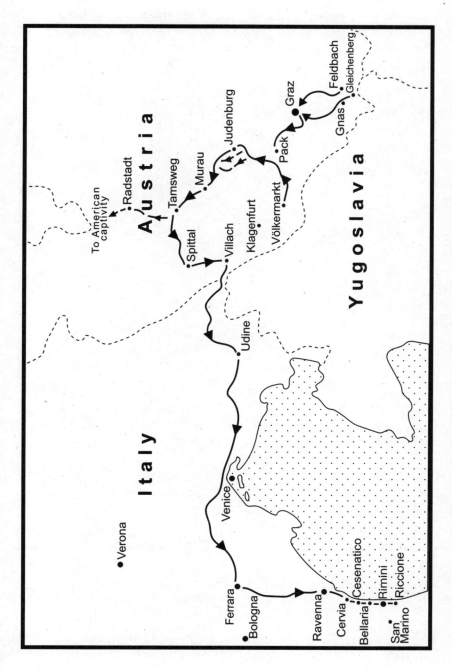

Map 3 The Division's route from the front to internment. Map created by Darian Picklyk.

IN THE MAELSTROM

INTRODUCTION

"All wars are fought twice, the first time on the battlefield, the second time in memory."

VIET THANH NGUYEN, *Nothing Ever Dies*, 2017.

The Galicia Division's creation was announced on 28 April 1943. From that moment until the present it has been one of the most controversial topics in Eastern European history. As opposing views have clashed and conflicting images of the force have confronted one another, two issues have remained dominant: the motivation of the soldiers who enlisted and their actions during the war. The men claimed to have taken German uniforms and weapons with the aim of opposing Stalin's regime and winning political recognition for Ukraine. Even at the war's end most hoped to join the Western Allies and to continue fighting the Red Army. However, the Division's critics have told the history from other perspectives. They have asked: Were the men Ukrainian soldiers or German mercenaries? Patriots or dupes? What did they hope to accomplish? Were they guilty of war crimes? Did they play a role in the Holocaust? The contest over this history has resulted in a large volume of documentation. The veterans alone produced seventy years of journalism, memoir writing, creative literature, and oral testimony, in which they described their experiences and challenged the stereotypes that portrayed them as captives of Nazi ideology or supporters of Hitler's plans for Eastern Europe. This long controversy, which is unique among German military formations, forms an integral part of the

Division's story. *In the Maelstrom* examines the most controversial issues: the reasons for enlisting, wartime actions, and the framing of narratives.

The force was created in 1943, mostly from volunteers. Since the Nazis did not wish to encourage Ukrainian hopes of statehood, initially they did not allow it to be called "Ukrainian." According to their racial policies Slavs were considered subhuman. German leaders therefore promoted the idea that the population of Galicia had been partially Germanized during 150 years of rule by Austria. When the Division was sent to the front in July 1944 it was named the 14th Waffen Grenadier Division of the ss (Galician no. 1). In November the "Galician" moniker was changed to "Ukrainian." Only at the end of the war, shortly before surrender to British and American forces, was a name change allowed to 1st Ukrainian Division of the Ukrainian National Army.[1] Although the force is sometimes referred to as the Ukrainian Division, this book uses the shorthand term "Galicia Division."

There were three categories of Waffen-ss units: German, Germanic, and foreign. They were respectively designated "ss," "ss-Freiwilligen," and "der ss." So, for example, they could be named, respectively, ss-Panzerdivision, ss-Freiwilligen Panzergrenadierdivision, and Waffen-Grenadierdivision der ss. The last translates as "Arms ... of the ss." Most soldiers in units of this third category were neither German nor Germanic and could therefore not be members of the ss (Schutzstaffel, or Protection Squadron).

The Division's recruits trained for eleven months and were deployed on 13 July 1944 against the Red Army. Outnumbered and lacking air support, they were trapped in the so-called Brody pocket. From ten thousand men sent to the front only about three thousand soldiers escaped. Most crossed the Carpathian Mountains at the Uzhok Pass, regrouped on Hungarian territory near Ungvár (today's Uzhhorod), and returned to the training ground in Neuhammer (now Swiętoszów in Poland). Here reinforcements were added from the reserve regiment, the so-called Galician ss Volunteer Regiments and other units. In October the reformed Division was sent to Slovakia to help put down an army revolt supported by two Soviet airborne brigades. Then on 26 January 1945 it was ordered to Slovenia to fight Tito's partisans. This necessitated a month-long trek across the mountains because the railway and main roads were blocked by people escaping westwards. A month later the force was rushed to Feldbach and Gleichenberg in Austria where, in the last weeks of the war, it held the front against the Red

Army and incurred heavy losses, with about sixteen hundred men killed or injured. When the war ended on 8 May it withdrew and surrendered to British and American forces in Austria. Ten thousand men were interned by the British in Italy. They were transferred to the UK in 1947 and released in 1949. About twelve hundred were interned in Germany by the Americans and released within twelve months.

In all, about twenty-five thousand Ukrainians served in the Division.[2] Its strength was around twelve thousand at any given time with another three thousand in the reserve regiment or undergoing training. Of the seven thousand men who disappeared at the battle of Brody in July 1944 some were killed or captured but others joined the underground resistance (the UPA) or melted into the population.[3] The second wave of recruitment in the spring and summer of 1944 was a conscription of all able-bodied men. At this time most recruits were forced into service or signed up to avoid being sent to work camps in Germany or to the Baudienst (construction service) in the General Government (Generalgouvernement, GG), to which Galicia had been assigned as one of five districts.

Researchers have focused on the Division's military history or accusations of criminality. However, many aspects of the wider story have remained unexamined. They include Galician society's support for recruitment, the nature of military training, the fate of teenage youth and nurses who were attached to the force, and the Volunteer Regiments to which some men who enlisted were sent. The postwar period has been particularly neglected. Little attention has been given to life in internment camps and emigration, and even less to the personal experiences of soldiers or their political views. By using memoirs, interviews, and archival materials the present account examines these facets of the history.

Of course, retrospective accounts have to be treated with caution. The earliest were produced in internment camps, where the men tried to explain to the British and Americans their reasons for enlisting and their refusal to be "repatriated" to the Soviet Union. In the years from 1947 to 1949 British authorities discussed transferring the men to the UK, granting them civilian status, and the possibility that some individuals had committed war crimes. The same issues were then re-examined in the 1980s by commissions of inquiry in Canada, Britain, and Australia. In postwar decades the émigré Ukrainian press debated whether the Division's creation had been justified and responded to Soviet and Western accusations. The contest over memory and history continues today, especially with regard to monuments, insignia, and commemorative practices.

The military formation's history has remained a sensitive topic for several reasons. It has been accused of anti-Jewish and anti-Polish actions. This account discusses specific accusations and summarizes recent debates. A number of the German commanders participated in the Holocaust prior to joining the Division. Some Ukrainian late-comers to the Division were also guilty of killing civilians, but the Division was not used either for rounding up or for killing Jews. It was formed as a front-line division on the understanding that it would not be a police formation. However, some enlisting men were sent to the so-called Galician Volunteer Regiments, which were in fact "police" formations, an issue that I discuss. It should also be noted at the outset that the men were aware of what was happening to Jews, as they made clear in interviews. Even though the machinery of the extermination camps was grinding to a halt by the time they were sent to the front, their military actions served to delay the Third Reich's collapse, thus preventing the rescue of remaining Jews. Consequently, they have been charged with playing an accomplice's role in the Holocaust. However, this should be set against another consideration. Many soldiers later stated that they enlisted precisely because they had witnessed the mass destruction of Jews, Poles, Ukrainians, and other populations. They wanted to be prepared, when the occasion presented itself, to fight in a Ukrainian army against all aggressors and hoped to do this at the war's end.

There is another major reason the Division has remained a sensitive topic. The existence of the force sheds light on an issue long veiled in silence – the enormous number of people inside Soviet borders who took German uniforms. General Ernst Köstring informed Himmler on 2 October 1944 that, prior to the invasion of 1941, there had been 100,000 Eastern volunteers and auxiliaries in the air force and navy, and that by 1944 the figure was "between 900,000 and 1,000,000" (Thorwald 1975, 228). Recent research has put the total number from within former Soviet territory in the ranks of the German army, Waffen-ss, and auxiliary police at 1.2 million (Młynarczyk et al. 2017, 168). After the war Western literature avoided this topic. Jürgen Thorwald stated in 1974 that many people simply assumed that these men "must have been nasty traitors, like Quisling, Mussert, or Dagrelle" (Thorwald 1975, xxi). Because Hitlerism was held in abhorrence, there was little interest in searching for distinctions within the German army or the Nazi system. Writers were "apt to condemn anyone who made any compromise with fascism for whatever reason," without looking more deeply into the question (xxii). Although a similar attitude is still prevalent today, there is now an awareness that, without examining the issue of motivation it is impossible to distinguish between different forms of collaboration or to explain why so many individuals from within the Soviet Union wore German uniforms, including an estimated 220,000 Ukrainians.

When the motivation of the Division's volunteers has been discussed the emphasis has been on ideology: the writings of Dmytro Dontsov, the rise of fascism, or the pronouncements of the Organization of Ukrainian Nationalists (OUN). However, soldiers joined under different circumstances, for various reasons. Many in the first cohort of volunteers from the summer of 1943 had completed their secondary education and were motivated by patriotism. They were convinced that their country needed a modern army if it was to break free from Russian rule. Their historical reference point was 1918 and they expected a similar scenario to be repeated: the major powers would exhaust themselves by fighting to a standstill, at which point the alliance between the West and Moscow would break down and the Division would form the nucleus of a Ukrainian army that would fight for independence. Soldiers in the second cohort from 1944 were taken as conscripts or joined because the alternatives appeared even worse: work in German labour camps and construction brigades, life among the forest partisans, or forced service in the Red Army's punitive battalions. A third cohort attached itself to the Division at the end of the war. It included people escaping from Germany or the Soviet Union. Some had served in police or guard battalions; others were avoiding arrest by the Gestapo; some were teenagers who had been sent to operate anti-aircraft batteries or train as medical personnel; and more than a few were civilians who did not want to return to life in the Soviet Union.

Perspectives on this history differ radically. Soviet narratives remained at the level of what Christopher Browning (1993, xx) calls "one-dimensional caricature." They simply denounced the veterans as Nazis, fascists, and war criminals. Any deeper discussion of fellow citizens in German uniform was taboo. This has remained the case in Russia until the present day, largely because the Galicia Division constitutes a challenge to the Kremlin's historiography, which demands the narrative of a united popular struggle against an external enemy. This dogma distracts from any deeper consideration of who wore German uniforms and why, and impedes investigation into the Soviet state's own criminality, which has remained an ultra-sensitive issue from the time of the Nuremberg trials in 1946 until the present. Western narratives have sometimes followed the Soviet template, resorting to the same language of demonization and repeating disproven accusations.[4]

The judgments of the Nuremberg's International Military Tribunal and the reports filed by the commissions of inquiry in the 1980s are also germane to any discussion of the Division.[5] In 1986, a Canadian commission of inquiry concluded that the Division should not be indicted as a group and that charges of war crimes against its members had never been substantiated – either in 1950 when they were first advanced or in 1984 when they were renewed before the commission. Although some historians have since argued that the Division's personnel "fought honourably as soldiers" (Melnyk 2016, 1:12), the charge of criminality continues to be levelled, particularly in the tabloid press and in digital trolling. As will be seen, the reasons have much to do with the image of the Waffen-ss as murderers and, more specifically, with the complicity of some soldiers in anti-civilian actions prior to their joining the Division.

In contrast, a positive narrative of the Division developed in the postwar Ukrainian diaspora and, to some degree, after 1991, in Ukraine. Versions of this narrative contrast starkly with the "soldiers-as-villains" image. They not only reject charges of criminality but assimilate the Division into an overarching story of national liberation. According to this view, practically all armed resistance to Russian rule, even in German uniform, can be justified.

Opposing perspectives have clashed. Victims of German aggression have naturally seen the force as complicit in Nazi criminality, specifically in the victimization of Jewish and Polish civilians, while the counter-perspective has cast the soldiers as patriots and pragmatists who grasped arms from the Germans because they wished to fight Stalin. Both views have sometimes calcified into tropes or memes. Often facilitated by a lack of research, simplified, even mythologized narratives have appeared. One scholar in Ukraine comments that "few historical questions in Ukraine have become as twisted as the history of the 'Galicia' Division and the Ukrainian volunteer movement" (Ponomarenko 2016, 7). While Western tabloids continue to equate the Division with the ss and Nazi savagery, exculpatory narratives present a picture of men forced to take the uniform of one imperialist power in order to oppose another.

Condemnatory accounts have drawn on a particular image of the ss, one that Heinz Höhne had already dismissed in *Der Spiegel* in 1966. He rejected the view of the ss as a monolithic force that controlled Germany and unleashed an apocalyptic racial war (Höhne 1966, 94–5). Instead, he argued that the stereotype of the ss as a state within a state, an organization whose members differed fundamentally from other human beings in their depravity, was an alibi for the rest of German society. During the Nuremberg trials Allied lawyers also found this approach convenient. They used it to separate the ss from other Nazis and to work with the assumption that the ss bore sole responsibility for the "criminal state" (96). After the appearance of Hannah Arendt's *Eichmann in Jerusalem* (1963), which discussed the "almost ubiquitous complicity" of the civil service, and studies such as George Stein's *The Waffen ss* (1966), this view could not be maintained (Arendt 1982, 18, 112–19). It became clear that the idea of a totalitarian state run by daemonic automatons, however useful for postwar German society and US military authorities, was a hallucination (Höhne 1966, 96–7). The ss was no longer seen as uniquely culpable. In later decades the search for guilty parties expanded, with the focus shifting to the German army (Heer or Wehrmacht) and Waffen-ss soldiers, including non-Germans, who were now often described in the same way as the ss – as brutes driven by a pathological psychology and primed for violence by Nazi propaganda or by endemic local anti-Semitism.

Meanwhile the Division's veterans in emigration had come to terms with the fact that they had pursued an illusory goal. Aware that they carried the guilt of association with a reprehensible regime and a war machine that was responsible for enormous suffering and destruction, they continued describing their experiences, analyzing personal motives, and justifying, or regretting, their decisions. Their writings and testimonies examine different aspects of life under occupation in ways that are far more complex than many Western researchers realize. However, as a result of stereotyping, writings on the Division have generally traded in stock images. At one extreme, the soldiers are seen as grotesque ss monsters driven by a *Blut und Boden* obsession; at another, as idealistic victims of an impossible choice. A more nuanced picture has only recently emerged, often as a result of gaps in the Division's history being filled by information from archives and personal testimonies.

For one thing, the veterans themselves did not view the Division in the same way. The cohort from 1943 experienced the war entirely differently from the so-called *kukurudznyky* – a term that comes from the Ukrainian word for corn or maize, *kukurudza*, and was used to describe locals taken in 1944 "from the corn-fields." The experience of men and women in the medical staff, or teenage boys and girls in the anti-aircraft defence, was also entirely different. Their military service was short and, by any reasonable standards, blameless. They spent a few months as conscripts or as child labour and sometimes saw no military action. Other men, however, were hardened fighters who had already accumulated a long and often murky history before they met up with the Division. Some had served in notorious units and had a past to hide.[6]

Many individuals had breathtakingly dramatic stories to tell, which are instructive in historical, political, and psychological terms. The rich texture of their personal accounts has often gone unrecognized because of a tendency to tar all veterans with the same brush or to exonerate them by linking every soldier to the cause of political independence. Both extremes have avoided complexities and contradictory evidence.

Most veterans were born in prewar Poland or Ukraine. Some had served in one or more military formation (Ukrainian, Polish, Soviet, German) and could recount stories of internment in Soviet or German camps. A number had served in the Red Army, had been captured by the Germans, escaped, and were arrested by Soviet forces because Stalin had decreed that no soldier could surrender. Forced into front-line action, they were captured again by the Germans and given the choice of starving or joining the Galicia Division. They chose the latter.

Some recruits were sent by the Germans to France, where they deserted and joined the Resistance. At the end of the war, the French government refused to hand them over to Soviet authorities for execution or imprisonment, and instead allowed them to join the Foreign Legion. A number of men had postwar careers in the Polish, French, British, and US armies. They are described as war criminals in some accounts and decorated heroes of the Resistance or Allied armies in others.

Most men passed through British or American POW camps in the immediate postwar years before building lives in communities around the globe.

To provide some of this detail and to capture the texture of individual lives *In the Maelstrom* makes extensive use of memoirs, which were published in the Division's two periodicals *Visti* (News, 1950–74) and *Visit kombatanta* (Combatant's news, 1961–2014) or in book form.[7] This literature has shaped the Division's image in the diaspora and post-Soviet Ukraine. A creative literature written by veterans has also influenced collective memory.[8] Although uneven in quality, it is frequently illuminating, especially when dealing with attitudes towards the Soviet Union and Germany, war, repatriation, the West, and international politics. It also provides an understanding of how perceptions of the war and international politics changed over time, both for the writers and readers. Such ego-documents and oral interviews, after due attention to their personal and temporal biases, are now widely used in scholarship. Later testimonies, when they are consistent with earlier ones, uncover "a firm core of shared memory" (Himka 2021, 92). This can be said of the written and oral testimony by the Division's soldiers. Individuals who came from different backgrounds, joined at various times, and often held different political views corroborated some basic facts for over fifty years. To dismiss their testimony as "nationalist" is to neglect a valuable source with the heuristic potential offered by personal experience.

Particular attention is paid to two war theatres: the ethnically mixed territories of prewar Poland immediately west of the Curzon Line (sometimes referred to in Polish as "Zakerzonie" and in Ukrainian as "Zakerzonnia") and Galicia (sometimes referred to as "eastern Galicia").[9] Most soldiers were from these two regions and saw action there. The war on these territories is described in quite different ways depending on the narrator's choice of frame and focus. The experiences of German or Soviet soldiers provide a contrast, of course, with those of individuals in the Polish or Ukrainian undergrounds, and with those of Jews who were trying to survive the Holocaust. The concluding section of this book suggests how different contexts continue to influence perceptions of the Division.

At the level of macro-history the account builds on previous research into military and political events.[10] At another level, eyewitness testimonies, interrogation files, oral interviews, and memoirs are used to distill a collective experience, a view of the past shared by larger groups.[11] Contrasting views are indicated by referencing other accounts, particularly those dealing with the Polish underground, Soviet partisans, or Holocaust.[12] An attempt is also made to convey the individual experience, which offers a detailed, "granular" picture of events and a "focalization" that only the personal voice can provide. It is hoped that these levels of narrative complement one another.

Research used *In the Maelstrom* draws on archival fonds in Ukraine, Canada, the UK, Germany, Poland, Italy, and the US. The aim is not to produce a detailed military history of the Division, a task that has been accomplished by researchers like Michael O. Logusz, Michael Melnyk, and Andrii Bolianovskyi. Rather, the focus is on the Division's "long" history, the controversies that pursued veterans after the war and that have been discussed in scholarship, journalism, and popular literature. Some little-known archival materials, memoirs, dissertations, and interviews are used to cast new light on the issues. The book also draws on studies of wartime violence, nationalism, and the Holocaust.[13] Micro-studies of violent conflicts in other European countries, such as Yugoslavia and Greece, provide some comparative perspective on how loss of legal and moral norms contributes to the spread of violence.[14] The populations west of the Curzon Line and Galicia, like many parts of wartime Europe, experienced waves of destruction, including mass deportations, arrests, and killings that traumatized local communities and affected the psychology of soldiers. As these studies make clear, it is not always easy to establish the degree to which political and social pressures, consent or constraint, governed decisions made by men and women. Nonetheless, there is now a considerable body of evidence about the attitudes of the Division's soldiers towards such issues as German propaganda, relations with the Germans who constituted over 11 percent of the Division, and possible outcomes of the war.

In postwar decades veterans modified their views of the war and the Division, partly because life in the West, Soviet Union, or Ukraine shaped their evolution and encouraged new narrative frameworks. The Ukrainian diaspora's need to shape a positive image of the past also affected these views. The former soldiers were continually asked whether the price paid for creating an army had been too high, whether they regretted the decision to serve in the uniform of the Third Reich, a regime responsible for so many atrocities in occupied Europe. *In the Maelstrom* describes how they answered these questions and how a struggle over the Division's legacy has continued. After surviving one maelstrom, that of war, the formation has remained in another, that of public controversy.

PART ONE
MOTIVES

1

GENESIS AND REASONS
FOR VOLUNTEERING

"There's only one moment when the bird of happiness alights
on the ground and must be grasped. If you miss it, you must wait
many years."

YURII YANOVSKYI quoted by Oleh Lysiak, *Vidlamky*, 1996

The Galicia Division went into combat in July 1944 as the fourteenth of thirty-eight Waffen-ss divisions.[1] The first four – the Leibstandarte Adolf Hitler, Das Reich, Totenkopf, and Polizei – had been created in 1939 and 1940 and contained only Germans. In 1940, a recruitment began of "ethnic Germans" (*Volksdeutsche*) living beyond the frontiers of the Reich. At this time "racially acceptable" Danish, Dutch, Norwegian, Finnish, Estonian, and Belgian volunteers were accepted into the 5th Wiking (Viking) Division and the 11th Nordland. In 1941, a legion of French volunteers was formed and became the Waffen-ss Charlemagne Division. When in 1943 the 13th Handschar Division was created out of Yugoslav Moslems, the barrier was broken to recruiting Eastern European Slavs, whom Nazi doctrine designated as subhuman, or *Untermenschen*.

The search at first was for foreign soldiers of "Germanic blood" who would help incorporate their countries into the "Greater Germanic Reich." Despite what Hannah Arendt has written about the immunity of the Dutch and Danes to anti-Semitism, the most successful enlistment was among these two nations (Arendt 1964, 169, 179; Gingerich 1997, 815–16). However, in late summer of 1940 Germans still constituted a majority among the troops. Some prospective non-German recruits were discouraged by the language barrier, others by the ideology, which projected the vision of a Greater Germanic Reich. Nor did the concept of racial solidarity play well in most occupied countries (Gingerich 1997, 825). As a result, when the Viking Division crossed the Soviet border at the start of Operation Barbarossa, only 1,142 of its 19,377 men were Germanic volunteers (recruits from Norway, Denmark, and Holland), although another 1,400 (primarily Dutch and Flemish volunteers) served in the Nordwest Battalion. Eventually the Dutch formed two divisions, the 23rd and 34th Waffen-ss.[2]

Soon after the invasion the German army began absorbing former Soviet soldiers. Recruited or conscripted Eastern units (Osttruppen) were incorporated into the army to guard lines of communication, fight partisans, or reinforce front-line positions. Hiwis (Hilfswillige, or Volunteer Auxiliaries) were employed in non-combat roles, as drivers, cooks, labourers, medical orderlies, porters, and storesmen. Local people were recruited for police work in what became the Schutzmannschaft battalions. These were assigned to border and rear-area security throughout the occupied territories. In total by the end of 1942 close to one million Soviet citizens were in German uniform or taking German orders (Bishop 2005, 69, 82).

Many Russians volunteered to fight Stalin's regime. The Russian National Army of Liberation (RONA) was formed in the autumn of 1941; the Russian National Patriotic Army (RNNA) came into existence in March 1942, expecting to become the nucleus of a future Russian army; the Military Union of Russian People (BSRN) was formed in April 1942 and became the 1st Russian ss brigade. However, best known was the Russian Army of Liberation (ROA), which recognized General Andrei Vlasov as leader. These armies absorbed volunteer battalions, companies, and squadrons, and eventually were designated as divisions of the Waffen-ss (the 29th, 30th and 1st Cossack) or the regular German army (650th Infantry) (Bishop 2005, 73–4).

The ethnicity of these Soviet citizens in the German military is not easy to establish, but it has been estimated that overall there were 300,000 Russians, 53,000 Cossacks (from the Don, Terek, Kuban, Orenburg regions, and the Urals), 221,000 Balts (including 87,000 Latvians in two Waffen-ss divisions and 15,000 Estonians), 220,000 Ukrainians, 50,000 Belarusians, 180,000 Turkmen peoples, 110,000 Caucasian peoples, 60,000 Tatars, and 5,000 Kalmyks (Młynarczyk 2017, 168).[3]

Most Ukrainian military formations were created without any political agreements with German authorities. The men were assigned guard, construction, and support duties (Wachschutz, Werkschutz, Bahnschutz, Baudienst, Hilfswillige) or were sent to the auxiliary police (Schutzmannschaften). Some underground formations made temporary arrangements with the Germans but also fought against them. These included the Polissian Sich formed in Volhynia in 1942, the UPA (Ukrainian Insurgent Army), and the Ukrainian People's Self-Defence (UNS), which was formed in Galicia in 1943 and then renamed the UPA. The only large Ukrainian military formation created as part of an agreement with the Germans was the Galicia Division.

Genesis

Many observers were aware that Nazi objectives in Ukraine were linked to the strategy of *Lebensraum*, or conquest and settlement of new territory. Hitler had already articulated this plan in *Mein Kampf* (*My Struggle*) in 1924, and Alfred Rosenberg in *Zukunftsweg einer deutschen Aussenpolitik* (Future path of German foreign policy) in 1927. Because Hitler was adamant that Ukrainians should not be allowed to bear arms, in 1941, prior to the German invasion, the Abwehr (German military intelligence) had secretly trained only two small battalions named Nachtigall and Rolland for diversionary and sabotage work, and "morale building" in the local population (Struve 2015, 179–80). The battalions were withdrawn and disbanded four weeks after the war began.

Only in 1943, when the tide of war turned against Germany, was the idea of creating a Ukrainian force activated. Otto Wächter, the governor of the Galicia district, initiated a discussion with Himmler on 1 March 1943 and was given permission to form the Galicia Division. The grand proclamation took place in Lviv on 28 April 1943 with a call for youth to join the struggle against Bolshevism, to fight for country, family, and a new Europe. Wächter tried to convince Himmler that the terms "Ukraine" and "Ukrainian" were appropriate and politically useful, but the latter prohibited their application to the Division.[4] Himmler also insisted that Ukrainians serving in the Division could not be referred to as "ss men" and that the Division would be a front line unit and not part of the Order Police (Melnyk 2002, 111; Melnyk 2016 1, 31).

A number of German officials opposed the Division's creation, correctly suspecting that Ukrainians intended to turn against them at the first opportunity. On 15 April 1944 in Kraków Wilhelm Koppe, the higher ss and police leader (HSSPF) of the General Government (GG), voiced his objection, noting the risk of recruiting from Ukrainians and Poles, and the mass desertions that had already occurred from the various Ukrainian police units. In fact, between the autumn of 1943 and February 1945 the number of men who escaped from the Division amounted to six hundred, a relatively low 3 percent of the force (Bihl 1987, 49, 51). However, desertions continued throughout the war, and, in its later stages there was even talk of murdering the German command and marching to a port on the Adriatic Sea to join the British (Pidhainyi 1951, 117–18). As will be seen, in August 1944, after being sent to France, a unit from the Division's reserve regiment mutinied and joined the Resistance.

The men who volunteered in the first wave of recruitment hoped that the force would become the nucleus of a Ukrainian army. Many also weighed the option of joining the UPA. Because they were not convinced that Ukrainians would have control of the Division, some recruits failed to appear when called up. On 10 October 1943 the no shows in Kolomyia numbered 967 out of 2,545; in the Lemko region 180 out of 400; in Stanislaviv, today's Ivano-Frankivsk, more that 100 out of 246; and in Otyniia 60 out of 84 (TsDAVOV, f. 3971, op. 1, spr. 23, ark. 42, quoted in Tovarianska 2008, 72).

Some prominent community leaders warned that the Germans could not be trusted and that the formation would complicate relations with the victorious Allies after the war (Melnyk 2016 1:34). However, Volodymyr Kubijovyč, who headed the Ukrainian Central Committee (UTsK), argued that the Germans would in fact be training a future Ukrainian army and that the force would in the interim provide leverage on German policy. This view proved persuasive.

The population of course opposed Hitler's ultimate aims, which included enslaving them. However, not everyone was enthusiastic about joining the forest partisans. Although Wächter maintained that the Division's creation would prevent a significant number of young people from entering or supporting the UPA, this proved not to be the case. The underground was continually supplied with weapons and goods stolen from the Division's storehouses and hundreds of soldiers deserted to the UPA. Both Wächter and the Ukrainian recruits were aware of a fundamental contradiction in German policy: it exploited Ukrainian nationalism to fill its ranks with local people but simultaneously denied or attempted to control this nationalism. German leaders failed to understand or appreciate the strength of national movements in Eastern Europe, a blindness that stemmed primarily from a faith in conquest, a sense of their own racial superiority, and a conviction that they could ignore the existence of other nations. In addition, those Germans who had some knowledge of Galicia's history tended to exaggerate the local population's attachment to the Austro-Hungarian imperial past.

Wächter had a better grasp of Ukrainian psychology than most Germans. On 28 April 1943, he sent a circular to his recruitment officers outlining how to encourage Ukrainian hopes without offering any guarantees. It read:

Statements that suggest any kind of brotherhood between Germans and Ukrainians are to be avoided.

Similarly, the impression is to be avoided that we are dependent on the help of Ukrainians.

Ukrainians may not be addressed as allies. All that should be said is that they will be treated in the same way as German soldiers.

Neither a positive nor a negative response should be given to the wish of Galician Ukrainians for an independent state. Should the case arise where this is not possible, it must be made clear that the fulfilment of the political aspirations of Ukrainians in Galicia can only be seen as a consequence of the new formation proving its worth and not as a premise of its existence.

Naturally we must avoid anything that could be taken to imply that we look on Galicia as our property, where we can do as we please. It should be strongly emphasized that we respect Galicia as the home of Galician Ukrainians. Any mention of settlement questions [German colonization] is therefore to be avoided. (Adapted from Melnyk 2002, 325).[5]

Reasons for Volunteering

The single most debated question in discussions concerning the Division has been why young people volunteered. In 1975 two researchers listed the following motives:

1. Ukrainian youth were leaderless, misinformed, misguided, and had little idea of what the Germans had in mind for them. They mistook the Division's very establishment as a sign of change in German policy toward Ukraine.

2. They looked on the formation as Ukrainian, saw it as strengthening the Ukrainian position in Galicia and even as the birth of a regular Ukrainian national army.

3. Some were motivated by their hatred for Russians to join a Division that was destined to fight on the Eastern Front.

4. Sympathizers of the UPA joined merely to be trained and lay their hands on arms or even to infiltrate the formation.

5. Immaturity.

6. Fear of being forced to work in Germany.

7. The search for adventure. (Bender and Taylor 1975, 19–20)

This list omits two dominant concerns in the first cohort of recruits: the recoil from Soviet practices and the drive for political recognition. Galicia had experienced a ruinous twenty-two months of Soviet occupation. As a reminder of the Soviet regime's brutality some soldiers even carried with them photographs of the bodies discovered in NKVD prisons in June and July 1941 (Melnyk 2016, 1:14–15).

Sectors of the population in Galicia and Western Ukraine (meaning also Bukovyna and Transcarpathia) accepted news of the Division's creation with enthusiasm. This was not because they sympathized with fascism or believed in German victory. In most cases the opposite was true: the defeat of Germany was expected and an army was seen as needed for protection at the war's end. Many hoped that the Division would play a role similar to that of the Sich Riflemen (Sichovi Striltsi) after the First World War. In 1917 this professional army, created largely from soldiers who had served in the Austrian military, became the core of a national army and fought for independence.[6] The songs sung by the Galicia Division had mostly been composed and sung by this earlier force; they give an indication of the mood among recruits. The most popular one begins: "The volunteers are marching, Like the Riflemen did before. Their helmets shine in the sun, a smile of freedom on their faces. Whoever's alive, join the ranks, to liberate and win our native land."[7] In 1918, after recognizing the Ukrainian People's Republic at the Brest-Litovsk Treaty, the Germans had also created the Blue Coats (Syniozhupannyky) and Grey Coats (Sirozhupannyky) – divisions that were formed out of Ukrainian POWs captured from the Russian army. These men were patriots who wanted to fight for a Ukrainian state.[8]

According to Kost Pankivskyi (1965, 216), the population and all leading politicians in Western Ukraine and in the emigration had long dreamed of a professional army with its own commanding officers. Because the interwar Polish government had prevented Ukrainians from entering officer schools, nationalist forces had in the 1930s tried to obtain military training in various countries. There was general agreement in society that in any major political conflict, when the decisive political moment arrives, foreign governments respect only a people and country with military capability: "In the depths of our hearts we were all guided by the idea that at the end of every war comes a time when tensions are relaxed; at that moment our soldiers could unfurl their flag and make their political demands" (220). The volunteers, according to Pankivskyi, expressed the Ukrainian desire to be a "partner, and not an agent of foreign powers" (216). The crucial argument was that the call issued by recruiters for a united front with Hitler's forces was a concession to the political conjuncture, a way of selling the Ukrainian case to the Germans by aligning with a common struggle against Bolshevism and the Soviet Union. In other words, the "strong" ideology was the call for national liberation and the "weak" one, adopted for convenience, was the celebration of an alliance with Germany.

In memoir literature and postwar interviews veterans often mention two scenarios that were uppermost in their minds at the time of recruitment. One envisioned the war being fought to exhaustion on all sides. Another

Figure 1.1 Volunteers marching in the parade, Lviv, 28 April 1943.

Figure 1.2 Women holding the Galicia Division emblem, Lviv, 28 April 1943.

focused on the expectation that Germany's defeat would lead the democratic West to open a new front against Stalin's totalitarian rule. In both scenarios the existence of a trained army, it was thought, would be of great value to Ukrainians. This was not as far-fetched as might appear from today's

Figure 1.3 Women in the parade. Lviv, 28 April 1943.

perspective. After the war General Reinhard Gehlen, who had run German military intelligence in the east, rebuilt his network and co-operated with the CIA before founding the West German intelligence service. Already in 1945 he considered the collapse of the East-West alliance to be only a matter of time and tried to reach an agreement with the Allies as rapidly as possible (Gehlen 1972, 9–10). In postwar years the Gehlen Organization, which included former members of the SS, worked with the Americans against the Soviet Union. Gehlen commented that Roosevelt "died in the knowledge that he had used Beelzebub to drive out the Devil" (10).

Another argument for the Division's creation focused on the inevitability of recruitment. The Germans, it was said, had already conscripted men and were preparing to form a division out of Ukrainians.[9] Some political leaders felt that under these circumstances it was better to develop a cohesive unit with a Ukrainian identity and command structure. The UTSK had opposed the first recruitment of Ukrainians in 1941, which attracted about two thousand men from supposedly racially appropriate individuals in the regions of Podillia, Pokuttia, and the Carpathian Mountains.[10] They had been distributed among various German units. Because there was no negotiated agreement, no control over their service could be exercised (Gehlen 1972, 221).

When in late 1942 Otto Wächter began promoting the idea of Galicia's unique identity and lobbying for the creation of a separate armed force with an eye to advancing his own political career, and perhaps even his personal rule over most of Ukraine, this prompted the UTsK early in 1943 to support the Division's creation while trying to win as many concessions from the Germans as possible. Pankivskyi (1965, 224) argues:

> Without exception leading circles in Warsaw, Prague and Berlin viewed the creation of an armed formation positively. No responsible agent in our national life was against the Division's creation. President A[ndrii]. Levytskyi and the military agents in the State Centre of the Ukrainian People's Republic [in exile], the leaders of our former political parties, all bishops with Metropolitan Sheptytskyi at their head, evaluated the creation of Ukrainian armed forces in the struggle with Moscow, albeit in the narrow and distorted form of a "Galicia" Division, as a serious and valuable political trump card.

Sheptytskyi's motivation has been debated. Dr Frédéric (real name René Martel), a Frenchman working with the German foreign ministry who had known the Metropolitan since 1928, reported that the latter told him in September 1943: "If the German defeats continue and there is a period of anarchy and chaos, we will be very happy to have a national army to maintain order and counteract the worst outrages until regular Soviet troops arrive" (Hentosh 2014; Magocsi 1989, 138). This statement has been cited as evidence of support for the Division, but it should be noted that Martel wrote what his superior Alfred Rosenberg wished to hear. There is evidence that the Metropolitan categorically refused to submit to pressure from both Wächter and Bisantz to support the force's creation. At one point he even had the latter removed from his office.[11] Significantly, neither Sheptytskyi nor Archbishop Slipyi formally "blessed" the Division during the service on 28 April 1943, and both avoided the military ceremonies. When asked by Martel whether Germany was worse than Bolshevism, Sheptytskyi answered that national socialism was more dangerous because it was attractive to the masses and exerted more power over young people. During this conversation he also condemned the killing of Jews (Hentosh 2014).[12] Sheptytskyi anticipated the Third Reich's collapse and hoped that the Division, as a disciplined army with chaplains, might offer the population

Figure 1.4 Men and women in the parade. Lviv, 28 April 1943.

protection against the intensification of violence that was expected after the German withdrawal. Volodymyr Kubijovyč's report of a conversation with the Metropolitan should therefore be treated with caution. He claimed that Sheptytskyi valued highly a professional military under Ukrainian control and told him: "there is almost no price that should not be paid for the creation of a Ukrainian army" (Kubijovyč 1970, 61). Sheptytskyi may also have felt that, by entering the Division, Ukrainians could be kept out of the auxiliary police or partisans and could be influenced by chaplains. During the solemn inauguration of the Division on 18 July 1943, as the first recruits were being sent to training, Reverend Laba stated: "You have the blessing of your parents and your Church. Therefore, go forth to your crusade not only for the motherland but also for the Christian faith and Christian morality, for freedom of conscience, and human culture, against the Horde invading our land like the Tatars [of old]" (HDASBU, f. 65, op. C-9113, t. 19, ark. 105-25). These comments can be read as a challenge not only to Nazi and Soviet doctrine but also to the OUN and local chauvinists.[13]

The UTSK set conditions for supporting the Division's creation: its Ukrainian character had to be reflected in the name, insignia, and commanding officers; it had to be part of the regular German army because the Waffen-ss did not allow religious care; it had to be fully mechanized, with

Figure 1.5 Governor Wächter salutes volunteers, Lviv, 28 April 1943.

Figure 1.6 Wächter and Bisantz, Lviv, 28 April, 1943.

tanks and planes; and all units had to be deployed only on the eastern front against Soviet forces.[14]

These demands were only partially met. The Division was named "Galician" and given the insignia of the lion rampant with three crowns, which had been the coat of arms of the Kingdom of Galicia-Volhynia from 1253 to 1349 and later was the emblem of Crown land under Habsburg rule. On 16 May 1944, when Himmler visited the force before it left for the front, he admitted that the designation "Ukrainian" would be more correct but stated that the name could not be changed at that time (Bender and Taylor 1975, 31). When, on 12 November 1944, the force was renamed the 14th Waffen-Grenadier-Division der ss (ukrainische 1), soldiers began attaching the trident to their uniforms, and General Fritz Freitag, for the first time, addressed the men as Ukrainians. Ukrainians, however, were not allowed to wear the ss runes. When the first issue of the Division's newspaper *Do peremohy* (To victory) appeared, the cover was censored and removed because it displayed a soldier with the runes (Tovarianska 2008, 35).

General Freitag insisted that all higher officers had to be German. With the exception of Paliienko and Pobihushchyi, Ukrainians were not appointed to any rank above captain.[15] The troops had to understand German commands but could speak Ukrainian among themselves. However, one principle of Waffen-ss formations, the lack of spiritual care, was broken: the Division was assigned Ukrainian Greek Catholic chaplains. Only Muslims in the Croatian Handschar Division had similar religious support – in the form of imams and mullahs.[16]

The utsk demand for the release of political prisoners, including arrested officers of the former Nachtigall and Roland Legions, was partially satisfied. Nachtigall had arrived with the invading Germans but had been withdrawn when its men complained about the arrest of oun-b leaders and the decision to include Galicia in the gg, which negated the idea of Ukrainian statehood. The soldiers of both Nachtigall and Roland (who numbered about 280 and 350, respectively) were then given the option of signing a one-year contract for service in Schutzmannschaft Battalion 201. They fought Soviet partisans in Belarus from March until November 1942, at which point the entire battalion rejected a contract that would have prolonged its service beyond 31 December. The men were disarmed, demobilized, and sent home without boots or coats, while the twenty-two officers were arrested on 5 January and kept in Lviv's Lonskyi prison (Pobihushchyi-Ren 1982, 99–101).[17] Nine accepted the option of entering the Division. The rest, including Roman Shukhevych, eventually escaped and joined the UPA (Kolisnyk 2009, 31).

Another partially fulfilled demand was for individuals who had fled work brigades in Germany or Ukraine to be amnestied. They were allowed a short grace period during which they could apply to join the Division. Other demands, such as for an improvement in the situation of the Ukrainian police or an easing of the economic exploitation, were ignored (Pankivskyi 1965, 227).

Sectors of Galician society put a considerable amount of pressure on youth to join. One veteran recalled the head of a school in Chortkiv leading the entire graduating class through town to the enlistment point, where he told them to sign up (Tovarianska 2008, 65). The final number of volunteers was 81,999, but this was a vastly inflated statistic. The recruitment commissions had been told to boost the numbers by enrolling everyone they could. Of the 53,000 who were told to report to the medical commission 42,000 turned up. From this figure only 27,000 were accepted and 1,400 were immediately released on appeal. In the end, a total of 19,047 were called up for service. Only 13,247 appeared, of whom 1,487 were rejected as sick or infirm. This meant that the real figure of volunteer recruits was actually 11,578 ([Haike] 2013, 21; Melnyk 2016, 1:69–70).

Some demands were met at the end of the war. Shortly before capitulation, senior Ukrainian officers were appointed. General Pavlo Shandruk took command, and the men who had been in officer training for over a year joined the force. The trident became the official insignia and the Division became the 1st Ukrainian Division of the Ukrainian National Army (UNA). The requirement that the force be deployed on the eastern front was fulfilled in so far as it was deployed against the Red Army and partisans who often had Soviet leaders and instructors. The Division was subordinated to the German Army (Heer), which decided where it would serve. Waffen-ss units, because they had received better training and equipment, were normally sent into battle at critical places, which was the case with the Division.

The Division's political importance was tacitly recognized when Sheptytskyi, as head of the Ukrainian Greek Catholic Church, was allowed to provide it with chaplains. These strengthened the force's Ukrainian character and counteracted national socialist propaganda. On Sheptytskyi's request, Reverend Vasyl Laba became the chief chaplain. He was also a member of the Military Board, the body created to maintain liaison with the community.

Governor Otto Wächter, like other German authorities, had until that moment ignored the Ukrainian Catholic Church. His request for chaplains put the hierarchy in a difficult position. It did not want to refuse requests for spiritual care but, at the same time, was reluctant to send its priests into an anti-religious German ss milieu or to give the impression that it approved the Division's creation. According to Laba, Metropolitan Sheptytskyi saw clearly the situation in which the Germans found themselves and "on one occasion said to members of the Military Board 'Gentlemen, you are allying yourselves with bankrupts'" (Laba 1952, 7–8). However, priests were already visiting the recruits at their training ground in ss-Truppenübungsplaz Heidelager (in Pustków, near Dębice in today's Poland) to serve mass, give sermons, and provide counsel. The Metropolitan received numerous letters, requests, and delegations from the men and was moved by their devotion to appoint Reverend Laba as vicar overseeing spiritual matters not only in the Division but also among the youth who had been drafted and the men who had been sent to guard military objects. Initially twelve, and eventually twenty, priests were attached to the Division.[18]

There is little doubt that most volunteers were motivated by patriotism and determined to obtain the military know-how their country required. They served in a foreign army but remained ready to turn against it at the opportune moment. However, whether such a turn was ever a real possibility would be debated in later decades.

The Division was given its own oath of allegiance, which mentioned the struggle against Bolshevism (a reference to the fact that it would fight on the eastern front) before mentioning loyalty to Hitler as commander of the military. This distinguished it from oaths taken by the ss and German army, which only pledged absolute allegiance to the person of Hitler as Führer of the German Reich. The Division's oath read:

I swear by God this holy oath, that in the battle against Bolshevism, I will give absolute obedience to the commander in chief of the German Armed Forces, Adolf Hitler, and as a brave soldier if it be his will I will always be prepared to lay down my life for this oath. (Melnyk 2002, 326)

When between 25 and 30 April 1945 the men took a second oath to the 1st Division of the UNA, they swore allegiance to the Ukrainian people and land:

I swear to Almighty God before the Bible and Cross that under the Ukrainian National Flag I will everywhere and always struggle with arms in hand, without sparing life or health, for my People and my native land Ukraine. Aware of the great responsibility of being a Soldier in the UNA, I swear to faithfully and unconditionally obey all orders of my commanders and to keep these orders confidential. May the Lord and the Blessed Virgin help me. (Hunczak 1993, 95)

The issue of motivation is, however, not a simple one. As many veterans later recalled, in the spring of 1944, during a time when the front stabilized for a few months, there were few alternatives available to young men who faced the Red Army's advance. They could join the forest partisans, something Bandera's wing of the OUN encouraged, but then they would have to conduct anti-Soviet and anti-German guerilla warfare with little training or support. Another alternative was to join the Baudienst, where they would have to dig trenches and do heavy labour on buildings, roads, and railways in wretched conditions. A third was to be shipped to Germany to work in slave-like conditions in factories, where they would be subjected to Allied bombing raids. A fourth was to remain in hiding until the Soviets came and conscripted them into the Red Army. This last alternative not only meant fighting for the detested collective farms, NKVD, and Stalin but also being driven into battle with poor equipment and almost no preparation. Such hastily conscripted punitive battalions (*istrebitelnye batalony*, sometimes translated as "destroyer" or "exterminatory" battalions) suffered heavy casualties.[19] The Germans were aware that conscription into the Red Army awaited any man left behind and, therefore, began capturing all men and sending them to work in Germany or forcing them into their military. In these circumstances, many individuals saw volunteering for the Division as their best chance of surviving the war. This consideration was probably the primary one for many men who joined or allowed themselves to be conscripted in 1944. In fact, about a third of Waffen-ss soldiers who joined at this late stage of the war were conscripts, some of whom were forced into the ranks at gunpoint (Khromeychuk 2013, 62).

It has been argued that volunteers who were not conscripts might not have realized the full scope of Nazi crimes (Khromeychuk 2013, 63). It is more likely, however, that many were aware of the desperate wartime situation, had witnessed the treatment of Jews, and drew the conclusion that whatever circumstances lay ahead it was better to be armed and prepared to fight.

2

COLLABORATORS AND CO-OPERATORS

In postwar decades the co-operation of Soviet citizens with German oc-cupation authorities received little scholarly attention. Soviet researchers were not allowed to acknowledge its scale or analyze its reasons because the official line was that the entire population had wholeheartedly supported a partisan resistance led by the Communist Party. Western scholars also showed little interest in the compromises that civilian populations had to make in order to survive. After the Soviet Union collapsed, a different ten-dency was observable in Ukraine and the Baltic states. The argument was advanced that all forms of resistance to Soviet rule were part of the struggle for freedom, and different forms of collaboration with the German occupa-tion were attempts to chart a path towards national sovereignty (Baranova 2008, 116).

There have been attempts to distinguish between co-operation and collaboration. The first has been defined as "unavoidable and involuntary contact" with the occupation and the second as "conscious and voluntary" co-operation with the aim of "doing harm to one's Fatherland" (Semiriaga 2000, 6). Some researchers have suggested that the concept of collabora-tion should be limited to the political sphere; it should, for example, be distinguished from the desire to survive during wartime. The different forms of contact with the occupying authority have been listed as ranging from the everyday (such as accompanied visits to the cinema), adminis-trative (participation in local government), economic (work in enterprises serving the needs of the occupation and population), and military-political (service in armed forces). One researcher argues that only the last can be viewed unequivocally as treasonous collaboration (10–11). However, even here planned desertion after obtaining training or forced conscription and the imperative of survival require consideration.

The German military and police distinguished between the functions assigned to local volunteers. *Hilfswillige* were used for non-combat purposes (blacksmiths, cooks, drivers, messengers, constructors). *Hilfspolizei* served mainly in the civil administration. When recruited into army units they became self-defence, or *Schutzmannschaften*. When they served at the front they were known as *Kampfverbande* (Baranova 2008, 122). The distinctions are important because collaboration was never a homogeneous and invariable category: some police tried to perform their duties with a commitment to public safety, while others saw the service simply as an opportunity for personal advancement, enrichment, or for revenging their family's suffering under Soviet rule.[1]

Although there were "ideological" collaborators who acted with enthusiasm, the issue facing most of the population was how to oppose German forces. Most chose to accommodate and co-operate until there was an opportunity for open opposition. The wait-and-prepare tactic characterized a wide range of political actors. It was, after all, the way Soviet apologists justified Stalin's adherence to the German-Soviet Non-Aggression Pact (the Molotov-Ribbentrop agreement) in August 1939, although in reality the secret protocols attached to the pact told a different story.[2] Stalin hoped that a German war against France and Britain would exhaust both sides and allow the Soviet Union an advantageous entry into the conflict at a later stage (Moorhouse 2014, 14). The bide-one's-time attitude characterized many militant groups throughout Europe, from the Chetniks in Yugoslavia to the UPA in Ukraine. Many men who joined the Galicia Division thought in similar terms. They gambled that an opportunity to turn their weapons against both Germans and Soviets would present itself. Nonetheless, observers have wondered how they reconciled their patriotism with serving a master as repugnant as Hitler or how they could deny that their service was a form of collaboration.

One answer can be found in the idea of nationalism as a universal proposition. In the nineteenth century, Giuseppe Mazzini first proposed that national self-determination, if good for Italy, should be good for everyone.

Interwar fascism was the distorted postwar heir to such thinking. However, while a fascist of one nation might in principle find common ground with a fellow fascist in another, no form of parity was acceptable to a national socialist. "Nazism," Snyder argues, "is about Germany and cannot be a model for others since both its form and content are specifically German" (Judt with Snyder 2012, 104). Ukrainian liberal patriots of the Mazzini type could to a degree align their desire for self-determination with their own fascist-leaning nationalists. However, both groups were compelled to resist German national socialists. The issue for all Ukrainian patriots was the same: how to steer a course towards self-determination by taking advantage of opportunities presented by the war.

A second answer can be found in the strong societal support for enlistment. To many Ukrainian Galicians the concept of collaboration immediately recalled recent history. Germany's greatest collaborator after the First World War had been the Soviet Union, which secretly helped it rearm and develop an air force. Between 1939 and 1941, the German-Soviet Non-Aggression Pact allowed Hitler to concentrate on conquering Western Europe and bombing Britain while Stalin provided him with enormous quantities of food, oil, minerals, and raw materials. The largest shipments were in fact delivered in 1941. In these years communists in the West were instructed to oblige Hitler by demanding that their own countries stay out of the war. In 1940 the Communist Party of Canada, for example, condemned its government, along with the "bankers and capitalists" who were promoting "imperialist war" (Kirkconnell 1944, 51–7). Similar contortions were practised by communist parties throughout the world (Morehouse 2014, 99–131). By 1941, the occupied European countries were seeking some form of accommodation with Hitler's regime, although some, like Poland, maintained governments in exile in London. Officially neutral countries also benefited from collaborative arrangements with the Third Reich. Sweden, for example, supplied huge quantities of iron ore, without which Hitler's weapons industry could not function, and permitted his troops to use its railways (181). Swiss banks offered the Nazis places to hide and then launder looted assets, gold, and profits from slave labour.

After 1939, many prominent Ukrainian figures hoped that the fallout from an anticipated German-Soviet war would serve their primary political aspiration, which was to escape Soviet rule. Only a few years earlier some four million of their compatriots had starved to death in the Great Famine of 1933–34, a catastrophe engineered by Stalin's collectivization policy and widely reported in Galicia's Ukrainian press. It was also well known that entire strata of intellectuals and cultural figures had been arrested and murdered in Soviet Ukraine in the 1930s. From 1939 to 1941, when the Soviet Union occupied what today are the Western Ukrainian oblasts of Volhynia (Volyn), Lviv, Rivne, Ivano-Frankivsk, and Ternopil, it arrested and deported to Siberia an estimated 190,000 citizens. In June 1941, as the NKVD beat a hasty retreat, it left over twenty thousand massacred people in twenty-two Galician and Volhynian prisons. Seventeen thousand of these victims were in the three Galician oblasts of Lviv, Ivano-Frankivsk, and Ternopil (Struve 2015, 214–15). Thirty-five hundred were killed in the three Lviv prisons, 2,000 in Lutsk, 600 in Sambor, 890 in Chortkiv, 574 in Ternopil, and 550 in Dubno (Morehouse 2014, 271). The massacres became symbols of the Soviet state's criminality and the population's suffering. They were used in agitation by the Germans and by Ukrainian nationalists, but they were also a reality that many people had witnessed personally.[3]

It is impossible to understand the events of the German occupation without examining the effects of this first introduction to Soviet rule. Brutal methods were applied throughout occupied territories with the purpose of decapitating potential political opposition. The massacre of Katyn also took place at this time. It involved the shooting of 21,768 Polish prisoners, who included not only officers but representatives of the prewar elite and administrative apparatus. Among them were 1 prince, 1 admiral, 12 generals, 81 colonels, 198 lieutenant colonels, 21 professors, 22 priests, 189 prison guards, 5,940 members of the police, and 1 woman (Morehouse 2014, 45). Simultaneously, the "Baltic Katyn" involved the execution, arrest, and deportation of 12,000 Lithuanians, 7,000 Estonians, and 7,000 Latvians. Meanwhile, in Bessarabia, an estimated 48,000 were arrested, with 12,000 deported and as many as 8,000 executed or murdered during interrogations (93).

The shootings in Galicia in the first week of the German-Soviet war were ordered by Vsevolod Merkulov, the deputy of the NKVD head Lavrentii Beria. On the day after the invasion Merkulov instructed his subordinates to check the prisons and compile lists of "those whom you deem necessary to shoot," and on the next day he ordered the execution of anyone accused of counterrevolutionary activity, sabotage, diversion, or any anti-Soviet activity (Morehouse 2014, 270). A veteran of the Galicia Division has described the mood in Stanislaviv (Pol: Stanosławów, now Ivano-Frankivsk) in the days after the war began on 22 June 1941:

The omnipotent NKVD worked without pause day and night. They began hunting for people on the town's streets. People fled and hid wherever they could, trying to survive until the Germans arrived. The German front was moving east quickly … In fact, two fronts were approaching: the German army from the west, and the Hungarians from the south, across the Carpathians. Because the Hungarian front was closer to Stanislaviv, they were the first to enter the town. The Bolsheviks left without major battles, but not without a legacy. Word quickly spread that a lot of our murdered Ukrainians had been found in the prison and surrounding buildings … My sister and I went to see the prison. I remember being alarmed even before entering the cellar where the corpses were laid out, because I heard the cries and weeping of women and mothers who had come to identify family members. The stench of decaying bodies carried far. It was impossible to breathe in the cellar without a handkerchief … I saw massacred, tortured young men, some with a bullet in the head … There were two lines of corpses arranged on the left and right side along the wall. Some heads were unbelievably deformed, probably beaten with a hard, blunt object. Some had been shot in the forehead. The clothing was torn and bloodied. All without exception had their heads shaved, looked starved, and had been stacked by other still living prisoners (perhaps friends). There were about 250 victims. A few days later more executed and tortured prisoners were found in the garden of the lawyer Lytvynovych, whose house and yard the NKVD had used for their needs and whom they had taken away. The bodies had been covered with a thin layer of earth. Obviously, the NKVD had been in a great rush. (Vysotskyi 1994, 13)

Like other people hoping to escape Soviet rule, Ukrainians believed that only Germany had shown any interest in destroying the hated Bolshevik system. Western European attitudes towards Stalin's regime appeared to them to be governed by wilful ignorance, sometimes compounded by the misconception, widespread in British communist circles, that the country was a free and compassionate society, a utopian socialist state. George

Orwell (2018, 90) in his 1946 essay "The Prevention of Literature" suggests that this illusion was due to "the poisonous effect of the Russian *mythos* on English intellectual life." The same illusion played a role at the end of the war, when tens of thousands of non-Soviet citizens were handed over to Stalin for immediate execution, an operation that remained concealed from the British public until the publication of Aleksandr Solzhenitsyn's *The Gulag Archipelago* in 1973 and Nikolai Tolstoy's *Victims of Yalta* in 1977.

Some form of collaboration, therefore, appeared to many people a reasonable reaction to what they had experienced from 1939 to 1941. In the weeks following the German invasion Soviet troops deserted in enormous numbers. Entire regiments switched to the German side.[4] Even men who had survived German POW camps, where an estimated 3.1 million of the 5.7 million captured soldiers died, were prepared to fight for the downfall of the Soviet regime (Snyder 2010, 180, 184). Stalin had proclaimed surrender to be an act of treason and abandoned these men. He informed the Red Cross that there were no Russian POWs: "The Russian soldier fights on till death. If he chooses to become a prisoner, he is automatically excluded from the Russian community" (Tolstoy 1977, 34). By refusing to recognize the Hague or Geneva Conventions and completely ignoring its own captured soldiers, the Soviet Union created another reason for desertion to the German side. Of all European countries, only the Soviet state witnessed over a million of its subjects enlisting in the enemy's army (48).

The vast majority did not collaborate for ideological reasons. Even when politics was a motivation, it was related to the experience of Soviet rule. Ideological alignment was impossible because the Nazis did not regard non-Germans as equals, while at the same time "no self-respecting non-German nationalist accepted the Nazi claim to German racial superiority" (Snyder 2010, 397). Most soldiers who fought for Germany were concerned with destroying the Soviet system, or simply surviving. We also now know from the novels of Vasilii Grossman and Alexander Solzhenitsyn that many Red Army soldiers went into battle hoping that their fight against fascism abroad would put an end to tyranny at home. For example, the protagonists of Grossman's war novel *Zhizn i sudba* (*Life and Fate*, written in 1959 but published in the West in 1980) compare Nazi to Bolshevik atrocities and hope that when hostilities end the Soviet regime will reform and become a different country. Mikhail Suslov, the Politburo's ideological chief, found the book dangerous because it might spark a discussion concerning whether the Soviet Union had a right to exist, and he declared its publication impossible for two hundred years.

Soviet deserters feared the NKVD, which continued to commit atrocities at the end of the war, especially against its own people. This was done not out of hatred for Nazis but because returning POWs had been branded as traitors. After the Red Army invaded Finland on 30 November 1939, the latter released and sent home Russian prisoners in March 1940. They were marched through Leningrad under triumphal banners announcing "The Fatherland Greets Its Heroes," then sent to railway sidings, put into wagons, and transported to slave-labour camps. Their conduct during the war was not the issue, nor did anyone suggest they had supported the enemy or imbibed an anti-social ideology: "It was the knowledge they had gained of the non-socialist world that constituted their crime ... It was inconceivable to Lenin's heirs that anyone could come in contact with non-socialist people and ideas and preserve their Marxist faith intact" (Tolstoy 1977, 396, 398). There were four million Soviet citizens in the Gulag when Germany invaded. The authorities sentenced another 2.5 million during the war, and between 1941 and 1943 at least 516,841 deaths were registered among Gulag inmates (Snyder 2010, 403).

According to one official Soviet account, 5,236,130 Soviet citizens were repatriated in 1945, of whom 500,000 were sent to labour camps.[5] Even men who had been behind enemy lines for a short time were suspected of treason. Knowing they would be called collaborators, some avoided returning at any cost. More than a few joined the Galicia Division, an estimated 10 percent of whom were Eastern Ukrainians, meaning they were Soviet citizens on 1 September 1939, as specified by the Yalta Agreement, and therefore liable to repatriation.

This intersection of victimhood and collaboration has been little analyzed. It is well known that many soldiers did not serve willingly and became instruments of the Nazi regime after suffering under the Soviet regime. They were often treated as Askari, the name for the black slave soldiers employed by imperial Germany in its East African colonies. While in German uniform some were imprisoned and executed when they refused assignments; others turned their weapons against the Germans when the chance arose.

The Co-operative Movement

There were also socio-economic reasons German authorities were initially welcomed. Many Ukrainian families were part of the co-operative movement that developed under interwar Polish rule and continued to exist during the German occupation, first in what Ukrainians called "Zakerzonnia" from 1939 to 1941 and then in Galicia in from 1941 to 1944. The co-ops were considered an essential part of the nation-building process and represented an ethos: the desire to bring societal change through economic success. When the Division was created, many parts of Galician society hoped that it would be a protective force against a repetition of disastrous Soviet socio-economic experiments and could help to force regime change in both Moscow and Berlin.

From 1939 to 1941, as the co-ops in Soviet-occupied Galicia were dismantled, their expansion continued under German occupation in "Zakerzonnia" (the Lublin, Przemyśl, and Lemko regions). Volodymyr Kubijovyč had studied the demography of these border communities in interwar Poland and had published several maps displaying their ethnic composition. One map from 1 January 1939, for example, shows pie-charts with the percentage of Ukrainians, Ukrainians using the Polish language, Poles, Polish colonists, Latynnyky (Roman Catholics who used Ukrainian), Jews, and Germans.[6] This research helped the co-ops identify potential areas of expansion in both "Zakerzonnia" and Galicia, and to support education, publications, and charity work in local communities. By the end of the 1930s, the Ukrainian co-ops represented a network of 3,500 enterprises, employed 15,000 people, and had 700,000 members (Markiewicz 2021, 7). They existed without state subsidies, by raising capital from membership dues. Their directors belonged to various political parties and their boards included many Ukrainian Greek Catholic priests.

The network was impressive. In 1936, Tsentrosoiuz (Central Union), which dealt in grain, meat, poultry, and eggs, accounted for 7.5 percent of all egg exports from Poland to European countries. Maslosoiuz (Dairy Union) accounted for 28 percent of the Galician dairy market (Sych 2000, 27, 31). Narodna Torhovlia (People's Trade) developed retail outlets for tea, coffee, cocoa, spices, fruit, and other food products, while Tsentrobank (Central Bank) acted as a credit union for co-op members. By 1937, the entire network constituted 27.3 percent of all co-ops in Poland and had expanded into factories for making bricks, cement, tiles, oil, metal, and chemicals.

The Polish government tried to prevent the network from penetrating markets in Lemko territory and Volhynia. It allowed the army to destroy or damage eight hundred Ukrainian co-ops in these areas during the Pacification campaign of 1930 (Sych 200, 46). Small, undercapitalized Jewish businesses also sometimes felt threatened by the success of Ukrainian enterprises.[7] However, the most vocal opponents were Polish activists in the Lublin voivodeship (province), who feared that mixed Ukrainian-Polish co-ops would become completely Ukrainian. In Tomaszów, Hrubeszów, and Włodawa counties Polish society expressed anxieties about its diminishing influence. Authorities described Ukrainian co-ops as "nationalist," a threat to state interests, and politically subversive. The head of Hrubeszów county, for example, informed the Lublin administration that a Ukrainian co-op in the village of Berest had bought soap from Tsentrosiuz and cigarette wrappers from a Ternopil firm (74). Lublin then notified the Polish co-op union Społem that their stores were selling cigarette papers made by a Ukrainian co-op. Trade with Ukrainian economic institutions was deemed to be "propaganda for the Ukrainian identity among the Orthodox in nationally mixed regions" – something that called for "serious control" (74). In 1934, the Lublin administration issued secret directives demanding the isolation of Ukrainian influences. Its assimilationist policies banned "purely Ukrainian" organizations and any literature originating in Volhynia or Galicia.[8] The culmination of this discriminatory policy was the destruction in 1938 of Ukrainian Orthodox churches in the Chełm region, partly because the priests were considered supporters of a Ukrainian identity. Later, in 1942–43, twenty-two Ukrainian co-op organizers would be assassinated in the Lublin district and 186 Ukrainian co-ops attacked, mostly in Chełm and Biłgoraj counties, as part of the Polish-Ukrainian conflict at that time (156, 278). During the interwar years in these towns and in Galicia there were also large Jewish communities, some of which contained fanatical supporters of communism.[9]

When Germany occupied Poland in 1939, there were between 357,000 and 700,000 Ukrainians in "Zakerzonnia" (Sych 2000, 59). Estimates varied depending on how national, ethnic, and religious criteria were applied, but it is clear that the largest concentration was in three areas: the northern area around Lublin and Chełm, the central area around Przemyśl and Jarosław, and the Lemko area in the southwest. The Lublin district was the most mixed. Although overall Polish villages were more numerous,

Ukrainians were a majority in Hrubeszów county, where the population distribution was 95,430 Ukrainians, 86,621 Poles, and 10,950 Jews. Moreover, local Ukrainian populations were boosted in 1939 by the arrival of twenty to thirty thousand refugees from Soviet-occupied Galicia, many of them cultural activists and co-op workers.[10] They helped to create the Aid Committees (Dopomohovi komitety), which united in April 1940 to form the Ukrainian Central Committee (UTSK) under Kubijovyč's leadership. At this time the Germans allowed some territories to be designated Ukrainian and for Ukrainians to be chosen as heads of towns and villages.

Although German "commissars" were gradually introduced into both Polish and Ukrainian co-ops, these were allowed to continue their work. On the other hand, Jewish co-ops (defined as run by Jews or with over a quarter Jewish membership) were closed down. The removal of this competition created a relatively favourable climate for other co-ops, especially in the early stages of occupation when requisitioning was not onerous. Moreover, Jewish property could be purchased cheaply, a situation that discouraged solidarity with the Jewish population and encouraged scoundrels to enrich themselves, as was the case throughout Europe wherever Jewish businesses were liquidated. Ukrainian co-ops extended their work and hired additional staff. Whether perceived or real, the advantages they enjoyed were an encouragement to remain silent about the ghettoization of Jews. However, it should be recognized that the Ukrainians of "Zakerzonnia" were a vulnerable, stateless people, with no government to represent their interests. While witnessing the fate of the Jews, they themselves lived in fear of deportation, ghettoization, or execution.

The threat was real. On 28 May 1940, Himmler issued a secret memo to a group of ss potentates, with instructions not to reproduce the text. Entitled "Some Thoughts on the Treatment of Alien Populations in the East," it outlined Hitler's policy towards Eastern European populations. The aim was to separate the various groups that inhabited the Polish state (Poles, Ukrainians, Belarusians, Jews, Gorales, Lemkos, Kaschubians) and then to extract the "racially valuable" from the "mush." The rest would be allowed to waste away. By applying this policy, over the next ten years the population of the GG would be reduced to a "low quality," leaderless mass, which Germany could use for its labour needs. Step by step the human stock of the East would be devalued. Jews would be removed first, either through "a large-scale emigration to Africa" or by being restricting "to a colony." Then the concept of Ukrainians, Gorals, and Lemkos would be made to "disappear" (Höhne 1969, 2, 313–14).

Himmler explained how national identities were to be destroyed: their vision of the future would be eliminated and their youth removed. "Racially valuable" children would be taken to the Reich and Germanized; the rest would be systematically stultified. Non-Germans would only be allowed four classes of basic schooling, where they would learn how to count up to five hundred, write names, and be told that divine law required them to obey the Germans and "be honest, diligent and well-behaved" (Höhne 1969, 314). The basic plan for national socialism's aims in the East had earlier been laid out in *Mein Kampf*, where Hitler noted that the Slav population of the Soviet Union, an inferior mass under the sway of Jewish Bolsheviks, had to be removed so that the German *Volk* could control the vast eastern vital space (*Lebensraum*) that stretched as far as the Urals. This conquered space would supply the Third Reich with food and raw materials. It would be populated by Germans; the native population would be deported or enslaved.

Under German occupation, Kubijovyč assumed leadership of the UTSK, the only permitted Ukrainian organization. He tried to obtain concessions in the social, economic, and educational fields – first after 1939 in "Zakerzonnia" and then after 1941 in Galicia. To do so he had to deal with some of the most monstrous figures in twentieth-century history: Hans Frank, Gottlob Berger, Kurt Daluege, Hermann Höfle, Odilo Globočnik, Friedrich Wilhelm Krüger, and Heinrich Müller. In most cases these interventions were mediated by Otto Wächter and the latter's aides, Ludwig Losacker and Otto Bauer. This triumvirate favoured a guardedly pro-Ukrainian policy. They opposed, for example, the Germanization of Lemberg (Lwów, Lviv) and came into conflict with Friedrich Katzmann, the city's SSPF. Losacker was demoted and almost shot for criticizing German occupation policy before being sent to a Waffen-ss penal battalion in Italy (Melnyk 2016, 1:335). With the help of this triumvirate Kubijovyč succeeded in winning some concessions, including a limited reprivatization and a suspension of German resettlement in areas bordering on the Galicia district (26–7).

During German occupation the ideology of the co-op movement to a large degree dovetailed with Kubijovyč's accommodationist rhetoric. Every individual was urged to take responsibility for an enterprise's success.[11] The movement's supporters encouraged expansion into urban areas. One article in *Krakivski Visti* (Kraków news) on 26 November 1940 stated: "The power of a nation lies not only in its nationally aware and organized villages, but also in its towns. As centres of trade, artisanal production and industry, these represent the pulse of the nation. Towns dictate their will to the masses and stimulate them. The quantity and quality of towns are how we measure a people's industrial and commercial civilization" (Lebishchak 1940).

After 1939, Polish society was shocked when Ukrainians were appointed to positions in rural and municipal administrations, and when Ukrainian co-ops separated from the Polish network Społem, many saw this as a case of Ukrainians taking advantage of a privileged position under German rule. By 31 December 1941, Ukrainian co-ops outnumbered Polish in the Chełm and Hrubeszów counties 150 to 139 and 205 to 113, respectively, although in the Lublin district as a whole Polish co-ops outnumbered Ukrainian 1,178 to 545. Nonetheless, Polish co-ops were instructed to boycott trade with the Ukrainian network (Sych 2000, 78, 85).

The situation was further inflamed by the arrival of Poles whose land in Galicia had been confiscated by the Soviet regime. These people were mostly colonists and military veterans who had been granted lands in the interwar years. Prior to 1939 they owned 11 percent of the arable land and, according to one researcher, constituted 80 percent of the large landowners in eastern Galicia and Volhynia (Dean 2000, 10). The Soviet regime also deported around 200,000 Poles and 70,000 Jews, along with 25,000 Ukrainians and 20,000 Belarusians from its newly acquired territories. It shut down private shopkeepers, 74.3 percent of whom were Jews (Sych 2000, 102, 105). The Polish community in Galicia, in particular its nationalistic element, was acutely aware that it had lost its former hegemonic status.

When Germany invaded the Soviet Union in 1941, both Poles and Ukrainians were drawn into the new administration. It has been calculated that during the war 260,000 to 280,000 Poles and Ukrainians worked for the occupation regime, mostly in local administration (Markiewicz 2021, 127). Poles still constituted a majority at many levels, and it was German policy to play them off against Ukrainians.[12] Fritz Arlt had in 1940 conceived of welfare work as a political means for splintering non-Germans. By controlling the distribution of material and financial aid the Germans aimed to prevent the development of any solidarity between the occupied populations (Markiewicz 2021, 48). They also retained the collective farms, which they renamed *Liegenschaften*, converting only 8 percent back into co-ops (Dean 2000, 108). Within the GG as a whole the Galicia district accounted for more than half these farms, 1,058 out of 2,016, and a third of all the agricultural land, with the greatest proportion in the Chortkiv, Lviv, and Ternopil counties (Sych 2000, 135). Germany allowed a limited restoration of the co-op network because the destruction of economic and commercial life under Soviet rule had left them with few short-term alternatives. German commissars were introduced on 5 March 1942, but until then the co-ops were largely self-governed. After this date, according to one researcher, a period of despoliation began. Vast amounts of grain and livestock were extracted, which reduced some of the rural population to subsistence farming and drove it to support the resistance movement (Dean 2000, 111–12).

In the GG, during the initial months of German occupation Ukrainians built a network of 4,078 coops, of which 3,217 were in Galicia (Sych 2000, 149). The first issue of the Ukrainian Co-op Union's newspaper, which appeared on 5 May 1942, outlined a strategy of unity in the interest of survival. Economic life, it argued, had to be maintained and developed, not sabotaged. However, acquiescence to German designs did not necessarily mean approval. The co-ops straddled the ground between legal and illegal work, collaboration and resistance. On the one hand, they fulfilled their quotas for the Germans; on the other, they supported charities, paid dues to the UTSK, and, like the Polish co-ops, supplied their underground with goods. Two Ukrainian co-op leaders, Andrii Palii and Mykhailo Khronoviak, joined the Military Board when recruitment to the Galicia Division began.

Ukrainian and Polish co-ops did not at first come into direct conflict in Galicia, but there was growing tension. *Lvivski visti* (Lviv news) on 18 February 1943 encouraged readers to buy from Ukrainian enterprises (Barychko 1943). By mid-1943 and early 1944 the Polish underground was calling for a boycott of "Ruthenian" co-ops, arguing that they represented "the Ukrainian identity that opposes us" (Sych 2000, 155). There was an anti-Semitic tone to some agitation. One report in *Krakivski Visti* on 16 May 1942 linked the disappearance of Jews from public life in Lviv during the first weeks of the German occupation with the growth of a Ukrainian administration, the revival of co-ops, and the reopening of their shops (Klenovych 1942).

By the end of the German occupation a socio-economic change had occurred in Galicia. This was due to the removal of Jews and Poles, and the reduced influence of Polish co-ops, which could no longer rely on state support. The demographic, economic, and political balance had shifted in favour of Ukrainians. Whatever their attitude towards Germany, many Ukrainians viewed "their" co-ops as proof that they could manage their own economic life and be agents rather than victims of change. The co-op commitment to daily work in the interests of economic betterment was a way of resisting foreign occupation, but it also expressed a faith in the gains that could be made under occupation. In the interwar period much of Ukrainian society had learned to work towards incremental gains. Its parliamentarians in the Polish Sejm and its co-operative movement taught it how to manoeuvre within a hostile political structure. When the Germans announced the creation of the Galicia Division, some observers interpreted this as a concession wrung from the occupier, a small victory of the colonized, one that could be used to advance Ukrainian interests.

3
KUBIJOVYČ, PANKIVSKYI, AND THE UKRAINIAN CENTRAL COMMITTEE (UTSK)

"That was our aim, to take our country back."
SOFI OKSANEN, *When the Doves Disappeared*, 2012

Within the Ukrainian community Kubijovyč was the key figure in the Division's creation. Born in 1900 to a Ukrainian father and Polish mother in Nowy Sącz in Poland's Lemko territory, he was raised a Greek Catholic. According to an accepted practice in mixed marriages, a son followed the father's religion and a daughter the mother's. The town was predominantly Polish and Jewish. As a boy Kubijovyč had good relations with Jewish classmates, who helped defend him against attacks from Polish youths. He later maintained close relations with some Polish school friends, even though they fought for different sides during the Polish-Ukrainian War in 1918–19 (Kubijovyč 1970, 11–12). Kubijovyč served in the Ukrainian Galician Army (UHA), then continued his studies and in 1923 obtained a doctorate in geography from Kraków's Jagiellonian University, with a specialization in the demography of the border regions separating Ukraine, Poland, Slovakia, and Belarus. This research displeased the Polish Ministry of Religion and Education, which suspended him and, in 1939, banned him from lecturing. The Kraków police came to arrest him on 1 September 1939, but the outbreak of the Second World War on that same day saved him from the notorious

Bereza Kartuzka prison. He remained in Kraków, on the German side of newly partitioned Poland. The Soviet state banned and destroyed his works when it occupied the eastern Galicia roughly up to the Curzon Line.[1]

According to Kubijovyč (1970, 38), 500,000 Ukrainians lived in what Germany now called the General Government (GG). Most of this population was in "Zakerzonnia" (lands immediately west of the Curzon Line), where refugees from Soviet rule now appeared, but there were also tens of thousands of earlier émigrés in Poland and neighbouring countries, who had come after the fall of the UNR. Germany immediately banned all Ukrainian political parties and cultural organizations except for the UTSK. As a well-known scholar with no party affiliation, Kubijovyč was appointed the UTSK's head in March 1940 and formally acclaimed at a meeting in Kraków that took place between 13 and 15 April 1940. He oversaw relief and cultural work, and represented the community in meetings with German authorities.[2]

Charity work focused on developing community kitchens and safe places for refugees, while cultural work focused on creating kindergartens, schools, youth groups, and helping churches. Kubijovyč maintained contact with Hans Koch (a historian born in Lviv, who had served in the UHA before becoming an advisor to the Abwehr), Alfred Bisanz (another former officer in the army), and Theodor Oberländer (the Abwehr's liaison with Ukrainians). They helped him obtain a building in Kraków, known as "Koch Place" (Kochstelle) among refugees who came there for help. It soon became the centre of Ukrainian life in the GG (Struve 2015, 97, 166–7). Kubijovyč wrote numerous letters and memos to German authorities explaining Ukrainian history, asking for aid in developing education and cultural life, and pledging Ukrainian support for Germany.[3] He met with Hans Frank, the governor of the GG, and wrote to the Gestapo's chief Heinrich Müller protesting the mistreatment of Ukrainians.

In his dealings with German authorities Kubijovyč "spoke Nazi" and adopted an obsequious tone, paying homage to Hitler and recognizing German superiority. According to Bisantz, the UTSK, initially at least, received funding from the Abwehr every month. Ukrainians received the same ration cards as Germans and were permitted radio receivers, something denied the Poles (Markiewicz 2021, 5). Other concessions included a degree of religious tolerance, the opening of gymnasiums (high schools) in Chełm and Jarosław, permission for some Prosvita reading rooms and theatres, and the transfer to Ukrainian use of a number of former Polish and Jewish properties, such as publishing houses. Kubijovyč's plan was to strengthen Ukrainian communities in mixed territories that he considered ethnographically Ukrainian. He advocated the removal of Jews and Poles from these regions. Although his ideas were not implemented, they contributed to anti-Jewish and anti-Polish feelings, and "showed a willful blindness toward the plight of the Jews" (104–5). It should be noted, however, that these regions had in the late 1930s suffered forced conversion to Roman Catholicism, social discrimination, and Polonization in education. Polish authorities tried to make them bastions of Polishness in the same way as Kubijovyč now wanted to make them bastions of Ukrainianness. In 1939, the civil administration of the Lublin voivodeship had even drawn up plans "to ethnically cleans the Ukrainian-inhabited regions" (12).

Perhaps Kubijovyč's most controversial decision, however, was to support the creation of the Galicia Division. He explained his motives in a letter to Vasyl Veryha from 5 December 1966:

> Basically, the question is clear. Ukrainians wanted to have armed units. After the outbreak of the German-Soviet war I wrote a memorandum on this matter and raised the question several times. But it was Governor Wächter who succeeded in negotiating permission for the Division, without asking Ukrainians. Therefore, at the outset, the organized Ukrainian community had no voice in the creation of this military unit. I intervened and after long negotiations with Governor Wächter succeeded in gaining some Ukrainian rights in the Division. In exchange I signed a call to the community to enter the Division, and in doing so became co-responsible for it. (LAC, MG 31, D203, vol. 12, file 54, V. Veryha)

In a letter to Volodyslav Vaskevych on 9 May 1975, he wrote: "all revolutionary undergrounds, including the Ukrainian and Polish, had to have a secure place, funds – a debt that had to be paid" (LAC, MG 31, D203, vol. 2). The faith in practical work, organization, order, and discipline underpinned Kubijovyč's thinking. It should be recalled, however, that although Wächter's approach was courteous (did they want a Division? would they co-operate in its creation?), the governor of Galicia made it clear that it would be raised forcibly if necessary and that "the reply could not be negative" (Pankivskyi 1965, 223).

On 28 April 1943, the Division's creation was announced with great fanfare in Lviv in the presence of German representatives from government, party, army, and police, alongside Ukrainian representatives from the churches, co-operatives, press, UTSK, and Military Board.[4] Kubijovyč stated: "Today is for Galician Ukrainians a truly historic day, because with today's state act one of the most sincere desires of the Ukrainian people has been realized, to take part in the armed struggle against Bolshevism. This desire, which has been expressed at various times since 22 June 1941 results from the conviction not only in leading circles but in the whole nation that Bolshevism is our greatest enemy and is bringing us not only material and spiritual ruin but also death as a nation" (Kubijovyč 1943a).

After the ceremonies, Wächter and others from the German administration attended a service in St George's Cathedral conducted by Yosyf Slipyi, the Coadjutor-Archbishop to the Metropolitan, who did not attend. Simultaneously, a strong campaign of agitation was mounted in the press. Older men, including former soldiers of the Sich Riflemen, marched to sign up in order "to set a good example." However, under various pretexts most immediately withdrew their applications, claiming that their work elsewhere had been deemed too important, which, of course, led to widespread ridiculing of the "reclaimed."[5]

On 29 April, *Lvivski visti* published Wächter's speech from the previous day. It stressed Galicia's role in defending Europe against Huns, Mongols, Tatars, and Turks, and the contemporary desire to fight Bolshevism ("Promova Hubernatora" 1943). Bisantz was quoted as welcoming the dawn of a new era in Europe, heralded by a great war of national liberation ("Nabir" 1943). On 6 May *Lvivski visti* printed Kubijovyč's speech from the previous day:

> The long-awaited moment has arrived when the Ukrainian people will again have the opportunity to come out with gun in hand to do battle against its most grievous foe – Bolshevism. The Führer of the Greater German Reich has agreed to the formation of a separate Ukrainian volunteer military unit under the name ss Riflemen's Division "Halychyna" [the Ukrainian for Galicia].
>
> Thus we must take advantage of this historical opportunity; we must take up arms because our national honour, our national interest, demands it. (Boshyk 1986, 183).[6]

Kost Pankivskyi, who headed the UTSK's Lviv office and acted as Kubijovyč's deputy, has described the positive attitude towards the Division's creation: "We wanted to let the world know that we existed and wished to live. There were various paths to expressing our desire. One of these paths was the Division" (Pankivskyi 1965, 215). Most official documents from the time contained the phrases "New Europe" and "brotherhood with the German people." However, Ukrainian recruiters privately informed the population that this was a German requirement, an act of lip service, and that the real motivation was the Ukrainian drive for statehood.

At a meeting of the UTSK on 10 December 1943, Kubijovyč stated that organizing the Division had been the year's most important act, although he admitted a serious shortcoming – the lack of a "clear positive political underpinning." He also pointed out that some of those called up never appeared, and he mentioned desertions (LAC, MG 31, D 203, box 18, file 21, 4). Six months later, at a meeting on 21 June 1944, he stated:

> Political sense demands the existence of a Division. Creation of armed forces in the forests is a utopia, a fantasy. The Division made it possible to expect an improvement of mutual relations with the Germans ... The most important thing now is the army, and the best school is the German army. At the moment several tens of thousands are on their way to the front. Besides the reserves there are 500 young candidates in officer training. Independently of the Division in various places we are living through mobilization. With the shifting of the front to the west, there are three possibilities: men will be taken into the German army, the Bolsheviks will mobilize them and spread them throughout the Red Army, or they will go into the forests. (LAC, MG 31, D 203, box 18, file 21, 3)

The key thing, he argued, was to provide training for thousands of young people who would learn military virtues, decisiveness, and endurance.

His aversion to the underground was linked to the spread of terrorism and mass murder in 1943, both in Volhynia and west of the Curzon Line. Because the call for desertions by the OUN-B (Bandera's wing of the Organization of Ukrainian Nationalists) had enjoyed some success, in the spring and summer of 1944 the UTSK organized a counteraction against what it called the underground's "demagogy" (Pankivskyi 1965, 247). "The

50 • MOTIVES

disintegration or collapse of the Division," according to Pankivskyi, would have been a blow not only to the UTSK, "but to us as a nation" (247).

When it realized that some volunteers to the Division had been diverted into police regiments for anti-partisan activity, the UTSK complained. In the summer of 1944 this eventually led to incorporation into the Division of men who still remained in these regiments. The wider society, however, did not appear concerned with the fact that some volunteers had been sent to police regiments, nor did German-controlled Ukrainian newspapers.

Pankivskyi headed the UTSK's efforts in Galicia for three years.[7] He saw eye to eye with Kubijovyč on the need for community work, warned of the dangers of anarchy, criticized the OUN-B's adoption of "Bolshevik methods" and its "belief that violence can achieve everything" (Pankivskyi 1965, 133). In postwar memoirs published in 1965 he expressed faith in the values of liberal democracy, which "were worth far more than the brutality of total-itarian tyranny, whether Bolshevik or nationalist" (135). Looking back on the war years, he wrote:

> Today we live in a time when not only Ukrainians but everyone tries to show that they always opposed the Germans and were enemies of Hitler, how they never had any contact with the Germans, but on the contrary played a great role in the resistance against them, how they were persecuted and imprisoned, and how they miraculously survived German occupation ... I write about cooperation with the Germans positively and assess various sides of that cooperation, whether it was useful for Ukrainians and amplified Ukrainian work in all areas of life. Without ignoring the criminal activity of Germans, especially the Gestapo and various German government officials, even when speaking of German ruthlessness and abuse, I also look at how much the Ukrainian people invited this by their thoughtless behaviour, by heedlessly provoking the Germans. (6–7)

These comments constitute his apologia for working with the Germans. He refused to glorify the "revolutionary" aspect of life, but, like his admired conservative thinker Viacheslav Lypynskyi, emphasized the "organiza-tional" aspect (8).

In his 1965 memoir, Pankiviskyi wrote that, during the first two months of occupation, Ukrainians did not view the Germans as aggressors but, rather, as liberators who, they hoped, would improve their situation. In the following months, he argued, the Galicia district remained an oasis of calm between other districts of the GG in the west and the Reichkommissariat Ukraine in the east. The successful harvest in 1942 improved the situation, and once the shock of executions and arrests in the first weeks had passed, people "learned how to approach the lower German representatives of power" (Pankivskyi 1965, 269). Only gradually, he wrote, did the Galician population learn about the brutal war in the east, the mass transportation of people to the Reich for work, the terror, and the Polish-Ukrainian struggle in Volhynia: "There was before the summer of 1943 no mass repression, an endemic feature of Hitler's regime, with its system of hostages, collective responsibility of families and communities, burning of villages, deliberate and unnecessary resettlement of people, killing of invalids, and so on. These things began in the third year of occupation" (271). According to Pankivskyi, the extermination camps for Jews were located outside Galicia's western border in the Lublin district, and therefore, presumably, people could choose to ignore their existence. He also euphemistically referred to the ghettoes in Galicia as "Jewish labour camps" and made only brief mention of the Lviv camp on Yanivska Street (Pol: Janówska), commenting that it employed guards composed of "criminals, *Volksdeutsche* and Soviet prisoners of war" (272–3).[8]

In his view, the attitude of Galicians changed fundamentally when Soviet partisan groups appeared in July 1943 and exposed the weakness of German rule. The news of defeats on other fronts and of Soviet advances in the east stiffened anti-German resistance among locals, and the anarchy in Volhynia began to spread to Galicia. At that point the OUN began a campaign of violence in Galicia and auxiliary troops serving the Germans responded by taking hostages and staging public hangings. Despite Metropolitan Sheptytskyi's powerful letters against murder and anarchy, personal vendettas multiplied, along with thefts in co-ops and stores, which were all justified with patriotic slogans. "As far as I know," Pankivskyi (1965, 289) wrote, "neither the leadership of the OUN, nor the command of the UPA distanced themselves from a single action, from a single killing."

This account raises numerous contentious issues, especially the degree to which the UTSK's work with the Germans served the population rather than the occupation, and the point at which co-operation became collaboration – the betrayal of conscience, moral norms, or the political cause. It is not clear that the community was so starkly divided between those who worked with the German administration and nationalist partisans, nor is Pankivskyi's silence on the mass murder of Jews credible.

His response to these criticisms was implicit in the assertion that "a whole people in its entirety cannot go underground, or move abroad ... People have to live, regardless of what the occupying power thinks and plans to do. Someone has to represent them" (Pankivskyi 1965, 434). The national interest "often demands that politicians choose the lesser of two evils and work with those who are enemies of our enemy, even though they are not our friends" (434–5). This, he insisted, was the accepted view in the first months of the German occupation, when no one suggested that fighting the Germans would benefit people. The Germans were seen as the most recent occupation force, through whom the situation might be improved. According to Pankivskyi, German plans for Ukraine were initially unknown and therefore could appear "no better or worse than those of our other occupants." The necessity of working for the Germans also provided Ukrainians with a chance to work for themselves, and the UTSK represented "a stage in nation building, the only possible one that existed under Hitler's rule" (445).

Volodymyr Yashan, who worked in the civic administration of Stanislaviv, has also left a memoir, which is based on notes he made when the Hungarians and Germans occupied the city in between 1941 and 1944. He recorded details of many German atrocities, political murders by the OUN-B, attacks by both Ukrainian and Polish partisans, the Kovpak raid in 1943, and the deportation and killing of Jews. Although his justification for collaboration resembled Pankivskyi's, he presented a much more harrowing account of the struggle to maintain some semblance of legality and order, which was everywhere undermined by arrests, executions, ghettos, assassinations, reprisals, food requisitioning, deportations, and violence by armed gangs.

The memoir points out that almost the entire Jewish population was killed: the city's overall population diminished from 53,000 in October 1941 (26,000 Jews, 20,000 Poles, 10,000 Ukrainian) to 43,285 in December 1942 (19,707 Poles, 16,499 Ukrainians, 604 *Volksdeutsche*, 80 Jews) (Iashan 1989, 59). From January 1942, each day 120 to 150 people – apparently Jews – were executed in the Stanislaviv prison on orders of the Gestapo chief Hans Krüger (77). These facts contradict Pankivskyi's assessment of the situation.

Nonetheless, it is clear from the memoirs of both Pankivskyi and Yashan that, after the initial illusions had dissipated, the population viewed the occupation with loathing. Part of Pankivskyi's argument in support of the Galicia Division's creation rested on the need for order and the desire to take advantage of opportunities. A military force, he suggested, would be required to prevent the worst expressions of disorder. This argument, however, was double-edged and contradictory: it was clear that the lawlessness was also a product of German rule. Nonetheless, many people associated the Division with hopes for protection, even salvation – from Bolshevism, German rule, and local criminality. They projected onto the soldier an idealized image of the warrior-saviour: he was to remove social evils and solve political dilemmas. Those who held this attitude did not see the Division's "collaboration" as blameworthy. Nor did creation of the force lessen their disgust with German brutality or their opposition to Hitler's plans for the Slavs.

The Ukrainian Central Committee

Kubijovyč argued that the Military Board had to do "everything possible" to recruit people to the Division. The Germans, he said, "have done something for us, so we have to do something for them" (TsDAVOV. F. 3971, op. 1, spr. 7, ark. 50). To understand his view of the repayable debt, it is instructive to glance at his summary of the UTsK's achievements.

On 7 and 8 January 1940, at a meeting in Chełm, he outlined the organization's goal of making "Zakerzonnia" a Ukrainian "Piedmont" through education ("Protokol zizdu Ukr. Dop. Kom. Liublynskoi oblasty," LAC, MG 31, D 203, vol. 18, file 1, 2). A year and a half later, when the Lviv branch was set up, he summarized the work accomplished in *Ukrainski shchodenni visti* (Ukrainian daily news), the organ of the Lviv city council, on 27 and 29 July 1941. The UTsK, he wrote, represented "the interests of the general mass of Ukrainians to the German authorities." It had sections devoted to organizational work, social security and labour, economic life, culture, youth and family, finances, schools, and communications. Separate committees dealt with the Ukrainian Catholic and the Ukrainian Orthodox Church (Kubijovyč 1941, 27 July).

He listed 26 Ukrainian Aid Committees (UDKs), 46 regional and 109 county delegate bodies, 965 trusted representatives (muzhi dovirria), and 235 fully employed paid staff. Membership dues or taxes were paid by all

54 • MOTIVES

members of the UDKs and all Ukrainian enterprises and institutions. The organization oversaw 914 schools (12 private) with 1,398 teachers and 91,789 children; 2 co-ed gymnasiums in Chełm and Jarosław with 35 teachers and 1,037 pupils; a teacher training school in Krynica (Ukr: Krynytsia) with 3 teachers and 160 students; 9 schools of agriculture with 23 teachers and 2,368 pupils; 6 schools of economics with 18 teachers and 203 students; and 7 schools of commerce with 32 teachers and 610 students. The Ukrainian Educational Society (UOT) supervised the work done by all previous cultural organizations, such as the Prosvita reading societies, which had been banned by the German government. It had 808 branches with 42,045 members, who organized 526 libraries, various self-education groups, women's sections, theatres, choirs, concerts, and help for the illiterate (Kubijovyč 1941, 29 July). All these activities were aided by the refugees from Galicia.

The UTSK created the Ukrainian Publishing House (Ukrainske Vydavnytstvo) and the newspaper *Krakivski visti*, which, under Kraków's more lenient censorship, printed information that could not appear elsewhere (Pankivskyi 1965, 296). However, the newspaper was still subjected to censorship. The editor had to report to German authorities and to face demands that some materials be printed.[9] It was clear to readers that the situation was worse for *Lvivski visti* (Lviv news), which had been set up by the Germans as their own periodical and published far more propagandistic and anti-Semitic materials.

In spite of censorship and paper shortages, the publishing house produced numerous titles, including literary classics banned in Soviet Ukraine. It was organized as a commercial union and returned all profits to the publishing fund. From December 1941 its offices were in Kraków and Lviv. The first city published the daily and weekly *Krakivski visti*, edited first by Borys Levytskyi (Lewytszkyj) and after 1943 by Mykhailo Khomiak (Chomiak); the daily *Kholmska zemlia* (Chełm land) edited by Stepan Baran; and the monthly *Vechirnia hodyna* (Evening hour), edited by Roman Kupchynskyi. Lviv published books, the monthly journals *Mali druzi* (Little friends), edited by Bohdan Hoshovskyi; *Doroha* (Path), edited by Yurii Starosolskyi and Olha Kuzmovych; and *Nashi dni* (Our days), edited by Ivan Nimchuk and Maria Strutynska. The publishing house enjoyed success because of a demand for the printed word and because Galicia's school system had finally allowed a Ukrainian publisher into the profitable textbook market.[10] The results were impressive. When, after spending the war outside

German-occupied territory, the Polish writer Paweł Hostowiec (pseudonym of Jerzy Stempowski) in 1946 saw the publication catalogue, he commented that "no people on the continent succeeded in doing as much for literature and publishing" in this period (Pankivskyi 1965, 349).

The UTSK's Lviv branch fostered national unity by consulting with Metropolitan Sheptytskyi on major issues. When in Lviv, Kubijovyč visited the Metropolitan to discuss German demands for food levies, work forces, and the Division's creation. The UTSK coordinated its hunger relief with the Greek-Catholic Church. War and Soviet collectivization had disrupted agriculture, resulting in starvation during the winter of 1941 and spring of 1942. The UTSK secured permission for individuals to transport across regional borders as much food as they could carry. It also rescued starving children in the Carpathians. In early 1942 some twenty-five thousand were temporarily resettled. Dmytro Paliiv headed this work from Lviv until the German police banned him from living in the Galicia district, but the most important work was done by peasants, who sacrificed food, transported the children to assigned places, and took them into their homes for several months (Kubijovyč 1970, 49). The organization also succeeded in releasing about thirty thousand Red Army POWs.

An estimated 250,000 labourers were shipped from the District of Galicia to Germany between September 1941 and October 1942 (Pankivskyi 1965, 209). The organization made efforts to help them in transit camps and to support their families. It distributed food and literature, and demanded adequate payment and vacations. In Pankivskyi's estimate, only a quarter of the workers saw any of the promised benefits, which included one to three weeks leave after a year's work and ten to twelve days unpaid leave in case of family emergencies. The UTSK was able to secure leaves for only one thousand workers (210). When people learned of work conditions they refused to work in Germany or for the Baudienst, which took people from the age of sixteen, even though the minimum was supposed to be eighteen (211). The UTSK tried to help this youth with lectures, books, newspapers, sporting exercises and games, collective visits to theatres and cinemas, and training courses. Local German authorities, who were primarily concerned with reducing the number of runaways, supported these efforts. From 1943 students were sent to this forced labour; all those born between 1921 and 1926 were told they had to serve six months if they wished to continue their studies (212). When work brigades for youth were first created in September

1941, police detachments compelled students to transport and bury executed people, mainly Jews. The UTSK's protest put an end to this use of youth labour. The organization also regularly sent memos to the German administration complaining about shootings, executions, and mistreatment.[11]

As in "Zakerzonnia" prior to the German-Soviet war, the relief work in Galicia after the summer of 1941 was accompanied by cultural and educational work. Regional committees raised money from local citizens through fund-raising drives, and, by 1943, the Lviv branch had a staff of four hundred (Pankivskyi 1965, 208).[12] It provided nine shelters for 286 individuals. In December 1943 its 1,366 community kitchens served 104,000 people (311). It ran 7 creches for 218 children, and 56 orphanages and safe houses. In August 1943 it found homes for 2,555 orphans and children of parents sent to work in Germany. Throughout the war the organization issued reports dealing with finances, field kitchens, resettlement, relief, and cultural work (courses, festivals, publications).[13] According to one estimate, a network of 4,173 Ukrainian primary schools was allowed to exist, along with twelve gymnasiums (under Poland there had been four) (Mohylov 2016, 19). These achievements, however limited, allowed the Germans to claim that the community enjoyed certain privileges and therefore had to support the war effort. One demand was for Ukrainians to serve in the Auxiliary Police.

Both Poles and Ukrainians competed to get people into positions of authority within the police forces in both "Zakerzonnia" and Galicia. Poles were often hired when previous experience was required, as was the case in the railway and criminal police (Mohylov 2016, 400, 407). When the Germans arrived, Ukrainians tried to create their own militia but lacked experience and training. Moreover, the Germans immediately used the militia for their own purposes, which included rounding up people for work, removing Jews from their homes, and requisitioning furniture.[14] In the Galicia district by mid-August 1941 the militia had been dissolved and a Ukrainian Auxiliary Police (Ukrainische Hilfspolizei) created. Its numbers in the district were capped at six thousand. The pay was low, the weapons old – often one rifle was allowed for two men with a maximum of ten bullets – and the behaviour of Germans towards the men was humiliating. The situation was, of course, anything but normal. Police were told to keep order among Poles and Ukrainians and to guard Jewish ghettoes in a country occupied by Germans who considered all these people subhuman and who were conducting genocidal policies. Local police had little power, but they did not face starvation, deportation, or forced labour, and many had hopes of later contributing to an armed struggle against both German and Soviet rule. Inevitably, however, unless they resigned or deserted, they had to obey the occupation's orders.

Ukrainian leaders supported the creation of a Ukrainian police force for the same reasons that the Polish government in exile supported the creation of its own police. These forces were seen as mitigating the German brutality towards local populations, providing insights into otherwise secret operations, supporting the resistance movement, and potentially playing a role in a future uprising (Młynarczyk et al. 2017, 167, 170).

A school for training police was opened in Lviv in November 1941 under the direction of Ivan Kozak, a former captain of the gendarmerie in the UHA and a lawyer during the interwar years. The UTSK made efforts to improve the training and conditions, but the main issue was, of course, whose interests the police served. The police found themselves subject to the whims of every German. Even so, Ukrainians viewed "their own" police as offering some degree of protection. On the other hand, most Poles, who, prior to 1939, had been hegemonic in Galicia, found the idea of a Ukrainian police force insufferable and acted towards it with uncontained hatred. The number of police killed by Poles, or as a result of vendettas between supporters of the Bandera and Melnyk factions, was, according to Pankivskyi (1965, 395–6), "exceptionally high."

Moreover, there was tension between the administration and the police. The former included many Poles who had "become Germans" in 1939 or 1941. Some were now classified as German citizens, or *Reichsdeutsche*, others as *Volksdeutsche*. When the Germans who had arrived in 1941 to work in the administration and the police began returning home, the "new Germans" replaced them, and a search began for anyone with German ancestry to fill positions.[15]

A comparable situation existed in other cities, such as Stanislaviv, the second largest in the district. Here the Hungarian occupation was initially unsure whether Germany would allow a Ukrainian state and therefore permitted the creation of a civil administration (Iashan 1989, 53–4). Volunteers set up relief agencies, a militia whose first task was to prevent stores from being robbed by Hungarian soldiers, a fire brigade, and committees to settle disputes related to the division of land and harvests. Initially, there were tensions with the OUN-B, which wanted to control all aspects of government, but after the Germans took over in the second week of August all previously elected or appointed people were removed, and on 14 and 15 September all known members of the OUN-B were arrested.

When a decision was taken to create the Galicia Division, a Military Board was appointed to serve as a recruitment team and to deal with publicity, complaints, and rumours. It consisted of thirteen prominent community figures selected by Kubijovyč, all of whom had served as officers in the Sich Riflemen and UHA. Alfred Bisantz was appointed as the board's head.[16] Stepan Volynets and Mykhailo Styranka edited *Do peremohy* (To victory), a weekly newsletter, the first issue of which came out on 23 December 1943 in Lviv. From July 1944 to January 1945 it was published in Kraków under the name *Do zbroi* (To arms). The board visited units in training and dispatched holiday packages and performing groups (Krokhmaliuk 1952, 7). Although formally subordinated to Governor Wächter, it was in close touch with Kubijovyč and the UTSK. Bisantz, who had been selected by the Germans to chair the body and represented their wishes, would frequently clash with other members.

4

MILITARY TRAINING: PROPAGANDA, CHAPLAINS, AND RELATIONS WITH GERMANS

"Obviously it would have been both futile and inexpedient to moralize about bayonet-fighting at an Army School."

SIEGFRIED SASSOON, *Memoirs of an Infantry Officer*, 1930

According to Reitlinger (1956, 77), by combining practical Prussian experience with the ideological training favoured by Himmler, the Waffen-ss developed an efficient system of military training. Breakfast was followed by weapons training, which was interrupted three times a week for a lecture on the inspiring life of the Führer, the ideology of national socialism, or the philosophy of racial selection. The principal textbooks devoted to Weltanschauung were Alfred Rosenberg's *Myth of the Twentieth Century* and Richard Walther Darré's *Um Blut und Boden* (Blood and Soil, 1940).[1] After lunch came drill, scrubbing, and cleaning: "On Sundays there was no church parade, for the ss had no chaplains, and Hitler liked to think that they were godless" (Reitlinger 1956, 78). By the time the Galicia Division was being formed, foreign recruits in the Waffen-ss outnumbered Germans, the training had been abridged to accelerate its completion, and the ideological focus had changed: it now emphasized European civilization's struggle against Asiatic Bolshevism. Moreover, the Division had chaplains and religious services.

The influence of German military propaganda on Ukrainian recruits has seldom been discussed. At a fundamental level it was in conflict with their aspirations for an independent state. They accepted the military training, but how were they affected by the ideological indoctrination? Before enlisting, their worldview had already been shaped by religious instruction, patriotic agitation, and public education. Interwar literature and community rituals, both urban and rural, were also strong influences. How soldiers processed the clash between values absorbed in homes and schools and the unfamiliar new concepts introduced in military camps is not easily answered.

The UTsK made its own pitch to the recruits. Because of its concern with desertions to the partisans, it published calls rejecting "internal anarchy" and destructive behaviour. One leaflet stated that "the strength of the people is created not in the forest but in regular detachments ... Human strength is merely wasted in the forest. Whoever goes into the forest has been lost to the people once and for all." The leaflet rejected the idea of a war against everyone – Germany, Bolsheviks, Poland, Romania, Hungary, and a significant part of Ukrainian citizenry – and called instead for discipline, order, unity, and collective work (UCRDC, Maleckyj Papers, "Viddil Kulturnoi Pratsi U. Ts. K. Propahandyvnyi viddil, 'Za lad i poriadok'"). On 26 February 1944, the Military Board sent out an appeal signed by thirty-six veterans of the struggle for independence between 1917 and 1920. It stated that the only path for a Ukrainian patriot was to serve in "a disciplined, militarily organized and trained formation" (Ponomarenko 2016, 62). However, the fear of mass desertions proved unwarranted. The Division's men could compare their own superior training and equipment with that of the partisans and were aware of how difficult conditions in the "forest" were.

Newspapers published agitation in line with German requirements. On 13 May 1943, *Lvivski visti* ran an account of how many men in various regions had volunteered. The same issue published a cartoon of Stalin wearing a crown and an armband with the hammer and sickle. His image was reflected in a mirror as a Jewish figure with the star of David and a dollar sign. On 3 June 1943, the newspaper printed another cartoon showing Stalin being crowned by a Jewish-looking secretary of the Communist International, an organization that had been dissolved at the time to avoid antagonizing the Allies.

The Division's own newspaper printed agitational materials alongside reports of army life. On 2 November 1944, for example, the lead article in *Do zbroi* was "Vira v Peremohu" (Faith in victory), a speech by Goebbels, which argued that Germany alone was leading the struggle against Bolshevism and for the revival of the European continent, that the Soviet Union had exhausted its material resources, and that the development of military technology and weaponry gave Germany the advantage.

However, soldiers also had to deal with the contrasting line carried by the OUN-B, which in 1943 argued: "Without a Ukrainian state, without a Ukrainian government there cannot be a Ukrainian army. German plans for the future involve the further exploitation of the people's physical strength, its destruction, and because of this our attitude [to the Division] can only be negative" ("Dovkruhy" 1943, 1).

Officer Schools

After completing three months of basic training, several hundred men were sent to officer schools, where they were exposed to another five months of intensive instruction. According to Oleksa Horbach, who attended the Waffen-Junkerschule "Braunschweig" from 13 July until 15 December 1944 and who after the war became a professor of linguistics at the University of Marburg, the basic subjects were applied philosophy, tactics and terrain, the ss and police, army, military duties, physical education, communication studies, technical weapons, engineer-sapper training, motorized vehicle training, riding and horse-drawn driving (Melnyk 2002, 335–6).[2]

Racial ideology had received little attention during the three months of basic training at Heidelager, so it struck men as a novelty when introduced in officer school. Several veterans later recalled lectures devoted to the national socialist worldview (the topic known as *Weltanschauung*). When the instructor presented material in the same way as he did to Germans, the men listened passively to the agitation about race, the destiny of the German people, and the soldier's political tasks, but they then began posing questions, particularly concerning the information that the "the East will be ruled solely by the German sword and plow." How, they asked, were these words, which suggested that there was no place for any people other than the Germans, to be understood? The questioning resulted in the topic's removal from further lectures (Ortynskyi 1951, 30). Moreover, the men pushed back against the indoctrination. Pavlo Hrytsak (1959, 18) recalled that "it took a lot of effort at times to convince the Germans that we had entered what was admittedly 'their' army not to fight for the 'New Europe' but for our own interests, which did not coincide with German ones. The Germans, who at first considered 'Galicians' a kind of German-Slavic *Mischlinge* (half-castes), were somewhat surprised by these views, but probably did not pay closer attention to them."

Under occupation the pervasive, steady drumbeat of propaganda in the press and during various parades and pageants affected the tone of all life. So did everyday encounters. Veryha (2007, 27) reports that while he was in administration (Verwaltung) school in Dachau, one day as the soldiers were marching to lunch they passed a group of men from the concentration camp who had to take off their caps in deference to the soldiers. This kind of experience worked to internalize aspects of Nazi ideology. Racism and xenophobia had, after all, been a feature of Dmytro Dontsov's writings since the later 1930s. At this time this pro-Hitler ideologist resided in Prague, wrote for the press of the ss-operated Reinhard Heydrich Institute, and published *Dukh nashoi davnyny* (Spirit of our past, 1944), in which he classified Ukraine's population according to four racial types: the Nordic, Mediterranean, Dynaric, and Oriental (ostiiska) (Erlacher 2021, 369, 375–8). In his study of the Order Police Christopher Browning (1993, 182) points out that, even if people came from social milieux relatively unreceptive to national socialism, "the denigration of Jews and the proclamation of Germanic racial superiority was so constant, so pervasive, so relentless, that it must have shaped the general attitude of masses of people in Germany, including the average reserve policeman." How it affected the Division's men is an open question. As Browning himself concludes, "human responsibility is ultimately an individual matter" (188).

The officer trainees were almost all graduates of gymnasiums (high schools), and their strong patriotism made them resistant to much German propaganda. They were accustomed to discounting government agitation under both Polish and Soviet rule and there is little evidence to show they were influenced by Nazi political theory, particularly when lectures mentioned the racial-biological inferiority of Slavs and superiority of Germans. While most recruits were prepared to accept the strict discipline in order to acquire knowledge of technology and military operations, this acceptance did not make them pro-German, still less pro-Nazi. Although propaganda stoked anti-Soviet and anti-Jewish attitudes, it is highly debatable whether the racial stereotyping produced the kind of psychological distancing that has been ascribed to "desk murderers" and designers of the Holocaust (Browning 1993, 163). In any case, "ideological education" in the Division's training camps differed significantly from the descriptions provided by Browning in his study of the Reserve Police Battalion 101. Instruction given the Division's officers avoided discussion of the superiority of the Nordic race, the German *Volk*, the purity of German blood, or the elimination of weak and inferior peoples (177–81).

An estimated total of six hundred officers and two thousand NCOs were given training, largely thanks to Dmytro Paliiv's insistence that such a cohort be developed. Kubijovyč (1985, 64) later wrote that Paliiv was his "unofficial representative" in the force and the only person with whom he could speak openly about the possibility of severing links with the Germans and transferring the Division to the Allies. According to Veryha (2006, 6), Paliiv hoped that German failures on the front would lead to a revolution in Germany, which would make peace with the Western Allies and then join them in opposing the Soviet Union.

As the Division completed training, on 15 and 16 May 1944, Himmler made a two-day visit to Neuhammer to inspect the force. During a reception for officers, he admitted that Galicians were really Ukrainians, appealed to both Germans and Ukrainians to support one another in combat, and then made two statements that have frequently been misquoted. Referring to Galicia, he said: "Your homeland has become even more beautiful – and I can safely say this – since it lost, through our intervention, those inhabitants who often sullied the name of Galicia, the Jews." He continued: "I know if I ordered the Division to wipe out the Poles in this area or that area, I would be a very popular man. But if I tell you or give you the order that the Division is to follow this or that route to the front in full battle order, and fight against the Russians, then that is what will be done" (UCRDC, Maleckyj Papers).[3]

Paliiv then responded in the presence of senior officers and Himmler's entourage: "Let it be permissible in your presence, Herr Reichsführer, for me to declare, that we Ukrainians are not preparing to slaughter the Poles and that is not why we voluntarily enlisted in the Division Galicia. But after observing German policies in Eastern Europe, we cannot fail to cite how you Germans continue to incite us against the Poles, and the Poles against us. Unfortunately, I feel that it is necessary to inform you that your politics in Eastern Europe are not correct and lead to nothing good. Forgive me for such an unpleasant rebuttal, but that is the way it is" (Logusz 1997, 166). A stunned silence followed. Most in attendance expected that he would be punished, but Himmler chose to ignore the comment. One senior German officer later approached Paliiv, shook his hand, and congratulated him.[4]

Melnyk has commented that Paliiv's impudent behaviour could not have gone unnoticed. A few days after this incident Himmler sent the following dispatch to the security police and sD, in which he once more disassociated Ukrainians from the ss:

> In the criminal report of the Reich Security Main Office of 26.5.44, reference is made to a Ukrainian ss man under item 2. This should be correctly defined as a Ukrainian serving in the combat units of the ss. I ask you to ensure that the term "ss man," which is so precious and highly esteemed by us, is avoided in all reports, as well as in all official and non-official announcements governing the people of foreign race which we today organize under the order of the ss. (Adapted from Melnyk [2002, 111])

The officer training has also been described by Dmytro Ferkuniak, who later served in the Division's Intelligence, Section 1c/a. He trained in Leshany, near Prague, together with Mykhailo Kachmar, Myroslaw Maletskyi (Maleckyi), and Bohdan Pidhainyi (Pidhainyj), all of whom were OUN-B members.[5] The training was from 6:00 a.m. to 6:00 p.m. daily and until noon on Saturdays, and once a week there was a night exercise from 10:00 p.m. until 1:00 a.m. Military films were shown from 8:00 p.m. to 10:00 p.m. three times a week. Each trainee had to complete assignments and read summaries of lectures. The training was intense, as is indicated by the fact that seventy-seven men were removed for inadequate performance (Ferkuniak 2003, 16–17).

It is telling that after returning to Heidelager, the officer trainees were placed under surveillance and treated as unreliable (Ferkuniak 2003, 18). The Germans had a network of informers, who had been promised promotions, easy service, and other benefits. Ferkuniak was aware of this because he was the only Ukrainian serving in counterintelligence, among whose tasks was interviewing POWs, exerting political control, and censoring letters. The other members in this service were Gunter Husbach, Fritz Nurmann, and Lieutenant Schenker (18).

Ukrainian officers either found themselves in secondary positions with limited powers of influence or were treated as service staff. They frequently expressed frustration with this treatment and with the incompetence of some of their German superiors. When the army was sent to the front, all senior infantry officers were Germans with the exception of Captain Mykhailo Brygider, who commanded the 1st Battalion of the 29th Regiment and Major Mykola Paliienko who commanded the heavy artillery. Major Yevhen Pobihushchyi commanded the 29th Regiment while it was in training.

Ferkuniak's characterization of the German command is damning. He describes General Freitag as a Prussian policeman who believed that knowledge of Hitler's *Mein Kampf* qualified him for membership "in the dominant race's elite" and viewed everything non-German as inferior (Ferkuniak 2003, 20). Lieutenant Shenker was a provocateur. A native of Przemyśl, he had been educated in Romania and knew Ukrainian and Polish. By posing as a friend of Ukrainians, he drew them into conversations and then denounced them to Freitag.

Dmytro Paliiv's service in Section 2a/b, which dealt with personnel issues, allowed him to prevent the trainee officers from being sent to the front for three to four months, which was the usual practice. Both Paliienko and Ferkuniak reminded Paliiv that the older officers had come to the Division to give younger men the opportunity of forming an officer corps (Ferkuniak 2003, 21). In this way the young officer corps avoided destruction at Brody.

Ferkuniak witnessed widespread corruption among the officers. Some goods assigned to Ukrainian soldiers, such as extra rations of cigarettes and alcohol, were distributed to Germans. Section 6a, which was responsible for provisions, was staffed exclusively by Germans. They had almost all come from the SD and dispatched packages of goods to their families. At one point, Section 1c received a report that an officer from provisions called Lentz had sent his wife a package with a note informing her that it contained 5 kilograms of sugar, 5 of pork, 1 of coffee, and 2,000 cigarettes, and that he had retained 1,000 cigarettes because of a problem at the post office. The commander, after seeing this letter, ruled that the goods had been legally obtained and that there was no prohibition against sending them (Ferkuniak 2003, 24).

Figure 4.1 Galicia troops in camouflage before Brody, July 1943. Petro Markevych with members of his company.

German officers knew little about Ukrainians. Captain Johannes Kleinow, who was in charge of field-replacement, mentioned in one conversation that he realized the men wanted to be known not as a Galician but as a Ukrainian division, but that this was "impossible and unwarranted" because "Ukrainians lived east of the Zbruch River, and most of the men in the Division were Galicians." Ferkuniak replied:

> I regret that you know so little about Ukraine and its people. According to your view, I ought not to call you a German, but use the name of the province from which you come. For example, "Brandenburger," "Saxoner," "Bavarian" ... All these provinces taken together constitute Germany. This gives you the right to call yourselves Germans. If this is so, then what prevents uniting all Ukrainian provinces into one state called Ukraine and a people called Ukrainians? I request that you do not call us Galicians any more, which suggests that you, gentlemen, wish to travel the path of our enemies, the Russians and Poles: divide and conquer. (28)

This discussion was reported to Berlin, and about three weeks later the Division's name was changed to "Ukrainian" (29).

Karl Zoglauer, who was in charge of Section 6, which dealt with cultural-educational work and propaganda, shortly before capitulation admitted that he knew little about Ukraine and its people and that all along he thought they were Russians. According to Ferkuniak (2003, 25), all officers in this section viewed Ukraine in terms of national socialist doctrine, as a future colony, and saw their task as suppressing national feelings and transforming the men into tools of Germany. Zoglauer wrote the speech that Freitag delivered after the battle of Brody, when the force regrouped in Serednie, near Hungary. In it the general stated that Ukrainians had not matured to the level of an independent nation and, therefore, had failed the test of combat. This, supposedly, was why he had resigned his command during the battle. After the report was read, Ferkuniak asked how it was possible that over 70 percent of the Ukrainian officers who "ran away" lay dead on the battlefield while over 90 percent of the German officers who "fought determinedly" were present in Serednie. The general, in a raised tone, replied: "What is written in this report is correct and requires no explanation" (53).

Training of Soldiers

Not all rank-and-file soldiers had poor relations with Germans. Veryha's company apparently got on well with their superiors. When a delegation led by Volodymyr Vashkovych complained at being called stupid (*blödes Volk*), the company commander explained that this was not meant as an insult to the Ukrainian people but was a common way for instructors to address all troops. Nonetheless, he told instructors to avoid such language (Veryha 2007, 15).

Discontent among soldiers was frequently fuelled by the knowledge that the Gestapo had arrested and shot their relatives, usually on the pretext of being members of the OUN. When Ferkuniak was asked to report on complaints in the Ukrainian population, he listed the following: Germans have come to Ukraine not to liberate people from Bolshevism or to fight alongside Ukrainians but to occupy the country and conquer a *Lebensraum* for themselves; Germans want to destroy Ukrainians by using the Division as cannon fodder; the Division's soldiers are traitors who have renounced their national name, may only be called Galicians, and are treated poorly;

mistakes in caring for the families and men are the result of ill will (Ferkuniak 2003, 31–2).

Heinrich Wiens was particularly hated. A member of the Gestapo, his appointment had been requested by Freitag, who wanted him to run counterintelligence in Section 1c/a and ferret out Bandera sympathisers. Knowing that Wiens was in charge of censoring letters, Ferkuniak told Kachmar, Maleckyj and Pidhainyi to warn the men about expressing political views or criticizing Germany in correspondence. As a result, letters began including praise for the Führer (Ferkuniak 2003, 22). However, a number of soldiers ended up behind bars for frankly stating their opinions.

Wiens came from the Mennonite colony in Molochna, near Zaporizhia, but had moved to the "Free City" of Danzig (today's Gdansk) in 1930. He was fluent in Ukrainian, Russian, and Polish, had been a member of the ss since 1931 and of the SD (the elite Security Service) since 1937. At one point he tried to arrest Mykhailo Kachmar and was only prevented from doing so by Paliiv's intervention (Melnyk 2002, 353). Wiens's past was sinister. He had participated in mass executions in the Einsatzgruppen D, where he had acted as an interpreter and section leader, and then in the Einsatskommando 12 in the Stalino (now Donetsk) area. He has been described as a sadist who despised Ukrainians, especially Galicians, and was even avoided by some fellow Germans because of his untrustworthy character. Unknown to the Gestapo, he had reportedly developed pro-Russian, pro-Polish, and pro-communist views. The OUN network within the Division considered him a Soviet agent. He disappeared at Brody.[6]

Rank-and-file soldiers were only given intermittent lectures on ideology. Aware of why the men had volunteered, the Germans focused on producing a fighting force. However, there were other reasons for the ineffectiveness of propaganda. Most men had a poor grasp of German, which meant that the lectures had to be conducted in Ukrainian. As a result, the content was filtered through instructors or interpreters. Ukrainian officers who gave the lectures subverted them, especially when they were confident that no informers were present. Another reason was the existence of counter-propaganda in the form of chaplains, church services, and covert instruction from "nationalist" educators within the force. German officers knew that these conversations were taking place and often turned a blind eye to them. As a result, Ukrainian soldiers, like non-Germans in the Waffen-ss generally,

Military Training • **69**

were "certainly exposed to less political and racial indoctrination than Germans" (Bishop 2005, 18).

Nonetheless, the ss leadership insisted that some indoctrination be given. In Heidelager there were lectures on the Third Reich's invincibility and national socialist ideology. These avoided any mention of the "inferiority" of non-Germans. According to Roman Kolisnyk: "Political education consisted of lectures by the company commander once a week, lasting about two hours. The whole company sat down comfortably in the shade of the trees and he talked, usually about the situation at the front and how the Führer would take care of everything. Our interpreter translated very loosely. It was a farce. Nobody cared what he said. Most dozed off" (Melnyk 2002, 57).

Ortynskyi (1951, 30) also describes the cynical attitude towards propaganda lectures: "One could hardly expect interest or active participation from men who were attuned to the message of statehood but were forced to listen to lectures about a new European order in which Ukraine would not be a state, while information from home indicated that it was to being treated as a colony." This political factor was probably crucial in blocking the propaganda. The men had their own agenda, commonly expressed by the phrase: "Grab the weapons, no matter who is handing them out!" (Pidhainyi 1951, 59).

Because the German command was concerned with the influence of the OUN and the UPA, before deployment at Brody the lectures focused on discouraging men from deserting to the partisans. Most men, however, were convinced of the need for a professional army. In Petro Lavruk's opinion, although soldiers were interested in the partisan struggle, the army was "very disciplined from top to bottom."[7] Even so, there was a continuing covert discussion about the relative merits of the army and the partisans, and "nationalists" of various persuasions conducted their own agitation. While the troops were in Heidelager, which was close to Galicia, both the OUN and the UPA sent people to talk to the soldiers. Later, when the training moved to other places, this contact became more difficult.

Some officers were unsure how to deal with lecture outlines that had been sent from headquarters. When Roman Dolynskyi was asked about this, his advice was to speak openly about issues if the instructor was sure of his men: "This was risky, but it was the only way in these difficult circumstances if we were to preserve the image of a national idea in the Division, as opposed to the desires of the Germans and our own Quislings" (Dolynskyi 1951, 104). At the moment of deployment, secrecy became more difficult because many *Volksdeutsche* from Silesia (Śląsk), Bukovyna, and Romania were sent into the Division. They frequently knew Polish or Ukrainian, so group conversations with Ukrainian soldiers had to be conducted separately, during free time and outside instructional hours.

Some lectures have survived from November and December 1944, the time when the Division was in Slovakia. The notes for a lecture on 4 December devoted to panslavism, indicated that this ideology was being spread "in the Balkans, mainly among the Bulgarians and Serbs" and was aimed at extending the influence of Moscow, which hoped to capture the Dardanelles. However, panslavism has no influence on Ukrainians, who have experienced both Russian and Polish oppression. The Slovaks, "who have not yet experienced the Russian knout and have not learned from personal experience what the Russian represents – whether the White of a hundred years ago or the Red of today – look favourably at the new promises. Many are unaware of what awaits them under Bolshevism." Another lecture, dated 17 November, was devoted to the Division's name change to 14th Grenadier Division der Waffen ss (ukrainische 1). It was explained that men from all parts of Ukraine had joining the force, which was now the military home for them all and therefore the term "Galician" had become too narrow. "Europe and the Reich" was a regular topic. In notes for a lecture dated 9 December listeners were to be told that "only the Reich under the brilliant leadership of Adolf Hitler can save the future of the European family of peoples from the pollution of Jewish elements and Bolshevik slavery." The Reich's soldiers "were fighting for the New Europe's future," which would preserve and develop the West's thousand-year-old culture. This new Europe would bring a better world order, one dominated "not by the false socialism of the Bolsheviks, which enslaves farmers, [takes] their property and lowers their human dignity to the level of working animals with no rights, but by the real socialism of free activity, which safeguards the sacred law of private ownership for every worker." The death of Sheptytskyi was an opportunity for a lecture stating that the Metropolitan had been hostile to the Bolsheviks but positively inclined towards the German state. The lecturer was to note that the Bolsheviks had destroyed churches or turned them into shops, cinemas, and clubs (ao, Veryha collection, copies in author's possession).

German propaganda was often countered by covert members of the OUN. The main representatives of the Bandera faction were Bohdan Pidhainyi, Myroslaw Maleckyj, Volodymyr Levytskyi, and Mykhailo Kachmar. According to Pidhainyi, all four maintained contact with Roman Shukhevych prior to Brody (Pidhainyi 1951, 113). However, there were many individuals in the force, like Vasyl Veryha, who were convinced that the Bandera faction had murdered Omelian Senyk and Mykola Stsiborskyi, two leaders of the Melnyk faction, in Zhytomyr on 30 August 1941, and that Bandera's supporters had unleashed a campaign of terror against this competing organization.[8] When Ivan Voloshchak (Woloschak) was informed by Bandera supporters in 1941 that this friend, a Melnyk loyalist, had been murdered for recruiting to this faction, Woloschak promptly quit the Bandera group and in 1943 enlisted in the Division.[9]

Vasyl Sirskyi (Wasyl Sirskyj) had joined the youth OUN in prewar years in the town of Sokolivtsi near Lviv but ran into conflicts with what he called "narrow-minded" people incapable of taking criticism: "They were all failures in life who had forced their way into the OUN."[10] When the German-Soviet war broke out, these OUN-B supporters erected triumphal arches, on which the new Leader (Vozhd) Stepan Bandera was portrayed sending greetings to the German Führer. In Sirskyi's estimation the Bandera supporters declared a "state of war" in the town, preventing anyone from leaving their house after 9:00 p.m. One man berated the local OUN-B chief: "Tell that to my horse, which can only graze at night because it has to work during the day." Local people were not permitted to remove parts from destroyed Soviet tanks, which were declared "property of the state." Shortly afterwards, the tanks were taken by the Germans. The OUN-B also immediately began a campaign against anyone who showed support for Melnyk or the Poles. As his main reason for leaving the party Sirskyi cited the dissemination of hatred and the political murders, which frequently initiated a cycle of vendetta killings.

On the whole, however, the existence of the UPA tended to unite members of the Division, who put aside difference in face of the larger struggle against Soviet forces. Whenever possible, soldiers funnelled arms to the underground. Ivan Bendyna spoke about personally giving away many weapons, including grenades and anti-tank mines.[11]

The Role of Chaplains

Another counter to German propaganda was provided by the priests. According to Wolf-Dietrich Heike, the presence of Christian chaplains virtually excluded direct Nazi propaganda because Bishop Yosyp (Joseph) Slipyi and Metropolitan Sheptytskyi had instructed priests "to negate any attempt at Nazi indoctrination" (Heike 1988, xix). Sheptytskyi had himself been a cavalry officer in the Austrian army, during which time he had witnessed violence against civilian populations by Poles, Germans. and Ukrainians. This experience had elevated his concern that the German defeat would be followed by widespread killing (Magocsi 1989, 17).

From the beginning, the priests were viewed by the ss as potential subversives. After the announcement of the Division's creation on 28 April 1943, Reverend Laba delivered a sermon in which he described the Galicia Division as a reincarnation of the Sich Riflemen.[12] An audio recording was made of the sermon and a translation forwarded both to Himmler and to Gottlob Berger, who oversaw Waffen-ss recruitment (Melnyk 2002, 28). Because figures in the ss complained that the chaplains would serve Sheptytskyi and the Vatican, the Reichsführer issued an order on 16 July 1943 that the Metropolitan was to be informed that the priests could stay if their influence was positive but would be removed if they "began to agitate" (33). As Sheptytskyi's representative, Laba listened to the admonishment and answered diplomatically that he would personally select the initial twelve clergymen. Although senior members of the ss continued to suspect the chaplains, their opposition was overridden by Germany's urgent need for military personnel. First Hitler, then Erich Koch, the head of the Reichskommissariat Ukraine, and then organizers of the various police forces, pretended that Galicians, who had spent over a century under Austrian rule, constituted a hybrid German identity. They were "ersatz Aryans," or *Mischlinge*, a form of German Métis. Simultaneously, however, these leaders reminded themselves that in 1918 Ukrainians had "betrayed" Germany and assassinated Field Marshal Hermann von Eichhorn. Hitler and Himmler referenced this event several times when Ukrainians were mentioned.[13]

The view that the chaplains opposed Nazi ideology has been challenged. In 1943 they attended a six-week ss Training Camp in Cernay (Germ: Sennheim), where, according to Ponomarenko, they were thoroughly indoctrinated and subsequently did the bidding of the German command.

Laba, according to this view, was trusted by the Germans to select chaplains who were relatively loyal to German rule, "otherwise they would not have been sent to the Division" (Ponomarenko 2018, 37).[14]

It is hard to agree with this judgment. As a field chaplain in the Austrian army, Laba had served on the Italian front and won several medals for courage. He disregarded orders to remain behind the lines in safety, insisting that the chaplain's place was with the troops. He survived poison gas attacks and administered spiritual and medical first aid to casualties from both the Entente's forces and those allied with Austria (Iwasykiw Silecky 2006, 19). While a POW in Italy, his fluency in Italian and Latin allowed him to act as a spokesman for the interned and to negotiate on their behalf. In 1919 he became a chaplain in the Sich Riflemen. Laba recruited chaplains to the Galicia Division based on their character traits, life experiences, and mental fitness. He selected highly educated men, leaders in their communities, who had experienced violence under Polish and Soviet rule. Reverend Iosyp Kladochnyi, for example, had since 1932 regularly visited fifteen prisons that contained people charged with political offences (Kladochnyi 1994, 67–9). Reverend Nahaievskyi had been imprisoned for two months during the so-called Pacification of 1930 and was one of the accused during a trial of fourteen nationalists in 1931 (Nahaievskyi 1955, 59). As a defender of Ukrainian rights he had been incarcerated in the notorious Bereza Kartuza prison on the eve of the Second World War. During the Soviet occupation of 1939–41 he was interrogated and beaten by the NKVD, escaped, and crossed the border to work in the Chełm area. He was then imprisoned by the Germans in April 1941 and freed on 15 June 1941, apparently on condition that he would work as a translator and mediator between detachments of the OUN and the 6th Army. He received Metropolitan Sheptytskyi's permission to do so (36). In the first weeks of the German-Soviet war he saw the murdered corpses in the NKVD prisons, an experience that convinced him to become a field chaplain: "I sensed that God and Ukraine, my subjugated homeland, demanded this of me" (36). Laba trusted Nahaievskyi and appointed him to serve in his place as the chief chaplain in both the Heidelager and Neuhammer camps. When sending him off, Laba warned that there was little hope of close co-operation with the Germans and that his role would be to act "in the name of the Metropolitan Andrei and our church." He reminded Nahaievskyi of the words Christ had spoken when sending the apostles out: "Be gentle as doves but cunning as serpents" (44).

Ponomarenko claims that *Weltanschauung* study was part of the course of instruction at Sennheim and that it included national socialist ideology. If this was the case, it is highly unlikely that the priests would have been influenced by its main ideas: the new Europe, the racial superiority of Germans, the history and economy of Germany. They had been recruited precisely to combat Nazi indoctrination. Reverend Nahaievskyi (1955, 38) wrote that the priests were not, in fact, subjected to an "ideological-political course," a statement that Ponomarenko (2018, 37) describes as "an outright lie." However, the Germans modified the instructions for Ukrainian officers, and even more so for chaplains. Nahaievskyi's comment can be understood as a dismissal of the "theoretical" instruction, which did not apply to priests, who were considered a "special group" with a good knowledge of Soviet psychology. According to Nahaievskyi: "We did not complete an ideological-political course. The Germans considered us immune to their propaganda and that of the Bolsheviks. All their speeches and writings about a 'New Europe' had no effect on us" (39). He recalls military drills, gymnastics, long-distance runs, jumping over barriers, crawling under barbed wire, climbing high fences. Theoretical studies included cartography, army formations, military strategy, classification, and theoretical use of weapons, especially Soviet (38). The chaplains were given pistols, but some, such as Vasyl Leshchyshyn, refused to carry them.

On one occasion the chaplains mistakenly entered a hall and heard the camp commander denouncing Pope Pius XII for encouraging the Italian government of Marshal Pietro Badoglio to break with Germany and capitulate to the Allies, an event that occurred on 8 September 1943. The priests, according to Ponomarenko (2018, 38), did not express their dissatisfaction openly. However, this information is taken from Nahaievskyi's own memoir (Nahaievskyi 1955, 39). Moreover, it is clear that, whatever their immediate reaction, the priests would not have been in a position to challenge such a characterization of the pontiff, nor, for that matter, would they have wanted to if they were opponents of German rule.

Each regiment and battalion had its own chaplain. They reported to Reverend Volodymyr Stetsiuk, who became the senior religious officer after Nahaievskyi was removed by Freitag. Reverend Levenets drew up the basic guidelines for the work of chaplains. They were to try to gain the trust of soldiers and to learn their characters so that they could influence the men at decisive moments. They were to help ensure that eligible relatives received support. If Ukrainian newspapers were not available, the daily German army report was to be translated into Ukrainian at least every other day. They were to develop strength of character and soldierly virtues in the men, to educate them concerning correct conduct among civilian populations, and to encourage cultural work through choirs, the press, and comradely gatherings. Masses were celebrated in Ukrainian every Sunday and on major religious holidays. They took the form of field services with sermons. These were always well attended, with thousands of men standing in ranks. The sermons allowed priests to strengthen Ukrainian patriotic attitudes (Iwasykiw Silecky 2006, 22; Melnyk 2002, 328).

Although Ponomarenko (2018, 38) states that the priests failed to raise issues with the Germans, this view is not supported by the literature. Reverend Levenets, for example, wrote a memo to the German command stating that as a spiritual advisor he often had to listen to complaints from soldiers. The problems he outlined were: unequal distribution of food and cigarettes, refusal of German soldiers to recognize or obey Ukrainian officers, abusive behaviour that included punching people in the face, spreading rumours that Ukrainians were about to desert to the partisans, and refusal to promote Ukrainians. The tactlessness of many German officers was widely reported, as was the fact that, unlike German soldiers, Ukrainians were arrested, degraded in rank, or executed for minor offences (Levenets 1971, 67–72). The priests regularly opposed the German command by defending the idea of a separate Ukrainian religious and national identity and by protecting soldiers from military tribunals.

The contents of some sermons by Levenets are available (Iwasykiw Silecky 2006, 37, 74–5). Nahaievskyi (1955, 35) describes the aim and content of his own lectures and sermons to the troops as being guided by Christ's words: "there is no greater love than when someone sacrifices his life for his friends." In Neuhammer, sermons were delivered in the presence of the whole Division, sometimes to six thousand to eight thousand men. They took place on Sundays and Christian holidays, whatever the weather, and presented a sight that could not fail to make an impression on German and other soldiers. On one occasion Nahaievskyi continued the service while bombs were falling in the area and troops were running for protection (50).

The chaplains performed marriages and funerals, visited the sick and wounded, comforted men imprisoned for various infractions, and often spent the last night with men who had been sentenced to execution. A number of men were saved from execution due to the intervention of chaplains (Iwasykiw Silecky 2006, 41–4).

The chaplains also acted as ambassadors for the Ukrainian cause among local populations. They did so with the Catholic population of Alsace, where the Sennheim camp was located. When priests visited local churches, parishioners expressed curiosity about their manner of making the sign of the cross and the fact that they did not kneel at certain points in the service. The chaplains soon made friends with parishioners and were invited to homes. Locals were particularly impressed by the choir, which was under the direction of Reverend Saprun, who had been director of the Institute of Folk Arts in Lviv: "At every opportunity we explained to the French and Germans about the struggle of the Ukrainian people to gain its sovereignty" (Nahaievskyi 1955, 40). Similar contacts with locals were made by priests in Slovakia and Styria (Austria), and in Tarbes (southern France), where a reserve battalion was stationed. Reverend Yulian Gabrusevych also reported establishing cordial relations with the local Czech population and their priest in Jince and Strančice (Gabrusevych 1994, 89).

Providing spiritual and moral support was an important aspect of the work. When funerals were conducted for fallen soldiers, the bodies had to be wrapped in tarps, identified, placed in graves, and a service held. Whenever possible, the chaplains tended the graves, affixed crosses with the names of the men, their dates of death, and the inscription "For the freedom of Ukraine." Sometimes graves had to be dug during heavy combat (Iwasykiw Silecky 2006, 44–5).

The chaplains also conducted discussions with the men. Nahaievskyi told soldiers that without an army no nation can gain its freedom. Although aware that a lively debate was taking place about joining the UPA, he concluded that most soldiers agreed with the argument that they should remain in the Division in order to "learn as much as possible about the military profession" (Nahaievskyi 1955, 51). Freitag wanted Nahaievskyi to become part of Section 6, which dealt with cultural education and propaganda, but the chaplain refused, explaining that his task was pastoral work, in which he would be "guided by the directives of my higher spiritual power" (56). The Section's head Zoglauer, formerly a carpenter from Bavaria and a Catholic turned atheist, asked Nahaievskyi several times whether he had read Rosenberg's *Myth of the Twentieth Century*. The priest replied that he had but thought the book "a compilation of thoughts from old German philosophers" whom he had already studied in gymnasium and theological academy, and since he had decided to become a priest the texts obviously had failed to make the same impression on him as they had on Zoglauer (60). When the latter demanded that the priest obey his instructions, Nahaievskyi responded that he considered it "foolish and unnatural for an atheist to tell a priest what he should say and what he should teach believers" (60).

Nahaievskyi (1955, 61) describes his own program of instruction as focused on a soldier's duties and virtues through description of heroic acts in Ukrainian history and negative traits among ancestors, among which he listed "drunkenness, rebelliousness and coveting worldly goods." These had led to the loss of the country's leading strata, which "because of miserable greed had gone over to the side of our enemies" (61). During one conversation, Freitag complained that the priest always spoke about Ukraine but forgot to mention that, without the "Führer and Reich," Ukrainians "would never achieve anything" (73). Nahaievskyi replied that he taught faith in God and religious principles because these countered atheistic Bolshevik propaganda and made Ukrainians into good soldiers. He also pointed out that the Gestapo's presence in the Division was counterproductive: it reminded the men that their fathers, brothers, and sons, even mothers and sisters, had been executed or hanged. He then asked that all men in the Division's prison be released immediately. A few days after this conversation, Paliiv warned Nahaievskyi that the general had complained of the latter's behaviour and had recalled the priest's previous arrest by the Gestapo. Soon after this Freitag secured the appointment of Reverend Stetsiuk as Nahaievskyi's replacement. The intervention of Laba and Paliiv probably saved Nahaievskyi from imprisonment in a concentration camp. One German officer even joked at the time that the offending chaplain would soon be sent to Dachau "for a long vacation" (77).

With these facts in mind, Ponomarenko's judgment appears harsh. The researcher draws on the minutes of interrogations conducted after the war with captured chaplains. Their recorded comments, for the obvious reason that they were obtained under duress, should be read with care, particularly when they describe Nahaievskyi's supposedly servile attitude towards the Germans and his interest "in petty arguments among German officers" (Ponomarenko 2018, 39).

At one point in his memoir, Nahaievskyi (2018, 60–1) comments: "Each field chaplain had to rely on his own abilities and strengths. None of us received any textbooks or instructions. Each acted in accord with his conscience, knowledge, character traits, nature, and temperament." Ponomarenko (2018, 38) characterizes this statement as evidence of the priest's "negligent" attitude towards his duties and suggests that it is a complaint against the church hierarchy. The researcher also characterizes the work of the chaplains in general as serving the Gestapo and Section 6, and suggests that Nahaievskyi's meetings with Zoglauer led to the delivery of "pro-fascist" sermons. As evidence, he states that, on 20 April 1944, a mass was served on the occasion of Hitler's birthday (39). Laba is described as enjoying great respect and confidence in the ss leadership, and Levenets's instructions on the duties of chaplains are described as "very similar to those of Soviet *politruks* and contemporary military psychologists" (38, 40).

Available literature does not support these views. The German command distrusted the priests, and during the encirclement at Brody, when Freitag lost his nerve and resigned his command, he may have shot both Paliiv and Stetsiuk (Nahaievskyi 1955, 84). The chaos of front-line action frequently provided an opportunity to remove disliked figures with impunity. Nahaievskyi comments laconically on this fact: "I know that German officers feared the Ukrainian soldiers more than enemy fire" (48). Veryha also describes a similar moment. After a German soldier had machine-gunned a group of ten captured Red Army soldiers, Veryha complained. Another German pointed his gun at Veryha and began cursing Ukrainians. Fortunately, the man was disarmed by a German NCO (Veryha 2007, 72–3).

Deteriorating Relations with Germans

Not all officers were unsympathetic to Ukrainian attitudes. Veryha's job in Neuhammer was to stamp letters registering the fate of fallen soldiers. Normally the stamp read "Fallen for the Führer and Greater Germany." The officer with whom he was working told him that particular stamp was inappropriate because "you are fighting for your homeland and not Greater Germany." He handed him a stamp that read "Fallen for the homeland" (Veryha 2007, 126).

However, relations with Germans were fraught from the start and deteriorated after Freitag was decorated for his "heroic" conduct at Brody. He began to spread the word that Ukrainian soldiers were traitors (Veryha 2007, 122). As already noted, a number of military authorities had opposed the creation of the Division. They continued to view the force with suspicion. Karl Wolfe, one of the highest-ranking ss officials within the Reich Main Security Office, stated: "We, within the RSHA, were against forming the Division. We did not believe in Ukrainian loyalties in regard to any co-operation with Germany. To us, it was apparent that we would only be training our enemies, who sooner or later would defect to the UPA" (Logusz 1997, 77). It was also well known that some men who had been implicated in anti-Gestapo activities had enlisted to obtain immunity from arrest.

The consensus among Ukrainians was that, in German eyes, the force was cannon fodder. Zahachevskyi recalled that every German acted towards Ukrainians as a superior. When he first arrived, he had been directed to the canteen for NCOs, but as he approached the server he was redirected to another place. At that point he understood that the canteen was only for Germans (Zahachevskyi 1952, 188). However, in spite of all the chicanery and humiliation, the Ukrainians "took to learning the craft of war with eagerness, even with passion," something he understood because he himself was prepared to pay a high price to gain military expertise. The Ukrainian soldiers joined "not for [the benefit of] the Germans and not to defend the Germans"; rather, they had put on a uniform they found repulsive "to gain military know-how so that at the crucial moment we could serve our fatherland" (189).

Because they doubted the loyalty of Ukrainians, when the attempt on Hitler's life occurred on 20 July 1944, training camps with Ukrainian soldiers were surrounded. This happened to the Division's reserve force stationed in Neuhammer and to the 6th Volunteer Regiment as it was leaving Tarbes. A secret instruction issued on 5 September 1944 ordered that only German officers were to serve in all regimental, battalion, and administrative positions, and that they were to constitute 60 percent of any communications staff (Veryha 2007, 131).

Conflicts also occurred during deployment. Petro Lavruk describes an incident during the fighting near Brody. The soldiers were approached by villagers who were complaining that the last of their cattle were being taken by Germans. The locals had to take the animals to pasture at night and hide them during the day. Milk, of course, was a crucial source of food, especially for families with children:

We ran across the fields to help. I saw a German leaving the village. I ran like a tiger, threw myself at him; he fell, I took his weapons and let him get up. He got on his knees and prayed. I saw he was very young, younger than myself. I took the bullets out of his pistol and gave it back. He tried to kiss my feet ... When we got back, the gendarmerie was arresting our officer. We drew weapons and told them to leave. They were astonished and drove off to Brody ... About fifteen minutes later two trucks with soldiers and the gendarmerie returned. They stopped opposite us on the road, we heard the command, they got off and advanced toward us in a line. The Soviet front fired at them and they retreated. They could not come for us because it was in a harvested field and they were unable to crawl 400 metres. At that moment, I was given the order by telephone to go toward Brody through the village. It was at that moment on 13 July that the front was penetrated. (UCRDC, oral history archive, Lavruk)

The start of the battle saved Lavruk from arrest. Shortly afterwards he witnessed a similar incident. The Germans were forcing people out of the villages as they retreated, taking whatever they needed without paying. Some soldiers were driving a pig in front of them. Lavruk and a friend jumped from their horses and returned the pig to its owner. The grateful villagers invited them into their home and gave them potatoes and sour milk. At this point, Lavruk recalled, "our hatred of Germans had grown to the point that if another confrontation occurred, no one would have restrained themselves" (UCRD, oral history archive, Lavruk).

As time passed, General Freitag developed a paranoia concerning his Ukrainian troops. When the Division was in Slovakia he granted each regimental and battalion commander the right to form a military tribunal (*Kriegsgericht*), allowing them to pass sentence on soldiers and to conduct executions. As a result, scores of men were shot by firing squad, mostly for trivial offences, but no German faced this punishment. Freitag also decided that one individual in each company had to produce regular monthly reports on conversations among the troops. These were collated, sent to regimental headquarters, and then to Section 1c/a, where Wiens was responsible for analyzing the data. Soldiers responsible for providing the information in most cases submitted fabrications. They would, for example, mention belief in German victory, in the new V rockets being produced, or would discuss minor issues like food, cigarettes, and alcohol, or commodities like soap, toothpaste, and shaving supplies. Melnyk (2002, 211) concludes that "the enterprise was effectively sabotaged and the reports were of no real benefit." There was one exception. Bohdan Pidhainyi wrote truthfully that, when the Division was sent to the front, he was afraid it would not fight for the "New Order in Europe," which had no meaning for Ukrainians. This report incensed the regimental commander Forstreuter, who summoned Pidhainyi. However, because Pidhainyi enjoyed a high profile and was popular among his countrypeople, Forstreuter feared punishing him and merely issued a verbal threat, saying: "You're a dead man" (366).

PART TWO

ACTIONS

5

BEYERSDORFF BATTLE GROUP, FEBRUARY–MARCH 1944

In February 1944, while still in training, the Division received an order to create a battle group, which would engage Soviet and Polish partisans in the Lubaczów (Ukr: Liubachiv) area south of Lublin and north of Przemyśl (Ukr: Peremyshl). Friedrich Beyersdorff, who was in command of the Division while General Fritz Freitag attended a course for commanders in Berlin, learned that two Soviet partisan groups had been activated, one under the command of Petro Vershyhora and another under Mikhail Naumov. They had penetrated the Lublin district and caused disruptions by cutting lines of communication, blowing up bridges, and destroying German garrisons. The two groups coordinated their actions with the Armia Ludowa (AL), a pro-communist Polish partisan group. The Division was instructed to deal with the threat. At the time, it had about 12,634 men in training, mainly in Heidelager, of whom ten thousand were Ukrainians and the rest Germans. The Beyersdorff Battle Group (*Kampfgruppe*) numbered around two thousand men (Logusz 1997, 145). Both German and Ukrainian officers were selected as commanders. Some of the latter had previously served in the UNR army, the UHA, or in the Polish and Soviet military, and a number had experienced partisan warfare, including Mykola Paliienko, Ivan Rembolovych, Yaroslav Kubashevskyi, Yurii Cherkashyn, and Roman Dolynskyi.[1]

Wolf-Dietrich Heike, the Division's chief of staff, objected to the assignment because the deployment was rushed, the training had not been completed, and the men were not prepared for anti-partisan warfare. In his postwar memoir he complains of difficulties during deployment and the lack of experienced commanders (Heike 1973, 62). The concerns about inadequate equipment and experience are echoed in soldiers' memoirs, which comment on boots unsuitable for the conditions and the slow movement of detachments, which had to transport wagons and heavy guns.

Several soldiers who served in the Battle Group have left accounts that present a different picture from Polish and Soviet reports. One problem stems from the fact that civilians often had a problem identifying forces. There were several groups in the area, including detachments of the 4th and 5th Galician Volunteer Regiments. Local people often confused these with the Division, referring to all three units in the same way – as the "Galicia Division" or the "Ukrainian ss." Beyersdorff's men were also supported by other forces, including a battalion from the 22nd and 26th Police Regiment ss, and it is thought that the 115th Landesschutzen Regiment may also have been involved, along with a reserve tank company (Heike 1973, 39–42; Melnyk 2002, 99).

The Battle Group left Heidelager on 16 February 1944 and headed for Lubaczów. The first train arrived, but partisans blew up bridges to the town, forcing the second and third to be diverted to Lviv while sappers repaired the line. In Lviv between 18 and 26 February the soldiers were greeted by representatives of the Military Board and family members. Their arrival caused excitement because this was the first glimpse for many people of uniformed Division soldiers and it marked the "debut" of its emblem. Soldiers attached the lion patch to their lower right sleeve; after June 1944, it would be fixed to the upper left sleeve. While in Lviv several men deserted, probably to join the UPA. As a result of the diversion to Lviv, the Battle Group formed in the area of operations only at the end of February.

Petro Vershyhora's Soviet partisans (known as the 1 Sydir Kovpak Ukrainian Partisan Division) operated in the counties of Lubaczów, Tarnogród (Ukr: Ternohorod), Biłgoraj (Ukr: Bilhorai), Zamość, and Tomaszów (Ukr: Tomashiv). Vershyhora worked with partisans of the pro-communist AL and until 27 February with Naumov, who then moved in the direction of Lviv. In all, there were approximately two thousand Soviet partisans supported by about one thousand to fifteen hundred Polish fighters. Beyersdorff's task was to surround the Soviet forces, then to squeeze the pocket and destroy them. However, the forested terrain and support from local Polish villagers who provided information about troop movements often allowed the partisans to escape their pursuers, who were slowed by heavy equipment and mined roads. The entire operation, which was the Division's first experience of military action, lasted less than a month and ended on 17 March, although some men remained in the vicinity of Biłgoraj-Zamość until 27 March. The Soviet partisan group was driven out of the GG in a northeasterly direction and Vershyhora reported the loss of four hundred men, although it is not clear how many were killed, wounded, or deserted (Ponomarenko 2016, 88). The Division suffered an estimated 10 killed, 13 wounded, and 10 men who disappeared without a trace, no doubt having deserted to the underground (Melnyk 2002, 99, 351).

Lubaczów's Ukrainian population had in recent months been attacked by the Soviet and Polish partisans. Its villages, which had seen arsons and the killing of community leaders, were organizing their own defence and were pleased by the Division's arrival. Polish villages in the area were also prepared for self-defence. Because the entire region lay along the ethnographic divide between Ukrainians and Poles, some towns and villages were almost entirely Ukrainian or Polish, and some had mixed populations. Cieszanów, for example, was predominantly Polish, while Tarnogród was split fairly evenly between the two populations. In a number of places considerable animosity had built up between the two communities. In 1938 the neighbouring Chełm area had suffered the destruction of Ukrainian Orthodox churches and forced Catholicization, and in 1939 it had been subjected to a "pacification" by the Polish army (Motyka 2011, 35–6). When in September 1939 Germany and the Soviet Union invaded, Polish soldiers had burned "every village" that fired shots at them, while Ukrainians burned Polish villages with Soviet approval (51). Since then antagonisms had been further exacerbated by the German occupation, which burned and murdered villages whenever it suspected that they helped partisans (72).

The situation was complicated by competition between Polish and Soviet partisan groups. The pro-communist AL, for example, accused the AK (Armia Krajowa, or Home Army), which recognized the émigré government in London, of using raids across the Bug (Ukr: Buh) River by small bands of Ukrainian nationalists as an excuse to unleash attacks on Ukrainian villages, thus spreading "terror and destruction" and shedding "innocent blood" (Gronczewski 1964, 112–14; Wołczew 1969, 164–5). The AL blamed the "reactionary" London government in exile for attacking "the peaceful Ukrainian population" in revenge for anti-Polish actions by the OUN-UPA (Wołczew 1969, 164).

The conflict between Ukrainians and Poles in the District of Lublin became particularly intense in the spring of 1944. Thousands of Poles had arrived from Volhynia in 1943, fleeing attacks by the OUN and the UPA. Simultaneously, the Germans had begun deporting Ukrainians from Tomaszów county, sending them to areas near Biłgoraj from which Poles had been removed (Wołczew 1969, 163). Polish fighters in the AK, Bataliony Chłopskie (Peasants' Battalions, BCH) and Związek Walki Zbrojnej (Union of Armed Struggle, ZWZ) began burning homes and demanding that Ukrainians leave the Hrubieszów, Tomaszów, and Zamość areas (165). Many Poles were convinced that the Germans were working with detachments of the Galicia Division (meaning, in most instances, the 4th and 5th Galician ss Volunteer Regiments) and the UPA.

The Germans in turn exacerbated conflicts by using one nationality against the other in accordance with the policy of *divide et impera*, which, from the first, had been a deliberate strategy. Hans Frank, the head of the GG, had already on 12 April 1940 used the term to describe his policy and repeated it on 16 December 1941 when he said: "Ukrainians are principally useful as a counterforce in relation to the Poles" (Torzecki 1969, 156). It appeared to many observers that, once the Jews had been exterminated, the Germans intended to remove the Poles and then the Ukrainians (156, 160).

In this situation local forces felt empowered to commit acts of violence on behalf of their communities or simply to plunder whenever the opportunity arose. Attacks on Ukrainian communities were reported to the UTSK's Kraków office on a regular basis. One letter, dated 4 February 1944, signed by Mykhailo Fedirchuk from the village of Horishnii Potik in Biłgoraj county, complained of robberies, the destruction of the local church, and the murder of thirteen people over the last year by "Polish bandits." Victims included local representative of the UTSK, the deacon, the priest, the district secretary with his wife and father-in-law, the village head, and ordinary villagers (Veryha 1980, 235–9). The murder of Ukrainian village heads and community figures continued throughout 1942 and 1943.[2]

In both communities there were people who did not support the armed bands, but the political middle ground was hard to find. The AK and the Polish government in exile were adamant that, after the war, not only "Zakerzonnia" but Galicia and Volhynia had to remain part of a reconstituted Polish state, while the OUN and the UPA insisted that territories with majority Ukrainian population should become part of an independent Ukrainian state.

Reports by the Galicia Division's soldiers describe what they witnessed in this war theatre.[3] Lev Stetskevych recalls marching past deserted Ukrainian villages. Their inhabitants had been persuaded to move to Soviet Ukraine in 1940 and the houses had then been burned by Polish partisans to prevent anyone returning (Stetskevych 1998, 29). Volodymyr Ketsun remembers seeing ruined houses with only chimneys still standing and comments on the hatred between Ukrainians and Poles, Roman Catholics and Orthodox (Ketsun 2013, 14). Yaroslav Ovad reports that when his company entered Tarnogród a day after Soviet partisans had been there they found that the administrative centre had been destroyed, the police had run away, the Ukrainian co-operative had been robbed and its building burned. Several Ukrainian village activists had been killed, but not a single Pole, and the Polish co-op building remained untouched. All prominent Ukrainians (the priest, teachers, doctor, lawyer, head of the co-operative) had fled, but the prominent Poles (the doctor, lawyer, teachers) had remained (Ovad 1999, 51).

The Battle Group participated in one major military action in Chmielek (Ukr: Khmelik), where about four hundred partisans confronted a similar number of soldiers from the Division, who were reinforced after two hours by three hundred men (Ponomarenko 2016, 65–6). Most of the time, however, the Division's soldiers chased partisan fighters with little success.

Because of the complex local situation, on 27 February, prior to the any action taking place, Beyersdorff issued special instructions on correct behaviour towards civilians. Soldiers were told the following: (1) They could not arrest civilians on their own. When required by military necessity, the suspects had to be apprehended and delivered to the command post. (2) Shooting at civilians was only permitted when they were armed and were attempting to use their weapons or when they tried to flee after being ordered to halt. (3) It was forbidden to beat and abuse any arrested individual. (4) It was strictly forbidden to plunder or to acquire any goods (Melnyk 2016, 1:165).

Orders with a similar blend of moderation and harshness were typically given by the German command in anti-partisan actions wherever the local population expressed different loyalties (Shepherd 2012, 143). Stetskevych confirms that the officers insisted on courteous conduct towards Polish civilians. He describes staying for several days in the area of Zwierzyniec, where "the Polish population tried to get to know our boys, to strike up conversations, to spread defeatism and to demoralize them, particularly through the agency of girls" (Stetskevych 1986, 69). He was aware that local Poles and Ukrainians detested one another but still got along well with the family of the estate administrator at whose place he was quartered, even though the latter encouraged him to desert. Stetskevych did not tell the Germans about this, knowing that the Poles "could not have done otherwise" (69). He was vexed, however, that the honeytrap diplomacy of Polish girls proved effective and led to several desertions.

Myroslav Holowaty recalled that Polish civilians tried to avoid the Battle Group, while Ukrainians welcomed it. He also wrote that sometimes locals did not have a sense of national identity, in his words, "did not know they were Ukrainians," and that a number of *Volksdeutsche* carried weapons and secretly "worked for the Poles." This made for a treacherous situation. One night, three Division soldiers were killed while sleeping. When the Division entered the village in search of the culprits, it looked for partisans, who could sometimes be recognized by the marks left on clothing after a gun had been fired. However, all the menfolk had left, leaving only women and children. The soldiers tried to avoid contributing to the cycle of revenge killings between Ukrainians and Poles. Because they feared surprise attacks, and did not want locals to get caught in firefights, the troops slept more often in the fields than in houses.[4]

Two incidents have been recorded in memoirs. On 2 March, scouting the area about seven kilometres from Tarnogród, Roman Dolynskyi stopped a sleigh coming from Biłgoraj. His reconnaissance party searched it and asked for documents. He reports:

> The sleigh, according to the documents, was transporting the local doctor, who was a *Volksdeutscher* Pole, a Polish hospital nurse, and a butcher, who acted as driver and was going to do some business in the co-operative. It appeared suspicious to me that immediately after the appearance of the partisan group these people were travelling freely through such a dangerous area along mined roads. I let them go without showing any suspicions but told two riders to use paths through the fields so as to get to the outpost ahead of the sleigh and indicated that these people should be checked at headquarters ... The

detainment was made by the Head of Intelligence, Lieutenant Ya., a former participant in the battles for Transcarpathia and an experienced officer. During the required search, he found on the doctor a pass issued by the underground and approved by Kovpak's headquarters. Having written up the appropriate report in the presence of the headquarter's adjutant [Mykhailo Kachmar] and another officer, and following wartime instructions, he ordered the doctor shot as a spy. (Dolynskyi 1957, 7–10, 6)

The sentence was carried out immediately. The nurse and butcher were held for questioning. According to Polish documentation, Ukrainians killed three other representatives of the Polish intelligentsia in Tarnogród.

The execution of the doctor, whose name was Krzyszkiewicz, was investigated because his friend the county commissioner (*Kreishauptmann*) sent letters to Berlin and the Division's headquarters complaining that an innocent man had been killed. Rumours of a court martial began circulating. Dmytro Paliiv and two members of the Military Board, Osyp Navrotskyi and Yevhen Pyndus, came to investigate the circumstances. However, no German commission was sent, which would normally have been the case in such a serious matter. After some time, it was revealed that the commissioner, who was responsible for provisions, had been sending the Division low-quality, often spoiled food. When Paliiv and Reverend Durbak inspected the storehouses, they discovered a large stash of hidden, high-quality supplies. The commissioner was accused of sabotage, fired, sent to Lublin, and the investigation into the execution was closed (Ponomarenko 2016, 82).

Poor provisioning led to a second major incident. In order to improve the food supply the adjutant Mykhailo Kachmar and two other men travelled to villages to buy chickens, geese, ducks, and other products. Requisitioning was strictly prohibited, but the village head was supposed to point out the richest farmers and these were to be paid according to state prices. Naturally, the farmers were unhappy because state prices were lower than market value. When the food supply was inadequate, this led to illegal requisitioning from the Polish population, which viewed this as confiscation or theft. At one point, the 2nd Company's commander Bohdan Sobolevskyi was informed that a pig had been stolen. Although he denied any knowledge, the 1st Company's commander admitted eating it with him. That same evening Sobolevskyi wrote several letters taking responsibility for the breach of discipline and then shot himself. In some places the "confiscation" of food products was widespread, a not uncommon feature of military campaigns.

Besides the shooting of Doctor Kryszkiewicz and the three other Poles in Tarnogród, one Polish woman was raped by a Ukrainian soldier. Beyersdorff wanted to execute the man without a trial, but Ukrainian officers convinced him to send the offender back to the Division, presumably for a court martial. It is not known what happened to him. Ponomarenko found no evidence that the Beyersdorff Group conducted "punitive actions" or applied the principle of collective punishment to the population (Ponomarenko 2016, 86). Heike, whose statement about "poor behaviour" seems to have been a reference to these incidents, also noted that it was the Division's practice to investigate all charges and, "if there was evidence, the guilty were punished" ([Haike] 2013, 44).

The Battle Group has been accused of destroying villages, killing innocent civilians, or shipping them off to Germany. Because in many instances the Division was not in the given location on the dates specified, these charges do not appear credible. Among them are attacks on the villages of Smoligów on 27 March 1944, Poturzyn on 1 April 1944, and Wicyń (Ukr: Vitsyn, now Smerekivka near Lviv) on 25 April 1944. Michael Melnyk has reviewed the daily situation reports dealing with antipartisan actions in Lublin district, which detail each action, including enemy losses, civilian losses. and German casualties. He has found no mention of the above places in the reports (Melnyk 2010; Melnyk 2016 1:169).

In discussing the actions of the Beyersdorff Group, Grzegorz Motyka (2011, 261), one of the most authoritative Polish researchers of this period, writes that it is "at least probable" that during the operations in March 1944 "the murder of civilians occurred." However, he produces no evidence and notes that attacks against civilians in two places might be attributable to the 5th Police Regiment of the PPT (Polizeihilfsdienst bataillone in German, or Pagalbinės policijos tarnyba). This was a Lithuanian group under the command of Franz Lechthaler, which fought Soviet and Polish partisans along the Bug River in March and April 1944 (261). Because several other German units operated in the area south and east of Lublin, including the 4th and 5th Galician Volunteer Regiment, it appears more likely that they were responsible for any anti-civilian actions that occurred.

6

DISTRICT OF LUBLIN AS WAR THEATRE: BATTALIONS, GUARDS, AND MUTINIES

In the Lublin district a number of police, guard, and anti-partisan battalions were composed of Ukrainians, some of whom joined the Division near the end of the war. Vasyl Tatarskyi and Orest Horodyskyi were both officers in Schutzmannschaft Battalion 204 and have left accounts. Tatarskyi joined the Division in September 1944 and Horodyskyi in March 1945.

Tatarskyi had been a soldier in the Polish army and, after the German invasion of 1939, was pressured by the Gestapo to inform on fellow Polish officers and fellow Ukrainians. When presented with the alternative of serving in Schutszmannschaft 204, which was composed of Ukrainians, he accepted. The battalion's men refused to wear swastikas and other German insignia, and after they protested the *Untermenschen* label were told they would be treated in the same way as Germans. Tatarskyi informs us that he reported a German who refused to salute him as his senior. As a result, the German was sent to the front (Tatarskyi 1983, 138).

The battalion trained in Heidelager alongside Schutzmannschaft Battalion 203, a similar Polish battalion with Polish officers. Tatarskyi even recognized one man with whom he had trained in the Polish army. After training was completed, the Ukrainian battalion was sent to do guard duty on Polish ethnic territory, while the Polish battalion was sent to Ukrainian territory in Chełm and Volhynia – an example of German divide-and-conquer tactics.[1] Tatarskyi's battalion guarded a concentration camp near Heidelager and escorted the Polish prisoners to and from work. The camp's inmates sometimes attacked and killed their Ukrainian guards. The battalion also guarded an estate about eight kilometres away (Tatarskyi 1983, 140–1). Polish partisans in the woods around Heidelager regularly attacked guard posts and prisons. In response the Germans organized surprise attacks against Polish villages and shot innocent people without any investigation. This happened in Brzeźnica near Heidelager, where on one night the Gestapo shot five Polish families, who, according to local inhabitants, had never taken part in any partisan actions (145).

When Tatarskyi received permission to visit his home in the area that Romania had occupied and named Transnistria, he witnessed a Jewish ghetto, where many Jews from Poland and Germany were held. The head of the local school showed him a textbook, which was to be used in teaching history. It described Transnistria as belonging to Romania for over a thousand years before being conquered by Moscow (Tatarskyi 1983, 143–4).

The Germans made some concessions to national feelings. On 4 June 1944, at Tatarskyi's request, the battalion was allowed to organize an evening commemorating Symon Petliura and Yevhen Konovalets. Mass was served, speeches were given by Horodyskyi and Ivan Danyliuk, a choir performed, and poems were recited. The event was even reported in *Krakivski visti* on 2 July 1944, with a note that Captain Tatarskyi opened the evening and the hall was "decorated with Ukrainian and German flags and portraits of leaders." However, when a man called Masliak was caught with OUN-B literature, a Captain Halanevych reported him to the Gestapo. Halanevych was trying to ingratiate himself with the Germans and could not be dissuaded from informing on Masliak. The latter was taken away but avoided punishment by joining the Galicia Division (Tatarskyi 1983, 145). Ironically, Halanevych also joined the Division shortly afterwards.

Later in the year both Tatarskyi and Horodyskyi escaped from the battalion and joined the Ukrainian Legion of Self-Defence (ULS) before being transferred to the Division. Tatarskyi (1983, 156) describes the situation as follows:

> The front was coming closer and closer and the Germans began making field fortifications and anti-tank barriers in the area. Seeing such preparations, people from the battalion began deserting. The first

to do so was Lieutenant I[van] Danyliuk with his entire field guard, armed with a heavy machine gun. After him Lieutenant Colonel O[rest] Horodyskyi deserted to the Melnyk Legion [ULS], which was stationed at that time near Miechów and was scheduled to go to Warsaw. I helped Horodyskyi desert, driving him there with his things. The Germans already distrusted our battalion and decided to disarm it. Using the pretext that the weapons needed examining by a specialist, they ordered the battalion to lay down its arms in an appointed place.

The Germans suspected Tatarskyi of abetting the desertions and planned to arrest him. Because of this he requested transfer to the Galicia Division. An experienced officer, who had already served in the Russian, UNR, and Polish armies, he was sent to Slovakia, served in Wildner's Battle Group, and from that moment shared the Division's fate. His own political orientation was to the UNR, and, after the war, he worked in Neu-Ulm and Munich for this government in exile, for which he was regularly denounced by the OUN-B, whose political chicanery and attempts to gain political control within the DP camps he exposed (Tatarskyi 1983, 186–90, 196–200).

Late in 1944 the ULS was directed by the Germans to Slovenia to fight Tito's partisans.[2] In March 1945 it was integrated into the Division. The Legion's story is complicated. It began as a partisan group loyal to the OUN-M. While fighting Polish and Soviet partisans in Volhynia near Kremenets (Pol: Krzemieniec) and Lutsk (Pol: Łuck) it was disarmed by supporters of the OUN's Bandera wing, who were trying to gain control of all partisan units. The Security Service (SB) of Bandera's OUN was at the time killing fighters in the underground who refused to subordinate themselves.[3] Some of the disarmed men approached Siegfried Assmuss of the German SD and negotiated an agreement to become a self-defence legion that would fight Soviet and Polish partisans.[4] According to the deal, they would serve under Ukrainian commanders and the Germans would provide them with weapons and intelligence (Hirniak 1977, 19–20). The force was incorporated into the Order Police as Schutzmannschaft Battalion der SD 31 but was commonly referred to as the Ukrainischer Selbstschutzlegion (Ukrainian Legion of Self-Defence). By the summer of 1944 it numbered around one thousand men and had about ten Germans attached to it as liaison officers (Radchenko and Usach 2020, 454).

At first it operated near Kremenets, Dubno, and Lutsk, coordinating its actions with Assmuss, who arranged for its safe passage through German forces. When it moved west and entered the Lublin district, Assmuss was killed in an ambush. His place as chief German liaison officer was taken by Heinrich Biegelmayer of the Lublin SD, who demanded that the force combat the Polish underground.[5]

Early in 1944, Oleksandr Kvitko became the group's commander, while Mykhailo Soltys remained its political leader.[6] Near Hrubieszów on 27 April 1944 it published a call "To All Volhynian Ukrainians":

> Your place is not in the miserable and hopeless emigration, not among beggarly refugees, not in the convoys of evacuation wagons or automobiles travelling west, not in the shameful crowd escaping from the Bolsheviks, not in senseless wandering among forest detachments. Your place is in the hard, concrete and fearless ranks of the Ukrainian Legion of Self-Defence. You should be here, where a military, organized struggle is taking place against Bolshevik and Polish imperialism! (UCRDC, 2016.7. B11, Military Board, Documents V. "Vidozva Do vsikh Ukraintsiv-Volyniakiv!")

According to Polish and Soviet accounts, the unit murdered Polish civilians in Pidhaitsi, Karczunek, and Edwardpole, near Volodymyr-Volynskyi. In retaliation for Assmuss's killing, on 23 July 1944 it is alleged to have killed forty-four people in the villages of Chlaniów and Wladyslawin. These accusations were made in the Soviet press in 1984 and were later examined by Polish and Ukrainian researchers (Styrkul 1984, 271; Radchenko and Usach 2020, 453–60, 471). In 2013 a number of articles in the Associated Press accused Mykhailo Karkots (Karkoc) of participating in these wartime atrocities, and in 2017 the Polish government announced that it would seek his extradition from the US to be tried for war crimes. He died in 2019 and the accusations were never tested in court (Radchenko and Usach 2020, 450). Despite discrepancies in various accounts, available information appears to confirm the culpability of key figures.[7]

The ULS viewed itself as using contacts with the Germans to defend the Ukrainian population from Soviet and Polish partisans (Kartots 2002, 158). It therefore refused some German orders. Soltys was arrested and executed for doing so. At one point, Biegelmayer ordered the unit disarmed. He also insisted on the unit's participation in putting down the Warsaw Uprising.[8]

Records list the presence of over one hundred ULS men in Warsaw, twelve of whom were killed in action and thirty-four wounded.[9] A Soviet researcher has accused the unit of being "among the butchers" (Styrkul 1984, 274–5). However, Radchenko and Usach found no evidence of war crimes. They note that the unit fought off at least ten assaults on the highway linking Warsaw to the district of Praga (Radchenko and Usach 2020, 454).

The accusation against Petro Diachenko in connection with the Uprising was made in the same Soviet publication and then repeated in the West at the time of the Deschênes inquiry. Diachenko had served as an officer in the Russian army during the First World War, then in the UNR's army from 1918, and the Polish army in 1939, where he was wounded, captured, and sent to a German POW camp. By 1941, when the German-Soviet war began, he had been released and was living in the Chełm area. He was contacted by the Ukrainian underground and agreed to serve, first as a military instructor and then as a commanding officer. His partisan group joined the ULS in Miechów and he took command of the force when it was in Warsaw.[10]

Members of the Galicia Division themselves expressed doubts about the biographies of some men in the ULS. Myroslav (Myron) Holowaty, in an oral interview, testified that, although he was informed of all the places in which the Galicia Division saw action and knew of no evidence of war crimes, he was "not sure" about the Legion. He had access to memoirs in which one soldier from the Legion described the military action in Warsaw. According to Holowaty, the text does not mention any brutality: "The Germans put them in a place where they were a kind of barrier preventing the Poles from crossing. There are some descriptions which mention preventing people from crossing by firing from a machine gun" (UCRDC, Holowaty). The Uprising began on 1 August and ended on 3 October, after sixty-three days.[11]

In October 1944, the Legion was removed from the list of Order Police units and sent to Kraków. On 12 January 1945, about five hundred men from the unit were sent to Zakopane to combat Polish partisans. The unit at that time discussed breaking through to Ukrainian territory and joining the UPA (Horodyskyi 1962, 23). However, they were sent through Czechoslovakia to Slovenia, where they joined the action against Tito's partisans.

By all accounts the ULS was well organized and trained. It had its own priest, Reverend Palladii Dubytskyi, its own propaganda section, which published the periodical *Ukrainskyi lehion* (Ukrainian legion), its own nurses and medical staff, and its own officer training school. Many of the Legion's members had been victims of the Nazis. Several, including at least one nurse, had been released from German prisons on condition that they join the unit. The nurse had been arrested for evading compulsory labour in Germany. One man agreed to join in return for the release of his brother from Majdanek concentration camp (Radchenko and Usach 2020, 460). Horodyskyi (1962, 22) describes the Legion as composed of "strong Ukrainian patriots whose participation on the German side was conjunctural." The force considered itself an independent structure with Ukrainian officers.[12] Others, however, have commented that it quickly "turned itself into a German weapon" (Radchenko and Usach 2020, 460).

On 5 March 1945, the morning on which the ULS was to be integrated into the Galicia Division, about 250 men who were dissatisfied with losing their status as an autonomous unit left with the intention of making their way to Ukraine (Hirniak 1977, 50; Karkots 2002, 164–5). Led by Roman Kyveliuk (alias Voron), the rebels contacted Yugoslav royalist and nationalist partisans (the Chetniks under General Dragoljub Mihailović) for help in crossing the River Mur by ferry. Within two days the rebel group had been surrounded by the Division's men and forced to return, with assurances that no one would be punished for trying to leave.[13] The Legion's merger with the Division took place on 9 March, after which the men were dispersed throughout the force. They were permitted to retain their ranks and, by all accounts, fought exceptionally well in ensuing anti-partisan action (Lysiak 1996, 69). Five of the rebels were imprisoned (Radchenko and Usach 2020, 465). Kyveliuk was summoned to the Division's headquarters by General Freitag and shot, reportedly for trying to escape.

Lysiak, who worked as a photographer and writer for the Division's newspaper *Do zbroi* (To arms), described the Legion as having a German major as official commander, a Ukrainian officer as semi-official commander, and Kyveliuk from the OUN-M as unofficial commander. This "should not surprise anyone," he wrote, because "similar mysteries" existed in all formations to which the Germans agreed (Lysiak 1951, 2).

A number of young people from the Chełm region, after serving elsewhere, also found their way into the Galicia Division at the war's end. Some were boys from Chełm's Ukrainian gymnasium. At the 1943 graduation ceremony, with members of the German administration in attendance, one boy was ordered by the school's director Stavnychyi to thank the Third Reich and the Führer on behalf of the new graduates for helping Ukrainian youth in their studies, and to promise that they would all gratefully join the ranks of the Galicia Division. The selected eulogist was unable to escape the task:

> I tried to get out of it, as best I could, explicitly and honestly telling Stavnychyi that there was no such gratitude and no one was preparing to join the Division, least of all myself, and therefore all these promises would simply be lies. The director encouraged me, saying that he himself was not enthusiastic about enlistment in the Division, that he knew the mood of young people, but for the gymnasium's continued success some smoke had to be blown into German eyes at the graduation. In the end I agreed and gave a speech in the required spirit, although I cannot remember whether it was in German or Ukrainian. Neither I, nor any of my friends signed up for the Division. At least not immediately. I went there eventually, but by a circuitous route. (K. 1963, 20)

Two of the gymnasium's graduates enlisted, one of whom was Orest Slupchynsky. Over a dozen others from the Chełm area ended up in the Division involuntarily, some after escaping forced labour in Germany.

A group of men recruited in 1941 by the ss was trained near Trawniki. These men served as auxiliaries and "indigenous collaborators" for Operation Reinhard – the murder of Jews in the GG – which was managed by Odilo Globočnik, the ssPF for the Lublin district. Three killing camps – Bełżec, Sobibór, and Treblinka – were built. In them, the Germans killed 1.5 million Jews, either in gas chambers or by shooting them in nearby pits (Black 2011, 2). The operation spanned the entire territory of the Lublin district and in 1943 spilled across the border into the Białystok district. Little is known of these police auxiliaries, who were called "Ukrainians" by their victims and commanders but came from many regions and were of different nationalities. Virtually none of the first Trawniki guards were from the region in which these murderous tasks were carried out (44).[14]

Trawniki men were stationed in various camps in the district. They helped put down the Warsaw Uprising and were in Lviv between January and September 1942, where they served as guards for the Yanivska (Janówska) Street Forced Labour Camp for Jews.[15] The plan to "Germanize" the Zamość region in the winter of 1942–43 was also implemented with the assistance of Trawniki-trained detachments. This disastrous project incited unrest and led to Himmler removing Globočnik from Lublin in late summer of 1943 and sending him to Trieste, along with most of the Operation Reinhard staff.

Some Trawniki men were later used as guards on estates throughout the Lublin district. They also supported the Security Police and gendarmes who were searching for Jews, pursuing partisans, transporting forced labourers, and protecting supply depots. Ivan Bogdanov, a veteran of Trawniki's NCO training program, recalled how he and his men, "along with a Ukrainian ss unit [perhaps a reference to the 5th Galician ss Volunteer Regiment] and a German police detachment," searched for partisans in the vicinity of Hrubieszów in March 1944. After partisans managed to kill two Trawniki men and wounded two others, a company detailed from Lublin burned down several settlements. Bogdanov recalls that one of them, consisting of fifty households, was completely destroyed along with its inhabitants: "These Polish citizens who ran out of the burning buildings were shot. I participated directly in this expedition and I shot at the Polish citizens … running out of their burning homes" (Black 2011, 42).

As will be seen in chapter 16, two men in the Galicia Division were trained at Trawniki.

Mutinies

Towards the end of the war there were several mutinies among soldiers in German service. About twelve hundred men from Schutzmannschaft Battalions 102, 115, and 118, which had been recruited from Ukrainians and were stationed in Belarus and Ukraine, became part of the newly created 30th Waffen-Grenadierdivision der ss (russiche 2).[16] They were sent to France on 18 August 1944 to the area of the Voges Mountains and the so-called Belfort Gap. Since northern and southern France had been invaded, this gap in the mountains was the only remaining channel for transporting men and supplies to Germany. The men had no desire to be used against Allied troops and contacted the Maquis. When the German command learned of the plot to desert, they began transporting the men to their garrison in Vesoul, either for imprisonment or execution.

However, on 26 August 1944, 460 men in what had earlier been Schutzmannschaft Battalion 118 shot their twenty-five German officers and NCOs in Valdahoul near Besancon. On the following day, 820 men in what had earlier been Schutzmannschaft Battalion 102 shot their 24 German officers and 70 NCOs near Vesoul. Most of the men who defected were Ukrainians.

A group from Battalion 102 also mutinied as their train stopped en route. A flare was sent up as a signal and the entire unit made off to the Maquis with equipment, arms, and horses. In response to the mutiny the Germans reportedly shot five officers and one hundred men who were not on the train. The remaining men from Battalions 115 and 118 were imprisoned by the Germans on 10 September 1944. They were freed by the Americans at the end of the war (Pasichnyk 1957, 8–11).

The French underground immediately integrated the escaped soldiers into the French Resistance (FFI) designating them the Batallion Ukrainien (BUK 1 and BUK 2). Informally the men called their respective units the "Ivan Bohun" and "Taras Shevchenko" Battalions. The larger BUK 1 fought the Germans in major battles at Confrancourt on 28 August, Semadon on 29 August, and Melin on 2 September. The unit helped to liberate Confracourt and Combeaufontaine. The smaller BUK 2 fought northwest of Besanson near Belmont, where it helped capture the town of Pontarlier. Today the men of the BUK 1 and 2 are considered heroes of the French Resistance. Several were awarded the Legion d'Honneur and the Croix de Guerre, and a monument has been erected to them in Confracourt.

The earlier history of these units has not been adequately investigated. Battalion 118 had been recruited in the Kyiv area, while Battalion 102 had been created in Kremenets near Ternopil and had served as a police auxiliary unit protecting military and transportation sites from Soviet partisans. It included former Soviet POWs, victims of Stalin's famine of 1932–33, and men who had been given a choice between enlistment and forced labour (Sorobey 2016). According to Dean (2000, 63), before its transfer to anti-partisan operations in Belarus the unit had participated in the mass execution of Jews in Kremenets in the late summer of 1942.

Both battalions completed training in October 1942 and were assigned to guard duty in Ukraine and Belarus. The 102 was at first stationed near Postavy and then Kopyl in Belarus. As a *Wach-Batallion* its duty was to guard railways and military installations. Its Ukrainian commander, Major

Rudnyk, was in contact with the Ukrainian underground, whose partisan armies in 1943 began attacking German police stations and prisons, and combating Soviet and Polish partisan groups. Rudnyk was ordered in November 1943 to conduct his battalion into Ukraine and join the UPA in the Kremianets-Rivne-Kostopil region, which had succeeded in pushing Soviet partisans north into Belarus. He planned to make his move on 12 December 1943, but he was injured in a battle with Soviet partisans on 6 December and the plan had to be delayed. In January 1944, because the Red Army front was advancing, the Germans decided to withdraw the battalion. It was sent on 2 February 1944 to Deutsch-Eylau south of Danzig (Gdansk) for a further six months of training. Although now officially named Schutzmannschaft Battalion 61, the men continued to refer to themselves as the Battalion 102 (Kosyk 1994, 3).

On 1 August 1944, the unit was combined with other Belarusian, Russian, and Cossack units to form the 30th Waffen-ss Grenadier Division (russische 2).[17] At that point it contained 820 Ukrainians and about 200 Germans. These Schutzmannschaft battalions have been accused of complicity in anti-civilian violence. Battalion 118 has, for example, been charged with participating in the murder of 147 people in Khatyn (Chatyń) in Belarus on 22 March 1943.[18]

American officers who had been parachuted to help organize the French Resistance fought alongside the BUK. Together with commanders in the Resistance they explained to French authorities that repatriation would almost certainly mean death for the men, who were now part of the French army and had made an important contribution to the liberation of France. Initially, French authorities considered disarming the men of BUK 2 and sending them to Marseilles, where they were supposed to board a ship for Odesa. However, they instead offered them the option of serving in the French Foreign Legion.[19] Most enrolled into General Jean de Lattre's 13th Demi-Brigade (13e Demi-Brigade de Legion Etrangère), which had fought in Norway, Syria, Africa, and Italy. Twenty men agreed to repatriation and were either executed or sent to the Gulag.

A few men from the BUK battalions came to Canada, including the highest-ranking Ukrainian officer, Major Leon (Lev) Hloba, who became a photographer for the *Hamilton Spectator*. His story came to light after his death on 31 December 2012 in Dundas, Ontario.[20]

Less well known is the fact that a group from the Galicia Division's reserve regiment also mutinied. It was led by Osyp Krukovskyi and Myron Protsakevych. Krukovskyi found himself in France at the outbreak of the Second World War, volunteered for the French army on 7 September 1939, and served until demobilized in 1940. He then returned to Ukraine, and in 1943 volunteered for the Galicia Division. He was sent to Tarbes as part of the reserve regiment, where he made contact with the French Resistance and prepared to desert with his fellow soldiers. However, someone informed on the group and they were arrested. When the train transporting them back to Germany was bombed near Tours, Krukovskyi and about forty prisoners escaped in the panic, taking horses and weapons with them. Krukovskyi created a Ukrainian partisan unit within the FFI-Tours, which was commanded by Legendre (known as Legrand in the Resistance) (Kosyk 1994, 36; Nebeliuk 1951, 199–200). These former Galicia Division soldiers helped to capture Loches, near Tours. Two died in the fighting. The group then fought alongside the Resistance from 30 August until 3 September 1944. At the end of the year Krukovskyi joined the French Foreign Legion, was wounded, and demobilized.

The story of how these units joined the Resistance and were decorated by the French as heroes illustrates some complexities of wartime history, which saw men change sides, sometimes more than once, while at times concealing their motivation and altering their biographies.

7

GALICIAN SS VOLUNTEER REGIMENTS

Four military formations with a total number of 6,112 soldiers bore the name Galician ss Volunteer Regiment (Galizische ss-Freiwilligen Regiment). They were numbered 4, 5, 6, and 7. A number 8 was planned but never created. The regiments were formed from men who had volunteered for the Galicia Division but were considered unsuitable, often because they did not make the height requirement of 165 centimetres. They were trained by the Order Police and placed under its commander Kurt Daluege. There were no Ukrainian officers in the regiments, and the Division exercised no control over them.

The Germans had discussed forming a police rifle division (to be called Polizei Schützen Division Galizien) but dropped the idea in March 1943 when they decided to create the Waffen-ss Galicia Division. However, as soon as it became clear that there were more volunteers than required for the twelve-thousand-strong Galicia Division, it was resolved to make police regiments out of the personnel excess. The name "Galician ss Volunteer Regiments" was chosen to camouflage the fact that these units served the Order Police. Subterfuge was required because the Germans had agreed that the Division's volunteers would only serve in front-line units.

The nomenclature led to considerable confusion. Although remnants of these regiments were only incorporated into the Galicia Division near the war's end, the men saw themselves as associated with the force. So did the Military Board, and so did the general population, which referred to the soldiers as "our ss men" (nashi eses-y), or simply as Galicia Division men. The numbering of the regiments contributed to the confusion. Since there were three regiments in the Galicia Division, originally numbered 1 to 3, it was natural to assume that the Volunteer Regiments 4 to 8 were to be added later. These four regiments were deployed before the Division itself, which suggests that the intention all along had been to rush them into police work.

Gottlob Berger, who supervised Waffen-ss recruiting, and Otto Wächter objected to the forming of police regiments. Himmler, too, was aware that there would be "undesirable political consequences" in the form of dissatisfaction among Ukrainians, so he ordered that "for psychological and political reasons" the regiments would be designated "Galizische ss-Freiwilligen Regimenter" (Melnyk 2002, 61–2). When on 9 February 1944 the 4th and 5th were assigned to anti-partisan action and placed under the control of HSSPF Wilhelm Koppe, Wächter once more protested in Kraków on 16 February 1944 (100, 352).[1]

However, the governor of Galicia skilfully manoeuvred Kubijovyč when the issue came up. In a letter to Kubijovyč from 15 December 1943 he explained that the Waffen-ss did not have the capacity to train all recruits and therefore police instructors had to do the job. He then added that it was impossible to say when the men would be able to join the Division because this question would be decided by higher military authorities, and, in any case, the regiments, like all formations, required an opportunity to prove themselves. He ended on a note of flattery, stating that the regiments made an excellent impression on him when he visited them in Alsace and southern France, that he was confident they would perform exceptionally well after a prolonged period of apprenticeship, and that Galician Ukraine would enjoy a full and active presence when the "beautiful goal" they had together embarked upon on 28 April was achieved (Veryha 2000, 1280–3). Wächter never mentioned a Ukrainian state or identity, or the fact that the regiments were being deployed in anti-partisan and police actions.

The soldiers in the 4th and 5th Regiments were given blank collar patches. They were sent the lion collar tabs and armshields after deployment in January 1944. Photographic evidence shows that some men, both Germans and Ukrainians, attached the latter, including Major Siegfried Binz of the 4th Regiment.[2] Therefore, people who saw the men naturally assumed they were part of the Galicia Division. However, the Volunteer Regiments trained for a much shorter time and had exclusively German officers. They were employed by the Order Police to guard communications, industries, roads, and railways, and to conduct reconnaissance patrols in search of partisans, armed groups, and saboteurs.

The 4th Galician SS Volunteer Regiment

Formation of the 4th Regiment began on 15 July 1943. With a strength of 1,264 men, it trained primarily near Zabern (now Saverne, Alsace), but its 3rd Battalion was sent for a time to Maastricht in the Netherlands. The regiment was led by Siegfried Binz, who had been decorated during the First World War and in 1941 served with ss Police Regiment 23 (to which his Police Battalion 307 was subordinated). He took part in anti-partisan actions in Belarus and executed Jews.[3] Heinrich Plantius led the regiment's 3rd Battalion. He had been a captain and adjutant in Police Battalion 306 in 1941–42 and took part in the destruction of the Jewish population of Pinsk.[4]

While in training, the 4th Regiment was visited by Mykhailo Khronoviat and Andrii Palii of the Military Board, which sent the men Christmas presents. The holiday was celebrated on 6 January 1944 in the Ukrainian tradition with *kutia*, a decorated tree, cards, a manger scene, and a play. After sixteen weeks of basic training, the men were pressed into action because of the critical situation created by the incursion of Soviet partisan groups. The regiment's 2nd Battalion was sent to the area near Brody in the second half of February, close to where the 4th Soviet Tank Army was located and where Petro Vershyhora's 3rd Sumsk Battalion had completed a raid on 15 February.

For propaganda purposes the regiment's 1st Battalion was sent to Lviv, where on 24 February it participated in a parade and was addressed by both Wächter and the Military Board's Yevhen Pyndus ("Na pole boiu" 1944). *Krakivski visti* described the men as "the first detachments of the Galicia Division on their way to the front" (ibid.). The regiment's 3rd Battalion left Maastricht on 19 February and was deployed in the Ternopil area.

The 4th Regiment was spread over an area of 170 kilometres directly behind the front line, stretching from Radekhiv northeast of Lviv through Zolochiv and Zbarazh to Shelpaky northeast of Ternopil. Radekhiv had recently been invaded by Soviet partisans against whom the UPA had been unable to make a response. The men were therefore welcomed. They began reconnaissance patrols, repaired roads, removed mines, and guarded railway lines. Meanwhile the Red Army was advancing along a broad front.

Throughout February and March the regiment fought Soviet partisans who were destabilizing the situation in the German rear and preventing supplies from reaching the front. The regiment confronted Naumov's cavalry unit of fifteen hundred to two thousand, which had been chased out of Poland on 27 February and gathered north of Zhovkva on 1–2 March. Naumov then retreated first to Stanislavchyk and then to the village of Hutysko northeast of Lviv. He then moved in the direction of Brody and on 22–23 March broke through the encirclement and moved to Volhynia. His losses were 147 killed, 299 wounded, and 96 unaccounted for (Ponomarenko 2017, 71).

Another partisan unit under Mikhail Shukaev, with approximately one thousand men, attempted to attack the oil production in Boryslav but was prevented from doing so by men from the 4th Regiment, who met it in Zaliztsi, northwest of Ternopil, on 9 March (Ponomarenko 2017, 71–2). On 20 March the Red Army attacked Brody, forcing the regiment into front-line action in several places. It fought the 13th Army near Stanyslavchyk and helped to stabilize the front on 9 April.

The regiment's 3rd Battalion found itself directly facing the Red Army advance. On 29 February it had chased the 1st Moldavian Partisan Unit in the Zbarazh area. When the Soviet attack on Ternopil began, the battalion had just arrived in the city. Surprised by the assault, it was badly mauled (Fricke 1986, 28, 44). Its men continued to fight in the following days and helped clear the city of Soviet troops between 9 and 11 March. Hitler had declared Ternopil a fortress and had forbidden any retreat. After the city was surrounded on 24 March, the garrison hung on for three weeks, then tried to break out on 15–16 April. Some 120 men of the 3rd Battalion were trapped in the city along with thirteen hundred troops and seven hundred wounded. Most men died in the breakout attempt. Of the fifty-five who made it out, two were Ukrainians from the 3rd Battalion (Ponomarenko 2018, 118). A number of men escaped to the UPA, while others were captured and pressed into the Red Army.

V. Petrovskyi was one of the latter. He was sent to the Baltic, where on 17–18 August he deserted along with about fifty others and joined the Galicia Division in Slovakia (Ponomarenko 2018, 120; Petrovskyi 1952, 8). The destruction of the 3rd Battalion was used in the OUN-B's agitation against joining the Galicia Division. Leaflets were distributed claiming that, on 5 March, the German officers had escaped, leaving six hundred Ukrainian soldiers to die in the city.[5] In fact, although the 4th Regiment had contacts with the UPA, there were few desertions and only about fifty men ended up in the underground. The men still remaining in the regiment were transferred to the Galicia Division on 17 June. Most became NCOs while in the Neuhammer training camp and then joined the Division in Slovakia.

Several accusations have been levelled against the 4th Regiment. The Polish underground spoke of the destruction of the villages of Yasenytsia (Pol: Jesienica Ruska) and Budky Neznanovski in the county of Kamianka-Strumylova (Pol: Kamionka Strumilowa) and the village of Pavliv (Pol: Pawłów) in the county of Radekhiv, supposedly because their inhabitants refused to leave Ukrainian territory. However, this may have been an evacuation of the civilian population from a front-line region (Ponomarenko 2018, 122). According to Ponomarenko, the statistics bear this out: throughout the entire period of the Second World War in the first village 40 Poles died out of an evacuated total of 500, in the second 21 out of 800, and in the third 41 out of 338. He considers the evacuations to have been a pragmatic action of the German army and rejects the claim that a war crime was committed (123).

Ponomarenko (2018, 70) describes the action in the Polish village of Zawonie, where the regiment's 1st Battalion destroyed part of Naumov's group, as "a successful liquidation of one, relatively small, Soviet partisan detachment." However, this information is contradicted by German reports, which indicate that twenty-two Polish civilians were killed by soldiers from the regiment between 2 and 6 March, and that, on 6 March, fifty civilians were killed and the village burned.[6] The 4th Regiment has also been accused of killing twenty-two people in the village of Khatky (Pol: Chatki) near Pidhaitsi (Pol: Podhajce) on 7 April 1944. According to Ponomarenko, no detachment of the 4th was in the area, but a UPA force may have been present (102).

Ponomarenko agrees that the villagers of Skazhenytsia near Zhukiv in Zolochiv county were removed by the 4th Regiment after an unspecified group destroyed eight Ukrainian farms and killed fifteen people on 3 March 1944 before leaving for the village of Wicyń (now Smerekivka). Polish sources state that between 1939 and 1945 a total of fifty-one people were killed in Wicyń (ten of whom are known by name) and 1,441 removed. "There is no doubt," writes Ponomarenko (2018, 102), "that a detachment of the 2nd Battalion of the 4th Regiment took part in this 'pacification,' which was in fact a deportation of the inhabitants, but did not involve their physical destruction."

There is, however, widespread agreement among scholars that the 4th Regiment was involved in a major atrocity in the village of Huta Peniatska (Pol: Huta Pieniacka) near Brody on 28 February 1944. Early Polish accounts and the memoirs of Dmitrii Medvedev, the Soviet partisan leader who was operating in the area, made no mention the 4th Regiment.[7] When in the 1970s the Ukrainian journalist Oleksandr Matla searched for eyewitnesses he concluded that the regiment's soldiers participated in the military action but not in the punitive action that followed (Matla 1978, 55). An NKVD special operations group assigned to sabotage and intelligence gathering under Boris Krutikov, and which was part of Medvedev's partisan force, left Huta Peniatska shortly before the destruction. Survivors (nineteen according to Medvedev and forty-nine according the Polish government in exile) found their way to Krutikov. Based on this information, Matla suggests that the action could have been provoked by Soviet partisans so as to report the inevitable German reprisal as an attack on civilians (60).

In February 1944 there were several partisan groups in Huta Pieniatska, including the 9th "Chkalov" Battalion, Krutikov's group, the village's self-defence group, which helped Krutikov when he tried to reach Lviv, and about one hundred Polish deserters from the German police forces. These forces also co-operated with the partisan groups of Hydzik (pseudonym "Czarnyi") and Jan Kurilowicz (pseudonym "Riszard") (Juchniewicz 1973, 328, quoted in Veryha 1980, 112; Chobit 2020, 258, 278). In all there were about five hundred armed men in what was a partisan stronghold that kept in touch with local AK headquarters in Brody. In late 1943 and early 1944 this armed village had repelled several attacks by Ukrainian groups.

On 7 March 1944, a week after the village's destruction, Mykhailo Khronoviat gave a report to the Military Board after visiting the 4th Regiment. He testified that during reconnaissance on 23 February two of the regiment's men had been fatally shot. Five days later the Germans conducted their attack, in which a company from the 4th participated. After subduing the resistance, they destroyed the village. This is Khronoviat's description of what happened:

> They set out from Koniushkiv and were in Zharkiv at 2 am on 28. II. 1944. Zharkiv is the last village before Huta Peniatska. At 6 am our advance began; the first patrol had 40 men ... They entered the village of Huta Peniatska after one hour of fighting and were in the village until 11 o'clock. Leaving the village, they took with them the two men killed on 23. II, who were naked and mutilated. The Poles [Mazury] of Huta Peniatska had a reputation: they abused Ukrainians, murdered our peasants, tore the jawbone out of one priest. The whole population

ran to the Catholic Church. They set fire to the village. The houses were stores for ammunition and began to crack as grenades went off. There were also some Jews hiding in the village. In the church they found one *Volksdeutscher*, whom the German commander let go after questioning. Our soldier said: "We shed blood and they are letting them go!" The reply was: "Don't be a fool, man! Why did you bring the *Volkdeutscher* to the commander?" The freed *Volksdeutscher* hung around the soldiers, looking everyone in the eye. He was told: "Go to hell and don't look for joy here!" (Kolisnyk 2009, 213–14)[8]

Khronoviat then stated that the Ukrainian company left and "a separate German unit completely pacified the village, leaving only the church" (214).

In Hunczak's (1993, 61) view, the village of 488 people had been transformed into an encampment of one thousand inhabitants and was attacking neighbouring Ukrainian villages, thus complicating the situation for the Ukrainian underground and for the Germans who were attempting to secure the region for their army's retreat.

Motyka (2011, 261–2) describes the village as a Polish place of self-defence against the UPA, in which a group of Jews had also taken refuge:

For a certain time, a group of Soviet partisans had also been stationed there. On the 23 February 1944 a reconnaissance party from the 4th Regiment appeared near the village. The Poles, thinking they were dealing with an UPA group disguised in German uniforms, attacked the aggressors, killing two of them (the first soldiers of the Division ss Galicia to be killed). The patrol was only saved from complete destruction by a detachment of the "Yastrub" UPA group, which attacked the flank of the Poles.

According to Motyka, the German punitive expedition on 28 February razed the village, murdering several hundred inhabitants. Based on survivor testimonies, the priest Jan Cieński produced an account describing how some people were shot, while others died in burning barns and houses. According to him, when the attack was over people from neighbouring Ukrainian villages arrived in wagons to take away cattle, horses, and pigs (Wolczański 1992–93, 70, quoted in Motyka 2011, 262).

The Polish underground stationed in Lviv reported the action in its survey of events for 5–11 March 1944 as follows:

The Germans sent out a punitive expedition composed mainly of detachments of the ss Division Galicia ... and several Germans ... They began by shooting at the village and sent up flare rockets ... Under this illumination brutal Ukrainians [dzicz ukraińska] burst into the houses, from which they dragged the inhabitants, took them to the local church, then sorted the men, women and girls into groups. The children were killed and thrown into the fire or burned alive. The others were led to the cemetery and either killed on the way or taken to buildings and shot, after which the buildings were set on fire. (*Kwestia ukrainska* 2003, 72, quoted in Motyka 2011, 263)

Initially the Polish underground was unsure who had been responsible and blamed the attack on the Secret Field Police (Geheime Feld Polizei) (PISM, Ministertwo Spraw Wewnetrrzych, Wydzial Spoleczny, *Sprawozdanie sytuacyjne z ziem wschodnich*, no. 12/44, 45, quoted in Veryha 1980, 113). A later situational report for April–May mentioned the "Schützendivision-Galizien" as co-operating with the UPA in murdering Polish settlements "in a bloody and bestial manner." It stated that as many as five hundred Poles may have died, that only forty-nine members of the village managed to escape. When the first soldiers arrived, the Poles thought they were disguised Ukrainian bandits and shot at them. In response, a "Ukrainian ss detachment from Podhorce [Ukr: Pidhirtsi] was sent, surrounded the village and began murdering people." Reportedly, the Ukrainian soldiers were mostly drunk and abused people "in a monstrous way, murdering them, for example, in the church while one of them played the harmonica." Most people were driven into barns, which were covered in petrol and then burned. The "macabre picture" resulting from this destruction was witnessed on 5 March by "a strong detachment of Soviet partisans who travelled through Huta Pieniatska" (PISM. Ministertwo Spraw Wewnetrrzych, Wydzial Spoleczny, *Sprawozdanie sytuacyjne z ziem wschodnich*, no. 15/44, A.9.III, 1/45, 24).[9] This report uses anti-Ukrainian tropes: playing the harmonica, drunkenness, and church burning appear to be embellishments to emphasize sadistic enjoyment and brutality.

Most Polish testimonies were anthologized between 1993 and 2004. When the Polish Institute of National Memory reviewed eyewitness accounts in 1997 it concluded that around one thousand people had been murdered by "a detachment of the ss Galicia with the participation of Ukrainian nationalists" from a number of neighbouring villages.[10] Some details in these accounts have been challenged (Hunczak 1993, 62; Bolianowski 2000, 218). In a recent book, Dmytro Chobit analyzes and compares Polish, Russian, Ukrainian, and German reports, and indicates the many errors they contain.[11] Most important, he indicates that the pacification was conducted by the 4th ss Polizei Division under the command of Friedrich Wilhelm Bock. Many of the soldiers in the punitive unit were *Volksdeutsche* from Silesia who knew Polish and spoke with their strong local accent. According to him, the fact that they were from this division has confused some commentators, making them think that the men were from the 4th Galician Volunteer Regiment or from the Galicia Division itself (Chobit 2020, 107–10, 284).

Nonetheless, it should be noted that all descriptions, including Khronoviat's initial report, agree that the village was destroyed and a war crime committed. The disputed issues have been whether the 4th Galician Volunteer Regiment participated in the destruction, whether the village contained an armed force or unarmed civilians, and whether local Ukrainians (the UPA or another group) were involved.[12] If the estimate of five hundred dead is accepted, it constitutes one of the largest wartime pacifications.[13] The presidents of both Poland and Ukraine recognized five hundred victims of the massacre on the occasion of its sixtieth anniversary on 28 February 2009.

German punitive actions regularly involved the burning of houses or even entire villages if they were considered to have harboured hostile forces. The Polish underground had at the time activated its forces, and the AK was preparing to initiate Operation Tempest (Burza), which was to take Lviv and demonstrate that Galicia should remain part of postwar Poland. The UPA and the OUN's self-defence groups were preparing to challenge Polish forces. As in "Zakerzonnia," some villages were almost completely Polish or Ukrainian, and some mixed. When Soviet partisan groups passed through Polish villages, they sometimes received food, clothing, medical help, and information. They also encouraged or provoked the Polish underground to take action. One Soviet partisan, Panas Kundius, demanded that Kazimir Voitsekhovsky (Pol: Wojcechowski) in Huta Peniatska not only supply

Soviet partisans with provisions but also conduct anti-German sabotage by destroying telephone connections. During their terrorist activities the Kundius group killed 447 Ukrainians, often village leaders and activists (Ponomarenko 2017, 83; Chobit 2020, 216).

Krutikov's group was in the village a total of fifty days throughout January and February while it recuperated after suffering defeat in a battle with the UPA. His men dressed as OUN or UPA soldiers, spoke exclusively Ukrainian, gathered information, and frequently murdered local Ukrainians, including captured guides who had been forced to conduct them. The purpose of these actions was to compromise the underground in the eyes of local inhabitants (Chobit 2020, 233, 245). While in Huta Peniatska, Krutikov's group reinforced itself, growing from thirteen to fifty men. Having received information of the imminent German attack, the group left on 22 February and travelled in the direction of Bilyi Kamin, leaving four partisans in the village (Ponomarenko 2017, 84–5).

Huta Peniatska served as a base from which nighttime attacks were mounted against Ukrainian villages, and from which assassinations of Ukrainian community activists were organized. In Yaseniv village the director of the school and the priest Martyn Baliuta were victims (Chobit 2020, 182–90). Shortly after he had given a fiery speech at a funeral, the latter was killed on his way to serve mass on Christmas day, along with his cook and driver. He was found with his jaw-bone ripped out, as Khronoviat mentioned. Such violence was endemic. When Kundius described his activity in the underground on 9 October 1944 in Kyiv, he stated that "Ukrainian Banderite priests" were "rabble" and expressed regret that "we had not killed them earlier, because now it is not allowed" (Ponomarenko 2017, 85). He admitted to torturing UPA members and murdering priests. It therefore appears credible that Huta Peniatska was a headquarters from which terrorist activity was initiated and that the 4th Regiment arrived to take revenge not only for the killing of two comrades, whose naked and mutilated bodies they found, but also for other atrocities.

Ponomarenko believes that Maksym Skorupskyi's UPA detachment, which had arrived from Volhynia, and a local self-defence group under OUN-B command participated in the destruction of Huta Peniatska. Because locals were aware of the upcoming punitive action they may have informed the UPA. According to the researcher, resistance in the village was quickly overcome, the cattle taken away, the houses burned, and 380 to

750 people killed. Such "pacifications" of "partisan villages" were common, and Ponomarenko (2017, 96) believes that the 4th Regiment along with two UPA detachments were responsible. Chobit (2020, 332–48) provides evidence that the destruction was accomplished by Friedrich Bock's 4th Police SS Division.

Ponomarenko (2017, 99–100) insists that soldiers of the UPA helped to destroy the village because they wanted to remove a strong Polish military point. In fact, Skorupskyi later admitted to co-operating with a Galician volunteer regiment, some of whose men requested acceptance into his UPA unit. He refused to take them because he was in a buffer zone between two fronts, cut off and unable to absorb new men (Skorupsky 2016, 253). In May 1944 he would be dismissed from his position as battalion leader and told to report to the OUN's SB – an indication, according to Ponoimarenko (2017, 100), that he would be shot for his co-operation with the Germans.

A second major accusation against the 4th Galician Volunteer Regiment concerns Pidkamin (Pol: Podkamień) and Palikorovy (Pol: Palikrowy). A Polish situational report from April–May suggests that the Germans sent a punitive detachment to conduct the destruction and that local groups later plundered the houses.[14] In Motyka's (2016, 261) view, the 4th Regiment under the command of Siegfried Binz "probably helped the UPA murder Poles" in the two locations. However, this description of events is doubtful because the OUN-B's documents place responsibility for the action on Maksym Skorupskyi's detachment. They state clearly that "our [namely, Skorupskyi's] battalion" did this on its own: "The Germans wanted to provide us with planes and two hundred Germans for this action. The battalion leader refused" (Ponomarenko 2017, 102). Binz may have offered Skorupskyi use of a German reconnaissance plane and a company of the 2nd Battalion, which was refused (102).

This raises the issue of how units from the 4th Galician Volunteer Regiment could have co-operated with the UPA. The regiment's 1st and 2nd Battalions were subordinated to the 4th Panzer Army, the overall military authority in this sector. An entry in this army's war diary (*Kriegstagebuch*) records the chief of the 13th Army Corps in his morning briefing for 3 May 1944 raising "the question of handling the UPA gangs (the so-called National Ukrainian Liberation Army), which continue to raid Polish citizens and destroy their property." He provides a reminder that German policy all along had been to destroy the UPA "root and branch" wherever possible. The briefing then orders the annihilation of "gangs that harm us (i.e., behind the front line, even if only by destroying Polish economic assets that are ultimately working for us)," but states that groups who "co-operate with us by fighting against Bolshevism" could be supported.[15] The suggestion here is that German military authorities did not tolerate UPA units attacking Polish residents and destroying property but that some decisions to co-operate were made locally depending on circumstances. It is worth noting that the terms "gangs," "bands," and "UPA" were used loosely to cover a range of groups, some of which were simply taking advantage of a situation in order to plunder. They operated independently or even in disregard of orders from a higher authority. As noted, Ukrainian sources attribute the Pidkamin atrocity to Maksym Skoruptskyi's rogue UPA group. Other accounts identify the perpetrators as soldiers of the Galicia Division, by which they mean the 4th Regiment, which both Polish and Ukrainian sources routinely describe as part of the Galicia Division.[16]

The 5th Galician SS Volunteer Regiment

The 5th Regiment was created at the same time as the 4th and its 1,372 men (as of 30 October 1943) trained at Toruń and Adlershorst near today's Gdynia. It incorporated the former 1st Battalion of the Police Rifle Regiment 32 (Polizei Schützen Regiment 32). Franz Lechthaler, a Schützpolizei officer, was appointed commander. He had previously led police battalions in Lithuania, including Reserve Police Battalion 11, which in 1941–42 participated in anti-partisan operations; the liquidation of the Jewish population in Latvia, Belarus, and Russia; and in guarding Soviet POWs.[17]

The 5th was composed mainly of Galicians from the Sambir, Drohobych, and Sniatyn areas. Reverend Ivan Durbak was the group's chaplain in the training camp until 23 December. Here they were visited by students from Vienna and performers from Lviv, who staged concerts for the men. Wächter, Bisantz, and Pindus also visited during Christmas celebrations in early January 1944.

The regiment never completed its sixteen weeks of basic training. It was placed under Wilhelm Koppe's orders on 9 February 1944 and sent to combat Polish and Soviet partisans near Lublin, Hrubieszów, and Chełm, where it supported the Beyersdorff Battle Group. Petro Vershyhora's 1st Ukrainian Partisan Division and Mikhail Naumov's partisan cavalry unit were in the area, each with approximately fifteen hundred to two thousand men. Another group of six hundred men led by I. Banov also entered the area to sabotage rail transport. The 5th Regiment found itself thrown into immediate action. Its 1st Battalion was sent to Chełm, its 2nd to Hrubieszów, and its 3rd to Biała Podlaska (Ukr: Bila Pidliaska). Near Tarnogród the 2nd Battalion fought Naumov's partisan unit, driving it towards the Lviv oblast on 28 February (Ponomarenko 2017, 152). It then joined the Beyersdorff Battle Group in tracking Vershyhora's partisan unit and participated in the battle near Chmielek (Ukr: Khmelik) on 4–5 March.

The 1st and 3rd Battalions were tasked with guarding against partisan attacks during the construction of defences along the Bug (Buh) River upstream as far as the village of Pisochne in the Lviv oblast. In mid-March, Vershyhora's division fought its way out of encirclement, crossed the river, and left the region. The 1st Battalion then took up position in bunkers along the river near Włodawa (Ukr: Volodava). On 16 April it returned to Chełm. The 3rd Battalion took up guard duties along the river near the village of Pisochne in the Lviv oblast. Another group was sent for garrison duties along the river in the villages of Mircze, Zagórnik (Ukr: Zahirnyk), and Dubienka (Ponomarenko 2017, 155). Good relations were established with local Ukrainian populations. The men were not allowed to requisition but this was not a problem in Ukrainian villages because people brought them food. In Polish villages the soldiers were in constant danger of attack from partisans, in search of whom they combed the woods.

Mykola Faryna has left an account of his experiences. When he set off with the first group of volunteers to the Division from Drohobych in July 1943 the train took them through Lviv and Warsaw to Torn. Through November and December they were employed guarding the railway line, which ran from Gdynia to Germany, and a large farm for angora rabbits, whose fur was being used to make underwear for the army (Faryma 2007, 82). In February 1944 they were transported to fight partisans. The train stopped forty to fifty kilometres outside Lublin because a railway bridge had been blown up. After the crossing was repaired the train stopped again at the next bridge, which was mined. The men marched the rest of the way through Polish and Ukrainian villages until they reached Chełm. They were assigned to watching the banks of the Bug to prevent partisans from crossing. They killed one man and lost one of their own in an accident, then were sent to Hrubieszów, where one afternoon a shoot-out took place in a cinema, from which Faryna escaped by crawling out of the theatre. He reports that the AK was active in the area and travelled openly in wagons, forcing the German garrison to hide. One morning his company marched towards a neighbouring German garrison along a road that passed between stacks of hay and straw. They found the garrison station destroyed and discovered corpses of murdered Ukrainian women and children who had worked in the local distillery. Suddenly from behind the stacks Polish and Ukrainian partisans began shooting at one another, and three of the regiment's men were wounded. With the aid of the UPA, one injured man was sent to a hospital in Lviv (83–4). Faryma's company was planning to shoot its German officers and desert to the UPA but was advised by a UPA contact that this would lead to the punishment of local Ukrainians in German detachments. The Germans no doubt learned of the plan because the company was ordered back to headquarters in Hrubieszów. Here the Gestapo arrested two men, disarmed the rest, and sent them in a goods train to a POW camp in Biała Podlaska. From there they were sent to Neuhammer, arriving shortly after the Division had set off for Brody (84).

Other detachments had similar experiences. After a Polish group burned part of the village of Prehoryłe (Ukr: Pryhorile), on 8 March a reconnaissance group was sent out. Locals informed that the attack had been the work of a BCh (People's Battalion) led by Stanisław Basaj with the help of neighbouring villagers, whom the locals recognized. The regiment then dispatched a detachment to Gołębie (Ukr: Holubie), where it was informed of approaching armed partisans. In the ensuing battle the partisans were driven off, but their trail went cold in the village of Kryłów (Ukr: Kryliv). Similar attacks, followed by chases, occurred regularly. The soldiers reported that many villages had been destroyed, especially on the right bank of the River Bug. One later wrote: "We saw ruins, corpses, and could not find out where the inhabitants had gone" (Faryna 2007, 163).

From 20 March the 5th Regiment's main assignment was guarding the boundary formed by the River Bug. Polish partisan groups active in this area frequently targeted Ukrainian villages and assassinated community leaders, whom they accused of collaborating with the Nazis. Between March and May of 1944, the regiment developed ties with the UPA. When the situation became more chaotic and the Germans lost control over the territory, about 150 men deserted to the partisans (Usach 2016, 69). At that point the Germans decided that the regiment was unreliable and withdrew it from service. On 22 April 1944, Himmler ordered the transfer of both the 4th and 5th to the Galicia Division.

The 5th Regiment therefore only saw large-scale action at the beginning of its deployment. Its main task was guarding the border and pursuing partisans. The 150 desertions to the UPA, a relatively high number, was due to the Red Army's approach, the German loss of control, and the intensification of the Ukrainian-Polish conflict in the Chełm area. The UPA was organizing a response to Polish attacks at the time. Oleksandr Lutskyi, the head of UPA-West (UPA-Zakhid), during his interrogation by the KGB on 1–2 August 1945 stated that the Polish underground in the spring of 1944 transferrred to the Chełm area a force that began annihilating Ukrainians in revenge for the UPA's attacks on Polish settlements. According to this transcript, the OUN's leadership took a decision to send UPA units with instructions to combat this force and destroy or drive out the whole Polish population from the Chełm region (Serhiichuk 2007, 1:542)

Members of the 5th Regiment had expected the Germans to use them in defence of the Ukrainian population. When this did not happen, desertions to the UPA increased, particularly in April and May. The soldiers left in groups, taking their weapons with them after killing their German officers (Melnyk 2009). However, there was a limit to the number of men the UPA could absorb, and most soldiers in any case preferred to remain in military service. In some cases the Germans were informed when desertions were imminent (Ponomarenko 2017, 183).

The intensification of the Ukrainian-Polish conflict in the Lublin district was partly due to developments elsewhere. Between 15 March and 15 April 1943 an estimated four thousand men in Volhynia had deserted to the UPA from Schutzmannschaft battalions. By December the UPA in Galicia also had approximately five to six thousand men with adequate military training. After its forces were pushed out of Volhynia in the spring of 1944, it reportedly sent six thousand men from Volhynia and Galicia to help with the struggle in Chełm, which intensified Polish-Ukrainian clashes (Serhiichuk 2007, 1:543).

The conflict had flared up in 1943 when the Germans began resettling Ukrainians in the Biłgoraj county on land from which Poles had been removed. The latter viewed these settlers as colonists and collaborators, and from January 1943 the Polish underground began shooting village heads, agronomists, and the UTSK's "trusted men." Transplanted Ukrainians were attacked, robbed, beaten, murdered, or forced to flee (Motyka 2011, 280). As thousands of Polish refugees arrived from across the Bug with stories of UPA atrocities in Volhynia, the Polish underground began describing its attacks on Ukrainian villages and Auxiliary Police stations as revenge for Volhynian massacres and resistance to German resettlement plans.

Ukrainians, as a minority in the district, were the weaker party. However, their presence in the Auxiliary Police, and the proximity of the 4th and 5th Regiments, gave them a limited advantage. When the UPA began operating in the Chełm area, the Polish population perceived this as a further strengthening of the alliance between the Germans, Ukrainian police units, and the OUN-UPA. The Polish underground responded by ordering the complete removal of all Ukrainian settlers and, on 10 March 1944, launched an "anti-Ukrainian offensive." Concentrated in Hrubieszów and Tomaszów counties, it was led by the AK and supported by the BCh under Stanisław Basaj (alias Rys). Police stations were destroyed, over a dozen Ukrainian villages were burned, and their populations murdered (Motyka 2011, 294).[18] On 21 March the leader of the AK's 21st Company in Tomaszów county, M. Pilarski (alias Grom), instructed his men "to make life insufferable for Ukrainians, so that they leave as soon as possible for the lands beyond the Bug or elsewhere. There must be no trade, no coexistence with Ukrainians; separate from them everywhere, and remember all the wrongs done to our people beyond the Bug and in Hrubieszów county" (Wołczew 1969, 165).

Detachments of the 4th and 5th Regiments operated in this highly charged environment until 9 June, when the last of the men were transferred to Neuhammer to begin their incorporation into the Galicia Division.

The 6th and 7th Galician SS Volunteer Regiments

The 6th and 7th Regiments saw little action. The 6th was created in August 1943 with a strength of eighteen hundred. Most of its recruits came from the Przemyśl and Lviv areas. It trained in southern France, in Pau and Tarbes near the Pyrenees, and its chaplain was Reverend Yohan Holoida. The 7th was created in August and September 1943 from elements of the disbanded Police Rifle (Polizei Schützen) Regiment 32 and from new recruits. It had 1,671 men. Initially it was stationed in East Prussia and was then sent for training to Bayonne and Orthez in southwestern France. Its chaplain was Reverend Danylo Kowaluk (Melnyk 2002, 63). Both the 6th and the 7th were dissolved at the end of the year and transferred to the Galicia Division. However, some men deemed unsuitable for combat duties were sent to other police battalions (Melnyk 2002, 70). A group of nine hundred remained in Tarbes as a reserve battalion and joined the Galicia Division on 23 May 1944.

Relatively good relations were established with French locals once these discovered that the men were not Germans and witnessed them attending church services or visiting Lourdes. At one point, a high-ranking German who was inspecting beach fortifications in Bayonne approached Reverend Kowaluk while the latter was conducting a funeral service and asked with a smile: "Since when do priests bury ss men?" Kowaluk explained who they were and the man then introduced himself as Field Marshall Rommel (Ponomarenko 2017, 225).

Since the area was remarkably quiet, the two regiments saw little action. However, according to Ponomarenko (2017, 230), the reserve battalion was drawn into one anti-partisan action and at least three regimental soldiers were killed by partisans. When the Military Board learned that the men had been used against the Maquis it protested vigorously and the soldiers were withdrawn. On 8 May 1944, six hundred left for Neuhammer. The three hundred who remained in Tarbes were removed on 7 July.[19] Several additional accusations against the Division or the Volunteer Regiments appear to be based on misinformation as these forces had not been created at the time of the alleged acts.[20]

As the above accounts indicate, the situation was complex. In areas where the 4th and 5th Regiments operated, there were numerous German units, some of which included Ukrainian troops.[21] There were also at least eight Soviet partisan groups, with an estimated total strength of forty-four hundred. Each group had orders to destabilize the rear. They were supported by twelve units, a total of 296 men who had been sent in with instructions to stimulate Polish groups to attack German forces (Ponomarenko 2017, 164). This war in the rear also involved local self-defence groups created by specific villages or towns. As a result, the evidence collected sometimes makes it difficult to distinguish between an armed clash, a punitive action, and an evacuation. Moreover, local conflicts frequently erased the distinction between combatants and civilians.

8

SLOVAKIA, SLOVENIA, AUSTRIA, AND THE UKRAINIAN NATIONAL ARMY, 1944–45

On 23 August 1944, as the eastern front approached Slovakia, a revolt against the pro-German government of President Joseph Tiso broke out. It was led by Defence Minister Ferdinand Čatloš, supported by Slovak army units under General Jan Golian, and assisted by two Soviet airborne brigades that landed behind German lines. These included twenty-two hundred soldiers of the 2nd Czechoslovak Independent Airborne Brigade, which had been formed by the Soviets from men who had served in the Slovak army and had been captured or had deserted (Melnyk 2016 1:42, 335). Altogether about forty-seven thousand soldiers participated in the rebellion, along with seven thousand partisans, who included Soviet commanders and specialists.

Slovakia

The Division's reserve regiment in Neuhammer was ordered to Slovakia and joined the Division between 15 and 17 October. It included about one thousand raw recruits, over half of whom were young people from Eastern Ukraine (Gotskyi 1951, 5). They were kept out of action. Forty Ukrainian nurses who had been trained in Krynica and then completed their instruction in German hospitals also arrived, but they learned that there were already enough German nurses and personnel who had been evacuated from

Ukraine. Although attached to the field hospital for a time, the Ukrainian nurses were forced to move further west. One thousand German NCOs were also sent to the Division, along with twenty-five hundred Luftwaffe ground personnel in training, who were mostly *Volksdeutsche* from Romania. A group of Ukrainians who had served in the 5th Waffen-ss Viking Division also arrived.

This last group came from the estimated one thousand men who had fought the Red Army east of Warsaw. They had been mobilized in February and May–June 1944. In February the Germans had announced a conscription of all men aged between twenty-one and thirty-five, and in May they extended this to men aged from sixteen to forty-four. In reality, they simply captured men in dawn raids and transported them further west. Many "volunteers" decided to join the Division rather than work for Albert Speer's Todt Organization, which oversaw civil engineering projects in Germany, usually the building of fortifications. In this way in June 1944 about five thousand men from the Buchach, Berezhany, and Pidhaitsi regions were taken into various Waffen-ss divisions. Many stated that they enlisted "because it was safer in the army than in the civilian population" (Ponomarenko 2018, 21).[1] Often these men did not wish to join the UPA and admitted they preferred the army to a hungry life avoiding German dragnet operations in the forests. Many were apolitical and concerned only with surviving the war. They were sent to Lviv, given a send-off under yellow-and-blue flags, accompanied by singing. On the rail trip Poles often shouted insults or turned naked behinds to the passengers. In the Viking Division they were allowed to wear the Galicia Division's lion on their collar and arm, and were integrated with eighteen-year-old Germans and with some Hungarians and Romanians who had been mobilized in similar fashion. Most Ukrainians were incorporated into the Westland Regiment but some were placed in the Germania, where they wore yellow-and-blue epaulettes. The insignia were a German concession to national sensibilities. The recruits trained for eight weeks, first in Heidelager, then Strašice near Prague. Local Czechs were at first suspicious, but the church attendance and singing as usual drew admiring crowds and invitations to homes. This led to discussions in which some locals tried to convince the recruits that the Soviet army was bringing democracy and that "the Russians" were "our people" and "brothers" (43).

The men were divided into two battalions of approximately 450 each and sent to the front along the Vistula and Narew Rivers near Modlin, fifty

Figure 8.1 Returning from church service in Slovakia, 1944.

kilometres north of Warsaw. Here they participated in intense fighting between 10 and 28 October. Despite being outnumbered and suffering heavy casualties, the Viking Division succeeded in holding the front. It is estimated that the Red Army lost over thirty thousand men during the entire action and that 150 to 170 Ukrainians serving in the Viking Division were killed (Ponomarenko 2018, 160). At least a dozen men were captured and sentenced to ten years in labour camps plus five years loss of rights and confiscation of property. One captured man, Roman Kraievskyi, was immediately mobilized into the Red Army, wounded on the 19 January 1945, and died the next day (163).

In November 1944, the remaining Ukrainians demanded transfer to the Galicia Division, a request that was probably supported by Wächter. On 4 November the commander of the Viking Division, Karl Ullrich, thanked the men for their service, praising them for conscientiously fulfilling their duties and holding the front against much more numerous enemy forces. On 17 November they joined the Galicia Division in Slovakia.

The Viking Division allowed a substantial force of Slavic background to mix with primarily German personnel on equal terms. The Ukrainians were spread throughout the formation, received the same treatment as Germans, had their own insignia, and swore their own oath of allegiance.

Meanwhile, in Slovakia a number of units had arrived to put down the army revolt that was threatening to cut off the German 8th Army's retreat. Besides the Galicia Division, these units included the 18th ss Horst Wessel Division, the Dirlewanger ss Brigade, the Schil Battle Group, and the East Turkish Waffen-ss.[2] The 178th Tatra Panzer Division, and the 208th and 209th Volksgrenadier Divisions were also present.

The Dirlewanger Brigade was one of the most notorious Waffen-ss units. Its commander, Oskar Dirlewanger, has been described as "perhaps the cruellest of all commanders of World War II" (Bishop 2005, 162). A decorated veteran of the First World War, he was a drunk and a sadist who had been imprisoned in the 1920s for sexual assault. He had suggested the creation of a special unit in which convicted poachers and other criminals could redeem themselves. The unit eventually became a brigade of sixty-five hundred men that included expelled police officers and ss men.[3] The East Turkish Waffen-ss Group numbered eight thousand men recruited in the Crimea and Caucasus. Their commander called himself Harun el-Raschid (born Wilhelm Hintersatz) after a famous early Ottoman Sultan. These two formations had a reputation for not taking prisoners (Ingrao 2011, 40–4).[4] Heike describes Dirlewanger as distinguishing himself by indiscipline, brutality, and foolish decision making. His men abused the civilian population and then laid the blame on the Division (Heike 1973, 152–3).

In Slovakia, the Galicia Division co-operated with anti-communist partisan groups who informed about the movement of hostile forces. There were strong anti-Bolshevik political sentiments among the predominantly Catholic Slovaks. A Catholic priest, Andrej Hlinka, had in 1913 founded the Slovenská Ľudová Strana (Slovak People's Party), which has been described as mixing "Italian-style fascism, Catholic orthodoxy, and traditionalism" (Bauer 1994, 62–3). The party's militia, the Hlinka Guard (Hlinkova Garda), was, according to Arendt (1964, 202–3), Catholic in outlook and exhibited the anti-Semitism of "clerical Fascists or Fascist clerics," which differed in both style and content from "the ultramodern racism of their German masters," meaning that it was interested in expelling, not exterminating, Jews.

Slovakia had in 1942 deported about fifty-two thousand Jews to Poland, a "resettlement" for which the Slovak government paid. These deportees were killed in Auschwitz, Treblinka, Bełżec, and Sobibór. However, thirty-five thousand Jews had been given permission to remain in the country. In 1944, Hitler decided that they were responsible for the uprising and instructed Himmler to resume the deportations. While the Slovak rebellion was being put down, 18,937 people were arrested, half of whom were Jews. Of these, 8,975 were sent to German concentration camps, while 722 were "specially handled" on the spot (Reitlinger 1956, 379). The remaining Slovak Jews survived, partly because the approach of the Red Army required the mobilization of all available forces and left few German troops for security police duties, and partly because international bodies such as the Swiss Red Cross intervened (379).

The Galicia Division set up headquarters in Žilina. Its task was to establish control in the region of Čadca, Ružomberok, Sv. Martin, Považska Bystrica, and Turzovka. It coordinated the anti-partisan operation, while protecting roads, railway lines, bridges, tunnels, factories, and weapons plants. The centre of the insurrection in Banská Bystrica was dispersed within a month, and the Division's battle groups then chased rebels in the Tatra Mountains, often with little success.[5] Oleh Lysiak (1996, 68) later recalled many night patrols and futile attempts to catch Soviet parachutists.

The memoirs of all soldiers indicate surprisingly good relations between the Division's soldiers and local Slovaks.[6] Heike (1973, 155) notes that there were almost no difficulties with civilians. Ukrainians and Slovaks spoke closely related languages and many locals had contacts with Ukrainians living across the border. The population realized that the soldiers were temporary visitors who were fighting against Soviet and communist rule. On occasions when the soldiers met sympathizers of the Slovak underground – for example, in taverns – the reported exchanges were tense but courteous. Several memoirs describe conversations with locals who were sympathetic towards Russians because they saw them as fellow-Slavs (Veryha 2007, 136).[7] According to Myron Matchak (1951, 9, 4), the Division's soldiers took advantage of every opportunity to explain to locals the nature of the "Bolshevik paradise in Ukraine." Since the insurrection was organized by communist forces, on more than one occasion the predominantly Catholic population greeted the Division warmly (Młynarczyk et al. 2017, 204).[8]

John Armstrong (1988, xxiv), while noting that Heike described military operations as being conducted with maximum concern for the "well-being of the fraternal Slav population," also indicates that a detailed investigation of the Division's operations in Slovakia was still required. The evidence is that Friedrich Wittenmeyer's Battle Group burned down Smerečany on 28 October and Ziar on the following day. After surrounding the latter village, the force fired from cannons. When the houses began burning, inhabitants were not allowed to put out the fires. Reportedly, those who tried to escape were fired upon by machine guns. A mother and child were killed. The action was apparently ordered because a German officer and friend of Wittenmeyer had been killed.[9]

The accusation that the Division committed a war crime in the Slovak village of Nižna Boca on 24 October 1944 was broadcast by Yorkshire Television (now ITV Yorkshire) on 7 January 2001 in a program entitled *ss in Britain*. The producers edited interviews with Pavlina and Eteli Bahmerova to suggest the Division's involvement. However, the two witnesses had in fact stated categorically that the Germans and a punitive unit of the Hlinka Guard had been responsible. When Mykola Mushynka from Prešov University interviewed the women, they vehemently protested that their testimony had been misused. The program avoided showing the monument to the dead, which gave the date of the killings as 24 October 1944, whereas the Division only arrived in the village on 26 October. Mushynka interviewed all the people whose testimony had been used in the program, both eyewitnesses and scholars, and researched the sources mentioned in the program, including studies published in Czechoslovakia. He found no evidence of involvement by Ukrainian troops, although neither he nor other historians denied that this and similar incidents had taken place (Mushynka 2001).[10] It appears that the program's producers were determined to link the Galicia Division to the incident and ignored the fact that other units in the area were the likely perpetrators. The program has been strongly criticized for "inaccuracies, innuendo and lack of objectivity" (Kormylo 2021, 96).[11]

Heike's history contains a record of the Division's military engagements in Slovakia. A professional soldier, he had fought in Poland and Western Europe before being transferred to the eastern front. From January 1944 until the surrender he was the Galicia Division's chief of staff. After the war he was interned by the British (until May 1947) on suspicion of being an SS commander, a claim he always denied. While imprisoned he wrote the first history of the Galicia Division on the basis of field diaries, maps, and personal recollections.[12] The account lacks many of the prejudices that German soldiers held concerning Ukrainians, although it is not free of condescending stereotypes.

In addition, Vasyl Tatarskyi and Myron Matchak have provided detailed accounts of Wildner's Battle Group. They describe attacks by Soviet airplanes in the days after their arrival on 28 September 1944 and an ambush by partisans near Banská Štiavnica. Their company was sent to guard the bridge and road near Krupina. Its initial action was against the Slovak army, which was being supported by Soviet air power (Tatarskyi 1983, 160). One action after 30 October provides an insight into conditions. As the Division's detachments climbed the mountains in pursuit operations, the partisans would cut telephone wires, which then required repairing, a procedure that went on almost the entire day. Some soldiers conducted reconnaissance patrols and brought back partisans, usually Slovak soldiers and officers:

> One time they brought me a Czech captain, who belonged to the Czech brigade that had been trained in far-off Baku and afterwards had been parachuted into Slovakia. He asked for a cigarette and when he saw me offering some Slivovitz to a nurse who was soaked-through with rain he overcame himself and asked for a cup. I gave him some. The nurse asked to be allowed to remain with our company. It was a

great temptation, but we had orders to send all prisoners to headquarters. Over the three days I spent in the mountains we had a lot of them. All those soldiers and civilians came to us themselves, because, wandering through the mountains in the dark, they stumbled upon our men. There was also no lack among them of Ukrainians, Frenchmen, Poles, and Germans – yes, Germans, and even Englishmen. (164)

Roman Dolynskyi has left a report of two Canadian bomber pilots shot down in Slovakia. They were in danger of being lynched by a local mob, which had been told by the German ss that the pilots were responsible for bombing women and children. According to Dolynskyi, twenty of the Division's soldiers stood with weapons drawn and refused to give the men to the Security Police or the mob. They conducted them safely to a POW camp for British, Canadian, and American soldiers, mainly pilots. Both pilots were aware that leaving them behind would have been a death sentence and thanked the Division's men for saving them (Dolynskyi 1951, 4–5).

The fullest account of the Division's stay in Slovakia belongs to Michael Melnyk (2016, 2:42–135), who records incidents of fraternization with the local population and with captured soldiers who were allowed to escape when the occasion presented itself.

Slovenia

On 21 January 1945, the Division was ordered to Slovenia, a journey of over six hundred kilometres that was made on foot because the railway line and main routes were restricted to traffic delivering supplies to the front. The men crossed Austria by taking snow-covered side roads and skirting the town of Gratz. They began operations near Maribor, where their assignment was once more to chase partisans, who had many units operating in the area. Here the local population was hostile and the search operations difficult, dangerous, and often unsuccessful.[13] The mountainous terrain, knowledge of local conditions, and guerilla tactics favoured Tito's partisans. Armstrong (1988, xxvi) comments:

Whereas the rank-and-file guerrillas consisted of Slovenes motivated at least partly by nationalist resentment of Nazi intentions (which included direct annexation to the Grossdeutsches Reich), complete control was exercised by Tito's communist partisan cadres. Consequently, Ukrainian soldiers were combating a real surrogate of their principal enemy, the Soviet regime. In fact, in his intention of annexing German-language areas around Klagenfurt (as well as Italian-speaking Trieste) Tito at that point outdid Stalin in intransigence. Tito's partisans engaged in a race with British forces moving up from Italy to occupy the coveted non-Slavic territories. Tito was prepared (at the risk of precipitating World War III) to fight the British to gain his objectives.

The political situation was complicated by the fratricidal conflict between belligerent ethnic and political groups, which was almost the entire cause of the 1.75 million dead, 11 percent of the population, that Yugoslavia suffered during the Second World War (Shepherd 2012, 1). The partisans were not readily identifiable, often did not carry arms openly, and murdered German prisoners and their native collaborators "in ways that defied all notions of internationally acceptable conduct" (4).

Conditions varied, however. Much depended on the terrain and relations between armed groups and the local population. The Galicia Division arrived in Slovenia at a time when the Serbian nationalist Chetniks were fighting fellow Serbs in Tito's partisans. This allowed for the Division to establish a "live-and-let-live" arrangement with the smaller bands of Chetniks who recognized the authority of the Serb general Dragoljub Mihailović but in many cases acted independently. On occasion, their detachments would be allowed to pass without conflict, and information about hostile forces was shared. During the war Slovenia had suffered less because the initial plan to "Germanize" northern Yugoslavia and deport Slovenes had been halted in the autumn of 1941 (Shepherd 2012, 93). Mihailović was supported by the British and the government in exile. His aim was to restore the old monarchical system and extend Serbian power within Yugoslavia, and his strategy was to restrict actions to low-key subversion and sabotage against the occupation while waiting for a moment when he would be aided by an Allied invasion. Tito's partisans, on the other hand, sought a revolution against the old order and the creation of a new state based on the principles of communism and Yugoslavism (145–6).

Most partisans supported Tito and were entrenched in the mountains south of the Drava River. The Division fought Tito's 14th Partisan

Division, generally by chasing partisan brigades over difficult, often snow-covered terrain.[14]

Some incidents in Slovenia were later noted by Lysiak, both in his novel *Za striletskyi zvychai* (The riflemen's custom, 1953) and his stories. He recalled that two soldiers had their throats slit while watching a film in the town of Maribor, and others were fired upon by partisans dressed as women (Lysiak 1953, 242). In his novel, the protagonist Reverend Bilenkyi (in reality Reverend Levenets) describes visiting a church in the town of Selica. The priest who answers the door is at first terrified, thinking that German-speaking armed men in ss uniforms are about to rob the church and maybe shoot him:

> When he saw me removing the vestments and chalice from a small suitcase carried by one of the soldiers he was astounded. After I removed the belt with the revolver and the soldiers left their rifles in the sacristy and knelt to help me serve mass, I heard a sobbing by the wall. The old parish priest was weeping loudly – roaring, not weeping. He attended the entire service and then invited me to his rectory. We had a long conversation. I do not think that the attitude of local residents was very hostile to us after that. (240)

Veryha (2007, 140–54) describes an encounter with the underground. Together with a colleague, he was captured and questioned but released when the partisans realized they were Ukrainians. Pylyp Trach also met with the partisans. There was talk at the time of breaking through to the "democratic world" and informing it of Ukraine's treatment by both the Soviet and Nazi dictatorships. The Germans had arrested and sent off to concentration camps several groups of soldiers and then disarmed the entire Division. Only when Wächter and other senior figures intervened were the weapons returned. These events spurred Trach's company to make contact with the Chetniks. They did so through the man at whose house they were quartered. When Trach told him that one of his sons had been killed by communist partisans and another by the Nazis, they found a common language. A meeting was arranged with a Chetnik commander, who complained that his forces had been betrayed by the West, which was now accusing them of "collaborating with the Third Reich" (Trach 1951, 5).

One incident in Slovenia involved a British air crew, which had been shot down on 17 October 1944. Sergeant Calder had been injured in the crash and was taken by partisans to a secret hospital, where he had one leg amputated and was left to recuperate. The British received a report that he had been killed by the Germans in March 1945. An investigation was launched and it was reported that the hospital had been discovered and burned, along with the patients, including Calder. The information, received on 31 May 1945, was that "the units which carried out this atrocity were from the 14th ss Division, who had committed similar atrocities before in the MARBOR area" (NA/PRO, WO, 108/107). Sergeant Parker had gone down in the same plane and had spent time with the injured man in the hospital. He last saw Calder on 10 March. On the following day, Parker was himself captured by men from the Galicia Division while hiding under a cliff and was taken to Ljubljana. After being released at the end of the war, he returned to the United Kingdom and was interviewed about the incident. In a report signed on 23 June 1945, he stated: "I myself have never witnessed any atrocities committed by the UKRANIAN [sic] DIVISION OR THE 14 S.S. DIVISION. The only building I saw burning was the last hospital I was in, and that was when I was being marched from the hills on the morning of me being captured. I could not say if any partisan patients were in the building at the time, and I could not say who ordered the hospital to be burned down" (ibid.). Parker, however, suspected that the Ukrainian guards who marched him off shot a local man of about forty-five, who could not keep up because of an injury: "The officer in charge of the guard ordered him out of the group, and with two guards went into the trees, then I heard rifle fire[.] I suspect he was shot, but I did not witness the atrocity" (ibid.).

In its concluding report from 3 September, the investigation stated: "Whilst it cannot be precluded that Sgt. Calder's hospital was, in fact, burnt down, it will be observed that the statement of F/Sgt. Parker does conflict with the original report upon which this enquiry has been based, since, though the hospital which he vacated was burnt, Sgt. Calder was certainly not therein at the time" (NA/PRO, WO, 108/107).

While the Division was stationed in Maribor, the OUN leader Mykola Lebed (alias Ruban) sent a message to Bohdan Pidhainyi instructing the Division to kill its German officers, fight its way to a port on the Adriatic Sea, and there await the arrival of the British. Given the military situation, this was impossible. However, it is interesting that the letter had been re-layed first through a UPA major named Ivan Butkovskyi (alias Hutsul), then through one of the Division's reporters. It had been sent at the beginning of March but reached Pidhainyi only at the end of April, when the Division was back on the eastern front in Austria. This illustrates the unrealistic nature of many plans, the rapidly changing picture on the ground, and the tenuousness of connections with the underground (Pidhainyi 1951, 117–18).

Altogether an estimated 156 Division soldiers were killed in action on Yugoslav territory, but the figure would have been much higher if unit commanders on both sides had not entered into truces and avoided contact (Melnyk 2016 2:176).

Austria and the Ukrainian National Army

Meanwhile, since November 1944, Pavlo Shandruk had been trying to ne-gotiate a change of the Division's name to the 1st Division of the Ukrainian National Army.[15] German authorities, however, insisted that the Division had to be part of a united force under the leadership of General Andrei Vlasov and the Russian Liberation Army (ROA), something that all Ukrainian leaders and the Division's soldiers refused to consider. The day after Vlasov issued his Prague Manifesto on 14 November 1944, over sixty thousand applications for service in the ROA were received, and thousands of Red Army deserters arrived daily with hopes of joining the force.[16]

It took until 12 March 1945 for Alfred Rosenberg to recognize the right of the Ukrainian National Committee to represent all Ukrainians in the Reich and therefore to bring together all Ukrainians in German military units under a single Ukrainian command. President Andrii Livytskyi of the Ukrainian People's Republic (UNR) in exile on 15 March ordered Shandruk to organize the Ukrainian National Army (UNA). The general then called a meeting of the hastily created Ukrainian National Committee on 17 March. Under the signatures of Shandruk, Kubijovyč, Oleksandr Semenenko, and Petro Tereshchenko, it announced that "By will of the Ukrainian citizens who now reside in Germany and other countries allied with it" the creation of the UNA had begun (Shandruk 1999, 170, 175–6).[17]

Shandruk had been a Russian army commander during the First World War, then joined the UNR's army and was made a general in 1920. In his memoir he describes relations with the Jewish population, recording, for

Figure 8.2 At the front by a bunker, Gleichenber, Austria, April 1945. Left to right: Roman Hankevych, Smuk, Yarolsav Rudyi, N.N., Stefan Maier, Solodkyi, N.N., Volodymyr Motyka (with back turned).

Figure 8.3 General Pavlo Shandruk.

example, that his unit, along with a group of Sich Riflemen, ended the pogrom in Proskuriv unleashed by Ivan Semesenko on 15–16 February 1919. This violence took around twelve hundred, mostly Jewish, lives. Shandruk caught and delivered for trial some of the perpetrators, although Semesenko himself was only arrested and executed in the spring of 1920 for disobeying Symon Petliura's orders, not specifically for the notorious pogrom. Shandruk (1999, 55) reports that the local Proskuriv rabbi thanked him for restoring order, and eight Jews joined his battalion. His men also restored order in the town, or shtetl, of Brailov, which suffered a pogrom on 10 July 1919. Here the local rabbi provided him with a document in Hebrew, saying: "If you ever find yourself in danger, show this letter to any Jew and you will receive whatever help can be offered" (56). Later, in the town of Kopaihorod, fifteen Jewish boys were caught firing at soldiers, after being encouraged to do so by a local Jewish tailor who thought that the men were preparing to murder Jews. Shandruk showed the letter to the rabbi, who told the boys to kneel and ask forgiveness: "We arrested none of them, but merely asked their families to take care of our wounded" (71–2). The memoir reports that Shandruk's soldiers received praise from the local Jewish community in the town of Ozaryntsi, where a delegation presented him with a scroll (90).

From 1926 Shandruk served as a contract officer in the Polish army with the rank of major. He co-operated with the Prometheus group, which brought together Poles, Ukrainians, and political figures from other nations to counter the Soviet threat. The Ukrainian section was headed by Roman Smal-Stotskyi and supported by Andrii Livytskyi as president of the UNR's government in exile. In 1939, when Germany and the Soviet Union invaded Poland, Shandruk commanded the 19th Polish Infantry Brigade. He was imprisoned and interrogated by the Gestapo from September 1939 to January 1940 after being denounced by the NKVD. In 1944, when the Germans began to search for a figure who could head a planned Ukrainian national committee and a Ukrainian army, they approached Shandruk. As a commander respected by all Ukrainian political groups except the pro-Soviet, he was in many ways an ideal choice.

When all Ukrainian political parties flatly refused to join General Vlasov's Committee for the Liberation of the Peoples of Russia (KONR) and the ROA, the Germans reluctantly gave up on the idea, which had been the brain-child of Fritz Arlt in the Reich Ministry for the Occupied Eastern Territories. The goal of General Shandruk and President Livytskyi was to rescue from forced repatriation as many Ukrainians stranded in Germany as possible. The majority had been sent there as forced labourers, but others had served, willingly or unwillingly, in various German forces. The likelihood was high that they would be executed or imprisoned if they fell into Soviet hands. With Livytskyi's encouragement, Shandruk agreed to head the Ukrainian National Committee, whose role he saw as offering practical help to Ukrainians at a time of crisis (Shandruk 1999, 176). Shandruk was particularly concerned with the fate of the Galicia Division. At the war's end he succeeded in guiding most of these men to the British and American zones, where they were interned as surrendered enemy personnel. Colonel Mykhailo Krat, a veteran of the First World War and the 1919–21 struggle for independence, was asked by Shandruk to become the Division's staff officer. On 6 May 1945, in headquarters at Felkermarkt, before returning to the front, Shandruk gave him instructions to "preserve the Division and military discipline and to prepare to participate in a new war, this time between the Western Allies and Moscow, which would certainly not wish to voluntarily leave the countries of Eastern Europe it has taken in the last military operations" (Krat 1979, 36).[18]

The idea of joining the UNA appealed to many men who wished to continue fighting Stalin's regime or who had been conscripted into German formations. Numerous forced labourers also saw service in the new army as a way of escaping their situation. To gather these men, Shandruk created a 2nd Division within the UNA, which immediately attracted two thousand volunteers. Realizing that thousands of teenagers, aged mostly from fifteen and seventeen, were serving in anti-aircraft forces, he decided to also take them into the UNA to help them reach the American and British zones (Shandruk 1999, 183). Simultaneously, other groups of Ukrainians scattered throughout Germany began asking to join the force.

It was unclear how the postwar situation would develop. Various rumours circulated. Some expected the Allies to declare war on the Soviet Union, then appeal to Red Army soldiers to desert and join the newly created Russian or Ukrainian forces. This was indeed part of the reasoning behind the plan hatched by Arlt and other German leaders, who foresaw the Reich's collapse and were hedging their bets. The rumours were not without substance. Under interrogation by the US army, Gottlob Berger on 5 June 1945 stated that the German government and troops had decided in the first days of March to withdraw to the mountains of Austria and to hold out there until they could come to an agreement with the Allies.[19] Moreover, Winston Churchill had at the time developed plans for Operation Unthinkable, a scheme to attack the Soviet forces in Germany or to confront and force them back. Churchill reportedly wanted to retain 100,000 German soldiers in combat-ready divisions. There were also fears that Tito would launch an attack on Trieste or southeastern Austria in order to extend his territory. The Division's soldiers may have figured in plans to prevent this. Archival documents on Operation Unthinkable make clear that plans for the "third world war" existed and had the potential of becoming reality (Walker 2013, 43–9; Bruns 2007).

Shandruk's efforts to rescue military forces under his command from Soviet capture faced several difficulties. The German front was collapsing on all sides, causing transportation and communication problems and making travel hazardous. The Galicia Division (now named the UNA) was still fighting the Red Army on the eastern front and would have to retreat to British and American lines on the western front.

After Shandruk created the UNA's 2nd Division, detachments of Ukrainian soldiers scattered throughout Germany began to arrive and were sworn in between 28 March and 25 April (Shandruk 1999, 175). Some of these men were unlucky. They were sent by the Germans to the front and their retreat was cut off. As a result, about 60 percent of the force was captured by Soviet troops in the final days of the war. The remainder made its way to the American zone (208). Some youths in anti-aircraft groups travelled south to join the Galicia Division, but those who were seventeen or younger were steered to DP camps in the Western zone. When Shandruk was finally able to join the Galicia Division on 25 April, the men took a new oath of allegiance and formally became the 1st Division of the UNA.

There was an immediate difficulty in explaining their identity to Allied forces, most of whom had not heard of the Galicia Division, let alone the UNA. In fact, because Ukrainian nationality was not recognized, numerous confusing problems arose when military personnel registered Ukrainians as Poles, Russians, or Soviet citizens. Shandruk (1999, 188) asked Smal-Stotskyi and the UNR's government in exile to use its contacts in General Anders's Polish Corps so that London would be informed of the Galicia Division's retreat and planned surrender. For this to be done Shandruk had to obtain Smal-Stotskyi's release from German prison. Arlt made the arrangement, and the Gestapo invited Smal-Stotskyi to its office, where it "very politely told him he was a completely free man" (188–9).

The number of people attached to the Division in the final weeks of the war swelled to over twenty thousand. This was because the reserve regiment arrived from Neuhammer, along with the youth from anti-aircraft training programs, and various other personnel who were temporarily attached.

The change of name was not merely a ploy to confuse the Allies or a pretence at severing relations with Germany: it was an important symbolic moment for the soldiers, who had in most cases enlisted to serve in a Ukrainian military formation. As soon as he joined the Division in Austria, Shandruk demanded recognition of the new name and use of Ukrainian insignia, such as the national flag and the trident, which was worn as a badge on the arm and cap. He had obtained German agreement that Ukrainians would be appointed to command positions but decided to delay making this change for practical reasons. Upon his arrival, a number of German officers made a point of ignoring him. He commented that some "orthodox Nazis" appeared to consider it beneath their dignity to report to a member of a "lower race," even one who wore a general's uniform (Shandruk 1999, 193). On 25 April 1945, Shandruk held a ceremony in which the men took the new oath, this time to God and Ukraine. The Germans officers had been notified that the force was now a Ukrainian formation, that General Shandruk was acting chief commander of all Ukrainian forces, and that in the event of the Reich's capitulation the Division was to break through to the western front. The instructions also stated that any German personnel who did not wish to serve under Ukrainians should be transferred to a reserve battalion: "Those who hate Ukrainians or who are hated by Ukrainians will not remain" (197).

Captain Mykhailo Lishchynskyi, who lost an arm at Brody and was now working in the Division's intelligence section, informed Shandruk on 2 May that some men expected to be separated into smaller groups to facilitate breaking through Soviet lines and joining the UPA in the Carpathians. Shandruk informed the Division that it was still facing the Red Army on the battlefield and was surrounded by strong German formations who, because they had nothing to lose, could allow the enemy to encircle and capture them. If that occurred few men would survive. Moreover, any unfriendly act vis-à-vis the Germans would cut off supplies. These considerations had obliged him to drop the idea of immediately replacing German commanders with Ukrainians. Shandruk (1999, 198–9) told the men that "only a highly developed imagination" could make them believe that, given the heavy concentration of Soviet forces in Austria, Hungary, and Slovakia, they might singly or in small groups cover the distance of six hundred kilometres to the Carpathians.

On 7 May, Otto Wächter met Shandruk at Klagenfurt and informed him that the war would end on the night of 8 May at one minute after midnight. Wächter, after losing his position as governor of Galicia, served as chief of the military administration in Italy and then in the Reich's Main Security Office in Berlin, where, together with Arlt, he tried to join Vlasov's ROA to Shandruk's UNA. He told Shandruk (1999, 202): "Now, General, you are the central figure in the action of saving the Division, and possibly all of us who are with you." The British were in Spittal and were moving towards Klagenfurt. Liubomyr Makarushka and Arlt were dispatched to make contact with them. Makarushka, previously a member of the Military Board, had joined the Division early in 1945 as liaison officer.

On 9 May at 3.00 a.m. the Division received its final instructions. After dismantling or burying its heavy weapons, it began a retreat. The sappers had constructed a bridge across the River Mur, which was successfully crossed. On the following day, in Judenburg, Makarushka brought written permission for the Division to move through British lines. British headquarters already knew of the 1st Ukrainian Division of the UNA, perhaps through Smal-Stotskyi's intervention (Shandruk 1999, 203).

Most troops marched to Spittal, Feldkirchen, and Klagenfurt, which were all in Carinthia in the British zone. They were then redirected to Udine in Italy. To get there they had to cross the Alps. For self-protection against marauders and Tito's partisans, they were allowed one rifle for every ten men, and officers were allowed to keep their pistols. All memoirs written by the Division's soldiers praise the British for their honourable and understanding behaviour in allowing this to happen. On their way to Italy the men met a ten thousand-strong column travelling in the opposite direction. These were mounted Don Cossacks under the command of General Helmut von Pannwitz and General Petr Krasnov. One of them shouted: "Brother-Ukrainians, where are you going? The war is not over for us yet! We are on our way to protect the Austrian borders against Tito. Why not join us?" (Dolynskyi 1979, 15). On 12 May, these men surrendered to the British at Judenburg, and, on 27 May, they were handed over to the Soviets. The officers were immediately shot, the generals publicly hanged in Moscow, and the soldiers sent to Siberia. In the Austrian town of Lientz, not far from Spittal, where the Division's soldiers were first held, there was another camp, with thirty-five thousand people of the various Cossack nationalities who had fought for the Germans. They, too, were handed over to the Soviets, together with their wives and children, and their German officers. Most were massacred.[20]

Not all the Division's soldiers ended up in the British zone. About twelve hundred men moved through Judenburg into the American zone in Auerbach, Darschmidt, and Regensburg. They were kept in an open field with almost no food for close to a month. Then the Americans sent them to a POW camp, from which most were released within a year. Ferkuniak has described their experience. Beyersdorff was angered by the German defeat and by the insubordination of Ukrainians at the war's end. He denounced them to the Americans as bandits, robbers, and rebels. In fact, he initially intended to shoot every tenth man for rebellion. Ferkuniak and the Ukrainian officers of course opposed this, stating that they were now POWs and subject to American law. Beyersdorff denounced them to the Americans as a gang of robbers, stating that he was no longer responsible for them (Ferkuniak 2003, 65). After he separated the Germans from the Ukrainians, on 1 June 1945 the latter were transferred to the Americans at gunpoint. At 8:00 p.m. Beyersdorff called Ferkuniak and announced: "Ukrainians got what they wanted; let them now see whether things will improve for them." Fernuniak replied that he considered his work in the Division's headquarters finished and announced that he was leaving to be with his Ukrainian comrades. The Ukrainians were confined to a narrow, damp area and their provisions removed. Realizing that the moment was critical, they set up their own camp guard and established an exemplary order, with military discipline, evening prayers, and Sunday services, which American soldiers attended. When Lieutenant Ortynskyi explained the reasons for German behaviour to the Americans, their tone changed. Beyersdorff then sent Wildner with three officers, eight NCOs, and seven soldiers to take over the camp. They were refused entry. Ferkuniak (2003, 68) announced: "The separation of Ukrainians and Germans conducted by the Germans without consulting the Ukrainians has to be seen as final, and a return to the subordination of Ukrainians to German commanding officers is not possible."

Already on the trek through Austria, Germans had begun leaving the force and returning home. General Freitag, who initially planned an escape to the mountains but could convince no one to accompany him, committed suicide on 12 May. Once the Division's surrender to the Allies was completed, Shandruk travelled to Munich to take up his duties as head of the Ukrainian National Committee. He visited DP camps, arranged safe passage for refugees, helped to free interned soldiers, and continued to advocate on behalf of the Division's men. Bishop Ivan Buchko in Rome was informed of their situation and contacted Pope Pius XII, who intervened with the Allies.[21] Buchko brought the desiderata of Ukrainian refugees to the Pope through the Congregation, then called Pro Ecclesia Orientali (now the Congregation of the Eastern Churches), which was headed by Cardinal Eugène Tisserant. The refugees included both Catholic and Orthodox Christians. Tisserant, a Frenchmen who had made his sympathies clear during the war, was respected by the Western Allies. He lobbied them through political and military contacts and, especially, through the Papal Secretariat of State, which appealed to Allied authorities all over Europe not to forcibly repatriate Ukrainians, including the Division, to the Soviet Union (McVay 2021). Shandruk received a letter from Buchko sent on 14 October 1945 informing him that thirty of the Division's men from the Camp 5C in Bellaria had been accepted for theological studies in Rome. The bishop noted that the greatest obstacle to this had been the presence in the camp of a Soviet repatriation committee (Shandruk 1999, 214). In May 1956, the general wrote a letter of thanks to the Pope, crediting him for saving the Division's soldiers "from certain death" and recalling that the Western Allies, "ignorant of the Ukrainian people's struggle for freedom and independence," had been "on the verge of handing them over" (214).

In Munich, Shandruk established contact with former Polish officers and colleagues in the Prometheus group. In the postwar period he continued to work with President Livytskyi and other members of the government in exile. On 17 March 1961, the Polish émigré government awarded Shandruk the Virtuti Militari decoration for his courage in rescuing a Polish infantry brigade in September 1939. The awarding committee consisted of General Władysław Anders; General Tadeusz Bór-Komorowski, who commanded the Warsaw Uprising of 1944; and President Edward Raczyński. In 1964 and 1965 a number of articles in Polish and Soviet newspapers denounced the committee and the recipient, but the selection was defended by Jerzy Giedroyc, the editor of the Polish journal *Kultura*, which was published in Paris. The US-based historian Marian Kamil Dziewanowski (1965, 106) wrote in the journal: "The actions of Gen. Shandruk not only during the September campaign but throughout the last war attest both to his strength of spirit and political judgement. The combination is relatively rare; he fought where it was possible and necessary, refrained from compromising and excessively risky actions, and saved what had to be saved: the threatened national substance. There are many painful and contentious issues between Poles and Ukrainians. But there are also matters that ought to be axioms for thoughtful people, not subject to emotional reactions but treated as long-term political categories. To these belongs the premise that the two nations undoubtedly share a common fate, and a threat to the existence of one is a mortal danger to the other. The example of General Shandruk shows that there are among the Ukrainians people who understand this axiom."

9

YOUTH SOLDIERS, WOMEN, AND NURSES

In early 1944, retreating German troops were everywhere in Lviv – in all the buildings, schools, institutes, with vehicles parked in every available square. The city's population of 300,000 swelled to 1 million. Meanwhile Ukrainian youth continued to attend unheated and partially ruined schools, supplied the city by transporting food from the countryside, delivered anti-German and anti-Soviet literature for the underground, and were hunted by the Gestapo and criminal police. Over the Christmas and New Year holiday many students were hosted by their Lviv friends because the Red Army's advance prevented them from visiting their families. Locally the criminal police contained a substantial contingent of Poles or Polish *Volksdeutsche* who made efforts to send Ukrainians to the Baudienst work camps, where the barracks were unsanitary and the rations meagre. Their dire situation, and in a few cases the idea of defending their homeland, attracted young people to the idea of joining the anti-aircraft forces.

In Germany teenagers from the Hitlerjungend were already being drafted into anti-aircraft defence units. They received three months training – soon reduced to six weeks – and were sent to the Luftwaffe, where they wore uniforms with the swastika and ss runes, and were promised medals for shooting down enemy aircraft. When this recruitment proved insufficient, it was extended to other nations, who were told that in a total war they had to play their part.

By the end of 1944, there were about 100,000 young men and women, exclusive of German nationals, in anti-aircraft units. Hungarians numbered 50,000, Russians 14,000, Latvians 7,000, Belarusians 3,300, Lithuanians 1,200, and Estonians 1,100. Women accounted for 10 percent of the total. Altogether about ten thousand Ukrainians were drawn into this force.[1]

Across Germany these Airforce Helpers (*Luftwaffenhelfer*) were under the command of Siegfried Nickel. Sometimes referred to as "ss Youth," they were considered trainees of the ss (*ss-Helfer or ss-Zögling*). In fact, they had nothing to do with the ss. Nickel used the term because he had visions of his own youth army, analogous to non-German divisions formed under the Waffen-ss rubric. The Luftwaffe rejected Nickel's attempts to interfere in its affairs and generally viewed the entire ss leadership with contempt for having avoided serving at the front. Nickel was despised for "playing at war" with children. When captured by American forces, some of the youth were at first considered real ss men and interned with them, but it was soon realized that both de facto and formally they were not.

From his office in Berlin, with a staff of hundreds of officers, Hitler Youth, secretaries, stenographers, and couriers, the energetic young Nickel recruited students of other nations into the war effort. He was subordinated to Alfred Rosenberg, the Reich minister for occupied eastern territories. Towards the end of the war, to escape the bombing of Berlin, Nickel moved his offices to Troppau, where he controlled a large store of textile goods, shoes, leather, and personal wares, such as knives, combs, shaving razors, soap, cigarettes, and tobacco. Within the structure devised by Nickel most national groups had separate organizations and were able to protect their youth from chicanery and exploitation. Ukrainians were not allowed to create such an organization.

The UTSK and the Military Board were taken aback when the campaign to recruit schoolboys was first announced. Both objected strenuously. When it became clear that recruitment could not be prevented, Zenon Zelenyi and Tymish Bilostotskyi were appointed to help the youth by organizing material, educational, and spiritual support, and by interacting with German authorities. Zelenyi was responsible for education on the Military Board. Bilostotskyi was an educational expert and an instructor in Plast (the Ukrainian Scouts), and Olha Kuzmovych (née Sheparovych) was a journalist, Plast activist, and publisher of youth materials.

Figure 9.1 Youth "recruits" with Wächter, Bisantz, and the Division's reporter Stepan Konrad, Przeworsk (Ukr: Perevorsk).

In February, the Germans announced that boys from the age of fourteen could be recruited to day service in anti-aircraft forces, and from fifteen to night service. Soon afterwards the population learned that girls from sixteen could serve (Pankivskyi 1965, 258). Nickel opened an office in Lviv in May 1944. He announced that the youth would be kept in their own groups and that, after eight weeks of training, they would be allowed schooling and religious guidance. Ignoring protests, Erich Koch and Heinrich Himmler decided that Eastern Ukrainians and Galicians should be kept apart and given different insignia: the first had a badge with a trident, the second with a lion. Ukrainian community leaders took the position that war was not for children, that the Hitlerjugend might feel a patriotic duty to serve but that Ukrainians did not feel the same way about their children (Zelenyi 1965, 19).

However, Bisantz planted an announcement over his own signature and those of Osyp Navrotskyi and Zenon Zelenyi in *Krakivski visti* on 2 July 1944 stating that the Military Board had begun recruiting youth from fifteen to twenty ("Zaklyk" 1944). An accompanying unsigned article encouraged parents not to deny children permission to enlist but to consider whether their child was safe at home. It promised education and security, and the opportunity "to fight for the good of our people" ("Molod" 1944). When confronted, Bisantz claimed there had been no time for consultation with other members of the board. A further article urging youth enlistment appeared in *Krakivski visti* on 23 July (K. 1944).

Zelenyi tried to get the Germans to comply with the promises they had made concerning youth welfare, but Nickel responded on 24 October 1944 by saying he would only communicate with Bilostotskyi. The latter kept a record of the locations to which students had been sent, corresponded with them, and attended conferences for leaders of the other youth groups. Kuzmovych kept in touch with young women in the camps.

The youth recruitment began when twenty-two German officers arrived in Lviv. Bizantz told the board on 20 April 1944 that the boys would live in good conditions, under the guidance of experienced officers, and that when they reached the age of eighteen they would enter the Galicia Division. To formulate its response, the UTSK invited sixteen prominent community members to a secret meeting on 24 April. This group decided to sabotage the campaign as much as possible by arguing its negative effects, insisting that the recruitment must be voluntary with a minimum age of sixteen and that teachers and religious advisors must be provided (Zelenyi 1965, 20–1).

The visiting German officers were given a tour of Lviv and a series of short lectures on Ukraine.[2] On 7 May the board was told that eight soldiers of the Division would help with the campaign, that the number of expected recruits had been raised from sixty to three hundred, and that the recruitment would be voluntary only in areas not threatened militarily. Educational and spiritual care would be allowed, but other requests were refused. Bisantz produced the text of a leaflet calling on youth to join the struggle for a new Europe, learn new languages, see new places, receive a salary, and continue their education. It ended with "Heil, Hitler!" Protests led to the removal of a couple of phrases, including the Hitler salute. Without further consultation, Bisantz published the leaflet over the names of Navrotskyi (representing the Military Board) and Zelenyi (representing the UTSK). The Division's lion emblem was included in subsequent leaflets addressed to parents, with the claim that the action was enthusiastically supported by the Board and the UTSK. One leaflet stated that, in Germany, "even ten-year-olds were contributing to the victory" as scouts for the air force and that fifteen-year-olds were serving in anti-aircraft defence (Zelenyi 1965, 225–9). Another leaflet informed young people that, as auxiliaries, they would be "fighting for the freedom of their homeland, which was threatened by Bolshevism"; that they would have the same quality of food, lodgings, and uniforms as German youth; that their futures were assured; and that their parents would receive aid (UCRDC, Maleckyj, "Ukrainska Molode! Tvoie mistse mizh namy!").

When the recruitment fell far short of expectations, the Germans resorted to force. If a personal identity card (*Ausweiskarte*) was demanded and could not be produced the individual was arrested and pressured to sign up. A group of boys in Drohobych was ordered to undergo a medical inspection in a cinema, then conducted under gunpoint to sealed trains and transported to training camps (Volchuk 2011, 161). In schools the recruitment was often accompanied by threats. Students were told to gather and "voluntarily" enlist if they wished to continue their studies. They had to decide immediately "whether they preferred a rifle or a shovel." Letters of complaint and appeals from parents flooded the UTsK. Although the latter's protests were mostly ignored or met with threats, they did extract permission for teachers and priests to visit the recruitment point in Przeworsk (Ukr: Perevorsk) and training centres in Central Europe.

In May, all able-bodied young men in Lviv were instructed to report to the Krakivskyi Hotel for a compulsory medical inspection. Those who were nineteen or twenty were sent for military service; younger boys were sent for anti-aircraft training. In mid-June, singing songs and accompanied by the Galicia Division's band, the first 210 teenagers were marched through Lviv with yellow-and-blue stripes on their caps and the lion emblem on their upper arms. They were greeted by Bisantz, Wächter, and other German dignitaries. Zelenyi spoke on behalf of the UTsK. Each young man received instructions on how to behave, a certificate, and a work book (Zelenyi 1965, 230–3). After a reception for parents and community figures, the group boarded trains travelling westward.

Once they reached the camps some boys spent weeks living in rail carriages. They were denied leaves of absence and their parents received no support. The behaviour of instructors was often inappropriate; some boys were struck in the face when they refused to do press-ups in the mud. One was arrested when he retaliated by punching the instructor; he was released after the UTsK intervened (Zelenyi 1965, 52). Several boys were as young as thirteen. Forty who had failed their medical examinations were sent to work camps in Germany (47).

Although the Germans were slow to allow the promised education, persistent efforts had some success. First Bilostotskyi and Olha Kuzmovych were permitted to visit the camps, then teachers and priests. By the end of July, seventy-seven hundred youth were in camps in Niepolomice, Przeworsk, and Krynica in today's Poland; Troppau (Opava) in Czechia; Eger in Hungary; Krems and Malta in Austria. Without informing German administrators a gymnasium program was created in Linz, Austria, with Nykyfor Hirniak as headmaster. He had been a commander in the Sich Riflemen and director of a school in Ternopil and was the brother of the famous Soviet Ukrainian actor Yosyp Hirniak. In addition, high school courses were offered in Aspern near Vienna by Mykhailo Rabii. The Linz school covered grades 4 to 7 and taught Ukrainian, German, Latin, history, geography, mathematics, physics, biology, and chemistry. Classes took place from 2:00 p.m. to 6:00 p.m. Students had to walk to them, sometimes several kilometres, often after bombardments. The enterprising Hirniak attracted boys who had come from all parts of Ukraine. Some of them were employed in the construction of an entire fake city, with running trains and sham factories belching smoke, all of which was lit up at night by the flick of a switch, while not far away the real city and factories were blanketed in darkness. Most boys worked as labourers in these Linz factories and several were killed during bombings. Priests came to conduct religious retreats, confession, communion, church services, and funerals.[3] By the end of August a team of twenty-two educators, four priests, and two doctors served the camps. The number of priests would rise to fourteen (Zelyeni 1965, 73).

There were problems. Teachers sent by the UTSK were sometimes kept in rail wagons, put on guard duty, or used as interpreters. It was only after strenuous complaints that some were even allowed into a camp and given food or clothing. Some teachers were chiefly interested in obtaining a document that allowed them or their families to leave Ukraine. German administration at first had insisted on only one priest serving every one thousand youths (Zelenyi 1965, 64–6).

Ten thousand books from Ukrainian Publishers (Ukrainske Vydavnytstvo) and twelve thousand copies of *Krakivski visti* were distributed. Over the course of a year the UTSK delivered 5,500 calendars, 6,500 prayer books, 400 books of carols, 1,000 textbooks on Ukrainian history and

Figure 9.2 Youth being taught to assemble a rifle in Malta, Austria, 1944.

Figure 9.3 Study session for youth. Malta, Austria, 1944.

geography, and 400 books describing Ukrainian holiday traditions. Olha Kuzmovych organized the publication of a small Ukrainian-German dictionary and phrase book, the journal *Doroha* (The Road), and brochures dealing with health and hygiene. Amusingly, when, during a meeting with the Germans, Bilostotskyi insisted on the need for literature, the surprised response from one lieutenant was that they had provided forty thousand German brochures, including a beautifully illustrated one about the life of Hitler (Zelenyi 1965, 158, 160). In January 1945, during the Christmas holidays, presents and visits were also successfully delivered.

A primary task for Bilostotskyi, Zelenyi, and Kuzmovych was locating the youth. This involved negotiating a maze of administrative bodies, which included Nickel's office, the Hitler Youth organization, the ss Supreme Command, the Gestapo, the police, the Ministry of Education, and the Luftwaffe, each of which was at loggerheads with the others. Keeping track of individuals was made more difficult because the cataloguing was done by Germans, who often recorded the names incorrectly, lost cards, or never filed them due to a hasty, often disorganized procedure. Since all nationalities

Youth Soldiers, Women, and Nurses • **149**

were filed together, it was hard to identify Ukrainians. On top of this, the students were moved from place to place, and some locations were treated as military secrets. Towards the end of the war Bilostotskyi was told by the Germans to burn his archive, with his correspondence and statistics (Bilostotskyi 2000, 141). Reverend Severyn Saprun, who visited many of the camps, had collected many photographs and, at the end of the war, deposited them for safe keeping in a monastery in Austria. They have never been found (Shnerkh 2004, 9).

Contact was lost with several groups, such as the 250 students in Tours, and the seven hundred in Holland. Altogether the groups were spread over 272 places, making it virtually impossible to stay in touch with all of them (Zelenyi 1965, 186). The mail was censored, but books were not, which allowed for libraries of one hundred to five hundred books to be delivered (188).

About half the boys were assigned duties in airfields and stone quarries or were sent to put out fires, mend telephone wires, dig trenches, and clean up rubble in bombed towns and cities. Some worked in factories for ten to twelve hours a day, enduring insults and beatings from foremen. The work was physically demanding and often beyond their capacity. Some worked the night shifts. There were no days off during the week. Although a leave after six months was promised, this was rarely granted. The term of service was supposed to be eighteen months but was extended to two years, by which time the Third Reich had collapsed.

Women and Nurses

When the drafting of young women began, it was opposed by practically the entire community. The press refused to print announcements, so notices appeared in German newspapers and a leaflet was printed on 20 July 1944 and distributed throughout refugee and transit camps. It had considerable success. Almost immediately, the first women recruits enlisted, convinced that they would be allowed to serve Ukraine. The Germans hired several of them as agitators. Sporting smart Youth-ss uniforms and armbands with the lion crest, they assured audiences of a better life in the force than the one they had to endure in work camps. At one point, more girls than boys began signing up, due in large part to the efforts of young women recruiters who successfully used the argument that the Galicia Division needed nurses.

There were women's camps in Neisse (now Nysa in Poland) and Budweis (now Ceske Budějovice in the Czech Republic). After a short course of instruction, the women were sent to various locations. Often they were assigned difficult and dangerous tasks. Usually they directed the projector lights or the listening apparatus for anti-aircraft flak guns. Some worked as nurses or in communications, but many were sent to work ten or twelve hours a day in factories.

The best-known work camp was Putnitz (now Poniec) on the Baltic coast, near Stralsund airport, where there were about three hundred Ukrainian women. Their only warm meal was a thin soup once a day, and the canned food was poor. During the harvest they were taken to work in fields and ate better food. They had no leisure time because Nickel rejected the idea of cultural education for women. The commander and camp doctor, a woman, had a paranoid suspicion that the workers had venereal diseases and demanded frequent inspections. The results were negative, but the self-esteem of the young women suffered. Eventually Bilostotskyi and other educators forced Nickel to remove this commander.

There were two deaths in the camp, one a suicide and the other an accident. The first was due to an unwanted pregnancy. When the man who impregnated a young woman from Central Ukraine disowned her, she threw herself under an automobile. He had in fact raped her, but the doctor recorded the cause of death as syphilis so as to avoid an investigation. She was buried by her friends. The fate of women in these forces was harder than that of men: they were sometimes attacked by men, who then took revenge when repulsed, often by forcing the women into the worst jobs or sending them to dangerous places. The most degenerate bosses or co-workers were guilty of rapes. The second death was an accident in which a woman jumped from a moving automobile and fell under its wheels.

Some of the worst conditions were in an armament factory hidden in the forest near Schliefe in southern Germany, where 150 women worked. They had to lift bags of ammunition powder, fill two thousand ordinances daily, and clean guns and bombs with chemicals. Because they worked in a damp concrete building, they developed rheumatic pains. They were never allowed any visits from educators. Labour was also hard in the transport sector, where the women had to load trucks with bombs. One of the most detested jobs was the difficult, dirty work of creating smoke screens during air raids by using a fogging apparatus.

Figure 9.4 Woman operating searchlight. From Zelenyi, *Ukrainske iunatstvo*, 1965.

Figure 9.5 Woman in anti-aircraft force. From Zelenyi, *Ukrainske iunatstvo*, 1965.

Few women were assigned to the work for which they had volunteered. About half were obliged to fill labour requirements in canteens, hospitals, factories, airports, barracks, and farms. When they worked in ammunition factories it was usually alongside women designated as Ost (Eastern) slave labour and they shared the same conditions. Only in a few cases did the UTSK's interventions make any difference. Olha Kuzmovych wrote letters of complaint about conditions, but they went unanswered and she eventually resigned her position.

There was a conflict in one camp between Western Ukrainians and Russian-speaking Eastern Ukrainians, and another when the ROA propagandists entered the camps. However, most Ukrainians ignored Vlasov's agitators; only seven out of three hundred women in Punitz (Poniec) joined the ROA (Zelenyi 1965, 88).

The Germans did not allow youth of other nations the same amount of food, pay, and care as they allowed their own, partly because years of education under fascism had left a legacy of intolerance. Ironically, this made it easy for foreign youth to reject national socialist ideas. Any pro-German tendencies, if they ever existed, disappeared as soon as young people saw the treatment of people wearing the Ost badge, which signified to Germans belonging to a lower, less valuable race.

When it was no longer possible to recruit youth in Ukraine, the focus shifted to "Zakerzonnia" and the Lemko region. In early October, Olha Kuzmovych learned that forty-eight nurses, who had completed their training in Krynica, had no support or prospects. Thanks to Kuzmovych, Tsiopa Palii, and Daria Sijak, they were evacuated. About half were transferred to Trenčín in Slovakia. Here some were put to work sewing army uniforms. A few found work in hospitals in Germany. Out of desperation several signed up for the anti-aircraft training, along with female students from the Krynica gymnasium who had been separated by the front from their parents, and some orphaned women with no means of support. These were sent to camps where they had to work in fields picking sugar beets and potatoes (Matsiv-Balahutrak 1994, 92). A number were sent to work in German hospitals, which were being bombed two or three times a day. These women never in fact succeeded in joining the Galicia Division (93).

The rest of the trained nurses, about twenty-five in number, were able at the end of the war to make their way to the Riccione camp, where they finally linked up with the Galicia Division's men. They included not only

Youth Soldiers, Women, and Nurses • 153

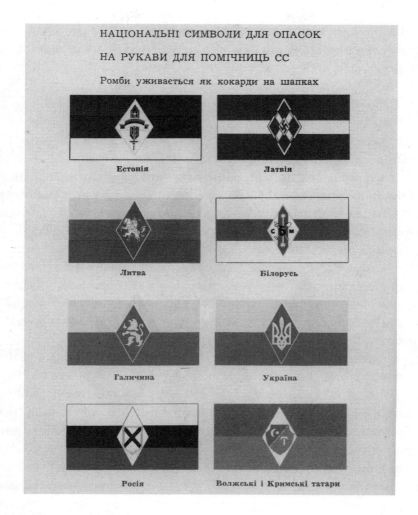

Figure 9.6 Armbands for groups in the "Youth SS." Ukrainians were separated into Galicia and Ukraine groups. Other groups: Estonia, Latvia, Lithuania, Belarus, Russia, and Volga and Crimean Tatars. The central diamond in each armband was used as a badge on caps.

the nurses from the Krynica course but several women from Volhynia who had served in the ULS. This last group joined the Division's men along with the rest of the ULS in March 1945. Twelve had been sent to work in Berlin, while six had remained to tend the wounded (Vazhna-Vankevych 1998, 82). These last retreated with the Division's men and became the first nurses in the Riccione camp. From that moment they shared the fate of the men interned in Rimini and travelled with them to the UK, where they found work in hospitals (86).

Service in the Anti-Aircraft Force

Half the recruited young men and women operated anti-aircraft batteries, machine guns, and search lights. In the last months of the war a secret order was issued, according to which boys were to be trained in fighting tanks. With the assistance of the German air force, which was not subject to Nickel's command, the UTSK succeeded in having this rescinded. However, reportedly 150 boys were trained and sent to fight in the streets of Berlin.

Despite the announcement of a new superweapon that would change the course of the war and the silence concerning military defeats, young people were not convinced by German propaganda. Nonetheless, the idea of military service appealed to those with few alternatives. They were paid one German mark per day, with half the wage entered into a savings book, and combat personnel in particular were well fed.

Eight hundred boys were sent from Eger to the western front, where the British and Americans were bombing underground petrol deposits. Two boys were shot by the Germans for taking canned food from a bombed plane. Even in places where the camp's educators succeeded in keeping the boys from military action, they were forced to dig trenches and often came under aircraft fire.

In Linz, the anti-aircraft batteries were located near factories to protect against American bombers. One boy of fourteen, O. Sahaidakivskyi, was known as the army's "youngest artillery man."[4] Even at the war's end he still "expected some *deus ex machina* to bring decisive change in favour of the German armed forces" (Zelenyi 1965, 190). His battery was near the army's headquarters and at one point he went looking for the general "to assure him that his group would defend him well." He was arrested and sent back to the battery (192). He recalled that most of the time the boys felt carefree and self-sufficient, but then suddenly German motorcycles appeared and they heard American tanks approaching. Someone told him that "Americans were good-natured people," whose soldiers behaved like children. This was reassuring and lessened his fear. On the night before Linz capitulated, the boys were ordered to retreat to the city and prepare

Figure 9.7 Reverend Severyn Saprun conducts mass near anti-aircraft gun, Vienna, 6 January 1944.

for street fighting, but the officers had no intention of doing so and told the boys to spike their guns.

Attitudes among the youth varied, but this boy's feelings, as later recorded, are instructive:

> As a fourteen-year-old I was an object of interest for several generals and lieutenants who visited us. I was "famous" as the youngest artillerist and this, obviously, made my case exceptional ... At first, I was assigned to telephone service in a bunker, but I was keen to work on the guns and eventually became a first cannoneer. In general, I thought only in terms of my group. I did not have any ideological or political ideas at the time. I very much wanted to see the front and even dreamed of a "heroic" death ... My general attitude toward the wartime conjuncture was romantic and idealistic, and I had a simple answer to complex problems: keep with your group, remember God, and everything will be alright. There was another alternative – flight – but that seemed to me unethical. (Zelenyi 1965, 191–2)

As bombings began to take lives, the antagonism between Nickel and the UTSK became intense. With the Third Reich in its death throes, Ukrainian community leaders began efforts to evacuate the young people. To the UTSK's credit, it never ceased pressuring the German administration through letters and visits or working to secure the release of youth from various camps throughout Germany and Austria. There were by the end of the war twenty-eight designated Youth-SS camps (Zelenyi 1965, 172). The number of Ukrainians in them (with either the lion or the trident badge on their uniforms) has been estimated at eighty-eight hundred boys and twelve hundred girls (116).

In the war's final months, these young people were caught up in the wave of refugees that was rolling westward in 1944 and 1945. Those travelling through Hungarian-controlled territory were robbed of their horses by retreating Hungarian soldiers and German Sonderkommandos (Special Units) or were forced to sell their remaining possessions cheaply to locals. Some soldiers handed out IOUs, which of course were impossible to cash. The Germans had some success in recruiting into the anti-aircraft force a number of stranded young people who had no food or shelter. There were also kidnappings. However, word quickly spread whenever an "inspection" was coming and the youth would scatter. Bilostotskyi purposely sent out agitators who did not believed in the cause or allowed the medical commission, which included Dr Mykola Kuzmovych, Olha's husband, to pronounced them unfit for service (Zelenyi 1965, 81–2). Even at this late stage in the war, Nickel's typical response to entreaties was that Ukrainians liked to declaim high-sounding patriotic phrases but were incapable of dealing with reality.

The Hungarian army was imprisoning people who, it claimed, were disguised Soviet partisans. In May 1944, Dmytro Ferkuniak was dispatched from the Galicia Division's camp in Neuhammer on a fact-finding mission. He travelled through Slovakia, Hungary, and the Pokuttia area of Ukraine. In his home town of Sokolivka he discovered a concentration camp with five hundred starving people, a number of whom he knew personally. The Hungarian commander told him that the captives would only be fed if they admitted to being POWs. Ferkuniak listed those who could not possibly have been Soviet partisans, but only twenty-nine were freed. He then travelled to Zhabie to find the German officer responsible for liaison with the Hungarian army and received his support. As a result, the camp was dissolved and the people freed (Ferkuniak 2003, 38–9).

Youth Soldiers, Women, and Nurses • **157**

In these final months, Bilostotskyi received many letters from the Troppau (Opava) camp complaining about the ROA's aggressive recruitment. Some letters were requests for transfer to the "Ukrainian Division" (Zelenyi 1965, 72). On 6 March 1945, Zelenyi and Bilostotskyi contacted Shandruk in Berlin and discussed how the youth could be transferred to the American, British, and French zones. In the end, the overwhelming majority were successfully directed to DP camps, although some ended up in the Soviet zone. Zelenyi was later informed by parents that these had not been punished because they had been forcefully taken by the Germans (194). However, later interviews indicate that a number of boys were sent to the Gulag, while others were summoned for questioning by the police on many occasions and treated as personae non gratae. Some young men who escaped to the West were recruited by Polish officers to the 2nd Corps of General Anders; others joined British forces and served in Palestine, Burma, and Malaya; a few entered the French Foreign Legion (see Volokh and Heva 1994; Shnerkh 2004).

Given the circumstances, the UTSK's work had some limited success. Its insistence on the principle of voluntary service probably helped to reduce the number of recruits. By demanding German adherence to promises, it was able to maintain contact with many students and provide some education, along with cultural and religious support. With the Luftwaffe leadership's help it blocked Nickel's plan to send boys into anti-tank combat. It also prevented Nickel from sending the youth into the ROA. Aided by some German officers, most of the youth found their way to the American zone, where they were directed to relief organizations.

Conditions in the camps often depended on the administration and local conditions, which in some were better than in the Baudienst. In many cases the youth were able to continue their education. In other camps conditions were terrible, especially when the commander was hostile towards Ukrainians. Usually they were best where military training was being conducted, and worst in work camps, where the youth slept on straw mattresses without blankets, had poor food, no change of underwear or soap, no books or teaching, and no contact with home. Illnesses, including typhoid, spread in these camps. Good clothes were stolen from new arrivals, and camp authorities appropriated clothing sent by the UTSK.

Overall, the constant complaints by Zelenyi, Bilostotskyi, and Kuzmovych had little effect. However, the organized visits and educational efforts offered some comfort. For example, the Christmas celebrations of 1945, which took place in about fifty locations, although only symbolic, were greatly appreciated and had a strong psychological impact. Like much of the Ukrainian community's relief work during the war, the help extended to youth was an effort to mitigate harm. Its success depended on generosity and support from many individuals whose stories have generally remained untold.

PART THREE

CAMPS

10

BELLARIA AND THE REPATRIATION CAMPAIGN, 1945

The resilience of the Division's soldiers would be repeatedly tested in Italy. While they were being transported to the first camps, some passers-by threw stones, shook fists, and showed by gesture that they would have their throats cut (Veryha 1984, 29). The soldiers commented wryly that only weeks earlier many of the stone-throwers had no doubt been enthusiastic supporters of Mussolini. In the first transit camp Reverend Mykhailo Ratushynskyi was roughed up and his liturgical objects thrown around. In Udine troops from the Palestinian Regiment (also known as the Jewish Brigade) were generally more sympathetic. Some had family roots in Western Ukraine and were curious to hear about life in that part of the world (30).

Having ditched their equipment and supplies before crossing the Alps, the men lived in semi-starvation throughout May and June. However, their great fear was deportation to the Soviet Union. For months they were unsure of their fate. It took some time to explain to the British who they were. Colonel Krat (whom Shandruk had promoted to the rank of general) and other officers protested being sent to a camp with German ss soldiers and tried to explain to puzzled British officers why as Ukrainians they were fighting against "their own government" (Veryha 1984, 33, 35).

Eventually, on 4 June 1945, the Division was moved to its own Camp 5C in Bellaria, about twelve kilometres north of Rimini. The German camps were guarded by men from General Anders's 2nd Polish Corps, while the Ukrainians were guarded mostly by British soldiers. Relations with Allied troops were civil. The Ukrainians were impressed by the British sense of "fair play." The first front-line British soldiers they met had saved some disarmed men from being slaughtered by irregulars by allowing them to keep some weapons on the trek to holding camps. In Bellaria and Rimini, the British soldiers on sentry duty stood to attention along with the mass of interned men when the Lord's Prayer or a patriotic hymn was sung during evening ceremonies. One British camp commander carried a copy of the Geneva Convention in his pocket for reference.[1] Polish army newspapers were occasionally available and the men discussed events with Poles from Anders Army, many of whom thought the Allies would go to war with Moscow and were shocked to learn that, on 5 July 1945, the Western powers had broken ties with the Polish government in exile and recognized Warsaw's pro-Soviet Provisional Government (Krat 1979, 43–4).

At the Potsdam Conference (17 July–2 August 1945) Stalin demanded that the Galicia Division be handed over to him, the only military formation to be singled out in this manner.[2] He was told that anyone within the 1939 frontiers of the Soviet Union who wished to return would immediately be allowed to do so and that any others who would go without the use of force would also be handed over. Soviet representatives in Italy were given complete freedom of movement to see anything, anywhere, and at any time in the camp where the Division's surrendered soldiers were being held.

At Potsdam Stalin also demanded a new Polish-Soviet border and received agreement that it would run roughly along the Curzon Line. Poland was compensated with German territory in the west. The Soviet delegation rejected the idea of supervised elections in countries occupied by the Red Army. It insisted on the partitioning of Germany and forced reparations. These would include withdrawals from Germany's national wealth (factories, land, machinery, machine tools, railway rolling stock, and foreign enterprises) and payments for ten years after the war's end. Ivan Maisky, the deputy commissar for foreign affairs, proposed that 80 percent of all German industry be withdrawn, meaning carried away physically and used as reparations payments (Byrnes 1947, 26).[3] Britain and the USA protested that destruction of the German economy would leave 80 million people starving and make future reparations impossible. The Soviet side also required continued shipments to the Soviet Union under terms of the lend-lease agreement, and the division of the German navy equally between the Soviet Union, the USA, and Britain.

Stalin had made similar territorial demands on Germany in 1939–40, when he grasped all territories east of the Curzon Line and discussed a division of the British Empire.[4] The secret protocols accompanying the German-Soviet Non-Aggression Pact of 23 August 1939 assigned Finland, Estonia, and Latvia to Stalin, and recognized his interest in Bessarabia. In 1940 Stalin invaded Bukovyna, an action that had not been agreed in the pact.

In 1945, the Soviets began dismantling entire German plants and industries and shipping them east, without consulting other powers. During negotiations in Paris held in February 1946 Molotov stated that the 475,000 displaced persons in the western zones of occupation included pro-Nazi Yugoslav Chetniks and Ustaše, Hungarian Salashists, Russian and Ukrainian White Guards, and members of General Anders's Polish Army, whom he described as "fascists." He claimed that these displaced persons constituted a "grave danger to the neighbouring democratic states" and should be urgently evacuated (Moorhouse 2014, 165).

The Galicia Division's soldiers followed these negotiations with keen interest. In their first place of internment near Venice, they lived in the open. To avoid the oven-like heat of the Sirocco winds, they dug holes, trenches, and ditches for protection. In the evenings the camp came alive with songs, games, and group discussions, whose main topic was what would happen next. The war in Japan continued and some men speculated that the Division would be used by the Allies on the Japanese front. The men boiled soup in primitive containers, sending up smoke from thousands of fires that created fantastic patterns in the evening Italian sky. The fusiliers had somehow managed to drag their field kitchen across the Alps and the hills of Carinthia. It now served the hospital, which was full of men who were sick or whose wounds had not fully healed.

Most men had their personal belongings taken from them by British troops during the first search. Camp rules were strict: for selling an army uniform to locals the punishment was eight days arrest and for going beyond the wires it was fourteen. Anyone caught stealing a uniform spent twenty-eight days in confinement. Recidivists could be sent to another camp and banned from returning. One man received twelve days for sticking his tongue out at the Soviet repatriation commission as it was being escorted by British authorities (Veryha 1984, 56).

There were rule breakers and trouble-makers, especially among those who had attached themselves during the retreat simply to escape Soviet troops. There were also individuals who had quit work on German farms, put on a soldier's uniform, and joined: "They later spread dissatisfaction, slander and gossip, and were the first to volunteer for return to the 'motherland.' The camp also contained people who could not give a clear explanation of how they had ended up behind prison wires. Some of these took an active part in camp society and in time made their way into leadership roles" (Zahachevskyi 1968, 200).

Throughout May and early June 1945 new groups of soldiers arrived almost on a daily basis, all claiming to be Ukrainians. They included Belarusians, Poles, Russians, and even Germans who thought that the Ukrainian camp would be a safer place than wherever they happened to be. There were also Ukrainian workers from Austria and Germany who had "volunteered" for the reserve regiment while it was in Austria. Many of these individuals were undisciplined, easily swayed by rumours, or influenced by the repatriation commission. As a result, the number of people in the camp fluctuated. On 16 June 1945, Camp 5C held 10,437. After the major repatriation of 17–25 July and the winnowing out of soldiers of other nationalities, such as the Germans, or a group of eight who went to the camp of the Kuban and Don Cossacks, the figure on 31 August was 9,316, which included 163 officers (Veryha 1984, 74).

Some combative types did not wish to submit to camp regulations. They were prone to indiscipline and frequently stole from the camp's food store. Younger soldiers suffered from hunger and some fainted during roll call. One died from eating unripe grain (Veryha 1984, 70). In Bellaria breakfast consisted of coffee and eighteen rusks (called *keksy*, or "cakes," by the men), soy, canned meat, and tinned margarine. American rusks from Sanitary Food Manufacturing in Saint Paul, Minnesota, were better quality and could be easily soaked in water. Two of them could be traded for one cigarette. Tobacco served as currency (67, 68).

A number of Eastern Ukrainians had entered the camps and hid their identities because they were liable to extradition under the provisions of the Yalta Agreement. One of them was the painter Leonid Perfetskyi, who attached himself to the Division in the last days of the war. He had been given a uniform but refused to wear it – the helmet and gas mask in particular – or to carry a rifle. Even the Germans treated him with respect, calling him "Herr Professor." He would gather up his sketching materials and go off, asking Oleh Lysiak to safeguard his uniform. He retained only a small gun in his pocket, saying: "If the Bolsheviks couldn't finish me off, a helmetless cavalryman of the 'Iron Division,' I will be able take care of myself now." When the painter returned, Lysiak would give him back his entire uniform (Lysiak 1996, 69). Another was the theatre scholar Valerian Revutskyi, who later taught at the University of British Columbia.[5]

Although lack of English translators and interpreters was initially a problem, the British army leadership was able to observe the men closely. It was impressed by their discipline and solidarity and soon gained a good understanding of their mentality and situation.

The Repatriation Campaign

The Division's main struggle was with efforts to hand it over to Soviet authorities. The Soviet repatriation campaign began in Mestre near Venice, where three thousand soldiers were first kept after surrendering. Unaware of the Yalta Agreement and the possibility of being sent back, seventeen soldiers admitted to being born in what, before 1 September 1939, had been Soviet territory. A map was placed on the table and each was told to indicate his place of birth. They were then informed that they would be deported. After their Ukrainian officer wrote to the British command explaining that the men were not Soviet citizens, even though they might have been born east of the 1939 border, they were allowed to join the others in Camp 5C. In order to coax men to return, Soviet agitators claimed that a general amnesty had been proclaimed and that they would all be pardoned. The Poles also screened men in the transition camps. They encouraged repatriation to Poland or recruitment into the 2nd Corps of General Władysław Anders, which had been formed in 1942 out of Polish citizens sent to Soviet concentration camps in 1939 and 1940. The 2nd Corps, which, by 1945, numbered 100,000, in fact contained hundreds of Ukrainians who had been arrested at the same time as the Poles and shared their fate throughout the war. One hundred and sixty-two soldiers from the Division volunteered to join the Anders Army (Veryha 1984, 135).[6]

On 15 June 1945, Camp 5C was instructed to made a card catalogue of all men in the camp, giving dates and places of birth. The men did this themselves.[7] Captain Levin of the British Army's Palestinian Regiment was attached as an instructor. He had escaped to Palestine from the Soviet Union in 1925; knew English, German, Russian, Polish, and Ukrainian; and was often able to distinguish Galician, Volhynian, and Eastern Ukrainian accents. Levin compiled a list of 199 candidates for repatriation, even though all the men denied being Soviet citizens. When General Krat protested Levin's aggressive interrogation methods, the latter was removed. Soon afterwards a statement was read to the assembled troops, explaining that no one would be forcibly sent to the Soviet Union. The Yalta Agreement was read to the troops and whoever wished to return was asked to step forward. Ninety-nine men did so. It appears, however, that only fifty-two actually went to the Soviet camp. Most were Eastern Ukrainians and had been part of the reserve regiment. Some may have been Russians who attached themselves to the Division in the war's closing stages.

In response to Soviet demands the British command registered each soldier's date and place of birth, and listed those who had been in the Soviet Union prior to September 1939. On 25 June, the register was completed and another 167 soldiers were persuaded to return, seventy-one from the reserve regiment. Some of these men had served in the Red Army or had been forcibly sent to work in Germany and, therefore, felt they would find a sympathetic ear (Veryha 1984, 137).

On 15 July, Major Podobedov and Lieutenant Tarasov from the Soviet repatriation commission visited the camp accompanied by British officers. Urging the men to return, they addressed each regiment in turn, while the men listened, standing at attention. Although the speeches were interrupted at points with exclamations and whistles, at the end of the day over six hundred people left the camp. Most were from the Buchach area and had been forcibly conscripted in 1944 (Krat 1979, 50). The commission then set up a tent outside the camp gates with a different captain from the Palestinian Regiment as translator. Ten soldiers entered at a time and each was asked whether he wanted to return. When no one agreed to leave, the commission demanded the removal of General Krat and Lieutenant Malets from the camp, supposedly because their presence did not allow the soldiers to express their desires. The commission argued that the officers were terrorizing the troops and preventing them from returning. It demanded that the men be interviewed separately outside the camp, with their belongings. This was allegedly because the men who wanted to be repatriated were afraid that "fascists" would lynch them when they returned for their possessions. The demand was satisfied and eventually one more soldier agreed to leave (51). The commission was now accompanied by two young women in short tight skirts who informed the men that the girls were waiting for them (Veryha 1984, 137).

In the second half of July the commission became more aggressive when a new British captain who supported repatriation became camp commander. The Soviet officers walked freely through the camp, took an interest in the publications produced by the men, and then demanded a list of all officers, especially those who had served in "White" armies. They were informed that there were no such officers. When Major Podobedov stated that Krat himself was one of them, the latter replied: "If you mean officers of the Army of the Ukrainian People's Republic in the years 1917–1921, then we were never 'Whites.' On the contrary, we fought for a free Ukraine both against the Bolsheviks and the 'Whites.'" Krat refused to provide a list, saying he was under British, not Soviet, authority (Krat 1979, 51–2).

At one point the new camp commander ordered an armed truck with machine gunners to escort two members of the commission into the camp. They were accompanied by several former soldiers of the Division who had earlier agreed to repatriation. Dressed in English clothes, these men distributed cigarettes and chocolates while conducting agitation. However, two of them jumped out of the vehicle and hid among the tents. Earlier, four others who had agreed to repatriation also returned. All these men had concluded that they were better off in the British camp (Veryha 1984, 146). On 24–25 July, after further interviews, another 108 agreed to go. Some ninety-six hundred men still remained. The Division's leadership sent memos to the British camp authorities on 26 July, and 9 and 10 August, explaining that the Division had agreed to fight only on the eastern front and giving reasons they refused to live under Stalin's rule.

Soviet authorities demanded that Captain Anatol Orlyk be handed over and searched for him throughout the camp. Some guards who had by then soured on the commission's behaviour turned a blind eye to the fact that Orlyk had been placed among the sick in the infirmary. On 7 August 1945, camp authorities repeated that there would be no forced repatriations but also stated that there was no guarantee the men would find a place in the British Empire (Veryha 1984, 149).

One day a Soviet officer saw a picture of dumplings on a willow falling into a dish. He complained of anti-Soviet propaganda, interpreting the image, correctly, as promises of the impossible. At this point the repatriation commission convinced the British authorities to transfer General Krat and other officers from Bellaria to nearby International Camp 12. Thirty-five men were taken away on 13 August; another 38 on the followed day, along with 51 NCOs; and 2 more were removed on 25 August (Revutskyi 2005, 42–53). These officers were only allowed to rejoin the other soldiers in March and April of 1946. The removal, however, did not have the effect the Soviet mission desired. Younger men who had completed secondary education created the Student Group (Studentska hromada), which constituted about one thousand men, or 10 percent of the camp. This educated group had been instructed by Krat to take over leadership in the event that all officers were removed. Along with the remaining senior men, they set about organizing camp life. A youth company (Iunatskyi kurin) was organized for the 288 youngest soldiers who needed to complete their education. Some older men shared their food rations with the youngest, realizing that they needed more nourishment. A cultural-educational team was formed and began planning a multifaceted program. The men signed up for high school classes, an art group, a workshop for artisans, a theatre group, and two choirs. Public lectures began and various courses were organized. These initially focused on practical skills, such as driving, mechanics, horticulture, mathematics, and language-learning. When the camp moved to Rimini in October, the range of courses expanded.

Meanwhile, the repatriation commission entered the camp every day with packages of propaganda, behaving as though it was the administration. The continual visits became a war of nerves. On 22 August, three more soldiers agreed to repatriation and on the following day another thirty-three. One British officer tried to pressure the soldiers by telling them that if they did not agree to repatriation they would be handed over to the Soviets and given ten years hard labour. General Filip Golikov arrived and the interviews outside the camp continued, but no more men agreed to leave.

Golikov was appointed head of the new repatriation commission on 24 October 1944. Nikolai Tolstoy describes him as "one of the most cowardly and incompetent" officers in the Soviet forces. From July 1940 he had been chief of the Intelligence Directorate of the Red General Staff and, through a series of blunders, had caused the arrest of the best counter-espionage agents operating abroad. He also bore a large share of responsibility for Soviet unpreparedness for war in 1941 because he had altered reports and played down legitimate fears of German intentions in order not to earn Stalin's displeasure. As a result of the disaster he had been dismissed from his command (Tolstoy 1977, 399; Morehouse 2014, 239).

Golikov was in charge of the Red Army's political administration; de facto, he was the army's leading KGB official. He announced to the men that he had been sent from Moscow and urged them to return to their "homeland." The interned soldiers responded that the repatriation commission did not contain anyone from their homeland: it included no Ukrainian speakers, nor anyone from Kyiv.

Behind the scenes, a different kind of repatriation was being conducted by the administration of counter-intelligence, SMERSH, and the NKGB. SMERSH, which operated against Soviet citizens abroad, was capturing, kidnapping, or murdering people whom it suspected of disloyalty. Many victims had never engaged in any fighting but were considered dangerous because they were well informed about the Soviet past or present.

Although the repatriation commission claimed that every man would be accepted as a son of the "motherland" and have a chance to redeem himself, the soldiers were better informed. One Ukrainian who had decided to return later recounted his experience. He described how the men were sent off with speeches, music, and banners, then at the collection point had been placed behind barbed wire: "Instead of music, there were loaded machine guns. The welcoming speech was full of curses and threats. Then interrogations began: this was no longer the army, this was the NKVD. They asked an endless number of questions, and after each reply the interrogator would shout 'You liar!' The food was atrocious. Nor did the conversations among the men sound very comforting: there was talk of the horrible fate of the preceding parties" (Tolstoy 1977, 375). This particular individual managed to escape by smuggling himself on board a returning American truck.

On 25 August at 9:00 a.m., when Soviet officers again demanded to see individual soldiers, they were met with unexpected resistance. The Ukrainian internal camp guards refused to open the gate to allow entry. Captain Andrii Sakovych was relieved of his guard command and Savelii Yaskevych was appointed in his place. At that point a mass protest occurred. Transports were waiting outside the gates to take away Sakovych and other officers, but the soldiers prevented them from leaving, prompting a member of the Soviet commission to complain that the officers in the camp had fomented a revolution. The Ukrainian officers met with the British command at 3:00 p.m. Yaskevych stated that he would only take command if he was given a guarantee that no more officers would be removed, that the Soviets would stop entering the camp, and that British officers would be present at any future meetings with the commission outside the camp. These conditions were accepted. After that, one further soldier agreed to repatriation on 7 September and one on 11 September (Veryha 1984, 163–4). A frustrated Red Army colonel was allowed to address the men. He cried to the wooden faces staring at him: "You are a grey mass … You have nothing to offer but your hands. The world doesn't want you. For them, you are rubbish. Be warned. Sooner or later the Soviet Union will have you" (Hills 1989, 14).

These experiences challenged the interned men to explain who they were and why they refused to live in the Soviet Union. They produced a memorandum on 28 August 1945, signed by ninety officers, which stated that Moscow viewed them "not only as enemy prisoners, but above all as political opponents" (Veryha 1984, 225–8).

The protest on 25 August 1945 was a turning point. Along with the intervention of Archbishop Ivan Buchko, who was the envoy of Pope Pius XII, and representations from Canadian and other Allied soldiers of Ukrainian descent, it succeeded in convincing the British that the interned men would never be reconciled to Russian-Soviet rule in Ukraine. The repatriation commission stopped bothering the men. By that time a total of 1,052 had agreed to be sent to Ukraine and 176 to join the 2nd Corps (Veryha 1984, 168). Some of those who agreed to repatriation intended to escape and join the partisan struggle; others believed the promise of amnesty. On 17 October 1945, the Division was transferred to a new camp in Rimini, a total of 9,308 men – 9,148 soldiers and 160 officers.[8]

In Italy the threat of deportation was constant. Soviet agents tried to kidnap men who had left the camp, whether on an official pass or illegally. All the while, the drumbeat of Soviet propaganda continued. Mykola Bazhan, a great poet who was forced to parrot the Kremlin's opinions, on 1 February 1946 told the UN's Committee for Social-Humanitarian and Cultural Questions: "The Germanized Ukrainian fascists, who find themselves in Germany, Austria and Italy, are a danger to peace in the entire world as long as they are not returned to the hands of justice" (United Nations General Assembly 1946, 15, quoted in Veryha 1981, 174). In his speech published in *Izvestiia* on 3 February 1946, he claimed: "In Italy in Camp 5c a formation under Lieutenant Krat of the German army has been created out of Ukrainian-German nationalists and Ukrainian POWs serving in the German army. Ukrainian citizens who desire to return to their motherland are beaten with sticks by officers under various pretexts" (Zahachevskyi 1968, 75).

There were individuals in the British government, like Anthony Eden, who favoured deportation. He had stated in July 1944: "If these men don't go back to Russia, where are they to go? We don't want them here" (Tolstoy 1977, 54). Eden admired Stalin and had been taken in by the latter's performance at a meeting in Moscow on 11 October 1944. On 17 October, both Eden and Churchill had agreed that all Soviet citizens should be returned "without reference to the wishes of the individual concerned" (73–4, 103). Like the British experts in the Moscow Embassy, they appeared to believe that the Soviet Union wished to co-operate with the Western Allies (428–9).

However, by July 1945 things had changed. British troops had witnessed scenes of horror as men handed over were instantly machine gunned. Major Denis Hills had overseen the repatriation of 1,651 Russian soldiers, whom he personally escorted on the New Zealand cargo ship, the *Arawa*. When it reached Odesa in February 1945, the men were immediately shot or sent to the Gulag. The *Duchess of Bedford* and two other ships had docked at Odesa in the first week of March 1945. NKVD officers marched the prisoners off the ship and out of sight. Two bombers then appeared in the sky, circling slowly, while a mobile saw-mill and its high-pitched blades were put to work. The sounds were used to muffle the shooting of the prisoners who had been taken off the ship (Tolstoy 1977, 129–30).

Hills had also witnessed the handing over of Don, Kuban, and Terek Cossacks (nationalities not recognized by the Soviet Union). British soldiers were ordered, in his words, "to club old men, women and children to get them into the transports."[9] Red Army machine gunners had immediately executed the men.[10]

This handing over of forty-five thousand Cossacks became an iconic moment. In order to justify it, internal British memos described them as "primitive tribesmen" who were "guilty of dreadful atrocities in Yugoslavia" (Tolstoy 1977, 274–5). Field-Marshall Alexander may have been given oral instructions by Churchill for the operation to proceed.[11] Certainly, General Keightley admitted that his orders to repatriate them came directly from Churchill (Dismukes 1996, 113).

Because the policy of handing over hundreds of thousands was a concession to Stalin, dissimilation was used by both the British and US political authorities to keep the facts out of the press and to misinform. The UK propaganda insisted that the men, women, and children were being returned because "they took up arms for the Germans," that they would be "put to work on the land," that they would be educated as "decent Soviet citizens," and that their lives were not in danger. The US press assumed that the people being forced back were traitors or deserters. In December 1945 the *New York Herald Tribune* printed an article under the headline "Renegade Reds Roam Balkans, Spread Terror." It explained that remnants of Vlasov's army were wandering "fully armed and desperate" around Austria and were murdering farmers from whom they stole food. The message was that these men were escaping justice and posed a danger to civilians and to American troops.

The US was repatriating both civilians and soldiers, even when these protested violently, and even if the people were not Soviet citizens. In Seattle, American soldiers threw men into trucks, subdued them with blackjacks and bayonets, and dumped them into Soviet ships where they fought with bare fists and disabled the engines (Epstein 1973, ix). The US policy in September 1945 was stated in *Handbook Issued by Headquarters, United States Forces, European Theater*: "No United Nations' National, stateless person ... or persons persecuted because of race, religion, or activity in favor of the United Nations, will be compelled to return to his domicile except for a criminal offence. Liberated Soviet Citizens ... are excluded from this policy ... and will be returned to the control of the USSR without regard to their individual wishes" (x). In fact, however, the British and Americans were repatriating all Soviet citizens in line with their interpretation of the Yalta Agreement (Dismukes 1996, 97).[12]

The policy was only stopped because of resistance from within the military. By July 1945, British officers, who were shocked that the Soviets were not honouring the Geneva Convention, had begun insisting that the Ukrainians should not suffer the same fate. The men interned in Rimini also found support from General Anders. The vast majority of the Division's soldiers were, after all, not Soviet citizens but, rather, had been citizens of Poland prior to the outbreak of the war. On 5 July, the Pope also appealed to the Allies against the forcible deportation of people against their will and the refusal of right of asylum (Dismukes 1996, 100).

Soviet operatives also began demanding the return of their own POWs, whom they had until then disowned. Moscow required that these men be given new winter clothing, including a change of underwear. When they were marched to the railway station in Odesa, their clothing and shoes were removed. Many were immediately imprisoned and loaded into railway wagons popularly known as Stolypin cars.

These cars were first produced prior to 1911 when Petr Stolypin was Russia's interior minister. In the 1930s they became the universal means of prisoner transportation. Solzhenitsyn describes them in his *The Gulag Archipelago* (1973), where he writes that the compartments held "thirty-five people, lying on top of one another, floundering, fighting" (Solzhenitsyn 1973, 493). Some individuals hung suspended between others, their legs not touching the floor. When people died, the guards hauled the corpses from under their feet.[13] The "slave caravans," as he calls them, had, since the 1920s, transported hundreds of thousands to Siberia, including entire nationalities. Evgeniia Ginzburg also provides a description in the chapter entitled "Car Number 7" of her *Journey into the Whirlwind* (1967). In it she recalls her own experience of being transported, along with seventy-six women. These transports shipped both the arrested and the repatriated to Siberia, where both groups became part of the Gulag nation.

Major Denis Hills was the British screening officer during several deportations. Operation Keelhaul took place in 1946. The term "Keelhaul" refers to a form of torture that involves tying someone up and repeatedly dragging them under the keel of a boat from one side to the other. The victim bleeds to death from the wounds inflicted by the barnacles on the keel – or is decapitated by them. Hills's personal account of this military operation was discovered in a hand-corrected carbon copy that had been sent to a group of Ukrainian Canadians (Nimenko 2016, 183). The document makes clear that the operation was arranged by British diplomats in order to maintain good relations with the Soviet Union.[14]

Operation Eastwind took place in 1947. It was the name given to a plan to transport and forcibly repatriate 170 men whom Hills selected in May 1947, two years after the end of the war, from the original list of Soviet citizens he had been given. He later claimed that the Division's men owed their lives in part to this "calculated last-minute token sacrifice of 170 Russians from other units to appease Moscow" (Nimenko 2016, 184). The victims were told they were being sent to another camp but were placed in specially prepared trains to prevent any suicides. All objects had been removed and all windows covered with grills. Restraining devices were provided to the British soldiers escorting the train: handcuffs, straightjackets, tear gas, truncheons, and firearms (206–7).[15] Hills has been described in later accounts as minimizing the deportations and deaths by drawing attention in an internal report to what was happening (Cesarani 1992, 113, 119;

Greenfield 2013). Nimenko (2016, 200), however, sees him as "the linchpin" in these operations.[16] Dismukes has quoted the US Army Headquarters directive in connection with Operation Eastwind. It authorized the use of firearms and stated: "Every effort will be made to return repatriates alive, but when no other means will prevent their escape, shooting becomes necessary, or if death occurs through natural causes, bodies will be delivered to the Russian authorities at destination" (Dismukes 1996, 106).

The backlash within the armed forces, which threatened to spill over into the press, put an end to similar measures, although politicians from the British foreign secretary Ernest Bevin to General Dwight D. Eisenhower continued to argue for their implementation.[17] However, soldiers found ways of evading or disobeying the orders. The various tactics included turning a blind eye to escapes, delaying action by asking for clarification of orders, the use of bureaucratic procedures to remove people from the deportation lists, or simply refusing to implement an order. It is estimated that, as a result of this protest, 500,000 Soviet citizens were able to escape repatriation (Dismukes 1996, 121–8).

Many Allied soldiers had come to know the imprisoned people. Some, like Reverend William Sloane Coffin, a US army officer who served as an interpreter, initially had little sympathy for them because they had fought for the arch-villain Hitler, who had invaded and pillaged their country, incarcerated their compatriots in labour camps, and put 6 million Jews to death (Coffin 1977, 73). However, Coffin soon came to know about the cruelties of collectivization and the mass arrests, shootings, and deportation. Like other military men, he came to sympathize with their plight and became increasingly uncomfortable with the words "traitor" and "deserter" as applied to them (Dismukes 1996, 115–16).

These episodes show why, during internment and for many years afterwards, the Division's veterans feared being sent back. Nimenko, who spent years researching his father's biography, discovered that the latter was from Dnipro in Eastern Ukraine and had escaped from a train transporting people to a work camp in Germany. Because he was good with horses he found work with a Galician farmer and assumed a new identity. When interviewed by the British, he claimed to have been born in the Galician town of Berezhany. After the war, he was unable to use the Red Cross Tracing Service to contact relatives because this would have put him at risk of deportation for lying to the authorities in Italy and to the Home Office.

On 17 June 1944, while Nimenko's father was working on the Galician farm, a group of forty Germans entered the village and were attacked by Ukrainian partisans. Two Germans died in the fight and the rest were captured. The partisans agreed to release them in exchange for a guarantee that the village would not be punished. However, on the following day, the Germans returned and burned four or five houses. According to Nimenko's father, they then put a boy of fifteen against the wall and asked if he was ready to fight with them because they would not leave him to be taken by the Russians to fight against them. The young boy refused and was immediately shot in the head. To avoid the same fate, the rest of the men "volunteered" (Nimenko 2016, 333).

While researching his father's life, Nimenko was directed to the individual who had in 2000 provided information for the Yorkshire Television program about the Division. This individual refused to give any details but pointed out that the film had accidentally been shown in Canada. Nimenko (2016, 361) writes:

I then asked him the title of the film, but he stuttered, mumbled and then said something quickly so that I couldn't understand him. I asked him to repeat himself, and he said, "The ss in Britain."

Now I understood his position and his reason for not telling me anything about the film. He obviously believed what he had researched would be released in England as a sensational documentary which would shock the average British person ... It seemed to me from the title alone that the film was aiming at one sided sensationalism rather than being a factual documentary. Documentaries like this can sometimes be "cheap telly," made to incite trouble rather than to reflect and understand very difficult and complex times in a balanced way. The motives of the makers can sometimes just be inflammatory.

Like a number of other *dyviziinyky*, Nimenko's father had survived the war and five years imprisonment, and had then been prevented from telling his story. The only narrative available in the Western media depicted the Division's men as perpetrators of heinous crimes.[18]

It was little known that about 150 Ukrainians who arrived in Britain in 1947 were given training as radio operators and spies and parachuted into

Ukraine by the RAF as part of Operation Integral. They were immediately captured, largely because they had been betrayed by Kim Philby, the British Intelligence officer who was working for the KGB and informing Moscow of all the flight details (Melnyk 2016 2:289–90).

Wasyl Nimenko, who has the same first name as his father, became a psychotherapist and worked extensively with soldiers, homeless people, and survivors of torture. In his view, physical and psychological damage from extreme stress can be profound, a fact that was recognized in 1980 when the term "post-traumatic stress disorder" was introduced. A number of men like his father found it difficult to speak about their wartime experiences, especially with their children, because they were trying to protect them from being damaged by their own traumas. The silence of Nimenko's father was not due to guilt or shame for having been in the German army. He always maintained that the Ukrainians fought for patriotic reasons, that they were motivated by strong anti-Soviet feelings and not pro-Nazi sympathies (Nimenko 2016, 68).

It is instructive to set similar accounts against Cesarani's (1992, 8) comment about the "quiet sojourn of Nazi collaborators and mass murderers in Britain." The researcher characterizes the MI5 and MI6 missions as recruiting from "DPs, including Axis collaborators and known war criminals," and thus makes Kim Philby's betrayals appear honourable. He quotes accounts that describe the Galicia Division as "exceptionally brutal" and guilty of "monstrous outrages" (6, 119–20).

11

RIMINI, 1945–47

After five months in Camp 5C in Bellaria, on 17 October 1945 the Division's men were transferred to a new camp on the grounds of an airport near Rimini. In the eighteen months that followed, they continued resisting attempts to deport them and worked to generate publicity for conditions in Ukraine. This period was formative: it provided them with the sense of identity that they would maintain in following decades. According to Vasyl Veryha (1980, 172): "Wherever they later found themselves, the *dyviziinyky* remained one of the most dynamic, best organized and most reliable groups in the Ukrainian community. Members of the 'Galicia' Division as a group did not betray or trample the Ukrainian ideals for which their parents died in the Liberation Struggles of 1917–20 or their brothers and sisters on all fronts fighting the occupants of Ukraine."[1] Volodymyr Gotskyi (1990, 192) would echo this view in 1990 when he wrote: "The Division did much more for our cause while imprisoned than in bloody battles on the eastern front … Our determined and proud stance in the face of the repatriation danger, our constant and frank demands, free of any trickery, in defence of our national principles, at every step and opportunity, both in prison camp in Italy and while working in Great Britain, created around us a degree of respect."

In Rimini the soldiers forged a collective spirit based on an image of themselves as the nation's defenders. One camp periodical stated: "We do not forget that a soldier's honour lies in the willingness to place himself in harm's way in defence of his people and country, to sacrifice his blood and even his life! We understand that the soldier's best virtue is his courage in battle, which demands resolution and decisiveness" (B.M., *Batkivshchyna,*

16 February 1947, quoted in Zahachevskyi 1968, 224). The men would spend the rest of their lives affirming that, in spite of their German uniforms, they had enlisted for patriotic reasons. Even though many veterans continued to doubt the wisdom of creating a Division, the time they spent in Italy deepened their commitment to Ukraine's liberation struggle. An editorial in their newspaper *Visti* later asserted: "Their soldierly spirit was further tempered, and the Division's men found ways of continuing without weapons the war for Ukraine's liberation" ("Obiednani" 1957, 1).[2]

Not everyone in Rimini's surrendered enemy personnel camp (SEP) was from Galicia. About 10 percent of the men were from Eastern Ukraine. The soldiers held different political convictions: there were supporters of the OUN-B, the OUN-M, the UNR, monarchist sympathizers of Hetman Pavlo Skoropadskyi's rule in 1918, and social democrats who in 1948 created the Ukrainian Revolutionary Democratic Party. About 90 percent of the interned men were Ukrainian Greek Catholics and 10 percent were Ukrainian Orthodox. In spite of these differences, they forged a unity that was later maintained in emigre organizations. Veryha (1980, 177) later wrote that the Division put down its arms without releasing its members from their duty to continue struggling in peaceful fashion for recognition of Ukraine's right to statehood.

Nonetheless, there were political tensions. One supporter of the OUN's Melnyk wing was murdered, allegedly by supporters of the rival Bandera wing (Budnyi 1979, 284). The latter group gained control of the camp's Prosvita (Enlightenment) society, through which it recruited people to the party. Later, in the UK, its numerical superiority allowed it to dominate the rank-and-file soldiers and the emigré community (283).

Initially, some camp guards in Bellaria and Rimini were British front-line troops. They allowed detainees to leave the camp and return. When replacements arrived from Britain, they were given orders to shoot anyone caught leaving and to subject anyone found outside the camp to a military trial. One member of the Division was shot and killed trying to leave the camp. On 10 February 1946 another was wounded in the leg near the perimeter fence (Budnyi 1979, 168–9). This prompted a delegation to visit the authorities. Discipline was harsher than in neighbouring German camps, where it was possible to leave without escort or permission from officers (Zahachevskyi 1968, 2034). One prisoner from an adjoining German compound was a driver who could move freely outside the camp. Every day he brought a loaf of bread for his own consumption. A prisoner in the Ukrainian camp arranged for him to throw a loaf over the fence each week in exchange for a blanket. On one occasion the loaf touched the top of one fence and dropped between the two wires. As the prisoner pushed through the wires to reach the bread, he was shot twice in the chest and died instantly. This caused anger because, even if he had managed to get through the wires, he would only have found himself in the other camp (Paziuk 1993, 126–7).

Articles in the Italian press claimed that the interned men had built a tunnel and were using it to leave the camp. This led to searches. In fact, those leaving and returning often did so in the refuse bins, which were emptied far from the camp. Others were given passes by various personnel, such as priests, translators, doctors, and work brigades, who loaned them to "tourists" on condition that they would be returned. Because the sanitation team, which removed rubbish from the camp at night, was the least supervised group, it became the main conduit through which trade with the outside world (mainly in food, tobacco, and alcohol) was conducted.

Escapes normally resulted from despair, when internees realized they would not be freed soon. Some went off to other parts of Italy, others crossed the Alps to join the French Foreign Legion, and a few travelled to Spain. Most, however, ended up in Germany and Austria. Estimates of how many escaped vary from three hundred to one thousand.[3] According to Zahachevskyi (1968, 209), "many ended up in the hands of Bolshevik agents and died a martyr's death. More than one died breaking his neck [falling] in the stony Alps. Nonetheless, escapes continued until the end of internment."

The Division set up its own internal guards. When camp rules were broken, because of theft, for example, there would be a trial followed by punishment, which might consist of twenty-five whacks or, in the case of recidivists, a trip to the cage known as the *kalabusha* (from the English "calaboose"). Internal punishment for stealing food from others could be severe. One soldier was punished with one hundred whacks and was required to return the food to the different companies and to apologize (Veryha 1984, 81). On one occasion, when an officer was discovered hiding boxes of rusks, cans of meat, margarine, and tobacco under his bed, he was banished from the camp. On 11 October 1945, several recidivist thieves were sentenced to forty-two days in another camp's "cage" and banned from returning (89). Men caught escaping were imprisoned in the *kalabusha*, although some breakouts were aided by the guards (Zahachevskyi 1968, 182). However, the

Figure 11.1 Judging an athletic competition, Rimini.

Figure 11.2 Blessing Easter baskets, 21 April 1946. Courtesy the estate of B. Maciw.

main reason for leaving the camp was to obtain goods for trade in the lively camp bazaar. Some individuals would sneak out regularly to barter for tobacco, wine, watches, and gold. Resourceful prisoners used the blankets they had been issued to make clothing and hats for sale.

The women's camp in Riccione contained twenty-five Ukrainian nurses (the male medical personnel had joined the Rimini camp), who had arrived from Carinthia in Austria, where the Division's last field hospital had been stationed. Most of the women were nineteen to twenty years old and had trained in Krynica after volunteering for the Division. Some were later transferred to a nearby civilian camp, leaving thirteen, six of whom worked in the hospital in Cezantico in the tuberculosis, x-ray, and other wards. One was assigned to be a translator.

The repatriation commission frequently appeared in Riccione with demands that the women leave. On one occasion, Soviet officers even brought completed papers for their "return to the homeland." This caused a panic, but the British guard telephoned his superior and learned that no permission had been given. From that moment the commission was not allowed into the Riccione camp (Cholkan 1979, 120).

Contacts between Riccione and Rimini were close. Men from Rimini would visit the nurses on most weekends, bringing literature and performing groups, and, on Sundays, the priests served mass. The women took part in plays and musicals staged in Rimini. The nurse Pavlia Fihurka-Plaviuk later described her experience performing in the operetta *Zaporozhets za Dunaiem* (The Cossack beyond the Danube):

The camp was a sea of symmetrically placed tents, with general order and cleanliness, and we were greeted on the way to the Camp Theatre by the pleasant smiling faces of the men. ... We were enthralled by the theatre building itself and marvelled that our brothers had been able to create such a remarkable building in such primitive conditions.

As far as I recall, our "guardians" transported us every day to the rehearsals ...

Finally, the impatiently awaited premiere took place, followed by a string of performances. What a contrast of feelings! The first Christmas in internment, behind barbed wire, in a foreign land, with yearning for one's relatives, for one's Homeland. And then the emotions of the performances themselves: the decorations, lights, music,

Figure 11.3 Ukrainian commanders with nurses from the Riccione camp.

song ... The theatre was completely packed with enthusiastic viewers, whose sparkling, tear-filled eyes and spontaneous applause are impossible to forget. It was like a wonderful dream! ... We could not at that time have experienced deeper emotions. (Pankiv 2005, 100–1)

Riccione was a stopping point for men leaving the camp or returning. The women hid those who were planning to escape until it was dark, allowing the "tourists" to change into civilian clothing and eat before setting off. In their turn, the men in Rimini collected money to support two nurses who were given the opportunity of studying in Rome (Cholkan 1979, 123). The nurses were among the first to be released after transfer to England (Zahachevskyi 1968, 187).

Seventy percent of the soldiers were younger than twenty-six, and three quarters were unmarried. They included not only engineers, doctors, accountants, lawyers, professors, and teachers but also tailors, bootmakers, carpenters, blacksmiths, and electrical workers. Their skills were put to use almost immediately. Because of pressure from the repatriation commission, everyone "instinctively understood that the worst possible outcome was to surrender to apathy and despair. This is why various courses, schools, lectures, choirs, concerts, a chamber and jazz orchestra, theatre, literary and other discussions were quickly organized" (Zahachevskyi 1968, 84). Major Yaskevych, who was appointed commander in the absence of other senior officers, proved to be a capable organizer and motivator. The camp soon became an enormous school, with classes for everyone, from the illiterate to university-level students. Professor Oleksandr Montsibovych, formerly of Lviv University, helped organize the high school and university courses. After ten months the high school (gymnasium) graduated 170 of 230 students. They studied six hours daily, from 9:00 a.m. until 4:00 p.m. The subjects were divided into four groups: classical languages and literatures; mathematics, chemistry and physics; humanities; history and geography (Iwasykiw Silecky 2006, 59–60; Revutskyi 2005, 25). Along the back portion of the camp an "experimental farm" grew tomatoes, cabbage, and other food.

Bishop Buchko and the Ukrainian clergy in Rome created a commission that oversaw the school and the exams. This allowed the results to be recognized by most universities to which the students applied after graduation. Cardinal Tisserant granted the high school official status on condition that clergy from the camp and the Vatican were allowed to preside over its academic affairs (Iwasykiw Silecky 2006, 60). The church and Ukrainian communities in the United States and Canada supplied books and materials. When the camp closed in April 1947, Buchko arranged for 247 men to continue their studies at universities around the globe: 52 in medicine, 36 in technology, 23 in agronomy, and 10 in the humanities (Iwasykiw Silecky 2006, 58). Twenty-five students found places in Spanish universities, where they studied languages, literatures, diplomacy, and international law. Their studies were funded by the University of Madrid's Catholic Aid Committee and by grants from the Spanish government (64–5). Under the Vatican's patronage a six-month school for deacons was organized in Rimini. Eighty students participated, of whom sixteen completed the full program and officially became deacons of the Catholic Church of the Eastern Rite (63).

The first general courses were in driving instruction, Italian, and English. Some British soldiers were invited to the English courses for conversational practice. All money had been confiscated from the soldiers, but some of it may have been returned by camp authorities for educational purposes. The German Office for POWs may also have contributed funding (Veryha 1984, 116). The Germans had their own aid organization, which in the first

Figure 11.4 Final high school exams in the theatre built by the Division's veterans, 30 July 1946.

weeks supplied the Ukrainian camp with books, writing materials, films, and German newspapers, including its organ *Die Brücke* (The bridge).

The Ukrainian Aid Committee in Rome helped to create a course in commerce. There were also courses in metalwork, tailoring, carpentry, shoe-making, masonry, hairdressing, electrical work, photography, auto-mechanics, and agriculture. British camp authorities created a team of two hundred mechanics to work on auto repairs. A workshop supervised all construction. It built a theatre, a Greek-Catholic and Orthodox church with belfries, a sports hall, an agricultural school, and a barrack for the Prosvita Society (Zahachevskyi 1968, 80–1). These were made out of available corrugated iron and wood. The results by some accounts were impressive, although Cesarani (1992, 103) mentions only one "primitively built church – a battered hut adorned by a cross." All materials were put to use. Packing papers were used for writing scripts and lectures. Boards from delivery crates and oil cans served in construction and decoration. Instead of church bells, steel rings with a melodious sound were used. The priests meanwhile provided services every Sunday with the participation of choirs. They visited the graves of soldiers, some of whom had died of wounds at the end of the war and others from tuberculosis, heart attacks, or in automobile accidents.[4]

On 7 April 1946, after General Krat and the senior officers returned to the camp, a university began functioning. Twenty-two lecturers offered classes in history, geography, economics, literature, languages, and sciences – each attended by three hundred to four hundred students. They took place in the camp theatre three times a week and lasted two hours (Revutskyi 2005, 20). The seats were made from container barrels. When electricity became more widely available, the communications team set up telephones and loudspeakers, allowing music to be broadcast from a central area. The phrase "shafa hraie" (literally "the music box is playing") became popular. It initially referred to a five-ton truck that was converted into a mobile studio with microphones inside and loudspeakers on top. The truck would park in the middle of the camp and the concert would begin. Metaphorically, the phrase came to mean "the show has begun," or "everything is in working order."

The artisanal shop had forty-four members, although officially there were 2,301 registered artisans in the camp.[5] One chemical engineer created the "Ukrainian gold" that became known far beyond the camp and was thought by some Poles to be gold stolen from Warsaw. The fake gold was made of brass pipes taken from dismantled cannon compressors. These were fashioned into rings and other "gold" products. The engineer devised a way of polishing the rings with sand and stone, then placing them on a roller, smearing them with a mastic he had invented. After repolishing they were stamped with 14 or 24 carat signs. Numerous Polish soldiers outside the camp asked for this gold, even after it was revealed to be fake.

The camp was surrounded by a high barbed-wire fence and ten watch towers with machine gunners. The men slept in tents whose entrances displayed embroidery-type patterns made of sand, clay, and crushed bricks. There were two main "streets," Lviv and Kyiv. Almost every tent was a beehive of creativity, part of a village in which each group demonstrated its skills and ingenuity:

Around one tent there was a garden with plants, sunflowers and carefully laid out pebbles. Another proudly showed off its sand path and wooden doors made out of food crates that were installed into the tent canvas. Then there was one with a trident and lion made of coloured glass. Further on, in a small square someone had laboured to build a miniature medieval castle with parapets, a defensive moat and a drawbridge ... The tents were not only dwelling places for camp inhabitants, but also workshops. Practically under every canvas something useful for the individual or group was going on: one tent was editing and publishing the regimental newspaper; a second was a tailor's shop; a third made metal or wooden boxes and tobacco cases; others marinated herring, boiled *varenyky*, mended watches, made rings out of real or fake "camp" gold. The merchandise was sold on the spot or taken to the camp bazaar, where anything could be traded for anything. The camp currency was the "dippable" or the "undippable" rusk, the "twist" of tobacco, or the dollar ... sent from America or Canada by an aunt. Money could be spent in the camp casino, which began running in the camp's last days, and where one could listen to "jazz," drink wine and play cards. (Volynskyi 1979, 134)

Public lectures were organized to mark important moments in history. There were talks on Ivan Mazepa and the battle of Poltava in 1709, the publication *Istoriia Rusov* (History of the Rus), the Lviv Uprising of 1 November 1918, and the execution of 359 soldiers of the UNR army at Bazar in 1921. Christmas, Easter, the Feast of St Nicholas, and all religious holidays were celebrated.

Newspapers arrived from abroad, including the Canadian *Novyi shliakh* (New pathway), *Ukrainskyi holos* (Ukrainian voice), *Kanadiiskyi farmer* (Canadian farmer), and the American *Svoboda* (Liberty). Wall newspapers begun appearing. The first issue of *Zhyttia v tabori* (Camp life) was produced in Bellaria on 1 September 1945 with the help of soldiers from the Polish 2nd Corps, who donated the printing paper (Revutskyi 2005, 33). A Gestetner machine appeared, probably sent by the nurses in Riccione (9). Numerous camp publications were "sponsored" by a particular regiment, group, or tent. They included *Visti* (News), *Osa* (Wasp), *Na varti* (On guard), *V nametakh* (In tents), *Taborovyi visnyk* (Camp news), and *Taborovyk* (Camper).

Performance groups did much to change hostile British and Italian opinion. The most successful were Stepan Huminilovych's choir Burlaka (Rover), Iliarii Kushnirenko's dance group, and Yaroslav Babuniak's bandura ensemble. A second choir, Slavuta, was directed by Osyp Holovatskyi and later by Yaroslav Havryliuk. It performed liturgical music and sang at most of the camp's church services.

The choir was influenced by Myron Lozynskyi, who had been a professional singer in Warsaw in the Juranga quartet, but Huminilovych himself had made a reputation in the 1930s in Lviv's jazz scene with Leonid ("Yabtso") Yablonsky's famous group, which played to mixed Polish, Jewish, and Ukrainian audiences. This group included Iryna Yarosevych (Jarosiewicz), who found fame on the Polish stage and screen as Renata Bogdańska. During the war she helped entertain the Polish armed forces and in 1948 married General Władysław Anders. Her brothers were the composer Ostap Nyzhankivskyi and the opera singer Oleksandr Nyzhankivskyi. Her father had been a chaplain in the Sich Riflement and served as a priest in Western Ukraine. In her youth, she and a third brother Anatol participated in Plast, the Ukrainian scouts who had been banned by Poland in 1935. Another brother, Stepan, was killed in 1944 as a member of the UPA.

Huminilovych's choir staged 104 concerts, 43 in the camp and 61 outside (35 for German, 15 for British, and 11 for other camps). On six occasions the choir, bandura ensemble, and dance group performed together. During a visit to a German camp the choir was surprised by the backdrop, which displayed a trident on an azure background, the symbol that in 1943 the Germans had forbidden (Veryha 1984, 98).

British soldiers greatly enjoyed the concerts and requests for performances immediately arrived from Cezena, Riccione, and other cities. Performances in Riccione on 9 and 12 September 1945 took place in the presence of British commanders of the 8th Army, including Field Marshal Harold Alexander, who attended the second concert. He had commanded the 15th Army Group at the battle of Monte Cassino and, in 1946, would be appointed governor general of Canada on the recommendation of the Canadian prime minister William Lyon Mackenzie King. Marshal Alexander publicly congratulated Huminilovych after the concert. In the following year the British army organized a tour for the choir, first through southern Italy around Naples and then through northern Italy. After transfer to the UK in May–June 1947 the choir was directed by Yarema Hordii (Yevhen Pasika). It gave thirteen concerts for Ukrainian and German POWs, and for English audiences. On 10 January 1948, for example, it performed in London's King George Hotel (Veryha 2006, 11).

The jazz group, called Ono, played at a ball for the British officers in Riccione on 12 September 1945. The payment for this performance allowed the group to buy several instruments. It also played for the 2nd Polish Corps and, on many evenings, for the British camp command, which had developed a taste for Ukrainian melodies and asked for them to be performed (Revutskyi 2005, 152).

The bandura orchestra directed by Volodymyr Domashivets and Osyp Holovatskyi organized weekly concerts and favoured Ukrainian composers. The music could be heard in the tents and by British and other soldiers in the neighbourhood (Revutskyi 2005, 99–100). There was also a vocal quartet, which put on about thirty performances, and a symphony orchestra, which performed its first concert on 24 September 1946. The camp's artisans made most of the instruments, including 42 mandolins, 3 balalaika, 2 violins, 2 baritone horns, 2 guitars, and 9 banduras (Zahachevskyi 1968, 140).

The art group Veselka (Rainbow) was formed in Bellaria by Volodymyr Kaplun. It made use of available materials, including barrels for storing heating oil, crates in which pears had been packed, and materials found on the beach. Using penknives and improvised chisels the artists made carvings and encrusted boxes, for which coloured electrical wire was used. At an exhibition in Riccione, the public was particularly impressed by the embroidery, hutsul-type wood carvings and encrusted works (caskets, axes, powder-cases, decorated boxes, cigarette holders, crosses, albums, and chess pieces). A number of works were presented as gifts to visiting dignitaries.

A stamp club of twenty-three members was formed on 1 May 1946 and issued twenty-eight stamp series, primarily for the inter-camp postal service. These have now become collector's items. The first series depicted life in the Rimini camp. Designed by Stepan Dytso and Roman Dudynskyi, it was printed on the *Die Brucke* press (Revutskyi 2005, 220). Later stamps portrayed Kyivan princes, Cossack leaders, and prominent political and cultural figures, such as Andrei Sheptytskyi, Mykhailo Hrushevskyi, Pavlo Skoropadskyi, and Symon Petliura. One series was devoted to the Division itself and featured the artillery, infantry, communications, and other groups (Zahachevskyi 1968, 146).[6]

The theatre performed not only well-known plays and musicals but also original musical reviews, such as *Rizdviana melodiia* (Christmas melody) and *Vesna ide* (Spring is coming).[7] The music for the latter was composed by Huminilovych to the words of the camp poet Yurii Forys. The Division's

Figure 11.6 Stamp produced in Rimini, 1946. Designed by Dmytro Dudynskyi.

Figure 11.5 Stamp produced in Rimini, 1946, "Ukrainian Camp Post Italy." Designed by Stepan Dytso.

Figure 11.7 Stamp produced in Rimini, 1946. Designed by Stepan Dytso. The figure symbolizes labour. Monte Titano is in the background.

Figure 11.10 Stamp produced in Rimini, 1946. Designed by Sviatoslav Yatsushko. It commemorates the anniversary of the Lviv Uprising on 1 November 1918.

Figure 11.8 Stamp produced in Rimini, 1946. Designed by Dmytro Dudynskyi.

Figure 11.9 Stamp produced in Rimini, 1946. Designed by Sviatoslav Yatsushko. It commemorates Metropolitan Andrei Sheptytskyi.

Figure 11.11 Theatre performance, Rimini. Francuzenko in female role in Borys Hrinchenko's *Na iasni zori*, 1946. Courtesy Ukrainian Historical and Educational Center.

nurses from Riccione performed the female parts, although when permission was not granted for them to travel, men took these roles. Up to eight hundred people attended the performances.

Most plays were directed by Stepan Stoliarchuk, who had worked in the Ivan Franko Theatre in Stanislaviv (Ivano-Frankivsk). Hryhorii Sosidka designed the sets (Revutskyi 2005, 114–27).[8] Some plays were directed by Ivan Verbytskyi, who was well known to Western Ukrainians from a political trial in 1928. He and Vasyl Atamanchuk were members of the paramilitary UVO (Ukrainian Military Organization) and had been tried for the 1926 assassination of Stanislaw Sobinski, the Polish superintendant of schools in the Lviv region.[9]

Sport played an important role, with football the most popular entertainment. A team with the camp's best players competed against other camps and developed an intense rivalry with German camps. Boxing, basketball, and table tennis also drew crowds.

While in Italy, the interned men had contact not only with British but also with Polish soldiers. The latter were far better equipped to understand the political complexities of postwar Eastern Europe. Those who had served in the 2nd Polish Corps had fought on the Allied side for their country's liberation and now faced the dilemma of whether or not to return to a communist-controlled homeland. There might have been several thousand Ukrainians in this army, although the figure is difficult to estimate because both Ukrainians and Jews from Galicia had enlisted as Poles and, in most cases, preferred to hide their identity (Danyliv 1952, 3).

The Corps had been recruited from men sent to the Gulag betweem 1939 and 1941. When it reached Palestine, it passed under British command and then participated in the defence of Tobruk and the Italian campaign, including the battle for Monte Cassino. Twenty soldiers from the Corps were interned in the Rimini camp. They were all from Śląsk (Silesia) or from Poznań and had won many Polish and British medals. However, they had no sympathy for Warsaw's communist regime. Their attitude to the *diviziinyky* was friendly, but they caused numerous problems for the British guards by refusing to appear for roll call and going on hunger strike. They blamed their imprisonment on the Polish secret service (Zahachevskyi 1968, 71–2).

Soldiers from the Corps had been among the first Allied troops to transport and guard the Division's men in Italy. Curious as to what the Ukrainians had experienced, they immediately offered cigarettes and struck up conversations. They also allowed some interned men to "disappear" from the camp, no doubt to facilitate defections to the Corps.

Ukrainians in the 2nd Corps regularly visited the Rimini camp. One such visit led to the reunion of a father serving in the Corps with his son in the Division (Revutskyi 2005, 34). Another prisoner had a younger brother in the Corps. While on guard duty, with machine gun in hand, the latter would talk to his older brother who sat on the grass as close to the wire as was permissible (Paziuk 1993, 131). A group from the Corps purchased and presented the Division with a Ukrainian flag and an official *hramota* (document) marking the day on which the flag was blessed. Soldiers from the Corps also attended a ceremony commemorating Symon Petliura, who in 1920 commanded the Ukrainian armed forces that fought alongside Polish armies against the Bolsheviks.

The political situation remained fluid. At the time Chang-Kai-Shek's forces were fighting Moscow-supported communists in China. Jewish nationalists were leading an underground struggle against the British in

Figure 11.12 Blessing the flag, 9,000 participants. Rimini, 25 May 1946. of B. Maciw.

Palestine. It was rumoured that Tito's partisans were preparing to capture Trieste and that Churchill was planning to use the Galicia Division to prevent this. On 5 September 1946, *Zhyttia v tabori* (Camp life) reported that ten Ukrainian soldiers had taken French citizenship and joined the Foreign Legion fighting in Vietnam.

However, the liveliest interest among Division's soldiers was stirred by the fate of the UPA, which continued its partisan struggle into the early 1950s. Mykola Lebed, a representative of Ukraine's Supreme Liberation Council (UHVR), which was the UPA's official leadership and voice in emigration, visited the Rimini camp in 1946. Although most interned men supported the resistance, they viewed Lebed's attempt to recruit them with suspicion. News had spread that during the summer Lebed had sent two officers from the camp to Ukraine on a mission. They had been killed. Lebed arrived with his book UPA (1946), in which he admonished the "ambitious leaders" who had been responsible for forming the Division and for "the 6,000 or more" victims at Brody (Lebed 1946, 93). He described the Division's organizers as careerists, political speculators, and agents, or "aging knights of the romantic *Chervona kalyna* idea, who had failed to grasp the realism of the present day and had tried to fit Hitler's Ukraine into Franz-Joseph's Austria." The *chervona kalyna*, or viburnum tree, was a symbol of the generation that had formed the Sich Riflemen within the Austrian military and had then fought for an independent Ukraine from 1918 to 1920. Lebed associated this entire generation with genteel, liberal-democratic views. He disparaged it for enjoying a comfortable life far from the front and for stealing funds donated by millions of common people (93). This did not go down well with the Division's soldiers, who had fought alongside these "genteel" older men, some of whom, like General Krat, were now their senior officers. Most of all, perhaps, it was Lebed's hypocrisy that rankled. He had sent soldiers to certain death, while suggesting that the ideal of freedom and democracy was ridiculously outdated in the age of Hitler's ruthlessness. Zahachevskyi (1968, 77) comments sarcastically that, if the men who had obeyed his orders could have risen from their graves, Lebed's trial would have been a short one.

Émigré attitudes towards the *dyviziinyky* varied. At a Ukrainian women's conference held on 30 August and 1 September 1946 in Feldkirch, Austria, Hanna Sobacheva gave a passionate, patriotic speech about the dangers posed to the interned men by the Soviet repatriation commission. As most women were "reaching into their handbags" for handkerchiefs to dry tears or for donations to fill the collection basket, Milena Rudnytska protested. She viewed the Division as part of the German ss, a group that had placed itself outside Ukrainian society and was partially responsible for German brutality. She criticized Kubijovyč who, in her view, "was in German service" (Knysh 1955, 31). This was not an unusual attitude. A Ukrainian women's organization in Canada expressed its fear, in *Novyi shliakh* on 27 June 1946, that "deserters, traitors or war criminals" would be transported to their country. However, Irena Knysh, who was present at the same women's conference, expressed the more common view: "All of us could not but view him [Kubijovyč] as a Ukrainian patriot, who at a difficult time for Ukraine took upon himself the enormous burden of responsibility for legal Ukrainian life, and did as much as he personally could ... In no way could we consider him a German lackey" (31).

In émigré and diaspora communities perceptions of the Division gradually became more favourable. This was in no small measure due to Bishop Ivan Buchko. In 1939, when he arrived in Rome from Lviv, the Vatican appointed him Apostolic Visitor of Ukrainian Displaced Persons in Europe.

On 31 May 1945, he helped to create the Ukrainian Aid Committee in Italy and dispatched priests to the Bellaria camp. When they arrived on 27 June 1945 they were moved by the fate of the soldiers, particularly of the teenagers. After receiving reports, the bishop had urged Pope Pius XII to protest their repatriation. Buchko visited Rimini on 2 December 1945. Since the British did not allow money to be sent to Rimini, the Aid Committee in Rome arranged for donations to be deposited in a Bank of Rome account. These were then passed on to the interned men, often by visiting priests (Vavryk 1979, 201).

The Vatican arranged for twenty-six men to attend the Pontifical College of St Josaphat in Rome. In the autumn of 1946 an additional group of thirteen arrived. In both cases, the authorities ignored the fact that the men had de facto "escaped" from the camp (Muzychka 2017, 93). The first students appeared on 21 November 1945. Twelve would become priests and six would complete doctorates. From the second group three entered the priesthood. Later, four more veterans enrolled in the college and became priests, while a further seven completed training for the priesthood elsewhere. In all at least twenty-six veterans took holy orders. A number had already contacted the Church while living in "Robinson Crusoe-like conditions" in Bellaria (6). Reverend Ivan Muzychka was one of them. He had been a member of the expeditionary forces (*pokhidni hrupy*) that the OUN sent into Eastern Ukraine in 1941 to agitate for an independent Ukraine. Although he had always dreamed of becoming a priest, the family's poverty had prevented him from entering the Lviv seminary. After volunteering for the Division he was accepted into the orchestra, where he played in the brass section. When he developed lymphadenitis and could no longer play, he served in the medical section (30).[10]

Muzychka agreed with Reverend Nahaievskyi that the job of military chaplaincy was poorly developed in Ukraine and that the Division's chaplains therefore had to improvise. He provided a spirited defence of the chaplaincy in his 2017 memoir:

The history of humanity's deliverance, the history of Old Testament Israel is everywhere linked to armies and military campaigns. The Lord Himself guides Israel's army, even its strategy, when the defence of this people, from whom the Messiah must come, is at issue. The liturgy is full of references to and prayers about warriors; there are military martyrs in the Christian calendar among the lists of saints; military terminology is used to describe the forces of angels. It appears that we spiritual workers are not so far removed from soldiery, and our nation's church leaders or monastic orders should respect soldiers in whatever army they serve, and should not harbour strange ideas about them, especially when they return from defeat in war. The soldier's fate demands respect and compassion. The soldier is an individual who is prepared to give his life for the great values of the people and Church. I do not mean that the priest or monk should wish to become a soldier and take up weapons. This is not his work before or during war. He battles alongside the soldier with different weapons, which save the soldier from losing his soul, but he stands by the soldier respectfully. Today's "liberation theology" in Latin America has created a type of priest who keeps automatic weapons among his spiritual books, and explosives or grenades with a literature that has nothing to do with the Gospel. I am not thinking of this kind of priest. I only wish for a respectful, courteous attitude toward armies and soldiery. (Muzychka 2017, 32)

The seminarians attended the Pontifical Urban University (Urbaniana), where they took courses in philosophy, history, and theology, which were mostly taught in Latin. According to Reverend Muzychka, the veterans brought a new spirit of mutual respect, collegiality, and comradeship to the Collegio Ruteno, a spirit they had acquired in the military. He credits the veterans with helping to change the stuffy legalism, patriarchal attitudes, and obscurantist views of the college's instructors, some of whom even blacked out art works in encyclopaedias, fearing that students' imaginations would be "tempted" (Muzychka 2017, 50–1, 77). The new students showed an aptitude for practical tasks. For example, they restored a villa that Metropolitan Andrei Sheptytskyi had bought in 1928 in Castel Gandolfo and which had been robbed and destroyed by Italian soldiers. They also transformed the college's musical repertoire by introducing a new sung liturgy, songs of the Sich Riflement, Mykhailo Verbytskyi's *Alleluia*, and Handel's *Messiah* (76). The veterans also lobbied for the college's change of name from "Ruteno" to "Ucraino" (68). Because the Germans had forced Ukrainians to sing at every opportunity during training at Heidelager, even in gas masks, Muzychka had soured on choirs, but he recovered his interest while in the college, where this art was not overemphasized: "In the following years people told us that in our time (the 'Division's') the choral performance and church singing was the best in the College's history" (79).

Ukrainian Canadians who visited Rimini included Anthony Hlynka, a member of Parliament, and Flight Commander Bohdan Panchuk, who headed the Ukrainian Central Relief Bureau in London. At this time the interned men began receiving invitations from relatives and friends in North America and South America. For example, the American Relief Committee received over one thousand affidavits from people in Canada and fifty from Argentina offering to help settle individuals (*Zhyttia v tabori* 2 July 1947, quoted in Zahachevskyi 1968, 241).

The interned Ukrainians jokingly called the Rimini camp "San Taborino" ("tabir" is the Ukrainian word for camp) because it was located close to San Marino, Europe's third smallest republic, which, like Camp 5C, seemed to live an independent life. When the time came to leave for the UK, the men traded tents and materials for oranges and lemons, then were transported by train to Po and Padua before boarding ships in Venice. Kolomatskyi, a great lover of antiquity, went to look at Padua's old walls and monasteries and missed his train. He had to walk the thirty-five kilometres to Venice, where he was picked up by military police and rejoined his comrades (Gotskyi 1990, 10, 13). On the ships the men slept on the inflated life-saving tires and listened to stories, some of which were told by a former UPA member, who described his experiences disarming retreating Hungarians, fighting Soviet partisans in the forest, and retreating through the Carpathians (22).

12

UNITED KINGDOM, 1947-49

The decision to transport the interned men to the UK and then to give them civilian status has been a prominent topic in discussions of the Division's postwar fate. The screening and civilianization process was debated within the British government in the 1940s and revisited in both Britain and Canada in the 1980s during the commissions of inquiry.

Although some government figures had been ready to deport the men, military officials who conducted the screenings argued that the overwhelming majority had signed up out of patriotic motivation. The impossibility of analyzing every individual biography was recognized, especially given the short time available before British forces were scheduled to leave Italy on 1 June 1947. Italy had signed a peace treaty with the Allies, including Russia, allowing them to extradite from Italy any of their nationals and any citizens of other nations who were accused of collaboration or war crimes. The authorities in London were aware that the Division's men could be sent to the Soviet Union, even though the Yalta Agreement did not apply to most of them. The danger was that the Italians might yield to Soviet and Polish pressure and deport the men.

On 21 February 1947, Haldane Porter wrote the report of the Refugee Screening Commission in charge of the Rimini Camp. He admitted the impossibility of screening all the men and that a cross section had been chosen. However, he expressed confidence that the overwhelming majority of internees had been born in prewar Poland and noted that the Commission had formed a generally favourable impression of the men as "decent, simple minded sort of people." Aware that some "real villains" might be sheltering in the force, the Commission paid attention to thirty men in the reserve regiment, among whom, as the camp leader had informed them, were some civilians who "had only attached themselves to the regiment shortly before its surrender, as a means of escaping from the Germans" (NA/PRO, HO/213/1851, Screening Commission Report, 21 February 1947, 2).[1] In interviews these men explained in which factories they had worked, but the Commission was unable to further research their testimony.

The report dismissed the Soviet claim that a minority was responsible for terrorizing the majority and preventing men from volunteering for repatriation. The only effect of the Soviet mission's visits, it said, had been to convince waverers never to return to the Soviet Union and to raise anxieties among men who still had relatives there. Haldane Porter made it clear that the Soviet government regarded the men as its citizens and would demand their forcible repatriation as war criminals when the Italian Treaty came into force (NA/PRO, HO/213/1851, Screening Commission Report, 21 February 1947, 3). Although no cross-examination had been possible, he considered it fair to assume that, "by and large the men are what they say they are and did what they say they did" (4). The Commission found that the soldiers were not "at heart pro-German," and it considered the fact that they had given aid and comfort to the Germans "to have been incidental and not fundamental." Their desire for an independent Ukraine the report found "naive and unreal" but nonetheless genuine. During the Soviet occupation of Eastern Poland in 1939–40 the families of many men had been taken to Siberia and appeared "to have suffered a good deal at the hands of the Red Army during the Russo-German campaign, and also on occasions at the hands of the Germans" (6–7). In its conclusion the Commission noted the "exemplary" behaviour of the men since their surrender and recommend "most strongly" that they should all be classified as DPs and immediately given protection from being handed over to the Soviet government (7).

Haldane Porter's summary was later denounced by Sol Littman (2003, 129) as "a masterpiece of bureaucratic report writing," which confessed to shortcomings but provided the conclusions desired by the government. The Commission, after all, only interviewed 219 people but conveyed the overall image of the Division's men as people who would cause no trouble if moved from Rimini (Khromeychuk 2013, 116). It would, of course, have been inconvenient for the government to find suspicious individuals, but the fact remains that no evidence against the men was provided at the time by Soviet authorities or, for that matter, at a later time by Littman. Khromeychuk correctly points out that the image of the men as simple and hard-working "peasant" types was part of a constructed narrative, one that Haldane Porter knew would play well with British authorities who were looking for potential agricultural and industrial labourers (109). However, this image was not inaccurate. Although the one thousand educated men in the Division, who were sometimes described as the flower of Western Ukraine's intelligentsia, often acted as the Division's spokesmen, the two propositions – that the Division had an educated elite and that it contained "simple" folk – were not incompatible. Nor was it inconsistent to call both groups naïve. Many "educated" men who became the Division's writers and intellectuals readily admitted later in life that they had been poorly informed about political issues when they joined the Division.

The Commission's report provided no accusations or evidence of war crimes. Nor did it offer any evidence that some of the men were liable for "repatriation" (in reality, deportation) under the Yalta Agreement. This information only came out later and concerned a small percentage. It is undeniable, however, that, after the massacre of the Cossacks, the British government wanted to avoid another potentially damaging scandal, and, more than likely, this pragmatic consideration played a role in shaping the report (Khromeychuk 2013, 114).[2] Another consideration was the need expressed in 1947 by British Intelligence to secure Russian speakers for MI6 and other services, and to recruit agents who could be sent into Ukraine (Dorril 2000, 205, 242).

The Foreign Office, in a secret telegram to its representatives in Rome, Moscow, Washington, Caserta, and Warsaw on 3 March 1947, recognized the difficulty of a satisfactory screening in the time available. It voiced concern that "a substantial proportion" of the interned would be found to have been Soviet citizens prior to September 1939 and therefore liable to repatriation. It noted that an order for forcible repatriation had not been given and, even if it had been, a full screening would still be necessary before the British could act "with any semblance of justice." As a result, the War Office concluded that the men had to be removed from Italy and suggested bringing them to the UK, where they could be screened in due course (NA/PRO, WR 694/1/48). The British authorities were confident that a few hundred at most were liable to repatriation under the terms of the Yalta Agreement. It was considered unlikely that Germany could accept them, and because the date for evacuating British forces from Italy was approaching, a decision was taken to ship the men to the UK.

Pressure to do so came from various sources. Bohdan Panchuk of the Central Ukrainian Relief Bureau (CURB) lobbied steadily on the Division's behalf. After a visit to Rimini he wrote a memo to the British government on 17 December 1946:

> They are very strongly and permanently Western minded. Many of them have relatives and friends in Canada and the United States and in countries in South America. They are all religious. The majority are of the Eastern Catholic (Byzantine or Uniate) faith and are strongly anti-communist. They are all educated and developed in the Democratic way of life. This is chiefly due to the Polish citizenship which most of them had, to their relations and communications with their friends and relatives in Canada and the United States prior to the war, and to their general Christian principles and Western mindedness. The majority of them are excellent agricultural and industrial labourers and potential colonists. Most of them come from peasant stock. The bulk of them are young men between 18 and 30 years of age, strong, virile and healthy. In consideration of the characteristics listed it is submitted that the personnel in this camp at Rimini would make most excellent immigration material both from the point of view of colonization and future citizenship and also from the point of view of any Western country's self-defence. (Kormylo 2021, 187)

In May and June 1947, two years after surrendering to the British, the men from the Rimini camp were transported on eight ships to England and Scotland. The first group disembarked in Liverpool on 20 May 1947 and was sent to camps in Sheffield, High Garret, Brentree, Ely, Horbling, and Woolfox.

In Horbling, Lincolnshire, they were housed in a camp from which Germans had recently been repatriated or released. One German prisoner soon gained fame. Bert Trautmann had been imprisoned in Ashton-in-Makerfield, near Manchester. Formerly a member of the Hitler Youth, he had served as an elite paratrooper, fought in Ukraine in 1941 and on the western front, earning five medals, including the Iron Cross 1st Class. After release from a POW camp, he became Manchester City's goalkeeper and, in 1956, helped the team win the FA Cup with a legendary performance.

Figure 12.1 Writers and editors of camp publications shortly before leaving Rimini for the UK.

Figure 12.2 Lodge Moor Camp, Sheffield.

Figure 12.3 "1976 Our Last POW." Copied by a Division POW from a painting left on the wall of Barrack D5, POW Camp 17, by German POWS, 1947.

Queen Elizabeth made him an Officer of the Order of the British Empire in 2004 for his work promoting Anglo-German understanding. However, when he was first selected for the team, twenty thousand people took part in a mass protest. Today only his football exploits are recalled and he is pictured in a football uniform, not as a German soldier.

The Division's men were sent to various camps in England and Scotland.[3] From the moment they stepped onto British soil they were reclassified from surrendered enemy personnel (SEP) to POWs. Individual British soldiers responsible for guarding them confiscated their belongings and bullied them. One sergeant was particularly vociferous, ripped off all badges, raged over details such as torn shoes, and confiscated belts and embroidered shirts (Gotskyi 1990, 57). Some of the Division's officers were reportedly incarcerated in London for complaining about searches and crude behaviour or for criticizing Britain in letters. Gradually, however, the interned men won over most guards, one of whom, an avid footballer, played on their team. The symphony, jazz orchestra, and best sports groups were successfully kept together. These became ambassadors in local communities. Approximately

United Kingdom, 1947–49 • **203**

120 officers were sent to Selby in Yorkshire, where, in accord with international conventions, they were not expected to work and were paid a small sum of four pounds and ten shillings each month (Mohylov 2016, 62–3).

The rank-and-file soldiers worked for the UK ministries of agriculture, labour, and military affairs but received almost no pay because deductions from earnings were made for transport, food, accommodation, and clothing. The hardest labour was harvesting, threshing grain, and digging canals, sewers, and ditches. Farmers on the whole were friendly. Many offered food and cigarettes. The Division's medics were protected personnel and not subject to forced labour.

Early British press reports generally carried positive accounts. The *Scotsman* on 24 May 1947, the *Scots Daily Express* on 28 May 1947, and the *Sheffield Star* on 3 June 1947 stated that the men had been checked before entry, were working in the agricultural sector, had studied various trades in Rimini, and had mostly been citizens of prewar Poland (Gotskyi 1990, 33–4). According to a *New Chronicle* report on 19 June 1947, the minister responsible had informed Parliament that the men had been screened and that no evidence of criminality had been found. Tracy Phillips wrote in the *Manchester Guardian* on 12 June 1947 that they had voluntarily surrendered, were idealistic, and, like their kin who had settled Canada, the United States, and Argentina, were good farmers with a strong sense of co-operation. He described the camps in England as models of cleanliness, discipline, and wise organization (Gotskyi 1990, 48). This was the official government line. Screening had been conducted with the men, beginning on 10 February 1945, at which time around a thousand were asked about their recruitment (whether it had been voluntary or forced) and wartime activity. In Rimini they had been visited by a five-person parliamentary committee led by Harold Macmillan, who, in 1957, would become the British prime minister. This committee held conversations with every twenty-fifth man in order to understand their way of thinking, particularly their attitude towards the Soviet Union and the Allies. Like British officers responsible for the Rimini camp, the committee had been favourably impressed.

In the UK camps enforcement of rules was gradually relaxed, although internally the men continued to maintain their own discipline. Several civilians who had ended up in the camps were criminals who had avoided repatriation by hiding among the soldiers, and some had been arrested for theft in Italy. The soldiers sometimes organized "Cossack trials" to teach culprits a lesson. Punishment might include a physical beating, having a cross shaven onto the head with an order not to hide it for a week. A thief was sometimes allowed to go unpunished if he agreed to be transferred to another camp (Gotskyi 1990, 79, 106).

Relations with German POWs in neighbouring UK camps were good. In Italy at the end of June 1945 there had been about 150,000 Germans in sixteen camps. Because of the strain on British resources, the Germans, who had the expertise and technical resources, constructed and to some degree managed many of the camps themselves. In the UK, visits to German camps took place on the occasion of religious holidays and during sporting competitions. There were, however, occasional incidents. In the UK, one *dyviziinyk* reportedly thrashed a German who called him a fascist in front of the English (Budnyi 1979, 162).

Towards the end of their stay in the UK, soldiers began receiving pay for their work, initially illegally through arrangements with local farmers who were happy to hire them. In the second year of their internment they were allowed to work in agriculture. Later, they began working in mills and garages, quarries, brick factories, and airports. The last location was considered the most desirable because it led to the discovery of useful materials: sewing machines, bicycles, and photo cameras, which were repaired and put to use. As in Rimini, loudspeaker systems were set up and regular concerts were broadcast in the camps.

Wall newspapers appeared, chapels were constructed, and theatres began to operate. The men organized lectures on various topics: the 1848 Spring of Nations, the English Trades Union Movement, Petliura, Konovalets (Gotskyi 1990, 95). Press rooms and libraries with materials in different languages appeared. Choirs were invited to English churches to sing prayers. As the fame of the main choir under Vsevolod Bohdan Budnyi spread, it began performing public concerts and receiving invitations to festivals. After the men were released it won first prize at a competition in Scunthorpe, to which it was invited. Budnyi also staged the operetta *Natalka Poltavka* and other musical productions in local Ukrainian communities (160–1).

Political solidarity remained a point of honour for veterans. However, the men supported various political parties and the competition between groups was already evident in Rimini, where the newspaper *Zhyttia v tabori* was known to be controlled by OUN-B and *Batkivshchyna* by the OUN-M. In the UK camps party politics became more pronounced, and, after the men were released, sectarian attitudes began to influence life.

Towards the end of internment, another screening commission was organized, after which the Ministry of Agriculture allowed the men to sign work contracts. By this time the men were preparing to integrate into British society or to emigrate from Great Britain to Canada, Australia, and other countries.

In 1949, when it was discovered that the British government was planning a deportation of men who were sick or invalids, the veterans issued a communique on 21 December 1948 and organized a protest. It was addressed to all Ukrainians in Britain and signed by Bohdan Panchuk, as head of the Union of Ukrainians in Great Britain, and by representatives of the Ukrainian Orthodox and Ukrainian Catholic churches. The communique called for a demonstration and protest actions, including a hunger strike in every camp with Ukrainians. This led to a story entitled "Unlucky Ukrainians" appearing in the *Manchester Guardian* on 29 December 1948. British authorities responded by explaining that only those men who wished to go would be sent to Germany ("Nepratsezdatni" 1949). In the end, eighty men went voluntarily, and the remaining 250 were allowed to stay, including the sick and invalids. A campaign was then organized to raise money for the care of men with long-term illnesses and for those incapable of working. The campaign led to the purchase of a property in Chiddingfold, Surrey, and its transformation into a care home. Over eight thousand individuals pledged small sums on a monthly basis over extended periods. The thirty-room home in a park-like setting was purchased on 11 September 1949 ("SUB" 1949).

In fact, a secret internal memo sent by the British Control Commission for Germany on 19 December 1948 had already warned that, because of a growing German refugee population, it was becoming difficult to dispose of foreigners by sending them to that country. Moreover, because conditions in the German refugee camps were "terrible," any proposal to send to Germany people incapable of work would be equivalent to "a sentence of extermination." The memo urged that the incurably disabled at least should not be sent away (UCRDC, Maleckyj, "Outgoing Secret Telegram to Concomb Lubbecke"). Fortunately, within a year the Chiddingfold home had assumed full responsibility for the twenty-two disabled veterans.

Panchuk was an effective lobbyist for the Division in the late 1940s. He argued that, although some individuals might have guilty records from before the Division's formation, the overwhelming majority of men would make excellent citizens. As a flight lieutenant in the Royal Canadian Air Force and an intelligence officer, his opinion carried weight. Moreover, in 1943 he helped to create the Ukrainian Canadian Servicemen's Association, traced over one thousand Canadian Ukrainians living in Great Britain, and brought them together (Kormylo 2021, 170).[4] Then, at the end of the war, he directed the CURB in London, and in the years between 1945 and 1952 he headed the Canadian Relief Mission for Ukrainian War Victims in Europe. He is also credited with helping thousands of Ukrainian refugees emigrate from Great Britain to Canada.[5] These credentials allowed him to exerted an influence on British authorities during discussion of the Division veterans' civilianization.

The military expressed the view that there would be "a hard core among the Ukrainians" who were liable for trial under the Nuremberg Laws. Lieutenant Colonel H. Faulk wrote to A.W.H. Wilkinson of the Foreign Office on 4 May 1948 that the real authority on the Division was Haldane Porter, who had conducted the enquiry in Italy:

I have spoken to Mr. Haldane Porter, and I understood him to say that in his view the members of the Ukrainian Division were volunteers to the Waffen ss. I have perhaps misinterpreted what he said, but if indeed it is so there is certainly a prima facie case for examining these men in the light of the Nurnberg [sic] judgment ...

You will wish perhaps to discuss the problem with M. Haldane Porter. If he can confirm your impression that the members of the Ukrainian Division started out as a normal field formation which was then automatically dubbed an ss formation without any option on the part of the members of the Division, the question would really solve itself. On the other hand that would require a second confirmation that the men in question were not already ss men before the Division received its new name. (Lieutenant Colonel H. Faulk to Mr. A.W.H. Wilkinson of the German Refugee Department, 4 May 1948. POW.1/F/3334)

Although the soldiers were, of course, not members of the ss or the Nazi Party, the letter shows that confusion between Germans in the ss and foreign soldiers in the Waffen-ss was an obstacle to civilianization, as was the issue of whether the men had volunteered.

Wilkinson, in his reply to Faulk on 1 June 1948, noted that, according to Haldane Porter, most of the men had volunteered for a Division "to which the Germans gave the title 'Waffen S.S.'" and that the Ukrainians had objected to this action by the Germans. Therefore, "there seems to be ample reason for regarding these men in a different light from persons who deliberately joined an existing Waffen S.S. formation." He suggested that the matter be closed and civilianization should proceed (NA/PRO, WR 1675/218/48).

Olesya Khromeychuk points out that, in letters to the British and Canadian governments, community organizations in both countries lobbied for civilianization by casting the Division's men simply as soldiers who fought on the eastern front against the Soviet Union. A "narrative featuring the 'Galicia' as a Wehrmacht Division was being used by officials both in Canada and the UK" (Khromeychuk 2013, 116). The Home Office began to prepare for civilianization after 12 January 1948, when the Home Secretary approved the idea "on the understanding that satisfactory assurances regarding the removal from the United Kingdom of those who were not recommended for civilianisation, or who had subsequently proved unruly or unsatisfactory, would first be obtained" (NA/PRO, WR 631/218/48, letter from Home Office (Aliens Department) to Wilkinson of Foreign Office, Whitehall, 25 February 1948.).

The remaining issue was a possible "hard core" who had committed war crimes. British authorities had no evidence of criminality. They had already searched for ways in which they could "dispose" of the Ukrainians otherwise than by giving them civilian status, and they were aware that by the late 1940s various countries were releasing soldiers who had served in the Waffen-ss. Non-Germans and those who had not been members of the ss or the Nazi Party were being civilianized and allowed to emigrate. Many members of the ss, including some who had been higher functionaries, were also being released, usually after going through a "denazification" process. The veterans of the Galicia Division, who had been screened at different times by Polish, Soviet, and British military authorities, expected to be released in the same way as these other groups. Therefore, even though the screening had not been as thorough as authorities would have liked, there appeared to be no reason to keep the men as prisoners or to investigate them further.

Canadian immigration law prevented men who had volunteered for the Waffen-ss from entering the country. It was only in 1950, after new legislation was introduced, that members of the Division were allowed to settle in Canada (Khromeychuk 2013, 142–4). In March of that year a decision was made to allow former Waffen-ss *Volksdeutsche* to enter Canada and various Western countries. At that point no legal grounds remained for not allowing the Division's men to emigrate. The Galicia Division's veterans were by then one of the last groups to whom the restriction on emigration still applied. Moreover, postwar politics had changed: attitudes towards Germany were being revised, the Cold War had begun, and many observers did not view the Division's anti-communist and anti-Russian credentials as a disadvantage.

The British Foreign Office assured the Canadian government on 5 September 1950 that there was no evidence of criminality or of the men being infected by Nazi ideology. It presented the soldiers as members of the 1st Ukrainian Division of the Wehrmacht, some of whom were survivors of the earlier "14th Galician Grenadier Division." This, the report said, was also a Wehrmacht unit that had "apparently" resisted German attempts to make it into an ss Division. The men, in short, had volunteered to fight the Red Army from nationalistic motives, and, although Soviet propaganda had depicted them as "quislings" and "war criminals," no specific charges of war crimes had been made against any member of the group (LAC, Immigration Branch, RG 76, vol. 656, file 1353802 1-2; reprinted in Boshyk 1986, 241–2). A similar note was sent to Canada House on 4 September 1950 by L. Scopes on behalf of the foreign secretary. Dorril has commented on this note: "Rarely have there been so many untruths in such a short statement." In his view the British government, and the MI6 specifically, took advantage of the available new legislation to transfer large numbers of inadequately screened people to Canada, Australia, and the US.[6]

PART FOUR
STORIES

13

STORIES OF CAPTURED MEN: INTERROGATIONS 1944–54 AND INTERVIEWS 1987–2012

The case files of about 280 captured soldiers who served in the Galicia Division or the Volunteer Regiments are today in Ternopil's SBU archive.[1] Many of the men took part in the battle of Brody and were captured near Ternopil and interrogated in the months following. The tapes and transcripts of a very different set of interviews conducted between the years 1987 and 2012 with over one hundred veterans can be found in Toronto's UCRDC. Whereas the Ternopil transcripts focus on establishing guilt, particularly of men who had joined the underground resistance, those in Toronto are more biographical and focus on political and historical contexts.

In the Ternopil files the charge against all the convicted men was treason, according to article 54.1a of the Ukrainian SSR's criminal code. Occasionally these files contain testimony by eyewitnesses about the behaviour of the men during the German occupation. Some files include pleas for clemency by men who were imprisoned or exiled. The pleas were refused in most cases, as were posthumous appeals for rehabilitation by relatives. One group of interviews concerns soldiers who joined the UPA, another concerns soldiers who blended into the population and were only arrested later when recognized, and a third concerns men who committed a crime prior to entering the Division. Several men were executed immediately following the verdict, but most received sentences ranging from ten to twenty-five years with confiscation of all property and an additional loss of rights for five years, which meant that the person had to continue living and working in Siberian mines and factories. We now know from published memoirs and the interviews in Toronto's UCRDC that there was a fourth category, albeit a rare one: men who survived, avoided arrest, and integrated themselves into Soviet civilian life. The Ternopil files show that the harshest sentences were given to men who, after Brody, fought in the underground.

Bohdan Onatskyi (born 1925) was arrested near Chortkiv on 23 February 1946 while hiding in a bunker (*kryivka*). He was sentenced by the secret police of the Ministry of State Security (MGB) and executed on 5 July. Mobilized into the Red Army in 1941, he had been taken prisoner by the Germans and agreed to join the Division in June 1943. After Brody he hid from Soviet authorities, escaped, made his way home, and joined the UPA in December 1944. He carried out expropriations from food stores in the Buchach area and was responsible for killing five men in a punitive (destroyer) battalion. Onatskyi was captured with a photograph of himself in a German uniform, a patriotic poem he had written, and a speech to compatriots urging them to fight for Ukraine's freedom. When in 1997 relatives asked for a review of his case, rehabilitation was denied (AUSBUTO, Onatskyi).

Antin Kachkivskyi (born in 1910 near Borshchiv) was sentenced on 26 January 1945 and immediately hanged. He joined the Division on 1 November 1943, trained near Aachen, fought at Brody, and, after hiding for two weeks, returned home on 8 August. He joined the UPA and was captured on 29 November 1944 after a five-hour battle during which one Soviet soldier was killed and five were wounded. He claimed that the UPA had threatened to punish his family if he did not join them. He described the twenty UPA members in his group, how they collected food from villagers and mobilized people for attacks on NKVD units (AUSBUTO, Kachkivskyi).

Ivan Kit (born in 1921) from Monastyrskyi county near Ternopil was sentenced to hang on 2 February 1945. He joined the Division in late 1943. After Brody he came home and joined the UPA. On 22 December 1944, he participated in attacks on the villages of Tovstobaby and Zavadovka (Pol: Towstobaby and Zawadówka), both in Monastyrskyi county. A Soviet commission that reported the attacks on the following day stated that 150 men had taken part in the assault on Tovstobaby, in which only Polish homes and individuals had been targeted, and provided a list of fifty-four victims, their ages (which range from four to seventy-eight), and the nature of their wounds. The report stated that a group of sixty UPA members then attacked Zavadovka, and it listed twenty-five victims, aged nineteen to sixty. Kit was captured on 14 January 1945 (AUSBUTO, Rusnak and Kit).

The two villages were predominantly Polish: in 1921 Tovstobaby had 2,024 inhabitants, a figure that included 1,579 Poles, 426 Ukrainians, and 19 Jews. There were Polish resistance groups in both villages. In Tovstobaby (named "Vysoke" since 1965, Pol: Wysokie) sixteen of the listed victims were soldiers and the rest were civilians. Later Polish descriptions report that two UPA fighters were also killed in the action, that the massacre was perpetrated by local villagers, and that twenty women arrived to take away valuables. When an armed group set off in pursuit of the perpetrators, it apprehended eight local men armed with knives and axes, who admitted to participating in the attack (Motyka 2018, 343).

Several files deal with men who had served in the 4th Galician ss Volunteer Regiment. For example, Mykola Hevko-Mymanskyi (born in 1914 in the Chortkiv area) was sentenced on 22 January 1945 to a firing squad, but after a review his sentence was commuted on 6 March 1946 to twenty years hard labour and five years loss of rights. When the Red Army retreated in 1941 he left the train on which he was a stoker, stayed behind, and found work as a labourer. He signed up for the Division in 1943, apparently because his factory manager informed him that a quota of workers had to enlist. Sent to the 4th Galician ss Volunteer Regiment, he trained in Maastricht, Holland, then fought partisans near Ternopil in February 1944. On 27–28 March 1944, as the Red Army approached, he left his detachment, joined a UPA group of sixty people, and was captured on 14 June 1944 after an armed struggle (AUSBUTO, Hevko-Mymanskyi).

Pavlo Zahainyi (born in 1909 in Mezhyhirtsia in today's Ivano-Frankivsk oblast) was sentenced to execution on 13 November 1944, but the sentence was commuted on 31 January 1946 to ten years hard labour. He volunteered for the Division in December 1943, trained in Bitburg near Trier for three months, and was sent to the 4th Galician ss Volunteer Regiment. His detachment fought at the front in March 1944 and near Zbarazh (Pol: Zbaraż). When the Germans retreated, he stayed behind, exchanged his uniform for civilian clothes, and was captured on 2 May 1944 (AUSBUTO, Zahainyi).

Stepan Karachek (born in 1923 in the Borshchiv area) was sentenced to death on 20 August 1945, but the sentence was commuted on 27 September to twenty years hard labour. He voluntarily left for work in Germany in June 1942 and, in the following year, volunteered for the Division. After training in France, and two weeks in Holland, he was sent to the 4th Galician SS Volunteer Regiment. In February 1945 he was part of a group that parachuted near Zbarazh with orders to disrupt Soviet partisan activities. He fought partisans near Ternopil, then joined the UPA and fought NKVD troops. Along with another UPA member, he was accused of beating the mother of a man who served in a punitive battalion to make her reveal her son's whereabouts. Karachek was confronted with a number of witnesses on 15 June 1945 (AUSBUTO, Karachek).

Harsh sentences were also given men who had served in the local militia or police prior to joining the Division. Adolf Moroz (born in 1922 in Horodyshche village near Kozlov in Ternopil oblast) was sentenced on 15 December 1944 to twenty years hard labour. In 1941, he voluntarily joined the militia in the town of Kozlov and served as a mechanic and driver. In November 1943, he was sent to Germany to train with the Division. He avoided capture at Brody but was arrested on 20 July 1944 when he came home. During the interrogation he admitted to driving the four Komsomol members to work. Witnesses confirmed that he had served in the militia for three or four weeks immediately following the German invasion and wore a yellow and blue armband. One witness stated that she saw him in July–August 1941 with rifle in hand escorting four Jewish members of the Komsomol who were carrying shovels. That same day the news spread that these people had been killed. Another witness testified that Moroz regularly drove around with the local police and people knew that he had killed three Jews (AUSBUTO, Moroz).

Yevhenii Luhovyi (born in 1906 near Chortkiv) was sentenced by military tribunal on 2 October 1944 to twenty years hard labour. He served in the local Auxiliary Police, where his job had been guarding a tobacco factory, but he also participated in attacks on Jews. On 3 March 1943, three Gestapo men tried to detain a Jewish factory worker called Zygmunt Rozman. When the man began to run, Luhovyi caught him and hit him over the head with a rifle butt. After that a member of the Gestapo set his dog on the man and shot him with a pistol. Witnesses confirmed the incident. One testified that, prior to joining the Division, Luhovyi guarded a camp for Jews. He signed up for the Division in 1943 but, after a month of training, returned to his village of Yahilnytsia, where he lived until his arrest on 10 May 1944. It is not clear whether he deserted the training camp or was rejected because of his behaviour (AUSBUTO, Luhovyi).

Antin Demydas (born in 1910 in the village of Dychkiv, Ternopil oblast) served in the Polish army in 1939 and then hid from the Germans in Kraków until 1941. Upon returning to Ternopil in September 1941 he joined the Auxiliary Police for two weeks. He guarded the Gestapo's premises and a hospital with wounded Soviet POWs. He claimed to have then hidden from the Germans for a year before again working for the police in September and October 1942. Armed with a rifle, he once more guarded the Gestapo building and hospital, and took part in arresting and convoying citizens. Witnesses recalled that he wore a dark blue police uniform with German insignia on his cap. In the summer of 1943 he sold yeast in a Ternopil store and in September 1943 was called up by the Division. In January he was granted a leave from the Heidelager training camp and never returned. For the next four years he lived with his mother in Radvalov near Buchach, and in 1948 he moved to Rohatyn. Arrested on 19 June 1951, he was sentenced on 18 September 1951 to twenty-five years hard labour. After Nikita Khrushchev denounced Lavrentii Beria as an "enemy of the people," Demydas wrote on 31 March 1954 to the procurator general of the USSR asking for clemency, claiming that he had been beaten in the Stanislaviv and Ternopil prisons to extract false confessions. He argued that, prior to 1944, he had been a Polish citizen and that, while in the German army, committed no crimes against the Soviet Union. The sentence was commuted on 19 October 1954 to ten years (AUSBUTO, Demydas).

Several men described how they deserted shortly before the Division went into action at Brody. Yaroslav Krasnopera (born in 1926 in Lviv) studied commerce in Zbarazh. His father came from a priest's family, worked as an artist until 1926, and then directed a co-operative in Zbarazh until arrested and sent to a labour camp in 1940. Yaroslav was never a member of the OUN and showed little interest in its literature. In Zbarazh he had a German relative whom he often met. During his interrogation he recounted an episode from the end of 1942, when the Gestapo in Zbarazh rounded up the town's Jewish population before taking them out of town and shooting them. The people were forced to gather in one spot. As he was walking to school, Yaroslav was stopped by the Gestapo and forced to join this group. He produced documents showing that he was a student at the gymnasium, but the Gestapo tore them up. Yaroslav then saw a German officer, told him he was Ukrainian, produced his passport, and was released.

He volunteered for the Division in 1943. Because of poor health he was only called up in December, then trained in Heidelager for seven months. He deserted in early July while the Division was at Lviv's railway station on the way to the front. Leaving the train, he changed into civilian clothes and walked to Zbarazh, arriving a month later. As he passed Zolochiv, he was wounded in the cheek by a bomb that exploded on the main road. When arrested and interrogated on 23 and 25 October 1944, Krasnopera admitted to joining the Division because he hated the Soviet regime and had been influenced by agitation conducted by his teachers. He apparently agreed to turn informer and was allowed to return to Zbarazh, where he established contact with other Division veterans. He then served in the Red Army and informed on people, characterizing their views and activities. The file does not indicate Krasnopera's later fate, but it appears that he continued serving as an informer (AUSBUTO, Krasnopera).

Mykhailo Poburennyi (born in 1900 in Chortkiv) was sentenced on 15 February 1945 to ten years imprisonment. He served in the Polish army between the years of 1922 and 1925. When called up for work in Germany, he refused, claiming illness. He was given the choice of working in Germany or joining the Division. He accepted the second alternative and was sent to Heidelager in September 1943. During interrogation he claimed to have deserted in June, shortly before Brody, but may have changed into civilian clothing after Brody and then come home (AUSBUTO, Poburennyi).

Several sentences were commuted on appeal when the men convinced authorities that they had only served in a support capacity or had been forced to enlist. Volodymyr Horbach (born in 1924 in Surokhiv village near Jarosław, Poland), worked on his father's farm, then as a metalworker and wood cutter. He voluntarily left for Germany in August 1942 and was employed for a while on automobile repairs near Köln before returning home. In October 1943 he volunteered for the Division, but, when called up in November, he hid for a while, until the village head threatened him with deportation to Auschwitz unless he reported for duty. In March 1944 he was sent to Neuhammer, where he worked in a unit doing automobile repairs, and on 1 June he was sent to the front near Brody. After being captured on 17 July near Zolochiv, he was allowed to work in factories in Ternopil and Zbarazh, then in 1948 he was sentenced to twenty-five years in labour camp. Because of his youth and the fact that as a mechanic he did not participate in military action, his sentence was commuted to seven years labour camp and three years loss of rights (AUSBUTO, Horbach).

Ivan Osmak (born in 1924 in the village of Surokhiv, Pol: Surochów, near Jarosław) was arrested in Ternopil and sentenced on 14 August 1948 to twenty-five years imprisonment. He joined the Division in February 1944 and was captured near Zolochiv in July 1944, where he was working in a field hospital. In 1955, his sentence was commuted to seven years imprisonment because of his youth and because his father Vasyl, who had been head of the village, had forced people to choose between work in Germany or joining the Division. Two men provided mitigating evidence. They stated that Vasyl Osmak, the village head, decided who had to surrender a cow and who would go to Germany for hard labour. He selected people for service in the Division by stating at the village council: "My son went and you can't?" The witnesses testified that the village head was in frequent contact with the Gestapo in Jarosław. The fact that his son, Ivan, did not participate in military action but served as a medic was taken into account. On appeal the sentence was commuted on 26 July 1948 to seven years in labour camp. Ivan escaped from his Siberian prison in 1947 and returned to the Zbarazh area before his case was reviewed on appeal (AUSBUTO, Osmak).

Mitigating circumstances were taken into account in the case of Mykhailo Dovbniak (born in 1911 in the village of Tysmentsia near today's Ivano-Frankivsk), who escaped capture after Brody by dressing in civilian clothes and claiming that he had been taken by the Germans to dig trenches. When he returned home he was arrested and a military tribunal was held on 14 November 1944. A witness who had hidden from the Germans for five months testified that Dovbniak was poor, had joined the Soviet collective farm, but then enlisted in the Division because the Germans promised him a good life and family support. He was sentenced to ten years hard labour (AUSBUTO, Dovbniak).

Volodymyr Lahish (born in 1925 in Ternopil) also appealed to mitigating circumstances and was sentenced on 8 January 1945 to ten years hard labour. He had worked building roads for the Baudienst in Ternopil from April 1942 when the Germans began forcing men aged twenty to twenty-two to work in this service for a year. Avoidance meant arrest and being sent to Germany. Lahish testified that the Baudienst provided a uniform, boots with wooden soles, pants, a shirt, and a cap, but no warm clothes such as a jacket or coat. The workers were fed twice a day, in the morning and evening, before and after work, and earned one zloty per day. He loaded coal onto trains, unloaded building materials, and cleared tracks. The work began at 5:00 a.m. and ended at 6:00 p.m. with one free hour for lunch. On Sundays work stopped at 1:00 p.m. The workers wore an emblem depicting a spade and pick axe. Ukrainian and Polish units were segregated. Lahish left because he found the work extremely hard. The police came for him in July 1943 and forced him to continue working until October, when he volunteered for the Division. He trained as a driver and joined the Division in February 1944. On 20 May 1944, he was sent to Lviv, then to Kraków on a two-week driving course. When he returned to Lviv, he discovered that his unit had left for the front. He asked a man for money to buy bread and milk, and for civilian clothes, and returned to Ternopil, where he was arrested (AUSBUTO, Lahish).

There is no information in the files as to why or how the confiscation of property, which accompanied almost every conviction, was administered, to what extent it affected the situation of families, whether it was a form of collective punishment or whether it provided an incentive for local authorities to enrich themselves. When these files in the Ternopil archive are compared with published accounts by captured men who returned from imprisonment, a different perspective emerges, especially concerning trial procedures, conditions of imprisonment, and relations with the underground.[2]

Roman Shumskyi, who after Brody spent a year in the UPA, disputed the witness testimony that was used to convict him to fifteen years hard labour and five years loss of rights. He was sent to the Norilsk camp above the Arctic Circle, where he worked on factory construction. He participated in the Norilsk revolt that broke out in 1953 after Stalin's death and witnessed the shooting by guards of two hundred prisoners (Ivankov and Romaniuk 2016, 255–60).

In the camps he met Danylo Shumuk, the longest-serving Ukrainian political prisoner, who provided him with a different perspective on the underground. Shumuk was from Volhynia and had already been imprisoned for five years and eight months under Polish rule for membership in the Communist Party of Western Ukraine. In 1941, as an "enemy of the people," he was forced into a Soviet battalion, captured by the Germans, and sent to a concentration camp near Poltava, from which he escaped. He joined the UPA, was captured, and spent a total of forty-two years in Soviet prisons.

An opponent of both fascism and Soviet-style communism, Shumuk looked for a third way. He supported a popular movement for democracy and self-determination. Two books outlining his evolution were written in Soviet prison camps and published in the West. They describe crimes committed by the three undergrounds – Soviet, Polish, and Ukrainian – all of which at different points co-operated with the Germans to have their local enemies removed. He is particularly revealing concerning the SB, the security service of the OUN-B, whose brutal actions and suspicion of Eastern Ukrainians drove away many people.

Shumuk's perspective on the camps is interesting. He also points out that many people in the camp administration had been Schutzmannschaft commanders under the German occupation: "Earlier they served the fascists and beat the communists, and then in the camps they served the communists and beat and abused whoever they needed to in order to survive. It was precisely this 'type' of person that the Chekists quickly took into service" (Shumuk 1983, 286). He also points out that, alongside principled and idealistic UPA fighters, there were many prisoners who, after serving in village self-defence groups formed by the OUN, had joined the NKVD's punitive battalions. He describes these individuals as "bandits and thieves who robbed and fleeced peaceful people and cooperatives, leaving nationalist literature in the places of their crimes, so that the crimes would be attributed to the organization" (357). These people co-operated with the Gulag administration and acted as a fifth column among the prisoners.

By the early 1970s, Shumuk had become one of the most respected leaders of the dissident movement. While imprisoned in the camps he met not only former members of the Division, the OUN, and the UPA but also people like Ivan Svitlychnyi, Nadia Svitlychna, and Iryna Kalynets, who belonged to the generation of the 1960s that was persecuted for defending human rights. They helped to smuggle out and publish his manuscripts, which are now classics of camp writing and dissident literature.

One of the best accounts of capture and captivity was published in Munich in 1959 by Pavlo Hrytsak (Hrycak). His father taught classical studies in Jarosław's Ukrainian gymnasium, which Pavlo completed in June 1943 before volunteering for the Division. His motives were patriotic, but already during training in the anti-aircraft artillery he expressed doubts about the political wisdom of forming a Division and its military feasibility. The fundamental flaw in the whole conception, in his view, was that Ukrainian personnel "was being drawn into the German war machine" and could defend Ukrainian interests "only as far as they coincided with German ones" (Hrytsak 1959, 66). Realizing that the force could not achieve Ukraine's military-political aspirations, he argued: "The Division by itself was of no use as an instrument of armed action, and it did not harm the Bolsheviks. It was needed by us only as a school and in this respect it fulfilled its general purpose. The 6,000 soldiers who after the catastrophe at Brody remained in Galicia were of great value. The hundreds of officers and NCOS who received training in the Division will also be of value" (66–7).[3] Whether they remained on Soviet territory or lived abroad, writes Hrytsak, these men helped to "develop cadres" and to educate people about Ukraine (68).

Hrytsak served his sentence in the coal mines of Stalinohorsk, 180 kilometres south of Moscow, where the prisoners included Russians, Belarusians, Estonians, and Tatars. He was amnestied and released as a Polish citizen when the great exchange of populations between Poland and the Soviet Ukraine began at the end of 1945 and early in 1946. Ironically, Polish authorities assumed that he was a captured Polish resistance fighter from the AK and allowed him to return to his native Jarosław and Przemyśl region, where Ukrainian cultural life had been destroyed and the UPA was fighting desperately to prevent mass civilian deportations. After immigrating to the US, Hrytsak studied at the University of Minnesota and then at Fordham University under Oskar Halecki, while simultaneously working in the Slavic Section of the New York Public Library. His promising career as a historian of the Galician-Volhynian state in the twelfth to fourteenth centuries was cut short when in 1958 he died of cancer at the age of thirty-two.[4]

A supplement and corrective to the Ternopil files is also provided by oral interviews with former *dyviziinyky* conducted in the years between 1987 and 2012 by the UCRDC.[5] Several interviewees describe how they were captured and served their sentences. These testimonies are fuller than the laconic Soviet interrogation files and were not given under duress. The fact that they occurred fifty years after the events needs to be taken into account, but they are often consistent with other testimonies gathered earlier.

Dionisii Pletsan (born in 1924 in Chortkiv) was captured, sent to Siberia, and then allowed to return to his home town.[6] He studied engineering, and he witnessed his father being arrested under Soviet rule in 1941 and people being executed in Chortkiv. He went to prison immediately after the Soviets departed: "There was a long pit into which they had thrown the bodies, but they had done this four days earlier. The earth was mixed with blood all along the pit. It was impossible to recognize anyone. People came from the villages looking for their relatives. I was the first into the place because we lived the closest." He recalled that, as soon as the Germans arrived, they shot thirty-five people, including a priest. Under German occupation he and his brother distributed nationalist literature. Since their farm was by the railway line, the literature could easily be unloaded from rail carriages, quickly carried through the corn fields, and hidden.

His brother joined the UPA but advised Dionisii to enter the Division, which he described as a Ukrainian army "with our priests, our medicine, a lot of Prague students, doctors." Dionisii recalled that most boys from the technicums and colleges signed up:

> We all decided to go with one aim, to struggle for Ukraine. Since we had almost all been in the underground, we were educated in a Ukrainian spirit ... We all went together as young people from the same football teams, choirs, orchestras. A few went into the UPA ... However, there were some individuals, whom I know well because they are still with us, who were opposed both to the UPA and to the *dyviziinyky*. They throw mud, tell lies. I had an encounter with one recently, a drunk who accused me of being a Bandera supporter. Another drunken Russian shouted at me in this manner. I always try to explain things to them. During Soviet rule we got this all the time. There were students in my company who had studied in Kraków, Prague and Breslau (Wrocław) in the universities and gymnasiums ... They were raised abroad but did not lose their sense of Ukrainian identity and they educated their children in the same way as the diaspora today educates its people.

Pletsan confirms other testimonies that those who systematically shot captured men were usually part of the Soviet security services: "When taken prisoner, we were shot. Not by men at the front, but by KGB men in the rear. When I was captured one of them grabbed me, but the soldier refused to let him take me, saying, 'what are doing shooting children?' I did not understand Russian, so when he said *patsan* [kid] I thought he was referring to my surname [Pletsan]. He told me where to hide quickly."

Pletsan spent over seven years working in copper mines near Baikal and Baikonur, the town from which the sputniks were launched. The work ruined lungs, which would get blocked or poisoned by gas. He describes workers "lying like breathless fish after coming out of the mines." In his estimate about eight thousand workers died there, were thrown into a mass grave, and covered with stones. Eventually, as an engineer he was appointed to a relatively high position, given an apartment, and asked to stay. However, he insisted on being allowed to go home.

Pavlo Lavruk (born in 1924 in Zahvizdi near today's Ivano-Frankivsk) was caught in a German dragnet operation and sent to a work camp in Germany.[7] Every family in the village had been ordered to send one person. His alternatives were serving in the police or escaping into the forest. Initially he tried living in the forest but came home because he was starving. He then joined the Division. His OUN leader told him he could do so and would be called upon later.

As a good horseman, he was sent on a special course, where he practised riding in a hall surrounded by mirrors so as to improve posture and technique. His comrades were less fortunate. He personally knew of seven recruits who tried to escape from Neuhammer and were executed.

When he was taken prisoner, a Red Army soldier immediately asked him whether he had a watch. His boots were removed and he walked barefoot. An NKVD man ordered all Russians and Ukrainians to step forward, but Lavruk was one of several who did not. Since he had torn off the lion insignia and had the same helmet as the Germans, he looked like one of them. The NKVD man approached and said: "You're a *khokhol* [a pejorative term for a Ukrainian]." He responded in German by shouting "What do you want?" and the officer moved on. The officer ordered the men who had stepped forward to be taken into a ravine and shot. While the executions were taking place, a senior officer drove by and commanded them to stop. The shootings continued until he fired several times from his revolver. Five of the Division's men came out of the swamp alive, one of whom had turned grey. Four years before the interview Lavruk succeeded in locating the ravine. When the mud was dried, the remains of the soldiers were found. After this discovery the local farmer refused to plough the land.

Lavruk was taken to Perm oblast in the Urals to work in the mines. The discipline was military. During interrogations he said nothing about being a student and an officer trainee, only that his horse pulled one of the

Stories of Captured Men • 223

batteries. In a year's time he was transferred to a mine where he worked with Finnish and Russian ROA men. On the morning of 18 March 1946, the gates were open and the guards disappeared. The commander told them they would work in the factory for six years as a special settlement.

Bohdan Kepeshchuk (born in 1921 in Luh near today's Ivano-Frankivsk) attended the local gymnasium but had to interrupt his education a couple of times because his father could not afford the tuition fees. His friends included the only Jew in the gymnasium, a boy named Koch, and some Poles. When Germany and the Soviet Union invaded Poland, there was mayhem in the town for a week, during which time people smashed state and military stores. Before he fled, the head of the Polish militia told people to take the flour and grain, otherwise it would be burned.[8]

The Red Army arrived on 17 September 1939 and "a few thousand Jews," who were probably members of the Communist Party of Western Ukraine, came out to greet it, carrying red flags. Poles and Ukrainians generally viewed this event as an entertaining theatrical performance, but a few days later the arrests and deportations began, everything disappeared from the stores and people had to queue all night for any goods. Each day files of prisoners were packed into freight wagons encased in barbed wire and deported. Those who were taken during the winter died in transit. Poles made up most of the first deportees, but Kepeshchuk's own family was also among those taken.

When the German-Soviet war began, the local population went to the prison to see the corpses, which had been buried in the courtyard and covered with asphalt. After exhumation, they were placed in coffins and taken to the cemetery. Photos of the funeral and cemetery were taken, but these were later destroyed when the Soviets returned.

Kepeshchuk decided to avoid the UPA and volunteered instead for the Division in June 1943. He trained in Brno, Heidelager, and Neuhammer and became a radio operator. There were four such operators in the headquarters and two or three in the battalion. When taken prisoner, he was sentenced to hard labour in mines, where he saw dead Romanians being thrown down a shaft. In Karaganda he met UPA members, then he was sent to Kengir, where prisoners were building an electricity plant and a factory.

There were two camps for men and one for women. The work regimen was brutal with no free time. After Stalin's death, on 16 May 1954, he participated in the uprising that was led by Ukrainians. When the guards began shooting people, he was hidden by the women in their camp. According to Kepeshchuk, Solzhenitsyn was mistaken when he wrote that the thousands of corpses were removed: they were thrown into pits that bulldozers covered with earth. From that time, the men were allowed to work without a convoy. They restored a bakery and rebuilt the barracks. In 1955, he married a Ukrainian from the women's camp, and in the following year they were allowed to live in the city.

Ivan Mamchur (born in 1925 in the village of Rokytno near Lviv) witnessed the Soviet invasion of 1939 and the persecution of his father as a *kurkul* (Rus: *kulak*), a synonym for "successful farmer." Soviet soldiers not only insisted on forced contributions but also stole their property, including the beehives, which they smashed for the honey. When his father saw that Ivan was suspected of OUN activity in school, he sent him to the Lviv seminary directed by Archbishop Slipyi. Here he studied Greek and Latin, but he disliked the constant prayers and asked to return to the gymnasium.[9]

When the Germans arrived he was sent to the Youth ss camp in Malta, Austria. The instructors were mostly Ukrainians, and the two hundred boys participated in sports; studied the histories of Ukraine and Germany, world geography, and topography; and received religious instruction from a Ukrainian Catholic priest. Early in 1945, they were sent to Slovakia to join the Division but were kept apart from the troops. On 2 May, as the war was about to end, he and a friend decided to return to Ukraine "to continue the struggle." He was captured by Czech partisans while trying to cross a bridge and was taken to a barracks, where he witnessed the Red Army execute a man from the ROA. Some Germans gave him civilian clothes. He and his friend claimed they had been transported to Germany as forced labour and were now trying to return. He felt that the Czechs acted humanely by providing field kitchens and helping the many displaced people. Soviet trains in the meantime rumbled by, taking away entire dismantled factories.

When he and his friend crossed the border, everyone was thrown to the ground and marched to a concentration camp. A boy from near Lviv had obtained a pass because he was small and looked young. The boys agreed that he would leave, then throw the document into the camp. In this way all three got out on one document, leaving at different times, one in the morning, one at lunch, and one in the evening. They got to Lviv on a cargo train, where they heard about dragnet operations and murders. Covered in lice and with nowhere to sleep, they met some boys hiding from the Red Army's press gang by spending nights in the woods.

They also met a group of UPA fighters who refused to take them, saying: "Boys, honestly, we're finished. We can't do anything. If you have a chance, study. Maybe, someday you can be useful." With his father's help Ivan obtained a temporary passport, studied in a technical school, and attended evening school to finish tenth grade. He and his friend distributed leaflets for the underground, still hoping that the US would go to war with the Soviet Union. They were arrested and confessed to being "in the Division." He spent three months in solitary confinement and was interrogated at night. For entertainment he caught flies and listened to the music they made in a can. He could only see the sky though a window high in the wall. A hole marked the spot where there had once been a toilet bowl. He slept on the floor. After being forced to stand for three twenty-four-hour periods in the interrogator's office, he was told to sign a two-hundred-page document. When he refused, he was prevented from sleeping at night. In December 1946 he was sentenced to ten years in prison and ten years loss of rights. Thirty others were sentenced at the same session. One UPA man was given the death sentence.

Ilko Havrysh (born in 1904 in Veldizh, now Shevchenkove in the Ivano-Frankivsk oblast) witnessed the Soviets requisitioning food products in 1939. They kept raising the number of forced contributions even when there was nothing left to take and, in 1940, began exiling people. He knew about Demianiv Laz, where hundreds of mutilated bodies were buried, because he could see the road leading to the place, the trucks bringing bodies, and the blood. At first, people thought the place might be a field kitchen, but after the Soviets left, members of the OUN went to look and opened the grave. Under 1.5 metres of clay they found corpses in hutsul jackets with their hands tied with wire.[10]

He joined the Division in 1943, suffered a shrapnel wound to the head, and was dragged from a trench when the dead and wounded were being collected. After three months in hospital, in April 1945 he retreated with the Division and tried to get to the American zone. In Linz, the Americans refused to take his group of about one hundred Division soldiers and instead handed them over to the Red Army. He escaped by climbing into a wagon that was returning to the American zone.

In the autumn he went back to Ukraine, claiming that he had worked for a German farmer. However, he was recognized by neighbours and had to hide with the UPA's partisans. Here he witnessed the execution of an eighteen-year-old and his father. The boy had quit the UPA because he was hungry and his father had told him that the partisans were doomed. Havrysh left the partisans after witnessing these executions. From that time he avoided both the underground and the authorities until, in June 1949, he surrendered to the police and admitted being in the Division. While in custody he saw former Bandera supporters who had become informers living in a special house on the prison grounds. These turncoats were summoned to identify men who had been caught and were suspected of supporting the UPA. After being moved between five prisons, he was sentenced in a two-minute hearing to twenty-five years hard labour.

Roman Korduba (born in 1921 in Khodoriv) finished gymnasium in 1942 under the Soviets, witnessed the arrest of teachers, and the introduction of Russian and the history of the Communist Party as compulsory subjects. When the Soviets fled, he saw the opening of prison cells and the recovery of bodies, some with large wounds on their breasts. He volunteered for the Division in June 1943 and was sent to Lauenberg in Germany for training as an NCO.[11]

Captured at Brody, he was sent to work in a coal mine between Moscow and Tula, where friends taught him carpentry. He was sent to the Urals in 1946 to work in the gold mines, then in 1950 was arrested, sent to Sverdlovsk prison, and interrogated for six weeks. In January 1951 he was sentenced to twenty-five years, previous years of imprisonment not included. The next thirteen years were spent in the northern Urals working in construction, where his carpentry skills were valued and enabled him to survive.

After being sent to Irkutsk, he was made a brigade leader and a professional worker. His sentence was reduced to thirteen years and he was released on 13 March 1955. He was given an internal passport in Sverdlovsk and allowed to return to Ukraine, where he studied and then worked as an accountant in Ivano-Frankivsk for thirty-five years.

Wolodymyr Molodecky (Volodymyr Molodetskyi, born in 1927 in Przemyśl) attended Polish schools in Kraków, where his father worked after obtaining a law degree. In 1940, Wolodymyr entered the Ukrainian gymnasium, which the Germans had allowed to open in Jarosław, then in 1942 he attended the Lviv gymnasium. He enlisted in the Division in 1943.[12]

He was captured at Brody with a group of ten people. Having suffered a concussion when hit on the head, he woke up in a barn surrounded by

German prisoners. There were no Ukrainians because they had all been shot. In a couple of days, the guards changed and an older German advised him to throw away his Waffen-ss jacket and pretend to be a German army soldier. He put on a regular army jacket and whenever the Soviets tried to question him screamed in German that he did not understand them. They were taken to a POW camp near Brody where he met Nestor Zhubryk, a comrade from the Division. They spoke in Polish and pretended to be Poles serving in the German army.

Along with other prisoners they were taken to Kyiv and paraded through the streets, while people screamed, cursed, and threw trash at them. They worked half the day and spent the other half being paraded. After that they were sent to work in the Donbas mines. In January 1945 an explosion killed most of the prisoners and the rest were sent to a camp near Minsk. Molodecky continued pretending to be Polish and used his aunt's last name, Pomorski. Since the aunt did not have children, he was hoping that, if contacted, she would realize that they were talking about him and would confirm that he was her son. Out of twelve hundred people who left for Minsk, only six hundred arrived. The rest died en route.

In Minsk he worked for six months on a collective farm, where ten to twelve people were harnessed in place of horses. A Belorusian beat them with a stick to make them plough the field. The majority of prisoners were Germans. They were given two hundred to four hundred grams of bread a day and half a litre of warm water with flour mixed into it. They worked ten- to twelve-hour days; his weight dropped to forty-nine kilograms. There was no medical care. When he contracted typhus, a doctor came to measure his temperature and then left. Most people died from the epidemic.

While working on the railway in Minsk he escaped by jumping on a tank that was being transported to Poland. After four days the train reached Brest-Litovsk. Here he was caught, sent back to the camp, and severely beaten. However, because the Polish communist government and the Soviet Union had agreed to an exchange of citizens, he was freed. He arrived in Kraków to find that his parents had left. In 1947, he walked through Czech territory, reached Munich, and reconnected with his sister, who told him that his parents were in Paris getting papers for immigration to Canada. He joined them. In Canada he completed a BA in political studies at the University of Toronto and an MA in Slavic studies at the University of Ottawa.

Vasyl Rezuniak (father's name Levytskyi) was from the village of Akreshory (Pol: Akreszory) in Bukovyna. In 1939 his uncle was arrested by Soviet authorities, but the OUN told him to enter the Komsomol and report on what was happening there.[13] At the start of the German-Soviet war he was drafted into the German army and sent first to Kraków, then to Bavaria, where he studied German, topography, armour, and military strategy. In the fall of 1942 he completed training and was sent to Lviv to patrol streets and work in counterintelligence, intercepting suspects. He was then sent to Czech territory where he studied in an artillery college for a year. After being injured at Brody, he was sent to a hospital near Przemyśl and then to one in Germany, rejoined the Division in Slovakia, fought in Austria, was injured, and was taken prisoner.

While he lay unconscious, a fellow soldier ripped the military emblems off his uniform and threw away his documents. Under interrogation he admitted to being an officer and a decision was taken to execute him. However, two older officers from Vinnytsia who were assigned the task allowed him to escape. He made his way to Germany, hid among Ukrainian workers, obtained civilian clothing, and registered in a DP camp. After three weeks he joined some young people who were being drafted into a paramilitary unit and sent to Odesa. Here he worked in a car repair shop until demobilized in March 1947. He then lived in barracks, where he was interrogated every other day. Luckily, he was surrounded by former Division soldiers who had served in Yugoslavia and had obtained documents certifying that they had fought together with Tito's partisans. With their help he avoided being sentenced or sent to Siberia.

He returned home in April 1947 and reconnected with friends who helped him get a job as a bailiff. His job was to confiscate the property of people sentenced by the military tribunals for anti-Soviet activities. However, instead of confiscating property he evaluated it and ordered relatives to reimburse the government financially. The only person who checked his work was a judge with no legal education. Rezuniak also served in a party committee charged with removing people's cattle and goods for failing to contribute towards government needs. He prevented the cattle being taken and even received commendations for humane application of the laws. In 1949–50 he worked for a year at the prosecutor's office, where he was able to reduce a number of penalties from imprisonment to volunteer work and a fine.

In 1950 he joined the Communist Party. He considered this a way of fighting the occupation regime from within, analogous to the way he had earlier joined the Komsomol on the OUN's instructions. While making public statements about the great contributions of the party, behind the scenes he worked to make progressive changes. One of the individuals with whom he worked was Vasyl Pavlychko, the father of Dmytro Pavlychko, who was a leading youth activist and later became a prominent writer and, after 1991, a member of Parliament.

Rezuniak eventually became a prosecutor. He concluded his testimony with the following: "for forty-nine years I worked among strangers never forgetting the military oath I took back in 1943 to be loyal to Ukraine and its people." He felt that throughout his life he had not served "a foreign nation" but had made "practical efforts" to help his own people and country.

14

ÉMIGRÉ PRESS AND THE PATRIOT IMAGE, 1951–74

"But somehow the newspaper men always kept the horrifying realities of the War out of their articles."

SIEGFRIED SASSOON, *Memoirs of an Infantry Officer*, 1930

In postwar decades the Division's veterans shaped an image of themselves as patriots. The force's main ideologist had at first been Dmytro Paliiv. A former Sich Rifleman, he had been on the committee that planned the armed uprising of 1 November 1918 in Lviv. Fiery and impulsive, he had favoured starting the revolution without waiting for "what Vienna had to say" (Kedryn 1986, 463). In interwar Lviv he became an influential journalist and was elected to the Polish Sejm, where he served between 1928 and 1930, from the UNDO party, which expelled him on 6 July 1933 for publicly criticizing its policy towards the government. He created the Front Natsionalnoi Iednosti (Front of National Unity) party, ran the newspaper *Ukrainski visti* (Ukrainian news) and the journal *Peremoha* (Victory). Paliiv was a strong political personality and an effective organizer, so much so that the OUN saw his party as a rival and sent a group to demolish his editorial offices (Knysh 1959–60, 2:99). By the late 1930s, he had become an ardent advocate of the need for a Ukrainian armed force and was among the first to enlist in the Division.

When challenged by the Polish underground, Paliiv expressed his belief in the need for developing professional military cadres in the following way: "The Poles will not disappear under Soviet rule, because they have allies in England and America ... We have no choice: we stand before the destruction of our nation. Do not think that we are working with the Germans for the victory of Germany. We simply do not want the victory of England, America and Poland over Hitler to send us to the grave. Therefore, we will defend ourselves. We have no choice: either we die like slaughtered rams, or we die in struggle. We prefer struggle" (Krokhmaliuk 1952, 6).

According to the journalist Ivan Kedryn, prior to the First World War Ukrainian society had either shunned the military profession or held it in contempt. As a result, both the Sich Riflemen and Ukrainian Galician Army lacked professionally trained officers (Kedryn 1986, 72). In part, interwar Galician society attributed the defeat of the 1917–20 independence struggle to this deficiency.

In 1943, Paliiv was dispatched by the UTSK and Military Board as political adviser to General Freitag and to serve as the liaison with Ukrainian officers. Heike (1973, 39) writes that Paliiv defended Ukrainian personnel "with skill and tact," in spite of frequent clashes with Freitag. After his death at Brody his persona acquired a legendary aura. He was lauded for his energy, civic courage, and passion for politics, and for being able to conduct political and journalistic activities while living from a modest income: he kept a guest house in the mountain resort of Krynica (Kedryn 1986, 462–3).

Although viewed as the Division's initial inspirational force, Paliiv never articulated its raison d'être in any depth. This was done by other veterans. After the war, Liubomyr Ortynskyj became an influential spokesperson. He had been arrested as a member of the OUN on 21 March 1939 and spent several months in Lviv's Brygidky prison. Freed by the outbreak of the Second World War, he crossed the Soviet-German border illegally and worked for the OUN, first in Warsaw and then in Vienna, where he became an officer in the Roland Battalion. In September 1941 the Gestapo arrested him along with the other officers. He volunteered for the Division in 1943 as a communications officer and was wounded at Brody. At the war's end, he found himself in the American zone and in the early 1950s lived in Munich, where he became a member of the Western Representation of the UHVR (Ukrainian Supreme Liberation Council). This group was the UPA's voice in the West

Figure 14.1 Front page of *Visti bratstva kol. Voiakiv 1 UD UNA*, July 1951, depicting Battle of Brody. Heading: "Glory to the fighters at Brody!" Caption: "You will win a Ukrainian State or die in the struggle for her. Yevhen Konovalets."

and had broken with the OUN-B. He began writing for the Division's journal *Visti* and, after moving to the United States in 1956, helped create the Brotherhood of Former Soldiers of the 1st Ukrainian Division of the UNA (Bratstvo kolyshnikh voiakiv 1 UD UNA) in 1961. Ortynskyj used his accreditation with the newspaper *Svoboda* (Freedom) to attend sessions at the UN in New York, where he monitored the Ukrainian Soviet Republic's participation in this body. He wrote for both organs of the Division, *Visti* and *Visti kombatanta*, but died only two months after his lead article appeared in the first issue of the latter (Ortynskyi 1961).

His most influential article appeared in 1951. It provided a justification for the Division and raised themes that would later be developed by others (see Ortynskyi 1951). He described the formation as a highly idealistic, well-trained, and disciplined army, which had come out of a long tradition of armed struggle in the name of statehood, a view echoed by Heike and Kedryn (Kedryn 1986, 150). Ortynskyj took the line that, over the centuries, subjugated peoples had created national legions within foreign armies in order to serve their own liberation struggles, arguing that an oppressed nation has the right to take weapons from a stronger power when the opportunity arises. The Galicia Division had been a gamble because it did not have the customary trappings of a legion – distinctive uniforms and insignia, and its own commanders. In his view, the risk had been worth taking because, despite its small military value, the Division had a political significance, which was why the Soviet Union had made such efforts to demonize it after the war. The Division stood alone among thirty-eight Waffen-ss divisions in garnering such a degree of attention from Moscow, including the torrent of deliberate misinformation.

Although the possibility of an armed coup similar to the one on 1 November 1918 never materialized, Ortynskyj argued that the Division's existence had drawn attention to the liberation struggle in Ukraine. Kedryn agreed; he later wrote that scores of civic activists emerged from the Division's ranks (Kedryn 1986, 151).[1] They included men who had served in the Ukrainian armies from 1918 to 1920, like Pavlo Shandruk, Borys Barvinskyi, and Mykhailo Krat, and many others who made significant contributions to émigré life in postwar decades.

Oleh Lysiak was another prominent spokesman for the Division. He wrote that the veterans saw the end of the war as concluding only the first chapter of their work. In the diaspora they continued explaining the situation in Ukraine (Lysiak 1951b, 11). Lysiak's article "Bytva bez lehendy" (Battle without a legend, 1951) points out that the defeat at Brody and the questionable political decision to fight in German uniform meant that the Division was never able to create a "legend" that could compete with that of the Sich Riflemen. Nor could Brody play a role in the national imagination comparable to Bazar or Kruty. However, the thousands who laid down their lives in the Brody pocket had demonstrated their desire to fight the Red Army's advance. They answered the call of community leaders, knowing they would never receive the recognition normally given a nation's defenders:

> The Ukrainian soldiers who took up their rifles calmly and without enthusiasm knew what they were doing, and were already prepared for the results of their act. Therefore, we make no demands on any of them; we merely affirm the facts. The Ukrainian soldiers who left the Red Army and crossed the front line to join the UPA partisans, those who went into the forests, the Division's soldiers who put on German helmets – were all doing their duty toward the future Ukrainian state. As for us, soldiers of the Division, we took up arms because we believed in defending our native land, even when we did not believe those who gave us these arms. (Lysiak 1951b, 9–10)

Most reminiscences and articles by veterans were unsentimental. These included early anthologies edited by Oleh Lysiak (1951a, 1974) and Vsevolod Budnyi (1979), and later memoirs by Vasyl Veryha and Roman Kolisnyk. Writers agreed that the Division, to use Kedryn's (1986. 149) words, had not created "its own legend," meaning it had not left a mark in literature. The force had no press bureau comparable to that of the Sich Riflemen, which produced an entire school of poets and song writers, novelists and musicians. However, Kedryn's observation was not entirely correct. The Division had its repertoire of marching songs, even though they were not created specifically for the force. They were folk songs, songs of the Sich Riflemen, or contemporary melodies that were given new lyrics. The most popular song, "Marsheruiut dobrovoltsi," was in fact written by Roman Kupchynskyi, the celebrated Rifleman. He had apparently produced the song for the short-lived Nachtigall Brigade, but the Division adopted it and Kupchynskyi's daughter Tania reworked the lyrics (Slupchynskyi 2003, 5). Reportedly, the song's author was delighted to learn of its success among the soldiers. In the 1990s the Division's songs were given new accompaniments by the leading composer Myroslav Skoryk and were performed by the Lviv Philharmonic Academy in July 1994 on the fiftieth anniversary of the battle of Brody (6).

The "lack of a legend" was part of the price paid for the association with Germany. The defeat at Brody deflated any remaining enthusiasm, as did the negative attitude of the underground, but above all it was the image of an alliance with Nazi Germany that dictated postwar discourse. The Division's spokespeople had to answer why they had accepted German uniforms and commanders. Western public opinion showed little interest in their justifications or experiences. This became even more the case when Holocaust studies developed in the 1970s and research focused on analyzing processes that had brought about the destruction of Jewish communities. The relative silence of the Division's memoirists, writers, and historians on this topic and on German atrocities reflected the embarrassment of the Division's spokespeople, who had to deal with their complicity in Berlin's drive not only to conquer but also to subdue and exterminate entire populations.

Voices in the Ukrainian press criticized the move to create the Division. Feliks Korduba in 1963 stated that the organizers had a poor grasp of the strategic military-political situation and of Hitler's plans. With hindsight he felt it was possible to say that organizing the Division had been a mistake, "because this ill-considered experiment cost the Ukrainian people very many sacrifices" (Korduba 1963, 6). He blamed the pro-German political orientation of Galician leaders, who saw what they wanted to see and therefore overemphasized Rosenberg's plans concerning Ukraine and failed to read the chapter on Ostpolitik in *Mein Kampf.* They had been influenced by Dmytro Dontsov, whose *Visnyk* (Herald) had agitated in favour of Hitler, Mussolini, and other dictators. As a result, Ukrainian youth "believed in Hitler's noble plans concerning Ukraine" (15).

Young people were prepared to rebel against Germany's policy of physical and material destruction, but they soon learned that the romantic idea of fighting a guerilla war in the forests with a few rifles, pistols, and grenades was a fantasy. All the same, the partisans had one advantage: a fanatical faith in the justice of their cause. Korduba took the line that the Germans created the Division both to weaken attraction to the UPA and to counteract the despair caused by Erich Koch's regime in Reichskommissariat Ukraine. After their defeats in Moscow, Africa, and Stalingrad, the Germans knew they needed Ukrainian recruits but offered no political agreements. Ukrainians had only one simple argument: "take the weapons!"

In Korduba's view plenty of observers rejected this pragmatic argument as false and harmful. They reasoned that the Division provided Ukraine's enemies with evidence of the population's Germanophilia, associated Ukrainians with a regime that was losing the war, and required them to shed blood for German interests. Ultimately, the Division had been a failed experiment. In his view, the comparison with 1918 was flawed because the two situations were entirely different. In the final reckoning, the Division's creation "had caused the Ukrainian people a great deal of harm" (Korduba 1963, 16).

In the 1960s Vasyl Veryha emerged as a prominent spokesman for the Division. Born in 1922 in the small village of Kolodribka south of Ternopil, he attended gymnasium in Zalishchyky and Kolomyia, volunteered for the Division, and became an officer. In 1946 he contributed to the Rimini newspaper *Batkivshchyna*. After immigrating to Canada in 1951 he completed a degree in library science at the University of Toronto and an MA in history at Ottawa University, worked as a university librarian, edited *Visti kombatanta* in the years between 1966 and 1973, and managed the Division's archive, which, after his death, was donated to the Archives of Ontario. He published several books on the Division, a number of memoirs, and many essays.[2]

An article from 1965 provides a concise summary of the case veterans had developed over two decades. "Analizuimo nashe mynule" (Let us analyze our past) was a response to the reprinting of a 1943 OUN-B publication that opposed the Division's creation on the grounds that it was a "German colonial formation." Veryha's reply tackled the charge by listing justifications for the Division's formation.[3]

Ukrainians wanted "sovereignty on their ancestral territories" and could accept neither the German idea of *Drang nach Osten* nor the Russian theory of a fusion of nations (Veryha 1980, 152). They viewed the policies of neighbouring countries as obstacles to their sovereignty. It was obvious that the international community did not recognize Ukrainians as a people, partly because the country had no national army. The world assumed that wartime armies were composed of people with heir own state: Poles, Russians, Romanians, Hungarians, Germans, and so on. Galicians asked themselves: What would happen if the war ended like the previous one? Would we be ready to meet a new 1918? The answer lay in the need to create a military formation that could respond to every political conjuncture. The Galicia Division was conceived as the core of a future Ukrainian army that was organized "not against the West, but against our deadly enemy, Moscow" (156). Beyond this, the creation of the Division was aimed at strengthening the situation of Ukrainians in German-occupied territories and opposing the influence of Poles, who were heavily represented "in all administrations and used their positions against the Ukrainian people" (156). Veryha argues that the force's creation led to "a considerable improvement in relations

Émigré Press and the Patriot Image, 1951–74 • **237**

between the Ukrainian population of Galicia and the German occupation regime" (161). Letters from the Division's soldiers bearing the "ss Feldpost" stamp and a return address helped people to arrange transportation, the forest partisans received a constant supply of instructors and soldiers, and by enlisting many people were able to escape the Gestapo, concentration camps, and work camps in Germany (160, 164).

In any case, he argues, young people did not have the option of remaining at home. They had to work in Germany for the Arbeitsdienst or at home for the Baudienst, and Ukrainians had no control over either agency. In the Division there was at least some possibility of community oversight. As for misreading the postwar scenario, Veryha indicates that no one could have foreseen the Allies allowing a totalitarian regime that covered a sixth of the earth's surface to exist alongside them (Veryha 1980, 157). In retrospect, he writes, the OUN-B's idea of the "forest" and the UTSK's idea of the Galicia Division both proved unrealistic, but neither group should be blamed for this.

Veryha supports the idea that the force had demonstrated Ukraine's opposition to Soviet rule and the country's willingness to shed blood in its struggle for freedom. He insists that the population did not see the Division as a party to German colonialism but welcomed its men as defenders. He agrees that the Division was the result of an understanding between representatives of the Ukrainian people and the occupation but argues that the collaboration had been arranged to combat another occupation – the Soviet one. Some form of collaboration had been practised by everyone. To get military training the OUN-B had collaborated, by agreeing, for example, to the formation of the Nachtigall and Roland Battalions. All groups manoeuvred to gain some advantage in the liberation struggle, but "everywhere," in his words, "the conjuncture was stacked against Ukraine," and there was no collaboration with any major power that would have brought a favourable result (Veryha 1980, 168). He offers the example of Poland, an ally of the West, which fought against the Germans and valiantly demonstrated its desire for independence but, in 1945, was sacrificed by the Allies to Moscow's will (Veryha 2002, 125).

As for the charge that the human losses were unjustified, he responds that no one had even tried to count the Ukrainian lives lost in German slave labour camps. If mentioned in Soviet or Western accounts, they were classified as "Russian" victims. Nor were Ukrainian losses among Soviet soldiers or civilians ever counted. The Division, however, was always identified as Ukrainian. This at least allowed it to signal to the West the population's anti-Soviet attitude. It was clear, he argues, to all observers that the Division was not fighting for the Third Reich's *Lebenstraum* in Ukraine but to better the situation of its own people (Veryha 2002, 126–7).

In the years from 1972 to 1974, thirty years after the Division's recruitment, the émigré journal *Ukrainskyi samostiinyk* (Ukrainian sovereigntist) regretted that a deeper, more searching analysis of the military formation's genesis and wartime history had not been produced. A series of articles asked whether the decision to create the force had not from the outset been an error. The exchange was triggered by the appearance of Wolf-Dietrich Heike's memoir (in an abridged Ukrainian translation in 1970 and in German in 1973) and by several ground-breaking publications on non-Germans in the German army and Waffen-ss.[4] Simultaneously, a number of books published in Soviet Ukraine and Poland accused the Division of various crimes, while Kremlin-inspired texts published in the West tried to link arrested Soviet Ukrainian dissidents to wartime nationalists.[5]

Volodymyr Vashkovych, a former officer in the Division, begins the discussion in *Ukrainskyi Samostiinyk* by pointing out that, although the OUN-B considered itself the dominant political group in wartime Galicia and publicly opposed the Division's creation, an entire generation of young people with completed secondary education responded positively to the call for volunteers. However, when the Division's creation was announced, no concessions were made to the idea of Ukrainian statehood, so much so that even the adjective "Ukrainian" was carefully avoided. Why, asks Vashkovych, did the Division's creators accept this? Were they simply deceived by the agenda of Bisanz, Wächter, and Himmler?

The explanation, he argues, is to be found in a residual sympathy for Germany, which had been nurtured by the interwar Galician press. It had extolled the "German" virtues of discipline, good economic management, and military strength, and had convinced readers that Germany's desire to revise the Treaty of Versailles made it a natural ally. The same press made no attempt to discuss Nazi Germany's intentions in the east or Hitler's plans as outlined in *Mein Kampf*. Although the wave of volunteers in 1943 might partly be explained as the result of a pent-up desire for action among youth, Vashkovych emphasizes the fault of community leaders.

The fault of course lay not just with Ukrainian Galician society. Western political and intellectual leaders in the 1930s were also guilty of appeasement, accommodation, and understatement, and in the years between 1939 and 1941 both the Soviet and Polish press muzzled criticism of Germany, while communist parties and Soviet apologists around the globe opposed the participation of Western powers in the war.

Vashkovych's second point is that Ukrainian Galician leaders must have been aware of the Division's limited military potential. To illustrate this point he makes some revealing comments about life in the Division after Brody. Some fought well, he argues, but much of the second recruitment was of a lower quality. It included conscripts and police or Schutzmannschaft units, some of which had guarded administrative and industrial sites or forced labour camps in Germany. These men fought poorly and sometimes fled in panic "at the first meeting with the enemy" (Vashkovych 1972, 1–2, 55). Several former Schutzmannschaft soldiers, he recalls, refused to follow orders, robbed civilians, and stirred up insubordination. One of them, a man called Zvarych, deserted his nighttime guard post, got drunk, and tried to rape a Slovak girl. He was disarmed but escaped the required court martial, or any punishment, because the German commander was courting popularity among soldiers by avoiding harsh decisions and relaxing discipline.

When the higher military authorities learned of these acts of indiscipline and of desertions, it dispatched letters, one of which was addressed to Lieutenant Colonel Karl Wildner. Vashkovych, who served in the latter's headquarters, was able to read its contents. The letter asked why no one had been shot to set an example. This communication resulted in someone being arrested and shot in almost every larger unit, "even for the smallest theft, such as [stealing] half a package of margarine" (Vashkovych 1972, 3, 35). The arbitrary executions caused outrage. Vashkovych personally ordered the release of one arrested man, who promptly deserted during the night. The next day Wildner condemned the ruthlessness of the German command and refused to act in the matter. The superior officer Bruderhofer, although infuriated by Vashkovych's behaviour, was powerless to do anything because the unit was stationed in forested mountains and it would have taken hours to arrest and convoy him. More important, at a signal from the Ukrainian officer, the soldiers would have liquidated their German command (35–6). In the end the order to shoot people for show merely created animosity towards the Germans and "a passionate desire to see them defeated" (36).

As a dutiful officer who wished to apply the rules and maintain discipline, Vashkovych was appalled by the laxity of Ukrainian officers, who preferred physical punishment to martial law even for serious offences. This, in his view, further contributed to the demoralization and led to self-serving, dishonourable behaviour among some men. He gives the example of German troops at one point sending Ukrainians as an advance party on a dangerous mission behind enemy lines while they themselves waited with no intention of following (Vashkovych 1972, 36–7).

Vashkovych made these revelations to undermine Heike's rather flattering depiction of the German officer corps and to show that belief in the Division's military capacity had been enormously exaggerated. The reorganized Division, he asserted, "had no chance of becoming the core of some larger military formation, because it could barely keep itself intact" (Vashkovych 1972, 38). In retrospect, he could find only one justification for forming the Division: that it saved the lives of thousands of young people, whose talents, commitment, and work for the Ukrainian cause made a difference wherever they later settled. The basic problem, from the start, was with the formation's unclear identity and future.

Osyp Bodnar provides a similar judgment. He asks how fighting for the German military could be reconciled with the goal of Ukraine's independence and urges veterans to produce memoirs that explain their point of view. In his opinion, a realistic record of events, no matter how controversial, was required to learn from the experience. He asks how veterans could argue that they were not fighting against Western powers but only against the Bolsheviks, and why they expected the Red Army to exhaust itself in the war against Germany or the West to turn against the Soviet Union. Were there any secret plans to contact the West or was this mere speculation? If the latter, then the Division's organizers had miscalculated badly and their compromises had not been justified (Bodnar 1974, 27).

Bodnar suggests that Ukrainian leaders were aware of German attitudes and could see that people were being conscripted into German forces and the Red Army or were escaping to the underground. Faced with taking a decision "for" or "against" the Division, they decided that it was better to fight for a Ukrainian illusion than for Bolshevik interests (Bodnar 1974, 28).

Community leaders had reasoned that service within a recognized military unit would at least bear witness to the armed struggle of Ukrainians. Political optics therefore explain why veterans considered the Division's renaming in the last weeks of the war (as the UNA) such an important moment: it advertised the fact that a Ukrainian military was fighting against the Soviet Union.

Bodnar agrees with Vashkovych that the effectiveness of any force depends on its belief in a cause. He himself had served five years in the Polish army, then fought in the German army near Stalingrad. Without faith in a just cause, he argues, military confrontation is a form of adventurism or service in the interests of a foreign power. In short, lack of faith in the Division's purpose had affected its military capability. The UPA, by contrast, even though it had no illusions about victory, at least had a clear goal: "to gain a sovereign Ukrainian state or die in the struggle." Bodnar (1974, 31) therefore questions the decision to create the Division and calls for serious a documentary study of wartime events – not panegyrics but "a cold analysis of facts and phenomena."

Kostiantyn Zelenko, a Canadian army officer who in the 1950s participated in NATO exercises in West Germany and then became a London-based historian, provides the most bracing assessment of the Division's genesis and achievement. He criticizes Heike's book for its superficiality but also dismisses accusations of Germanophilia or collaborationism. If these terms were to be applied, he argues, one should also admit that a million Russians and other Soviet citizens served under German banners and that half of nearly forty Waffen-ss divisions were raised in Western Europe. The relevant question is why so many men enlisted, even from countries that had lost their independence to German invaders. At the time of this discussion, David Littlejohn's *Patriotic Traitors* (1972) and Jurgen Thorwald's *The Illusion: Soviet Soldiers in Hitler's Armies* (1975) had appeared and historians in other countries had begun to raise the painful question of local collaboration.[6] Zelenko argues for a fuller appreciation of the wartime context, including the fact millions of Ukrainians fought in the Red Army.

Like Vashkovych and Bodnar, Zelenko is most interested in the political conception behind the Division's formation. After asking what vision drove its organizers, whether this vision was realistic and whether in retrospect the unit's creation could be justified, he concludes that the force was a German division formed from Ukrainian soldiers. All the higher officers were German, which distinguished it from Andrei Vlasov's divisions, which had non-German commanders at every level (Zelenko 1972–73, 11–12, 29). Although the Galicia Division was allowed to train, by his calculation, some 250 to three hundred officers and two thousand NCOs, it had no influence on how the force was to be deployed within the German war machine. There was only a vague general agreement that it would fight on the eastern front. Historians, he argues, were in agreement that there had not been any real possibility of the Soviet Union's immediate collapse. However, even if this had occurred, a Ukrainian army would have been created out of the tens of thousands of experienced officers and the millions of men in the Red Army (30).

Zelenko's conclusion is that Vlasov had envisaged a coup within the Soviet Union and an uprising against Stalin's tyranny, but supporters of the Division had nurtured even more illusory hopes: a change of attitude within the German leadership and the emergence of a conflict between the Allies and the Soviet Union. However, Nazi Germany remained a totalitarian state ruled by a Führer. To be sure, in 1944 a new conception and ideological line had been developed by Reinhard Gehlen, Gottlob Berger, Fritz Arlt, and Otto Wächter, who were ready to mobilize national armies among Eastern Europeans. However, as historians have pointed out, this never became a realistic part of Germany's Ostpolitik. As Reitlinger (1960, 353) comments, the only concession made to Slavs at the war's end was to admit they were sufficiently human to be allowed to die on the front in place of Germans. Nor was the switch to joining the Allies a genuine possibility. Although Vlasov's army did turn against the Germans in Prague in the final days and preserved the city, the Allies delivered him to the Soviets for execution.

All three contributors to *Ukrainskyi samostiinyk* condemned Ukrainian political leaders for not having a better grasp of Germany's real intentions and the Division's prospects. They admitted that enthusiasm for creating "one's own" army had been palpable, but in the long run the liaison with the brutal regime had proved to be an error. Zelenko (1972–73, no.1, 29) summarizes the reasoning given for creating the Division as emotional, contradictory, and illogical. In his view Germany had used the force in a hopeless attempt to plug a hole in the front near Brody, then in anti-partisan warfare in Slovakia and Slovenia, before dispatching it to hold back the collapsing front in Austria. A number of men were also sent to other war zones without their consent or that of the Division. Several were exploited for appalling purposes. For example, he notes that one veteran described to him how, in November and December of 1944 near Bydgoszcz, he had been sent on a course dealing with poison gases. During the training, naked Soviet POWs were placed in wire cages and sprinkled with mustard gas to demonstrate its effects. The prisoners, no doubt, included Ukrainians (30). Zelenko also warns against the fascination with martyrdom, arguing that sending schoolboys and students to fight at Kruty in 1918, or untrained and unequipped youth to fight in the Carpathian Sich in 1939, were lamentable acts that doomed young men to destruction (31).

The Ukrainian leadership, he insists, should have at least obtained firm political and military guarantees from the Germans, and he characterizes as "a gross simplification" the postwar claim by the Brotherhood of Former Soldiers that they fought for Ukrainian statehood (Zelenko (1972–73, no. 1, 35). Like Vashkovych and Bodnar, he concludes that fighting in German uniform for a German cause negatively affected troop morale (36). However, he also defends the Division against unwarranted attacks. In a letter to the *Spectator* in 1978 he points out that many attacks on the Division – such as the claim that they exterminated Jews and Poles and suppressed the Warsaw Uprising – were driven by "tendentiousness, inaccuracy and prejudice" (Zelenko 1978).

His assessment of the decision to create a Division was challenged by veterans. Kost Hirniak replies that the soldiers knew they were part of a foreign army but nonetheless saw themselves as fighting for the Ukrainian cause. He argues that attributing a lack of motivation to the volunteers was a mistake based on retrospective awareness. The struggle for Ukrainian statehood had over the generations taken many forms and had not always been successful, but each generation had grasped available opportunities (Hirniak 1974, 171).

The arguments used in this debate from the early 1970s were repeated in the émigré press in later decades. Most commentators agreed that the Division's political significance had outweighed its military role but that this conclusion had only become possible with the benefit of hindsight. They pointed out that, in democratic societies, there was a greater liberty of choice, but squeezed as Ukrainians were between two totalitarian systems their options were severely limited, and it remained unclear at the time how the war's endgame would play out.

15

POETRY AND MEMOIRS

Creative literature played an important role in constructing the Division's postwar image. It became the prism through which the veterans themselves and much of the Ukrainian public viewed the Division.

Several poets made reputations in Rimini. Their work expressed the yearning for their country and families, which they blended with political commitment and youthful optimism. Volodymyr Biliaiev produced reminiscences of his native Kyiv and wistful poems in which the exile gazes over the sea and recalls home:

> And so I stand, gaze drowning in the distance,
> Where a conical sail rocks –
> Suddenly it opens my eyes and heart,
> Believe me, to another world.
> I loved that world so much,
> The flood of yellowing grainfields
> Flowing far beyond the horizon –
> In a flash of undying love
> I recognize in the conical sail
> A poplar in my sad-winged fatherland.[1]

Andrii Lehit (real name Vorushylo) was from Korsun-Shevchenkivskyi near Kyiv. Born in 1916, he published his first poems in a local newspaper in 1935. After completing a degree in the philology faculty of Kyiv Pedagogical Institute, he taught Ukrainian language and literature for two years, then was mobilized into the Red Army in 1939. He was taken prisoner by the Germans in 1941 but escaped, went home, and found work as a teacher and proof-reader. He moved to Galicia and, in the autumn of 1944, to Slovakia, where he joined the Division.

Lehit wrote for the camp's periodicals and then published three collections of poems in the UK.[2] In one poem he describes the *Ubermensch* covered in Satan's blood who "executed and hung the people and took millions into captivity" (Lehit 1958, 20).[3] Much of his work is marked by pessimism and by images of beautiful, unattainable women. "Bilia moria" (By the sea) was written in Rimini:

Azure sky, golden sun,
Wind cradling silver sea waves.
A heart blossoms with joy
In a land with no misfortune, grief.
No one's to be seen,
Far in the distance San Marino.
I look around: a splendid seniorita
Approaches, a proud nymph
Of unseen beauty that smites me,
A goddess Phoebe descended from Athens,
of antique stature, with unbraided hair,
With blue sky reflected in her eyes,
A Madonna, glorious and precious.
Amazed, I call: "O, lovely girl!"
She stretches out a delicate arm and
Begs me: "Signore, mi dia pane!"[4]

Yurii Forys completed gymnasium in Przemyśl. His poetry collection *Z moikh dumok* (From my thoughts, 1945), published in Rimini, expresses the feelings of a soldier who left home to "win freedom" and now yearns for loved ones (Forys 1945, 6–7). "Otche nash" (Our father) asks the Lord to destroy the "Red Satan" who has turned the world bloody. When that occurs, "we will build a kingdom of Truth, Freedom and Love, for future generations" (8).

Bohdan Bora (Borys Shkandrij) completed gymnasium in Stanislaviv in 1940 and, after taking courses in pedagogy, began teaching in his native village of Pavlivka. He signed up for the Division in 1943 and trained as an officer, rejoining the force late in the war. He wrote poetry as a school-boy and admired émigré poets like Oleksandr Oles and Yevhen Malaniuk, and Soviet Ukrainian lyricists of the 1920s. He published two collections in Rimini and two in the UK.[5] His work moves between elegy and civic protest. Some poems, such as "Moia doba" (My age), aim to capture the strange mixture of terror and hope that for many in this generation characterized the war years:

My age – so huge
My age – so terrible.
Unfettered and savage as the night,
Then bright as a rainbow
My age …
My homeland – ray of sunshine and beauty,
Then ominous lightning bolt
Like blade of sword and scythe.[6]

The juxtaposition of hope and anger runs through his poetry. The mingling of eschatological visions with dreams of returning home were to remain popular in the emigration for several decades. The journalist Mykola Frantsuzhenko (Francuzenko, pseudonym Virnyi) describes Bora's work as "the confession of an entire generation swaddled in the fire and blood of the Second World War" (Virnyi 2005a, 173). The poetry was also popular because it projected a sense of vulnerability, an image of youth's wounded sensibility, and a child-like impulse to protect and save. The choice of strict classical forms, such as the sonnet, and careful attention to metre and rhyme, also carried an implicit message – the importance of structure and attention to detail as a way of ordering emotion and providing a defence against trauma.

"Liubov i hniv" (Love and anger) marries patriotism with personal modesty:

I'll walk the ascetic's path of modesty,
Grown tired, will quietly depart without a word,
And high above under the azure tent
Will lay my head upon a small white cloud.

No need for wreathes, no salvia bouquet,
Just a low dignified bow and spark of warmth
For Maria, the mother who gave me to my people.[7]

Although these more personal lyrics are among his best, it was the civic poetry with its strong rhythms and wish-fulfilling sentiments that was frequently reprinted in émigré journals and books. For example, "Mii son" (My dream) introduces the 1963 issue of *Samostiina Ukraina* (Independent Ukraine) dedicated to the Division:

A bravura march. The regiments set off ...
This, this is my dream!
Their banners retreat
There – over the horizon ...

Steel horseshoes spark stones,
The earth resounds like a bell.
Winds continue combing thoughts ...
O, this is my dream!

Behind, the day disappears in dust,
Ahead – the fresh distance
And the yearning there – on the horizon
In a star wreath – like a coral bead.

The division's regiments march on and on,
While home dreams its distant dream,
And Kyiv in a golden mirror
Is a drunken vision of revolt.

Horseshoes spark cobbles,
Shrapnel rips from bullets ...
Gun barrels roar with laughter
Bringing joy, hope and torment!

A bravura march. The regiments enter,
From the crowd, from windows, wreathes ...

Nothing more do I want,
Just this, just this – my dream![8] (*Samostiina Ukraina* 16, no. 4
[April 1963]: 1)

Vitalii Bender (real name Mykhailo Martiuk) was one of the Division's best memoirists. Born in 1923 near today's city of Dnipro, he completed secondary education in the Donetsk and Luhansk oblasts. In 1941 he was drafted into the Soviet army, was twice wounded, and then captured by the Germans. To escape a POW camp, in October 1944 he agreed to join the Division while it was in Slovakia. His first stories appeared in Rimini.[9] Later he published a novel dealing with life in the Division entitled *Marsh molodosty* (March of the youth, 1954), and two books of memoirs *Frontovi dorohy* (Front roads, 1984) and *Stantsiia Puhalovska* (Puhalovska station, 1984). From in Neu-Ulm, Germany, from 1954 to 1957 he edited *Ukrainski Visti* (Ukrainian news), the organ of the Ukrainian Revolutionary Democratic Party, which had a social-democratic orientation and which Bender joined in 1949. Its readers were mostly from Central and Eastern Ukraine. Bender also worked in the monitoring section of BBC radio.

Frontovi dorohy describes life in the Red Army from the summer of 1941 to the spring of 1944. It is his best work; a vivid portrait of young mine workers and villagers who serve at the front. None have seen much of the world. The narrator develops a bond with Hrudko from Vinnytsia, based on a mutual interest in jazz, ballroom dancing, and films. After being captured and rounded up by the Germans, they escape and make their way east by avoiding the main roads and carefully approaching villagers for food. One man informs them that German soldiers "are even worse than ours" and that they should be wary of the police, which contains "many sensible lads" who will help with advice and food but also nasty types who in order to ingratiate themselves with the new authorities "will immediately take you to the Germans" (Bender 1984a, 25–6). The locals had hoped for something better. They are shocked to see POWs being starved. Doubt and fear have returned. The man tells them that the house from which he was expelled in 1931 now belongs to the village head, whose wife fears that he will ask for its return.

The narrator compares attitudes towards the dead. He has seen a newsreel in which Soviet soldiers destroy the crosses on German graves, chopping them up with axes, and cheerfully throwing them onto a bonfire around which they warm themselves. Although he understands the vengefulness, "all the same the scene with crosses gave me an unpleasant, if not revolting, feeling" (Bender 1984a, 84). He compares this newsreel with a British one, in which there was not a single downed enemy plane. Instead, viewers saw fire crews working to put out flames, people taking ruins apart and saving anyone trapped inside:

> The calm on the faces of Londoners was impressive. They worked without unnecessary hurry, without panic. The ending showed the soldiers' canteen, troops dancing with girls, drinking beer, playing cards around tables, smoking cigarettes. They all had nice haircuts, were clean, wore wonderful uniforms. We especially admired their short, belted jackets ... English soldiers looked like dignified, valued human beings. And look at us: shaved heads, sunken eyes, unbrushed teeth because there's nothing to clean them with, unshaven faces because there are no razors, short shapeless coats that hang as though made not for young people but for for scarecrows, clothes held together with ropes instead of belts. And not the faintest hope of beer, fragrant cigarettes or dances! (Bender 1984a, 85–6)

After returning to their own lines, the two friends are imprisoned as suspected spies. When the Germans renew their advance, the Soviet officers disappear and both men walk out of prison.

In the winter of 1943 they are again back on the front line, where they witness soldiers wounding themselves so as to be sent home. Knowing that a shot from close range leaves a mark, some prefer "voting" for a trip home by lifting their hand above the trench, hoping to have a finger removed by an enemy bullet (Bender 1984a, 251). Civilians who have spent time under German occupation are called "black shirts" or "blackskins" because of their civilian clothing. They are driven into battle ahead of troops and suffer enormous casualties. The narrator thinks that this is a form of punishment for having remained under enemy occupation. He reports rumours of captured policemen and village heads being hanged in market places. The lynchings were stopped in the summer or 1943, but anyone who served in the occupation's administration was quickly tried, given twenty years, and sent to punitive battalions. If they survived the war, they ended up in the Gulag.

The presence of the PPZh is also described. These initials are a play on PPSh (*pulemet-pistolet Shaposhnikova*, the Shaposhnikov machine gun), which was a short gun resembling those used by Chicago gangsters in the 1930s. A PPZh (*pokhodno-polevaia zhena*, campaign field wife) was a nurse or female soldier who lived openly with an officer. It was a term of abuse, uttered in a whisper.

Because Soviet soldiers were not allowed to surrender, the narrator realizes that he will inevitably face questioning about having been taken prisoner. When he is captured by the Germans a second time, he mulls over his options and decides that, during Germany's death throes, armed men are the ones with the best chance of survival: "It doesn't matter whose weapons, German or Soviet, as long as they're weapons" (Bender 1984a, 274). He agrees to enlist in the Division.

Bender's *Stantsiia Puhalovska* (1984) describes life in a small settlement in the Donbas during the period of *liknep* (*likvidatsiia nepysmennosti*, eradication of illiteracy). The book covers the Ukrainization of the 1920s and Stalin's rule in the 1930s. In school, along with reading classics of Ukrainian literature, children learn songs they believe are folk tunes but are in fact compositions of the Sich Riflemen. During May Day festivities they attend obligatory marches and are required to listen to speeches full of words like "Dniprelstan," "Five-Year Plan," "industrialization," "bourgeoisie," "Comintern," "collectivization," and *kurkul*. Afterwards everyone runs off as quickly as possible, throwing the banners and posters into the mud, over fences, and onto piles. The narrator recalls one old man urinating onto a pile, while bystanders roar with laughter and applaud: "This both amazed and disillusioned me. It turned out that many people went to the demonstration without an uplifting festive feeling or passion in their hearts" (Bender 1984b, 67). For many the holidays are simply an opportunity to drink for two days. In 1933, however, there was no parade, either on 1 May or in November, to celebrate the October Revolution. The famine had killed off the population and demoralized city leaders (67).

The book describes popular entertainment in the 1930s: films, radio music, tangos, and the songs of Petro Leshchenko (Bender 1984b, 76–82, 99–112). The idea of the Ukrainian language as "unfit for tenderness" has been instilled in the narrator, so when he first hears Leshchenko sing he is stunned by "the soulful voice and masterful accompaniment" (111).

Bender's (1954) *Marsh molodosty* was written in England between the years 1949 and 1953. It describes the Division's time in Slovakia and

Slovenia, focusing on tensions between men from Eastern and Western Ukraine. Captain Siroshtan, an Easterner, has taken over an unruly unit. Chyhovskyi, a Westerner who, between 1939 and 1941, was forced to study Marx and Lenin, at first distrusts him. Chyhovskyi accepted the arrival of Hitler's troops as the dawn of a new age. Then came disillusionment and disorientation. Friends joined the underground or began to serve the new masters. Chyhovskyi bided his time. In 1943, reassuring himself that the Division could renew the famous traditions of the Sich Riflemen, he was one of the first to sign up and was sent to officer school. He dislikes Easterners for their unpolished manners, their tendency to argue with superiors and to take liberties when, first, permission ought to be obtained.

Siroshtan, on the other hand, has come to the Division from the UVV, a force recruited by the Germans in the late stages of the war mainly from Eastern Ukrainian POWs, in the same way as General Vlasov's ROA was raised from captured Russian soldiers. Siroshtan had been arrested by the GPU in the 1930s and sent to work in the Siberian gold mines, where he witnessed how many workers were killed or crippled. At the war's outbreak he was given the option of joining the Red Army and took it.

Siroshtan is a good commander and respected by his men. He proves his worth when one company mutinies, robs a Slovak family, and creates panic in the village. The family had expressed pro-Russian sympathies and, after drinking, the soldiers smashed some dishes and took a watch and money from the owner. The company now refuses to give up two soldiers who are threatened with courts martial. Siroshtan is able to defuse the situation.

While the Division is in Slovenia, he meets another Eastern Ukrainian, one of an estimated 2.4 million *Ostarbeiter* who were sent from the territory of present-day Ukraine to work in the Reich. This man was imprisoned in a concentration camp after hitting a farmer with a pitch fork, but he escaped and joined a partisan group in Slovenia. Here he witnessed Soviet officers taking control of the group and local partisans handing over captured soldiers to the Yugoslavian secret service to be tortured and killed (Bender 1984b, 8). This Easterner has himself been captured by the Galicia Division. He trusts neither side, hates Germans, and believes that the Division is merely another German trick. Although he sees that there is no way back to the Soviet forces or the partisans, he refuses to join the Division. Nonetheless, he is pleasantly surprised to see a fellow Easterner leading a group of mainly Galician soldiers.

The narrator makes clear that Siroshtan's company does not mistreat captured men or civilians. The troops are disciplined and approach their work "with a sense of honour" (Bender 1984b, 69). This depiction of Easterners was perhaps written to influence readers who came from Western Ukraine and had reservations about their Eastern compatriots.

Roman Kolisnyk published many articles on the Division and a number of books. His *Ostannii postril* (Last shot, 2011) is one of the best fictionalized memoirs of life in the Division (Kolisnyk 2011). It deals primarily with events in Slovakia, Slovenia, and Austria but incorporates flashbacks to earlier periods. The text references Erich Maria Remarque's (1929) *Im Westen Nichts Neues (All Quiet on the Western Front)*. In one section towards the end of the book, the narrator agrees with Remarque's attitude towards war, depicting it as a dismal, cynical business. Like the German novelist, Kolisnyk follows the fate of four friends: Stefko, Myrosko, Yarko, and himself. In the end, the narrator's friends are killed, leaving him to tell their story.

The reader observes recruitment, training, interaction with German officers and local civilians, and behaviour during combat. When in Slovakia the soldiers meet naively pro-Russian locals, who are impressed by the fact that the Ukrainians are Catholics, attend church, and recognize the Pope. The local priest is appalled to learn that the church is persecuted in the Soviet Union and repeats that he is familiar with "a different kind of Russian." He is assured: "When they arrive, you'll see for yourself" (Kolisnyk 2011, 149). In Slovenia. Kolisnyk describes captured soldiers being killed by Germans and partisans. As in Remarque, food, hunger, the brutality of basic training, and the foolishness of higher officers receive attention.

Soldiers ask themselves why they signed up. Initially they volunteered for patriotic reasons. The narrator recalls his gymnasium teacher Professor Hrytsai delivering an impassioned lecture that recalled the days of the Sich Riflemen, assuring pupils that history would repeat itself and that the moment to take up arms had arrived (Kolisnyk 2011, 46). Remembered by the narrator at the end of the war, this passage serves as ironic counterpoint to the uninspiring depiction of life in the army, which is a constant struggle with German officers who demand total subordination and who do not understand that the men are Ukrainians, not "Galicians." Kolisnyk's attitude toward *Weltangschauung* instruction echoes other accounts:

Forstreuter began speaking calmly and slowly, explaining the military situation. The more he talked, the more he was carried away by his own words about the "most talented Führer," the "struggle for life and death with the Jewish-communist hordes of Asia and the eventual German victory," the "great comradeship and heroic deeds of Waffen-ss soldiers," the "new Europe and the special role that the ss and we ourselves would play in it." Vretsona translated the talks for us. He did not translate but adapted Forstreuter's lectures, as Kotliarevskyi did Virgil's *Aeneid*. Sometimes Vretsona introduced a joke here and there, at which point Forstreuter, who did not expect such a reaction to his serious political conclusions, would look suspiciously at Vretsona, who with an innocent face would spread his arms, as though asking forgiveness from the entire company for failing to understand political nuances. Sometimes Vretsona would ignore the captain's words and "read his own lecture," full of enthusiasm and optimism about our division being the embryo of a Ukrainian army, filling us with faith in ourselves. In those moments a different enthusiasm filled the soldiers and Forstreuter glowed with pleasure, thinking that we found his ideas uplifting. (78–9)

There are unexpected moments of fraternization. One occurs in the spring of 1945, when the Division's Captain Kuk and the Red Army's Captain Pliushch agree to meet and exchange Easter baskets. Kuk tells his men that Pliushch "is just as much a Ukrainian as you and I; we are children of the same people" (Kolisnyk 2011, 245). With snipers from each side watching in case of treachery, the two captains exchange the traditional greeting "Christ is risen! Truly he is risen!" They swap baskets, shake hands and kiss one another (245–6). This recalls a similar moment during the First World War when Ukrainians in the opposing Austrian and Russian armies celebrated Easter together. A photograph of the event was published in *Chervona kalyna* (Red viburnum), the interwar journal of Ukrainian veterans (249). Some time later, Kolisnyk describes a battlefield scene in which a sniper from the Division who accompanied Kuk has Pliushch in his sights but does not shoot.

Later two soldiers make contact with their countrymen on the Soviet side and secretly visit them to bring back soup. The Division's front-liners turn a blind eye, but the returning men are noticed by a German officer, arrested, and executed for "communicating with the enemy, thus undermining army morale and discipline in the struggle for the fatherland" (Kolisnyk 2011, 252). Such moments of fraternization were common in Austria, where Ukrainians faced each other on both sides of the front. They are recorded in written and oral accounts.[10]

An ironic moment occurs when the Division is finally renamed the 1st Division of the UNA. As the men swear allegiance to Ukraine, they are given badges with the trident, which everyone attaches to their caps, including German officers. The emblem, as the narrator remarks, had been forbidden until that moment (Kolisnyk 2011, 257).

Oleh Lysiak, the Division's most popular prose writer, served in the force's press corps first as a photographer and then as a correspondent, in which capacity he was often close to the front line.[11] According to him, the training of correspondents consisted of leafing through photos from the front and filming football matches. They learned the use of firearms and "how to crawl through mud on their bellies" (Lysiak 1996, 65). He recalls the Ukrainians teaching their Swedish, Walloon, Flemish, Dutch, and French fellow-trainees how to sing the Division's song "Khloptsi pidemo … za Ukrainu, za ridni prava" (Boys, let's go … for Ukraine, for its rights) (66). On one occasion his fellow correspondent Myron Levytskyi (who later gained fame as an artist) lost contact with his detachment and spent a week behind Soviet lines, When he made it back successfully, "the German command was not sure whether to shoot him as a deserter or decorate him for bravery" (66).

Lysiak provides many revealing details. He informs us, for instance, that one of his reports for *Lvivski visti* (Lviv news) had a line from a partisan song removed. The censor excised the words: "the fettered are throwing off their chains." Lysiak also describes a meeting with a man from the 4th Galician ss Volunteer Regiment, one of the handful who survived the siege of Ternopil. The writer also informs us that Konstantin Simonov, the Russian novelist, had been a reporter on the Soviet side during the siege. According to Lysiak (1996, 67), when Simonov asked a Soviet officer about the enemy, the reply was: "they fight remarkably well."[12]

In postwar years, Lysiak worked with Oleksa Horbach, Liubomyr Ortynskyj, Stepan Konrad, Liubomyr Rykhtytskyi, and Yevhen Shypailo on the Division's periodical *Visti* and the Munich-based *Ukrainska trybuna*

(Ukrainian tribune), which was published under licence from the United States Military Authorities. In 1953, he immigrated to Philadelphia, where he was employed by the newspaper *Ameryka* (America) and wrote for *Ukrainskyi samostiinyk* (Ukrainian independentist), which appeared in Munich between the years 1957 and 1975.

Several editors recognized Lysiak's talent. Zenon Tarnavskyi, who under German occupation edited *Ukrainska trybuna* (Ukrainian tribune), encouraged the author to record his experiences, as did Mykhailo Ostroverkha, who was attached for a time to the Division's team of journalists. Lysiak's war diaries were later used to produce two novels and a collection of stories. He also edited an anthology of articles about the battle of Brody, a history of twentieth-century Ukrainian theatre, and composed radio sketches and stage performances. In Philadelphia, he worked as a lawyer and financial inspector.[13]

The writer grew up on Virmenska vulytsia (Armenian street) in Lviv. In 1918, as a five-year-old, he witnessed the revolutionary struggle for the city, wandered among sailors festooned with bullet belts, found cartridges near dead soldiers and placed them on streetcar lines to watch them explode like fireworks. He saw mutilated corpses of high school students from the Cadet Corps and the bodies of drowned Red Guard soldiers (Lysiak 1996, 29). In 1932, he heard the ringing of bells throughout the city in protest against the execution of two young OUN members, Vasyl Bilas and Dmytro Danylyshyn, who killed a policeman during a failed "expropriation" (robbery) attempt.

His father sent him to a Polish school, where students learned about the bloody eighteenth-century peasant uprisings against Polish rule and read Henryk Sienkiewicz's *Ogniem i mieczem* (With fire and sword, 1883–84). In the 1930s he witnessed the destruction of the Maslosoiuz co-op store, the burning of the Shevchenko Society's bookstore, and the rioting of Polish crowds who smashed windows in Ukrainian homes shouting "Give us the young hogs!" (*kaban*, meaning young hog, was a derogatory term for a Ukrainian) (Lysiak 1996, 30). He joined the OUN's expeditionary forces (*pokhidni hrupy*) and witnessed the execution of his friends when the mass arrests of OUN-B members began on 15 September 1941. In 1943, he belonged to an underground group directed by Yaroslav Starukh (alias Stiah or Obukh). At that time the OUN opposed the creation of a German-led division. Soon afterwards Starukh was arrested and Lysiak lost contact with the underground for several weeks. He saw recruitment posters for the Division on streets with the words "Don't Weep, but Fight!" (Ne rydai, a dobuvai!), the same slogan that was on the medals of the Sich Riflemen. When he learned from friends that the Gestapo was looking for him, he decided that the best place to hide would be in the Division: "In any case, I was waiting for some sort of justification, because as a young man looking for 'action' I wanted to join the army" (60).

In his postwar fictionalized memoir, Lysiak records events from the soldier's point of view, taking care to avoid pathos. *Za striletskyi zvychai* (In the riflemen's footsteps, 1953), published in eight thousand copies, was a bestseller by émigré standards and garnered many positive reviews. Like Kolisnyk's *Ostannii postril*, it follows the lives of a group of friends from Lviv: Bohdan Garan, Anatol Rudych, Roman Denysiuk, and Vasyl Balytskyi. Other characters include Mrs Grets, who arranges safe houses in Lviv for the OUN, and the female protagonists Natalia Berezynska and Mira Valytska. The action begins in 1943 at a time when officers of the former Nachtigall and Roland Battalions remain locked up in the Lontskyi Prison and the call goes out for young men to volunteer for the Division. The four friends enlist. Garan, the only OUN-B member among them, has been instructed by the organization to join. He is sceptical of the recruitment and rejects the "romanticized" image of war associated with the Sich Riflemen. In time, however, he realizes the motivational value of the Riflemen's history.

Several real individuals can be recognized behind their fictional names.[14] German officers are given their correct names: Freitag, Beyersdorff, Renberger, Kleinow, Forstreuter, and Wiens. A number of scenes retell events from published materials. For example, Khronoviat's report is used to describe events at Huta Peniatska, but Lysiak's narrative focuses on the deaths of the Ukrainian soldiers and leaves out the killing that came after the military action. In the spring of 1944 he was attached as a cameraman to the 4th Galician ss Volunteer Regiment. Here he wrote his first report and began his career as a correspondent (Lysiak 1996, 9).

Za striletskyi zvychai describes a confrontation with German soldiers who are prevented from stealing cattle shortly before the battle of Brody, the same incident recorded elsewhere in written and oral testimony (Lysiak 1953, 118–23). Lysiak also confirms the large number of executions for minor transgressions that took place in Slovakia and Slovenia, and the discussions with Slovak civilians who were convinced that the Russians were "brother Slavs" and "good" people (105, 182, 206).

Like Kolisnyk, he has an eye for paradox and irony. General Freitag's speech blaming the Ukrainians for the defeat at Brody is recalled, along with the angry response of Harmider (Brygider), who in Bisantz's presence demands that the general be removed for losing his nerve and resigning his office (Lysiak 1953, 163–4).

The novel reproduces Beyersdorff's bad-tempered parting speech at the war's end, which Olshtynskyj (Ortynskyi) is forced to translate. As Beyersdorff quits the Division, he states that the Germans had "fought shoulder to shoulder" with Ukrainians, but the latter could not be made into soldiers because they were "robbers and bandits" and desired all along "to escape our command" (Lysiak 1953, 320). He orders the German officers and men to move to one side of the meadow, which is surrounded by American tanks. Beyersdorff then announces: "I am returning your criminals and thieves. We wanted to try them in our military court; now let them go to you!" The narrator continues:

> From behind the lines several soldiers appeared with hands tied behind their backs. They were led by gendarmes with machine guns.
> "They're going to shoot them ... shoot them! Here at the front!" someone in the back whispered hysterically. "And us, us too ..."
> From the green tanks, machine guns barrels were raised; semicircular shell cartridges were lifted; metal locks of machine guns clacked. The barrels lifted and slowly pointed toward the defenceless column, which the Germans had now quit. (Lysiak 1953, 320)

When the momentary vision of a mass execution passes, Beyersdorff tells the Ukrainians to keep to one side of a meadow between the three hills on which the tanks are placed; guns will open fire on anyone who crosses this boundary. Olshtynskyi comments that, until that moment, he had not fully understood the Germans: "Even the Gestapo in the Vienna prison did not teach me what I learned this evening" (Lysiak 1953, 321). The event symbolizes the final break from the illusion of being comrades in arms (*Waffenkamaraden*) with the Germans. It is the final abandonment of Ukrainians by frustrated and defeated German soldiers. Lysiak's version was later confirmed by Ferkuniak's account of this event.[15]

The book describes the fighting at Brody, Straden, and Bad Gleichenberg in Austria. The last confrontation provides a moment of restrained pathos when the unheroic death of a simple, reliable hutsul soldier is described in Tolstoian fashion (Lysiak 1953, 254–5). In a later essay Lysiak also describes the fraternization with enemy soldiers in these last days. The fusiliers in Huliak's company exchange Easter greetings and gifts with delegated soldiers from the enemy side, who apparently are from the Kamianets-Podilsk Rifle Regiment. In Roman Herasymovych's company, one soldier plays melodies on his harmonica for nearby Soviet troops on the front line and receives encouragement from them – "Hey, Galician, play something more!" – until they warn him: "That's enough, the *politruk* is coming" (Lysiak 1996, 70). Lysiak was told by a German officer not to write about this incident or about the Division's being renamed the UNA (72).

The protagonists know that their war will not end on 8 May 1945. The narrator reminds readers that most veterans continued the struggle to free their homeland by working in literature, journalism, education, and scholarship. In the final pages, Garan observes the graves of English heroes buried in Westminster Abbey and realizes that the label "ss" will follow the men of the Galicia Division for the rest of their lives and that they will be taunted by the question: "Who told you to enlist?" Like the Polish soldiers who fought on the British side, many men feel they have wasted their lives (Lysiak 1953, 334). Garan at that moment recalls his initial reaction to the recruitment, his refusal to "fight for margarine," to be "an agent," or to carry the "red viburnum ballast" (334). He agonizes over whether it was the correct decision, whether gaining military expertise for the revolution's "dirty work" was ever a realistic goal, and whether there had been other alternatives. In the end, he concludes, if he were offered the opportunity to live life again and experience its every mistake, pain, and misfortune in the same way – he would gladly accept the offer (335).

The opening and closing scenes of Lysiak's second fictionalized memoir, *Liudy taki, iak my* (People like us, 1960), portray former members of the underground who now live in the United States. The focus is not on the Division but on a group of men and women who, during the war, were drawn into the Lviv underground. They include the Kurhanskyi family, whose father is a veteran of the UHA, his three sons who are all murdered by the Germans, and his daughter who ends her life in a Soviet concentration camp in Karaganda. The chief protagonist is Stakho (Yevstakhii) Maryniak. At the beginning of the novel he is an apolitical student in a Polish high school. Because of his ability as a soccer player he makes the

Poetry and Memoirs • **259**

local Polish team, in which he witnesses anti-Ukrainian and anti-Jewish behaviour. He becomes friends with a Jewish boy, Yakiv Vizel, after defending him from a physical attack, and it is Vizel who tells him he should not be afraid of admitting his Ukrainian identity. When Stakho is drafted into the Polish army, he helps a Ukrainian called Vasyl Remega to avoid arrest by hiding the latter's copy of the illegal OUN publication *Surma* (Bugle). After the German invasion Stakho is thrown into a POW camp from which Remega, an OUN member, rescues him. Stakho's soccer skills propel him into a German team, and this allows him to deliver messages for the OUN wherever the team travels. When the German-Soviet war breaks out, his "Ukrainization" has been completed and he joins the UPA.

Much of the book's interest lies in the process of political radicalization among young people. This applies not only to Stakho but also to Vizel, who, under German occupation, assumes a new name and helps the Ukrainian underground as a doctor. It also applies to a Frenchman who escapes POW camp and finds his way into the UPA. At the end of the novel Stakho and the Frenchman are killed attempting to send a radio broadcast to the West.

Women are also politicized. They keep safe houses, act as couriers, and gather information. Their lives are particularly difficult because they have to manoeuvre in complex political situations while avoiding the advances of German and, after 1944, Soviet officers. Under German occupation they witness arrests by the Gestapo and the execution of fighters in the Resistance whose bodies are left hanging in the streets. They develop conspiratorial skills, learn to use false IDs, passwords, and secret messages. Detecting spies becomes part of their daily existence. The Resistance conducts assassinations, one of which leads to the killing of German officers in charge of the Yanivska Street concentration camp. When the Soviets return, the women are hounded by the NKVD, and all three heroines, Oksana Kurhanska, Katria Taran, and Rita Haidai, end their lives in a Karaganda concentration camp.

This background of suffering and sacrifice is contrasted to the comfortable life of emigrés in the US. The message is that in the West former members of the underground should support the Resistance. The emigrés help UPA fighters, who continue to arrive in the West and work with radio programs to broadcast information about Ukraine. All of this, however, does little to influence Western opinion. Another important message is that Jews, Poles, and Western Europeans can be allies in the liberation struggle.

Vidlamky "Shybky u vikni" (Fragments of "The window pane," 1996) is a collection of stories and essays written in postwar decades. Like the fictionalized memoirs, they represent an attempt to come to terms with a generational experience. The passage of time has allowed Lysiak to reflect on the complexities of the Ukrainian identity. His generation grew up in Lviv among Poles and Jews; they spoke Polish, or a Ukrainian heavily laced with Polish. In fact, the identity of some of his fictional characters appears more Polish than Ukrainian. *Vidlamky* develops this theme. He comments on the peculiar Lviv dialect: a mixture of Ukrainian, Polish, German, Yiddish, and local urban banter, a language with roots in the city's interwar cabarets, songs, wit, and humour. It reflected a collective historical experience: life under Austro-Hungarian, Polish, Soviet, and German rule.

Hybridity is a feature of this generation's identity. Individuals change political convictions, as his Polish-Ukrainian and Jewish-Ukrainian protagonists demonstrate. The fluid, evolving nature of their views is reflected in the clouded, naïve reasoning behind their motivation as soldiers or freedom fighters. In one piece, written in 1993 on the fiftieth anniversary of the Division's creation, he offers a retrospective: "It was clear after Stalingrad that the Third Reich would fall and in my opinion even the organizers in the Military Board no longer believed in Germany's victory (what, in any case, would this victory have given us?). Not without cause, voices were raised (even in the legal sector) arguing that we should not expect any 'universals' [declarations of independence] or a Ukrainian army" (Lysiak 1996, 55).

However, service in the Red Army or in German labour camps and factories was a less attractive option. The Division, after all, offered an opportunity to escape the SD and Gestapo. Lysiak recalls that political leaders were enthusiastic about the force in the spring of 1943 because they were "finally" getting weapons, including artillery, and real training. The dominant opinion at the time was that "someone had to go" because the UPA was not a viable alternative. Lysiak does not present the UPA's weakness as justification. He argues that young people enlisted because they hoped that at the war's end both antagonists would be exhausted and their army would play a role in the struggle for a state. In his view, both the UPA and the Division represented two paths to the same goal (Lysiak 1996, 55).

Fifty years later, this argument was still controversial, and Lysiak posed the question: Did the Military Board expect Germany to change its plans concerning Ukraine? Was it expecting Berlin to do a deal with the Allies and turn against the Soviets? The decision to enlist had been a leap into a void, into a dubious and unclear future. Already in 1954 Bohdan Pidhainyi had written in *Ukrainskyi samostiinyk*: "The Division was an enormous piece of foolishness [nisenitnytsia] meant only to serve the career of the Governor of Galicia, Wächter" (quoted in Lysiak 1996, 55). Lysiak had immediately challenged this, stating that the soldiers saw themselves as fighting and dying for Ukraine, not for Wächter's career. Pidhailnyi replied:

> Thanks to the political awareness and position taken by the Division's soldiers and officers we came out of that adventurism [avantura] with honour, without staining the reputation of the Ukrainian soldier. Therefore, there is no difference between the former soldiers of the USS [Sich Riflement], the UPA, and the Ukrainians in the Red Army – all of whom fought and died for Ukraine. But there is a difference in the conceptions, and this is the issue. We are not today discussing whether we, soldiers of the Division, were ready to die for Ukraine. This is clear and incontrovertible. The problem is with the political conception, which is something different. I today as a front-line officer of the Division insist: the creation of the Division on the German side in those political circumstances was politically foolish. We should and must learn a lesson from this. (Quoted in Lysiak 1996, 56–7)

In 1993, Lysiak was still mulling the issue. On the one hand, he argued, the soldiers went to fight "for Ukraine," for "its rights," in the footsteps of the Sich Riflemen. On the other hand, the justification for creating the Division was dubious. Like Ivan Kedryn and many others, he still found the idea problematic. Nonetheless, like his fictional protagonists, when asked whether under the same circumstances he would again enlist, his answer was positive. He quoted Yurii Yanovskyi's classic novel *Chotyry shabli* (Four swords, 1930), a work of revolutionary romanticism describing the armed struggles of 1918–20, where the author writes: "There's only one moment when the bird of happiness alights on the ground and must be grasped. If you miss it, you'll have to wait many years" (Lysiak 1996, 57). In 1993, Lysiak concludes: "Fifty years ago we thought this moment had arrived for us young people, and we could catch this bird" (57).

Several stories and essays in this collection also deal with the postwar period. The author describes the wretched conditions faced by the

Division's men in the American POW camp. After being separated from the Germans, they were reduced to eating pickles and grass. The field kitchen shot a horse and made a soup from the meat. Lysiak (1996, 72) and his fellow correspondent Lutskyi made their escape and "became civilians." He notes that, within a couple of years, they were writing for émigré publications and helping to create *Visti*. At that time, Oles Honchar's trilogy *Praporonostsi* (Flag bearers, 1946–48) appeared in Ukraine. An example of Soviet myth-making, it was awarded the Stalin Prize in 1948. Lysiak's *Z striletskyi zvychai* was conceived, at least in part, as a response to it.

In his last stories Lysiak tries to covey the complexities of human fate. He reports the remarkable true story of two brothers, Hnat and Hryhorii Rohek, who end up fighting on opposite sides. Hryts was born in Wilkes-Barr near Scranton, where his father worked in the interwar years. Both boys then lived in Poland. Hryts was in Danzig (Gdańsk) studying engineering when the Germans invaded and took him into the Wehrmacht as an interpreter. He was captured by a Polish detachment near Przemyśl.

By chance his younger brother Hnat was serving in this detachment. Later, Hnat was captured by the Germans and sent to a POW camp, from which he was released following the intervention of the UTSK. He, too, was forced to become an interpreter for the Germans, then signed up for the Galicia Division, was sent to France for training, and then to Monte Cassino, Italy, where he was told to broadcast agitation to Polish soldiers.

By that time Hryts had returned to the family farm, where he was arrested by the Soviets as an ex-German soldier and was sent to Siberia, where he joined Anders Army. He found himself in Monte Cassino on the other side of the front, listening to his younger brother's voice broadcasting German agitation. The younger brother on the German side was wounded and sent to a hospital in France, where the Americans found him, set him to work in the kitchen, and then made him a GI. He ended up on the River Elbe. Here he met his American-born older brother fighting in the Anders Army. They were reintroduced to one another by a bewildered American officer who was unable to understand the situation.

The older brother Hryts went on to serve five years in the French Foreign Legion and immigrated to Canada. In 1952 he became a corporal in the Canadian Royal Rifles and joined the UN peace-keepers in Korea. Here he once more met his younger brother Hnat, who had immigrated to the United States and joined the 172 Pennsylvania Division. Both men served under the UN flag before being forced to retreat by North Korean forces (Lysiak 1996, 133–7).

Equally complicated is the story of Osyp Khoma. Born in Vienna, he grew up in Stanislaviv but fell in love with the sea when he was in Gdynia and joined the merchant navy. He visited New York on twenty-four occasions, decided to try his luck in the city as a professional boxer, and became a star pugilist after knocking out the German Herbert Runge in Warsaw. The former world champion Benny Leonard became his trainer. The war broke out while he was in Gdynia on a trip to Europe. He was taken into the Polish army and defended the city until taken prisoner by the Germans, at which point the UTSK intervened to obtain his release.

In 1943, Khoma joined the Division, fought his way out of the encirclement at Brody, and was captured near Lviv. He was sent to Siberia but, as a former Polish citizen, was repatriated to Poland. Here he joined the UPA company of Stepan Stebelskyi (alias Khrin) and fought in the Lemko region, where Karol Swierczewski, the former Red Army general and then deputy defence minister in the Soviet-installed Polish government, was killed. Khoma was in the UPA group that broke out to the West in 1947 and made it to the Mittenwald DP camp. He began boxing again and immigrated to Connecticut, where he worked as an estate manager. Many Ukrainians in the postwar émigré generation were familiar with similarly astonishing peripatetic biographies.

16

POPULAR FICTION

The first popular literature by veterans was printed on a Gestetner machine in Bellaria and Rimini.[1] The periodical *Osa* (Wasp) began appearing on 12 June 1945 and featured the caricatures of Orest Slupchynskyi (Slupchynskyj, alias Go-Go).[2] Volodymyr Kaplun, a writer and artist, signed humorous letters to the editor as Fedia Yushkyi.[3] The camp had its own conversational language, which included words derived from Polish, German, English, Italian, and Lviv's urban argot. When Slupchynskyi republished the collected issues of *Osa* in 2013, he included a dictionary of terms.[4] The term *selepko* was coined by soldiers to describe themselves. Yurii Tys popularized it in his *Shchodennyk natsionalnoho heroia Selepka Lavochky* (Diary of the national hero Selepko Lavochka, 1954), which became the Division's version of Jaroslav Hašek's *Good Soldier Svejk*.

In Rimini, Vasyl Davydiak (pseudonyms Vasyl De-Vu, Misko Makolondra, Kronikous) was a favourite performer. He came out of Lviv's literary-artistic scene, worked for the camp's youth publication *Iunatskyi zryv* (Youth revolt), the theatre, and the *Shafa hraie* radio broadcasts. His character creations Misko Makolondra and Hryts Maznytsia (performed by Mykola Maliuzhynskyi) were favourites both in the camp and later at literary gatherings in Canada (Zahachevskyi 1968, 132).

Oleksii Devlad (pseudonym Zaporozhets-Devlad) was also known for his humorous stories. Born in 1885 into a family that had for generations worked as ferrymen (*lotsmany*) near today's city of Dnipro, he was the oldest *dyviziinyk* and "enlisted" in order to escape the Soviet Union. Devlad had written about the Dnipro ferrymen in 1927, when he met the scholar

Figure 16.1 General Mykhailo Krat. From Orest Slupchynskyi's *Zibralasia Kumpaniia* (1946). The caption reads: "He led us to the camp, like Moses led sons of the kahal – Moses brought the stones ... He got the rank of general."

Figure 16.2 Portrait of the writer Oleksii Devlad (Zaporozhets) by Volodymyr Kaplun, Rimini camp, 1946. From Zaporozhets-Devlad, *V odvichnii borotbi*, 1955.

and writer Viktor Petrov, who was researching the culture of river workers during an expedition of the vuan (All-Ukrainian Academy of Sciences) Ethnographic Commission. A team from the Dnipropetrovsk Historical-Archeological Museum made the study in consultation with the scholar Dmytro Yavornytskyi. Devlad, who was a founder of the Dnipro ferrymen's *artil*, or co-operative association, was a consultant (Andrieiev 2012, 50). In the following year he helped the commission collect historical and ethnographic materials and wrote a study of the ferrymen's ancient and unique association.[5] The Dniprelstan dam was built at the time and soon flooded a vast area, putting an end to the association and profession.

His *Obiznalys* (They became acquainted, 1948) appeared in Rimini in one hundred copies (Zahachevskyi 1968, 126, 172). A farce reminiscent of Gogol's story "Christmas Eve," it portrays an incompetent, conceited village head. The story *Harbuzova misteriia* (Pumpkin mystery, 1956) was published in Argentina, where Devlad settled after the war. It satirizes the collective farm system. Comrade Yakubets, the head of one farm, decides to save money by feeding the workers exclusively with pumpkins, which are plentiful. They are served three times a day, each time prepared differently. Meetings and study sessions take place, but a secret party council makes the real decisions. The fear of authority is pervasive, fuelled by denunciations and arrests, but the tone is semi-serious, in the spirit of Orwell's *Animal Farm*.

At one point the farmers protest; curse Stalin, the Communist Party, and Soviet power; sing songs calling for the tsar's return; and lament their poverty. However, they eventually disperse and learn to prepare pumpkins in various ways. Complainers are removed and the head is praised for his success in cutting costs. The party's hypocritical ideology and rhetoric are exposed, as are its view of ruthlessness as a virtue and its readiness to blame all complaints on the stupidity of farmers. Although people laugh at the head behind his back, their behaviour is servile. Sycophants multiply after NKVD agents remove outspoken critics.

The farm saves money by not having to purchase products, and the authorities lavish praise on the head, who begins to dream of a promotion, an apartment, electricity, and a servant. His own family eats meat and a varied diet. When one village child dies he refuses to see the mother. Strange rumours begin to circulate about a new kind of person being born, with short arms, small mouths, no brain, one eye in the back of the head – perhaps the kind of creature that can survive on this diet. Then a mass pregnancy occurs, for which the head is blamed. The women beat him and fight among themselves over slanders concerning the pregnancies. Eventually it turns out that the diet has led to mass stomach problems and unhealthy swellings.

Evstakhii Zahachevskyi was best known for his memoir *Spohady frontovyka* (A front-liner's memoir, 1952), but he also produced two popular novels about the Division. *Lvivska bratiia* (Lviv brotherhood, 1962) describes life in Lviv and Przemyśl in 1939. The hero, Roman, works for the underground, smuggling information across the border. He and the other young protagonists have grown up together in Lviv, watched their Ukraina team play soccer, and attended demonstrations and the *hahilky* (spring celebrations) at Easter. When the Division's creation is announced, they are overjoyed that at last they will have their own army and can "pummel

Popular Fiction • **267**

the Russkies (kropyty katsapa)" (Zahachevskyi 1962, 168). Roman joins the Division in Neuhammer, announcing that they are not going to war to fight for the Germans but for their own cause: "It's not for us here to decide ... whether we should or shouldn't be on the German side. There are other people who have thought long and hard before deciding to create the Division" (174). Zahachevskyi's second book, *Ii rehit ne liakav* (Her laughter was not frightening, 1975), depicts life on the front line, especially during Brody. Various protagonists are presented, some as young as seventeen. A number speak in the jargon of Lviv's street apaches (*batiary*). A few have previously served in the Polish army. Combat is presented without heroics, and many stories end in an individual's death. A couple of Lviv apaches, Filko and Milko, enlist together and remain inseparable. Both books recreate the social and political atmosphere of the day and the psychology of Lviv's teenagers. They are closely related to the fictionalized memoirs of Bender, Kolisnyk, and Lysiak but are less successful at capturing the reader's imagination and lack the critical insights found in Zahachevskyi's memoir.

Stepan Liubomyrskyi (real name Liubomyr Rykhtytskyi) began publishing stories in *Zhyttia v tabori* under the pseudonym Elerson. He completed the Drohobych gymnasium and studied in the Lviv Polytechnical Institute. After the war he moved to Chicago, contributed articles to the veterans' journal *Visti*, and continued publishing fiction until his death in 1983.

According to a Rimini colleague, Liubomyrskyi received better quality food, including thicker soup, supposedly because he worked for the "English service." What function he served was a mystery. Whenever friends entered the English service's tent he was busy on a typewriter, no doubt composing his first three novels (Zahachevskyi 1968, 123). Nine more followed, all tales of espionage and adventure focused on the political underground in Ukraine.[6] More than any other writer he created the myth of a courageous, principled Ukrainian Resistance fighting in dangerous conditions against a ruthless enemy. The structure of this fiction is an eschatological showdown between good and evil with one teleogogical drive – the Soviet regime's collapse.

In the 1950s, he published *Pid molotom viiny* (Under war's hammer, 1955–56), which covers life in Galicia under the Soviet occupation of 1939 to 1941 and the early months of the German occupation in 1941. This second part is particularly interesting for its depiction of how the NKVD prisons were opened and murdered bodies discovered, and how the Ukrainian militia was hastily established. The chief protagonist is Bohdan Dub, a member of the OUN, who becomes deputy head of the militia in a Galician town. His strained relations with the Germans are described, leading to his arrest in the final pages, but the tensions between the Ukrainian police and the Germans are only part of the plot. There are Polish nationalists who pass themselves off as Ukrainians in order to infiltrate the police, Soviet spies who have remained active, and mafia-like gangs of criminals of different nationalities who compete among themselves and are inexorably drawn into political struggles. As in the film *Casablanca* (1942), it is never clear who is loyal to what cause, or what turn the political situation might take. There is anger in the local population and a desire to punish not only those who have collaborated with the Soviet occupation but also their entire families. Daria Vashkivska is such a victim. When a voice from the crowd objects to her being blamed for her brother's behaviour, someone cries:

> "Look at that! An advocate! Go defend the Jews, over there, where the Germans are driving them along the street, see?! ...
> Indeed, at that moment the Germans were leading several dozen educated Jews with armbands. Each held a large broom and bucket. They were being led somewhere to clean up. People watched in silence, as though confounded.
> "Look, look, there's old rabbi Birnbaum ...
> "And Professor Ainleger"
> "Look, old Vegner, who owns three buildings in the centre" ...
> "All of them well heeled" ...
> "What a fate," sighed someone.
> "Why didn't they leave? They could have gone with the Bolsheviks."
> "Leave? That's easy to say. Just try and leave for somewhere today!"
> (Liubomytskyi 1955–56 2:92)

The novel depicts this confusing period. The crowd distrusts or brushes aside the new militia and is ready to drag off anyone it perceives as responsible for the suffering inflicted by the Soviets. Some groups blackmail or browbeat the militia. The Germans order it to bring all weapons to them, while the underground demands that the same weapons be secretly delivered to their organization.

Most of Liubomyrskyi's works, however, deal not with the war itself, but with the period between 1945 and 1950, when the UPA is fighting against

Popular Fiction • **269**

the second imposition of Soviet rule in Galicia. *Khai rossudyt mech* (Let the sword decide, 1948) is notable for dealing with women in the UPA, who often serve as couriers. Their patriotic motivation and brutal treatment in NKVD prisons constitutes the main plot line. The author's fascination with the mechanisms and excitement of underground work – coded messages, disguises, assassinations, and infiltration of enemy organizations – suggests that his work for the "English desk" might have been influenced by the recruitment of soldiers for MI6's operations in Soviet-occupied territories.

Early in 1946 the OUN had begun recruiting "messengers" from the Division's soldiers in Rimini and sending them to Poland, often with the help of US intelligence. At that time, the West German, British, and American intelligence services were also recruiting and sending men. Expecting military confrontation with the Soviet Union in Europe, the British co-operated with the OUN-B based in Munich to obtain military intelligence. They were particularly interested in the Kremlin's atomic capability, which became evident in 1949. A so-called K-3 operation was formed in that year, and about ten groups were parachuted into Poland and Ukraine by the British between 1951 and 1955. Two of the Division's soldiers, Bohdan Pidhainyi and Bohdan Matsiv (Maciw), were involved in training the K-3 operatives who were sent as couriers to make contact with the underground.[7] The Americans in turn supported the rival UHVR group, which was also based in Munich.

Liubomyrskyi romanticized the UPA, which he promoted as a symbol of militant struggle for a noble cause. His later novels were published in Canada and Britain by Novyi shliakh (New pathway), Homin Ukrainy (Echo of Ukraine), and Ukrainian Publishers. The first was an organ of the OUN's Melnyk wing, the other two of the Bandera wing. Both political organizations distanced themselves from the Division but embraced the idea of the UPA as a pan-Ukrainian resistance movement conducting a heroic struggle against Germans and Soviets. Two of the author's works on this topic, *Zhorstoki svitanky* (Cruel dawns, 1947) and *Nikoly ne zabudu* (I'll never forget, 1984), were made into feature films in Canada in 1966 and 1969, respectively.

Zhorstoki svitanky, completed in June of 1946, describes anti-UPA operations conducted by the NKVD in the Carpathian Mountains. Female Russian agents have been sent to infiltrate the Resistance but are successfully unmasked. One of the heroes, Petro Verbiv, states: "Our dawns are cruel. Fate has not spared us its blows; it is tempering us in preparation for even harder tasks. We have to understand that serving for a thousand years at the border of two worlds, at the border of two epochs, is not an easy task; such duty demands of us much more than of every other people" (Liubomyrskyi 1947b 2:232). He believes that the country's resurrection will eventually occur and will shake the world, which will understand how much it owes Ukrainians. With this novel the theme of self-sacrificing devotion to the cause of independence became a leitmotif in all the author's works.

Mizh slavoiu i smertiu (Between glory and death, 1948–49) describes the Ukrainian Resistance within the Soviet Union. London's attaché in Moscow has been sent an agent called Bohdan Borbenko who has links with the UPA and encourages the British to use them. The UPA's network even stretches as far as the Soviet scientists who have developed the atomic bomb. Realizing the regime's nature, these scientists would rather destroy their laboratory than allow the military to obtain its secrets. Borbenko unmasks the attaché's secretary, Mr Scott, as a Soviet informer. The attache's daughter Elli (Elizabeth) Nordson urges her father to trust the Ukrainians. Because Britain's own agents have been assassinated, she encourages him to use the UPA's network. However, the attaché refuses, saying: "I cannot speak to them. If the Bolsheviks learn about such a conversation, a war will break out. And I am not sure myself whether the Ukrainians will not inform them of such a meeting, because precisely such a war is in their interests. They want it, knowing that only such a war will give their people freedom" (Liubomyrskyi 1948, 179). Elli, however, trusts the Ukrainians. They are, she says, "fighting the enemy, while England trembles before it" (178–9). Borbenko confides in her:

> One can respect an enemy, but not one that is so base, treacherous and cunning. Compared to the spirit of my people, the spirit of Moscow is very dismal. I am sorry that I cannot be a worshipper of Russian [moskovskoi] literature, or the Russian [moskovskoi] soul, but I hate slavery, and Moscow is an eternal prison-house ... As long as it exists, it will be a symbol of the worst subjection ... It has been educated in this way for centuries, and no one will root this out because it has completely seeped into the Russian [moskovsku] soul! Moscow cannot be any different. (110)

Popular Fiction • **271**

He argues that the entire system has to be destroyed and a common effort must be made to improve society, "in the same way as Christianity once revived the old Roman world and breathed a new better content into it" (110). He is proud that Ukraine refuses to bow its head before this enemy, maintains its spirit, and believes in eventual victory.

In the final pages London tells the British attaché that it desperately needs information on Soviet atomic capability. He begins searching for Borbenko to establish links with the Resistance. An anonymous caller from the UPA informs him that Soviet troops have begun massing on the Manchurian border and that an international conflict is about to erupt.

Plemia vovkiv (Wolf tribe, 1951) was completed in 1948. An underground called "Wolves" has succeeded in penetrating the Soviet atomic industry. When the Anti-Bolshevik Union of Peoples calls for an uprising, the "Wolves" lead a popular revolution. They are in touch with the scientist Yuliian Yuliienko, who works in a special facility in Perm and has developed a ray with great destructive potential. The "Wolves" encourage him to hide this discovery from Soviet authorities.

The Resistance is well organized. It has penetrated every level of the Soviet administration, including the Politburo, and is supported by millions of people who await the decisive conflict. Ukraine, which has always been known for a spirit of insubordination, plays a prominent role in this militant underground. When the armed uprising begins, thousands flock to it and the revolutionaries gain the upper hand in Ukraine. Negotiations are held between all nations who have taken part in the struggle.

The novels describe the UPA in heroic terms and show how the revolt of nationalities will be a crucial factor in the Union's collapse. Perhaps as compensation for the Resistance's "defeat" at the time of writing, Liubomyrskyi depicts its "victory" in the future. However, he also presents the reader with challenges. One of the more interesting aspects is the dialogue between two kinds of Ukrainian patriot: one who feels the Soviet Union must be dissolved immediately and another who is prepared to work for change within the system. These confront one another in verbal exchanges towards the end of each book. In *Mizh slavoiu* it is Nataliia, the daughter of a Kyiv professor, who feels that speaking Russian (albeit poorly) rather than Ukrainian is not an issue. She does not consider Russian culture foreign because she has been raised to see it as the common currency of people living in the Soviet

Union. This provokes Bobrenko to state that young Ukrainians will have to reach national consciousness after a long spiritual struggle that will crystallize their character and soul (Liubomyrskyi 1948, 161).

But conversions occur. In *Plemia vovkiv* it is Rozumovskyi, a Ukrainian member of the Politburo, who undergoes one. He realizes that he has been mistaken in supporting the Union and that, by doing so, he has betrayed his own people and country. When arrested, he informs the secret service that the population of Ukraine, including the part that is not Ukrainian by nationality, has gone through a spiritual transformation. A new, great revolution is approaching, one that the Kremlin will not be able to prevent (Liubomyrskyi 1951, 166). The officer, Lieutenant Marchenko, who is of Ukrainian nationality and has until then fought against the underground, also switches sides and agrees to take up arms against the regime (418–19).

Taiemnyi front (Secret front, 1952) tells the story of Soviet kidnappings and executions in France at the end of the war. It portrays a Ukrainian woman who betrays the underground. In the conclusion two NKVD men guilty of executing four Ukrainians are shot, and although the traitor Vira is allowed to go free she must bear the shame of her actions. The hero tells her: "For three hundred years the Russians have murdered us and over the course of this long period not once has generosity and mercy been understood by them in the way we and the rest of the world do. ... No, they always understand them as weakness and a reason to strike us even harder. This is the terrible and logical truth. This is our enemy's nature" (Liubomyrskyi 1952, 147).

Liubomytskyi's last novels deal with contemporary Ukraine and are influenced by the struggle of the dissident movement for human and civil rights. *Slidamy zapovity* (In the testament's footsteps, 1985) presents this generation. The author states that people with the courage to protest state-organized crimes have appeared over the last decade (Liubomytskyi 1985, 74). He mentions Levko Lukianenko, Vasyl Stus, Viacheslav Chornovil, and Mykola Rudenko, whom he describes as idealists struggling for a democratic Ukraine in which national rights are respected. Even though their tactics are non-violent and they recognize no organized political party, they are preparing the future revolution (39).

Sviatomyr M. Fostun was born in 1924 near Stanislaviv. In postwar years he published several historical novels and essay collections.[8] His *Zviduny stepovykh kohort* (Explorers of the steppe cohorts, 1972), for example, is set in 1648, during the signing of the Treaty of Westphalia that ended the Thirty Years' War. Bohdan Khmelnytskyi's legion of twenty-five hundred Cossacks has fought against the Spanish and Habsburg Empires on the side of France, helping to capture Dunkirk. The men have served as mercenaries so as to gain Western military expertise. Khmelnytskyi intends to raise an army of fifty thousand and then pressure the Polish king to restore Cossack rights and privileges. Cardinal Mazarin, who realizes that Poland is in decline, allows the Cossack army to return to Ukraine. He predicts a bright future for the country and believes that Khmelnytskyi, together with Frederick Brandenburg of Prussia, will overturn the old European order and institute a new one. Before they leave, Khmelnytskyi tells his men:

> We signed up not because we sought fortune, silks, atlases, and star-headed steeds. We went to improve our knowledge of the martial art, to master the Western military profession. And we achieved this. In two years of service we and our Cossacks have learned ten-fold more about military affairs than the Poles and Turks know. We have travelled through much of the world, seen Western Europe, brought glory to the Cossack sword in many battles and have not dishonoured the Cossack name. Those who do not know us well, think that we are simply mercenaries, *condottieri*. But Prince Conde [Louis II de Bourbon] knows better, as does Paris, as do the Poles. (Fostun 1972, 35)

The theme and treatment are not original. Fostun drew heavily on Yurii Kosach's *Rubikon Khmelnytskoho* (Khmelnytskyi's Rubicon, 1943), which is set in Danzig (Gdansk), where the Cossacks have arrived after fighting in Flanders and in which a European coalition is organized by Cardinal Mazarin.

Fostun's most revealing work is probably *Shliakhamy smerty* (Roads of death, 1976), which deals with the Second World War. It portrays Oleh Vyshnevyi, who attends Warsaw University and then in 1939 returns to his native Volhynia after the German invasion. "His own people" tell him to join a German military unit to obtain the desired training and skills. He serves on the eastern front, apparently in Chełm and Volhynia. After deserting in 1943, he becomes a captain in the UPA, is captured by the Germans during a shoot-out, and sent to a concentration camp. As a form of punishment, he is then sent to the front-line special services Battalion 138 (Sonderbatallion), given two months training, and dispatched on various dangerous missions. The novel describes brutal acts by the German and Soviet armies and includes descriptions of demoted German officers and Ukrainians. At one point the main protagonist joins a group sent behind enemy lines. Dressed in NKVD uniforms and carrying false identification, their mission is to bring back news of enemy troop strength and disposition. During this assignment they witness the ugly behaviour of Red Army soldiers who rape women. The novel shows the horrors of war as witnessed by a Ukrainian who has in a short space of time served in three different military forces.

After the war Fostun lived in Wimbledon, in southwest London. He admitted to the *Daily Telegraph* in 2003 that he had been a guard at the Trawniki concentration camp but denied any role in killings (Foggo 2003a, 2003b, 2003c). In 2015, a British researcher told the press that he suspected Fostun of having witnessed the massacre of Jews in the Białystok ghetto in August 1943 (Elgot 2015). Fostun died in a car crash in 2004, shortly after the allegations were made. Although these were never tested in court, they renewed speculation concerning war criminals in the Division. Two men, Fostun and Hryhorii Osovyi (Grigorij Osowoy), have been identified as Trawniki-trained guards who later joined the Galicia Division.[9]

Bearing this earlier history in mind, it appears that Fostun's *Shliakhamy smerty* may have been, in some degree at least, a fictionalized wartime biography. His attachment to the Galicia Division came late in the war and the novel hints at his activity prior to joining. In Britain, Fostun became secretary of the Association of Ukrainians in Great Britain, editor of the newspaper *Ukrainska dumka* (Ukrainian thought) and of the Association's publishing house in the years between 1977 and 2004. In later life he developed a mania for self-aggrandizement. To the amusement of the Division's veterans, he promoted himself to the rank of major and, on his trips to Ukraine, appeared in a self-fashioned uniform.

Yurii Tys (real name Krokhmaliuk) was a staff officer in the Division from late 1944. In 1928 he completed an engineering degree in Vienna and shortly before the war published his first novel. After the war he lived in Buenos Aires, produced ten books, including several historical novels, a play, and collections of short stories. He also wrote two studies of military strategy and a Spanish-language history of the Division.[10] He was critical of the Division's creation. In his UPA *Warfare in Ukraine* (1972) he wrote: "Experience has shown that peoples seeking national liberation may fruitfully create their own military units within the framework of other, alien armies only if they are guaranteed eventual full state independence. In the absence of such a basic understanding, serious conflicts and antagonisms are inevitable between captive peoples and any invader or occupier" (Tys-Krokhmaliuk 1972, xi).

The patriotic adventure story was his preferred genre, and his most widely read book was the science fiction novel *K7: Fantastychne opovidannia* (K7: A fantastic story, 1964). It portrays a family of diapora Ukrainians who are scientists and engineers but remain deeply concerned with the fate of Ukraine. The grandparents and parents have experienced the DP camps. The grandmother was a member of the OUN, and her husband was in the Division, fought at Brody, and met his death in the partisan underground. Semen, an atomic engineer, belongs to the third, youngest generation. He is committed to the liberation struggle and works with his uncle Pavlo, who owns an engineering factory and laboratory. Together they have developed remote controlled mini-rockets and have discovered a fuel made from a rare mineral named K7. They manufacture the rockets in a secret facility in South America.

One rocket is sent to Moscow and drops leaflets demanding that the Kremlin withdraw its military and administrative personnel from Ukraine, free all political prisoners, and allow the national republics to declare independence. The Russian media agency TASS denies any knowledge of the mysterious missile or the leaflets. It claims that disinformation is being spread by Ukrainian nationalists, whom it describes as "enemies of progress and peace, whose goal is to destroy the friendly coexistence of the USSR's people" (Tys 1964, 48). However, additional rockets explode and disintegrate over European and American cities, spreading leaflets. Finally, a rocket destroys the Ministry of State Security (MGB) building in Moscow. Thousands of Russian agents are sent out to search for the source of the rockets and the atomic-like fuel.

To escape the net tightening around them, Semen and his two friends, Panko and Haska, use a large rocket powered by the superfuel to leave the Earth in search of K7 on other planets. They travel through space, visit the moon and Venus, and are pursued for a time by a Russian rocket. Eventually they find a planet composed entirely of K7 and discover beneath its surface the mysterious ruins of a lost civilization. They load up with the superfuel and return to Earth to rejoin Uncle Pavlo. Russian paratroopers have been dropped from a plane and are searching for their underground facility, but the guards, who are members of a secret OUN group, succeed in capturing the intruders.

Because their location has been discovered, the friends are forced to activate their plan for launching a series of rockets. They destroy Moscow's command centres. Chaos spreads in the Soviet Union and the UN announces plans to send international troops to Ukraine and other Soviet republics to maintain order until a legal government can be formed. The remnants of the OUN in Ukraine put out a call to reject the presence of these international troops because the UN's intention is to restore rule from Moscow. Russian military and administrative personnel are forced to leave Ukraine, which becomes a free and independent country. The space travellers come to witness the declaration of independence on Kyiv's St Sophia Square. Their rockets and K7 fuel protect the country from its enemies. Ancient treasures, which have over the generations been taken from Ukraine and kept in Moscow's museums, are returned. Uncle Pavlo is appointed head of a new Ukrainian research centre.

The novel reveals how some émigré nationalists imagined the future and compensated for their own political disappointments. The description of space travel and exploration of new horizons perhaps also represents an admiring tribute to the diaspora, which succeeded in making its way in unfamiliar places and adapting to difficult circumstances. Above all the narrative reflects Cold War anxieties about the Kremlin's long reach, the presence of spies and subversives, and the fear that Western powers were ready to submit to Soviet pressure. The message to younger readers is that the struggle continues, albeit in new and unexpected forms, and that the diaspora has a valuable role to play.

Roman Korotko was born in 1935 and was a student in Rohatyn when in the 1950s he heard of a sensational murder committed during the war. He researched the story and published it in the form of the novel *Provokatsiine vbyvstvo* (Murder provocation, 2013), slightly altering the real names. It was conceived as a tribute to the national liberation movement and published on the seventieth year of the UPA's creation and the Division's founding.

Mykhailo Dovhaniuk, the main protagonist, is from a village near Rohatyn. He is nineteen and has only completed primary school. After joining the Galicia Division in 1943, he is captured by Soviet troops during the final retreat through Austria. During interrogation he claims to have enlisted to obtain food and clothing, and that he never fired a shot against the Red Army. Threatened with execution, he agrees to become a Soviet agent and is provided with an alibi: he is to claim that he spent the war working for a German farmer. He then becomes an informer, is sent back to Ukraine, and told to make contact with the UPA.

Dovhaliuk gradually infiltrates the Resistance, spends time in its safe houses and hidden bunkers, and makes contact with its leaders. His handler, Captain Anosov of the MGB, assigns him tasks of increasing difficulty and danger. He betrays UPA cells and kills two members of the underground. The narrative reveals the UPA's methods of avoiding detection and the Soviet tactics.

Both sides often behave ruthlessly. UPA leaders and members of the SB suspect treachery everywhere and execute suspects. One member of the underground admits his suspicion that the SB has itself been infiltrated and is killing anyone it suspects. Provocateurs in the SB are agents of the NKVD. Soviet search parties disguise themselves as UPA fighters and commit atrocities. Informers work in pharmacies and clinics, and report people who ask for medicines and bandages that might be for wounded underground fighters. Most shockingly, when Dovhaliuk is sent to Kyiv for further training he is told that he can murder NKVD operatives. General Svertsov instructs him that to gain the trust of the OUN-UPA and to penetrate its centre he can kill rank-and-file NKVD men and up to ten officers (Korotko 2013, 231). Mykhailo is told to boast about his service in the Galicia Division, about being at Brody, and about receiving tactical training in the Division.

He realizes that he must murder one relatively significant figure not on the list of untouchables. When he sees that his first handler, Amosov, whom he despises, is not on the list, Mykhailo murders him. His new handler, Major Buhaiov, is happy to have Amosov removed because he covets the latter's post in the NKVD's regional directorate. Eventually, Dovhaliuk is assigned to track down the UPA leader Roman Shukhevych and the OUN leader Roman Kravchuk, who handles Shukhevych's contacts with the emigration.

The local OUN leader Shpak (real name Zenovii Blazhkiv) and his deputy Zenon Dyr act with particular violence. It turns out that Shpak was originally a fanatical believer in an independent Ukraine but sold himself to the enemy and is now destroying the underground movement from within. He issues orders to kill "informers" who are in fact innocent people.

In the denouement, two SB men reveal that Dovhaliuk is a Soviet agent. The latter has become brazen and developed a sense of invincibility. Local people, however, recall that he was never popular. Even as a child he was a "lost sheep," unprincipled, easily led astray, and behaved like a thug. It turns out that he did not join the Division out of patriotic motives but because he was told that the Germans paid well. In the end the SB executes him.

Zenon (real name Yaroslav Haluha) and his commander Vii (real name Yevhen Smyk) are underground leaders in the Rohatyn area. Both have served in the Division and both are liquidated by the treacherous Shpak and Dyr, who themselves were once members of the Division. After he is exposed, the Soviet regime provides Shpak with a new identity and allows him to live quietly in Lviv. Dyr murders his security detail and reveals the underground's hiding places. He too is allowed to start a new life in Lviv after he is exposed, becoming a cloakroom attendant at the Intourist Hotel, where he hands out coats and hats for tips, thus continuing his servile behaviour. The last lines are an admonishment and a warning to the reader not to go against their convictions or serve the enemy, because any individual who does so is forever branded and will not receive forgiveness "even after death" (Korotko 2013, 413).

Despite this ending, the most lasting impression left on readers is the presence of spies and apostates at the underground's centre and the startling revelation that they are former members of the Division. This makes the text an antidote to simplistic depictions of the war or the partisan struggle. The reason for such a critical depiction of the armed resistance lies in the post-1990 publication of archival sources dealing with the UPA. The author used transcripts of KGB interrogations published in *Litopys Ukrainskoi Povstanskoi Armii* (Chronicle of the UPA), which provide him with information about the protagonists in his novel. He also used interviews with villagers in his native Cherche, in which provocateurs posing as SB men killed twenty-two people, supposedly for betrayal ("Provokatsiine" 2013). The author benefitted from archival materials and provided both the aliases and real names to demonstrate the ruthlessness of the struggle and the cynical tactics employed.

PART FIVE
REAPPRAISALS

17

COMMISSIONS OF INQUIRY AND POSTWAR TRIALS

"As for me I find it disgusting to beat the other man's breast, in the manner of our judge-penitents."

ALBERT CAMUS, *Actuelles III*, 1958

Most of the Western public first learned of the Galicia Division when three government inquiries in the 1980s investigated whether war criminals had entered Canada, the UK, and Australia. Press coverage at the time focused attention on the Division and expressed shock that the men were citizens of these countries, assuming at least initially that they had all been guilty of atrocities. The inquiries dismissed these accusations. The Deschênes Commission produced its report in 1987 and the Hetherington-Chalmers inquiry in 1989.[1] In Australia a similar inquiry led in 1986 to a report by Andrew Menzies.[2] The findings throw light on discussions about the Division.

The Canadian and UK inquiries, after examining accusations, rejected the "criminal by definition" charge that had been levelled against all individuals who served in the Waffen-ss. Soviet authorities had argued that the men were traitors and "criminals in a generic sense" because they had fought against the Soviet state (Cesarani 1992, 57). The International Military Tribunal at Nuremberg had declared the Waffen-ss to be a criminal organization. It stated: "Units of the Waffen-ss were directly involved in the killing of prisoners of war and the atrocities in occupied countries. It supplied personnel for the Einsatzgruppen, and had command over the concentration camp guards after its absorption of the Totenkopf ss, which originally controlled the system" (Deschênes 1986, 286).[3] However, the Deschènes Commission in 1986 found that this evidence was not relevant to every Waffen-ss division or every individual who had served in these forces. It recalled that, already on 31 May 1948, Flight Lieutenant Bohdan Panchuk, who headed both the Ukrainian Canadian Servicemen's Association and the Central Ukrainian Relief Bureau, had stated in a memo: "In accordance with the general policy for all non-German 'foreign' units, the unit was termed Waffen S.S. This should not, however, be mistaken for the actual German S.S. in which only 'pure bred' Germans could serve. The Ukrainians were permitted to have priests in their units, they were not given any S.S. identity marks whatsoever and the terminology of their ranks and titles were those of the Wehrmacht" (255). Panchuk pointed out that the Nuremberg Tribunal did not go into fine distinctions but declared the ss in general "a criminal organization" and a participant in war crimes and crimes against humanity (257). Despite this fact, the Tribunal imposed certain limitations and recognized exceptions.

The Deschènes Commission stresses: "Membership alone in the Waffen ss does not, in itself, amount to a crime under international law; it must be membership as qualified by the Tribunal in Nuremberg. It implies either knowledge or participation" (Deschênes 1986, 257). The Commission report, quoting Calvocoressi (1947), also states: "No individual can be punished without first having specific charges brought against him personally and without being brought before a court of law" (257). This was a blow to some members of the Jewish community who had argued the a priori criminality of all Division members.[4]

When the Deschènes Commission issued its report, it noted: "Between 1971 and 1986, public statements by outside interveners concerning alleged war criminals residing in Canada have spread increasingly large and grossly exaggerated figures as to their estimated number" (Deschênes 1986, 249).[5] Sol Littman and Simon Wiesenthal were singled out as particularly persistent in advancing the figures of three thousand and six thousand (248).[6] Concerning Wiesenthal's accusations, the Commission states:

> As already outlined, evidence of participation had not been forthcoming in 1950. In 1984, Simon Wiesenthal had supplied a list of 217 former members of the Galicia Division who, according to him,

"survived the war and [were] not living in Europe." Since then the Commission has tried repeatedly to obtain the incriminating evidence allegedly in M. Wiesenthal's possession, through various oral and written communications with Mr. Wiesenthal himself and with his solicitor ... but to no avail: telephone calls, letters, even a meeting in New York between Mr. Wiesenthal and Commission Counsel on 1 November 1985 followed by further direct communications, have succeeded in bringing no positive results, outside of promises. (257)

The report explains that, of the 217 names supplied, 187 never set foot in Canada, 11 came to Canada and died, 2 came to Canada and left for another country, 16 had no prima facie case, 1 was not located (258). The RCMP also received the same list in 1984 from Wiesenthal. It conducted its own independent inquiry but could find no evidence of war crimes against the thirty-one individuals on Wiesenthal's list of individuals who might have entered Canada (258).

On the issue of knowledge, the report stated that it could not be inferred that every individual must have known of slaughter on a gigantic scale, especially since "it is acknowledged the Division was used only in combat on the Eastern front from the middle of 1944" (Deschênes 1986, 258). The report affirms that the burden of proof was on the prosecution. It concludes that the Division should not be indicted as a group. Its members had been individually screened and charges of war crimes had never been substantiated, either in 1950 or in 1984 when they were again renewed and examined by the Commission. Membership in the Division was insufficient to justify prosecution and no case for revocation of citizenship or deportation could be made. The denunciation of 217 officers of the Division by Simon Wiesenthal had put the RCMP and the Commission "to a considerable amount of purposeless work" (258).[7]

The public campaign against the Division had peaked in the mid-1980s during the inquiry, with most accusations coming from the Simon Wiesenthal Center in the United States and Sol Littman in Canada. Littman wrote in the July 1983 issue of *Saturday Night*:

Ultra-nationalist Ukrainians, Byelorussians, Georgians, Lithuanians, and Estonians formed their own ss units. Members of the Ukrainian Halychyna ss division helped put down the Warsaw ghetto uprising.

Some of those who took refuge in Canada were among the many non-Germans who volunteered as concentration camp guards. Others were members of the punitive units and of the Einsatzkommandos that slaughtered thousands of Jews; still others were civic and state officials in puppet governments that did the Nazis' bidding. Some acted out of hatred for the Russians, some out of hatred for communism, some out of a naïve belief that the Germans would help them regain national freedom. All demonstrated an unquestioning acceptance of the centuries-old anti-Semitism endemic in their countries.

Aware of the fate that awaited them at the end of the war, they fled to Canada. Some were granted entry on forged papers. Many relied on subtle name-changes to confuse the immigration department's primitive filing system. There is reason to believe that many passed through with the connivance of Canadian officials, acting on their own or in collaboration with American intelligence units such as the CIA. Communism had been the new menace.

In any case the Canadian government had been reluctant to honour requests for their extradition. (Littman 1983, 23)

The Division's legal representation issued a Statement of Claim in the Supreme Court of Canada on 2 November 1983 in connection with this article, but the Deschènes Commission's ruling of 1986 effectively settled the issue.

Littman had previously, on 8 June 1980, alleged in the *Toronto Sunday Star* that the Division committed what he called "some of history's ugliest deeds." On 17 August 1980, the newspaper was compelled to publish a retraction, in which it indicated that there was no record of the Division having engaged in atrocities or other war crimes; that its members had been individually screened by the American, British, and Canadian authorities after the war and before admission to Canada; and that none were found to have committed any crime at all.

In a speech given in 1997 Littman (1997) repeated some of his charges in a modified form. He also reiterated them in his *Pure Soldiers* (2003), where he disagreed with the Nuremburg Tribunal's decision not to assign collective guilt (Littman 2003, 44). This text quotes from Soviet propaganda booklets, such as Styrkul's *We Accuse* (1970).[8] Similar accusations had earlier been made by Petro Kravchuk (pseudonym Marko Terlytsia) in his *Pravnuky pohani: ukrainski natsionalisty v Kanadi* (Evil grandchildren: Ukrainian nationalists in Canada, 1960), and his "Hanebna richnytsia" (Shameful anniversary, 1973).[9] These Soviet publications, it should be noted, are diatribes full of factual errors. With the exception of Styrkul, they offer no evidence. Styrkul had been given access to KGB files, but whatever evidence he provided was relevant either to the 4th and 5th Volunteer Regiments or to the Ukrainian Legion of Self-Defence and had in part already been produced by the Division's members themselves. He makes no attempt to distinguish the regiments from the Galicia Division but refers to them, perhaps deliberately, as the "ss Halychyna Division" (Styrkul 1984, 269, 279).

Specific accusations of participation in anti-civilian violence had earlier already been made against the Division. A number of publications in the 1960s and 1970s indicated involvement in atrocities against Polish civilians.[10] German and Polish scholars have checked and rejected a number of these accusations. The charge that the Division was involved in putting down the Warsaw Ghetto Revolt in 1943 (which Littman repeats in the article quoted above) and the Warsaw Uprising in August 1944 were rejected by historians between 1962 and 1982.[11] Refutations of the latter charge had already, in 1952, been published by two Ukrainian researchers in the Polish journal *Kultura* (Culture) (Ortynskyj 1952, 109–16; Lewyckyj 1952, 74–82). Ortynskyi and Lewyckyj pointed out that, when the Warsaw Uprising broke out on 1 August 1944, the Division had just been crushed at Brody on 21–22 July 1944 so could not have taken part. However, as has been noted earlier, one company of the so-called ULS under the command of Petro Diachenko was in Warsaw. This Legion was independent of the Galicia Division but fused with it at the end of the war in March 1945.[12]

It should also be mentioned that, at the end of June 1944, just before the Division set off for the front at Brody, ten men were sent to Warsaw from the school for NCOs at Pozen (Pol: Owińska). After a protest by Bohdan Pidhainyi, the Division's liaison officer in the school, nine returned. As Polish speakers the men had been assigned to General Vlasov's forces for translation work but had been kept with the Germans, who were unsure what to do with them and sent them back after three weeks. They took no part in the action, but one of them, Klymiuk, was a native of Warsaw and had tried to get to the home of his parents, from whom he had not heard anything even before the outbreak of the Uprising. He was killed on the street by a sniper (Veryha 1980, 127).[13]

The troops that Himmler and Bach-Zelewski sent to put down the Warsaw Uprising of 1944 were substantial. They included four thousand men of the Dirlewanger Brigade, three or four battalions of the German regular police under the supervision of police general Reinefarth, and part of the 22nd ss Cavalry Division, which was recruited in Hungary from ethnic Germans. But the largest individual force was the Kaminski Brigade. The German High Command had permitted Bronislav Kaminski in 1942–43 to run his own government in Lokot (now in Briansk oblast, Russia) behind the lines of the Central Army Group (Kleist 1950, 200–1; Reitlinger 1956, 375). His RONA army of fifteen thousand men was withdrawn in the autumn of 1943 and accepted into the Waffen-ss. A regiment of seventeen hundred men was sent to Warsaw and withdrawn after three weeks because of its atrocious conduct. Kaminski was arrested, accused of looting (he had a penchant for jewellery and luxury goods), and shot (Littlejohn 1994, 310–11).

The most commonly raised charge of anti-civilian violence against the Division concerns the Beyersdorff Battle Group in February and March of 1944, the actions of the 4th Galician Volunteer Regiment in Huta Peniatska in February 1944, and those of the 5th Galician Volunteer Regiment around Hrubieszów and Lublin in May 1944 (Littman 2003, 77). The background to these war crimes has been described (see chapters 5 and 7). Another crime in the village of Semenivka (Pol: Siemianówka) near Lviv region on 26 July 1944 has also been attributed to the Division, but this does not appear correct because the Division had suffered near annihilation at Brody four days before, and survivors were retreating across the Carpathians into Hungary, Slovakia, and Poland. One serious accusation has also been raised concerning the Division's behaviour in Slovakia in August–October 1944, but, as already indicated, the evidence in this case is questionable (see chapter 5).

A suggestion has also been made that some soldiers were used to round up Jews in Brody in February 1944 (Pohl 1997, 365). It is possible that this, and similar events, occurred, but the evidence so far accumulated does not support the claim that, as a military formation, the Division was involved in anti-Jewish violence (Khromeychuk 2013, 74). Nonetheless, it should be noted that in wartime situations there are always "AIMs" (accidents, incidents, and mavericks). All such events, of course, require investigating. However, many charges have mistakenly been brought against the Division based on the fact that the perpetrators spoke Ukrainian, wore German uniforms, or were assumed by witnesses to be members of the Waffen-ss. As has been indicated, the issue of uniforms is more complicated than might initially appear. Ukrainians in the Division were not allowed to wear the ss runes, whereas Germans and *Volksdeutsche* were. The Division's lion and three stars badge was issued in 1944 and was worn not only by the Division's men but also by soldiers in the 4th and 5th Galician ss Volunteer Regiments. Not all soldiers in these regiments chose to wear it, but some did, including Germans. The evidence in all reported cases therefore requires careful sifting.

On the other hand, the charge that some men participated in anti-civilian violence prior to joining or being attached to the Division, either as members of police units, guards, or guerrilla fighters, is "highly credible" (Khromeychuk 2013, 75). Although never tested in court, it appears convincing with reference to some individuals in the ULS, the Galician ss Volunteer Regiments, and men who served as camp guards.

It is also well established that some units that fought alongside the Division had a history of violent, even sadistic behaviour. The most notorious was the Dirlewanger Brigade, which participated in the counter-insurgency operations in Slovakia. Moreover, a number of the Division's German officers had led police battalions in the first two years of the German-Soviet war. Some Ukrainians who had served in police units also joined the Division in the last stages of the war. Therefore, although as a unit the Division was formally cleared of participation in war crimes, the biographies of several individuals who were absorbed into the force after serving elsewhere indicate criminal behaviour.

It should be noted, however, that a number of the most notorious units who served alongside the Division, such as the Dirlewanger Brigade, were not composed of Ukrainians at all and were never part of the Division. The criminal behaviour of this particular group was never denied by the Division's memoirists and historians (Veryha 1980, 9–10). Nor have these writers denied the criminality of Ukrainians in the RONA under the command of General Bronislaw (Mieczyslaw) Kaminski or in the ROA of General Vlasov. Both these military formations were present in Warsaw in 1943 and 1944. The memoirs are much less forthcoming, however, when mention is made of the ULS, men who served in Schutzmannschaft battalions or local police forces. In these cases the individual biographies need researching.

Some memoirs written by men who served in the Ukrainian Schutzmannschaft Battalion 204, which was stationed at the Heidelager ss training grounds and was transferred to the Galicia Division in January

1944, have already been discussed (see chapter 6). However, relatively little is known about these men or the activities of the battalions (Bender and Taylor 1975, 39–40).

It will be recalled that only three thousand of the Division's eleven thousand soldiers managed to break out of the Soviet encirclement at Brody. The remainder were either killed, taken prisoner, or joined the UPA. The Division was then reconstituted from the remainder, members of the Galician ss Volunteer Regiments, the reserve regiment, and new recruits. According to a memorandum on the Division prepared in May 1948 by Bohdan Panchuk, "Ukrainians who had previously been drafted to other German units were offered the opportunity to 'volunteer' for transfer from these German units to the Ukrainian Division" (LAC, RG76, v. 656, f. B53802, pt. 1, Memorandum re: Ukrainian "Divisia Halychyna," 31 May 1948, 4).

Alti Rodal has pointed out that the reconstitution of the Division after the battle at Brody provided an opportunity for integration into the Division of persons who needed to hide a war criminal background.[14] Eight thousand men joined the three thousand remaining from the earlier formation, and one thousand German officers were also added (Heike 1973, 125). It also cannot be ruled out that some anti-partisan activities by the Beyersdorff Battle Group, or later in Slovakia and Slovenia, might have supported anti-civilian violence by German security forces in these locations.

The decision by the Deschênes inquiry and the Heatherington-Chalmers Report to exonerate the men who served in the Division from collective responsibility for war crimes was therefore essentially correct. No credible evidence was produced against the Division. Already in 1945 Polish officers had examined the force in connection with the Warsaw Uprising of 1944, and in Rimini in 1946–47 the Division's members had been questioned by both Soviet and British officers. However, because a detailed investigation of each biography was not made at the time or when the veterans were given civilian status, the lack of this further layer of detail has allowed speculation about criminal behaviour to shadow later discussions.

British screening procedures at the end of the war have been criticized as superficial because they did not conduct a micro-analysis of each soldier's activity both before and during service in the Division. There appears to have been no attempt to separate those who joined late in the war or who had a pre-Division military history (Khromeychuk 2012, 64).[15] This has provided an excuse for some already disproved accusations to

Commissions of Inquiry and Postwar Trials · **289**

be repeated at regular intervals. British tabloids, for example, printed sensationalist stories at the time of the Hetherington-Chalmers investigation. Headlines like "Do Nazi War Criminals Live on Your Street?" were placed above photos of goose-stepping German troops.[16] The press has been described as going "wild" at the time and the media as being "saturated by the war crimes issue" (Cesarani 1992, 193, 216). Robert Maxwell's Mirror Group of newspapers produced a "torrent of disclosure," and the press was aided by the "unstinting help of top Soviet legal officials" (199, 206).[17] Ten years after the Hetherington inquiry, the British documentary *The ss in Britain* aired on the History Channel in Canada on 24 September 1999 (see chapters 8 and 10).

Exaggerated, even hysterical, reports have been used as cover for political projects. Since the Division's members provided effective criticism of the Soviet regime, the latter retaliated by portraying the Division as a criminal group composed of society's dregs. Moreover, in order to discredit *émigrés* and diaspora groups, including intellectuals, scholars, and politicians whom it perceived to be critical of its policies, Kremlin propagandists have sometimes linked them to the Division.

This tactic was used in the 1960s and 1970s when the Ukrainian *émigré* community mobilized in defence of dissidents, supported the publication of the *Encyclopedia of Ukraine* and created university chairs. It was replayed around 1983 on the fiftieth anniversary of the Great Famine (Holodomor) of 1932–33 when the diaspora supported the publication of Robert Conquest's (1986) *Harvest of Sorrow*. The value of the guilt-by-association tactic lies in its not requiring scholarly scrutiny: lurid headlines intercut with photographs are sufficient to throw a shadow on any critical voice. The tactic has been employed to discredit politicians and to intimidate scholars and journalists. In the 1960s, under the name "active measures," it was used by Soviet authorities to drive a wedge between Ukrainian and Jewish communities. The anti-Ukrainian aspect included charges of nationalism, anti-Semitism, and wartime atrocities; the anti-Jewish aspect included attacks on Judaism, Zionism, and Israel. Today, the tactic is used to establish an association between the Division and the diaspora whenever the Russian government feels it necessary to undermine or deflect a particular criticism or to prevent co-operation between its opponents.[18]

Tracing all members of the Division who came to the West proved difficult. Already in 1948 Panchuk suggested in a memorandum that many members of the Division did not end up in Rimini but attached themselves to DP camps and resettlement efforts:

> A large number of soldiers from the Division itself did not go to Italy but stayed behind in Austria. Of these about 5,000 went straight into civilian life and became DPs, having joined with their families or relatives or friends who had also evacuated westward as refugees, while about another 3,000 were taken by the Americans as POW [sic], kept as POW from a minimum of 6 months to a maximum of 1 year and subsequently released as civilians. These latter also became DPS and went into DP camps. Of those who went across to Italy and were subsequently interned in the SEP cage at Rimini, about 1,000 to 1,500 left the camp during the 2 years in Italy. Most of these made their way across the Alps back to Austria or Germany; others "settled" in Italy. (Quoted in Deschênes 1986, 382)

Panchuk's statistics can be questioned. There appears to be no evidence that five thousand "stayed behind" and then went into civilian life, and his figure for escapees from Rimini is several times higher than most estimates. Understandably, the Canadian government was hesitant to allow the men into the country. Initially, it viewed service in the enemy's armed forces as sufficient justification to disbar them, the more so because it was concerned that some individuals might be listed as war criminals, either by the Soviet Union or according to Canada's own standards. However, as already described, policies for Germans and *Volksdeutsche* were relaxed a couple of years after the war, and when the Baltic Waffen-ss units were cleared for entry in 1948, there were no reasonable grounds to refuse entry for Ukrainians (see chapter 13). After 25 September 1950, applicants were admitted through regular procedures "notwithstanding their service in the German army" (Deschèsnes 1986, 407). Deschènes concluded that it was likely that "at least some persons who had served with Nazi-sponsored Ukrainian police/militia units used in killing actions in 1941–1942 found their way into the ranks of the Division either before or after the Battle of Brody," but he found no evidence that these men came to Canada (408).

The British had also brought back to the UK members of Anders's Polish army who did not wish to be repatriated to a communist Poland. The nucleus of seventy-four thousand men in the Polish army had been created from men released from Soviet captivity. They had been joined by former members of the 30th Waffen-ss Division, who had been transferred to the army and had fought against the Germans in Italy in 1945 (Dean 2000, 153). According to the Hetherington report, fifty thousand men in the Polish army had previously served in the German armed forces (Hetherington and Chalmers 1989, 37). In 1952, approximately ninety thousand Poles remained in the UK as civilians, and 10,487 ex-Polish soldiers had entered the United States (Dean 2000, 209). It has been suggested that many of these men had served in Schutzmannschaft battalions or as local police chiefs (154). Any thorough screening of postwar immigrants to Britain and other countries would have been compelled to examine the biographies of all these men who had served as Allied soldiers. It would have had to rescreen the ninety thousand European Volunteer Workers who immigrated to Britain between 1945 and 1950 and the 400,000 DPs who had entered the United States by 1952 (155).

Cesarani accused the British government of stonewalling and conniving in the escape of individuals against whom there was damning evidence. He describes the Home Office as being "obliged to stomach the settlement of several hundred infirm men and reluctant workers due to another round of spirited lobbying by Panchuk" (Cesarani 1992, 130). He characterized Yorkshire in the 1950s and 1970s as a hotbed of anti-Soviet politics led by "members of the pro-Nazi regime that held power briefly in Lvov in June 1941" and whose allegiance to the "ideals they held" while in the Waffen-ss remained unyielding (131). This information was no doubt news to the men described as ruling Galicia, however briefly, as it was to researchers of the period. It reflects the tone of Cesarani's book, which omits mention of national independence as part of the diaspora's "ideals," cites Philby's description of the OUN-B as "darlings of the British," and describes the Anders Army as full of Polish turncoats and Ukrainian and Belarusian collaborators (156, 181). As Tony Judt (2008, 34) writes, there is a "present-minded primness" to Cesarani's tone, which is often "unintentionally funny and self-revealing."

The Deschènes Commission in 1987 isolated twenty serious cases for examination and another 139 where further investigations might be warranted (Troper and Weinfeld 1988, 297). The Hetherington-Chalmers report in 1989 concluded that three men in Britain should face prosecution because there appeared to be a realistic prospect of conviction based on the evidence available. It recommended another three cases for further investigation and seventy-five more for examination in greater detail (Cesarani 1992, 305). It appears that none of these cases referred to wartime service by the Division's soldiers. One case involved a Division soldier who had been accused of serving as a guard at Trawniki (202).

Although the legal case against the Division was rejected, expressions of outrage continued. In 1950, the Jewish case for excluding the Division from entry to Canada had rested on two points: that the Division was both a volunteer and an ss unit (Troper and Weinfeld 1988, 74). These points have been repeatedly raised since the inquiries ended, without, however, examining them in any depth. The tabloid press and some researchers have relied on innuendo. Cesarani (1992, 26) , for example, describes the counter-insurgency operation in Slovakia as "particularly vicious," suggesting that the Division was responsible, and Nachtigall is described as murdering "large numbers of Jews" in June 1941. Without providing any references he also claims that, in 1944, eighty-nine officers of Nachtigall and Roland joined the Division after being imprisoned since December 1941 and that five disbanded Schuma battalions were transferred to the Division at this time (30–1).[19]

Wartime Culpability and Western Courts

The issue of wartime culpability has proved troublesome for Western legal systems. In 1997 the *Toronto Star* reported that, although "more than 1,000 suspects were investigated" during the Canadian inquiry into war crimes, only one man, Jacob Luitjens, had been deported in 1992 to Holland, where in 1948 he had been convicted in absentia for being a Nazi collaborator (Tesher and Vienneau 1997). After the war many German officers and officials entirely avoided punishment, and individuals guilty of the gravest war crimes received remarkably light sentences. Some went on to have noteworthy careers. Browning reported that only fourteen members of the Reserve Police Battalion 101 whom he interviewed in the 1960s were indicted. Five were sentenced to between five and eight years. In 1972, after a lengthy appeal process, the convictions of two were upheld, while those of two more were reduced. The rest received no sentence (Browning 1993, 145).

A number of the most culpable units in the Waffen-ss, such as the Viking Division, which committed most of the atrocities in Ukraine in the month of July 1944, avoided public exposure. An asymmetry developed in the treatment of accused or sentenced Germans and Ukrainians. Theodor Oberländer, the advising officer of the Nachtigall Battalion, had from 1938 been commissioned by the Abwehr as an intelligence operative to work in foreign sabotage. At the time he "viewed Poland as a region overpopulated by poor, useless Poles and Jews" and advocated a divide-and-conquer strategy for the country that would pit minorities against one another before installing German rule (Markiewicz 2021, 25). Towards the end of the war he joined the staff of Vlasov's ROA. After the war he provided the US military with information until 1949, went through the denazification process, and entered politics. In West Germany he served as Konrad Adenauer's minister for expellees, refugees and war injured, remained a member of Parliament until 1965, and lectured on refugee issues. Eventually he was "outed" and forced to resign his government position, but the manner in which evidence was used against him has been described by Nikolai Tolstoy as a classic example of the KGB's disinformation techniques. In 1960 he was sentenced in absentia to life imprisonment by an East German court. However, the evidence against him was cooked up by a Soviet special commission. He was not responsible for the massacre of thousands of people in Lviv jails in 1941, nor for instigating the murder of the exiled Ukrainian resistance leader Stepan Bandera in 1959. These were Soviet fabrications (Tolstoy 1986b, 16). In 1993, a West German court declared his conviction null and void.

In postwar years Wolf-Dietrich Heike, the Galicia Division's chief of staff, studied agricultural science and industrial management and then, from 1950 until his retirement in 1973, worked for Audi Motor Cars, first as assistant director, then as chief of personnel and administration, and subsequently as company director. He co-founded and headed the German Association for Employers, and the Bavarian Red Cross. No journalist or researcher appears to have found this career path remarkable. Like the Division's Ukrainians, Heike was never a member of the Nazi Party or the ss.

Konrad Adenauer, who was chancellor of the Federal German Republic from 1949 to 1963, ended the denazification process in 1951. All former officials except for the most egregious offenders were able to return to their jobs in the civil service. By 1951, amnesty legislation had benefited 792,176 people, including three thousand functionaries of the SA, the ss, and the Nazi Party. Although in 1950 it was revealed that Adenauer's secretary of state Hans Globke had played a major role in drafting the anti-Semitic

Nuremberg Race Laws, he was retained. The chancellor pressured the Allies to free all war criminals in their custody and demanded the release of seven men convicted of war crimes at Nuremberg and imprisoned in Spandau Prison. As a result, two were released: one in 1954 and one in 1955. General Reinhard Gehlen, who had run Hitler's anti-Soviet military espionage, rebuilt his intelligence-gathering network after 1946 and for twenty-two years served first the US and then the West German government.[20]

After the war, military and civilian authorities had separated the ss leadership from other captured Nazis, working on the presumption that the ss was "a state within a state, responsible only to itself, the terror of German bureaucrats and the force that impelled them to tyranny and cruelty" (Reitlinger 1956, 452). Like Hannah Arendt, Reitlinger described this view as a myth that was useful to defendants with no past in the ss. It obscured the fact that the massive machinery required to drag millions of people to concentration camps could not have been handled without the various offices of the Ministries of the Interior, Transport, Finance, Economics, Labour, Armaments, the high military commands, and the Foreign Office (452).[21]

The International Military Tribunal in Nuremberg charged twenty-one people with "crimes against peace" – that is, of having planned and launched a war of aggression in violation of international law. Twelve were hanged, three acquitted, and the rest imprisoned. In so-called successor trials American prosecutors shifted towards accusing perpetrators of crimes against humanity. On 9 December 1948, the UN General Assembly voted to recognize genocide in international law in order to deal with the Holocaust and other examples of mass murder by governments.

In total, German courts dealing with Nazi-era crimes secured only about sixty-six hundred convictions, around forty-six hundred of which had been handed down during the occupation period immediately after the war. After 1958 the total number of people convicted in West Germany amounted to about 560 people. Most of the accused were given amnesties; the rest generally received lenient sentences. One hundred and seventy were given life sentences, but most were imprisoned for less than two years (Douglas 2016, 14, 151, 233).

Former Nazis served in West Germany's judiciary and were reluctant to pursue crimes committed by their colleagues.[22] Another issue was the accessory defence, which allowed the accused to plead they had been forced to comply with criminal orders. Ironically, this defence was used by Bohdan

Stashynsky (Staschinsky), the KGB assassin of Stepan Bandera and Lev Rebet, who defected in 1961. He received a sentence of eight years imprisonment (Douglas 2016, 186–7). Ninety percent of former Einsatzgruppen members were found to have acted as accessories, including those who had commanded units and personally shot people. SS guards who had herded victims into gas chambers or pushed them into gas vans used the same defence. It was held that "the person who fires the weapon is a murderer only if he does so out of 'inner conviction' with the regime's genocidal politics" (189). Numerous death camp functionaries were acquitted on the basis that there was no evidence they had killed Jews with their own hands.

This defence could no longer be used when, in 2009, John Demjanjuk was deported from the US and tried in Munich. Earlier, in 1977, intense media attention had been focused on his case. He was accused of being a Trawniki man, extradited to Israel in 1986, convicted and sentenced to death in 1988, then released in 1993 when the Supreme Court ruled that he was not Ivan the Terrible.[23]

At the time of the trial, few observers had doubts – neither Tom Teicholz in *The Trial of Ivan the Terrible* (1990) nor Philip Roth in *Operation Shylock* (1993). Roth describes how the trial was broadcast in its entirety on radio and TV, how sitting among high school students and staring at the man in the dock, an observer sees in him "an embodiment of the criminal sadism unleashed by the Nazis" (Roth 1993, 32). He imagines the cruel behaviour of the man who bludgeoned prisoners with an iron pipe, tore open pregnant women with his sword, drove nails through their ears, once took a drill and bored a hole right in someone's buttocks, "screaming in Ukrainian, shouting in Ukrainian, and when they didn't understand Ukrainian, shot them in the head" (60). The observer ridicules the suggestion that survivors who identified the man could all be lying or wrong – which in fact turned out to be the case (65).[24]

Eventually it turned out that the OSI (Office of Special Investigations) had withheld evidence, thus engaging in prosecutorial misconduct. By that time Demjanjuk had spent seven years in an Israeli prison, five of them under a death sentence – far longer than the sentences most Holocaust perpetrators in Germany received. At the time of their trials, however, service as a concentration camp guard had not by itself been considered a crime.

Sixteen years after his Jerusalem sentence was quashed, Demjanjuk was removed from the US a second time and retried in Germany. Although considered a small cog in a vast machine, he was convicted in 2011 and sentenced to five years imprisonment for serving as a guard at the Sobibor death camp. The roster of Trawniki men detailed to Sobibor was produced with Demjanjuk's name on it (Douglas 2016, 131, 213, 277, 291). This was enough to convict him, because historians testified that Sobibor, like Treblinka and Bełżec, was an extermination facility and the guards had some degree of choice. For example, about one thousand of the five thousand men who trained at Trawniki deserted. Demjanjuk was released on appeal and died shortly afterwards (253). It soon became clear, however, that the main "evidence" had been manufactured by Moscow as part of the KGB's Operation "Retribution" (sometimes translated as "Payback"). The discrepancies in testimony, forged documents, and KGB reports have convinced some researchers that Demjanjuk was neither at Sobibor not at Trawniki (Bertelsen 2021, 125–9).[25] According to this research he was drafted into the Red Army, incarcerated in a German POW camp, used as forced labour, and then served as a bodyguard in Vlasov's Army. His case became "the most successful KGB operation" in a series of efforts to divide the Ukrainian and Jewish communities (93). The Office of Special Investigations was spoon-fed forged information from Soviet sources. It portrayed Demjanjuk as a war criminal "without any crtedible evidence," even though it had been warned by the CIA about the fraudulent nature of the documents in its possession (108, 111, 124).

Demjanjuk's trial in Germany was a turning point after which a defendant could no longer plead having been a replaceable cog in an exterminatory machine. By that time, the Nazi leaders had retired or died, mostly in West or East Germany. Some sixteen hundred former Nazi scientists immigrated to the US, and another one thousand found employment in the CIA, the Soviet Union, or East Germany (Bertelsen 2021, 32).

Ideal solutions and commensurate judgments may, of course, be impossible, but this legal history raises questions about pursuing prominent criminals not only in Nazi Germany but also in the Soviet Union and Russia. If state-sponsored crimes can no longer be treated with leniency and anyone involved in the German war machine can be prosecuted, does this logic not apply universally?[26]

After the inquiries of the 1980s, amendments that allowed use of evidence, such as video recordings and extradition of citizens, were introduced to the Criminal Codes of Canada, the UK, and other countries. Under the new legislation, investigations of Nazi war criminals continued into the twenty-first century, and twenty-seven convictions were obtained worldwide between 1 January 2001 and 31 March 2004, mostly of concentration camp guards. A number of countries, such as Norway and Sweden, refused to examine accusations because of statutes of limitations on murder cases (Zurof 2004, 5). Even after the Soviet Union's collapse, it appears that no one was ever prosecuted for crimes committed in the name of that state.

This legal history has affected attitudes towards the Division. The geography of the Holocaust, particularly in the Lublin and Galicia districts, meant that a number of men who joined the Division at the war's end had been in close proximity to where Jews, Roma, and other populations had been rounded up and transported to camps. They were aware of the fate of Jews and, if they were in German service, were in some degree complicit. However, collaboration with criminal states and complicity in their crimes are elastic terms that include or exclude whole categories of people.[27] As for the Soviet Union, legal niceties were never a consideration. Collaboration was interpreted in the broadest terms and culpability assigned even to men who had been taken prisoner by the Germans. One enormous irony is that the Soviet state had signed the secret protocols with Hitler in 1939, thus partitioning Eastern Europe, providing the German economy and military with supplies, and making the Second World War possible.

When Justice Robert Jackson, the chief US prosecutor at Nuremberg, opened his case, he stated: "We have no purpose to incriminate the whole German people. We know that the Nazi party was not put in power by the majority of German votes. If the German people had willingly accepted the Nazi programme no Storm Troopers would have been needed, no concentration camps, no Gestapo. The German people should know by now that the people of the United States hold them in no fear and in no hate" (Jackson 1945). This argument – that only the top sliver of the Nazi Party was to be held responsible – could no longer be made after 2011, when new legislation around the genocide issue was introduced in Germany and other jurisdictions. The inadmissibility of the "small cog" defence has affected attitudes towards the Galicia Division, but in many instances not towards Soviet history. Outrage has its myopias.

18

REASONS RECALLED:
LAST INTERVIEWS, 1987–2012

Over 120 interviews were recorded with the Division's veterans between 1987 and 2012.[1] The men were asked to describe their family origins and education, their experiences during the Soviet occupation of Galicia from 1939 to 1941, and their service in the Division. Most were from Galicia, but a number came from "Zakerzonnia." All entered the force while in their early twenties and, when interviewed, were mostly in their seventies.

All discussed their motives for enlisting. They emphasized family influences, the "lessons" of 1918, and their reluctance to join the forest partisans.[2] No doubt, after fifty years, each of the men had repressed, forgotten, or reshaped parts of their experience. It may also be argued that, by the time of the interviews, they had settled on a common narrative, a collective memory that had been developed in memoirs and personal testimonies. However, their statements, when corroborated by other testimonies, accounts, and documents, make it clear that the primary motivation for signing up in 1943 had been to fight Stalin, Russia, and Bolshevism, and to create a military formation that would struggle for Ukraine's independence.

During the recruitment drive German propaganda emphasized the 1918 theme, in this way it dexterously played upon the Ukrainian desire for statehood and an army. Wächter, in his speech on 28 April 1943, reproduced in *Krakivski visti*, proclaimed:

Under protection of German military forces in the Baltic, Belarus and Ukraine, which still held out against the East, when the German Kaiser's regime collapsed, a move toward creating a state order could proceed. The attempts to create Ukrainian statehood were possible only thanks to this living rampart in the East. At that time Galician Ukrainian detachments took part in selfless and costly struggles after they had already fought for years in the bravest Austrian regiments under the leadership of predominantly Austrian officers of German and Ukrainian nationality. ("Promova na urochystomu derzhavnomu akti" 1943)

Individuals from the Military Board and UTSK developed this theme. Mykhailo Khronoviat of the Military Board stated: "After the First World War we entered the military struggle against our enemy under the flags of Austrian regiments, and in addition created the volunteer Legion of Sich Riflemen. In 1918, after the war had ended for others, we quickly created the UHA and then fought for two years against Moscow's Bolshevism" ("Promova chlena Viiskovoi Upravy Inzh. Khronoviata" 1943).

In private conversations members of the Military Board explicitly called the Division the nucleus of a Ukrainian army. The link to 1918 and the struggle for independence was explicit or implied in almost every speech. General Viktor Kurmanovych called upon former officers and soldiers in the UHA to sign up ("Promova henerala Viktora Kurmanovycha" 1943). Volodymyr Kubijovyč called upon citizens "to complete the great promise made in 1918" (Kubiiovych 1943b). In his "Ukrainian Citizens!" printed on the front-page of *Krakivski visti* on 6 May, he lauded veterans of the war for independence: "You who have travelled the difficult but heroic path of the UHA best understand what is entailed by an unequal struggle" (Kubiiovych 1943c).

Many of the men interviewed fifty years later recalled this message that Ukraine would need an army at the war's end. Andrij Sternyuk (born 1917 in Dobriany near Lviv) explained: "Our goal was to fight the Bolsheviks on the eastern front and we were prepared for negotiations if a conflict developed between the Soviets and the Allies ... We knew from *Mein Kamp* that Ukraine was supposed to become a colony and Hitler would not give us Ukraine."[3] Myroslav Bihus (born 1910 near Rohatyn) said he was convinced that the post-1918 experience would be repeated: "We believed that Germany would do a deal with the US and together the two would go east, because Bolsheviks were enemies of humanity."[4]

The scenario of a war that exhausted Germany and the Soviet Union, followed by Western powers turning against Moscow, was a repeated theme. Petro Savaryn (born in 1926 near Buchach) recalled his father telling him: "maybe the two devils will exhaust themselves, and an opportunity will appear to help people."[5] After the US entered the war, Volodymyr Malkosh (born on 12 January 1924 in Przemyśl) thought that a confrontation between West and East was inevitable.[6] For all of these men, the experience of the First World War and ensuing struggle for independence resonated powerfully.

The Germans also used 1918 as a reference, although for them it represented Ukrainian perfidy. Hitler had spoken of General von Eichhorn's assassination in Kyiv in 1918 as a "stab in the back" by Ukrainians and the reason they should not be allowed to bear arms.[7] At the time of the Division's formation, Gestapo and ss leaders also recalled this event and protested that the force would betray Germany at the first opportunity. When Kubijovyč first lobbied for the creation of the Division in 1941, Hitler, along with figures in the ss like Martin Bormann, had opposed the idea for the same reason.[8]

This attitude was confirmed by a number of interviewees who recalled that, throughout the war, German officers in the Division viewed mass desertions as a threat. Mychailo Mulyk, for example, noted that Germans occasionally commented: "we know why you are joining; you want to get weapons, which you will use against us."[9]

Most interviewees asserted that the prospect of joining the forest partisans was unattractive. Their enlistment in the Division was an implicit rejection of the oun-b's position, which was that they should join the armed underground.[10] Almost immediately, however, without commenting on the appropriateness of the Division's creation, the oun-b began sending men into the force with instructions that they should join the partisans at an appropriate time.[11]

Although it has sometimes been asserted that the Division's creation represented an attempt to undermine the partisan movement, or was inspired by the oun-m, this opinion was vigorously challenged by interviewed veterans, who insisted that there were different political views within the Division and a continual discussion (out of German earshot) about the advisability of joining the UPA. Several men reported that they had been instructed by the OUN-B to join, but most stated that they enlisted of their own accord. A number made the point that partisan warfare and service in the Division were both paths to the same goal.

Mychailo Mulyk (born in 1920 in Horozhenko near Ternopil) had initially been told by his local OUN-B leader not to enlist, but a week later the man ordered him to sign up without informing anyone, saying: "We need our own people in it." Mychailo was a member of the organization's SB with responsibility for checking three villages for Soviet and German informers and for gathering information. In the Division his company contained an equal numbers of Bandera and Melnyk supporters. Moreover, his father had told him that an independent Ukraine could not be won without paying a price, that the UPA was not an army, and that only a nation with a professional army is taken seriously in international relations. Mychailo became a radio operator, an expertise, he noted, that "the forest" could not provide.

Several interviewees had already contacted partisan units, who informed them that the "forest" could not feed or clothe them, or provide military training and expertise. Mykhailo Filitovskyj (born in 1922 in Pasichnia near Stanislaviv) was discouraged by forest partisans from joining them; they told him to gain military skills that could be used in the future.[12] Eugene Humesky recalled that he knew about the UPA in 1943 but considered it poorly organized. His friends joked about its having "one rifle on a string for ten people."[13]

Liubomyr Zakharyasevych (born on 25 November 1927 in Sianky [Pol: Sianki]), now in the Lviv oblast, made his decision to join after a conversation with Roman Shukhevych. The OUN leader, whom he knew through family connections, had escaped from the Germans and gone into hiding. They met unexpectedly in 1943, when Liubomyr attended a family gathering. Shukhevych advised him to enter the Division to learn how to be a disciplined officer and told him to encourage others to do the same. Shukhevych had himself completed higher officer training in both the Polish and German armies – one of few people in the OUN and UPA with this level of qualification.[14]

On the other hand, there were those who planned to escape to the UPA. Dmytro Humeniuk (born in 1925 in Bili Oslavy near Deliatyn) intended to train with the Division and then leave. His father, who had run away from home in 1918 to join the battle against the Poles for Lviv and to serve in the UHA, volunteered for the Division in 1943, and Dmytro did so in 1944. They went to gain expertise that could be used to train local partisans: strategic and technical training, and knowledge of modern weapons. When the Division set off for Brody both deserted and organized a partisan group in their village. They disarmed Hungarian soldiers who were retreating in 1944 and fought Soviet forces as members of the UPA.

When asked about pro-German sentiment, the interviewed men generally reported that in 1943 there had been a great deal of naive enthusiasm around the prospect of a Galicia Division but that the mood was not the same as in 1941. Although German rule in the Galicia district had not been as brutal as in the Reichskommissariat Ukraine, the widespread savagery and contempt for Slavs had turned almost the entire population against the Germans. Political leaders, including those from both wings of the OUN, had been imprisoned; arrests and executions were taking place everywhere; and all hopes of German support for statehood had evaporated. The population lived with "Nur fur Deutsche" signs in stores, restaurants, and public transport. It had witnessed the treatment of Jews, who were first confined to ghettoes, then executed and buried in mass graves in woods outside urban centres. Deportations to work camps in Germany; requisitioning of livestock and food; draconian punishments, such as the execution of one hundred local men for every German killed; and the refusal to disband the collective farms (now called *Liegenschaften*) had embittered almost the entire population.

By 1943, Hitler's social Darwinist beliefs were seen as a direct threat to Ukrainians. He had stated that "life is a constant, terrible struggle, which serves to preserve the species – someone has to die so that others may survive" (Hitler, *Monologe*, 25–26 September 1941, 71, quoted in Ullrich 2016, 61). This alarming message was understood by Ukrainians as a warning that they had to stand up for their own people during a brutal episode in history. Perhaps most important, by 1943 it had become evident to many observers that the US's entry into the war on 7 December 1941, the Wehrmacht's surrender at Stalingrad on 2 February 1943, and the defeats at Kursk in July and August 1943 presaged Hitler's defeat. Germany's weakened position and retreat across all fronts, as many realized, was the reason permission had been granted to create the Division.

The charge of Germanophilia was rejected by the interviewees. Petro Savaryn recalled that under German occupation he witnessed what happened in the ghetto in Stanislaviv, along with the barbaric treatment of Jews and the local Slavic population. One day, the Gestapo appeared on stage during a concert and began arresting performers and members of the audience. He was able to escape down a drainpipe from the second floor gallery.[15] Twenty-six students were taken during this round-up and shot. He had no illusions about German behaviour and recalled that, in 1943, people were saying "this will not last long."

Vasyl Paliienko (born in 1926 in Poděbrady, Czechoslovakia) had been among people in Kolomyia who were forced to watch the execution of six boys accused of sabotaging a threshing machine.[16] Ostap Sokolsky (born on 18 September 1925 in the village of Zavaliv) confirmed that there was no love of Germans among Ukrainians. He recalled witnessing Germans striking in the face anyone who did not move aside on the sidewalk.[17]

The interviewed men recalled that community attitudes had played an important role in shaping their attitudes and expectations. Veterans who had served in the Austrian army could affirm the value of Austrian or Prussian military traditions. These "lessons" were emphasized in memoirs and in journals like the popular illustrated Lviv monthly *Litopys Chervonoi Kalyny* (Chronicle of the red viburnum). Ukrainian politicians in Galicia expressed disappointment with the Paris Peace Conference and the postwar order that had assigned the eastern part of Galicia to Poland. The newly created Polish state had guaranteed Ukrainians territorial autonomy and cultural rights, but it later reneged on the promise. Galician Ukrainians were also aware that General Haller's seventy-five thousand-strong Polish army had been trained and equipped in France, and had been used at the time of the Conference to breach Ukrainian lines, thus giving Poland a strong negotiating position and military superiority in the Polish-Ukrainian war. As a result, Ukrainian society's claims to statehood had been brushed aside.

Twenty years later collective consciousness recalled the end of the First World War as a failed opportunity to gain independence, a crucial moment in history that had led to the contemporary impasse. Tens of thousands had participated in Ukrainian armies from 1918 to 1920, and disabled veterans, who numbered around ten thousand in Eastern Galicia, were generally honoured as patriots and exerted an influence in literature, art, theatre, journalism, and education. They could be seen in their ubiquitous kiosks selling goods (Vynnyk 20, 131). As former enemy combatants, veterans were excluded from the new state's welfare system. Polish narratives and political rituals cast them as enemies of the state, while Ukrainian narratives saw them as freedom fighters. Interwar Ukrainian writers in Galicia and Central Europe often rehearsed the idea of an unfinished struggle for independence.[18]

Supporters of the Division used the cultural memory of 1918, which has been called the recruitment campaign's most successful "manipulation" (Bihun 2018). Because ten of fourteen members on the Military Board were veterans of the UHA, this strengthened the impression that the Division represented a rebirth of the earlier force.[19] The campaign even included parades in which hundreds of former Riflemen marched to enlist.

Interwar community rituals also served to reaffirm the "lessons" of 1918. As a student in the Przemyśl gymnasium, Volodymyr Malkosh recalled that, during Whitsuntide, a procession would be organized to the neighbouring village of Pikulice (Ukr: Pekulychi), where there was a cemetery with graves of Sich Riflemen and a hospital that had served the UHA and the UNR army. Wreathes were laid at the graves and a religious service conducted. About twenty thousand participated in what became an annual demonstration of national solidarity. The procession carried a trident crowned with thorns and Ukrainian flags, which the police tried to remove. Independence Day (22 January) was celebrated, and there were annual commemorations of Kruty, where three hundred student cadets were destroyed by a Bolshevik force of four thousand on 30 January 1918, and of Bazar, where 359 soldiers were executed by Bolshevik forces on 22 November 1922.

Mychailo Mulyk recalled that, in the late 1930s, the destruction of the Riflemen's graves coincided with the agitation by Polish priests for people to speak only Polish. One Whitsuntide, prior to the annual procession in commemoration of fallen soldiers, the cemetery grave was scattered. Mychailo and other children rebuilt the grave with their own hands and fashioned a cross out of the branches of an acacia tree. Three policemen tried to prevent them from singing during the graveside ceremony, arrested several boys, and kept them overnight at the police station.

Liubomyr Zakharyasevych recalled attending a memorial service for the Riflemen in Lviv at St George's Cathedral on 1 November 1938, with Metropolitan Andrei Sheptystskyi presiding. Patriotic songs like "Ne pora" (The time has passed) were sung during the street parade in which the school children participated and which was broken up by club-wielding Polish police.[20]

Perhaps the strongest motivation for enlistment was family history, which provided both war experiences and stories of postwar persecution or discrimination. For example, the uncle of Eugene Humesky (born 1921 in Staryi Sambir) had served in the Austrian army and was wounded in 1914 during the assassination of Archduke Franz Ferdinand in Sarajevo. Eugene's father had served as a magistrate until 1934, when he was dismissed by the Poles for his work in the Ukrainian community, which involved organizing Prosvita reading societies, choirs, and schools. He was forced to move from place to place working as a choir conductor and arranger of musical compositions.

Myroslav Bihus's father also served in the Austrian army and was wounded in 1916 and 1917. Subsequently, he served in the UHA, was interned by the Poles, and then was prevented from finding work because of government discrimination against UHA officers. He eventually set up a credit union; became the book-keeper for the Maslosoiuz co-op, with responsibility for thirty-two villages; and taught in a Ukrainian school. He had been a member of the paramilitary UVO in the early 1920s before joining the legal parliamentary party UNDO. Myroslav himself was refused various jobs because of his father's military career and was eventually hired by his father-in-law, another veteran of the UHA, who had created a tanning factory and business.

Paternal or family example and advice frequently proved decisive. Vasyl Paliienko was the son of a captain in the UNR army who had commanded a battery from 1918 to 1922 and had then been interned by Polish authorities. When Poland allowed the exiled UNR government to send sixty former officers to its army for contractual employment, Vasyl's father agreed to be one of them. In 1939 he fought alongside the Poles, as did almost all Ukrainian contract officers. Vasyl cited his father's experience as the reason he enlisted in the Division.

The uncle of Yevhen Myhas (born on 24 August 1924 in Burshtyn) had been a captain in the Riflemen. He often spoke of his military service and was frequently arrested by the police. The family had a photo album of the Riflemen, which Yevhen loved to examine as a child. When the Division's creation was announced, he imagined that it would resemble this force. Before enlisting he consulted the director of his school, another former Rifleman, who encouraged him to join.[21]

Mychailo Mulyk's father had been a Rifleman and a member of the UVO. In 1920, he hid from the Polish police and was only allowed to come home when the family paid off the authorities, although he remained under observation. He was active in the Prosvita reading society, where he performed in a number of theatre productions, and subscribed to several newspapers, including *Narodna sprava* (People's cause) and *Nash chas* (Our time), which he would read to acquaintances on the street while describing his army experiences. He took Mychailo to see the former home of Colonel Dmytro Vitovskyi, the Ukrainian political and military leader who organized the uprising of 1 November 1918 that initiated the Polish-Ukrainian war.

The grandfather of Liubomyr Zakharyasevych (born in 1927 in Sanok) was a successful businessman who founded the Maslosoiuz co-op in Galicia; built a dairy, cement factory, and church; and headed a credit union. His son, Liubomyr's father, served in the Austrian army, then became an officer in the Riflemen, UHA, and UNR army. He was a magistrate in all four armies, and at one point met up with the legendary Marusia (Oleksandra Sokolovska), the Ukrainian Joan of Arc who fought alongside the UNR army and the Sich Riflemen in 1919.[22] In 1923, when he returned to Galicia, he was arrested and barred from most jobs, which forced him to work as a labourer. He was rearrested in 1939 and imprisoned in the notorious Bereza Kartuzka camp. Liubomyr's uncle had also been an officer in the Riflemen and was also jobless after the war. The family library contained histories of Ukraine and its military, and the patriotic children's book *Syn Ukrainy* (Son of Ukraine), which the Polish government had banned.

During the First World War, the father of Ivan Mamchur (born in 1925 in Rokytno near Lviv) served on the Italian front with the Austrian army and then, in November 1918, joined the UHA, where he was in the field gendarmerie and was tasked with mobilizing youth. He often described the army's retreat towards Stanislaviv in the face of General Haller's Polish army, the Chortkiv counter-offensive, and his internment in a Polish POW camp, where, like many other soldiers, he contracted typhoid.

A number of recruits to the Division had close family connections with political and military leaders. Andrij Sternyuk was the son of a priest who was active in the local Prosvita and credit union. His uncle had married Yevhen Konovalets' aunt. Andrij often met Konovalets's father and younger brother Myron. The latter travelled to his assassinated brother's funeral in

Rotterdam in 1938 and described the event when he returned. The sister of Andrij's brother-in-law was Olha Basarab, who was treated as a martyr by Ukrainian society after 1924 when she was either murdered or committed suicide in a Polish prison. Andrij therefore grew up listening to conversations about noble fighters for independence.

Not all family members were supporters of the OUN. The father of Bohdan Buchak (born on 1 March 1923 in Nove Selo near Ternopil) was a member of the Radical Party, to which the writers Ivan Franko and Vasyl Stefanyk had belonged. A veteran of the Austrian army, he founded a reading society, choir, and co-operative, and spent much of his time reading the press to local people while discussing politics. Buchak's father warned against Hitler and any expectations that the Germans would agree to a Ukrainian state. In his view, "being a patriot was not enough" – one also "had to be a politician." Bohdan recalled his father saying that it was easy to light a spark but a mistake to whip people up when there was no achievable goal. It was partly for this reason that Bohdan never joined the OUN. Although his father disapproved of the Division's formation, Bohdan felt that some form of military service was unavoidable. He saw his other choices as joining the UPA or being conscripted into the Red Army.[23]

Personal experiences were also a factor. Many interviewees recalled suffering slights or abuse because of their nationality. Andrij Sternyuk recalled that, as a ten-year-old, he took part in a procession after a memorial service for the Riflemen. It was attacked by Polish mounted police, and he was found crying on a bench outside Lviv University by a woman who led him back to the school residence. The residence barricaded its doors and opened all windows because stones were thrown at them for several nights. The younger boys had to be escorted to and from school by several strong boys who walked in front and back carrying metal bars. As part of his school uniform he wore a *mazepynka* (the cap worn by Ukrainian soldiers during the First World War) and, because of this, was on several occasions hit over the head by Polish youths. Later, when he entered gymnasium, during the daily forty-minute train ride to and from home he was forced, along with other Ukrainian boys, to travel in the passageway because the Poles would not allow them into the carriages. These formative experiences were additional "evidence" for many young people that only independent statehood could bring improvements, a message that for many was reinforced during the Soviet occupation of Lviv from 1939 to 1941.

Some interviewed men vividly recalled witnessing the horrors of Soviet occupation. Sternyuk witnessed the exhumation of mass graves in the Lontskyi prison, where mutilated bodies were found after the hasty Soviet retreat: "The prisons were opened on 1 and 2 July [1941]. Jews were made to clean earth from the corpses. Fires were burned to cover the stench. Thousands of bodies were taken to Lychakivskyi cemetery where they were buried in mass graves ... We saw one wagon after another piled with bodies, many already decomposed."

Volodymyr Malkosh witnessed the effects of the 1939 Soviet occupation in Przemyśl. A seventeen-year-old friend was shot and thrown into a salt mine simply because he had made a radio. Volodymyr summarized his thinking in 1943 as follows: "Our leadership grasped the idea of creating a Division. We did not know what the OUN was saying, but could see that all officers of the UNR army and the Riflemen supported the Division's creation. We decided to join. The alternative was 'the forest' [UPA], but it was small, far off in the woods, and not everyone wanted to go there without weapons and training." After weighing his options, he decided to volunteer because he felt that at that moment Ukraine's fate was being decided, and that freedom and a better life would only be possible after independence.

These were typical biographies of the first cohort of volunteers to the Galicia Division. Generally, their family members had served in Ukrainian armies, had been active in enlightenment societies and in organizing community life, and had suffered discrimination. The young people themselves had witnessed Soviet behaviour, knew that neither the UPA nor the Division could defeat the Red Army, but hoped that these two forces could play a part in the inevitable East-West confrontation.

Bohdan Stasiv summarized their position as a strategic choice. He knew that Germany had lost the war and that only the approaching end had spurred it to allow the Division's creation. He was aware that the Poles, Ukrainians, and Balts were threatened by Soviet totalitarianism and that all these countries hoped that, after Germany's collapse, the West would strike at the Soviet state. As for wearing the German uniform, he responded: "So what? What uniform did our fathers and grandfathers wear? Polish, tsarist, Russian, Soviet, Romanian, Czech, Hungarian ... Why look at the uniform? ... What counted was what was in your heart and whether you had a weapon in your hands. If you had Ukraine in your heart and a weapon in your hands then who were you? A Ukrainian soldier."

He made his strategic choice fully aware of what he considered to be perfidious German behaviour. One acquaintance, who had witnessed Hitler's refusal to support Carpatho-Ukraine in 1939, told him: "Damn the Germans! Our heart was in Berlin for twenty-five years. It would have been better if it had rotted there!" The hope in 1943 was that Germany, not Hitler, would become an ally. He viewed the Division not as evidence of an ideological union but as a military alliance. In defending the Division, Stasiv commented: "We did not collaborate or cooperate with their administration against our own people. Not a single Ukrainian was shot by our Division. It was a military union with an agreement to fight only on the eastern front." He also cited General von Brauchitsch's advice to Hitler that the Soviet Union would only be defeated if some limited independence was granted the Baltic nations and Ukrainians. Even though Hitler ignored this suggestion, Stasiv maintained, it was clear to the *dyviziinyky* that, within the German military leadership, there were disagreements concerning Ukraine. Volunteers to the Division hoped that these disagreements would turn in their favour. After all, following the defeat at Stalingrad the idea that only Germans could carry arms had been dropped and the Waffen-ss began openly recruiting Eastern Europeans. According to Stasiv, at that moment young Ukrainians felt that an opportunity to bear arms had finally arrived. In his view, not since the First World War had there been such a chance for Ukrainians to create their own army.

There was also a category of recruit for whom joining the Division was a survival strategy. This was especially true of conscripts in 1944. As a schoolboy Ostap Sokolsky witnessed the Holocaust in Berezhany and the hanging of twelve oun members in Pidhaitsi on 28 July 1943. On that day some young men were preparing to leave for one of the Division's training camps. After seeing the hangings, half the recruits escaped to join the upa even before reaching the train that was to transport them. Ostap was forced to join in March 1944. He would have gone to the upa, but the front had moved and he was cut off. In Lviv he had an opportunity to escape from the train heading for the Division's training camp but decided not to because, by then, he had accepted the argument that Ukrainians needed military know-how and weapons. The liberation struggle from 1918 to 1920, he felt, had been lost because of these deficits.

Petro Balahutrak (born in 1912, from Kryvche [Pol: Krzywcze] near Borshchiv) also tried to avoid service. In the 1930s, he had gone to France, where he could earn money to support his engineering studies. In 1940, he was picked up by the German Labour Office (*Arbeitsamt*) and sent to work in Hamburg, where he cleaned cannon bores. After escaping to Kraków and Lviv, he joined the Division when all other options had been exhausted. He could not go to the UPA because transportation lines had been cut and, in any case, a UPA leader had told him that "the forest" could not feed or arm any more people (UCRDC, Balahutrak). Balahutrak's case is interesting because he was well aware of Nazi ideology, after witnessing life in Germany and reading *Mein Kampf* while he recovered in a Hanover hospital from a factory accident. The book, he realized, completely negated any possibility of Ukraine's existence. Upon returning to Galicia he had several conflicts with people who voiced strong sympathies for Hitler and the Germans; they refused to believe his report about the contents of *Mein Kampf* (which they had not read) or about the treatment in Germany of foreigners and German citizens alike.[24]

Some later recruits were simply dragooned into the army. Myron Martsinowsky (born in 1925 near Buchach) worked with his father as a blacksmith until the spring of 1944. He was captured, along with hundreds of others, in an early morning roundup. A number of soldiers conducting the operation wore the Galicia Division's insignia and he recognized one man as a local. Myron was given two months instruction as a driver and mechanic but claims he received no military training. He was then issued a Galicia Division uniform and attached to the Viking Division. After two days in a bunker he was taken prisoner by the advancing Soviet front. A Red Army major ordered his immediate execution along with five comrades, but the Ukrainian Red Army soldiers entrusted with the execution led the men into a wood, told them to run, and shot to the side. According to Myron's account, he did not understand German (his instructors in driving school were all Ukrainians), nor did he ever fire his rifle. His two older brothers, who were conscripted along with him, had been killed when they left the bunker to try and get food and water. Eventually, Myron was recaptured and on 17 November, six months after being conscripted, was sentenced to ten years hard labour. Ironically, his training as a driver allowed him to survive both the building of the Minsk-Moscow highway, where he drove a heavy truck, and forest cutting in Siberia, where he drove a train. Both jobs were relatively easy compared to the work allotted to most prisoners.[25]

Mykhailo Dydyk (born in 1924 in Kalne near Ternopil) tried to escape service in the Baudienst in 1943 but was captured by Ukrainian and

German police and taken to a camp in Świętosławice, Poland, where he was guarded by Poles for seventeen days. He recalled being beaten daily. He was freed when partisans attacked the camp. Hardly able to walk, he declined an offer to join the partisans. Eventually he made his way home, was again forced to dig ditches and trenches, and escaped a second time. Around 16 June 1944, with the Red Army approaching, he was faced with the choice of either joining the UPA in the Carpathians or serving in the Division. He chose the Division rather than waiting to be pressed into the Red Army. He was sent to join the Viking Division's Westland Company on the Belarusian front. After being injured, he was sent to the Galicia Division in Slovakia. Captured at the end of the war, he was sentenced to Siberia.[26]

The men of this later cohort expressed a much more negative attitude towards their military experience. They also spoke more frankly about the Holocaust. The most harrowing description came from Ostap Sokolsky, who was forcibly conscripted in March 1944. He recalled that, in November 1942 on his way to the Berezhany gymnasium, he witnessed German soldiers, together with local Ukrainian police and Polish railway police, surrounding the ghetto and leading Jews out of the main gate towards three enormous pits that the Baudienst had dug about one kilometre out of town. He stated that the shooting was done by Germans, but Polish and Ukrainians police served as guards, preventing escapes. A couple of Germans led the Jews, one hundred at a time, with a thick rope around each group. Anyone who stepped beyond the rope was shot. People prayed, wailed, and cried. Some who were no longer able to walk were shot along the way. At the killing site the people were undressed, made to place their valuables (mainly watches and glasses) into a separate pile, and then five people at a time were told to stand on a board above the pit. A single ss man shot them, trying to kill five people with one bullet. Those in the pit who were still alive were sprayed with machine gun fire in a zig-zag motion. An estimated two thousand people were killed. For two days blood came from the pit and had to be covered with lime. Sokolsky at the time was living on a hill opposite the site and, although he tried not to look, could not fail to see and hear what was happening. According to locals, about eighty-six people escaped from the pit to the forest. The locals were terrified and kept quiet. Sokolsky attended gymnasium until February 1944. In March the Red Army captured his village of Zavaliv and immediately pressed him into service. A German counter-attack retook the village and he was told he could either work in

Germany, dig trenches, or join the Division. He joined the Division's reserve regiment in May–June 1944.

It is difficult to judge to what extent postwar discourse, particularly around the time of the commissions of inquiry in the 1980s, influenced later testimonies by the Division's veterans. A number of men mentioned that, to the best of their knowledge, the unit was not involved in any police work and had not committed any war crimes. Although, as noted, several interrogation files in the Ternopil SBU archives indicate criminal behaviour, these acts were committed by men while they served in the local police, prior to joining the Division, or after Brody, when they joined the partisans. Interviewed veterans were laconic when mentioning the killing of Jews, perhaps understandably so in light of the charges levelled against them in the press, although several spoke frankly about what they had witnessed. A number had Jewish acquaintances. Sokolsky, for example, mentioned that, in order to avoid the compulsory two years of service in the Baudienst, a Jewish doctor gave him instructions on how to bring about a temporary high fever and, on one occasion, injected him with a substance that had this effect. As a result, Sokolsky was able to avoid the Baudienst and complete the Berezhany gymnasium.

During the interwar period, Galician society integrated the earlier wartime experiences into its collective (inter-personal) and cultural (literary and institutional) memory. An important aspect of this was the emergence of narratives that portrayed the outside world in 1918 as indifferent to Ukrainian statehood. Although the Brest-Litovsk Treaty negotiations of 1918 had included a secret clause in which Germany and Austria agreed to create an autonomous Ukrainian state in Galicia, this was forgotten when the war's fortunes turned against the Axis powers. Nonetheless, in interwar years Ukrainian leaders continued to cite this agreement, along with President Woodrow Wilson's Fourteen Point Declaration of 8 January 1918, in which he indicated that nations of the Austro-Hungarian empire would be allowed autonomous development. They also referenced the proclamation of a Ukrainian state on 1 November 1918 by the Ukrainian National Council (Ukrainska Natsionalna Rada) after it captured Lviv.[27] Most of the 1943 recruits indicated in their interviews that they hoped for a similar political opportunity to present itself after the fall of the Third Reich. They were convinced that only Ukrainian society's military capability had compelled the Entente powers to even consider Galician autonomy at the Paris Peace Conference.

Members of the Galicia Division were aware that the Sich Riflemen and the UHA had fought under their own colours, in their own army, for a declared state. However, the Division's soldiers were not able to emulate this experience. They fought in German uniforms and were only able to rename their formation the UNA in the final weeks of the war. Nonetheless, the interviews demonstrate that, for most men, the motivation for joining had been a desire to serve Ukrainian society's political aspirations. Half a century later, many presented the hope of playing a role in the war's endgame as the primary reason for volunteering.

19

ACCOMPLICES, TRAITORS, AND FOES: THREE NARRATIVE PERSPECTIVES

"Communist dictators resorted to violence and torture no less than any other dictators."

TONY JUDT, *Reappraisals*, 2008

Any discussion of the Galicia Division's history intersects with competing war narratives. Three in particular – those dealing with the Holocaust, Soviet partisans, and the Polish underground – cast the Division's soldiers in the role of villains and shoehorn their biographies into one of three categories: accomplices, traitors, or foes.

The Division has been linked to the Holocaust through individuals who, prior to joining the force, served in police battalions or as guards in concentration camps. Several German officers, including General Freitag, Friedrich Dern, and Franz Magill, had been guilty of war crimes between 1941 and 1943 before being assigned to the Division. Two Ukrainians who joined late in 1944 have been identified as Trawniki guards, and some men came from battalions such as the Schutzmannschaft 201 and the USL, which have been linked to the Holocaust.

Evidence directly connecting the Division to the guarding, transporting, or shooting of Jews has not been produced. The two large waves of killings, in 1941 and in 1942–43, had already occurred before the Division went into action in July 1944, and the extermination camps in the "Zakerzonnia" were

Accomplices, Traitors, and Foes • 315

by then closing. Indirectly the force was of course linked to the Holocaust because the capture of Jews and their transportation to camps, either from ghettoes or from other parts of Europe, was still taking place, and some of these operations, as in Slovakia, were not far from where the Division was deployed. By holding the front against the Red Army the Division was allowing these actions to continue. However, whether the force shared the same degree of responsibility as administrators and bureaucrats who organized the Holocaust and devised its machinery, or the military units that operated it, is an issue that requires consideration. Their level of involvement might be compared to front-line soldiers in other abhorrent systems. Red Army soldiers were aware of the Gulag and Stalin's mass murders, although they, like other front-line troops, were far less complicit than the NKVD and the thousands of administrators and bureaucrats who organized and ran the system.

The Division's soldiers knew of the killing of Jews, even if some might not have been fully aware of its enormous scale. Before enlisting, a number of men had witnessed the shooting of Jews in their home towns. They later recorded these episodes in memoirs and oral interviews, although the descriptions do not form a prominent part of their recollections. This is perhaps understandable given the threat of deportation and legal action they faced in the postwar period, but in some cases it may reflect the trouble articulating the clash between humane instincts and German policies – a psychological gap that Browning remarked upon when investigating interviews with the men of the Reserve Police Battalion 101. He commented that they "did not seem to be conscious of the contradiction between their feelings and the essence of the regime they served" (Browning 1993, 74). Most of the Division's soldiers, however, expressed revulsion at the scenes they witnessed and certainly showed no sympathy for Hitler, the "New Europe," Germany's plans for conquering Slavs, or for the exterminatation of the Jewish population.

Veryha describes witnessing the killing of Jews in the town of Tovste on 10 June 1943, which occurred on the same day that young men were registering for the Division. As he left the church, he learned that the Germans were rounding up Jews in the ghetto: "Some young Jews were trying to escape and the Germans were shooting at them as they ran in the town's streets. Walking home from the church I saw two young Jewish women lying dead on the bloodied pavement of the town's sidewalks. The sight was oppressive. Here a completely innocent person lay on the pavement shot like a dog, simply because she did not belong to the *"Herrenvolk"* but to the Semitic race" (Veryha 2007, 10).

Veryha witnessed another "Jewish action" during which the Germans gathered close to two thousand people in a square near the centre of his town, forced them to sit in rows, and then led them in groups of two hundred to the Jewish cemetery, where they were executed. He was struck by the fact that the Jews knew what awaited them but walked meekly to the cemetery accompanied by armed Germans and police. He also met a Jewish woman who was being hidden by the Ukrainian family with whom he was staying, knew that Ukrainians caught delivering food to the Jewish ghetto were being shot, and recalled people commenting that, once the Germans had removed the Jews, they would come for the Ukrainians. At the time, information was also circulating about the inhuman treatment of Poles in other parts of the GG. However, even before the German occupation the population had witnessed mass atrocities under Soviet rule, when first Poles and then Ukrainians had been deported or executed. Veryha's revulsion at what he witnessed led to this conclusion: "All this convinced me even more that we had to have our own army, which at the appropriate moment would become the foundation of a new Ukrainian army, well trained and with weapons, something the 'forest' could not provide. This made my decision to enter the Division firm and irrevocable" (10).

How deeply the Holocaust affected the Division's soldiers is not easily established. In their testimonies the men do not analyze the German treatment of Jews, nor do they discuss in any detail the involvement of local police in the rounding-up, guarding, and killing, or the fact that anti-partisan activities might have been directed against Jews and non-combatants hiding in forests. An estimated 1.5 million Jews were murdered under German occupation in what is today Ukraine, a fact that the country's scholarship is still processing. Although educational programming has spread a general awareness of the Holocaust, detailed studies written in English, German, and Polish are often not widely available, and in Western Ukraine there is as yet no equivalent of Warsaw's POLIN (Museum of the History of Polish Jews).

Lack of awareness about the Holocaust poses an obstacle to better understanding the psychology of the Division's soldiers. It is clear that the force was part of a profoundly anti-Semitic structure, the Waffen-ss, which broadcast the myth of Judeo-Bolshevism, an ideological construct employed to crystallize both political and cultural fears. Soldiers were exposed to it in their *Weltanschauung* lessons, in speeches and newspaper articles. There was, perhaps, no possibility of publicly opposing the propaganda during the war, but there are also few records of the soldiers doing so in private. The propaganda was publicly challenged only after the war – for example, in Lysiak's novels and in memoirs that discussed the fate of Jewish friends, colleagues, and comrades in arms.[1] At the same time, it should be noted that the men were focused on obtaining military training. Their agenda was anti-Soviet, not anti-Jewish.

In postwar years the primary concern of veterans was to shape a narrative that explained their reasons for joining and how they had survived. In today's Ukraine museum, exhibitions tend to integrate the Division's history into longer narratives dealing with the nation's military history or its liberation struggle. The latter often attempts to combine different legacies by presenting "all Ukrainians fighting in the Second World War (nationalists and those in the Soviet army) as part of a mythical anti-fascist coalition based upon Ukrainian patriotism" (Kuzio 2007, 10). Such an approach de-emphasizes or entirely omits the Holocaust, which, as Svetlana Aleksievich has reminded us, made the Second World War different from all other wars. In her words: "Human beings discovered something they had not suspected about themselves" (Drakokhrust 2021).

Veterans' memoirs adhere to this overarching narrative of national liberation. The postwar writings seldom reflected upon the war's brutality or that Germany had declared the conflict in the east a "war of extermination." The "Barbarossa Decree" signed by General Wilhem Keitel, head of the Wehrmacht office in the War Ministry, on 13 May 1941, a month before the invasion, declared: "Bolshevism is the mortal enemy of the National Socialist German people. It is against this subversive world view and its carriers that Germany is fighting. This battle demands ruthless and energetic measures against Bolshevik agitators, irregulars, saboteurs, and Jews, and the total eradication of any active or passive resistance" (Shepherd 2012, 70). The decree removed the actions of German soldiers towards Jews and Slavs from the jurisdiction of military courts and explicitly approved collective reprisal against entire villages (Browning 1993, 11). In their memoirs and interviews Ukrainian veterans emphasized the German army's anti-Bolshevism but for the most part avoided discussing its anti-Semitism and anti-Slavism.

A second set of narratives, mainly generated by Soviet and Russian scholars, has described wartime opponents of Stalin's regime as heinous traitors and despicable deserters. This category of villain includes 53,000 Cossacks (who formed two divisions of General Helmut von Pannwitz's 15th ss Cossack Cavalry Corps and served in General Timotei Domanov's militia); 180,000 Azeris and Turkmen peoples (who helped form the 162nd Turkoman Division); 110,00 Georgians, Armenians, and other Caucasians; 60,000 Crimean Tatars; and 100,000 or more soldiers who wore the ROA insignia. Among these "traitors" were older figures, men like General Petr Krasnov, who spent the interwar years in Germany and France.

The idea that opposition to Stalin's regime could be the product of spontaneous resistance movements that were neither pro-Nazi nor pro-Soviet was considered a dangerous heresy by Soviet authorities, partly because of the fear that such movements could rally support for regime change. Russian historians have made little distinction between oppositionists, collaborators, and deserters. All opponents of Stalin's regime have been termed collaborators, traitors, and fascists, and collectively described as "mostly criminals, scum of society, people without honour and conscience" (Krinko 2004, 154). Their collaboration was generally attributed to character defects, fear, ambition, greed, or hatred. Analysis rarely went beyond calling them class enemies, bourgeois nationalists, or stooges of Western powers. It was assumed that they must have been seduced by foreign intelligence services and were therefore traitors – history's antiheroes.

In the last two decades Russian media reports have floated new narratives. Krasnov's *Za chertopolokhom* (Behind the thistle, 1927) was republished in 2002 and 2009, and Aleksandr Dugin, Russia's leading fascist thinker, expressed admiration for the general's ideas, among which was the conviction that the *Protocols of the Elders of Zion* was a genuine document. The book appealed to Vladimir Putin's circle because of its hostile stance towards Western democratic norms and values, and its call to protect the state and social harmony by using violence against dissenters. Vladimir Sorokin satirized the book in his novel *Den oprichnika* (Day of the oprichnik, 2006).

The interest in anti-Soviet movements produced a softer terminology concerning collaborators. Such phrases as "co-operation with the enemy" and "enforced or willing aid to a hostile power" appeared in publications (Krinko 2004, 155). In 1996, Pannwitz was officially rehabilitated and described as a noble figure respected by Cossacks, and, in 2001, Russia's top military court dropped the charge of anti-Soviet agitation and propaganda under which Vlasov had been found guilty, although it rejected an attempt to rehabilitate him. The media reported that the line between traitor and patriot was becoming blurred "as evidence mounts that Vlasov may have changed sides in a bid to give his countrymen a better life than the one they had under Stalin" (Korchagina and Zolotov 2001).

However, anti-Soviet movements in Western parts of the Soviet Union have not been allowed a similar apologia. Any reassessment of them presents a threat to the dominant Russian nationalist narrative, which refuses to admit that non-Russians had legitimate grievances or suffered national oppression. To avoid drawing attention to this fact, the Galicia Division has rarely been discussed in Russia, except in scurrilous terms. Moreover, the government has continued to persecute researchers who expose human rights violations and deaths intentionally caused by the Soviet state. In 2012, it passed a law requiring NCOs to renounce all funding from abroad or else register as "foreign agents." The Memorial Society was criticized for investigating crimes committed under Stalin and was shut down in 2021. The historian Yurii Dmitiriev, a member of Memorial, was arrested and sentenced to thirteen years imprisonment on bogus charges. Authorities continue to describe any interest in wrongdoing by the Soviet state, particularly during wartime, as damaging to Russia's international image.

Despite fifty years of denial, shortly before the state collapsed in 1990, the Soviet government admitted that it had in 1940 murdered Polish POWs in Katyn and other sites (Etkind et al. 2012, xxv). Photographic evidence of people murdered by the NKVD in prisons during the Red Army's hasty retreat in 1941 is now available on the internet ("Rasstrely" 2020). Katyn and the prison murders have become iconic moments in Soviet history. However, they represent only a small aspect of the state's wartime criminality. The extent of the Red Army's atrocities has also become better known in the West from Anthony Beevor's *Berlin – The Downfall: 1945* (2002). Using Soviet sources, the book describes mass rapes and wanton destruction. An estimated 100,000 rapes occurred in Berlin alone, and 1.4 million in German territories, resulting in the death of 240,000 women. Beevor calls this wave of criminality "the greatest phenomenon of mass rape in history."[2] Although Western authorities complained to Stalin about the behaviour of his troops, the Soviet leader refused to take any action.[3] In postwar decades German women would refer to the Red Army Memorial in Berlin as the Tomb of the Unknown Rapist.[4] The crimes of the Red Army were not mentioned at the Nuremburg trials. Soviet prosecutors at Nuremberg even used fabricated evidence in an attempt to blame Katyn on the Germans.[5]

Another omission from Soviet accounts of the war were atrocities committed by red partisans. Recently, a number of researchers have produced studies (Dean 2000, 119–47; Gogun 2016; Tisetskii 2017). Here, for example, is how one commissar of a partisan unit in 1943 complained about the behaviour of his men: "Upon entering the villages, they carried out practically a general confiscation of cattle and property and killed the male population in revenge for killed saboteurs" (Gogun 2016, 112). This happened in the village of Bilchaky (near Liudvypil, Rivne oblast), where almost the entire village was burned in June 1943, and in the village of Zapruda (near Sarny raion, Rivne oblast). These reports of partisan atrocities have sometimes been overlooked because, as with German "pacifications," the murder of civilians could be passed off as the suppression of armed military resistance.

Some acts of violence, of course, had nothing to do with political or military necessity but were committed for personal reasons, such as vengeance, jealousy, or material gain. All armed detachments had an opportunity to commit such crimes and to settle scores with neighbours. Police, partisans, NKVD troops, marauders, and pillagers were all guilty. Local conditions frequently governed the reasons for this violence and its level of ferocity. Russian scholarship has not been able to challenge the established myopic focus on "traitors" in accounts of the Second World War.

A third set of narratives has examined the Division in the context of the Polish-Ukrainian conflict. The focus of these narratives has mostly been on the Beyersdorff Battle Group in the Biłgoraj area, the 5th Galician ss Volunteer Regiment in the Lublin distict and the 4th Galician ss in Galicia district. The internecine struggle between Ukrainian and Polish communities exploded in Volhynia in 1943, spread to Galicia in 1944, and then engulfed the Ukrainian population of Poland from 1944 to 1947. Polish and Ukrainian undergrounds fought one another, with the involvement of German troops, Polish and Ukrainian police groups, Soviet partisans, and Red Army forces. All groups relied upon or compelled assistance from local populations, which were often victimized.

The conflict was fuelled by deportations and population transfers, which pitted local populations against one another. The scholarly focus has been on the Volhynian massacres in 1943, but the destruction in "Zakerzonnia," from which many Galicia Division soldiers came, was equally devastating.

Ihor Hałagida, who has made a study of the number of Ukrainian victims in the Lublin district under German occupation, indicates that the most ruthless Ukrainian-Polish conflicts and the greatest number of killings occurred in the Hrubieszów and Zamość counties between 1942 and 1944, in large part because the Germans had begun to remove local populations (Hałagida 2019, 249).[6] From November 1942 to August 1943, 110,000 Poles (including 30,000 children) were expelled from 300 settlements, mostly in Zamość county. Over 11,600 were killed during resistance; many of the 58,000 who escaped joined the underground. The plan had been to settle 13,000 Germans and Volksdeutsche colonists on the farms of the displaced and simultaneously to resettle 18,000 Ukrainians as a barrier between Poles and Germans. The entire project, dubbed *Aktion Zamosc,* was a disaster and "turned Lublin district into into an ethnic war zone" (Markiewicz 2021, 184).

The intercommunal violence, much of it due to robbery by armed gangs, took on mass proportions. The eighteen thousand Ukrainians who had been forcibly resettled on lands taken from Poles were targeted both by gangs and the underground, which, on 22 January 1944, issued an order to sabotage the resettlement (Hałagida 2019, 255, 262–3). The worst massacres took place in March and April 1944. In a coordinated action beginning on 9 March, at least forty-nine Ukrainian villages were destroyed in the Tomaszów Lubelski area and 1,385 to 2,500 inhabitants were killed (267–8). Altogether in the Lublin district in March and April, 2,343 Ukrainians were killed, including 874 women and 433 children. The vast majority – at least 2,228 – were victims of the Polish underground. Since most were men over the age of fifty, women, and children, it was clear they had been targeted because of their nationality. In total, under German occupation, at least 4,484 Ukrainians were killed in the district. Although German troops and Soviet partisans were responsible for a number of these deaths, 3,700 to 3,800 were victims of the Polish-Ukrainian conflict (275).

Most Western and Polish scholarly accounts consider the killing of Poles in Volhynia in 1943 to have been a planned ethnic cleansing by the UPA. Some Polish narratives, however, are examples of "atrocity literature" produced for popular consumption. When dealing with war crimes, whether in Volhynia, Galicia, or "Zakerzonnia," this literature tends to condemn without closer investigation.[7] As a result, some incorrect reports based on hearsay have been recycled, sometimes by unscrupulous media campaigns, or even guided by tweets from the Russian Embassy in Canada.[8] Placing sensationalist articles has been a tactic in publicity wars. It was part of the USSR's disinformation playbook in the 1970s and 1980s, when attacks against the Division were designed to drive a wedge between the Ukrainian and Jewish communities, who were at the time defending arrested and imprisoned Soviet dissidents.[9]

Polish researchers have now published a series of serious scholarly investigations into atrocities against Polish villages. These have rejected often-repeated accusations against the Division and verified others, as already noted, concerning the 4th and 5th Galician Volunteer Regiments.

Nonetheless, the clash of Polish and Ukrainian undergrounds remains a contentious topic. Poles began organizing their armed resistance in 1943. Best known is the Home Army (AK, or Armia Krajowa), but the People's Army (AL, or Armia Ludowa) and the Peasants' Battalions (BCh, or Bataliony Chłopskie) were also active. The AK was loyal to the London-based government in exile, while the AL was an arm of the Soviet intervention; and the BCh, although partially integrated into the AK, often recognized the authority of a local commander. Polish communities in rural areas created strongholds for the purpose of self-defence and turned to the AK for help. If this force did not appear, the villages often asked Soviet partisans for protection. By 1944, Moscow was denouncing troops loyal to the London-based Polish government as "fascist" and arrested them when it gained control of a territory.

There was also a Polish "Dark Blue Police" that served the Germans.[10] Early in 1943, after Ukrainians deserted from German police units in Volhynia, they were replaced with about twelve hundred Poles, who were used in anti-partisan operations (Markiewicz 2021, 153). Soviet partisans reported that, in Volhynia and Galicia, the Germans used Poles against Ukrainians in the same way as in "Zakerzonnia" they used Ukrainians against Poles (Zajączkowski 2017, 136–7, 141).

In February 1944 the AK activated Operation Tempest, which aimed at capturing Lviv and larger urban centres as soon as the Germans left. The AK's 27th Wolyn (Volhynia) Division, a force of seven thousand to nine thousand men, was guilty of several atrocities. Soviet forces, for example, reported that it sent a special battalion to Ukrainian villages. With red ribbons attached to its clothing it called the villagers together, ostensibly for "political-educational work," then murdered them and burned the village. According to Soviet partisan reports, these actions were designed to

Accomplices, Traitors, and Foes • **323**

spread information about "Soviet bestiality" in the local population. They took place as part of Operation Tempest in February and March of 1944 in villages that were considered UPA bases or that were being punished for attacks on Polish settlements (Zajączkowski 2017, 147–8). Not infrequently, Polish informers denounced Ukrainian nationalist activity to provoke German reprisals (154–5). The UPA used a similar tactic (Motyka 1999, 200; Zajączkowski 2015, 331–3).

When, on 10 March 1944, the 27th Division attacked Ukrainian settlements, this was taken as a signal that Ukrainians were to be removed as a hostile population (Huk 2018, xxvii). The massacre at Sahryn, committed on that day, now plays a symbolic role in Ukrainian memory, similar to Huta Peniatska in Polish. At least 606 people were killed, almost all Ukrainians, including 231 women and 151 children (Hałagida 2019, 270–1). However, most scholars note that the scale and intensity of the massacres committed in 1943 in Volhynia against Polish civilian populations was greater than the violence west of the Curson Line.

After the AK was dissolved on 19 January 1945, some of its units began co-operating with the Polish army and groups like the People's Armed Forces (NSZ, or Narodowe Siły Zbrojne). Several atrocities took place in the ensuing months, including in the Ukrainian village of Wierzchowiny (Ukr: Verkhovyna) near Lublin, where on 6 June 1945 a detachment of the NSZ along with the Polish army murdered 196 people. Massacres took place in Piskorowice (Ukr: Pyskovorychi) near Rzeszów, where on 17 April 1945 between 160 and 400 Ukrainians were killed by the National Military Organization (NOW, or Narodowa Organizacja Wojskowa), and in Pawłokoma (Ukr: Pavlokoma) near Przemyśl on 3 March 1945, where between 150 and 500 people were killed.

The new Polish-Soviet border was ratified on 5 February 1946, at which time Poland ceded to the Soviet Union 90 percent of the territory the latter had occupied in 1939. The new communist government in Warsaw then co-operated with Moscow and Kyiv in a massive population exchange, which was in effect an ethnic cleansing. West of the Curzon Line it removed the Ukrainian population between the rivers San (Ukr: Sian) and Bug (Ukr: Buh). The deportations ended with the violent expulsion of the entire Lemko population in Operation Vistula (Akcja Wisła) in 1947.

Once the Allies had signed the Yalta Agreement, between 4 and 11 February 1945, and accepted the new Polish-Soviet border, the London-based government lost relevance. However, some Polish partisans refused to accept the communist government in Warsaw, regrouped, and on 2 September 1945 created Freedom and Independence (WiN, or Wolność i Niezawisłość). In 1945, a shared pro-Western and anti-Soviet orientation created the foundation for co-operation between the UPA and WiN. The two came to an agreement in the area southeast of Lublin, where they conducted joint actions against NKVD outposts until Operation Vistula in the fall of 1947.[11]

Joint operations became possible because the balance of forces between Ukrainians and Poles in Tomaszów county was roughly equal and the local Polish political administration was supportive. Moreover, the WiN had decided that a military victory was not possible and no longer insisted that Volhynia and Galicia had to be part of postwar Poland. This territorial demand had been a cornerstone of Polish policy since the beginning of the war, in fact since the creation of the new Polish state in 1918. The Ukrainian underground argued that, if the Polish government had agreed to agrarian reforms that allowed greater Ukrainian ownership of land, and to Galicia's autonomy, a Polish-Ukrainian conflict could have been avoided (Huk 2018, 22).

The UPA's leadership had already realized in the autumn of 1943 that its decision to unleash an attack on the Polish population of Volhynia was a costly error and issued statements condemning the violence. The Polish underground made similar attempts to reign in the violence.[12] Civilians were, however, drawn into a brutal "war-within-a-war," which then became a "war-after-the-war."

Operation Tempest's attempt to gain control of Galicia and reincorporate it into a postwar Poland collapsed on 27 July 1944. On that day all Polish flags in Lviv were removed, Polish divisions were disarmed, and arrests began (Huk 2018, 64–5). Poles were mobilized into the Red Army. 11,713 men and 1,712 women were taken from the Ternopil area alone; an estimated 45 percent joined voluntarily, but most were captured in dragnet operations (Haidai et al. 2002, 74). They were absorbed into the 1st Polish Army (Pierwsza Armia Wojska Polskiego), known as Berling's army. In February 1945, 292 punitive battalions were created from the local population, forty-four of them in Ternopil. Poles were often the majority in these forces.

Overall, partisan forces on both the Ukrainian and Polish side were formidable. A Polish intelligence report from 21 June 1944 put the number of UPA fighters at forty thousand (PISM, A.48.4/B1, doc. 45). AK support in Ukraine has been estimated at ten thousand, and in Poland itself at several hundred thousand.

Simple perpetrator-victim narratives are confounded by these wartime complexities. Although the tendency in contemporary Russia, Poland, and Ukraine has often been to romanticize local partisan movements, not everyone – either during or after the war – accepted the image of partisans as heroes and liberators. In spite of the widespread postwar awareness that partisan conflicts had contributed to lawlessness and violence, this issue became a taboo topic in public discussions, except when it was used to demonized the "Other."

The pervasive wartime violence was sometimes invoked as a justification for the Galicia Division's creation. The idea that the force could help maintain stability and preserve economic and cultural life made some sense in the maelstrom of conflicts, and Ukrainian soldiers in German uniforms were welcomed in many places. At the same time, many of the Division's soldiers, even though they would not have admitted it later when the "patriotic" narrative became dominant, enlisted in the Division precisely to escape the surrounding violence and to survive the war.

20

MONUMENTS AND MEMORY

Thirty kilometres from the Rimini camp, in Cervia, a cemetery was created for thirty-nine soldiers of the Division who died in Italy, many from injuries suffered during the war. The headstone on the grave of each soldier was a cement cross with the words "To those who fought for Ukraine's freedom" written in both Latin and Ukrainian. The individual's name, rank, and date of death was inscribed on a metal plate made of casings from cannon shells found near an anti-aircraft bunker. Each plate was cut, flattened, and polished by the camp's master metalworker Yaroslav Kuchynskyi, and the camp engraver Petro Cholii fashioned the inscriptions.

Cervia would not be the permanent resting place for these men. By agreement with the West German and Italian governments, in 1966 a large cemetery for thirty-six thousand soldiers was created in the Apennine Mountains near the Futa Pass (Passo della Futa), fifty kilometres north of Florence. The graves here were placed around a road that moves in an upward spiral towards a hilltop with a monument and a crypt for church services. Markers from various cemeteries, including the Cervia cemetery, have been built into the crypt's walls. Within this cemetery the remains of the Ukrainian soldiers are on the twenty-third field, which has a memorial plate located in its centre (Budnyi 1979, 145–6).

The typical marker on Ukrainian military cemeteries is the Petliura cross, named after the Petliura medal, which was instituted on 22 May 1932 by the High Command of the UNR army and confirmed by the president in exile, Andrii Livytskyi.[1] This type of cross, with its embedded trident, is found on the graves of many soldiers who fought for the UNR and

Figure 20.1 Cemetery in Cervia where 39 Division soldiers who died in Italy were buried. They are now reburied in Passo della Futa.

Figure 20.2 Inscription on Cervia monument: "To fighters for Ukraine's freedom." This monument is now embedded in the crypt in Passo della Futa.

individuals who belonged to that generation. Examples can be seen in the cemetery in the Wola suburb of Warsaw, in Tsebliv near Sokal, Ukraine ("Neznanomu" 2021), in the Yanivska Cemetery, Lviv, and in South Bound Brook, New Jersey. Whenever these crosses were destroyed during Soviet times, the marker and wording were restored.

This cross is now the standard one for soldiers' graves. The Ukrainian government's Institute of National Memory website recommends the design for its military cemeteries. It has been used, for example, in the large Kherson cemetery.[2] In recent times a similar design has appeared on sites where victims of Bolshevik terror are buried. One such cross marks the place in Vinnytsia where people were executed in the autumn of 1922 ("Na Vinnychchyni" 2020). Another has been erected in Sandarmokh (part of the Solovki archipelago in the Arkhangelsk oblast of Russia), where around 7,000 people of many different nationalities, including 677 Ukrainians, were executed in 1937. The largest group, consisting of 1,111 people, was shot on 4 November 1937, on the twentieth anniversary of the "October" Revolution.[3] Today this form of cross has become popular in Ukraine as a monument marking respect for the country's defenders against Russian military aggression in the Donbas.

Many markers on the graves of Galicia Division veterans copy this design and retain the traditional statement that the soldier died fighting for Ukraine's freedom or independence. Some have a modified version of the cross with a different inscription. The monument to the Division's soldiers in Gnas, Austria, has the words in German: "To the Unknown Soldier" (Sharko 1990, 54). A graphic of the same Petliura cross accompanied obituaries in the Division's journals.

As in many military cemeteries, the soldiers are often buried together with individual crosses spaced at regular intervals. This is the case in the village of Chervonyi near Zolochiv in Lviv oblast, where a cemetery for six hundred soldiers of the Galicia Division was recently created. Its central monument is a small chapel. The cemetery site is symbolic and is used as a place of commemoration, but when the remains of Galician soldiers are found, they are reburied there. There is also a cemetery in Ozhydiv near Brody, which is now the scene of an annual commemoration on 22 July, the date when many soldiers were captured or shot near this location. Like the Lychakivskyi Cemetery in Lviv, these sites in Ukraine have become "places of memory," where various groups pay respect to the dead, recall the past,

Figure 20.3 Monument to all fallen Ukrainian soldiers in St Andrew's Cemetery, South Bound Brook, New Jersey.

Figure 20.4 Base of monument to fallen soldiers in South Bound Brook, showing the UNA's emblem (lion) next to the UNR's emblem (Petliura Cross).

and conduct rituals. However, most veterans of the Galicia Division are buried in graveyards in Austria, Canada, the US, the UK, Italy, and Germany.

The cross that became the Division's postwar emblem is symmetrical and more closely resembles what is known as the Cossack cross, a design of Byzantine origin already found on Cossack graves from the seventeenth and eighteenth centuries. In later centuries an adaptation of this design was used for military medals, including the Prussian and German Iron Cross, the British Victoria Cross, and the Russian Imperial Cross of St George. The Polish Virtuti Militari version, with a lion rampant and three stars on a shield in the centre, became the badge of the 1st Division of the UNA. It is on the monument in the cemetery in Oakville, Ontario, and on many gravestones.

The defacing and destruction of monuments, particularly graves of soldiers who fought in Ukrainian armies, has taken place since the revolutionary struggles of 1917–20. Such vandalism has occurred far beyond

Figure 20.5 Mykola Francuzenko (Frantsuzhenko) interviewing Jack Palance, with Ulas Samchuk in foreground. At the unveiling of the Shevchenko monument, Washington, 1964. Francuzenko worked for Voice of America and Radio Free Europe.

the boundaries of Ukraine and has almost always been politically motivated, even when the sites or monuments have no connection to military history but merely represent a Ukrainian cultural figure, such as Taras Shevchenko or Oleksandr Oles.

Recently a newspaper reported graffiti on a memorial at the St Volodymyr Ukrainian Cemetery in Oakville, Ontario, which was created in 1984 and includes the graves of UPA soldiers as well as members of the Galicia Division. Some of the latter are buried with other family members. There is a memorial stone dedicated to the 1st Division of the UNA, with its postwar emblem, the symmetrical cross with a lion rampant in the centre. The wording on the monument, in Ukrainian, English, and French, reads: "To those who died for the freedom of Ukraine." Beneath are the words: "In memory of combatants from the 1st Division of UD-UNA and those who fought in defence of Brody in 1944." Brody was often referred to during postwar commemorations as symbolizing the struggle against the Soviet state (Maletskyi 1981, 115). Similar wording is now sometimes used in Ukraine. In 2002, for example, the city of Ivano-Frankivsk recognized the men as "fighters for freedom and independence."

Monuments and Memory • 331

Figure 20.6 Monument to the Division's soldiers in St Volodymyr Cemetery, Oakville, Ontario.

Most incidents of vandalism have press coverage as their objective. An article in the *Ottawa Citizen* on 17 July 2020 describes the Oakville monument as an obelisk to Nazis and the ss. It includes a photograph taken late in the evening, which made the marker appear large and menacing but which hid the cross and the wording (Pugliese 2020).[4] The article states that the men took an oath to Hitler, killed "Poles, women and children as well as Jews," and greeted Himmler's speech in 1944 with cheers. It alleges that the Division killed hundreds of Polish civilians in 1944 in the village of Huta Peniatska, fudging the fact that the 4th Galician Volunteer Regiment was likely responsible. The phrases "some Ukrainians dispute" and "only small elements from the unit" indicate that the reporter was aware of this. There is no mention of the fact that the Nazis viewed the Slavs as racially inferior, that the force had Christian chaplains, or that the destruction of

Huta Peniatska was recognized on 28 February 2009 in a commemoration attended by the presidents of Poland and Ukraine.[5]

The point in this kind of article is of course not to sift evidence but to stir outrage. The repetition of words like "allegations," "accusations," and "Waffen-ss" is done for this purpose. There is no reference to the Waffen-ss on the cemetery marker: it is provided by the reporter. The article does not quote the actual wording, nor does it try to explain why the soldiers were ready to bear the stigma of association with the German army and Hitler's abhorrent regime.

An article in the *Winnipeg Free Press* on 2 November 2017 notes that tweets from the Russian Embassy had claimed that the Oakville monument glorified Nazis. The same article mentions Chrystia Freeland, who at the time was Canada's minister of foreign affairs. It describes her grandfather as a Nazi collaborator who edited a Ukrainian-language newspaper that published "anti-Semitic rants and encouraged volunteers to join the 14th Waffen ss Galizien Division" (Taylor 2017). It then refers to the annihilation of the Warsaw Jewish ghetto, to the massacre in Huta Peniatska, where "children were killed by having their heads smashed against trees," all because the residents "had been harbouring Jews," and to the Nachtigall battalion as "responsible for the murder of between 4,000 and 6,000 Jews." In case readers had missed the reference to Freeland, it is repeated two more times.[6] The journalist's authority for these "gory details" is Christopher Hale, whom the article describes as an "award-winning historian."

Hale's book proposes a novel theory – that Himmler "imagined a future ss Europa which had dispensed with the NSDAP and its leader Adolf Hitler and was chopped up into ss-ruled provinces" (Hale 2011, 438). According to Hale, Himmler's master-plan was to remove both Hitler and the Nazis, and to rule by means of the ss. This is a reworking of the idea that the ss was a state within a state, run by an elite of savage soldiers. The difference is that Hale makes non-Germans central to his conspiracy. Their military training is described as "packaging" nationalism and anti-Semitism, a form of indoctrination that produced "foreign executioners" from all Europe (131).

Although the book describes crimes committed by numerous Waffen-ss units, it offers no new information on the Galicia Division. Nachtigall, the Lviv pogroms of 1941, and Huta Peniatska are all invoked. For good measure Khmelnytskyi's responsibility for the killing of Jews in the seventeenth century is recalled, along with Petliura's for the violence in 1919

(Hale 2011, 157). Presumably, the point is to demonstrate that Ukrainians have continually exhibited an endemic anti-Semitism and to discredit their attempts to assert an independent and democratic state. Hale has difficulty both linking Nachtigall to the Lviv pogrom and providing evidence of the Division's war crimes (173). He therefore describes the link to the Trawniki men as "crucial." Readers are informed that the individuals who trained at Trawniki, "including Mr Fostun and other Ukrainian volunteers who would later serve in the ss 'Galicien,' liquidated the Warsaw ghetto in April 1943" (338, 343). In this way Fostun's name is used to connect the Division, the concentration camps, and the Holocaust. Huta Peniatska is attributed to the Division, as is Nižna Boca in Slovakia. Hendy's report is the source for the latter accusation (362, 406–7). No countervailing evidence is provided and no deeper investigation attempted.

The mottos "fought for freedom" and "defended Ukraine" have irked the researcher Per Rudling, who goes beyond associating the Division with Nazi ideology and suggests that the veterans living in North America belonged to a silent, secret brotherhood that resembled those created by former German and Swedish Waffen-ss soldiers (Rudling 2012, 334). The most widespread conspiracy theory of this nature is ODESSA (Organisation der ehemaligen ss-Angehörigen). In 1945, the myth of a powerful organization of former ss members that had transferred stolen Nazi gold to Argentina and that was building a "Fourth Reich" had already been investigated and dismissed as baseless by British and US intelligence. It resurfaced in the press in 1962 and was publicized by the British novelist Frederick Forsyth in his *The Odessa File* (1972). It was then picked up by the Austrian Nazi hunter Simon Wiesenthal and by the World Jewish Congress in 1996–97 (Dorril 2000, 95–7). Elements of the hoax are believed to have originated within the British intelligence community to justify prolonging the existence of "Special Operations" capability at the end of the Second World War (98). Academic research has demonstrated that the networks of former ss men were, in fact, small and "far from powerful or centralized" (Steinacher et al. 2017, 321). In the chaotic postwar months they operated briefly and spasmodically, supplying forged papers to help their members stay alive and evade arrest, and then faded into oblivion (Dorril 2000, 102). Scholars who have described surviving European Waffen-ss associations show how far removed their self-image was from that of "Galicia" soldiers (see Hurd and Werther 2017, 332–55).

The Division's veterans did not show the slightest interest in these groups, in the Waffen-ss "anthem," or in a European "Germanic" crusade. If they had even heard of "Blue Mountain" celebrations they would have found them ridiculous. The idea of a neo-Nazi "transnational discursive space" was a concept entirely foreign to them, even at the time of enlistment. After the war the *dyviziinyky* assimilated culturally into Western society and identified with its mainstream values. Although politically conservative, they were strong supporters of democratic norms, and in Canada, for example, of multiculturalism, a policy officially announced on 9 October 1971.[7] One needs only to read the articles of their spokesmen, people like Petro Savaryn and Myroslaw Maleckyj, to become convinced of this. The latter headed the Brotherhood in the years between 1964 and 1973 and 1979 and 2001, and edited *Visti kombatanta* from 1974 to 2001. His articles from the journal were republished in *Bez illiuzii* (Without illusions, 1981) and *Priorytety* (Priorities, 1996). They are commentaries on democracy, minorities, personal and collective rights, and the collapse of empires. After the declaration of independence in 1991, he criticized the "integral nationalists" as well as those who attempted to introduce from abroad the idea of voluntarism, writing that their "empty phrases" had long lost their sheen. In his view, the glorification of oun leaders "served only Russian imperialists," who find it convenient to narrow the struggle for independence to one small group or party and to deny its broad support in the population (Maletskyi 1996, 93).

Maleckyj favours the liberal patriotism of Mazzini and warns of the dangers posed by all tyrannies. Of particular interest are his reflections on the rights of minorities. He considers it axiomatic that political states are never monoliths but are always composed of different nationalities (Maletskyi 1996, 142). It is crucially important therefore for Ukraine to pay attention to its minority communities, such as the Polish and Jewish. Already in 1987 during the Deschênes Commission inquiry he wrote: "There can be no doubt that the Jewish people were greatly victimized and suffered enormous moral, material and physical losses during the Second World War. This is absolutely true, as is the fact that those people still alive who were guilty of perpetrating the evil should be punished" (194). Maleckyj stresses the importance of rationally understanding political processes and the danger of mythologizing the past or manufacturing cultural heroes for partisan purposes.

European neo-Nazi re-enactments and revivals, although a fascinating topic for contemporary Western researchers, were ignored by the Division's veterans. Ironically, today's transnational neo-fascism can be most closely linked to the Russian right, in particular to Alexander Dugin, who has long been obsessed with the Third Reich, Eurasianism, and mystical nationalism (Clover 2016, 151–74, 277–305). Current scholarship demonstrates the Russian elite's links to this ultra-right movement (Laruelle 2015; Shekhovtsov 2017, 163–205). It also shows how the fascist "neo-Eurasian" network is being used in Russia's war against Ukraine (Borysenko et al. 2017; Di Pasquale 2021, 267–84).

Surprisingly, Rudling can find no "overt" indication that the Division was dedicated to Ukrainian statehood. He repeats that the men "faithfully" served the Führer and dispensed anti-Semitic propaganda "until the very last days of the war" (Rudling 2012, 360). He attributes the destruction of Huta Peniatska to the the 4th Galician Volunteer Regiment but, like many commentators, conflates this unit with the Galicia Division (352–4). The desire to uncover a conspiracy leads him to statements that border on the bizarre, such as the claim that "a center of former Waffen ss-Galizien veterans in London sought to establish a military dictatorship in Ukraine" (364). The source for this information, which is presented as indisputable fact, is the KGB interrogation in 1954 of an arrested member of the underground.

Dubious Polish accounts are described as "rather shrill," and Sol Littman's scurrilous attacks as "partly written in form [sic] of polemics" (Rudling 2012, 336). On the other hand, the Deschênes Commission's report is described as "now a quarter century old and written before Soviet archives were made available" (336). The researcher hints at coverups and material still to be revealed. One can only hope that further materials will indeed become available and that a clearer picture emerges both of the Division and all its members.

It is tempting for journalists and researchers to follow established patterns by repeating rhetorical phrases and code words, and to insinuate direct or indirect connections. Sometimes, however, these established patterns are the product of disinformation campaigns. One disinformation strategy relies on repetition, often by creating "informational cascades" that make use of tabloid newspapers as well as internet postings. By isolating these patterns, it is possible to identify a particular constellation of arguments that together generate "rhetorical elements capable of shaping a certain perception or opinion" (Kragh 2021, 330). The use of tropes – repeated and familiar but unexamined images – is frequently encountered in propaganda. It can also be observed in what has been called "postmemory," or the transmuting of history into myth (Hirsch 2008).

One recent book describes the technique of "gaslighting," a tactic that avoids problematic referents directly but, instead, evokes them by innuendo and allusion (Danesi 2020, 114). The gaslighting effect is produced gradually and repetitively through dog whistles and by invoking perceived enemies. It avoids accountability by not providing concrete references. A metaphor is considered real evidence, even when it conjures up a false referent. Danesi explains: "There is no such thing as a *unicorn*. But the word still conjures up the image of a horse with a single straight horn jutting out from its forehead. We get this image from mythic stories, of course. But the fact that it pops up in the mind via the word impels us to accept it as having some hidden significance, even though we know it is an imaginary referent" (119–20).

What I take to be the mainstream channel of research – from Reitlinger in the 1950s; Höhne and Stein in the 1960s; through Weale, Melnyk, Bolianovskyi, Khromeychuk, and Ponomarenko; to the recent volume of essays edited by Böhler and Gerwarth; and the study of collaboration by Markiewicz – refuses the caricature of non-German soldiers in the Waffen-ss. It does not try to stereotype them as psychopathic criminals, mentally unstable fanatics, or monsters but, rather, attempts to analyze the reasons for volunteering and to contextualize events within social, economic, and cultural history. The overall findings are clear: Himmler decided to open up his "Black Order" to non-Germans and non-Nordic volunteers only after realizing that German rule could not be established by exterminating 30 million Slavs, erasing national identities, bringing in German settlers, and "Germanizing" local populations. Most Eastern European "volunteers" strongly opposed these plans and had little interest in Nazi ideology. They had their own agendas, which, in the case of Ukrainians, did not include becoming Germans or fighting Western democracies. By 1944 the bulk of the combat units could often barely speak German, were "at best, dubiously motivated," and "in no military sense could they ever be described as a *corps d'élite*" (Weale 2012, 307). A wealth of information concerning the issue of motivation and German-Ukrainian relations can be found in the literature and testimonies of war witnesses – participants and survivors. This archival evidence challenges researchers who rely on the "generic" image of a pan-European Waffen-ss conspiracy.

Ukrainian veterans created the Brotherhood of Former Soldiers in Neu-Ulm in 1949. Its centre was first in Munich, moved to New York in the late 1950s, and then to Toronto in the mid-1960s. The organization's original purpose was to strengthen Ukrainian identity in the diaspora. Through grants it supported university students, scholarship, and book publishing. In 1991, it also contributed to the erection of a monument to the Division's soldiers in the village of Yaseniv near Brody. This was blown up in the same year and then restored (Kutyshenko 2019, 21). The Brotherhood's journalists and memory keepers wrote about political events in *Visti kombatanta* but gradually shifted their focus from the Division's own history to wider community concerns. Contributors commented on the USSR, visits to Canada by Soviet dignitaries, the dissidents of the 1960s and 1970s, the explosion at Chernobyl, the Deschênes Commission, and numerous other issues. Several veterans demonstrated considerable political acumen and became prominent figures in diaspora life. Vasyl Veryha, for example, became secretary of the World Congress of Free Ukrainians, while Petro Savaryn became president of the Progressive Conservative Association of Alberta, chancellor of the University of Alberta and president of the World Congress of Free Ukrainians. However, as Olesya Khromeychuk points out, the Division's soldiers were just over eight thousand out of more than 200,000 postwar DPs of Ukrainian origin who prefered to remain in the West (Khromeychuk 2013, 169). Because this DP generation was familiar with many aspects of Soviet life and made its views known, it became a bugbear for the Kremlin's propagandists. All émigré or diaspora figures who criticized Soviet policies had the pro-Nazi slur attached to them by Kremlin propagandists in an effort to discredit their views.

In 1992, the Brotherhood set up branches in Lviv, Ternopil, Ivano-Frankivsk, and Drohobych. The years that followed saw the publication of several books on the formation in Ukraine. Aimed at a popular audience, this literature tried to affirm the Division's patriotic image.[8] Nonetheless, contemporary Ukrainian attitudes towards the force have varied. Both personal recollections and historical narratives have often clashed (Khromeychuk 2012, 2016; Marples 2008–09; Himka 2005, 2009).

The contemporary war cannot be ignored in this context. Russia has demonstrated that it is prepared to invade Ukraine, dismember it, and erase its cultural identity, while ignoring all international agreements, conventions, and norms that are marks of a civilized society. The need for an army capable of opposing military intervention has contributed in Ukraine, in a few circles at least, to a more positive image of the Galicia Division. The *dyviziinyky*, after all, consistently warned of Russia's aggressive intentions and of the need for military preparedness. The issue, however, is a broader one. In current circumstances contemporaries are willing to draw inspiration from any historical group that preached militant resistance to Russian imperialism. The present moment has stimulated interest in armed struggles of the past.

Despite efforts made by veterans, the "servants of Hitler" image has remained attached to the Division and prevented its recognition as a patriotic formation. On 9 April 2015, the Ukrainian Parliament failed to include it in a list of twentieth-century organizations and armed forces that had contributed to the struggle for independence, which was declared on 24 August 1991 ("Zakon" 2015). In contrast, the UPA and OUN appeared on the list. At the same time as it presented the list, Parliament made it illegal to publicly deny the legitimacy of Ukraine's twentieth-century struggle for independence. It characterized denials as affronts to the memory of those individuals who had been part of the listed groups and to "the dignity of the Ukrainian people" (ibid.)

Recent "memory wars" around the globe have raised similar questions concerning what monuments and commemorations are socially acceptable. Statues to Canada's first prime minister, John A. Macdonald, have been toppled and vandalized because he is held responsible for policies that victimized Indigenous populations. Louis Riel, the founder of the province of Manitoba and leader of a rebellion by the Métis people, was hanged for treason in 1885, but two statues in Winnipeg now honour him and an annual public holiday is named after him. His armed struggle against the government is today viewed as contributing to shaping Canada's history.

Many memorials erected in previous times are now seen as problematic because the figures and events they mark can be simultaneously celebrated and condemned. A statue of Winston Churchill has been spray-painted with the words "racist" by individuals who consider him a war criminal and imperialist. In the last few years numerous monuments associated with imperial and colonial pasts have come under scrutiny because they represent figures accused of racism, anti-Semitism, or chauvinism. Although plaques or other markers to the Division are not in public spaces but, rather, on sites where the men are buried, the message of these markers – whatever the

Figure 20.7 Monument to General Andrei Vlasov in Nanuet, New Jersey, with the ROA emblem and flag.

Figure 20.8 Close up of Vlasov monument showing three flags. Carved into the side are the words "To those who fell in the struggle for a free Russia."

wording – is contentious. The conflict over how to interpret any gravestone or marker, particularly in Eastern Europe, is in fact part of the wider debate over how to characterize not only a particular military formation but also the history of the Second World War.

Two monuments in the Russian Orthodox cemetery in Nanuet, New York, have not so far been subject to as much vitriolic comment as the Division's, although they represent equally controversial service in the German army. One is dedicated to General Andrei Vlasov and his ROA, the second to the Russian Protective Corps (Russkii Korpus), which was created in Serbia, served in the German army in the years between 1942 and 1944, and, at one point, included over seventeen thousand men. The two monuments are the focus of annual religious commemorations. Vlasov's portrait is on the first monument, along with the ROA insignia and the words "Died in the Struggle for a Free Russia 1941–1945." The unit's flag flies in the background. The monument to the Russian Corps is a chapel-like structure with a plaque

Figure 20.9 Monument to the Russian Corps, Nanuet, New Jersey.

that states: "To the Soldiers of the Russian Corps" who "died on the field of battle 1941–45." In Russia's Rostov oblast, in Elasnsk Stanitsa, there is also a monument to General Petr Krasnov, who commanded eighteen thousand Cossacks during the war and wore the Ribbon of Saint George, a Russian imperial symbol, over his German uniform.

A controversy recently took place in Ukraine over the Division's emblem, the golden lion and three crowns. The legal question was whether reproduction or display of the symbol broke a law banning propaganda for "communist and national socialist totalitarian regimes" ("Symvolika" 2020). In 2020, a court of appeal ruled that it was not a Nazi symbol and allowed its use, along with the name 1st Ukrainian Division of the UNA. In fact, since 1945 only this symbol and name have been used by veterans in their publications and commemorations, and on many graves.

Today the dual naming – as the 14th Waffen-ss Galicia Division and the 1st Division of the UNA – reflects different views of the formation and its place in history. Collaboration with the German army was considered a regrettable necessity at the time of enlistment. It was described as such in private correspondence during the war and also in all postwar literature and oral testimony. After the war the association with Germany was a badge of shame from which veterans tried to distance themselves by downplaying or avoiding imagery that recalled the German military, including the ss runes. Although these were stamped on the Division's standard-issue helmets, they were never shown in graphics, books, or journals produced by the veterans. Nor were they ever seen at the funerals and commemorative ceremonies they organized or on the monuments they erected. The emblem of the UNA, the national flag, and the "fought-for-Ukraine" moniker up to a point succeeded in "rebranding" the Division. Nonetheless, scholars have noted, although it was created towards the end of the war "and thus did not participate in the most infamous crimes of the Nazis, which had already been committed, it shared the notoriety of the Waffen ss in the post-war period" (Khromeychuk 2013, 62). There is an irony in the fact that when created the force was not allowed to use the term "Ukrainian" or to display the trident, and that Himmler insisted that the soldiers could not be referred to as ss men. Today this last designation is often the primary one attached to the formation.

In postwar years, by fashioning a patriotic narrative with appropriate imagery, the veterans to some degree, at least in their own minds, "became" what they wanted to be from the start and then projected this desired identity onto the Division's entire existence. In this way one type of imagery superimposed itself upon another. This may be considered an attempt to manipulate institutional memory; if so, it was largely unsuccessful. The Waffen-ss mark pursued the men in emigration, continually requiring explanations and expressions of regret. The two sets of images today represent the dual identity. After all, even at the time of the first enlistment the soldiers were simultaneously referred to as members of the "Waffen-ss," the "Ukrainian division," and "our boys." The ambiguity has persisted.

Reactions to a parade that took place on 28 April 2021 illustrate the contest over legacy. This date, on which in 1943 the Division's formation was announced in Lviv, had never previously been marked, much less celebrated, and no march had ever been held in Kyiv. The event therefore appears to have been a provocation. The young people who participated may have seen themselves as historical re-enactors; a few may even have identified with national socialism, although more likely they saw the event as a form of epatage. Whatever the case, they were condemned in the press, which pointed out that such performances have no place in a democratic society. The Division's veterans would themselves have been dismayed by an attempt to assert the link to Nazism, which today, again ironically, serves to discredit the idea of Ukrainian independence. Some participants in the parade may have felt they they were countering the pro-Russian march that was to take place on 9 May – a parade that allows its participants to praise Stalin, celebrates the Soviet "conquest" of Western Europe, and glorifies the idea of Russian supremacy.

Whatever the case, Ukraine's president and Ministry of Foreign Affairs both condemned the parade of 28 April 2021 on their websites.[9] Commentators underlined the message that the Division's creation represented a tragic moment in Ukrainian history, a time when millions of citizens were drawn into the armies of warring states. The dominant opinion was that the Division's history had to be studied and discussed, not celebrated.

The two competing parades illustrated different political reflexes. The one marking the Division's proclamation can be seen as a misguided anti-colonial and anti-imperial response; the pro-Russian march can be seen as an attempt to reassert an empire's claims. The massing of Russian troops along Ukraine's borders and the fear of losing sovereignty gave rise to the first reflex. As the war with Russia has shown, Ukrainians overwhelmingly believe that they have a right to defend their statehood and to resist external aggression. In this context the Division's history, in some minds at least, serves as an example of commitment to armed struggle. However, the present context differs vastly from that of 1943. Today the country is an internationally recognized independent state. It is not an aggressor in the war, nor is it aligned with aggressor states with genocidal intentions. Its patriots, who come from many backgrounds and creeds, are committed to building a democratic society. They do not wear foreign uniforms or march under foreign flags.

For these reasons, despite the grim reality of war with Russia, the history of the Galicia Division has resonated only to a limited degree with the

Figure 20.10 Reburial of a Division soldier's remains. Chervone, 19 July 2015.

Figure 20.11 Anniversary of Brody. Chervone, 24 July 2005.
Left to right: Mykhailo Mulyk, Volodymyr Malkosh, Yurii Ferentsevych, Ivan Mamchur.

citizens of Ukraine. Nonetheless, the force's controversial, complex, and long story presents contemporaries with a range of lessons and challenges, and obliges them to consider how a previous generation reacted when trapped in the maelstrom of war.

21

CONCLUSION

It is a well documented but insufficiently emphasized fact that Nazi leaders were reluctant to arm Ukrainians and Russians, fearing that these would turn their weapons against German forces (Böhler and Gerwarth 2017, 19, 39). The German command was aware that Ukrainians had volunteered for the Galicia Division with the aim of creating their own army and state. Internal tensions and power struggles within the Division's officer corps provide evidence of this.

Recent research has indicated differences between and within Waffen-ss formations. Although the combination of anti-communism and patriotism was common, it expressed itself in various ways. The primary goal for Ukrainians, as for some Baltic and Flemish volunteers in Waffen-ss units, was the creation of "their own state." This was not a postwar afterthought but served from the beginning as the Galicia Division's raison d'être, a fact confirmed by documentary evidence from the period and by later memoirs and interviews. Whereas many Estonians, for example, took the option of fighting in Finnish uniforms, Ukrainians saw the German uniform as their only available option, a fact they lamented both when entering the force and in later years. When the "uniforms" of the Western Allies became available, more than a few men took them. One researcher has summarized the current state of research on the force in the following way: "The division was neither an ss police unit nor an ss extermination unit, and thousands of its Ukrainian volunteers were neither pro-Nazi, nor sympathetic to the Nazi cause. Instead, most of them were undeniably anti-Soviet, anti-colonial, and pro-Ukrainian" (Młynarczyk et al. 2017, 208).

As the present account shows, the motives for enlisting were various, ranging from patriotic fervour to physical survival. They were largely dictated by circumstances, in which the confusing fog of war and the desire for self preservation figured strongly. These factors, mixed with a wish to defend the homeland, nationalist agitation, and the urge to take revenge for horrors witnessed during the Soviet occupation of 1939–41, shaped the mental horizon of the Division's members and frequently governed their choices. Why were the Germans able to convince many Ukrainian leaders that a Waffen-ss army was to their benefit? The answer to this question lies partly in the fact that key figures such as Alfred Bisantz and Hans Koch were themselves natives of Galicia, had served as senior officers in the UHA, and had maintained contact with Ukrainian comrades in this force. Their lobbying was influential. Perhaps more importantly, figures like Dmytro Paliiv, who had played a role in the seizure of power in Lviv on 1 November 1918, argued persuasively that in the Ukrainian bloodlands a hard power pragmatism was required, one that harboured no illusions about German intentions but was steadfastly focused on developing Ukrainian military capacity. This fixation on hard power can also be attributed to Kubijovyč, who in public consistently called for supporting the anti-Bolshevik crusade.

The Ukrainian Galician élite was aware of German perfidy. Some individuals had read *Mein Kampf* and knew of Hitler's plans for Ukraine as a *Lebensraum*. Everyone had witnessed the Nazi betrayal of Carpatho-Ukraine in 1939, which allowed Hungary to occupy the territory, and the Molotov-Ribbentrop Pact, which allowed the Soviet Union to invade Galician territory. However, many Ukrainian opinion makers in Galicia chose to ignore these facts. In some cases they appear to have been swayed by the image of a powerful Germany that could inflict damage on the Soviet enemy. In other cases they were influenced by the conditions that had been offered Ukrainians in the Galicia district. For these individuals the German policy of co-opting a traditional élite contrasted favourably with the policy of repressing it, which they had witnessed under Soviet rule. Whatever hopes they had in Germany were dashed. In the last months of the war the question became how to extricate the Galicia Division from German service. The troops themselves considered many scenarios: escaping to join the UPA in Ukraine, offering to serve the Allies, or surrendering as soon as possible to the British and Americans in the hope that they would not be handed over to Soviet authorities.

The question of how volunteers to the Division in 1943 squared awareness of Nazi war crimes with their choice still requires study. Research that combines anthropological, psychological, and political approaches can probably provide insights. Although Christopher Browning, in his *Ordinary Men*, suggests that deliberate or politically induced amnesia offers some degree of explanation, it is clear that a rather different framing of the issue is required in the Division's case. Many men joined the force precisely because they had witnessed the slaughter of Jews, Poles, and fellow-Ukrainians (the latter in the Red Army, the nationalist underground, and the civilian population). Their motivation, while mixed, included the desire to avoid becoming helpless victims with no way of defending themselves. Hence the slogan "grab weapons from anyone giving them out." There are silences in the accounts Division members gave after the war. Veterans frequently did not dwell on the killing of Jews, which they all knew about and had witnessed. However, they also often failed to mention the bodies of hanged men from the Ukrainian underground, which were on public display in many towns and which they could not fail to have seen. Many men did mention these details. The reluctance of others to dwell on them does not necessarily mean that they played a part in these atrocities.

The Division's attempt to hold back the advance of the Red Army on Galicia in July 1944 was framed by the Germans as a defence of their country and local community. Rhetoric to this effect was used by the Ukrainian press when the Division was sent into battle at Brody. In emigration it remained the main argument for the force's creation. Later, when the Division held the front in Slovakia, a similar justification was used. It was subsequently argued that, by slowing the Red Army's advance, the force allowed many civilian refugees to escape to the West and to avoid the Soviet occupation. However, this holding operation also prevented a more rapid defeat of Germany and an earlier liberation of the remaining Jews who were being shipped to death camps. Although no evidence has emerged of the Division's direct involvement in the killing of Jews, in this respect the force played a role in the machinery of the Holocaust.

The force was, of course, part of a notorious anti-Semitic structure, the Waffen-ss, and German army. The fact that these men served in the German military, photographs of them in uniform, and accusations of war crimes have provided material for polemics over several decades. Far more has been written about the Division, which, after all, was a relatively small unit of little military significance, than about other units in German service. The explanation for this imbalance can be found in Ukraine's economic and political importance and Russia's obsession with subordinating its neighbour. Because of the population's size and the widespread loathing of Soviet rule that existed prior to 1941, Moscow was disturbed by the spectre of a professional Ukrainian army that set the country's independence as its ultimate goal. Such a force was potentially able to mobilize people, especially since tens of thousands were already part of underground networks committed to political and military resistance. In contrast, the parallel story of the 15th SS Cavalry Corps under the leadership of General Petr Krasnov and General Helmut von Pannwitz (formed from the 1st and 2nd Cossack Divisions) and Andrei Vlasov's ROA have proved considerably less troubling to Russian politicians and media. These formations were ignored in the post-1991 period, along with monuments and celebrations in their honour, because the goal of both military formations was to remove Stalin and Soviet rule but to retain Ukraine as a part of Russia. The revival of Russian nationalism and authoritarianism after Putin came to power in 2000 has produced a climate that is more favourable to both Krasnov and Vlasov.

A broader perspective on military formations during the war would situate the Division within the range of German-organized units raised from Eastern European peoples. It would compare different attitudes in the German army towards these military formations, particularly towards those raised from Ukrainian and Russian populations. Despite the numerous polemics devoted to German-sponsored formations, such a comparative framework has rarely been employed. Partly because of this, many valuable sources still await exploration. Perhaps the most important difficulty facing researchers is the challenge of framing narratives in ways that readers who approach the Second World War from different perspectives can understand and agree upon.

My original title for this book was "High Price for an Army." The phrase was used by Kubijovyč, who, before he began lobbying for the Division, visited Andrei Sheptytskyi. Allegedly the Metropolitan placed great value on a professional military under Ukrainian control and stated: "There is almost no price that should not be paid for the creation of a Ukrainian army" (Kubijovyč 1970, 61). The attribution of this phrase to Sheptytskyi is doubtful, at least in the way Kubijovyč presents it, but the phrase resonated with Kubijovyč and many other Ukrainian community leaders. From the very first days of the recruitment campaign and until the end of their lives the soldiers and many members of the Ukrainian community continued to ask themselves whether the price paid for such an army had been too high. The soldiers obtained military training and equipment but the force's Ukrainian identity was not formally recognized until the end of the war, when it began removing itself from the German military. During the war it had little military significance. Although after the war the veterans played a role in the drive for statehood by supporting the diaspora community and advocating for independence, they had to do so under a heavy burden – the opprobrium that came with having fought alongside Hitler's armies. For decades the Kremlin's propagandists were able to dismiss opposition to its rule by exploiting this association with Nazism. Not surprisingly, political activists in the Ukrainian community, including many *dyviziinyky*, asked themselves whether the decision to create the force had been correct and the price they paid for obtaining weapons had been exorbitant.

Ukraine's independence came in 1991, but there have been three subsequent invasions by Russia: Crimea and the Donbas in 2014, and the full-scale war of 2022. These have demonstrated that the Ukrainian population's desire for a sovereign state would inevitably be met by Russian military intervention – a fact that the Division's soldiers recognized in 1943 and warned against throughout their lives.

Notes

Note on Usage

1 For a list of corresponding ranks in the Waffen-ss, the German army (Heer or Wehrmacht), Ukrainian forces; and the Red Army, see Ivankov and Romaniuk (2016, 769–70). For correcponding ranks in the US army, see Stein (1966, 295).

Introduction

1 In correspondence during April 1943 it was referred to as the ss-Freiwilligen-Division "Galizien" or the Galizische Division. In his proclamation on 28 April 1943, Otto Wächter referred to it as the ss-Schützen-Division "Galizien." From July until October it was referred to as the 14th Freiwilligen-Grenadier-Division der ss (galizische 1). Between 22 October 1943 and 27 June 1944 it was designated as the 14th Galizische ss-Freiwilligen-Division. From 27 June 1944, shortly before entering combat, it was named the 14th Waffen-Grenadier-Division der ss (galizische 1). Following the battle near Brody, on 12 November 1944, it was renamed the 14 Waffen-Grenadier-Division der ss (ukrainische 1). On 15 April 1945 it became the 1st Ukrainische Division der ukrainischen National-Armee.

2 [Haike] (2013, 11) calculated that altogether thirty-two thousand people served. However, he may have included in this figure various groups only briefly attached to the formation at the end of the war, which included non-Ukrainian units such as the twenty-five hundred young men from the Luftwaffe training programs. According to some reports, Germans made up about 11 percent of the Division, but Tys-Krokhmaliuk, who served as a staff officer, saw the statistics for November 1944. These listed nineteen thousand soldiers of whom thirty-one hundred, or 16 percent, were Germans (Tys-Krokhmaliuk 1983, 59).

3 Estimates vary but it is generally thought that between one thousand and three thousand disappeared into the underground. An unknown number were killed, captured and shot, or sentenced to the Gulag. For a discussion of the numbers, see Logusz (1997, 257–61).

4 Soviet accounts of all Ukrainian nationalist forces, such as Styrkul (1984), are focused on allegations of war crimes. This is also the focus of accounts by Cesarani (1992); Littman (2003); Hale (2011); and Rudling (2012). Despite the wealth of accessible and verifiable material on the Division, it has been pointed

352 · Notes to pages 8–12

out that many of these accounts are littered with factual inaccuracies (Melnyk 2016, 1:11).

5 During the tribunal twenty-two men faced accusations of conspiring to commit a "crime against peace" (namely, of launching a "war of aggression"), "war crimes," and "crimes against humanity." Ironically, the Soviet judges and prosecutors were themselves guilty of staging show trials during the 1930s. The Soviet delegation denied knowledge of the secret protocols signed between Hitler and Stalin in 1939 (which allowed the war to begin and Poland to be divided). The delegation also tried to pin the Kalyn massacre of twenty-two thousand Polish officers on the Germans. See Hirsch (2020, 296–344).

6 Oleksa Babii, for example, was an OUN-M supporter who travelled to Kyiv with the Sonderkommando 4A of the Einsatzgruppe C, which was involved in the murder of thousands of people, including thirty-four thousand Jews at Babyn Yar. Babii had to escape from the Germans when they began arresting OUN members. He first organized a partisan group in Volhynia, then joined the Galicia Division in November 1943 and was killed in action at Brody (Radchenko and Usach 2020, 243).

7 Among the best wartime memoirs are Zahachevskyi (1952); Hrytsak (1959); Pobihushchyi (1982); Bender (1984a); Ferkuniak (2003); and Veryha (2007). For descriptions of internment camps, see Zaporozhets (1952); Zahachevskyi (1968); Gotskyi (1990); Stetskevych (1998); and Sydorenko (2002).

8 Of particular interest are the writings of Lysiak (1953, 1960, 1996); Liubomyrskyi (1948, 1951, 1953); Kolisnyk (2011); Lazurko (1971); Tys-Krokhmaliuk (1964, 1982); and Bora (1972, 1982).

9 Interwar "eastern" Galicia was comprised primarily of what are today the Lviv, Ivano-Frankivsk, and Ternopil oblasts of Ukraine. In the years between 1921 and 1939 they were the Lwów, Stanislawów, and Tarnopol voivodships of Poland, and the territory was sometimes refered to as Eastern Little Poland (Małopolska Wschodnia). "Western" Galicia is now part of the Małopolskie voivodship in Poland with Kraków as its main city.

10 See, in particular, Heike (1973); Logusz (1997); Bolianovskyi (2000); Melnyk (2002 and 2016); Ponomarenko (2016 and 2017); Khromeychuk (2013); and Markiewicz (2021).

11 For examples, see Lysiak (1951 and 1974); Budnyi (1979); Revutskyi (2005), and Ivankov and Romaniuk (2016).

12 For examples of Polish accounts, see Siemaszko (1971); Motyka (2006 and 2011); Motyka and Wnuk (1997). For Soviet partisan behaviour, see Gogun (2016); Baranova (2008). For the Holocaust, see Pohl (1997); Dean (2000); Friedländer (2008); Black (2011); Struve (2015); Kopstein and Wittemberg (2018); and Himka (2021).

13 The many relevant studies of wartime violence include (Pohl 1997 and 2007); Dean (2000); Golczewski (2010); Mick (2011); Struve (2015); Zajączkowski

Notes to pages 12–21 • **353**

(2015); Snyder (2015); Kiebuzinski and Motyl (2016); Kopstein and Wittenberg (2018); Motyka (2018); and Himka (2021). For recent archival research on the Galicia Division and wartime violence, see Ponomarenko (2017). For recent innovative use of memoir literature and the Division, see Nimenko (2016); Rohde (2017); Hrymych (2017); Sands (2021); Shnaider (2021) [Šnajder (2016)]. For dissertations on the Division, see Shnerkh (2004); Iwasykiw Silecky (2006); Tovarianska (2008); Khomiak (2017); Kutyshenko (2019); Vereshchaka (2019); and Kormylo (2021).

14 See, for example, Shepherd (2012); Bergholz (2016); and Gerolymatos (2016).

Chapter One

1 It was designated on 27 June 1944 as the 14th Waffen-Grenadier-Division der ss (galizische 1). There were thirty-nine Waffen-ss divisions, if Helmuth von Pannwitz's Cossack 1 (Kosaken 1) is included.

2 An estimated 50,000 so-called Germanic volunteers joined the Waffen-ss: 23–25,000 Dutchmen, 10,000 Flemings, 6,000 Danes, 5,000 Norwegians, and smaller numbers of Swedes and Britons (Bohler and Gerwarth 2017, 12, 42). There were also 6,600–13,000 Italians (93). The number of Western European volunteers for the front was, however, higher: 13,000 French, 47,000 Spanish, 40,000 Dutch, 22,000 Flemish, and 16,000 Walloons (81, 94, 148).

3 Others have estimated the total number of Ukrainians in various German uniforms as 250,000 (Bhil 1987, 31; Neulen 1985, 342).

4 For an English translation of Wächter's letter to Himmler from 30 July 1943, see Melnyk (2002, 326–7). For Wachter's archive, see https://collections.ushmm.org/search/catalog/irn85067#?c=0&m=0&s=0&cv=0.

5 The instructions continued: "Drastic insults to Bolshevism, the Soviets and the Russians have also to be curbed. It must be realized that the local populations have had their own experiences with the Soviets, not all of which have been unfavourable. For this reason, the proven disadvantages and faults of Bolshevism should be pointed out in a clear and factual way. A position can be adopted against the Poles in as far as, unlike the Ukrainians, they have not understood their European responsibility in the fight against Bolshevism. This should be accentuated in such a way as to flatter Ukrainian conceit. Under no circumstances must insults be made against the Poles" (Melnyk 2002, 325).

6 The Legion of Ukrainian Sich Riflemen (Ukrainski Sichovi Striltsi) was formed in 1914 as part of the Austrian army and fought on the Russian front. Its emblem, like the Division's, was a lion rampant. Men of the Legion helped form the Sich Riflemen (Sichovi Striltsi) in 1917, which expanded into the Ukrainian Galician Army (Ukrainska Halytska Armiia, UHA) in 1919.

7 Marsheruiut dobrovoltsi, iak kolys ishly striltsi. Hraiut ikh sholomy v sontsi, usmikh voli na lytsi. Khto zhyvyi, khto zhyvyi, v riad stavai, v riad stavai, vyzvoliaty-zdobuvaty ridnyi krai.

354 · Notes to pages 21–9

8 In 1938, General Viktor Zelinskyi described their reasons for taking arms from a potentially treacherous Germany in terms similar to those used five years later by supporters of the Galicia Division (see Zelinskyi 1938, 33, 35, 38).

9 There were already Ukrainians in the German armed forces. The Ukrainske Vyzvolne Viisko (UVV), like the ROA, was created to draw Ukrainians into the German army. However, it was not a separate force and did not have its own commanders. Various security sections throughout the front were simply given an identification badge on the left sleeve – a shield in light blue with the letters UVV embroidered in gold (Littlejohn 1972, 328). The UVV was composed of former Red Army soldiers eager to escape POW camps or to fight Stalin. There may have been as many as seventy-five thousand Ukrainians who wore the UVV badge (Khromeychuk 2013, 50; Bolianovskyi 2003, 576–7).

10 The UTSK's Lviv branch had at first functioned independently as the Ukrainian Homeland Committee (UKK). In 1942, it was transformed into a branch of the UTSK, whose centre remained in Kraków.

11 I would like to thank Liliana Hentosh for providing this information.

12 Sheptytskyi instructed Studite monks to rescue Jews. During the war he wrote nine pastoral letters affirming the sinfulness of all killing, informed the Pope about what was happening to Jews, and wrote a letter of protest to Himmler in February 1942 in which he complained of German behaviour (Skira 2019, 47–9). Although on 1 July at the request of the self-proclaimed Ukrainian government he issued a brief pastoral letter recognizing the new government and thanking the German army for bringing liberation from the Soviets, he made his recognition contingent upon all citizens being treated in a Christian manner. When he realized there would be no Ukrainian state he rescinded this recognition in a second letter issued on 5 July. I thank Reverend Athanasius McVay for providing this information.

13 My thanks to Reverend Athanasius McVay for this information and reference. For more on Sheptytskyi's attitude towards the Division, see Krawchuk (1997); Himka (2012, 102); Hentosh (2014).

14 For a list of the demands as presented by the UTSK, see Melnyk (2016, 1:34–5).

15 For the list of officers, see Bolianovskyi (2000, 177–82).

16 Namely, the 13th Waffen-Gebirgs Division der ss Handschar (kroatische 1).

17 The men wanted to be stationed in Ukraine and refused to be used for further anti-partisan work or to conduct requisitioning from the population. Roman Shukhevych reportedly stated that he would not send his men to "rob" the population (Kalba 1992, 72). The last straw came when the German commander prevented him from freeing forty-five Soviet Ukrainian POWs.

18 They were Vasyl Laba, Roman Lobodych, Severyn Saprun, Mykhailo Levenets, Yosyp Karpynskyi, Vasyl Leshchyshyn, Yosyf Holoida, Yosyp Kladochnyi, Volodymyr Stetsiuk, Vsevolod Ivan Durbak, Emanuil Korduba, Danylo

Notes to pages 30–9 • **355**

Kovaliuk, Sydir Nahaievskyi, Bohdan Levytskyi, Liubomyr Syvenkyi, Oleksandr Babaii, Oleksandr Markevych, Mykhailo Ratushynskyi, Yuliian Gabrusevych, Ivan Tomashivskyi. A number of these men accompanied the soldiers from training camp to front line service and to internment abroad. Laba reports that they were generally treated with respect by German authorities. Volodymyr Stetsiuk, however, was shot and killed near Brody by an ss officer (Laba 1952, 8).

19 On this issue, see Pyliavets (2021).

Chapter Two

1 For example, the various duties conducted by Belarusians in German service – crime prevention, guard duties, and anti-partisan warfare – are described in L. Golubovich, "Belarusskie kolaboratsionnye sili," HIAL, Dallin Collection, box 6, file 3. The author calculates that 40 percent were captured Red Army soldiers, 10 percent had served in the Polish army, 40 percent were recruited from the local population, and 10 percent were deserters from Soviet partisan units (p. 13).

2 The secret protocols reveal that the Soviet leader was engaged in an aggressive land grab. Along with other evidence of German-Soviet collaboration, they were first published by the US State Department in 1948 in a document collection. See Sontag and Beddle (1948).

3 For reports and testimonies, see Kiebuzinski and Motyl (2016).

4 One of the first was Major Nikita Kononov's Soviet 436th Infantry Regiment, which became the 102nd Cossack Regiment and fought against the Red Army and Soviet partisans (Tolstoy 1977, 40).

5 Another estimate puts the number of repatriated at 5.5 million. Those sentenced to death or twenty-five years hard labour constituted 20 percent of this total, those sentenced to five to ten years constituted 25 to 30 percent, and those sent to work as conscripts in the Donbas and other areas constituted 15 percent (Tolstoy 1977, 409).

6 Polish military colonists, or *osadnicy* (war veterans and their families), were awarded large landholdings in order to bolster the Polish rural population in the country's southeastern territories. For a version of the map, see Kubijovyč (1953). He had earlier published *Atlas Ukrainy i sumezhnykh kraiv* (Atlas of Ukraine and adjacent countries, 1937) and *Heohrafiia Ukrainy i sumezhnykh zemel* (Geography of Ukraine and adjacent lands, 1938 and 1943), and contributed statistical surveys to Ukrainian, Polish, and Czech journals. Together with Arkadii Zhukovsky he later produced *Map and Gazeteer of Ukraine*, which was published as part of the *Encyclopedia of Ukraine* (Toronto: University of Toronto Press, 1984). For a list of his publications, see Kubijovyč (1970, 129–34).

7 There were in that year 7,812 Polish, 3,510 Ukrainian, 773 Jewish, and 759 German coops (Sych 2000, 37–8).

356 · Notes to pages 39–41

8 Its instructions read:

The Polish population should feel master in any nationally mixed territories.

Ukrainian youth after completing high school must be directed to higher studies not in Lviv but to higher educational institutes in other Polish cities.

The Orthodox must be steered toward Polonization. The use of Polish should be required in religious teaching and in sermons … The printing of religious texts in Polish should be encouraged.

Ukrainian nationalists must be prevented from giving instruction in the Orthodox religion. Instead, clearly loyalist clergy with no national orientation, or those aligned with the state power, should be supported.

The network of Orthodox parishes should not be greater that the number genuinely required for the satisfaction of religious needs.

Polish colonists who represent a positive element should be given rights of ownership as quickly as possible.

Cooperatives as a platform for Polish-Ukrainian cooperation should be strongly supported, and the tendency to create purely Ukrainian coops and maintain contacts with Lviv should be paralyzed. The entire coop movement should be orientated toward Warsaw. (Sych 2000, 75)

9 In interwar years Isaac Bashevis Singer lived both in Bigoraj and Galicia before moving to Warsaw. He describes both the anti-Semitism and the Jewish fanaticism of the time: "I knew for a fact that Jewish youths in Russia also tortured and killed innocent people in the name of the Revolution, often their own Jewish brothers. The Jewish communists in Biłgoraj predicted that when the Revolution came, they would hang my uncle Joseph and my uncle Itche for being clergymen, Todros the watchmaker for being bourgeois, my friend Notte Schwerdscharf for being a Zionist, and me for daring to doubt Karl Marx. They also promised to root out the Bundists, the Poale Zionists, and, naturally, the pious Jews, the Orthodox. For these small-town youths it had been enough to read a few brochures to turn them into potential butchers. Some of them even said that they would execute their own parents. A number of these youths perished years later in Stalin's slave camps" (Singer 1986, 47).

10 According to official statistics taken in 1940, the Ukrainian population of Lublin district had grown within a year by fifty thousand. It included 1,779,363 Poles, 270,014 Ukrainians, 244,053 Jews, 24,910 *Volksdeutsche*, 3,190 *Reichsdeutsche*, and 6,532 people of other nationalities (Sych 2000, 60).

11 At a conference of Ukrainian co-ops held in Jarosław on 13–14 July 1941, the head of the united co-ops, Yuliian Pavlykovskyi, stated: "we have to show that in all conditions we know how to take an active approach to life and to grasp every opportunity to organize and accomplish the assigned work," to demonstrate that "we know how to work without mistakes and misunderstandings," to organize and lead "the economic-commercial sector of the entire population" (Sych 2000, 80).

Notes to pages 42–51 • **357**

12 For a list of Poles and Jews in each sector of the GG administration, see Sych (2000, 131). The relative numbers of Poles to Ukrainians were, respectively, 5,215 to 2,823 in forestry; 26,500 to 13,000 in education; 105,010 to 16,500 in railways; and 10,980 to 3,937 in the police.

Chapter Three

1 Proposed by the British foreign secretary Lord Curzon in 1919 as a potential border between Poland and the Soviet Union, it became the demarcation line when Hitler and Stalin invaded Poland in 1939.

2 At the end of the war he was arrested by the Americans and interrogated for two months, then settled in Sarcelles near Paris where he edited the *Entsyklopediia ukrainoznavstva* (Encyclopedia of Ukraine, 1949–84). By mutual consent he and his wife Celine separated on 31 July 1944. They married in 1929 but had lived apart since 1941. Kubijovyč continued to support his two daughters, Irena and Maria. His wife, who did not want to leave Poland, died in 1973. Kubijovyč married Daria Sijak in 1975 (LAC, MG 31, D 203, vol. 1, file 1).

3 Much of the correspondence by the UTSK is reproduced in Veryha (2000).

4 The news had already spread. Three days earlier, on 25 April, in a village near Morshyn, Kubijovyč made the announcement that permission to create the Division had been granted. I am grateful to Yaroslav Hrytsak for this information.

5 According to the records of the Military Board, fourteen hundred were deemed valuable for other occupations and therefore "reclaimed" ([Haike] 2013, 21). Some volunteers in this first wave of recruits were not sent to the Division but to four Galician SS Volunteer Regiments.

6 This speech appeared in *Krakivski visti* on 16 May 1943. Another version appeared in *Lvivski visti* on 6 May with "Bolshevism" preceded by "Muscovite-Jewish" – an adjective not in the original version. The Lviv newspaper was an official organ of the Press and Journal Publications Branch of the General Gouvernment and was managed by Georg Lehmann, a Nazi official in charge of the press in Galicia. The Kraków paper was the organ of the Ukrainian Publishers, a commercial enterprise with ties to the UTSK. Censorship in Kraków was less intrusive (Bozhyk 1986, 185).

7 From September 1941 he was head of the Ukrainian Homeland Committee (UKK). It existed as an independent organization until 28 February 1942, when it was dissolved by the Germans, who wanted only one organization for Ukrainians. From 1 March 1942, he was Kubijovyč's deputy and head of the UTSK's Lviv section. On 19 July 1944, he left Lviv to work from Przemyśl.

8 For this information Pankivskyi references the report of a Polish commission in *Biuletyn Głównej Komisji Badania Zbrodni Niemieckich w Polsce*, Warsaw, 1946.

358 • Notes to pages 54–7

9 Mykhailo Chomiak had trained as a lawyer in interwar Poland but was prevented from practising because of his Ukrainian background. He worked as a reporter for the largest Ukrainian newspaper in Galicia, the Lviv *Dilo* (Task). When the Second World War began he discussed with Metropolitan Sheptytskyi the possibility of Ukrainian-Polish co-operation in resisting Soviet and German rule.

10 In the years from 1940 to 1943 it put out 1,239 issues of periodicals (dailies and weeklies) in 13,215,000 copies; 124 issues of four monthlies in 2,283,000 copies; 455 books in 3,600,000 copies; 42 school publications in 710,000 copies; and 71 issues of notes, cards, and pictures in 790,000 copies. The daily *Krakivski visti* was published in runs of 18,000 to 24 000, and its weekly editions in runs of 20,000 to 26,000; the weekly *Kholmska zemlia* (Chełm land) was published in runs of 2,000 to 4,000; and various monthly children's magazines were in runs of 10,000 to 45,000 (Pankivskyi 1965, 348).

11 See LAC, MG31, D 203, vol. 18, file 10. For the UTSK's reports of shootings of Ukrainian population by German forces, executions in prisons of Ukrainians, shootings by Polish police and by unknown groups in the years from 1940 to 1943, see LAC, MG31, D 203, vol. 18, file 11.

12 The minutes of meetings held from 29 to 31 January 1943 give an idea of the work's scope. They record conferences with German administrative personnel dealing with the feeding of urban and rural populations, the selection of labourers for work in the Reich, the legal status of labourers in the Reich, schools and the founding of a Shevchenko Institute, re-privatization, food quotas, the taking of cows as a levy from those with little land, the incorporation of small land holdings into large farms, and "respect for the security and rights of Ukrainian citizens" (Pankivskyi 1965, 1).

13 All minutes of meetings in the years 1939 to 1944, along with reports from its regional offices, are available in LAC, MG31, D 203, vol. 18, file 1.

14 The Ordnungspolizei formed the first "native" units for policing and security. Schutzmannschaft (Self-defence) or Schuma batallions were created as police units under the local HSSPF (Higher SS and Police Leaders) and were given designations based on duties to be performed: "Wach-" for guarding installations and depots; "Ersatz-" or "Stamm-" for replacement and training services, respectively; "Pionier-" for engineering work; "Front-" for front-line duty. After May 1943 the "Schuma" designation was dropped and "Polizei-" was used instead.

15 The task, called "die Refassung der Deutschen," was assigned to institutions like the Race and Settlement Administration (Rasse- und Siedlungs-amt) and the State Commissar for Strengthening German Folk (Reichskommissar fur die Festigung des deutschen Volkstums) (Pankivskyi 1965, 405).

Notes to pages 58–64 • **359**

16 Yevhen Pindus was deputy-head and Osyp Navrotskyi chief of the secretariat. Health was the responsibility of Volodymyr Bilozor, who in 1910 had participated in the struggle to found a Ukrainian university in Lviv. Zenon Zelenyi, a gymnasium teacher in Lviv, who had finished Polish officer training, was given responsibility for youth. Culture and education were assigned to Mykhailo Kushnir and Stepan Volynets. The lawyer Ivan Rudnytskyi headed the legal section. Liubomyr Makarushka, an economist and elected member of the Polish Sejm from the UNDO party, was responsible for the officer section. Mykhailo Khronoviat supervised recruitment and Andrii Palii the welfare of families. Both had been leaders of the co-op movement. Reverend Vasyl Laba, a former chief chaplain in the Ukrainian Galician Army (UHA) and a professor in Lviv's Theological Academy, was given charge of spiritual guidance. Yurii Krokhmaliuk headed the historical-military section. Makarushka and Krokhmaliuk enlisted in the Division in June 1944 (Veryha 2006, 15–16; Krokhmaliuk 1952, 6).

Chapter Four

1 Himmler was provided with a rationale for creating the Waffen-ss by the theories of Darré, who argued that Germanic types could be found almost anywhere and not simply among the Nordic nations, among whom the initial recruitment of Danes and Norwegians for the Viking Division took place.

2 For another description, see Mohylov (2016, 32–5). Mohylov was among eighty men who completed Junkerschule training and were then selected for ten weeks of further instruction. In total his training lasted a year and three months, and he only joined the Division in the last ten days of March 1945 when it was stationed in Austria (32–8, 50).

3 An English translation of Himmler's speech can be found in Melnyk (2002, 329–30). For the original, see BA-KO. R 52 III/3c. Soviet propaganda has deliberately misrepresented Himmler's words. Oleksandr Vasylenko, in *News from Ukraine* on 20 May 1986, stated that Himmler congratulated the Division on ridding the Ukraine of Jews. According to Styrkul (1984, 275) the Division slaughtered the Polish population during the Warsaw Uprising and was praised by Himmler for its ruthlessness. Such inaccurate reports have often portrayed the Division as a product of Nazi ideology.

4 The exchange was first reported in *Visti* 5–6 (1968): 42–3. See also Logusz (1997, 464); Melnyk (2002, 354,129). Paliiv's response is omitted in many descriptions of the incident.

5 He describes the training as comprised of strategy, tactics, weapons, organization of the Division, terrain, map reading, drawing plans, shooting, rules of punishment in the army, intelligence, bookkeeping. The program's practical side consisted of use of light and heavy weapons, familiarity with field artillery, anti-tank fighting, anti-aircraft fighting, command of platoons,

companies and battalions, intelligence, billeting, digging defensive positions, advance and retreat (Ferkuniak 2003, 16).

6 See Logusz (1994, 34); and Melnyk (2016, 1:372). Reverend Mykhailo Levenets described Wiens as an ss officer who dealt with desertions, censorship, and the elimination of OUN activists. See UCRDC, oral history archive, Levenets, video interview with Reverend Mykhailo Levenets conducted by Jurij Darewych in Paris on 24 February 1987. See also Rempel (2010, 540–9).

7 UCRDC, oral history archive, audio interview with Pavlo Lavruk conducted on 26 October 2007 in Ivano-Frankivsk by Oksana Tovarianska, tape no. 478.

8 UCRDC, oral history archive, video interview with Vasyl Veryha conducted on 12 April 1989 by Jurij Darewych in Toronto, tape 29.

9 UCRDC, oral history archive, audio interview with Ivan Woloschak conducted by Stephan Ilnyckyj on 4 November 1989 in London, UK, tape 37.

10 UCRDC, oral history archive, audio interview with Vasyl Sirsky conducted by Iroida Winnickyj on 15 February 1989 in Kitchener, Ontario, tape 52.

11 UCRDC, oral history archive, audio interview with Ivan Bendyna conducted on 7 August 2016 by Yurij Maniukh in Radelychi village, Lviv oblast, tape 346.

12 Laba stated: "On this day of celebration, the Ukrainian people's army is resurrected. The Sich Riflemen return to join the Ukrainian people's army, restoring a link that was severed twenty years ago. At this decisive time we receive from the German government weapons that will let us join forces with the renowned German army and its allies, and to take part in the battle against Bolshevism (Adapted from Melnyk [2002, 28]).

13 For example, when Felix Steiner, commander of the 5th Viking Division, suggested using Ukrainians in the war and granting them autonomy, Himmler responded: "Do not forget that in 1918 these splendid Ukrainians murdered Field-Marshal von Eichorn" (Steiner 1963, 179, quoted in Melnyk 2002, 20).

14 Altogether, thirteen chaplains were selected: Yurii Vanchytskyu, Ivan Holoida, Ivan-Vsevolod Durbak, Osyp Karpinskyi, Yosyf Kladochnyi, Danylo Kovaliuk, Emanuil Korduba, Mykhailo Levenets, Bohdan Levytskyi, Vasyl-Vsevolod Leshchyshyn, Roman Lobodych, Isydor Nahaievskyi, and Severyn Saprun. The last, an older man, was assigned to the so-called Ukrainian Youth ss. Kovaliuk, Holoida and Karpinskyi were assigned to the training camps in southern France. Durbak served with the Beyersdorff Battle Group. Volodymyr Stetsiuk, who did not attend the Sennheim course, replaced Nahaievskyi as the chief chaplain shortly before deployment. Seven chaplains were sent with the army to Brody: Stetsiuk, Leshchyshyn, Durbak, Kladochnyi, Levytskyi, Levenets, and Karpinskyi. In the days before the engagement Karpinskyi was released for aiding the escape of a soldier who had been sentenced to execution. Stetsiuk was reportedly shot by Freitag during the battle for refusing an order. Kladochnyi was later captured and sentenced to ten years, Leshchyshyn to twenty-five years. Both men were amnestied in 1955 (Ponomarenko 2018,

Notes to pages 85–95 · **361**

39–400). In all there were twenty-one Ukrainian Greek Catholic chaplains and two Ukrainian Greek Orthodox. Some, like the two Orthodox priests, were attached to the Division in the last weeks of the war. For a full list, see Ponomarenko (2018, 41–2).

Chapter Five

1 Paliienko, who commanded the artillery regiment, was the Division's most experienced and respected Ukrainian officer. Dolynskyi had served in the UHA and then the Red Army. Ponomarenko reports that he joined the Communist Party (Bolshevik) of Ukraine and in the years from 1932 to 1934 worked for the Kharkiv party committee with responsibility for grain procurement. From 1923 to 1934, he apparently gathered information for the Berdychiv GPU (secret police). In 1935, he was arrested in connection with the dissenting Communist Party of Western Ukraine and sentenced to five years (Ponomarenko 2016, 19).

2 On 22 January 1944, the UTSK listed the total number of targeted killings at five hundred, most of them in Hrubeszów county, but others in Zamość, Chełm, Biłgoraj, and Tarnogród (Veryha 1980, 101). According to researchers in Poland, in the second half of 1942, 382 Ukrainians died at the hands of Poles while 316 were killed by Germans or by Polish and Ukrainian Hifspolizei units during pacifications in response to partisan raids. In 1943, 616 Ukrainians were killed by non-Germans, while 127 died at the hands of German police or Ukrainian Hifspolizei units (Markiewicz 2021, 187).

3 See, especially, Ovad (1999); Stetskevych (1998); Dolynskyi (1957); Ketsun (2013); Dliaboha (1968); Prypkhan (1989); and Vrublevskyi (2016). See also the manuscript by Mykhailo Dliaboha in AO, Veryha Collection, "Italy-Rimini. POW camps – Ukrainian division Galicia."

4 UCRDC, oral history archive, audio interview with Myroslav (Myron) Holowaty recorded in Toronto on 11 November 2010 by Oksana Tovaryanska, tape 439.

Chapter Six

1 Horodyskyi states that Battalion 203 was composed of Poles who were considered *Volksdeutsche*: "The Polish police Battalion 203 operated in the Chełm region and Volhynia; it was destroyed in February 1944 by Soviet troops and was sent to the Alps for recuperation. The battalion's commanders received a special letter from Himmler thanking them for the 'work' they accomplished" (Korchak-Horodyskyi 1994, 12).

2 The ULS is sometimes mistakenly referred to as the Volhynian Legion, although this term was never used by its members and was never an official designation (see Karkots 2002, 182).

3 For the actions by the OUN-B, see Hirniak (1977, 14); Skorupskyi (2016, 128–9, 134, 152–4, 169, 180, 188).

362 · Notes to pages 95–7

4 Its leader during the negotiations was Mykhailo Soltys (alias Cherkas) (Karkots 2002, 108–14).

5 According to a letter to the editorial board of *Visti Kombatanta* dated 22 August 1985, some men were sent for training to Heidelager in February 1944 and from there to the Galicia Division. A number were sent to Police Battalions 204 and 207 (UCRDC, Maleckyj Papers, letter from Volodymyr Gotskyi, 22 August 1985).

6 At this time the group reportedly issued a number of anti-Polish and anti-Jewish leaflets (Radchenko and Usach 2020, 459, 465–6).

7 Styrkul referred to Horodyskyi's account but also had access to closed archives. He corroborates some details in Horodyskyi and some in Polish and Soviet sources. He refers to the unit as the 31st Punitive Detachment and states that Soltys was a policeman in Lutsk, where he displayed zeal in the destruction of the town's Jewish ghetto (Styrkul 1984, 255). He also informs us that the Abwehr sent men from the ULS behind enemy lines as sabotage experts and radio operatives and that the unit fought Dmitrii Medvedev's Soviet partisans in December 1943. According to him, in Pidhaitsi in late December the ULS shot a group of three hundred Jews and then a group of Poles (258). He also accuses the ULS of killing Polish civilians in the village of Buiany, near Torchyn. Karkots (alias Vovk) is accused of destroying the village of Karczunek, which had two hundred households, and the villages of Edwardpole, Koloniia Ameryka, Lasków, and Smoligów (251, 264). Mykola Medvetskyi (alias Khrin) is accused of burning villages and killing Poles in Kivertsi and Bilyn (263). Teodor Dak is accused of murdering several people in the Hrubieszów county, including in his native village of Tudorkovychi. These accusations had earlier appeared in the Polish *Gazeta Zielonogorska* on 28 and 29 March 1970 (265). For the accusations, see Radchenko and Usach (2020). For an account of the ULS by one of its leaders, see Karkots (2002).

8 After the war a French military commission unsuccessfully sought Biegelmayer's extradition for crimes committed in Lorraine. In 1960, the Federal Republic of Germany tried him for his participation in the destruction of 42,000 Jews in Lublin on 3-4 November 1943. He was acquitted due to insufficient evidence (Radchenko and Usach 2020, 456, 458).

9 I am grateful to Michael Melnyk for sharing this information, which comes from the APL and from a letter by Orest Horodyskyi to Michael Melnyk on 23 November 1998.

10 Oleksandr Kvitko was the ULS's chief of staff. He had been a commander of the Kyiv regional police and had worked with German intelligence. Volodymyr Herasymenko (Gerasymenko) commanded the ULS later in 1944.

11 For further details on the Legion's history, see Melnyk (2002, 368). He interviewed Fedir Tsymbaliuk and used an unpublished manuscript by Orest Horodyskyj (Horodyskyi) entitled "The Organisation, Formation and History

Notes to pages 98–102 • **363**

of the Volhynian Self-Defence Legion, 1943–45." See also the substantial documentation in IHRC 1182, Michael and Nadia Karkoc Collection, boxes 24–6. For reports of the Legion's activities and responses to accusations against the Legion made in the Soviet press, see especially box 24, item 7, and box 25, item 29.

12 Melnyk has reported that the Legion absorbed a few former officers of the Galicia Division who had been discharged because of insufficient qualifications or their age: "The Legion had its own NCO school at Kłaj near Kraków and had a number of nurses who served as medical personnel. It was well equipped with several horses, radio equipment and a mixture of German and Soviet weaponry including a light infantry support gun, mortars and heavy machine guns. Its members wore standard pattern German uniforms with no distinguishing insignia" (Melnyk 2002, 368).

13 Heike describes the incident slightly differently. According to him, the men entered forested Chetnik-controlled terrain: "The Chetniks wanted to get rid of these uninvited guests, in whom they did not have the slightest interest and from whom they expected no benefit." The Chetniks continually informed the Division's command in Maribor of the legion's movements ([Haike] 2013, 139–40). The most complete account of the incident is provided by Horodyskyi (1962, 23–6), who was one of the rebel group.

14 These men were often Soviet POWs. Their nationality included ethnic Germans, German-speakers, soldiers of non-Russian nationality, and Russians (Black 2001, 6–7). Only late in 1942 were civilians recruited for service at Trawniki. This recruitment included Ukrainians residing in Galicia and Podolia (February, April 1943), in the Lublin district (June–July 1943), and a small group of Poles from the Lublin and Galicia districts (November 1942–January 1943) (7). The total number of men who served in the Trawniki system in 1943–44 was four to five thousand (7).

15 Black (2001, 30) reports that in the Yanivska Camp these men "participated directly in several large-scale massacres, the first of approximately 2,000 Jewish prisoners on May 25, 1943." One thousand more Jews were shot on 25 and 26 October and three thousand on 19 November in a ravine behind the camp. Trawniki men served at other camps throughout the Reich (40).

16 There was also a 29th Waffen-Grenadierdivision der ss (russiche 1), which was turned over to the army of General Andrei Vlasov before it ever saw action. After they mutinied, the rest of the men in the 30th were removed to Germany, reconstituted as a brigade, and had their name changed from "russiche 2" to "weissruthenische 2.

17 In German: 30 Waffen-Grenadier Division der ss (russische Nr. 2). Some of the men who found their way into BUK 2 appear to have been part of the 115th Schutzmannschaft Battalion. After the 102nd and 118th deserted, the rest of the Division was immediately withdrawn to Germany, disarmed, and

364 · Notes to pages 102–9

incorporated into work brigades, which were employed to dig trenches and construct fortifications. The remaining Russians in the 30th Division were soon afterwards incorporated into General Vlasov's forces.

18 For the 30th Waffen-ss in France, see also Dean (2000, 151–4).

19 Two hundred and thirty of the 350 men took the offer (Sorobey 2016).

20 After Hloba's death in 2012, his sister discovered documents relating to her brother's wartime life. These materials are now in the UCRDC. For accounts of the battalion, see Rohde (2017) and Sorobey (2016).

Chapter Seven

1 For Wächter's letter to Himmler on 30 July 1943 laying out his objections to using the men in police battalions, see Melnyk (2002, 326–7).

2 I am grateful to Michael Melnyk for this information.

3 On 9 January 1945 he was transferred to the 29th Waffen-ss Division, surrendered to American troops in Austria, and apparently died in 1945. US documentation lists him as a war criminal (Melnyk 2002, 62).

4 Plantius was arrested in 1962 and sentenced to four years in prison. Several German officers who were later transferred to the Galicia Division also served in police battalions. They included Friedrich Dern and Franz Magill, who were both later charged with war crimes. Magill was convicted in 1964 for complicity in the murder of 5,265 people in Belarus (Melnyk 2002, 67–8, 349). He had commanded the ss 2nd Cavalry Brigade operating near Pinsk and the Pripet Marshes, and had received the following order from Himmler on 2 or 3 August 1941: "All Jews age 14 or over who are found in the area being combed shall be shot to death; Jewish women and children shall be driven into the marshes [where they would drown]. The Jews are the partisans' reserve force; they support them … In the city of Pinsk the killing by shooting shall be carried out by cavalry companies 1 and 4" (Friedländer 2008, 208; Dean 2000, 32–5). General Freitag, had himself served in police brigades that in 1941 operated alongside the Einsatzgruppen directly under Himmler's control (Melnyk 2002, 64).

5 One leaflet, dated 26 June 1944, stated that out of six hundred men only forty had survived a battle with Soviet forces on 5 March 1944 in the village of Dobryvoda near Zbarazh (Usach 2016, 69–70).

6 For German documentation, see BA-L (copies in USHMM), B 162/20005-20007, and B 162/28950. Polish eyewitness reports are from 1968, 1975–76, and 1987–88. They identify the soldiers variously as the "Ukrainian army," "44th Division," "Vlasovites," "44th ss Division-Nachtigall." The Polish and German summaries refer to the troops as the 14 ss Galicia Division, not as the 4th Galician ss Volunteer Regiment. For Polish research, see Kisielewicz (2011).

7 For Medvedev's (1963) memoirs, see his *Silnye dukhom* (Strong of spirit).

Notes to pages 110–15 · **365**

8 For a photocopy of the original, see AO, Wasyl, Veryha Collection, F 1405-56-139, TBN: 2A, Lead no. 0919-053, Ostroverkha, Mykhailo, Protocols.

9 The Polish Ministry of Internal Affairs received regular bulletins that were filed *Sprawozdanie sytuacyjne z ziem wschodnich* (Situational report from the eastern region). The most relevant are no. 12.44 and no. 15.44. The first is identified as covering March 1944 and the second as covering April–May, 1944.

10 For the Institute of National Memory's collected documentation, see BA-L (copies in USHMM), B162/28.449.

11 Chobit deconstructs Polish accounts, including the misattribution of photographs, on pages 15–77, analyzes Russian and Ukrainian accounts on pages 78–116, and provides a detailed reconstruction of events based in large part on new archival information.

12 This information has been challenged by Chobit (2020, 111–13), who points out that Maksym Skorupsky's UPA group only arrived in the area on 20 March.

13 Michael Melnyk has referenced a report by Thaddeus Bor-Komorowski, the commander in chief of the AK, sent in an encrypted telegram from Warsaw to London on 23 March 1944, which states that units of the Galicia Division burned down the village of Huta Peniatska and murdered about one hundred inhabitants. He has suggested that the Soviet partisans and many of the village's inhabitants may have succeeded in leaving (Melnyk 2010).

14 The report notes that a detachment of the SS Galicia Division was stationed in Pidkamin on 10 March and remained there for five days. A UPA group, "which had clearly been given a free hand," surrounded a Dominican monastery in which many Poles from nearby destroyed villages had taken refuge, and an exchange of fire began. When a German detachment, which was returning from a punitive expedition, arrived at 1:00 p.m. on 12 March, it ordered the people to leave the monastery or be bombarded. The people left and were killed by "Ukrainian bands," who together with the German detachment massacred the town's Polish population. The report mentions the "cynical" co-operation of the Germans with the UPA (PISM, Ministertwo Spraw Wewnetrrzych, Wydzial Spoleczny, *Sprawozdanie sytuacyjne z ziem wschodnich*, no. 15/44, A.9.III, 1/45, 24).

15 NAUS, KTB PzAOK 4, 3.5.1944, T313, Roll 391, frames 8682005–8682006. I am grateful to Michael Melnyk for bringing this document to my attention.

16 A "detachment of the Division SS Galizien" is blamed for the Pidkamin massacre in Szczesniak and Szota (1973, 127). Testimonies collected in Bąkowski (2001) refer variously to the perpetrators as "Ukrainian Legion SS Galizien" and the "Division SS Galicia." Some testimonies also identify people from neighbouring villages as participating in the destruction and theft. They or the villages they came from are named. Sometimes perpetrators are referred to as Banderites, Ukrainian nationalists, or the UPA. For similar Polish eyewitness reports, see Komanski and Siekiera (2006, 560–1, 582–611). Ukrainian

reports also referred to the 4th Regiment as part of the Galicia Division. The Ukrainian Aid Committee (UDK) in Kraków reported: "On 29 February a detachment of the ss Div. 'Galicia' was combing the woods near the Polish village of Huta Peniatska, a place where Bolshevik paratroopers were most frequently dropped. When the search parties of the ss groups approached the village they were met with unexpectedly intense rifle fire that killed two and badly wounded a third. In response to this, a detachment of the ss surrounded the village and conducted a pacification" (PAA, M. Chomiak Collection, 85, 191, fol. 59, sheet 358, item 55/3).

17 After the war he was prosecuted and given a six-year sentence.

18 For a description of these actions, see Motyka (2011, 284–99).

19 The only other mention of clashes with Allied troops occurred in Slovakia and Slovenia, where the Division's soldiers captured some British and American airmen who were dropping supplies for partisans (see chapter 8). Melnyk (2016, 1:339) points out that the presence of Allied airmen was incidental and "at no point during its history did the Galician Division or any of its affiliated units ever engage in combat with organized military force of British or American origin."

20 Pontolillo, for example, refers to atrocities on 24 June 1943 in Majdan Nowy near Zamość; 1 July 1943 in Kaszów near Kraków; 3 July 1943 in Majdan Stary near Zamość; and 15 August 1943 in Zagaje south of Kielce. Since the first trainloads of volunteers to the Division only left Lviv to begin training on 17–18 July, none of these charges is valid.

21 According to Jurado (1998, 196–209), units in the German army identified as Ukrainian included 70 Schutzmannschaft battalions; 7 Police Rifle (Polizei Schützen) regiments; 12 Ordnance, Special Purposes, Construction, Security and Engineering battalions (often identified as Ukrainische batallionen); 3 Volunteer Service (Freiwillige Stamm) divisions; and 1 Anti-Tank Brigade (Panzer Jagr Brigade Frei Ukraine).

Chapter Eight

1 In June, posters throughout Ukrainian, Polish, and German villages announced their choices as follows: (1) Joining the Galicia Division; (2) Joining the German army; (3) Joining the youth ss; (4) Working for the Todt Organization that was employed in military and engineering projects. The population was aware that the Red Army was also taking all males between the ages of fifteen and fifty and sending them to the front (Ponomarenko 2018, 21).

2 In German: 18 ss-Freiwilligen Panzergrenadier Division Horst Wessel; ss Sturmbrigade Dirlewanger, which, on 20 February 1945, was renamed the 36 Waffen-Grenadier Division der ss; Osttürkische Waffenverband der ss.

3 In Lublin, Dirlewanger's men behaved like an "outright extermination unit," terrorizing and blackmailing the ghetto, but in spite of Dirlewanger's many

Notes to pages 124–7 · **367**

crimes, Gottlob Berger promoted him all the way to major general. This occurred partly because the unit was wholly German (Reitlinger 1956, 174).

4 Ingrao describes in detail the atrocities committed by the Dirlewanger Brigade, which became a symbol of Nazi cruelty. He points out that, because of the difficulties of indictment under German law, its members were rarely brought to trial after the war (Ingrao 2011, 182–5). In fact, a number entered politics in both West and East Germany. Several became members of the Central Committee of the Socialist Unity Party in East Germany, and at least nineteen became founders of the Stasi (193).

5 The Galicia Division formed three battle groups. The first under Karl Wildner, who had served in the Slovak army, took part in putting down the military revolt in the Banská Bystrica area. His group succeeded in driving these forces into the hills. The second, under Friedrich Wittenmeyer, was sent to secure the railway line and highway east of Ružomberok. It drove the partisans into the Tatra Mountains. A third battle group operated south of this city but met little opposition.

6 One of the most detailed accounts is by Michael (Mykhailo) Paziuk, who was conscripted in May 1944 at the age of sixteen and sent to join the Division in September (Paziuk 1993, 48–90).

7 Veryha's account confirms good relations and that one of the first orders on arrival was to behave correctly because Slovakia was an ally. When one of the Division's men died in a battle with partisans the entire village came to the funeral (see Veryha 2007, 128–38).

8 For a contradictory viewpoint, see Rudling (2012, 357).

9 I am grateful to Martin Rapák for this information, which is based on his archival research on the Division's time in Slovakia. Per Rudling provides some further sources on the action in Slovakia without giving details. He also references Hendy's unreliable television program (Rudling 2012, 357–8).

10 For a discussion, see Khendi (2001) and Mushynka (2001). For a report on the research he conducted, see Mushynka (2000). The twelve-page report and a translation into English are available in the UCRDC. His taped interview with the two women in Slovakia is also available (UCRDC, 2015.7.E, 2).

11 Michael Melnyk (2010) supports this analysis: "As for the killing of civilians in Slovakia, I have been to that region myself and the people who gave the testimony used in the documentary *ss in Britain* (which incidentally I took part in) stated that their testimonies were edited and were not presented accurately. I can confirm that of four hours of interview with me less than three minutes was used and this too was edited in such a way that it presented an entirely different picture."

12 For his comments on the time in Slovakia, see Heike (1973, 140–66). For the English-language translation, see Heike (1988, 73–90).

368 · Notes to pages 128–40

13 According to one testimony, the ULS, which was active with the Galicia Division in Slovenia, suffered eight killed and fifteen injured in one action (Radchenko and Usach 2020, 472).

14 Action against the 6th Slovenian National Liberation Assault Brigade "Slavko Šlander" has been analyzed in Štiplovšek (1971). See also Heike (1973, 167–93).

15 Shandruk was officially appointed head of the General Staff of the UNR Army by the UNR's government in exile on 3 November 1944. The order was signed by President Andrii Livytskyi and General Mykhailo Omelianovych-Pavlenko ("Nakaz Holovnoi komandy Viiska i floty U.N.R.," UCRDC, Maletskyi files).

16 The first point of the Prague Manifesto called for "the equality of all peoples of Russia and the real right for national development." The manifesto also called for the liquidation of forced labour and collective farms, the liberation of political prisoners, and an end to state terror ("Vlasov and the Russian Liberation Army" 2010).

17 For a translation of the declaration, see Boshyk (1986, 200–1).

18 These two older commanders were aware that their role was simply to rescue as many of the men as possible from annihilation. An indication of this is that their gravestones in South Bound Brook Cemetery note their rank and service in the UNR army but make no mention of the Division.

19 NAUS, SAIC/X/7, 5 June 1945.

20 British forces handed over thirty-nine thousand Cossacks in the summer of 1945, supposedly to ensure the release of thousands of Allied POWs taken into custody by the Red Army during its advance westward. British soldiers were aware of the many suicides among Russians before the exchange was completed. One British soldier recalled: "We made the strongest possible representations to the authorities that the Ukrainians should not be given a similar fate ... I very well remember entering the camp with the Soviet delegation and seeing the thousands of Ukrainians, many of whom were boys in their early teens and old men, fleeing in blind terror from the parade ground to avoid the eyes of the three Russian officers who accompanied us" (Falconer 1974). For further information, see Bethel (1974a and 1974b). The accounts by Solzhenitsyn (1973) and Tolstoy (1977) are mentioned later in this chapter.

21 See Assistant to the President's Personal Representatives at Vatican City (Tittmann) to the Secretary of State, 5 July 1945, memo, https://history.state. gov/historicaldocuments/frus1945Berlinv01/d528. The US branch of the Division's Brotherhood of Former Soldiers, on 30 September 1955, wrote an official letter of thanks to Pius XII for his intervention (AAV , Segr. Stato, an. 1950 segg., tit. Popolazioni, pos. 35, f. 22r). Shandruk followed this with his own personal letter of thanks (AAV, Segr. Stato, an. 1950 segg., tit. Stati e Corpo Diplomatico, pos. 1224, f. 2–5.). Reverend Athanasius McVay has graciously shared these documents with the author.

Chapter Nine

1 See Zelenyi, "Summary" 5, manuscript in Zelenyi Fonds, UCRDC. Much of the information provided in this chapter is drawn from Bilostotskyi (2000) and Zelenyi (1965), and from manuscript versions of these two books, written in 1945, which are in the Zelenyi Fond in the UCRDC.

2 Lasting from 22 April to 4 May, the topics covered included history, geography, politics in Galicia, economics, education, interwar youth organizations, and national symbols. Presenters included Mykhailo Dobrainskyi, Olha Kuzmovych, Tsopa Palii, Yurii Starosolskyi, and Zenon Zelenyi. Zelenyi argued with one of the visitors that Ukrainians could not be German patriots because they were being imprisoned for expressing their own patriotism and their youth organizations were banned. The visitor did not protest because he had been informed that Galicia "was a tough nut to crack and great opposition should be expected from the youth, parents and citizens" (Zelenyi 1965, 18–19).

3 The visiting priests included Severyn Saprun, Stepan Koliankivskyi, Roman Zakrevskyi, Myroslav Oleshko, and Stepan Figol. They gave church services and talks, and published literature for the camps.

4 For his testimony, see Zelenyi (1965, 189–94).

Chapter Ten

1 UCRDC, audio interview with Stepan Ilnyckyj conducted on 15 July 1993 in Kyiv, tape no. 263.

2 See Ambassador in Italy (Kirk) to the Acting Secretary of State, telegram, 25 July 1945, Foreign Relations of the United States: Diplomatic Papers, https://history.state.gov/historicaldocuments/frus1945Berlinv02/d1165.

3 He specified the iron and steel, engineering, metal, and chemical industries, and he wanted aviation plants, facilities for the production of synthetic oil, and all other military enterprises and factories to be withdrawn in their entirety.

4 When Molotov spoke to Hitler in Berlin on 13 November 1940, the latter had suggested the British Empire's division: Germany would look to the west and the Soviet Union to the east, meaning Iran, the Persian Gulf, and the Arabian Sea. Molotov asked for Finland, Bessarabia, and Bukovyna (Byrnes 1947, 288–9). Ribbentrop and Molotov then discussed dividing the world into spheres of influence (Moorhouse 2014, 199–209). These talks broke down when the Soviet side made increasing demands.

5 Revutskyi put on a uniform and entered the camp, where he contributed to educational work. His "voluntary" attachment was dictated by the fact that he was from Eastern Ukraine and was being pursued by the Soviet repatriation committee. His presence in Rome, which was teeming with Soviet agents, could have been discovered. Bishop Ivan Buchko advised him to hide in one of the two camps holding Ukrainians, either the civilian one or the one for the

370 • Notes to pages 165–71

Division's soldiers. He chose the latter. Reverend Mykhailo Vavryk drove him to Rimini and he took the place of another veteran who had recently "chosen freedom" (Slupchynskyi 2013, 5).

6 The Polish 2nd Corps had from 26 November 1944 collected materials and eyewitness reports on atrocities committed by the Soviet Union, on its labour and concentration camps, and on its persecution of minorities. These materials were shared with the government in exile in London and are now in the HILA. On the purpose and extent of the collected materials, see the letter from the headquarters of the Corps, HILA, Wladyslaw Anders, box 77, file 87, 13 September 1944. The 2nd Corps saw itself as representing the Polish people, and, until the Allies broke contact with the government in exile on 6 July 1945, viewed itself as the sole sovereign Polish army.

7 The original list is available at the Association of Ukrainians in Great Britain, 49 Linden Gardens, London, WH 4HG. It can also be found also online at: https://obd-memorial.ru/html/info.htm?id=85316040&page=124&p=71. My thanks to Michael Melnyk for this information.

8 For memoranda justifying the Division's formation and its ideals, see: Memorandum to the English Command in Italy signed by Mykhailo Krat and Viktor Malets, 18 May 1945 (Veryha 1984, 195–9); Memorandum about the 1st Ukrainian Division, motives and ideas animating formation and conduct of Division, 18 May 1945 (Veryha 1984, 201–8); Mychajlo Krat, letter to British Command of the POW Camps, 26 June 1945 (Veryha 1984, 213); Letter signed by ninety soldiers of the Ukrainian Camp 5-C to the Chief Command of the Prisoners Camps in Italy, 28 August 1945 (Veryha 1984, 225–8).

9 This information comes from Hills's own account, which was sent to the Ukrainian Veterans Association in Britain on 11 May 1988. The entire report is reprinted in Nimenko (2016, 178–7).

10 The fate of the forty thousand Don, Kuban, and Terek Cossacks and the five thousand voluntary refugees from the Caucasus is described in Tolstoy (1977, 130–40, 161–248, 306–9). Many of the men were not Soviet citizens. They had fought the Bolsheviks in from 1918 to 1920, had been decorated by the Tsar and the British government, and since then had lived abroad. About eleven thousand of the people handed over were women, children, and old men (Tolstoy 1977, 272).

11 In his second book on the topic, Nikolai Tolstoy accused Harold Macmillan of being the British official most directly responsible for knowingly and surreptitiously delivering seventy thousand Cossacks and Yugoslav citizens to Soviet authorities and to Tito's forces. British authorities were aware that the Cossacks in most cases had never been Soviet citizens and, therefore, did not fall under the provisions of the Yalta Agreement (Tolstoy 1986a, xvii–xx). The fact that the Galicia Division avoided this fate was likely due to the fact that most men had been citizens of Poland prior to the war and Churchill feared a mutiny in the Polish army serving with the British (93).

Notes to pages 172–85 • **371**

12 For US guidelines on the repatriation of Soviet citizens issued in January 1946, see Boshyk (1986, 202–8).

13 His chapter "The Ships of the Archipelago" describes a typical journey in such a car in the 1940s and early 1950s (Solzhenitsyn 1973, 489–532).

14 The British refused researchers access to the files of Operation Keelhaul and later claimed that these files had been destroyed. They also refused the United States permission to make the files public (Tolstoy 1977, 431–5). On Keelhaul and the role of Hills, see Dismukes (1996, 103–6).

15 On Operation Eastwind, see also Tolstoy (1977, 364–71) and Dismukes (1996, 106–10).

16 In 1989, in the *Spectator*, Hills claimed to have helped the POWs elude deportation to the Soviet Union. To what degree his article was a way of justifying his actions and alleviating a sense of guilt still requires elucidation. Between 1945 and 1947, while interrogation and screening officer in Italy, he was court martialled three times for drunken behaviour and was stripped of his rank as major. In 1975, while living in Uganda, he called Idi Amin a "black Nero" and a "village tyrant" and referred to the British community there as "spies." Amin sentenced him to death by firing squad. The Queen personally intervened, and Foreign Secretary James Callaghan flew to Uganda. Hills was put on an RAF flight back to Britain (Nimenko 2016, 353–4).

17 On Bevin and the intransigence of British political authorities, see Dismukes (1996, 80–1); on Eisenhower's agreement to continue repatriation even when it became clear that the soldiers were no longer willing to carry out the operations, see Dismukes (1996, 93–4, 129–32).

18 It is worth, in this context, reflecting upon what Nikolai Tolstoy (1977, 449) describes as the "latent sadism that so often appears to have impelled Western adherents of Soviet dictatorship." He is referring to an article in the *Times* on 31 December 1943 that exhulted over the public hanging of German prisoners in Kharkiv.

Chapter Eleven

1 See also AO, Veryha Collection. Especially interesting are documents in this collection on the Division's time in Italy. They contain materials in Ukrainian, German, and English justifying and explaining the Division's existence.

2 The periodical's full title is *Visti Bratstva kol. Voiakiv 1 UD UNA* (News of the Brotherhood of Former Soldiers of the 1st Ukrainian Division of the UNA).

3 Zahachevskyi (1968, 209–13) puts the overall number of escapes at one thousand. Krat (1979, 64–5) quotes the figure of 300, the number of repatriated men at 990, and the number of men who joined General Anders' Polish Corps at 155.

4 The Division's cemetery was in Cherviia, just north of the camp, where thirty-eight soldiers were buried. In 1963 the cemetery, along with the German

372 · Notes to pages 185–94

war dead, was transfered to Passo della Futa near Florence, where there are about thirty thousand graves. The graves of Ukrainian soldiers are in a separate spot, as was the case in Chervia, and have their own monument.

5 These included 675 metal workers, 427 wood workers, 192 textile workers, 425 leather workers, 396 food workers, and 108 construction workers.

6 Sviatoslav-Ihor Yatsushko and Oleh Ostrovskyi designed most of the stamps (Revutskyi 2005, 134).

7 Plays included *Martyn Borulia* by Ivan Tobilevych, *Ukradene shchastia* (Stolen happiness) by Ivan Franko, *Na iasni zori* (To the bright stars) by Borys Hrinchenko, *Oi, ne khody, Hrytsiu* (Hryts, don't go courting) by Mykhailo Starytskyi. The comedies included *Upiemosia bez vyna* (We'll get drunk without wine), *Triokh do vyboru* (Choice of three) by V. Martynevych, *Amerykanets* (The American), and *La Locandiera* (Mistress of the inn) by Carlo Goldoni. The musicals included *Zaporozhets za Dunaiem* (The Cossack beyond the Danube) and Carlo Goldoni's comic opera *Mirandolina.*

8 The best known actors included Zenon Haiovskyi, Yevstakhii Mykush, Mykola Frantsuzhenko (literary pseudonym Mykola Virnyi), Mykhailo Hryniuk, Roman Mamalyga, and Mykola Markevych. In the 1950s, in Leicester, England, several individuals from this group formed a theatre company that toured Ukrainian community centres in Britain with performances of *Yasni zori* (Bright stars) and *Marusia Bohuslavka* (Revutskyi 2005, 154).

9 Sobinski had banned use of the word "Ukrainian," demanding that "ruski" be used. He insisted that all accounting schools conduct their work exclusively in Polish. The assassins were in fact Bohdan Pidhainyi and Roman Shukhevych. Atamanchuk and Verbytskyi had been sentenced to death, but the Supreme Court of Poland revoked the verdict. After a new trial, they were given long prison terms. Sobinski was treated as a Polish hero, but the Polonization of schools slowed after the assassination. On Pidhainyi's terrorist activities, see Knysh (1986 1:176–9, 580).

10 Reverend Ivan Muzychka was born on 15 November 1921 in the village of Pukov near Rohatyn. He completed the Rohatyn gymnasium in 1941, which had been opened thanks to the efforts of the Ridna Shkola Society and for which the publisher Ivan Tyktor, an alumnus of the school, provided grants. The school was closed under Polish rule between 1930 and 1933 for its "strong Ukrainian spirit." He also worked for a Ukrainian co-op in 1939 and completed a course in accountancy. From 1940 he served as a deacon in Stanislaviv and taught in the village of Putiatyn and in his native Pukov. He attended the Rohatyn Teachers' Seminary in 1942. In the Division he wrote the music to the Division's song "Do boiu" (To battle). In Rome he directed the college choir and became the first editor of the college publication *Alma Mater.* He graduated with a doctorate in divinity in 1953, after which time he served as a priest in the UK in Rochdale, Wolverhampton, and Birmingham. He moved back to

Rome in 1975, became rector of the Ukrainian Catholic University, and edited its publication *Bohoslovia* (Theology). From 1991 he taught courses in theology in various cities in Ukraine and died in Rome on 22 February 2016.

Chapter Twelve

1 See also NA/PRO, Military, LACAB/RSc/RIC, Porter, David Haldane, 1947, "Refugee Screening Commission Report on Ukrainians in Surrendered Enemy Personnel (SEP) Camp No. 347 Italy." Haldan Porter's report is now available in Luciuk (2021, 165–74) and Boshyk (1986, 233–40).

2 For a discussion of the Haldane Porter report, see Khromeychuk (2013, 113–19).

3 They included Sheffield and Selby in Yorkshire; Diss and Fakenham in Norfolk; Braintree in Essex; Reversby, Boston, and Sleaford in Lincolnshire; Bury St Edmunds in Suffolk; and Langar in Nottinghamshire (NA/PRO. HO 170/1948, "Release of Ukrainian Prisoners of War for Civilian Employment, 28 July 1948). In Scotland there were forty-three camps and hostels for POWs and DPs (Kormylo 2021, 19).

4 Peter Kormylo has shown that Ukrainians in Britain constituted several distinct groups. Some were in the Royal Air Force and Royal Canadian Air Force. They had come during the war to the Scottish airfields that were used as training bases. Another group consisted of Ukrainians among the twenty thousand people in the Polish Armed Forces, who often arrived via France, Italy, and the Middle East. They were officially given Polish citizenship, which allowed them to avoid "repatriation" to Soviet-controlled territory. A third group consisted of the DPs and European Voluntary Workers. And a fourth consisted of the Division's soldiers (Kormylo 2021, 172–3). After the war the Division's men would play a key role as a mobilizing group within this diverse Ukrainian community by developing its self-image through cultural events, performances, and commemorative rituals.

5 The Panchuk family had emigrated from Bukovyna to Canada in 1896 and settled on a farm in Gardenton, Manitoba. Bohdan Panchuk grew up on a farm near Saskatoon, became a teacher and then a flight commander in the Royal Canadian Air Force. For his story, see Panchuk and Luciuk (1983).

6 Dorril has also indicated that Kim Philby, in his role as the senior British Intelligence officer in North America, persuaded the Canadian authorities to make an exception to the blanket exclusion of former members of the Waffen-ss (Dorril 2000, 240-2).

Chapter Thirteen

1 They are in the Ternopil oblast Archive of the State Security of Ukraine (AUSBUTO) because the cases were processed in Ternopil. In most but not all instances the files are under the individual's name and are stored in fond F. 6 r.

2 For written accounts, see, especially, Hrytsak (1959) and Ivankov and Romaniuk (2016).
3 These figures have been disputed. In the 1951 anthology *Brody*, Ortynskyi (1951, 31) estimates that four thousand had died at Brody and that there were one thousand invalids. The total number of soldiers who disappeared into the UPA has generally been estimated at between six hundred and one thousand. Hryniokh (1951, 47) offers the number six hundred. For a list of fourteen Ukrainian officers in the Division who later served in the UPA, see Usach (2016, 82–3).
4 On Hrytsak's biography and bibliography, see (Wynar 2008).
5 See UCRDC, oral history archive, Toronto. Some interviews are also examined in chapter 16.
6 UCRDC, oral history archive, audio interview with Dionisii (Denys) Pletsan conducted by Oksana Tovaryanska in Chortkiv on 7 September 2006, tape no. 496.
7 UCRDC, oral history archive, audio interview with Petro Lavruk conducted by Oksana Tovaryanska in Ivano-Frankivsk on 26 October 2007, tape no. 478.
8 UCRDC, oral history archive, audio interview with Bohdan Kepeshchuk conducted by Yurii Maniukh in Ivano-Frankivsk, tape no. 351.
9 UCRDC, oral history archive, audio interview with Ivan Mamchur conducted by Yurii Maniukh in Ivano-Frankivsk, tape no. 199. For his memoirs, see Mamchur (2009).
10 UCRDC, oral history archive, audio interview with Ilia Havrysh conducted by Yurii Maniukh in Ivano-Frankivsk, tape no. 183.
11 UCRDC, oral history archive, audio interview with Roman Korduba conducted by Yurii Maniukh in Ivano-Frankivsk, tape no. 140.
12 UCRDC, oral history archive, video interview with Wolodymyr Molodecky conducted on 6 February 1992 in Toronto by Iroida Wynnyckyj, tape no. 152. For his memoirs, see Molodetskyi (1952, 1983, 1998).
13 UCRDC, oral history archive, audio interview with Vasyl Rezuniak conducted by Yurii Maniukh in Rohatyn, tape no. 203.

Chapter Fourteen

1 This article by Kedryn first appeared in *Svoboda*, 15 March 1983.
2 For a list of his articles between 1966 and 1986 in *Visti kombatanta*, see Fedorovych (1987, 4–5).
3 The article to which Veryha was responding was entitled "Dovkruhy ss Striletskoi Dyvizii 'Halychyna'" and appeared in *Biuleten* 11 (1943); it was reprinted in *Suchasnist* (October 1963) and in Hunczak (1993, 132–5). Veryha's response appeared as "Analizuimo nashi mynule" in *Nasha Meta* 12–22, 27 March to 19 May 1965; it was reprinted in Veryha (1980, 146–71).

Notes to pages 238–45 • **375**

4 See Heike (1970 and 1973). An English translation appeared in 1988. For works on non-Germans in the German armed forces or Waffen-ss, see Littlejohn (1972); Solzhenitsyn (1973); Bethel (1974a and 1974b); and Thorwald (1975).

5 See Terlytsia (1960); Kravchuk (1973); Danylenko (1970); Dmytruk (1972 and 1974); and Styrkul (1982 and 1984). Terlytsia's real name was Petro Kravchuk. He was a leader of the Ukrainian Communists in Canada and was rewarded for his propaganda with trips to Ukraine, visits to Crimean beaches, and financial incentives. He denied the famine, calling it an invention of bourgeois nationalists. Under the pseudonym "Terlytsia" he later wrote a tendentious and poorly researched attack on émigré nationalists entitled *Here Is the Evidence* (Terlytsia 1984). Klym Dmytruk (real name Klyment Halskyi) was a major in the KGB who came from the Zhytomyr region. He wrote two anti-religious pamphlets: *Svastyka na sutanakh* (Swastika on cassocks, 1973) and *Bezbatchenky* (The fatherless, 1974). The latter was subtitled: "The truth about the participation of Ukrainian bourgeois nationalists and the church hierarchy in preparing the attack of fascist Germany on the USSR." For examples of Polish texts, see Szczesniak and Szota (1973); Maslovskyi (1975). For a summary of the Division's response to Soviet diatribes and early Polish accusations, see Veryha (1980, 60–91, 5–50, and 92–140). On Styrkul, see chapters 3 and 15.

6 At this time Vojtech Mastny (1971) produced *The Czechs under Nazi Rule: The Failure of National Resistance, 1939–1942*, and the Polish émigré journal *Kultura* discussed the cooperation of the Home Army (the Armia Krajowa, AK brigades) with the Germans (Siemaszko 1971, 202).

Chapter Fifteen

1 A ia stoiu, u dal vtopyvshy zir,
De konusne hoidaietsia vitrylo –
Vono ocham i sertsevi, povir,
U myt raptovo inshyi svit vidkrylo.

Ia tak toi svit liubyv,
Tu povin poloviiuchykh khlibiv.
Shcho hen perelyvalasia za ovyd ...
U spalakhu nevhasnoi liubovy
Ia vpiznaiu u konusi vitryla,
Topoliu batkivshchyny sumnokrylu ... (Virnyi 2005b, 180–1)

2 See Lehit (1958, 1974, and 1990).

376 · Notes to pages 245–7

3 Ibermensh u krovi sataniv
I ohnennu rozbryzkuvav slynu …
Vin rozstriliuvav, vishav narod,
U iasyr svii zabyrav miliony.

4 Blakytne nebo, sontse zolote,
Kolyshe viter sribni khvyli moria.
U hrudiakh sertse radistiu tsvite,
Shcho v kraiu tsim nemaie zlydniv, horia.
Zhyvykh liudei ne vydko tut nide,
Hen-hen syniut hory San-Marino,
Dyvlius nazad: do mene hordo ide,
Nemov rusalka, pyshna syniorina.
Mene vrazha nebachena krasa,
Nemov z Aten ziishla bohynia Feba,
Antychnyi stan, rozpletena kosa,
V ochakh blystyt blakytnyi vidblysk neba.
Nemov madonna, pyshna, doroha.
Ia z dyva kryknuv: "O, divcha kokhane!"
Vona tenditnu ruku prostiahla
I blaha mene: "Signore, mi dia pane!" (Virnyi 2005b, 185)

5 For the Rimini collections, see Bora (1946 and 1947). For the later collections,
see Bora (1972 and 1982).

6 Moia doba taka velyka
Moia doba taka strashna.
Mov nich, rozhnuzdana i dyka,
To znov, iak raiduha iasna

Moia doba …
Moia vitchyzna, iak promin, sontsia i krasy,
To znov, iak blyskavka zlovisna,
Iak lezo shabli i kosy. (Virnyi 2005a, 170)

7 Proidu dorohy skromnosty asketom,
Vtomyvshys, tykho y movchky vidiidu,
I vysoko pid holubym nametom
Cholo na bilu khmarku pokłady.

Vinkiv ne treba, ni puchka shavlii,
Lyshe dostoino, z iskroiu tepla,

Vklonitsia nyzko materii, Marii,
Iaka mene narodovi dala. (Virnyi 2005a, 177)

8 Bravurnyi marsh. Polky ruzhaiut …
Otse, otse – mii son!
Shpaliry lysh nazad vtikaiut,
Tudy – za nebosklon …

Stalni pidkovy kamin kreshut,
Dudnyt, iak dzvin, zemlia.
Vitry dumky i nadali cheshut …
O, mriia tse moia!

Pozadu den shchezaie v pyli,
Speredu – svizha dal
I tuha tam – na neboskhyli
V vinku zirok – koral.

Idut, idut polky dyvizii,
Daleko mriie dim,
I Kyiv v pianim zryvi vizii,
V svichadi zolotim.

Pidkovy iskry kreshut z bruku,
Shrapneli rvutsia z kul …
Vid shchastia, spodivan i muky
Nesetsia rehit dul!

Bravurnyi marsh. Polky vizdzhaiut
Vinky z iurby, z vikon ..
Nichoho bilshe ne bazhaiu,
Lysh tse, lysh tse – mii son!

9 See, for example, Bender (1947).
10 See, for example, Huliak (1952, 4–7).
11 The other correspondents were Stakho (Stanislav) Kravchyshyn, who specialized in radio reporting; Stepan Konrad; Yurko Kopystianskyi; Myron Levytskyi, who became a well-known painter and decorator of church interiors in Canada and Australia; and Oleksandr Lutskyi, who became a leader of the Ukrainian Congress Committee of America (ucca).
12 It is not clear to which passage Lysiak is referring, but Simonov, in one report from 1945, mentions that the story "Pered atakoi" (1944) was written a few days

378 · Notes to pages 255–64

before Ternopol fell: "At that time hard battles continued for almost a month in Ternopil, and long after a note had appeared about the fight for Ternopil with nothing further in the newspapers for three weeks, one could feel in the air an impatient anticipation. The whole country waited in silence for Ternopil to be taken" (Simonov 1956, 496–7).

13 For the edited collection, see Lysiak (1951a); for the novels, see Lysiak (1953 and 1960); for his collection of stories and essays, see Lysiak (1996); for the book on Ukrainian theatre, see Lysiak and Luzhnytskyi (1975).

14 Yurko Piddubnyi is Bohdan Pidhainyi, Maretskyi is Myroslaw Maleckyj, Kramar is Mykhailo Kachmar, Mykhailo Harmider is Mykhailo Brygider, Olshtynskyi is Liubomyr Ortynskyi (Ortynskyj), Yurko Hrozbetskyi is Bohdan Hvozdetskyi, M.Kh. is Mykola Khronoviat, L. M. is Liubomyr Makarushka, and Mykhailo Hostronyz is Mykhailo Ostroverkha.

15 See chapter 5.

Chapter Sixteen

1 The periodicals included *Visti* (News), *Batkivshchyna* (Fatherland), *Zhyttia v tabori* (Camp Life), and the weekly newsletter *Osa* (Wasp). Different regiments and companies produced their own newspapers: *Na varti* (On guard) by the 3rd Regiment; *V nametakh* (In tents) by the 4th; *Taborovi visti* (Camp news) and *Mokre riadno* (Wet rag) by the 5th; *Taborovyi visnyk* (Camp herald) by the artillery; and *Taborovyk* (Camper) by the technical group (Virnyi 2005, 158).

2 The caricatures were republished as *Zibralasia kumpaniia* (The company gathered, 1946). They included cartoons of General Mykhailo Krat, Colonel Roman Dolynskyi, Major Savelii Yaskevych, Lieutenant Yevhen von Nikitin, Reverend Ivan Bilanych, Reverend Emanuil Korduba, Lieutenant Kostiantyn Melnyk, Captain Mykhailo Kashchuk, Captain Mykhailo Dliaboha, Lieutenant Luka Klevchuk, Volodymyr Pobidynskyi, Professor Valeriian Revutskyi, Stepan Stoliarchuk, Captain Volodymyr Liakhotskyi, Stepan Huminilovych, Yevhen Psika, Yaroslav Babuniak, Yaroslav Pankiv, Captain Bohdan Pidhainyi, Bohdan Lytvynovych, Orest Horodyskyi, Volodymyr Gotskyi, Liubomyr Rykhtytskyi, Semen Fediuk, Mykola Volynskyi, Vsevolod Budnyi, Volodymyr Kaplun, Markiian Fesolovych, Yurii Forys, Vasyl Davydiak, Borys Shkandrii ("Bohdan Bora"), Lieutenant Roman Turko, Serhii Sokhtskyi, Osyp Syvenkyi, Roman Kovalskyi, Volodymyr Kishko, Professor Oleksander Montsibovych, Roman Rudenskyi, Bohdan Levytskyi, Ivan Rubych, Roman Fedyshyn.

3 Kaplun was from the village of Kryve in Radekhiv, studied art with Pavlo Kovzhun and Mykhailo Osinchuk, was sent in June 1944 to the Viking Division, and fought on the Narva River. Markiian Fesolovych (Em-Ef, e-M-F) also worked on the publication. A technician in a milk factory in Zbarazh, he volunteered in July 1943 and fought at Brody.

Notes to pages 264–81 • **379**

4 Among them were *bekerai* (fantastic, unreal land), *bekher* (drinker, aluminum military cup), *ity na banitsiiu* (go into exile), *kalabush* (calabouche, punishment cage), *paskar* (salesman, usually of illegal goods), *piko bello* (height of perfection), *pustytysia liafshritom* (to run), *richionista* (one who often visits Riccione), *selepko* (simpleton), *favl aut* (foul out, ball out of play), *faflega* (food, Ger: Verpflegung), *fifak* (adventure seeker), *shafa* (radio), *shite arsh* (soldier idiot, Ger: Schutze Arsch), *shtemp* (shame) (Slupchynskyi 2013, 171–2).

5 In 1929, Devlad presented Petrov with a signed map of the Dnipro rapids (Andrieiev 2012, 51). In 1955, he published a collection of historical essays that included this essay but without the map. See "Dniprovi Porohy" in Zaporozhets-Devlad (1955, 80–112). For the essay and map of the rapids, see Devlad, O.S., "Shliakhy ta stezhky cherez porohy," in *Materialy do vyvchennia vyrobnychykh obiednan, Vyp. 1. Dniprovski lotsmany*, 113–24, Kyiv: Vseukrainska Akademiia Nauk, 1929. For his report on the Dnipro rapids, see Devlad, O.S. "Shliakhy Dniprovymy porohamy – Lotsmanska Kamianka Dnipropetrovkoi okruhy, lypen 1929," Naukovyi arkhiv Instytutu arkheolohii NAN Ukrainy, f. 18, spr. 163 (1929) (Andrieiev 2012, 51).

6 See Liubomyrskyi (1951, 1952, 1953, 1955–56, 1977, 1984, 1985, 1993).

7 I am grateful to Olena Maciv for this information. On these operations, see also Plokhy (2015, 28–32). For how the operation was betrayed within Poland, see Hałagida (2005).

8 *Plemia nepokirnykh* (Insubordinate tribe, 1971) and *Vohon z Kholodnoho Iaru* (Fire from the cold ravine, 1996) deal with the Decembrists in Ukraine. *Nad Halychem hrymyt* (Tumult over Halych, 1973) is set in medieval Kyiv, and *Nas rozsudyt Boh* (The lord will judge us, 1985) deals with Pavlo Polubotok's resistance to Peter the Great of Russia. For his essays and journalism, see Fostun (1971a, 1974, 1988, 1993).

9 The first guards who trained at Trawniki were 1,250 Soviet POWs who volunteered. Later, in June and July 1943, one thousand were recruited from the District of Lublin. In total about five thousand served. For a discussion of Trawniki men, see chapter 6.

10 For his fiction, see Tys-Krokhmaliuk (1937, 1954b, 1954c, 1955, 1958, 1959, 1961a, 1961c, 1964). For the military studies, see Tys-Krokhmaliuk (1954a, 1961b, 1972). For a bibliography of his articles in *Visti kombatanta* between 1961 and 1985, see Fedorovych (1987, 43–4).

Chapter Seventeen

1 The findings of the first are discussed in Troper and Weinfeld (1988, 294–338), the second in Cesarani (1992, 247–67).

2 The report responded to allegations that individuals who had committed crimes during the Second World War had entered Australia. As a result of the

report, the Australian government committed to setting up a special investigations unit, which would look into details related to some seventy named persons. See Parliament of Australia (1987, 496–501).

3 Armstrong is quoted in this context: "Himmler adopted the practice of awarding nominal Waffen ss status to personnel in other branches of his appanage, either for administrative reasons or to protect them from conscription. In 1944, for example, some 40,000 of the 600,000 members of the Waffen ss were employed in other components of the ss organization. More than half of them were assigned to the ss Economic and Administrative Main Office (ss-Wirtschafts und Verwaltungshauptamt or WVHA), which ran the concentration camp system. Although the concentration camp personnel were not under the command of Army or the Kommandamt der Waffen ss, they wore Waffen ss uniforms and carried Waffen ss paybooks. Furthermore, there was a relatively limited but nevertheless continuous exchange of personnel between concentration camp staffs and the combat formations of the Waffen ss throughout the war. In short, the denials of the ss apologists notwithstanding, there existed a connection between the Waffen ss and the concentration camps" (Deschênes 1986, 248; Armstrong 1963, xxxii).

4 The Commission indicated that the Canadian Jewish Congress had already in 1950 provided a list of ninety-four suspects from the Galicia Division. "Unfortunately," the Commission stated, "no witnesses were offered in support of the allegations, and in exactly half the cases not even a first name was given to help identify the suspects" (Deschênes 1986, 251). On 25 September 1950, the president of the Canadian Jewish Congress, Samuel Bronfman, wrote that "each individual who was a member of the Halychyna Division ought to be stamped with the stigmata that is attached to the entire body of the ss" (252). The Commission, however, agreed with the opinion of M. Yves Fortier: "If the only allegation against a resident of Canada is that he was a member of the Galicia Division that is not an individual which we consider should be made the subject of an investigation by your Commission. If the allegation is that while he was a member of the Division, he committed atrocities at such-and-such a place, if there is evidence of the committing of atrocities alleged in the information which was conveyed to us, then that person becomes of interest to your Commission" (254).

5 The relevant chapters of the Commission's report are: Chapter V, "Relaxation of Restrictions on the Admission of Volksdeutsche and German Nationals," 204–15; Chapter VII, "Security screening, 1950–1951," 228–34; Chapter VIII, "Relaxation of Security Screening Guidelines with regard to Former Members of the Nazi Party, Wehrmacht and Waffen ss, and Nazi Collaborators, 1948–1953," 235–62; Chapter XII, part 3. "Admission of the Ukrainian Halychyna (Galician) Waffen-ss Division," 366–408. For a summary of the Deschênes findings, see: http://galiciadivision.ml/lib/veryha-eng/do2.html.

Notes to pages 282–5 • **381**

6 On Littman and the changing "parade of numbers," see Troper and Weinfeld (1988, 140–52 and 190–1).

7 The report examined individual cases, which it identified only by numbers, although it is clear that many were officers in the Division. It states, typically, in each case: "No evidence that the subject had entered Canada," "the Berlin Documentation Center ... had a record of the subject which confirmed only his membership in the Galicia Division of the Waffen-ss," "the Commission requested Mr. Wiesenthal to provide additional information with respect to the subject, and was advised that he was unable to do so," "it is recommended that the file on the subject be closed." In all, 776 cases on the Master List were looked at and reported on in this manner. The original Master List had been compiled from names provided by the Wiesenthal Center in Vienna (219 names) and Los Angeles (63), the Canadian Jewish Congress (and Profesor Irwin Cotler) (209), Sol Littman (171), B'nai Brith Canada (and David Mathas) (100), the Department of Justice Canada (81), the Canadian Holocaust Remembrance Association (54), the Israel Police (M. Russek) (54), the Jewish Federation of New Jersey (R. Krieger) (49), the USSR (43), and Ephraim Zufoff (29 names) (Deschênes 1986, 47–8).

8 Other Soviet propaganda booklets from the time include Danylenko (1970); Dmytruk (1973 and 1975); and Maslovskyi (1975). Dmytruk was a major in the KGB called Klymentii Halskyi. He was of Polish origin, from the Zhytomyr region, and had himself been accused of war crimes in the Lviv region, where he reportedly murdered prisoners and fabricated "cases" as required by the KGB. See *Ukrainskyi visnyk*, vol. 6 (Baltimore: Smoloskyp, 1972), 165–6, quoted in Veryha (1980, 77). Dmytruk falsely claimed that Sheptytskyi and the Ukrainian Catholic Church hierarchy were largely responsible for the Division's creation, calling them traitors and enemies of the people: "In spite of all the efforts of the clergy, the recruitment of volunteers dragged on" and "by 5 July only a few hundred collaborators had signed up" (Dmytruk 1970, 201, quoted in Veryha 1980, 78).

9 John Kolasky, a fellow communist who broke from the party, has explained that Kravchuk held paid positions and received dividends from businesses controlled by the Soviet government and the Canadian Communist Party. These included the Globe Tours travel agency, which had a monopoly on tours to Ukraine; the Taras investment company, which owned several business locations in Toronto; and the Ukrainska Knyha bookstore. He personally profited from all these (Kolasky 1979, 212–14).

10 See Madajczyk (1965, 6–7); Juchniewicz (1968, 153); Juchniewicz (1973), 27; Szcześniak and Szota (1973, 121–30); Klukowski (1958); and Siemion (1971, 287–8).

11 For example, Krannhals (1962) lists every military formation but does not mention the Division or any Ukrainian force. Neither does Kirchmayer (1964) or Lovell (1970). The latter writes: "no one anywhere has affirmed that

the formations of the Division ss-Galicia or even the detachments of the Ukrainian police were involved in putting down the Warsaw Uprising; all Polish sources ... list only the Vlasovite 'Cossack-Brigade' and Kaminsky's RONA brigade (Lovell 1970, 70). Torzecki (1982), a Polish historian who has done archival research on the Division, also supports the argument that its members did not participate in the suppression of the Warsaw Uprising.

12 See also the Polish archive in Lublin: Lublin Ortk, I/524/23, AGR MSW 185, APL.

13 See also the internet discussion: https://soc.culture.polish.narkive.com/ E8hmKdwD/ukrainian-waffen-ss-and-the-warsaw-uprising.

14 The author is grateful to Alti Rodal for this information and for the opportunity to consult her unpublished manuscript "The Ukrainian 'Halychyna' (Galician) Waffen-ss Division," chapter 12, part 3. See also Alti Rodal, "Nazi War Criminals in Canada: The Historical and Policy Setting from the 1940s to the Present," unpublished study by the Director of Historical Research, Commission of Inquiry on Nazi War Criminals in Canada (Deschênes Commission), LAC, RG 33, 1986, Rodal Report. See also AO, Veryha Collection, F1405-56-139, B 822 590.

15 The Military Board burned the Division's archive to prevent its falling into Soviet hands, and Colonel R. Campbell-Preston, the commanding officer of the 80th (Scottish Horse) Medium Regiment, RA, reportedly persuaded the Division's men to destroy all compromising indications of citizenship after he had learned of the forceful repatriation of the Cossacks (Khromeychuk 2013, 64).

16 For a description of the press reporting in Britain, see Cesarani (1992, 190–224); and in North America, see Troper and Weinfeld (1988, 73, 140–52, 90).

17 After his death in 1991 it was revealed that Maxwell had served more than one secret service, including the KGB, and had flattered Eastern European dictators. His death occurred after the revelation of a massive theft of pension funds, and his companies filed for bankruptcy in 1992.

18 For a discussion of Russian active measures, see Bertelsen (2021).

19 On the forces incorporated into the Division in 1944, see Melnyk (2016 1:152–3, 231; and Melnyk 2016 2:22–3, 33, 61, 219).

20 For an account of the general's career and his legendary postwar organization, see Gehlen (1972).

21 In Reitlinger's view, the first Nuremberg Tribunal made a serious error when it judged the ss to be a criminal organization: "If such a judgement were to be made at all, it should have been made on the German nation as a whole, instead of providing the German nation with a convenient scapegoat" (Reitlinger 1956, 452).

22 Up to 80 percent of judges in the highest appellate court had served in the judiciary or as state officials in the Third Reich, and prominent jurists who

Notes to pages 298-5 • **383**

had served the Nazis retained professorships or became influential lawyers specializing in Nazi-era crimes (Douglas 2016, 175).

23   In 1988, the Israeli court convicted John (Ivan) Demjanjuk of being Ivan the Terrible, who operated in Treblinka. Judge Levin, at the end of his ten-hour reading, stated: "we determine unequivocally and without the slightest hesitation or doubt that the accused, Ivan John Demjanjuk, standing trial before us, is Ivan who was called Ivan Grozny" (Teicholz 1990, 296). Shortly after the Soviet Union collapsed, evidence emerged that the real Ivan the Terrible had been a man named John Marchenko, who had died. Demjanjuk was released. In his book, Yoram Sheftel, Demjanjuk's lawyer, points out that the Soviet Union was aware that Demjanjuk was not Marchenko. So was the US Office of Special Investigations, which was in possession of relevant documents as early as 1978, when the first charges were brought, and who withheld this information from the defence until the prosecution's case collapsed (Sheftel 1994, 326-7).

24   To Roth's credit, another observer or persona offers a different, more disturbing and painful view, by arguing that the country needs the trial and dramatization of the Holocaust because most Jews were not choosing to live in Israel (Roth 1993, 83). For a view of the Holocaust as binding together Jews of different backgrounds, see Judt (2012, 125-6).

25   For more on Operation Payback, see Luciuk (2021, ix-xiii, 135-7, 193-8).

26   The principle of universality – that an act committed by one person must be regarded as criminal if committed by another – was already raised in 1946. One commentator stated that crimes against peace, war crimes, and crimes against humanity had been committed by the Soviet Union. He enumerates a long list of these crimes and notes that the Soviet regime was using "the same methods as did the Nazis against the millions of people on the territories it has occupied, or which come within its sphere of influence" (Gallus 1946, 31).

27   Arendt (1982, 117, 123) controversially points out that Jews also served as administrators, police, and executioners in the German concentration camps, and Douglas (2016, 66) notes that very few of them were brought to trial.

Chapter Eighteen

1   See UCRDC, oral history archive, "Interviews with Veterans of the 14th Waffen SS Division Galicia."

2   Of the audio and video interviews reviewed, thirty-eight were conducted in North America, mostly in Toronto; ten in Western Europe; and forty-five in Western Ukraine. They were semi-structured: individuals were asked to present their life stories, to state why they joined the Division, and to describe their experience. Twenty-eight interviews were taken by Oksana Tovaryanska as part of an MA thesis. The others were taken by researchers or community volunteers, two of which were conducted in German with Wolf-Dietrich

384 • Notes to pages 300–1

Heike, the rest in Ukrainian. For a description of how Tovaryanska identified the interviewees in Ukraine and how they were conducted, see Tovaryanska (2008, 11–14).

3 The names of the interviewees are presented as they are recorded in the UCRDC's Oral History Archive. The interviews have been digitalized. In most cases there is no written transcript. The audio interview with Andrii Sternyuk was recorded in Ivano-Frankivsk by Yurij Maniukh, tape 342, n.d.

4 UCRDC, oral history archive, audio interview with Myroslav Bihus conducted on 25 January 1996 in Toronto by Victor Susak, tape 280.

5 UCRDC, oral history archive, audio interview with Petro Savaryn conducted on 22 June 1990 in Edmonton by Peter Smylski, tape 129. For his memoirs, see (Savaryn 2007).

6 UCRDC, oral history archive, audio interview with Volodymyr Malkosh conducted in Ivano-Frankivsk by Jurij Maniukh, tape 184, no date. For his memoirs, see Malkosh (2007).

7 Himmler reacted similarly to statements by ss military chieftains urging abandonment of the dogma of the "subhuman" Slav and the "New Europe" concept: "Discussions of a United Europe are nothing more than empty blather. There can be no talk of including Ukrainians and Russians in this Europe. I forbid once and for all any form of support for this approach, which the Fuhrer unequivocally rejects" (quoted in Radchenko and Usach 2020, 458).

8 At a conference held at his headquarters on 16 July 1941, Hitler stated: "the security of the Reich depends on there being no foreign military forces west of the Urals ... No one in those parts may ever again be permitted to bear arms except the Germans ... Otherwise they will inevitably turn against us some day. Only the Germans may bear arms, not the Slavs ... not the Cossacks, not the Ukrainians ..." (quoted in Thorwald 1975, ix).

9 UCRDC, oral history archive, audio interview with Mychailo Mulyk conducted in Ivano-Frankivsk by Yurij Maniukh, tape 186, n.d.

10 The OUN's Bandera faction in its *Biuleten* 3 (1943) insisted that, "without a Ukrainian state, without a Ukrainian government there cannot be a Ukrainian army ... The Germans are planning continued exploitation, this time of physical force of the people, its further destruction and our position to this can only therefore be negative." See photocopy in Bihun (2018).

11 Within the Division these men formed a secret network, which included Bohdan Pidhainyi, Mykhailo Kachmar, Myroslaw Maleckyj, Sviatoslav Levytskyi, and Mykhailo Brygider (Usach 2016, 65).

12 UCRDC, oral history archive, audio interview conducted with Mykhailo Fitilovskyi in Ivano-Frankivsk by Yurij Maniukh, tape 179, n.d.

13 UCRDC, oral history archive, audio interview with Eugene Humesky conducted on 7 June 1996 in Toronto by Victor Susak, tape 323.

Notes to pages 301–10 • **385**

14 UCRDE, oral history archive, audio interview with Liubomyr Zakhariasevych conducted in Ivano-Frankivsk by Yurij Maniukh, tape 187, n.d.

15 The incident occurred on 14 November 1943 during a performance of the operetta *Sharika*, by the composer Yaroslav Barnych, which deals with the love of a Sich Rifleman for a girl from Transcarpathia. One hundred and forty people were arrested. After a show trial in the theatre on 17 November, twenty-seven men and three women were sentenced to death. At the public execution, forty Ukrainian policemen and German Schutzpolizei held back the crowd (Bondarev 2017).

16 UCRDC, oral history archive, video interview with Vasyl Paliienko conducted in Toronto on July 1989 by Jurij Darewych, tape 6.

17 UCRDC, oral history archive, audio interview with Ostap Sokolsky conducted in Toronto by unnamed interviewer, tape 11, n.d.

18 Interwar literature on the failed independence struggle was produced by numerous currents, Ukrainian Catholics, supporters of the parliamentary party UNDO (Ukrainian National Democratic Association), and the OUN. Prominent writers like Yevhen Malaniuk, Yurii Lypa, Leonid Mosendz, and Ulas Samchuk reinforced a message of militancy and respect for military organization. On the last three writers, see Shkandrij (2015, 191–8, 207–43).

19 Several German figures were highly visible during the Division's creation. Among them Colonel Alfred Bisanz, who headed the Military Board, Severin Beigert, and Hans Koch. All were natives of Galicia and had served as senior officers in the UHA. Their presence strengthened the impression that the Galicia Division would be a continuation of the earlier military formation. I am indebted to Roman Waschuk for this observation.

20 The words of the song are from a poem by Ivan Franko, with the refrain "Ne pora, ne pora, ne pora, Moskalevi y Liakhovi sluzhyt" (The time has passed for serving the Russian and the Pole).

21 UCRDC, oral history archive, audio interview with Yevhen Myhas conducted in Ivano-Frankivsk by Jurij Maniukh, tape 180, n.d.

22 Oleksandra Sokolovska's company had over one thousand fighters, one of whom was the writer Klym Polishchuk, who produced several novels describing events during the Ukrainian Revolution of 1917–21.

23 UCRDC, oral history archive, audio interview with Bohdan Buchak conducted on 18 May 1995 in Kozova by Yaroslav Statskyj, tape 334.

24 In the 1930s, Hitler and Nazi ideology were discussed favourably by Dmytro Dontsov and critically by a number of other groups. Most in the Ukrainian Galician elite took a decision to overlook the most brutal aspects of the Nazi regime, partly because of Germany's perceived dominance in European politics, and partly because of the expectation of obtaining some limited advantages. Unlike the Soviets, who applied a policy of elite repression and replacement in 1939–41, the Germans sought, initially at least, to co-opt traditional elites.

386 · Notes to pages 310–21

25 UCRDC, oral history archive, audio interview with Myron Martsinowsky conducted on 4 May 1995 in Buchach by Yaroslav Statskyj, tape 328.

26 UCRDC, oral history archive, audio interview with Mykhailo Dydyk conducted in village Kryve, Ternopil oblast by Yaroslav Statskyj, tape 337, n.d.

27 This information was made available in many interwar publications. See, for example, Lozynskyi (1970, 25–46 [orig. pub. Vienna, 1922]); and Kuzma (1960, 13–38 [orig. pub. Lviv, 1931]). There was also a substantial interwar literature about the military operations conducted by Ukrainian forces. Among the most popular were: Tiutiunnyk (1923); Dotsenko (1932); Omelianovych-Pavlenko (1929 and 1940 [orig. pub. 1929–32]); Bezruchko (1932); Horlis-Horskyi (1935).

Chapter Nineteen

1 For a recent account of OUN members saving Jews, see (Dzhulai 2021).

2 See Beevor (2002a and 2002b). The author's books were banned in Russia in 2015. See also Hitchcock (2003) and Berlin (2015). Heike Sander and Barbara Johr directed the film *BeFreier und BeFreite* (1992), which interviewed German women raped in Berlin by Soviet soldiers.

3 See: "Frau, Komm!" (2009); Johnson (2002); "The Red Army's WWII Horror Orgy" (2002).

4 For an image of the Berlin memorial, and for the diary of Vladimir Gelfand, a young Jewish lieutenant from Central Ukraine who wrote with extraordinary frankness about this aspect of the war, see Ash (2015).

5 Moscow continued to deny responsibility for the crime of Katyn and to withhold evidence until the end of the Soviet Union's existence in 1990. For an analysis of the cover-up, see Etkind, Finnin et al. (2012).

6 Hałagida states that only 5 Ukrainians were killed in 1940 and 18 in 1941, 9 of whom were killed by German police, but over the next two years a minimum of 3,184 were victims in Hrubieszów and 1,195 in Zamość. They included 31 village heads and 19 municipal administrators, 35 village council chairs, 38 trusted men and 10 workers of the Ukrainian Aid Committee (UDK), 15 co-op workers, 22 members of the clergy (20 priests, 1 monk and 1 deacon) of the Ukrainian Orthodox or Ukrainian Greek-Catholic Church, 12 cantors, 9 agronomists, 4 shoemakers, 71 Ukrainian police in German service, and 9 soldiers in various German formations (Hałagida 2019, 249).

7 See, for example, Piętka (2015, 193–9); Prus (2001, 2005, and 2007).

8 For the Russian embassy's instigation of stories, see Smith (2017) and Luciuk (2020). Recently released SBU archives demonstrate that the Ukrainian KGB took credit for placing Sol Littman's articles in the *Toronto Star* on 8 November 1984 and 25 January 1985, which led to the creation of the Deschènes Commission in February 1985. See Danylenko (2017, 198). For an analysis of Soviet "active measures" against the Jewish and Ukrainian dissi-

Notes to pages 322–8 • **387**

dents in the 1970s, which also aimed at dividing these two communities in the diaspora, see Bertelsen (2020).

9 For an analysis of this issue, see Bertelsen (2021).

10 The name comes from the dark blue uniforms that were issued to this police force. It included approximately 12,500 men between 1943 and 1944 and was frequently deployed during Operation Reinhard. According to information provided by the Polish resistance, up to 10 percent of the Dark Blue Police and the Polish criminal police may have been collaborators. See Młynarczyk (2017, 169–79).

11 Representatives of the UPA and WiN met on 31 November 1945, 6 December 1945, and 25 January 1946. Their most successful joint action was in Hrubieszów on 4–6 May 1946. For minutes of the UPA-WiN meetings, see Huk (2018, 29–64). For the Hrubieszow action, see Huk (2018, 40–4). The six-hundred-strong Rysia Battalion of Stanisław Basaj was also active in the area. He professed allegiance to the BCh but operated independently and was responsible for a series of murders. In an interview conducted in 1994, the WiN leader Marian Głębiowski admitted that Basaj should have been "liquidated" (78). After perpetrating mass murders on 10–11 March 1944 in Szychowice, Lasków, and Sahryń, Basaj left for the forests of Bilograj (80).

12 One appeal printed in *Dziennik Zolniera* (Soldier's diary) on 17 June 1943 called on Poles not to speak of the *dzicz hajdamacka* (Haidamaka savages) or to call Ukrainian Catholic priests by the derogatory *popy*: "There is no doubt that in the Ukrainian case the Polish side has committed many mistakes, which later took revenge on us. Of course, the Ukrainians, who sought support from the enemies of Poland, also committed equally many mistakes" (PISM, A.9.V/43).

Chapter Twenty

1 The first issue of the cross was in Poland, with the marker "J. Kweksilber – Warsaw" on the reverse, the second in Germany, the third in the United States. See: https://www.emedals.com/ukraine-republic-an-order-of-symon-petliura-c-1945.

2 See https://uinp.gov.ua/memorializaciya/sektory-viyskovyh-pohovan-ta-typovi-nadgrobky. For a photograph of the military graveyard in Kherson from 2016, see https://uinp.gov.ua/memorializaciya/sektory-viyskovyh-pohovan-ta-typovi-nadgrobky.

3 Among them were the following writers, academics, and theatre figures: Mykola Zerov, Les Kurbas, Mykola Kulish, Antin Krushelnytskyi, Valerian Pidmohylnyi, Pavlo Fylypovych, Oleksa Vlyzko, Valerian Polishchuk, Hryhorii Epik, Marko Voronyi, Oleksa Slisarenko, Mykhailo Yalovyi, and Matvii Yavorskyi. The evidence against the victims was fabricated, the dates of death falsified, and the executions kept secret for decades. It was not until 1997

388 · Notes to pages 331–42

that the place of execution was found, and in 2005 a cross with the inscription "Murdered Sons of Ukraine" was placed on the site ("Buty elitoiu natsii" 2017).

4 In fact, the marker is almost an identical monument to the one on the grave of the Sokolovskyi family, several of whom fought and died in the independence struggle between 1917 and 1921. Marusia (Oleksandra Sokolovska) was considered a Ukrainian Joan of Arc; she fought alongside the army of the UNR and the Sich Riflemen in 1919 (for images see Sviryn [2011]). The similarity of markers is, no doubt, part of the attempt to make connections between periods.

5 For a response to the Pugliese article, see Luciuk (2020).

6 Taylor and Pugliese are both regular contributors to *Esprit de Corps*, which bills itself as a Canadian military magazine. An article for the magazine by Richard Sanders states that Freeland "began her career with jobs for publications promoting the WWII Ukrainian Waffen ss Galicia as heroic 'freedom fighters'" and that both she and her grandfather "worked for the same far-right, Ukrainian-Canadian publications in Edmonton." The only publication Sanders mentions is the *Encyclopedia of Ukraine*, which "romanticises ethnic-cleansing Ukrainian fascists as ethnic anticommunists and whitewashes their complicity in the genocide of Jews, Poles, Roma and communist partisans who were backing the Red Army" (Sanders 2021). The malicious nature of these charges and their defamatory intent will be clear to any reader who consults the *Encyclopedia* or its online articles, or who examines Freeland's career as a journalist and politician. She was an editor of the *Financial Times* and published *Sale of the Century* (2000), which describes Russia in the 1990s, and *Plutocrats* (2012), which examines the growth of a wealthy and powerful "super class" in recent decades.

7 For the policy and its impact of Ukrainian scholarship in Canada and the United States, see Prymak (2015).

8 For examples, see Slaboshpytskyi and Stetsenko (1994); Midzhak (1994); Sirskyi (2000); Kalba (1999, 2008); Slaboshpytskyi (2008); Kolisnyk, Matsiv, and Mukha (2009); Matsiv (2009); Burtyk and Panchenko (2016). Their purpose was to provide a positive image of the Division as a military formation at war with the Soviet Union. Other books at the time also contextualized the war as a struggle against external aggressors. See, for example, Mukovskyi and Lysenko (1997) and Viatrovych (2012).

9 The president's message appeared on 30 April and was removed on the next day. It stated that permission had not been given for the parade and condemned "all propaganda for totalitarian regimes, in particular the national socialist one, and attempts to revise the truth about the Second World War." The message carried a reminder that the Ministry of Foreign Affairs had already condemned any glorification of the Waffen-ss and that "propaganda for totalitarian regimes" was forbidden in the country (President 2021).

References

Archives

AO	Archives of Ontario, Toronto
APL	Archiwum Panstwowe w Lublinie, Lublin
AAV	Archivio Apostolico Vaticano, Rome
AUSBUTO	Arkhiv Upravlinnia Sluzhby Bezpeky Ukrainy v Ternopilskii Oblast (Archive of the Administration of the Security Service of Ukraine in Ternopil Oblast)
BA-KO	Bundesarkhiv, Berlin (formerly German Military Archive, Koblenz)
BA-L	Budesarkhiv Aussenstelle Ludwigsberg
HDASBU	Halyzevyi Derzhavnyi Arkhiv Sluzhby Bezpeky Ukrainy (State Archive of the Security Service of Ukraine), Kyiv
HILA	Hoover Institution Library and Archives, Stanford University
IHRC	Immigration History Research Center, University of Minnesota
LAC	Library and Archives of Canada, Ottawa
NA/PRO	National Archive (formerly Public Records Office), London
NAUS	National Archives of the United States, Washington
PAA	Provincial Archives of Alberta, Edmonton
PISM	Polish Institute and Sikorski Museum, London
TsDAVOV	Tsentralnyi derzhavnyi arkhiv vyshchykh orhaniv vlady i upravlinnia Ukrainy (Central State Archive of Higher Organs of Power), Kyiv
UCRDC	Ukrainian Canadian Research and Documentation Centre, Toronto
USHMM	United States Holocaust Memorial Museum Archive, Washington

Published Sources

Adamski, Łukasz, Grzegorz Hryciuk, and Gregorz Motyka, eds. 2017. *Sowieci a polskie podziemie 1943–1946: Wybrane aspekty stalinowskiej polityki represji*. Warsaw: Centrum Polsko-Rosyjskiego Dialogu i Porozumienia.

Andrieiev, Vitalii. 2012. *Viktor Petrov: Narysy intelektualnoi biohrafii vchenoho. Monohrafiia*. Dnipropetrovsk: Herda.

Arendt, Hannah. 1982. *Eichmann in Jerusalem: A Report on the Banality of Evil*. Rev. and enlarged ed. New York: Penguin Books. Orig. pub. 1963.

Armstrong, John A. 1963. *Ukrainian Nationalism*. 2nd rev. ed. New York: Columbia University Press.

-. 1988. "Introduction," xiv-xxvi. In Heike, *Ukrainian Division "Galicia."*

Ash, Lucy. 2015 "The Rape of Berlin," BBC News, 30 April 2015, https://www.bbc. com/news/magazine-32529679.

Bąkowski, Władysław. 2001. *Zagłada Huta Pieniackiej*. Kraków: Biblioteka Zloczowska.

Baranova, Olga. 2008. "Nationalism, Anti-Bolshevism or the Will to Survive? Collaboration in Belarus under Nazi Occupation of 1941–1944." *European Review of History* 15, no. 2: 113–28.

Barychko, V. 1943. "Za mitsnyi kupetskyi stan." *Lvivski visti*. 18 February.

Bauer, Yehida. 1994. *Jews for Sale? Nazi-Jewish Negotiations, 1933–1945*. New Haven: Yale University Press.

Beevor, Antony. 2002a. *Berlin – The Downfall: 1945*. London: Viking Press. Published in the US as *The Fall of Berlin*, 2002.

-. 2002b. "They Raped Every German Female from Eight to 80." *Guardian*, 1 May.

Bender, Vitalii [Donchak, Donchenko, real name Mykhailo Martiuk]. 1947. *Navzdohin za vorohom*. Rimini: N.p.

-. 1954. *Marsh molodosty*. 2 vols. Munich: Vydavnytstvo "Dniprova khvylia." Rep. Kyiv: IUnivers, 2005.

-. 1984a. *Frontovi dorohy*. Toronto: Suzhero-Dobrus.

-. 1984b. *Stantsiia Puhalovska: Povist-Roman*. Toronto: Suzhero.

Bender, Roger James, and Hugh Page Taylor. 1975. *Uniforms, Organization and History of the Waffen-ss*. San José, CA: R. James Bender.

Bergholz, Max. 2016. *Violence as a Generative Force: Identity, Nationalism, and Memory in a Balkan Community*. Ithaca, NY: Cornell University Press.

Berlin, Lucy. 2015. "The Rape of Berlin." *bbc.com*, 1 May.

Bertelsen, Olga. 2020. "Ukrainian and Jewish Emigres as Targets of KGB Active Measures in the 1970s." *International Journal of Intelligence and Counter-Intelligence*, 26 May, https://doi.org/10.1080/08850607.2020.1750093.

-, ed. 2021. *Russian Active Measures: Yesterday, Today, Tomorrow*. Stuttgart: ibidem-Verlag

Bethel, Nicholas. 1974a. "A Brutal Exchange." *Spectrum*, 7 January.

-. 1974b. *The Last Secret: Forcible Repatriation to Russia, 1944–47*. London: Deutsch.

Bezruchko, Marko. 1932. *Sichovi striltsi v borotbi za derzhavnist*. Kalish: Voienno-istorychne t-vo.

Bihl, Wolfdieter. 1987. "Ukrainer als Teil der Streitkrafte des Deutschen Reiches im Zweiten Weltkrieg." *Osterreichische Osthefte* 29: 28–55.

Bihun, Ihor. 2020. "Velykyi blef: Kampaniia naboru v dyviziiu 'Halychyna' iak manipuliatyvna tekhnolohiia." *Istorychna Pravda*, 3 May, 2018, https://www. istpravda.com.ua/articles/2018/04/28/152370/.

Bilostotskyi, Tymish. 2000. *Spomyny*. N.p.: nakladom Bratstva kol. Voliakiv 1-oi UD UNA.

References • **391**

Bishop, Chris. 2005. *Hitler's Foreign Divisions: Foreign Volunteers in the Waffen-ss 1940–1945*. London: Amber Books.

Black, Peter. 2011. "Foot Soldiers of the Final Solution: The Trawniki Training Camp and Operation Reinhard." *Holocaust and Genocide Studies* 25, no. 1: 1–99. French translation *Revue d'histoire de la Shoah* 2 (2012): 337–401.

Bodnar, Osyp. 1974. "Dotsilnist stvorennia Dyvizii 'Halychyna'." *Ukrainskyi samostiinyk* 25, no. 10: 26–31.

Böhler, Jochen, and Robert Gerwarth, eds. 2017. *The Waffen-ss: A European History*. Oxford: Oxford University Press.

Bolianovskyi, Andrii. 2000. *Dyviziia "Halychyna," Istoriia*. Lviv: Lvivskyi Natsionalnyui Universytet imeni Ivana Franka.

–. 2003. *Ukrainski viiskovi formuvannia v zbroinykh sylakh Nimechchyny (1939–1945)*. Lviv: Lvivskyi nasionalnyi universytet im. I. Franka.

Bondarev, Ivan. 2017. "Khronika odnoho rozstrilu, 1943." *Istoriia Plastu*, https://100krokiv.info/2017/11/hronika-odnoho-rozstrilu-1943/.

Bora, Bohdan [Borys Shkandrij]. 1946. *U viriiu*. Rimini: Zhyttia v tabori.

–. 1947. *V dorozi*. Rimini: Zhyttia v tabori.

–. 1972. *Tverd i nizhnist: Vybrani poezii*. London: Spilka Ukraintsi u Velykii Brytanii.

–. 1982. *Buremni dni: Zbirka poezii*. Toronto: Bratstvo kol. voiakiv 1-oi Ukrainskoi Dyvizii UNA i Obiednannia buv. voiakiv ukraintsiv u Velykii Brytanii.

Borysenko, Veronika, Mascha Brammer, and Jonas Eichhorn. 2017. "The Transnational 'Neo-Eurasian' Network and its Preparation of Separatism in Ukraine, 2005–2014." In *Transnational Ukraine? Networks and Ties That Influence(d) Contemporary Ukraine*, ed. Timm Beichelt and Susann Worschech, 225–48. Stuttgart: ibidem-Verlag.

Boshyk, Yuri, ed. 1986. *Ukraine during World War II: History and Its Aftermath: A Symposium*. Edmonton: Canadian Institute of Ukrainian Studies, University of Alberta.

Browning, Christopher R. 1993. *Ordinary Men: Reserve Police Battalion 101 and the Final Solution in Poland*. New York: Harper Perennial.

Bruns, Roger. 2007. *Almost History: Close Calls, Plan B's, and Twists of Fate in America's Past*. New York: Barnes and Noble.

Budnyi, Vsevolod B., ed. 1979. *Rimini, 1945–1947: Persha Ukrainska Dyviziia Ukrainskoi Natsionalnoi Armii u Britanskomu Poloni v Italii. Zbirnyk 1*. New York: Bratstvo kolyshnikh voiakiv Pershoi Ukrainskoi Dyvizii Ukrainskoi Natsionalnoi Armii.

Burtyk, Ivan, and Oleksandr Panchenko, eds. 2016. *Druha Dyviziia UNA: Entsyklopediia voiennoi doby: UNK, UNA, 2-ha Dyviziia UNA, Protypantserna bryhada "Vilna Ukraina," UVV, UVK, UDP u borotbi za voliu Ukrainy v podiiakh, personaliiakj, spohadakh, rekonstruktsiiakh, versiiakh ta informatsiiakh: istoriia*. Hadiach: Vydavnytstvo "Hadiach."

"Buty elitoiu natsii ... Do rokovyn rozstriliv v urochysshchi Sandarmokh." 2017. 26 October, http://www.uinp.gov.ua/informaciyni-materialy/vchytelyam/metodychni-rekomendaciyi/buly-elitoyu-naciyi-do-rokovyn-rozstriliv-v-urochyshchi-sandarmoh.

Byrnes, James F. 1947. *Speaking Frankly*. New York: Harper and Brothers.

Calvocoressi, Peter. 1947. *Nuremberg: The Facts, the Law and the Consequences*. London: Chatto and Windus, London.

Cesarani, David. 1992. *Justice Delayed*. London: Mandarin.

Chobit, Dmytro. 2020. *Zahybel Huty Peniatskoi 28 liutoho 1944 roku. Knyha persha. Trahediia. Naukovo-populiarne vydannia*. Kyiv: Vydavnychyi dim Ukrainska kultura.

Cholkan, Liubov. 1979. "Posestry." In Budnyi, *Rimini*, 117–23.

Clover, Charles. 2016. *Black Wind, White Snow: The Rise of Russia's New Nationalism*. New Haven, NJ: Yale University Press.

Coffin, William Sloane. 1977. *Once to Every Man a Memoir*. New York: Stratford Press.

Conquest, Robert. 1986. *The Harvest of Sorrow: Soviet Collectivization and the Terror-Famine*. New York: Oxford University Press,

Danesi, Marcel. 2020. *The Art of the Lie: How the Manipuation of Langue Affects Our Minds*. Guilford, CT: Prometheus Books.

Danylenko, S.T. 1970. *Dorohoiu hanby i zrady: Istorychna khronika*. Kyiv: Naukova dumka.

Danylenko, V., ed. 2017. *Vlada URSR i Zakordonni Ukraintsi (1950–1980-ti rr.): Dokumenty i materialy*. Kyiv: Smoloskyp.

Danyliv, Teodor. 1952. "Ukraintsi v II-omu polskomu korpusi hen. Andersa." *Visti Bratstva kol. Voiakiv 1 UD UNA* 10–11: 2–3.

Dean, Martin. 2000. *Collaboration in the Holocaust: Crimes of the Local Police in Belorussia and Ukraine, 1941–44*. New York: St Martin's Press.

Deschènes, Honourable Jules. 1986. *Commission of Inquiry on War Criminals. Report. Part 1: Public*. Ottawa: Canadian Government Publishing Centre.

Di Pasquale, Massimiliano, and Luigi Sergio Germani. 2021. "Russian Influence on Italian Culture, Academia, and Think Tanks." In Bertelsen, *Russian Active Measures*, 263–308.

Dismukes, Donna. 1996. "The Forced Repatriation of Soviet Citizens: A Study in Military Obedience." MA thesis, Naval Postgraduate School, Monterey, California, https://core.ac.uk/download/pdf/36701975.pdf.

Dliaboha, M. 1968. "Boiova hrupa Baiiersdorfa." *Visti Bratstva kol. Voiakiv 1: UD UNA* 131: 101–3.

Dmytruk, Klym [real name Klyment Halskyi]. 1974. *Bezbatchenky: Pravda pro uchast ukrainskykh burzhuaznykh natsionalistiv i tserkovnykh iierarkhiv u pidhotovtsi napadu fashystskoi Nimechchyny na SRSR*. Lviv: Kameniar.

–. 1973. *Svastyka na sutanakh*, Kyiv: Vyd-vo polit. Lit-ry.

References • **393**

Dolynskyi, Roman. 1951. "Lytsarska tradytsiia." *Visti Bratstva kol. Voiakiv 1: UD UNA* 6 (8): 4–5.

–. 1957. "Boieva hrupa Baiersdorfa (Prychynok do istorii 1 UD UNA)." *Visti Bratstva kol. Voiakiv 1: UD UNA* 3-6: 10–14, and 7–10: 6–12. Rpt. Kyiv-Vinnytsia: Istorychnyi klub "Kholodnyi iar," 2012.

–. 1979. "Z frontu za droty polonu." In Budnyi, *Rimini*, 13–21.

Dorril, Stephen. 2000. *MI6: Fifty Years of Special Operations.* London: Fourth Estate.

Dotsenko, Oleksander. 1932. *Zymovyi pokhid (6.XII,1919– 6.V.1920).* Warsaw: Pratsi Ukrainskoho Naukovoho Instytutu.

Douglas, Lawrence. 2016. *The Right Wrong Man: John Demjanjuk and the Last Great Nazi War Crimes Trial.* Princeton, NJ: Princeton University Press.

"Dovkruhy ss Striletskoi Dyvizii Halychyna." 1943. *Biuleten*, rik III, ch. 11: 1–5.

Drakokhrust, Iurii. 2021. "'Mashina Stalina zhiva': Svetlana Aleksievich – o voskresshem proshlom." *Radio Svoboda*, 10 May, https://www. svoboda.org/a/31244211.html?fbclid=IwAR11qAQp75JpEHfZqntWI-d8PHc5uafHkop8-kkDmz9tnHI7m8nWDT5jWa_0.

Dziewanowski, M.K. 1965. "Pamietniki gen. Szandruka." *Kultura* (June): 103–6.

Dzhulai, Dmytro. 2021. "Represovani pravednyky: Iak chleny OUN riatuvaly umanskykh ievreiv." *Radio Svoboda*, 9 May, https://www.radiosvoboda.org/a/ nachionalisty-yaki-riatuvaly-yevreiv-oun/31244271.html.

Elgot, Jessica. 2015. "The UK Man Who Tracks Britain's Living War Criminals, Just Don't Call Him a Nazi Hunter." *Huffington Post*, 29 January.

Epstein, Julius. 1973. *Operation Keelhaul: The Story of Forced Repatriation from 1944 to the Present.* Old Greenwich: The Devin-Adair Company.

Erlacher, Trevor. 2021. *Ukrainian Nationalism in the Age of Extremes: An Intellectual Biography of Dmytro Dontsov.* Cambridge, MA: Ukrainian Research Institute, Harvard University.

Etkind, Alexander, Rory Finnin, et al. 2012. *Remembering Katyn.* Cambridge: Polity Press.

Falconer, John. 1974. Letter. *Sunday Times*, 13 January.

Faryma, M. 2007. "Moia sluzhba v 5-mu halytskomu dobrovolchomu polku." *Visti kombatanta* 2: 82–4.

Fedorovych, Vasyl, ed. 1987. *Visti kombatanka: Index, 1961–1985.* Toronto: Visit kombatanta.

Ferkuniak, Dmytro. 2003. *Spomyny z zhyttia v Dyvizii "Halychyna" i v poloni 1943–1947.* Ivano-Frankivsk: Lileia-NV.

Foggo, D. 2003a. "London Man Denies Role in ss Massacres." *Daily Telegraph.* 26 January.

–. 2003b. "'Wimbledon Academic' in Nazi War Crimes Inquiry." *Daily Telegraph.* 9 February.

–. 2003c. "Police to Use NHS Records to Find Nazi War Criminals." *Daily Telegraph*. 22 June.

Forys, Iurii. 1945. *Z moikh dumok*. Bellariia: Vydavnytstvo Ukrainskoho Taboru Polonenykh v Italii.

Fostun, Sviatomyr M. 1971a. *Na krylakh zhyttia: Etiudy*. London: S.M. Fostun.

–. 1971b. *Plemia nepokirnykh: Povist iz chasiv dekabrystskoho rukhu v Ukrainia*. London: Obiednannia buvshykh voiakiv ukraintsiv u Velykii Brytanii.

–. 1972. *Zviduny stepovykh kohort: Istorychna povist*. Buenos Aires: Iuliiana Serediaka.

–. 1973. *Nad Halychem hrymyt: Istorychnyi roman*. London: Soiuz ukraintsiv u Velykii Brytanii. Rep. Lviv, 1999.

–. 1976. *Shliakhamy smerty: Povist z chasiv II svitovoi viiny*. Buenos Aires: Vydavnytstvo Iuliana Serediaka.

"Frau, Komm!" 2009. *Pictures from History*, https://pictureshistory.blogspot. com/2009/10/frau-komm-rape-german-women-ww2.html.

Fricke, Gert. 1986. *"Fester Platz" Tarnopol 1944*. Freiburg: Verlag Rombach.

Friedländer, Saul. 2008. *The Years of Extermination: Nazi Germany and the Jews, 1929–1945*. New York: Harper Perennial.

Gabrusevych, Iuliian. 1994. "'Bachyv ia, bachyv, ranenoho druha' … Spomyn polovoho sviashchennyka." *Visti kombatanta* no. 2: 89–91.

Gallus, Gallieni. 1946. *Nuremberg and After*. Newton Mount, WS: Montgomeryshire Printing and Stationery Co.

Gehlen, Reinhard. 1972. *The Service: The Memoirs of General Reinhard Gehlen*. New York: World Publishing Company.

Gerolymatos, André. 2016. *An International Civil War: Greece, 1943–1949*. New Haven, NJ: Yale University Press.

Gingerich, Mark P. 1997. "Waffen ss recruitment in the 'Germanic Lands,' 1940–1941." *Historian* 59, no. 4: 815–30.

Ginzburg, Eugenia Semyonovna. 1967. *Journey into the Whirlwind*. New York: Harcourt Brace Jovanovich.

Go-go [Orest Slupchynskyi]. 1946. *Zibralasia kumpaniia' … Zbirka kryvyl i kryvuliok*. Rimini: Redaktsiia "Osa," Vydavnytstco "Batkivshchyna."

Gogun, Alexander. 2016. *Stalin's Commandos: Ukrainian Partisan Forces on the Eastern Front*. London: I.B. Tauris. Orig. pub. *Stalinskie kommandos: Ukrainskie partizanskie formatsii: maloizvestnye stranitsy istorii, 1941-1944*, Moscow: Tsentrpolifgraf, 2008.

Golczewski, Frank. 2010. *Deutsche und Ukrainischer, 1914–1939*. Paderborn: Ferdinand Schöingh Verlag.

Gotskyi, Volodymyr. 1951. "Na Slovachchyni." *Visti Bratstva kol. Voiakiv 1. UD UNA* 9: 5-6.

–. 1990. *Na druhomu etapi (Spomyny)*. London: Obiednannia buvshykh voiakiv Ukrainy u Velykii Brytanii.

References • **395**

Greenfield, Richard. 2013. "Denis Hills: Post-Yalta Whistle-Blower Later Sentenced to Death by Idi Amin." *Independent,* 17 July.

Gronczewski, Edward. 1964, *Wspomnienia "Przepiórki."* Lublin: Inne.

Haidai, Oleh, Bohdan Khavarivskyi, and Volodymyr Khavas. 2002. *Predtecha: Polkyi rukh Oporu na Ternopilshchyni 1939–1941 rr.* Ternopil: Pidruchnyky i posibnyky.

Hałagida, Igor. 2005. *Prowokacja "Zenona": Geneza, Przebieg a Skutki MBP o Kryptonimie "C-1" Przeciwo Banderowskiej Frakcji* OUN *i Wywiadowi Brytyjskiem (1950–1954).* Warsaw: Instytut Pamieci Narodowej.

–. 2019. Liudski vtraty sered ukraintsiv u Liublinskomu dystrykti (zhovten 1939-lypen 1944): Poperedniii analiz statystychnoho materialu." *Naukovi zapysky Ukrainskoho Katolytskoho Universytetu* 13, seriia Istoriia, vypusk 3, 232–78.

Hale, Christopher. 2011. *Hitler's Foreign Executioners: Europe's Dirty Secrets.* N.p.: The History Press.

Heike, Wolf-Dietrich. 1973. *Sie Wollten Die Freiheit: Die Geschichte der Ukrainischen Division, 1943–1945.* Dorheim: Podzun.

–. 1988. *The Ukrainian Division "Galicia," 1943–45: A Memoir.* Toronto: The Shevchenko Scientific Society.

[Haike, Volf-Ditrikh]. 2013. *Ukrainska dyviziia "Halychyna": Istoriia formuvannia i boiovykh dii u 1943–1945 rokakh.* Ternopil: Mandrivets. Orig. pub. Toronto: Bratstvo kolyshnikh voiakiv 1-oi ukrainskoi dyvizii UNA, 1970.

Hale, Chrisopher. 2011. *Hitler's Foreign Executioners: Europe's Dirty Secret.* N.p.: The History Press.

Hentosh, Liliana. 2014. Pro stavlennia Mytropolyta Sheptytskoho do nimetskoho okupatsiinoho rezhymu v konteksti dokumenta z kantseliarii Alfreda Rozenberha. *Ukraina moderna,* 17 October, https://uamoderna.com/shafka-dok/hentosh-sheptytsky.

Hetherington, Sir Thomas, and William Chalmers. 1989. *War Crimes: Report of the War Crimes Inquiry.* London: Her Majesty's Stationery Office.

Hills, Denis. 1989. "You Are the Grey Mass." *Spectator,* 23 December.

Himka, John-Paul. 2005. "War Criminality: A Blank Spot in the Collective Memory of the Ukrainian Diaspora." *spacesofidentity* 5, no.1: 9–24.

–. 2009. *Ukrainians, Jews and the Holocaust: Divergent Memories.* Saskatoon: Heritage Press.

–. 2012. "Christianity and Radical Nationalism: Metropolitan Andrei Sheptytsky and the Bandera Movement." In *State Secularism and Lived Religion in Soviet Russia and Ukraine,* ed. Catherine Wanner, 93–116. New York: Oxford University Press.

–. 2021. *Ukrainian Nationalists and the Holocaust:* OUN *and* UPA's *Participation in the Destruction of Ukrainian Jewry, 1941–1944.* Stuttgart: ibidem-Verlag.

Hirniak, Kost. 1974. "Ukrainska Dyviziia 'Halychyna': Boiova pidhotovka Dyvizii," 159–74. In Lysiak, *Brody*.

–. 1977. *Ukrainskyi lehion samooborony: Prychyny do istorii*. Toronto: Nakaldom starshyn i voiakiv lehionu.

Hirsch, Francine. 2020. *Soviet Judgment at Nuremberg: A New History of the International Military Tribunal after World War II*. New York: Oxford University Press.

Hirsch, Marianne. 2008. "The Generation of Postmemory." *Poetics Today* 29, no. 1: 103–28.

Hitchcock, William I. 2003. *The Struggle for Europe: The Turbulent History of a Divided Continent, 1945 to the Present*. New York: Doubleday.

Höhne, Heinz. 1966. "Der Orden unter dem Totenkopf." *Der Spiegel*, 10 October, 94–107.

–. 1969. *Der Orden unter dem Totenkopf: Die Geschichte der ss*. 2 vols. Frankfurt am Main: Fischer Bucherei.

Horodyskyi, Orest. 1962. "Dva dni v partyzanstvi (Prychynky do istorii Ukrainskoho Legionu Samooborony)." *Samostiina Ukraina* 15, no. 7 (161): 22–6.

Horlis-Horskyi, Iurii. 1935. *Spohady*. Lviv: Iu. Horlis-Horskyi.

Hrymych, Maryna. 2017. *Antropolohiia viiny: Case Study: Dyviziia "Halychyna."* Kyiv: Duliby.

Hryniokh, o. D-r Ivan. 1951. "Dyviziia 'Halychyna' y ukrainske pidpillia," 39–58. In Lysiak, *Bii pid Brodamy*.

Hrytsak, Pavlo. 1959. *Vezhi i kulemety (Spojady z Dyvizii i bolshevytskoho polonu)*. Munich: Bratstvo kol. voiakiv 1-oi Ukrainskoi Dyvizii una, 1959. Rpt. Lviv, New York, 1995.

Huk, Bogdan, ed. 2018. *upa i win w walce z totalitaryzmem, 1945–1947: Dokumenty Wspomnienia*. Przemyśl: Stowaryszenie Ukraińskie Dziedzictwo.

Huliak, Stefan. 1952. "Velykden na fronti." *Visit* nos. 4–5: 4–7.

Hunczak, Taras. 1993. "U mundyrakh voroha," *Viisko Ukrainy* 9: 6-151. Rep. Brody: Prosvita, 2003. In Eng. as *On the Horns of a Dilemma*. New York: University Press of America, 2000.

Hurd, Madeleine, and Steffen Werther. 2017. "Waffen-ss Veterans and Their Sites of Memory Today." In Böhler and Gerwarth, *Waffen-ss*, 331–55.

Iashan, Vasyl. 1989. *Pid brunatnym chobotom: Nimetska okupatsiia Stanislavivshchyny v Druhii svitovii viini, 1941–1944*. Toronto: New Pathway.

Ingrao. Christian. 2011. *The ss Dirlewanger Brigade: The History of the Black Hunters*. New York: Skyhorse Publishing.

Ivankov, Ihor, and Mykhailo Romaniuk, eds. 2016. *Ukrainska dyviziia "Halychyna" (Lvivshchyna): Istoriia, spohady, svitlyny*. Lviv: Dukhovna vis.

References • 397

Iwasykiw Silecky, Arianna Lesia. 2006. "Fathers in Uniform: The Greek Catholic Chaplains of the 14th ss Galicia Division." MA research project. Department of History, University of Alberta.

"Jackson Opens Nuremberg Trial."1945. *British Morning News*, 22 November.

Johnson, Daniel. 2002. "Red Army Troops Raped Even Russian Women as They Freed Them from Camps," *Telegraph*, 24 January, https://www.telegraph.co.uk/news/worldnews/europe/russia/1382565/Red-Army-troops-raped-even-Russian-women-as-they-freed-them-from-camps.html.

Juchniewicz, Mieczyslaw. 1968. "Z działalności organizacyjno-bojowej Gwardii Ludowej w obwodzie lwowskim PPR." *Wojskowy przegląd historyczny* 13, no. 4: 112–61.

–. 1973. *Polacy w radieckim ruchu podziemnym i partyzanckim, 1941–1944*. Warsaw: Wydawnyctwo Ministertwa Obrony Narodowej.

Judt, Tony. 2008. *Reappraisals: Reflections on the Forgotten Twentieth Century*. New York: Penguin Press.

Judt, Tony, with Timothy Snyder. 2012. *Thinking the Twentieth Century*. New York: Penguin Press.

Jurado, Carlos Caballero. 1998. *Breaking the Chains: 14 Waffen-Grenadier-Division der ss and Other Ukrainian Volunteer Formations, Eastern Front, 1942–1945*. Halifax: Shelf Books.

K., Mykola. 1963. "A iak bulo na Kholmshchyni [Letter to Orest Horodysky from 6 March 1963]." *Samostiina Ukraina* 16, no. 1 (170): 20–1.

K., O. 1944. "Iunaky ss – pomichnyky protyletunskoi oborony." *Krakivski visti*, 23 July.

Kalba, Myroslav. 1992. *DUN (Druzhyny Ukrainskykh Natsionalistiv)*. Detroit: Vydannia Druzhyn Ukrainskykh Natsionalistiv.

–. 1999. *My prysiahaly Ukraini: DUN 1941–1943*. Lviv: Naukove Tovarystvo im. Shevchenka.

–. 2008. *Nakhtigal v zapytanniakh i vidpovidiakh*. Lviv: Halytska vydavnycha spilka.

Karkots, Mykhailo [Michael Karkoc]. 2002. *Vid Voronizha do Ukrainskoho lehionu samooborony*. Rivne: TsOV "Kalihraf."

Kedryn, Ivan. 1986. *U mezhakh zatsikavlennia*. New York: Naukove Tovarystvo im. Shevchenka.

Ketsun, V. 2013. *Spomyny dyviziinyka*. Adelaide: Nasha hromada.

Khendi, Dzhulian [Julian Hendy]. 2001. "Hrupa esesivtsiv 'Halychyna' – daleko vsia Ukraina." *Den*, 14 July.

Khomiak, Oksana V. 2017. "Reprezentatsiia voiennoho dosvidu v pamiati veteraniv dyvizii 'Halychyna' (1943–2013)." PhD diss., National University of the Kyiv Mohyla Academy.

398 • References

Khromeychuk, Olesya. 2012. "The Shaping of 'Historical Truth': Construction and Reconstruction of the Memory and Narrative of the Waffen ss 'Galicia' Division." *Canadian Slavonic Papers* 54, nos. 3–4: 443–67.

–. 2013. *"Undetermined" Ukrainians: Post-War Narratives of the Waffen ss "Galicia" Division.* Bern: Peter Land.

–. 2016. "Ukrainians in the German Armed Forces during the Second World War." *History: The Journal of the Historical Association* 100, no. 343: 704–24.

Kiebuzinski, Ksenya, and Alexander Motyl, eds. 2016. *The Great West Ukrainian Prison Massacre of 1941: A Sourcebook.* Amsterdam: Amsterdam University Press.

Kirchmayer, J. 1964. *Powstanie warszawskie.* Wyd. 4. Warsaw: Ksiazka i Wiedza.

Kirkconnell, Watson. 1944. *Seven Pillars of Freedom.* London: Oxford University Press.

Kisielewicz, Andrzej. 2011. "Zapomniana tragedia Zawonia." *Uważam Rze.*

Kladochnyi, Iosyf. 1994. "Na sluzhbi narodu: Otets D-r Kladochnyi, avtobiohrafiia." *Visti Kombatanta* nos. 5–6: 67–9.

Klenovych, V. 1942. "Stanislaviv vchora i nyni." *Krakivski visti,* 16 May.

Kleist, Peter. 1950. *Zwischen Hitler und Stalin, 1939–1945: Aufzeichnungen.* Bonn: Athenäum-Verlag.

Klukowski, Zygmund. 1958. *Dziennik z lat okupacji Zamojszczyzny, 1939–1944,* Lublin: Lubelska Spoldzielnia Wydawnicza.

Knysh, Irena. 1955. *Pershi roky na emigratsii (Z nedavnoho mynuloho): Proekt za zberezhennia intelektualnoi spadshchyny ukrainskoi emihratsii.* Winnipeg: V-vo Kultura i Osvita.

Knysh, Zynovii. 1959–60. *Pered pokhodom na skhid: Spohady y materialy do diiannia Orhanizatsii Ukrainskykh Natsionalistiv u 1939–1941 rokakh.* 2 vols. Toronto: Sribna surma.

–. 1986. *Varshevskyi protses OUN na pidlozhzhi polsko-ukrainskykh vidnosyn tiiei doby.* 2 vols. Toronto: Sribna surma.

Kolasky, John. 1979. *The Shattered Illusion: The History of Ukrainian Pro-Communist Organizations in Canada.* Toronto: PMA Books.

Kolisnyk, Roman. 2009. *Viiskova Uprava ta ukrainska Dyviziia Halychyna.* 2d rev. ed. Kyiv: Naukove tovarystvo im. Shevchenka v Kanadi, Yaroslaviv Val. Orig. pub. Toronto, 1990.

–. 2011. *Ostannii postril, Erika.* Kyiv: Iaroslaviv Val, 2nd ed. Orig. pub. *Ostannii postril: Dolia odnoho voiaka.* 1989. Toronto: Obiednannia ukrainskykh pysmennykiv Slovo.

Kolisnyk, Roman, Bohdan Matsiv, and Leonid Mukha, eds. 2009. *Dyviziia "Halychyna" v zapytanniakh i vidpovidiaklh veteraniv.* Lviv: Halytska vydavnycha spilka.

Komanski, Henryk, and Szczepan Siekierka, eds. 2006. *Ludobójstwo dokonane przez nacjonalistów ukraińskikh na Polakakh w Wojewódstwie Tarnopolskim, 1939–1946*. Wrocław: Nortom.

Kopstein, Jeffrey S., and Jason Wittenberg. 2018. *Intimate Violence: Anti-Jewish Pogroms on the Eve of the Holocaust*. Ithaca, NJ: Cornell University Press.

Korchagina, Valeria, and Andrei Zolotov. 2001. "It's Too Early to Forgive Vlasov." *St Petersburg Times*, 6 November.

Korchak-Horodyskyi, and Orest [Horodyskyi]. 1994. *Zamist vyhadok: Ukrainska problematyka v zakhidnykh polityko-dyplomatychnykh dzherelakh. Dokumenty, retsenzii, spohady*. Ivano-Frankivsk: Pereval.

Korduba, Feliks. 1963. "Stratehichne polozhennia 1942–43 (Do 20-oi richnytsi stvorennia 1 UD UNA." *Samostiina Ukraina* 16, no. 4 (170): 6–16.

Kormylo, Peter. 2021. "Is the Term 'Diaspora' of Limited Use When Referring to Scotland's Ukrainian Community?" PhD diss., University of Glasgow.

Korotko, Roman. 2013. *Provokatsiine vbyvstvo: Roman*. Lviv: Triada plius.

Kosyk, Wolodymyr. 1994. *Les Ukrainienes dans la Resistance Francaise*. Paris : Publications de l'Est Europeen, https://mairie-confracourt.fr/wp-content/uploads/sites/679/2017/12/Les_Ukrainiens_dans_la_Resistance_Francaise_Wolodymyr_KOSYK_Publications_de_l_Est_Europeen_19944942.pdf.

Kragh, Martin. 2021. "Russian Influence Operations in Scandinavia: The Case of Sweden's Largest Tabloid *Aftonbladet*." In Bertelsen, *Russian Active Measures*, 309–50.

Krannhals, H. von. 1962. *Der Warschauer Aufstand 1944*. Frankfurt: M. Bernnard and Graefe.

Krat, Mykhalo Gen. 1979. "U novii diisnosti." In Budnyi, *Rimini*, 35–46.

Kravchuk, Petro. 1973. "Hanebna richnytsia." *Zhyttia i slovo*, 21 May.

Krawchuk, Andrii. 1997. *Christian Social Ethics in Ukraine: The Legacy of Andrei Sheptytsky*. Edmonton: Canadian Institute of Ukrainian Studies Press, Metropolitan Andrey Sheptytsky Institute of Eastern Christian Studies, and the Basilian Press.

Krinko, E[vgenii]. F[edorovich]. 2004. "Kolaboratsioinizm v SSSR v gody Velikoi Otechestvennoi voiny i ego izuchenie v rossiskoi istoriografii." *Voprosy istorii*, no. 11: 153–64.

Krokhmaliuk, Iurii. 1952. "Viiskova uprava." *Visti kol. Voiakiv 1 UD UNA* 10–11: 5–7.

Kubiiovych [Kubijovyč], Volodymyr. 1941. "Ukraintsi v Heneral Hubernatorstvi: Nova diisnist pislia rozvalu Polshchi," *Ukrainski shchodenni visti*, 27 and 2 9 July.

–. 1943a. "Promova Providnyka UTSK Prof. Kubiiovycha." *Krakivski visti*, 1 May.

–. 1943b. "Shliakh do nashoho Svitloho maibutnoho." *Lvivski visti*. 6 May.

–. 1943c. "Ukrainski Hromadiany!" *Krakivski Visti*, 6 May.

–. 1953. "Etnichni hrupy Pivdennozakhidnoi Ukrainy (Halychyha) na 1.1.1939 r. Chastyna 1." *Zapysky Naukovoho Tovarystva imeny Shevchenka* 160. London: Obiednannia buvshykh Voiakiv Ukraintsiv u Velykii Brytanii.

–. 1970. *Meni 70*. Paris-Munich: Naikove Tovarystvo im. Shevchenka.

–. 1985. "Dmytro Paliiv." *Visti kombatanta* 1 (1985): 61–5. Orig. pub. *Suchasnist* 1984.

Kutyshenko, O.V. 2019. "Samoreprezentatsiia veteraniv dyvizii 'Halychyna' u materiialakh ukrainskoi presy Kanady druhoi polovyny XX-ho stolittia." MA thesis, Ukrainskyi Katolytskyi Universytet.

–. 2007. "Ukraine: Coming to Terms with the Soviet Legacy." *Journal of Communist and Transition Politics* 14, no. 4: 1–27, https://doi.org/10.1080/13523279808415388.

Kuzma, Oleksa. 1960. *Lystopadovi dni, 1918 r. Iz shkitsamy*. New York: Nakladom vydavnychoi kooperatywy "Chervona Kalyna." Orig. pub. Lviv 1931.

Kwestia ukraińska i eksterminacja ludności polskiej w Malopolsce Wsodniej w świetle dokumentów Polskieko Państwa Podziemnego, 1942–1944. 2003. Ed. Lucyna Kulińska. Kraków: Adam Roliński.

Laba, V. o. d-r [Rev. Vasyl Lada]. 1952. "Dukhovna opika nad striltsiamy 1-oi DU." *Visti Bratstva kol. voiakiv 1-oi Ukrainskoi Divizii UNA*, nos. 10–11: 7–8.

Laruelle, Marlene. 2015. *Eurasianism and the European Far Right: Reshaping the Europe-Russia Relationship*. Lanham: Leington Books.

Lazurko, Roman. 1971. *Na shliakhakh Ievropy*. Chicago: Bratstvo kolyshnikh Voiakiv 1 UD UNA.

Lebed, Mykola. 1946. *UPA ii genez, rist i dii u vyzvolnii borotbi Ukrainskoho Narodu za Ukrainsku Samostiinu Sobornu Derzhavu*. N.p.: UHVR.

Lebishchak, Ivan. 1940. "Rozbudovuimo nashi remisnychi kadry." *Krakivski visti*, 26 November.

Lehit, Andrii [Vorushylo]. 1958. *Za drotamy: Persha zbirka poezii, 1945–1948*. Neu Ulm: Ukrainski visti.

–. 1974. *Chym sertse bylos*. London: N.p.

–. 1990. *Vybrani poezii*. London.

Levenets, [Revn. "Mykhailo]. Zvidomlennia pro vidnoshennia v Dyvizii – 29-yi polk." *Visti kombatanta* 6 (1971): 676–72.

Lewyckij, Boris [Borys Levytskyi, Borys Lewytszkyj]. 1952. "Ukraińcy a likwidacja Powstania Warszawskiego." *Kultura* no. 6: 74–82.

Littlejohn, David. 1972. *The Patriotic Traitors: A History of Collaboration in German Occupied Europe, 1940–1945*. London: Heinemann.

–. 1994. *Foreign Legions of the Third Reich*. Vol. 4: *Poland, the Ukraine, Bulgaria, Romania, Lithuania, Finland and Russia*. 2nd printing. San Jose: R. James Bender Publishing.

Littman, Sol. 1997. "Transcript of Sol Littman's Tryzub and Swastika Speech, 31 August," http://willzuzak.ca/lp/littma99.html.

–. 2003. *Pure Soldiers or Sinister Legion: The Ukrainian 14th Waffen-ss Division.* London: Black Rose Books.

Liubomyrskyi, Stepan [Elerson, Liubomyr Rykhtytskyi]. 1947a. *Son litnoi nochi.* Rimini: n.p.

–. 1948. *Mizh slavoiu i smertiu: Sensatsiinyi roman.* Augsburg: Vyd-vo PU-HU. Rep. as *Mizh slavoiu i smertiu: Povne vydannia u triokh tomakh* 3 vols. Munich: Dniprova khvylia, 1953.

–. 1948–49. *Khai rozsudyt mech: Povist z vyzvolnoi borotby UPA v triokh chastynakh.* 3 vols. Malin: Nakladom Ukrainskoho Vydavnytstva v Belhii K. Mulkevych.

–. 1951. *Plemia vovkiv: Roman.* Winnipeg: Novyi shliakh.

–. 1952. *Taiemnyi front.* Munich: Vydavnytstvo Dniprova khvylia.

–. 1953. *Doba strakhit: Roman.* Winnipeg: Nakladom Ukrainskoi natsionalnoi vydavnychoi spilky. Rep. Toronto: Homin Ukrainy, 1984.

–. [Khortytsia, Mykola]. 1953. *Velyka hra.* Munich: Dniprova khvylia.

–. 1955–56. *Pid molotom viiny.* 4 vols. Munich: Dniprova khvylia.

–. 1977. *Prometeiv vohon: Roman.* London: Ukrainska vydavnycha spilka.

–. 1984. *Nikoly ne zabudu: Roman.* Toronto: Homin Ukrainy.

–. 1985. *Slidamy zapovitu: Politychnyi roman-visiia.* 3 vols. London-Toronto: Ukrainian Publishers Ltd. and Homin Ukrainy.

–. 1993. *Armiia neskorenykh: Politychnyi roman.* Toronto: Homin Ukrainy.

Logusz, Michael O. 1994. *Battle of Brody, July 1944.* Toronto: Veterans' News.

–. 1997. *Galicia Division: The Waffen-ss 14th Grenadier Division, 1943–1945.* Altglen, PA: Schiffer Military History.

Lovell, J. 1970. *Polska, jakiej nie znamy: Zbiór reportarzy o mniejszościach narodowych. Kraków*: Wydawnnictwo Literackie.

Lozynskyi, Mykhailo. 1970. *Halychyna v rr. 1918–1920.* New York: Vydavnytstvo "Chervona Kalyna." Orig. pub. Vienna: Ukrainskyi sotsioilohichnyi instytut, 1922.

Luciuk, Lubomyr Y. 2020. "Dechesnes Commission Confirmed War Criminal Numbers 'Grossly Exaggerated.'" *Whig Standard*, 12 August.

–. 2021. *Operation Payback: Soviet Disinformation and Alleged Nazi War Criminals in North America.* Kingston: The Kashtan Press.

Lysiak, Oleh, ed. 1951a. *Brody: Zbirnyk stattei i narysiv.* Munich: Vydannia Bratstva kol. Voiakiv Pershoi UD UNA. Rpt. 1996 and 2003.

–. 1951b. "Bytva bez legendy." In Lysiak, *Brody*, 7–14.

–. 1953. *Za striletskyi zvychai: Roman.* Munich: Vydannia Bratstva kol. Voiakiv 1-oi Ukrainskoi Dyvizii UNA.

–. 1960. *Liudy taki, iak my: Povist.* Toronto: Nakladom vydavnytstva Homin Ukrainy.

–. ed. 1974. *Bii pid Brodamy: Zbirnyk stattei u trydtsitylittlia.* 2d rev. ed. New York: Vyd. 1-oi Ukr. Dyvizii Ukr. natsionalnoi armii.

–. 1996. *Vidlamky "Shybky u vikni": Zbir stattei, opovidan, narysiv i reportazhiv.* Toronto: Visti kombatanta.

Lysiak, Oleh, and Hryhor Luzhnytskyi, eds. 1975. *Nash teatr: Knyha diiachiv ukrainskoho teatralnoho mystetstva, 1915–1975.* New York: OMUS.

Matchak, M. 1951. "Z boiv kurenia 'Vildner.'" *Visti Bratstva kol. Voiakiv 1.* UD UNA, no. 9: 3–5; 10: 3–4.

Madajczyk, Cz. 1965. *Hitlerowski terror na wsi polskiej, 1939–1945: Zestawienie wiekszych akcji represyjnych,* Warsaw: Panstwowe Wydawnictwo Naukowe.

Magocsi, Paul Robert, ed. 1989. *Morality and Reality: The Life and Times of Andrei Sheptytsky.* Edmonton: Canadian Institute of Ukrainian Studies, University of Alberta.

Maletskyi, Myroslav (Myroslaw Maleckyj). 1981. *Bez iliuzii. Komentari.* Toronto: Nakladom Bratstva Kol. Voiakiv 1-oi Ukrainskoi Dyvizii UNA.

–. 1996. *Priorytety: Statti.* Kyiv: Vydavnytstvo Rada.

Malkosh, Volodymyr. 2007. *Ukrainska dyviziia "Halychyna" v svitli "lehionovoi" polityky XX storichchia.* Ivano-Frankivsk: Lileia-NV.

Mamchur, Ivan. 2009. *Nas dolia svitamy vodyla: Storunky perezhytoho.* Lviv: Afisha.

Markiewicz, Paweł. 2021. *Unlikely Allies: Nazi German and Ukrainian Nationalist Collaboration in General Government during World War II.* West Lafayette, IN: Purdue University Press.

Marples, David. 2008–09. "Beyond the Pale? Conceptions and Reflections in Contemporary Ukraine about the Division Galizien." *Journal of Ukrainian Studies* 33–4: 337–50.

Maslovskyi, V. 1975. *Zhovtoblakytna mafia.* Lviv: Kameniar.

Mastny, Vojtech. 1971. *The Czechs under Nazi Rule: The Failure of National Resistance, 1939–1942.* New York: Columbia University Press.

Matla, Oleksandr. 1978. "Sprava Huty Pieniatskoi i dzherela." *Visti kombatanta* 1: 55–61.

Matsiv, B. 2009. *Ukrainska dyviziia "Halychyna": Istoriia u svitlynakh vid zasnuvannia u 1943 r. do zvilnennia z polonu 1949 r.* Lviv: Zhuravlynyi klych.

Matsiv-Balahutrak, Stefa. 1994. "Spohad medsestry." *Visti kombatanta* 2: 91–3.

McVay, Rev. Dr Athanasius D. 2021. "General Pavlo Shandruk to Pope Pius XII." *Annales Ecclesiae Ucrainae,* 8 May, https://annalesecclesiaeucrainae.blogspot.com/2021/05/general-shandruk-to-pius-xii.html.

Medvedev, Dmitrii. 1963. *Sylni dukhom.* Kyiv: Radianskyi pysmennyk. Orig. *Silnye dukhom.* Moscow: Voennoe izdatelstvo Ministerstva Soiuza SSR, 1951.

Melnyk, Michael James. 2002. *To Battle. The Formation and History of the 14th Galician Waffen-ss Division.* Solihull: Helion and Company.

–. 2009. Comment by Melnyk. *Axis History Forum,* 24 September, https://forum.axishistory.com/viewtopic.php?t=96959&start=180 .

–. 2010. Comment by Melnyk. *Axis History Forum*, 28 February, https://forum. axishistory.com/viewtopic.php?t=163468.

–. 2016. *The History of the Galician Division of the Waffen-ss*. 2 vols. Stroud, UK: Fonthill.

Mick, Christoph. 2011. "Incompatible Experiences: Poles, Ukrainians and Jews in Lviv under Soviet and Nazi Occupation, 1939–1944." *Journal of Contemporary History* 46, no. 2: 336–63.

Midzhak, Oleksa. 1994. *Pomsta komunistam: Poryv: Pravda pro Pershu Ukrainsku Dyviziiu (UNA) "Halychyna" (Statti, narysy, spohady)*. Lviv: Osnova.

Młynarczyk, Andrzej, Leonid Rein, Andrii Bolianovskyi, and Oleg Romanko. 2017. "Eastern Europe: Belarusian Auxiliaries, Ukrainian Waffen-ss Soldiers and the Special Case of the Polish 'Blue Police.'" In Böhler and Gerwarth, *Waffen-ss*, 165–208.

Mohylov, Mykola. 2016. *Spohady pobratymiv-dyviziinykiv z Berezhanshchyny*. N.p.: n.p.

"Molod u borotbi za nashe maibutnie." 1944. *Krakibski visti*, 2 July.

Molodetskyi, Volodymyr. 1952. *U boiu pid Brodamy 28.I. - 28. VII. 1944: Spomyny ukrainskoho artylerysta protypantsernoi zbroi*. Toronto: Ukrainske vydavnytstvo Dobra Knyzhka.

–. 1983. *Polumiani dni. Avtobiohrafichna povist*. Toronto: Bratstvo kol. Voiakiv 1-shoi Ukrainskoi Dyvizii Ukrainskoi natsiionalnoi armii.

–. 1998. *U rukakh "vyzvolyteliv." Avtobiohrafichna povist*. Toronto: Bratstvo kol. Voiakiv 1-shoi Ukrainskoi Dyvizii Ukrainskoi natsiionalnoi armii (Rep. Kyiv 2020).

Moorhouse, Roger. 2014. *The Devil's Alliance: Hitler's Pact with Stalin, 1939–1941*. New York: Basic Books.

Motyka, Grzegorz. 1999. *Tak było w Biesycydach: Walki polsko-ukraińskie, 1943–1944*. Warsaw: Oficyna Wydawnicza Volumen.

–. 2006. *Ukraińska partyzantka 1942-1960: Działalność Organizacji Ukraińskich Nacjonalistów i Ukraińskiej Powstańczej Armii*. Warsaw: Instytut Studiów Politycznych PAN Oficyna Wydawnictwo RYTM.

–. 2011. *Od rzezi wołyńskiej do akcji "Wisła": Konflikt polsko-ukraiński, 1943–1947*. Krakow: Wydawnictwo Literackie.

Motyka, Grzegorz, and Rafal Wnuk. 1997. *Pany i rezuny: Wspólpraca AK-WiN i UPA w latach, 1945–1947*. Warsaw: Oficyna Wydawnicza Volumen.

Mukovskyi, I.T. and O. Ie. Lysenko. 1997. *Zvytiaha i zhertovnist: Ukraintsi na frontakh Druhoi svitovoi viiny*. Kyiv: Kryha pamiati Ukrainy.

Mushynka, Mykola. 2000. "Zvit pro naukowo-doslidnu ekspedytsiiu v s. Nyzhnia Botsa (Nizna Boca) okr. Liptovskyi Mykulash (Slovachchina)." 12 May. UCRDC.

–. 2001. "Vynni, tomy shcho ukraintsi?" *Den*, 18 August.

Muzychka, o. Ivan. 2017. *Z Rimini do Rymu: Spohad*. Lviv: Artos.

"Na pole boiu." 1944. *Krakivski visti*, 5 March 1944.

"Nabir do ss. Striletskoi Dyvizii Halychyna pochavsia." 1943. *Lvivski visti*, 4 May.

Nahaievskyi, Isydor o. 1955. *Spohady poliovoho dukhovnyka.* Toronto: Vydavnytstvo Ukrainska knyha, 1955.

"Na Vinnychchyni vidkryly memorialnyi znak zhertvam bilshovytskoho teroru." 2020. *Ukrainskyi Instytut Natsionalnoi Pamiati*, 21 October, https://www.uinp.gov.ua/pres-centr/novyny/na-vinnychchyni-vidkryly-memorialnyy-znak-zhertvam-bilshovyckogo-teroru.

Nebeliuk, Myroslav. 1951. *Pid chuzhymy praporamy.* Paris-Lyon.

"Nepratsezdatni poloneni zalyshaoutsia u V. Brytanii." 1949. *Ukrainska dumka*, 7 January.

Neulen, Hans Werner. 1985. *An deutscher Seite: Internatsionale Freiwillege von Wehrmacht und Waffen-ss.* Munich: Verlag Universitas.

"Neznanomu voiakovy." 2021. https://www.facebook.com/Незнаному-воякови-716789091792120.

Nimenko, Wasyl. 2016. *Searching in Secret Ukraine.* Hitchin, UK: Goalpaths Books.

"Obiednani i nadali." 1957. *Visti kol. Voiakiv 1 UD UNA* no. 3–6: 1.

Omelianovych-Pavlenko, M. 1929. *Ukrainsko-polska viina, 1918–1922.* Prague: Nakladom Merkur-filmu.

–. 1940. *Zymovyi pokhid, 6.XII.1919—5.V.1920.* Prague: Stilus. Orig. pub. in 3 vols. Kalish, 1929, 1930, 1932.

Ortynskyi, Liubomyr (Ortynskyj). 1951. "Persha ukrainska dyviziia na tli politychnykh podii Druhoi svitovoi viiny." In Lysiak, *Brody*, 13–38. Rep. In *Visti kombatanta* no. 5–6 (1986): 5–34.

– [Ortynskyj, Lubomyr]. 1952a. "Prawda o Ukraińskiej Dywizji." *Kultura* no. 11: 109–16.

–. 1961. "Krok vpered." *Visti kombatanta*, nos. 1–2: 7–8.

Orwell, George. 2018. "The Prevention of Literature." In his *Politics and the English Language and Other Essays*, 83–114, Faded page ebook #20180223.

Ovad, Iaroslav. 1999. *Bo viina viinoiu.* Lviv: N.p.

Panchuk, Bohdan, and Lubomyr Y. Luciuk. 1983. *Heroes of Their Day: The Reminiscences of Bohdan Panchuk.* Toronto: Multicultural History Society of Ontario.

Pankiv, Iaroslav. 2005. "Ansambl 'Burlaka' (Spohad)." In Revutskyi, *Rimini*, 96–110.

Pankivskyi, Kost. 1965. *Roky nimetskoi okupatsii.* New York-Toronto: Kliuchi.

Parliament of Australia. 1987. Government Response to Menzies Report on Nazi War Criminals. *Senate Hansard.* 24 February, 496–501, https://parlinfo.aph.gov.au/parlInfo/search/display/display.w3p;query=Id:%22chamber/hansards/1987-02-24/0035%22.

References • 405

Pasichnyk, Iu. 1957. "Ukrainskyi 115-yi i 118-yi kureni v borotbi z sovietskoiu dyversiieiu (Uryvok iz shchodennyka z 1941-44 rr)." *Visti Bratstva kol. Voiakiv 1. UD UNA* nos. 11–12: 8–11.

Paziuk, Michael. 1993. *Victim of Circumstance: A Ukrainian in the Army of the Third Reich.* Wrexham, WS: Bridge Books.

Petrovskyi, V. 1952. "Do istorii 4-ho politsiinoho polku." *Visti Bratstva kol. Voiakiv 1 UD UNA* nos. 6–7: 8.

Pidhainyi, Bohdan (Pidhainyj). 1951. "Dva shliakhy – odna meta." In Lysiak, *Brody*, 59–64.

Piętka, Bohdan. 2015. *Nacjonalism Ukraiński od Bandery do Majdanu.* Warsaw: Capital.

Plokhy, Serhii. 2016. *The Man with the Poison Gun: A Cold War Spy Story.* New York: Basic Books.

Pobihushchyi-Ren, Ievhen Polk. 1982. *Mozaika moikh spomyniv.* Munich: Nakladom avtora i Obiednannia buvshykh Voiakiv Ukraintsiv u Velykii Brytanii. Rep. Ivano-Frankivsk: Lileia-NV, 2002. Ukr. trans. Pobihushchyj-Ren, Colonel Evhen. 1982. *My Life's Mosaic.* London: Association of Former Ukrainian Combatants in Great Britain.

Pohl, Dieter. 1997. *Nationalsozialistische Judenverfolgung in Ostgalizien, 1941–1944: Organisation und Durchführung eines statlichen Massen verbrechens.* Munich: R. Oldenbourg Verlag.

Ponomarenko, Roman. 2016. *Boiova hrupa "Baiersdorf."* Tenopil: Mandrivets.

–. 2017. *Halytski dobrovolchi polky ss, 1943–1944: Istoriia bez prykras.* Ternopil: Mandrivets.

–. 2018. "Vyshkil kapelianiv Dyvizii Visk ss 'Halychyna' v Zennhaimi ta ikh zluzhba u Dyvizii (1943-1945 rr.)." *Historical and Cultural Studies* 5, no. 1: 35–43.

Pontolillo, James. 2009. *Murderous Elite: The Waffen-ss and its complete record of war crimes.* Stockholm: Leandoer and Ekholm.

President of Ukraine. 2021. "Shchodo aktsii u Kyievi do richnytsi stvorennia dyvizii ss 'Halychyna'," 30 April, https://president.gov.ua/news/shodo-akci-yi-u-kiyevi-do-richnici-stvorennya-diviziyi-ss-gal-68225. Viewed 30 April 2021, removed 1 May 2021.

"Promova Hubernatora d-ra O. Vekhtera." 1943. *Lvivski visti,* 29 April.

"Promova chlena Viiskovoi Upravy Inzh. Khronoviata." 1943. *Krakivski Visti,* 1 May.

"Promova na urochystomu derzhavnomu akti u Lvovi 28.IV. tsr." 1943. *Krakivski Visti,* 1 May.

"Promova henerala Viktora Kurmanovycha." 1943. *Stanislavivske slovo,* 16 May. Photocopy provided in Bihun 2020.

"Propovid o. D-ra Vasylia Laby." 1943. *Krakivski Visti,* 1 May.

"Provokatsiine vbtvstvo: tema zradnytstva." 2013. *V holos*, 23 February, https://vgolos.com.ua/news/quot-provokatsijne-vbyvstvo-quot-tema-zradnytstva-nbsp_107907.html.

Prus, Edward. 2001. *ss-Galizien. Patrioci czy zbrodniarze?* Wroclaw: Nortom.

–. 2005. *Zapomiany Ataman: Taras Bulba-Boroweć (1908–1981)*. Wroclaw: Wydawnyctwo Nortom.

–. 2007. *Banderomachia: Lźe rząd Stećki na tle Rzeczywistości*. Wroclaw: Wydawnictwo Nortom.

Prymak, Thomas M. 2015. *Gathering a Heritage: Ukrainian, Slavonic, and Ethnic Canada and the USA*. Toronto: University of Toronto Press.

Prypkhan, R. 1989. "Spomyny." *Visti kombatanta*, nos. 5–6: 70.

Pugliese, David. 2020. "Graffiti on Monument Commemorating Nazi ss Division Being Investigated as a Hate Crime by Police." *Ottawa Citizen*, 17 July.

Purves, Grant. 1998. *War Criminals: The Deschenes Commission*. Political and Sociel Affairs Division. Revised 16 October. E. The Report of the Deschenes Commission, 1. General, http://dsp-psd.pwgsc.gc.ca/Collection-R/LoPBdP/CIR/873-e.htm.

Pyliavets, Rostyslav. 2021. "Chorna pikhota: Skilky 'chornosvytnykiv' snyshchyv Stalin?" *Istorychna pravda*, 10 May, https://www.istpravda.com.ua/research/2015/02/16/147351.

Radchenko, Serhii. 2020. "The Biography of the oun(m) Activist Oleksa Babii in the Light of His 'Memoirs on Escaping Execution' 1942." *Journal of Soviet and Post-Soviet Studies* 6, no. 1: 237–76

Radchenko, Yuri, and Andrii Usach. 2020. "'For the Eradication of Polish and Jewish-Muscovite Rule in Ukraine': An Examination of the Crimes of the Ukrainian Legion of Self-Defense." *Holocaust and Genocide Studies* 34, no. 3: 450–77.

"Rasstrely zakliuchennykh vo Lvove i v Zapadnoi Ukraine v iune-iule 1941 goda. Ka keto bylo." 2020. *Poshtivka.blogspot.com*. 9 March, https://postivka.blogspot.com/2020/03/Lviv-tragedy-masacra-1941.html?m=1.

Reitlinger, Gerald. 1956. *The ss: Alibi of a Nation, 1922–1945*. Melbourne: Heinemann.

Remarque, Erich Maria. 1929. *All Quiet on the Western Front*. Boston: Little, Brown, and Company.

Rempel, Gerhard. 2010. "Mennonites and the Holocaust: From Collaboration to Perpetuation." *Mennonite Quarterly Review* 84, no. 4: 507–49.

Revutskyi, Valerian Revutskyj, Valeriyan], ed. 2005. *Rimini, 1945–1947: Persha Ukrainska Dyviziia Ukrainskoi Natsionalnoi Armii u Brytanskomu poloni v Italii – Materialy do istorii dyvizii. Zbirnyk II*. Kyiv: Smoloskyp. Orig. New York: Bratstvo kol. Voiakiv 1 UD UNA, 1979.

References • **407**

Rohde, Matt. 2017. *When Eternities Met: A True Story of Terror, Mutiny, Loss, and Love in a Disremembered Second World War.* Union Bridge, MD: Pencil and Barn.

Roth, Philip. 1993. *Operation Shylock: A Confession.* New York: Simon and Schuster.

Rudling, Per Anders. 2012. "'They Defended Ukraine': The 14th Waffen-Grenadier-Division der ss (Galizische Nr. 1) Revisited." *Journal of Slavic Military Studies* 25, no. 3: 329–68.

–. 2020. "Rehearsal for Volhynia: Schutzmannschaft Battalion 201 and Hauptmann Roman Shukhevych in Occupied Belorussia, 1942." *East European Politics and Societies and Cultures* 34, no. 1: 158–93.

Sanders, Richard. 2021. "Is the Esprit de Corps on Trial for Being on Target against Nazism?" *Esprit de Corps,* 6 April, http://espritdecorps.ca/commentary/is-esprit-de-corps-on-trial-for-being-on-target-against-nazism#comments-606c82512f5865252100a57d=.

Sands, Philippe. 2021. *The Ratline: The Exalted Life and Mysterious Death of a Nazi Fugitive.* New York: Alfred Knopf.

Savaryn, Petro. 2007. *Z soboiu vzialy Ukrainu: Vid Ternopolia do Alberty.* Kyiv: KVITs.

Semiriaga, Mikhail. 2000. *Kollaboratsionizm: Priroda, tipologiia i proiavleniia v gody Vtoroi mirovoi voiny.* Moscow: Nauka.

Serhiichuk, Volodymyr, ed. 2007. *Roman Shukhevych u dokumentakh radianskykh orhaniv derzhavnoi bezpeky (1940–1950).* 2 vols. Kyiv: Haluzevyi Derzhavnyi Archiv Sluzhby Bezpeky Ukrainy, Instytut natsionalnoho derzhavoznavstva Ukrainy.

Shandruk, Pavlo. 1999, *Syly doblesti: Memuary.* Kyiv: Vyshcha shkola. Published in English as *Arms of Valor,* 1959.

Sharko, V. 1990. "Na mohylakh v Avstrii." *Visti kombatanta* no. 3: 54.

Sheftel, Yoram. 1994. *Show Trial: The Conspiracy to Convict John Demjanjuk as "Ivan the Terrible."* London: Victor Gollancz.

Shekhovtsov, Anton. 2018. *Russia and the Western Far Right: Tango Noir.* London: Routledge.

Shepherd, Ben. 2012. *Terror in the Balkans: German Armies and Partisan Warfare.* Cambridge, MA: Harvard University Press.

Shkandrij, Myroslav. 2015. *Ukrainian Nationalism: Politics, Ideology, and Literature, 1929–1956.* New Haven, NJ: Yale University Press.

Shnaider, Slobodan 2021. *Midna doba.* Kyiv: Nora-druk. Orig. Šnajder, Slobodan. *Doba mjedi.* Zagred: TIM Press, 2016.

Shnerkh, Serhii. 2004. *Obmanuti Nadii. Spohady kolyshnikh iunakiv viiskovoho formuvannia ukrainskoho iunatstva protyletunskoi oborony.* Lviv: Misioner.

Shumuk, Danylo. 1974. *Za skhidnym obriie: spomyny.* Paris: Perrsha Ukrainska Drukarnia u Frantsii. Published in English as *Life Sentence: Memoirs of a*

Ukrainian Political Prisoner. Edmonton: Canadian Institute of Ukrainian Studies, 1984.

–. 1983. *Perezhyte i peredumane: Spohady i rozhumy ukrainskoho dysydenta-politviaznia z rokiv blukan i borotby pid troma okuratsiiamy Ukrainy (1921–1981)*. Detroit: Ukrainski visti.

Siemaszko, Z.S. 1971. "Najwyższy czas mówić głośno." *Kultura* 1–2, nos. 280–1: 100–3.

Siemion, L. 1971. *Z lat okupacji hitlerowskiej na Lubelszczynie*. Lublin: Wydaw. Lubelskie.

Simonov, Konstantin. 1956. *Povesti i rasskazy*. Moscow: Gosudarstvennoe izdatelstvo khudozhestvennoi literatury.

Singer, Isaac Bashevis. 1986. *Love and Exile: An Autobiographical Trilogy*. New York: Farrar, Straus and Giroux.

Sirskyi, Vasyl. 2000. upa *i Dyviziia "Halychyna" fakty i fantazii*. N.p.: nakladom avtora.

Skira, Iurii. 2009. *Poklykani: Monakhy Studiiskoho Ustavu ta Holokost*. Kyiv: Dukh i litera.

Skorupsky, Maksym. 2016. *On Attack and in Retreat*. Ostroh: Publishing House of Osron Academy National University.

Slaboshpytskyi, Mykhailo, ed. 2008. *Ukrainska dyviziia "Halychyna": Istoryko-publitsystychnyi zbirnyk*. 3rd ed. Kyiv: Iaroslaviv Val.

Slaboshpytskyi, Mykhailo, and Valerii Stetsenko, eds. 1994. *Ukrainska dyviziia "Halychyna": Istoryko-publitsystychnyi zbirnyk*. Kyiv: Bratstvo kolyshnikh voiakiv 1-oi UD UNA.

Slupchynskyi, Orest [Slupchynskyj, Go-Go]. 1946. *"Zibralasia kumpaniia" ... Zbirka kryvul i kryvulok*. Rimini: Vydavnytstvo Batkivshchyna.

–. [Gogo]. 2003. *Pisni shcho Dyviziia spivala*. Bratsvco kol. Voiiakiv 1. Musical editing and piano accompaniment Myroslaw Skoryk. Ukrainskoi Dyvizii Ukrainskoi Natsionalnoi Armii.

–. ed. 2013. *Humorystychno-Satyrychnyi zhurnal "Osa": Bellaria-Rimini, Italiia, 1945–1947*. Lviv: Nakladom Bratstva Kolyshnikh Voiakiv 1-oi Ukrainskoi Dyvizii Ukrainskoi Natsionalnoi Armii.

Smith, Marie-Danielle. 2017. "Russia Tweets about 'Nazi' Monuments in Canada amid Ongoing Concerns over Political Interference." *National Post*, 25 October.

Snyder, Timothy. 2010. *Bloodlands: Europe between Hitler and Stalin*. New York: Basic Books.

–. 2015. *Black Earth: The Holocuast as History and Warning*. New York: Tim Duggan Books.

Solzhenitsyn, Aleksandr I. 1973. *The Gulag Archipelago, 1918–1956: An Experiment in Literary Investigation, I-II*. New York: Harper and Row.

Sontag, Raymond James, and James Stuart Beddle, eds. 1948. *Soviet-Nazi Relations, 1939–1941: Documents from the Archives of the German Foreign Office.* Washington, DC: Department of State.

Sorobey, Ronald. 2016. "Ukrainians Fight for France." *Military History Now*, 29 November, https://militaryhistorynow.com/2017/07/30/double-cross-how-a-battalion-of-ukrainian-ss-volunteers-mutinied-and-joined-the-french-underground/.

Stein, George. 1966. *The Waffen SS: Hitler's Elite Guard at War, 1939–1945.* Ithaca, NY: Cornell University Press, 1966. Rpt. 1984.

Steinacher, Garald, Immo Rebitschek, Mats Deland, Sabina Ferhadbegovič, and Frank Seberechts. 2017. "Prosecution and Trajectories after 1945." In Böhler and Gerwarth, *Waffen-SS*, 284–330.

Steiner, Felix. 1963. *Die Armee der Geachteten.* Gottingen: Plesse.

Stetskevych, Lev. 1998. *Iak z Berezhan do Kadry: Spomyny z Dyvizii.* Ternopil: Dzhura. Rep. Lviv, 2003.

Štiplovšek, Miroslav.1971. *Slandrova brigada.* Ljubljana, Maribor: Knjižnica in POS 10.

Struve, Kai. 2015. *Deutsche Herrschaft, ukrainischer Nationalismus, antijudische Gewalt: Der Sommer 1941 in der Westukraine.* Berlin: De Gruyter Oldenbourg.

–. 2020. "The OUN(b), the Germans, and Anti-Jewish Violence in Eastern Galicia during Summer 1941." *Journal of Soviet and Post-Soviet Studies* 6, no. 1: 205–35.

Styrkul, Valerii. 1982. *SS Vovkulaky.* Lviv: Kameniar.

–. 1984. *We Accuse.* Kyiv: Dnipro Publishers.

"SUB kupyv osseliu dlia invalidiv." 1949. *Ukrainska dumka*, 11 September.

"Symvolika dyvizii SS 'Halychyna' ne nalezhyt do natsystskoi: rishennia sudu." 2020. *Ukrainskyi prostir*, 26 September,

Sviryn, Ihor. 2011. "Horbuliv i Marusia Sokolovska, lehendarna poliska otamanka Marusia," *I Ts Polissia*, http://www.polissia.eu/2011/04/gorbuliv-marusya-otamansha-sokolovska.html.

Sych, Myroslav. 2000. *Ukrainska kooperatsiia v Halychyni pid chas II Svitovoi Viiny.* Lviv: NTSh. Orig. Sycz, Mirosław. *Spółdzielczosść ukraińska w Galiciji w okresie II Wojny Światowej*, Warsaw, 1997.

Sydorenko, Natalia. 2002. "Taborovi budni viiskovopolonenykh na brytanskykh ostrovakh (1947–1950)." In *Persha ukrainska Dyviziia ukrainskoi natsionalnoi armii: Istoriia stvorennia ta natsionalno-politychne znachennia. Materialy Naukovo-praktychnoi konferentsii. Dopovidi ta povidomlennia*, 127–46. Lviv: Novyi chas.

Szczesniak, Antoni B., and Wieslaw Z. Szota. 1973. *Droga do nikąd: działalność organizacji ukraińskich nacjonalistów w Polsce.* Warsaw: Wydawnyctwo Ministerstwa Obrony Narodowej.

Tatarskyi, Vasyl. 1983. *Pid chotyrma praporamy: Spohad.* Munich: Nakladom avtora.

Taylor, Scott. 2017. "Nazi Monuments Uncomfortable Canadian Truth." *Winnipeg Free Press*, 2 November.

Teicholz, Tom. 1990. *The Trial of Ivan the Terrible: State of Israel vs. John Demianjuk*. New York: St Martin's Press.

Terlytsia, Marko [Petro Kravchuk]. 1984. *Here Is the Evidence*. Toronto: Kobzar Publishing.

–. 1960. *Pravnuky pohani: Ukrainski natsionalisty v Kanadi*. Kyiv: Radianskyi pysmennyk.

Tesher, Ellie, and David Vienneau. 1997. "A War Crimes Unit at War with Itself." *Toronto Star*, 2 November.

"The Red Army's WWII Horror Orgy Worse Then Thought." 2002. *Rense.com*, 25 January, https://rense.com/general19/redarmy.htm.

Thorwald, Jürgen. 1975. *The Illusion: Soviet Soldiers in Hitler's Armies*. New York: Harcourt Brace Jovanovich. Orig. pub. in German, 1974.

Tisetskii, Andrei. 2017. "Za porogom pobedy (Frontoviki i partizany vne zakona), 1944–1955: Istoriko-kriminologichekoe issledovanie." *BramaBY.com*, 25 December, https://bramaby.com/ls/blog/history/5801.html.

Tiutiunnyk, Iurii. 1923. *Zymovyi pokhid 1919-1922 r.* Kolomyia: Trembita.

Tolstoy, Nikolai. 1977. *Victims of Yalta*. London: Hodder and Stoughton. Published in the US as *The Secret Betrayal*.

–. 1986a. *The Minister and the Massacres*. London: Century Hutchinson Ltd.

–. 1986b. *Trial and Error: Canada's Commission of Inquiry on War Criminals and the Soviets*. Toronto: Justinian Press.

Torzecki, Ryszard. 1969. "Niektóre aspekty hitlerowskiej polityki wobec Ukraińców (1940–1944)." *Z dziejów stosunkow polsko-radzieckich* 5: 155–60.

–. 1982. *Dzieje Najnowsze, Rocznik XIII, 1981*. Warsaw-Krakźw-Lódz: Polska Akademia Nauk, Instytut Historii.

Tovarianska, Oksana Volodymyrivna [Tovaryanska]. 2008. "Dyviziia 'Halychyha' ochyma ii kolyshnikh voiakiv." MA thesis, National University of the Kyiv-Mohyla Academy.

Trach, Pylyp. 1951. "Nasha zustrich z 'Chetnikamy.'" *Visti Bratstva kol. Voiakiv 1 UD UNA*, no. 4: 5.

Troper, Harold, and Morton Weinfeld. 1988. *Old Wounds: Jews, Ukrainian and the Hunt for Nazi War Criminals in Canada*. Markham, ON: Viking.

Tys-Krokhmaliuk, Iurii [Tys, real name Krokhmaliuk]. 1954a. *Boi Khmelnytkoho: Viiskovo-istorychna studiia*. Unich: Vydannia Bratstva kol. Voiakiv 1-oi Ukrainskoi Dyvizii UNA.

–. 1954b. *Markiza: Istorychne opovidannia*. Winnipeg: I. Tyktor.

–. 1954c. *Shchodennyk natsionalnoho heroia Selepka Lavochky*. Buenos Aires: Vyd-vo Iu. Serediaka. Rpt. 1982.

–. 1955. *Reid u nevidome: Dyvni pryhody znatnoho molodtsia pana Mykol Pretvycha*. Buenis Aires: Vyd-vo Iu. Serediaka.

–. 1958. *Zhyttia inshoi liudyny: Povist.* Munich: Ukrainske vyd-vo.

–. 1959. *Konotop: Opovidanna.* Toronto: Nakladom vyd-va Homan Ukrainy.

–. 1961a. *Na svitanku: Biohrafichna povist z zhyttia Marka Vovchka.* Chicago: Vydavnytstvo Mykoly Denysiuka.

–. [Tys-Krojmaluk, Jorge]. 1961b. *Guerra Libertad: Historia de la Division "Halychyna" (D.U.1) del Ejercito Nacional Ucranio (1943–1945).* Buenos Aires: Biblioteca del Instituto Informativo – Editorial Ucranio.

–. 1961c. *Zvidun z Chyhyryna.* Buenos Aires: Vydavnytstvo Iuliiana Serediaka.

–. 1964. *K7: Fantastychne opovidannia.* Toronto: Nakaldom Vydavnytstva "Homin Ukrainy."

–. 1972. UPA *Warfare in Ukraine: Strategical, Tactical and Organizational Problems of Ukrainian Resistance in World War II.* New York: Society of Veterans of Ukrainian Insurgent Army.

–. 1983. "U shtabl dyviziii." *Visti kombatanta*, no. 2: 56–64.

Ullrich, Volker. 2016. *Hitler: Ascent 1889–1939.* New York: Alfred A. Knopf.

United Nations, General Assembly, Third Committee Official Records of the first part in the first session. Summary record of Meetings, 11 January–10 February 1946. London: Church House.

Usach, Andrii. 2016. "Dyviziia 'Halychyna,' Orhanizatsiia Ukrainskykh Natsionalistiv ta Ukrainska Povstanska Armiia: Do pytannia pro vzaiemovidnosyn (1943-1944 rr.)." In *Ukrainska dyviziia "Halychyna" (Lvivshchyna): Istoriia, spohady, svitlyny*, ed. Ihor Ivankov and Mykhailo Romaniuk, 61–83. Lviv: Dukhovna vis.

Vashkovych, Volodymyr. 1972. "Z pryvodu knyhy pro ukraińsku dyviziiu 'Halychyna.'" *Ukrainskyi samostiinyk* 23, nos. 1–2: 50–5; no. 3: 35–8.

Vazhna-Vankevych, Olia. 1998. "Spomyny medsestry." *Visti kombatanta*, no. 2: 81–6.

Vavryk, O. dr- Mykhailo. 1979. "O plinennykh…" In Budnyi, *Rimini*, 192–204.

Vereshchaka, M.V. 2019. "Rozhliad sotsiokulturnoho protsesu adaptatsii veteraniv dyvizii 'Halychyna' u emihratsii v Kanadi (1948–1960-ti)." MA thesis, Ukrainskyi Katolytskyi Universytet, Lviv.

Veryha, Vasyl. 1965. "Analizuimo nashi mynule," *Nasha Meta* (issues 13-22), 27 March to 19 May. Rpt. in Veryha (1980, 146–71).

–. 1980. *Dorohamy Druhoi svitovoi viiny: Legendy pro uchast ukraintsiv u Varshavskomu povstanni 1944 r. ta pro Ukrainsku Dyviziiu "Halychyna."* Toronto: Novyi shliakh. 2nd rev. ed. Toronto: Shevchenko Scientific Society in Canada, 1981; 3rd rev. ed. N.p. [Toronto]: Kanadske naukove tovarystvo im. Shevchenka, Nakaldom Bratstva kol. Voiakiv I-oi UD UNA, 1998.

–. 1984. *Pid sontsem Italii: Voiaky Ukrainskoi Dyvizii "Halychyna" Pershoi Ukrainskoi Dyvizii Ukrainskoi Natsionalnoi Armii v Brytiiskomu tabori polonenykh "5Ts" u Belliarii, Italiia, cherven-zhovten 1945.* Toronto: Naukove tovarystvo imeny Shevchenka.

–, ed. 2000. *The Correspondence of the Ukrainian Central Committee in Cracow and Lviv with the German Authorities, 1939–1944.* 2 vols. Edmonton: Canadian Institute of Ukrainian Studies.

–. 2002. *Za mezhamy batkivshchyny: Zbirnyk naukovyckh statei i dopovidei.* Lviv: Instytut im. I. Krypiakevycha NAN Ukrainy.

–. 2006. *Za ridnyi krai, za narid svii, abo Khto taki dyviziinyky?* Kyiv: Vydavnytstvo imeni Oleny Telihy.

–. 2007. *Pid krylamy vyzvolnykh dum: Spomyny pidkhorunzhoho dyvizii "Halychyna."* Kyiuv: Vydavnytstvo imeni Oleny Telihy.

Viatrovych, Volodymyr. 2020. *The Gordian Knot: The Second Polish-Ukrainian War, 1942–1947.* Toronto: Horner Press, 2020. Orig. pub. *Druha polsko-ukrainska viina, 1942–1947.* Kyiv: Vydanychyi dim Kyievo-Mohylianskoi akademii, 2012.

Virnyi, Mykola [Frantsuzhenko, Francuzenko]. 2005a. "Bohdan Bora – Liudyna z pidniatym cholom (11 Kvitnia 1920 r. – 20 serpnia 1997 r.)." In Revutskyi, *Rimini*, 170–9.

–. 2005b. "Ospivuvach poryviv molodykh." In Revutskyi, *Rimin*, 180–7.

"Vlasov and the Russian Liberation Army." 2010. A Journey through Russian Culture. Wordpress.com, 22 June, https://russianculture.wordpress.com/2010/06/22/vlasov-and-the-russian-liberation-army/.

Volchuk, R. 2011. *Spomyny z peredvoiennoho Lvova ta voiennoho Vidnia.* Kyiv: Krytyka.

Volokh, D., and V. Heva. 1994. "Zolotyi iuvilei iunatskva." *Svoboda*, 3 August.

Volynskyi, Mykola. 1979. "Z letu ptakha." In Budnyi, *Rimini*, 124–34.

Vrublevskyi, Roman. 2016. "Vin buv nam iak tato." In Ivankov and Romaniuk, *Ukrainska dyviziia "Halychyna,"* 144–7.

Vynnyk, Oksana. 2018. "Postwar 'Normalization': The Reintegration of Disabled Veterans to Civilian Life in Interwar Lviv." PhD diss., University of Alberta.

Vysotskyi, R. 1994. *Spohady dyviziinyka.* Chicago: Misioner.

Walker, Jonathan. 2013. *Operation Unthinkable: The Third World War – British Plans to Attack the Soviet Empire, 1945.* The Mill, Brimscone Pass, Stround: The History Press.

Weale, Adrian. 2012. *The ss: A New History.* London: Abacus. Orig. pub. 2010.

Wolczański, Józef. 1992–93. Korespondencja arcybiskupa Bolesława Twardowskiego z arcybiskupem Andrzejem Szeptyckim w latach, 1943–1944. *Przeglad Wschodni*, t. II, z. 2.

Wołczew, Wsiewołod. 1969. "Przyczynek do stanowiska ugrupowań obozu londyńskiego na Lubelszczyźnie wobec kwestii ukraińskiej." *Z dziejów stosunków polsko-radzieckich. Studia i materialy* 5: 161–9.

Wynar, Lubomyr. 2008. "Istoryk Pavlo Hrytsak: Zhyttia i tvorchist (U 50-littia smerty)." *Naukovi zapysky Natsionalnoho uniwersytetu Ostrozka akademiia: Istorychni nauky*, Vyp. 11, 205–21.

References • **413**

Zahachevskyi, Evstakhii. 1952. *Spohady frontovyka: Odyseia siroho "koliaboranta."* Munich: Vydannia Bratstva kol. Voiakiv 1-oi Ukrainskoi Dyvizii UNA.

–. 1962. *Lvivska bratiia: Povist perezhytoho.* Toronto: Vydannia Bratstva Kol. Voiakiv 1-oi Ukrainskoi Dyvizii UNA.

–. 1968. *Beliariia, Rimini, Anhliia.* Chicago-Munich: Bratstvo kolyshnikh Voiakiv 1 UD UNA.

–. 1975. *Ii rehit he liakav: Opovidannia z chasiv druhoi svitovoi viiny.* Buenos Aires: Vyd. Iu. Serediaka.

Zajączkowski, Mariusz. 2015. *Ukraińskie podziemie na Lubelszczyźnie w okresie okupacji niemieckiej 1939–1944.* Lublin-Warsaw: Instytut Pamięci Narodowej.

–. 2017. "Stosunki polsko-sowieckie na Wołyniu 1943–1944 w świetle dokumentów czerwonych partyzantów." In Adamski et al., *Sowieci a polskie*, 105–62.

"Zakon Ukrainy: Pro pravovyi status ta vshanuvannia pamiati bortsiv za nexalezhnist Ukrainy u XX stolitti." 2015. *Vidomosti Verkhovnoi Rady,* 19 June, article 190, 1351.

"Zaklyk." 1944. *Krakivski visti,* 2 July.

Zaporozhets-Devlad, Oleksii [Devlad, Did Pasichnyk]. 1948. *Obiznalys: komediia na try dii.* Buenos Aires: Peremoha.

–. 1952. "Zaklyk 'dodomu': spohad z anhliiskoho polonu." *Visti Bratstva kol. Voiakiv 1 UD UNA* no. 12: 3-5.

–. 1955. *V odvichnii borotbi.* Buenos Aires: N.p.

–. 1956. *Harbuzova misteria: Humorystychna povist.* Buenos Aires: N.p., 1956.

Zelenko, Kostiantyn. 1972–73. "Shche pro dyviziiu 'Halychyna.'" *Ukrainskyi samostiinyk* 23, nos. 11–12 (1972): 26–32; 24, no. 1 (1973): 25–32; 24, no. 2 (1973): 30–41.

Zelenko, Constantine [Kostiantyn]. 1978. "The Ukrainians." *Spectator,* 6 May.

Zelenyi [Zelenyj], Zenon. 1965. *Ukrainske iunatstvo u vyri Druhoi svitovoi viiny.* Toronto: Nakladom Bratstva kol. Voiakiv 1-oi Dyvizii Ukrainskoi Natsionalnoi Armii.

Zelinskyi, Viktor Gen-Polk. 1938. *Syniozhupannyky.* Berlin: Nakladom "Ukrainskoho Natsionalnoho Obiednannia" v Nimechchyni.

Zurof, Efraim. 2004. *World Investigation and Prosecution of Nai War Criminals: An Annual Status Report.* Jerusalem: Simon Wiesenthal Center.

Index

Adenauer, Konrad, 293–4
Alexander, Field-Marshall Harold, 171, 187
American Relief Committee, 196
Ameryka, 255
Anders, General Władysław, 136, 140, 165, 187; and Soviet Repatriation Commission, 172
anti-Semitism, 15, 43, 54, 60, 125, 316; accusations of, 332–3, 338, 347
Arendt, Hannah, 9, 15, 125, 294
Arlt, Fritz, 42, 134-5, 138; new ideology at war's end, 242
Armia Krajowa (AK), 87, 119, 322; estimated strength, 325
Armia Ludowa (AL), 87, 322
Armstrong, John, 126, 128
Assmuss, Siegfried, 95–6
Austria: Galicia Division in, 132–40
Auxiliary police, 7, 56–7, 118–19, 214, 219, 322

Badoglio, Marshal Pietro, 74
Balahutrak, Petro, 309–10
Baliuta, Martyn, 113
Bandera, Stepan, 71, 293, 295
Baran, Stepan, 54
Barvinskyi, Boys, 233
Basaj, Stanislaw, 117
Bataliony Chłopskie (BCH), 88, 117, 322
Batkivshchyna, 236
Bauer, Otto, 41
Bazhan, Mykola, 170
Bender, Vitalii, 248–52

Bendyna, Ivan, 71
Berger, Gottlob, 41, 72, 105, 242; and German withdrawal to Austria, 135
Bevan, Ernest, 174
Beyersdorff Battle Group, 85–92, 115, 256, 288; accusations against, 286; and Polish–Ukrainian conflict, 320; reports by soldiers, 89–92
Beyersdorff, Friedrich, 84; in American Zone, 139; portrayal in fiction, 257
Biegelmayer, Heinrich, 96
Bihus, Myroslav, 300, 305
Biliaiev, Volodymyr, 244
Bilostotskyi, Tymish, 143, 145, 147, 149–50; and agitators for youth force, 156; complaints about ROA, 157
Binz, Major Siegfried, 105, 114
Bisantz, Alfred, 24, 46, 48, 346; and Military Board, 58; youth recruitment, 145
Bock, Friedrich Wilhelm, 112
Bodnar, Osyp, 240–1, 243
Bogdanov, Ivan, 100
Bogdańska, Renata (Iryna Yarosevych, Jarosiewicz), 187
Böhler, Jochen, 336
Bolianovskyi, Andrii, 336
Bór-Komorowski, General Tadeusz, 140
Bora, Bohdan (Borys Shkandrij), 245–8
Brody: Battle of, 5, 78, 80, 107, 288–9; Brotherhood of Former Soldiers of the 1st Ukrainian Division of the

UNA, 232, 243, 337; in fiction, 256–7; soldiers captured after battle, 211–19
Browning, Christopher, 7, 62–3, 315, 347
Brygider, Mykhailo, 65, 257
Buchak, Bohdan 307
Buchko, Bishop Ivan, 140, 170, 183; aid for Division POWs, 193–4
Budnyi, Vsevolod, 234
BUK battalions, 101–2, 363n17

Camp 5C in Bellaria, 161–70, 177, 194, 196; publications, 264
Camp Riccione, 152, 181–2, 187–8
Camp in Rimini, 177–96; artists, 188; escapes, 179, 371n3; grave sites, 326; performance groups, 186–8, 204; publications, 186, 192, 204–5, 264; screening commission, 197–9; sport, 190
Camps for POWs in Britain, 200–5; British newspaper reports about, 202; performing groups, 204; planned deportation of interned, 205; relations of interned with Germans, 204
Canadian Relief Mission for Ukrainian War Victims in Europe, 206
Catloš, Ferdinand, 121
Central Ukrainian Relief Bureau (CURB), 206, 282
Cesarani, David, 176, 184, 290–1
chaplains, 27, 72–8
Cherkashyn, Yurii, 85
Chetniks, 129–30, 163. See also Mihalovič
Chobit, Dmytro, 112–14
Churchill, Winston, 171; and Operation Unthinkable, 136, 192
Cienski, Rev. Jan, 110
collaboration, 31, 53; ethnicity of, 16–17; former Soviet citizens in German uniforms, 6–7

Committee for the Liberation of Peoples of Russia (KONR), 134
Communist Party of Canada, 33
Communist Party of Western Ukraine, 223
Congregation of Eastern Churches (Pro Ecclesia Orientali), 140
Conquest, Robert, 289
cooperative movement, 38–44
Corrin, Rev. William Sloane, 174
Cossacks, 139, 199, 318; Don, 138, 171, 164; Kuban, 164, 171; Terek, 171
cultural memory of 1918, 304–8
Curzon Line, 162–3, 323

Daluege, Kurt, 41, 104
Danesi, Marcel, 336
Danyliuk, Ivan, 94–5
Darré, Richard, Walther, 59
Davydiak, Vasyl, 264
Dean, Martin, 101
Demjanjuk, John, 295–6, 383n23
Demydas, Antin, 215
Der Spiegel, 9
Deschenes Commission, 97, 281–8; 335, 337, 381n4
Devlad, Oleksii (Zaporozhets-Devlad), 264–6
Diachenko, Petro, 97
Die Brücke, 184, 188
Dirlewanger Brigade, 124, 286–7
Dirlewanger, Oscar, 124–5
Dmitriev, Yurii, 319
Do peremohy, 58
Do zbroi, 58, 61, 98
Dolynskyi, Roman, 69, 85, 90, 128
Domanov, General Timotei, 318
Dontsov, Dmytro, 62, 235
Doroha, 54, 148
Dorril, Steohen, 208
Dovbniak, Mykhailo, 217
Durbak, Rev. Ivan, 91, 116

Dubytskyi, Rev. Palladii, 98
Dugin, Aleksandr, 318, 335
Dydyk, Mykhailo, 310–11
Dziewanowaski, Marian Kamil, 140

Eden, Anthony, 171
Eisenhower, General Dwight, 174

Faryna, Mykola, 116–17
Faulk, Lieutenant-Colonel H., 206–7
Ferkuniak, Dmytro, 64–8; and
  Beyersdorff, 139; fact-finding
  mission, 156
Fihurka-Plaviuk, Pavlia, 181
Fitilovskyj, Mykhailo, 301
Forstreuter, Hans Otto, 81, 253, 256
Forsyth, Frederick, 333
Forys, Yurii, 245
Fostun, Sviatomyr, 272–4; mentioned
  in article, 333
Frank, Hans, 41, 46, 88
Frantsuzhenko, Mykola
  (Francuzenko), 246
Freedom and Independence (win), 324
Freitag, General Fritz, 27, 67, 74, 84,
  231; and chaplains, 76; portrayal
  in fiction, 256–7; relations with
  Ukrainians, 78, 80; suicide, 139–40
French Resistance (FFI), 101–3, 120.
  See also BUK battalions
Front of National Unity party, 230

Gabrusevych, Rev. Julian, 76
Galicia Division, 5, 351n2; and
  Allied soldiers, 131, 161–3, 165,
  178–9; civilianization, 5, 207;
  commemoration of, 329; desertions
  from, 18; emigre attitudes towards,
  193; entry to Canada, 208; genesis,
  17–23; and Holocaust, 314, 347;
  insignia, 27–8, 340–1; interrogation
  and sentencing of captured

soldiers, 211–20; military training,
  59–71; monuments to, 328, 337;
  name change, 4, 17, 25, 67, 132,
  254, 340–1; oath of allegiance,
  29–30; postwar interviews, 297–313;
  reasons for volunteering, 20–3;
  reception of propaganda, 60–3,
  68–9, 317; relations with Germans,
  78–81, 178–9, 302–6; screenings,
  288; witnessing treatment of Jews,
  302, 311, 315; volunteers, 8–10, 28
Galicia ss 4th Volunteer Regiment,
  88, 92, 104–15, 121; accusations
  against, 285–7, 335; captured men,
  213; in poetry and memoirs, 244–63
Galician ss 5th Volunteer Regiment,
  88, 92, 100, 104–5, 115–21;
  accusations against, 285–7, 331;
  soldiers' reports, 116–18
Galician ss 6th Volunteer Regiment,
  104, 119–21
Galician ss 7th Volunteer Regiment,
  104, 119–21
Gehlen, General Reinhard, 23, 242,
  294
Geneva Convention, 36, 162, 172
German court sentences for Nazi
  crimes, 294
Gerwarth, Robert, 336
Giedroyc, Jerzy, 140
Ginzburg, Evgeniia, 172
Globke, Hans, 293
Globočnik, Odilo, 41, 99, 100
Golian, General Jan, 121
Golikov, General Filip, 168–9
Gotskyi, Volodymyr, 177
Great Famine (Holodomor), 34
Grossman, Vasilii, 36

Hałagida, Ihor, 321
Hale, Christopher, 332
Hamilton Spectator, 102

Havrysh, Ilko, 225–6
Heike, Wolf-Dietrich, 293; on
    chaplains, 72; his history of the
    Division, 240–1;
objection to deployment, 85–6, 92; on
    time in Slovakia, 125–27, 233, 367n12
Hetherington-Chalmers Inquiry, 281,
    288–90
Hevko-Mymanskyi, Mykola, 213
Hills, Major Denis, 171, 173–4, 371n16
Himmler, Heinrich, 72, 105; secret
    memo, 40–1; visit to Division, 63–4;
    and youth soldiers, 144; speech to
    Galicia Division, 359n3
Hirniak, Kost, 243
Hirniak, Nykyfor, 147
Hirniak, Yosyp, 147
Hitler, Adolph: Mein Kampf, 41, 65,
    235, 238, 299, 310, 346; attitude to
    Ukrainians and Slavs, 72, 300,
    302; and independence for Baltic
    nations and Ukrainians, 309
Hlinka, Andrej, 125
Hlinka Guard, 125–6; attitudes towards
    Stalin, 35
Hlynka, Anthony, 196
Hloba, Major Leon (Lev) 102
Höfle, Hermann, 41
Höhne, Heinz, 9, 336
Holocaust, 3, 6, 11–12, 63, 235;
    awareness of, 316–17; and
    Demjanjuk trial, 383n24; geography
    of, 297; scholarship on, 352n12;
    sentences of perpetrators, 295;
    soldiers linked to, 314–15, 333, 347;
    and UN 294; witnesses to, 309, 311.
    See also Jews
Holoida, Rev. Yohan, 119
Holowaty, Myroslav, 90, 97
Honchar, Oles, 262
Horbach, Oleksa, 61, 254
Horbach, Volodymyr, 216–17
Horodyskyi, Orest, 93–5, 98
Hoshovskyi, Bohdan, 54

Hostowiec, Paweł (Jerzy Stempowski),
    55
Hrytsak, Pavlo (Hrycak), 62, 219–20
Humeniuk, Dmytro, 301–2
Humesky, Eugene, 301, 305
Hunczak, Taras, 110
Husbach, Gunter, 65
Huta Peniatska (Huta Pieniacka),
    108–14, 286, 323, 331–3, 335

Jews, 297; deportation from Slovakia,
    125; relations with Division's
    soldiers, 312; in Stanislaviv (Ivano-
    Frankivsk), 52; violence against, 134,
    214, 286; welcoming Red Army, 223
Judt, Tony, 290

Kachkivskyi, Antin, 212
Kachmar, Mykhailo, 64, 68, 71, 91
Kalynets, Iryna, 219
Kaminski Brigade, 286
Kaminski, Bronislav, 286–7
Karachek, Stepan, 213–14
Karkots, Mykhailo (Karkoc), 96,
    361n2, 362n4, 362n7
Katyn Massacre, 34, 319–20
Katzmann, Friedrich, 41
Kedryn, Ivan, 230, 233–4, 261
Keighley, General Charles Frederic, 171
Keitel, General Wilhelm; and
    Barbarossa Decree, 317
Kengir Uprising, 223–4
Kepeshchuk, Bohdan, 223–4
Ketsun, Volodymyr, 89
KGB, 118, 169, 176, 375n5, 382n17;
    assassinations, 295; disinformation
    techniques, 293, 296, 381n8; files,
    285; at the front, 221; interrogations
    by, 278, 335; and Russian embassy,
    386n8. See also NKVD
Kholmska zemlia, 54
Khomiak, Mykhailo (Chomiak), 54,
    358n9
Khromeychuk, Olesya, 199, 207, 336–7

Khronoviat, Mykhailo, 43, 106, 109–10, 112; agitation for Division, 299
Kit, Ivan, 212, 386n8
Kladochnyi, Rev. Iosyp, 73
Kleinow, Johannes, 66, 256
Knysh, Irena, 193
Koch, Erich, 235
Koch, Hans, 46, 72, 346; and youth soldiers, 144
Kolisnyk, Roman, 69, 234, 252–4, 256
KONR. *See* Committee for the Liberation of Peoples of Russia
Konrad, Stepan, 254
Koppe, Wilhelm, 105, 115
Korduba, Roman, 226
Korduba, Feliks, 235
Korotko, Roman, 276–8
Kosach, Yurii, 273
Kowaluk, Rev. Danylo, 119–20
Kozak, Ivan, 57
Kraievskyi, Roman, 124
Krakivski visti, 41, 54, 94, 106, 297, 299; and youth recruitment, 144–5, 147
Krasnopera, Yaroslav, 215–16
Krasnov, Petr, 138, 318, 340, 348
Krat, General Mykhailo, 135, 166–8, 170, 185, 193, 233; promotion to general, 161
Krüger, Friedrich, Wilhelm, 41, 52
Krukowskyi, Osyp, 103
Krutikov, Boris, 109, 113
Kubashevskyi, Yaroslav, 85
Kubijovyč, Volodymyr, 18, 25, 38, 45, 105; accommodationist rhetoric, 41, 4–8; creation of Division, 47, 49, 53, 299–300; creation of UNA, 132; criticism in emigration, 193; and Dmytro Paliiv, 63; *Kultura*, 140, 285; and Military Board, 58; and Sheptytskyi, 55, 348
Kundius, Panas, 112–13
Kupchynskyi, Roman, 54, 234
Kurilowicz, Jan, 109
Kurmanovych, General Viktor, 299

Kuzmovych, Olha, 54, 143, 145, 147–8; complaints about treatment of youth, 157; and women recruits, 152
Kuzmovych, Mykola, 156
Kvitko, Oleksander, 96
Kyveliuk, Roman, 98

Laba, Rev. Vasyl, 25, 28–9, 73, 77; sermon on 28 April 1943, 72
Lahish, Volodymyr, 217–18
Lavruk, Pavlo, 69, 80, 222–3
Lebed, Mykola, 131–2, 192–3
Lechthaler, Franz, 92, 115
Lehit, Andrii, 244–5
Leshchyshyn, Vasyl, 74
Levenets, Rev. Mykhailo, 74, 130, 360n6
Levin, Captain, 165–6
Levytskyi, Borys (Lewytszkyj), 54; on Warsaw Uprising, 285
Levytkyi, Myron, 254
Levytskyi, Volodymyr, 71
Lishchynskyi, Mykhailo, 137
Litopys Chervonoi kalyny, 253, 303
Littlejohn, David, 241
Littman, Sol, 198, 282–5, 335, 381n6
Liubomyrskyi, Stepan. *See* Rykhtytskyi
Livytskyi, Andrii, 132, 135, 327
Losaker, Ludwig, 41
Luhovyi, Yevhenii, 214
Lutskyi, Oleksandr, 118
Lvivski visti, 43, 48, 54, 60, 254
Lysiak, Oleh, 98, 125, 130, 233–4; on dissidents of 1960s, 219; and Perfetskyi, 164–5; portrayal of Germans, 256; portrayal of women, 259; prose, 254–63

Mackenzie King, William Lyon, 187
Maisky, Ivan, 162
Makarushka, Liubomyr, 138
Malets, Lieutenant Viktor, 166, 379n8
Maletskyi, Myroslav (Maleckyj), 64, 68, 71, 334

Mali druzi, 54
Malkosh, Volodymyr, 308
Mamchur, Ivan, 224, 306
Markiewicz, Paweł, 336
Martel, René (Dr Frédéric), 24
Martsinowsky, Myron, 310
Matchak, Myron, 125, 127
Matla, Oleksandr, 109
Matsiv, Bohdan (Maciw), 269
Mazzini, Giuseppe, 32–3
Medvedev, Dmitrii, 108–9, 362n7, 364n7
Melnyk, Michael, 64, 80, 92, 128, 336, 351n4, 353n4, 353n5, 359n3, 360n12, 363n12, 365n13, 366n19, 367n11
Memorial Society, 319
memory wars, 6, 11, 298, 304, 312, 323, 338, 341–2; memory keepers, 337; military cemeteries, 326; military insignia, 323; Polish Institute of National Memory, 112; postmemory, 326; Ukrainian Institute of National Memory, 328, 365n10
Menzies Inquiry, 281, 379n2
MI5, 176
MI6, 176, 199, 269
Mihailovič, General Dragoljub, 98, 129. *See also* Chetniks
Military Board, 28–9, 43, 53, 58, 104, 109, 120, 304; agitation for Division, 299; and end of war, 260–1; and Freitag, 231; and youth recruitment, 144-5
Military Union of Russian People (BSRN), 16
Molodecky, Wolodymyr (Molodetskyi, Volodymyr), 226–7
Molotov, Viacheslav, 163, 369n4
Molotov-Ribbentrop agreement, 32–3, 163, 346
Monte Cassino, 187, 262
Montsibovych, Oleksandr, 183
Moroz, Adolph, 214

Motyka, Grzegorz, 92, 110, 114
Müller, Heinrich, 41, 46
Myhas, Yevhen, 305
Mulyk, Mychailo, 300–1, 304, 306
Mushynka, Mykola, 126
Muzychka, Rev. Ivan, 194–6, 372n10

Nachtigall Battalion, 27, 237, 291, 293
Nahaievskyi, Rev. Isydor, 73–8, 194
Narodna sprava, 306
Nash chas, 306
Nashi dni, 54
National Military Organization (NOW), 323
National Socialist ideology, 33, 61–3
Naumov, Mikhail, 84, 86, 106, 108, 115
Navrotskyi, Osyp, 144
New York Herald Tribune, 172
Nickel, Siegfried, 143–4, 150; conflict with UTsK, 156–7
Nimchuk, Ivan, 54
Nimenko, Wasyl, 174–6
NKVD: massacres in 1941, 34–5, 109. *See also* KGB
Norilsk Revolt, 218
Novyi shliakh, 193
Nuremberg International Military Tribunal, 8–9, 281–2, 284, 294, 297; convictions by, 294; Nuremberg Laws, 206
Nurmann, Fritz, 65

Oberländer, Theodor, 46, 293
ODESSA conspiracy theory, 333. *See also* Waffen-SS
Office of Special Investigations (OSI), 296
Onatskyi, Bohdan, 212
Operation Eastwind, 173–4, 371n15
Operation K-3, 269
Operation Keelhaul, 173, 371n14
Operation Reinhard, 99–100
Operation Retribution (Payback), 297
Operation Tempest (Burza), 112, 323–4

Index • **421**

Operation Vistula (Akcja Wisła), 323–4

Orlyk, Anatol, 167

Ortynskyi, Liubomyr, 69, 231–3, 254, 257; in American Zone, 139; on Warsaw Uprising, 285

Osa, 264

Osmak, Iva, 217

Osovyi, Hryhorii (Grigorij Osowoy), 274

Ostroverkha, Mykhailo, 255

OUN, 67, 69, 88–9, 112–13; German execution of, 309; recruiting in camps, 269

OUN-B, 58, 64, 71, 95; in Division, 301; instructions to join Division, 301; publishing, 269; in Rimini Camp, 178; Shumuk on, 218

OUN-M, 71, 98 in Rimini Camp, 178; publishing, 269;

Orwell, George, 36

Ottawa Citizen, 331

Ovad, Yaroslav, 89

Palestinian Regiment (Jewish Brigade), 161, 165

Palii, Andrii, 43, 106

Palii, Tsiopa, 152

Paliiv, Dmytro, 63–5, 68, 77–8, 91, 346; as the Division's spokesperson, 230–1

Paliienko, Major Mykola, 27, 65, 85

Paliienko, Vasyl, 303, 305

Panchuk, Flight Commander Bohdan, 196, 205–6, 282, 288–9

Pankivskyi, Kost, 21, 24; on German occupation, 49–53

People's Armed Forces (NSZ), 323

Peremoha, 230

Perfetskyi, Leonid, 164–5

Petliura, Semen, 134, 191

Petrovskyi, V., 107

Philby, Kim, 176, 290

Phillips, Tracy, 202

Pidhainyi, Bohdan, 64, 68, 71, 81, 131–2; and decision to create Division, 261;

training K-3 operatives, 269; and Warsaw Uprising, 285

Pilarski, M., 119

Pletsan, Dionisii, 219

Pobihushchyi, Major Yevhen (Ren), 27, 65

Poburennyi, Mykhailo, 216

Podobedov, Major, 166–7

Poles, 18, 38, 40, 47, 185; archive of, 369n5; and Camp Rimini, 188, 191; and Ferkuniak, 66; in Galicia, 42–3, 46, 52, 56–7, 108–9, 142; and OUN-B, 71; and Palii, 63–4; and Sheptytskyi, 72 Polish Army 2nd Corps, 136, 157, 161–3, 165, 262; in UK, 289–90; archive of, 369n5

Polish 1st Army (known as Berling's), 324

Polish government in exile, 88, 109, 162, 322, 324

Polish–Ukrainian conflict, 303, 320–3, 356n8; in District of Lublin, 88–90, 92. *See also* Poles

Ponomarenko, Roman, 74, 77–8, 108, 114, 120, 336, 361n1, 366n1

Pontifical College of St Josaphat in Rome, 194

Pontifical Urban University, 195

Pope Pius XII, 74, 140, 170; and Repatriation Commission, 172, 194

Porter, Haldane, 197–9, 206

Potsdam Conference, 162

POWs: German 183; Soviet, 36–7, 172–3; transfer to UK and civilianization, 206–8

Ukrainian, 170, 197–205

Protsakevych, Myron, 103

Pyndus, Yevhen, 106

Rabii, Mykhailo, 147

Raczyński, Edward, 140

Radchenko, Serhii, 97

Ratushynskyi, Rev. Mykhailo, 161

Red Army, 7, 10, 166, 170–1, 240, 263; atrocities, 319–20; awareness of

Gulag, 315; captured soldiers, 213; in German service, 355n1; north of Warsaw, 124; occupation of Galicia, 223; Poles mobilized into, 324; punitive battalions, 30; and Rebet, Lev, 295; soldiers handed over to, 225; in UVV, 354n9

Reitlinger, Gerald, 59, 242, 294, 336

Rembolovych, Ivan, 85

Repatriation, 37; US policy, 172, 371n12. *See* Soviet Repatriation Commission

Revutskyi, Valerian, 165

Rezuniak, Vasyl, 228–9

Rodal, Alti, 288

Roland Battalion, 27, 231, 237, 291

Rommel, Field Marshall, 120

Rosenberg, Alfred, 59, 76, 143, 235

Roth, Philip, 296

Rudling, Per, 333, 335

Rudnyk, Major, 102

Rudnytska, Milena, 193

Russian Army of National Liberation (RONA), 16, 286

Russian Corps (Russkii korpus), 339–40

Russian Liberation Army (ROA), 134, 287, 293, 348; recruitment of youth, 157

Russian National Patriotic Army (RNNA), 16

Rykhtytskyi, Liubomyr (Stepan Liubomyrskyi), 254, 267–72; portrayal of dissidents, 272

Sahryn Massacre, 323

Sakovych, Andrii, 169

Samostiina Ukraina, 247

Saprun, Rev. Severyn, 75, 149

Saturday Night, 283

Savaryn, Petro, 300, 303, 334, 337

Schenker, Lieutenant, 65

Semenenko, Oleksandr, 132

Senyk, Omelian, 71

Shandruk, Pavlo, 132–41, 157, 161, 233; commanded Polish infantry brigade, 134; contact with Polish officers, 140; Virtuti Militari medal, 140-1

Sheptytskyi, Metropolitan Andrei, 24–5, 28–9, 55, 304, 348; and Castel Gondolfo, 195; and chaplains, 72; used in German propaganda, 70; letters against murder, 51, 354n12

Shukaev, Mikhail, 107

Shukhevych, Roman, 28, 71, 301

Shumskyi, Roman, 218

Shumuk, Danylo, 218–19

Shypailo, Yevhen, 254

Sienkiewicz, Henryk, 255

Sierczewski, Karol, 263

Skorupskyi, Maksym, 113–14

Sijak, Daria, 152

Simonov, Konstantin, 254

Sirskyi, Vasyl (Wasyl Sirskyj), 71

Skoryk, Myroslav, 234

Slipyi, Archbishop Yosyf, 24, 72

Slovakia; anti-German revolt 121; Galicia Division in, 125–8, 333

Slovenia; Galicia Division in, 128–32

Slupchynsky, Orest, 99, 264–5

Smal-Stotskyi, 136, 138

Sobacheva, Hannah, 193

Sobolevskyi, Bohdan, 91

Sokolsky, Ostap, 309, 311

Soltys, Mykhailo, 96

Solzhenitsyn, Aleksandr, 36, 173, 224

Sorokin, Vladimir, 318

Soviet partisans, 11, 27–8, 85–7, 89, 95–6, 101–2, 105–6; atrocities by, 320; on German tactics, 322; at Huta Peniatska, 109–11, 113; support for Polish villages, 322; Ukrainian fight against, 196, 213–14; Ukrainians accused of being, 156

Soviet Repatriation Commission, 163–4, 166–70, 181–2, 193–4, 198

Index • **423**

Soviet propaganda, 284–5, 381n8; disinformation, 293; by Kravchuk (Terlytsia), 284; by Styrkul, 284–5
Spectator, 243
Stalin, 168, 218, 315; concessions to, 171; demands of Germany in 1939–41, 163; demands at Potsdam, 162; Jewish supporters of, 356n9; resistance to, 3, 8, 318; Stalin Prize, 262; Western attitudes towards, 35
Starosolskyi, Yurii, 54
Starukh, Yaroslav, 255
Stashynsky, Bohdan (Staschinsky), 294–5
Stasiv, Bohdan, 308–9
Stebelskyi, Stepan (Khrin), 263
Stein, George, 9, 336
Sternyuk, Andrij, 299–300, 306–8
Stetsiuk, Rev. Volodymyr, 74, 77
Stetskevych, Lev, 89
Strutynska, Maria, 54
Stsiborskyi, Mykola, 71
Styranka, Mykhailo, 58
Suslov, Mikhail, 36
Svoboda, 232

Tarasov, Lieutenant, 166
Tarnavskyi, Zenon, 255
Tatarskyi, Vasyl, 93–5, 127
Teichilz, Tom, 296
Tereshchenko, Petro, 132
Thorwald, Jurgen, 241
Tiso, President Josef, 121
Tisserant, Cardinal Eugène, 140, 183
Tito, Josip Broz, 128–9, 136; described in fiction, 251; his partisans, 4, 95, 97, 128–30, 138, 192, 228
Todt Organization, 122
Tolstoy, Nikolai, 36, 168, 293
Toronto Sunday Star, 284; *Toronto Star*, 292
Trach, Pylyp, 130
Trautmann, Bert, 200–2
Tys, Yurii (Krokhmaliuk), 264, 274–6

UHVR. *See* Ukrainian Supreme Liberation Council
Ukrainian Aid Committee in Rome, 184
Ukrainian Canadian Servicemen's Association, 282
Ukrainian Central Committee (UTSK), 18; and recruitment, 23–7, 60; work of, 46, 53–8; and youth recruitment, 146–7
Ukrainian Central Relief Bureau, 196
Ukrainian Greek-Catholic Church, 28–9, 55, 178, 184
Ukrainian Legion of Self-Defence, 94–8; in Soviet accusations, 285, 362n7; women nurses, 153
Ukrainian Liberation Army (UVV), 251, 254n9
Ukrainian National Army (UNA), 132, 135; creation of 2nd Division, 136; desire to join the UPA, 137; retreat from front, 136
Ukrainian National Committee, 132, 135, 138, 140
Ukrainian Orthodox Church, 39, 178, 184; destruction of churches, 87
Ukrainian People's Republic (UNR), 167, 186; in exile, 132; in Rimini Camp, 178
Ukrainian Revolutionary Democratic Party (URDP), 178
Ukraine's Supreme Liberation Council (UHVR), 192, 231
Ukrainska dumka, 274
Ukrainskyi lehion, 98
Ukrainskyi samostiinyk, 238, 242, 255
Ukrainski shchodenni visti, 53
Ukrainska trybuna, 254–5
Ullrich, Karl, 124
ULS. *See Ukrainian Legion of Self-Defence*
UN, 263; General Assembly on genocide, 294
UNR. *See* Ukrainian People's Republic
UPA (Ukrainian Insurgent Army), 69, 71, 88, 107–8, 110; attitude of

Division to, 301–2; desertion to, 118, 260; Division's soldiers in, 211, 213–14; estimated strength of, 325; and Huta Peniatska, 112–14; joint operations with WIN, 324; KGB interrogations of, 278; in Lemko region, 263; and Renata Bogdańska, 187; and Rimini, 196; and UHVR, 192; UPA–West, 118; in Volhynia, 119, 321, 324

Usach, Andrii, 97

UTSK. *See* Ukrainian Central Committee

Vashkovych, Volodymyr, 67, 238–41, 243

Vechirnia hodyna, 54

Vershyhora, Petro, 84, 86–7, 106, 115–16. *See also* Soviet partisans

Veryha, Vasyl, 62, 71, 78, 130, 234; as Division spokesman, 236–8, 337; on Rimini Camp, 177; witness to killing of Jews, 315–16

Viking (Wiking) Division, 15–16, 122–4, 292, 310–11

Visti, 10, 232, 254, 262

Visti kombatanta, 10, 233, 334, 337

Vlasov, General Andrei, 16, 138, 172, 242; contemporary reassessment of, 318–19, 348; Nanuet monument to, 339; in Prague, 132, 242; recruitment of women Voitsekhovsky, Kazimir (Wojcechowski), 112

Voloshchak, Ivan (Woloschak), 71

Volynets, Stepan, 58

von Brauschitz, General Walther, 309

von Pannwitz, General Helmut, 138, 318, 348

Wächter, Otto, 18–19, 24, 28, 41, 105, 130; decision to create Division, 261, 298–9; and Kubijovyč, 47; meeting with Shandruk in Austria, 138; new ideology, 242 Waffen-SS;

recruitment in Western Europe, 15–16, 353n1, 353n2; types of units, 4, 380n3

Warsaw Ghetto Revolt, 285, 333

Warsaw Uprising, 97, 99, 140, 243, 285–6

Weale, Adrian, 336

Wiens, Heinrich, 68, 80, 256

Wiesenthal, Simon, 282–3, 333, 381n7

Wildner, Karl, 239; in American Zone, 139; his Battle Group, 95, 127

Wilkinson, A.W.H., 206–7

WIN. *See* Freedom and Independence

Winnipeg Free Press, 332

Wittenmeyer, Friederich, 126

Wolfe, Karl, 79

Yalta Agreement, 164–6, 172, 199, 323

Yanovskyi, Yurii, 261

Yashan, Volodymyr, 52–3

Yaskevych, Major Savelii, 169, 183

Yorkshire Television program *The SS in Britain*, 126, 175, 289

youth soldiers, 142; in anti-aircraft force, 154–6; camp conditions, 157; camp in Malta, Austria, 224; insignia, 153; nationality of, 143; postwar fate, 157–8; women, 149–54

Zahachevskyi, Evstakhii, 179, 193, 266–7

Zahainyi, Pavlo, 213

Zakerzonnia, 11, 38, 152, 314; population of, 46; soldiers from, 297; as war zone, 320–1

Zakharyasevych, Liubomyr, 301, 304, 306

Zelenko, Kostiantyn, 241–3

Zelenyi, Zenon, 143–5, 157

Zhyttia v tabori, 192

Zoglauer, Karl, 67, 76–8

ZWZ (Union of Armed Struggle), 88